CAMBRIDGE LATIN AMERICAN STUDIES

EDITORS
DAVID JOSLIN JOHN STREET

4

BRITAIN AND THE ONSET OF MODERNIZATION IN BRAZIL

1850–1914

THE SERIES

BRITAIN
AND THE ONSET OF
MODERNIZATION
IN BRAZIL
1850-1914

BY

RICHARD GRAHAM
Associate Professor of History
University of Texas at Austin

CAMBRIDGE
AT THE UNIVERSITY PRESS
1972

Published by the Syndics of the Cambridge University Press
Bentley House, 200 Euston Road, London, NW1 2DB
American Branch: 32 East 57th Street, New York, N.Y.10022

Library of Congress Catalogue Card Number: 68-21393

ISBN: 0 521 07078 3 clothbound
0 521 09681 2 paperback

First published, 1968
Reprinted, 1972

First printed in Great Britain
at the University Printing House, Cambridge
Reprinted in the United States of America

TO ANN

MAPS

CONTENTS

PREFACE

A transformation began in Brazil during the period from 1850 to 1914, and this book examines, as one theme within that story, the relationship of the British to the onset of this revolutionary process. By 1914 Brazil had done no more than begin to modernize; but it had begun. And perhaps the effort needed to start along this way was greater than that required to continue, for I am not merely speaking of economic development, but of modifications in the social structure and alterations of individual beliefs and attitudes, that is, of changes which have facilitated further changes down to our own day.

The British were among the major actors in this drama. They contributed directly to the spread of coffee culture which disrupted the ancient economic patterns of Brazil. They also provided much of the 'infrastructure' and some of the capital for industrialization. They wrought major changes in Brazil's labor system and were among the agents of diffusion for a more 'Western', European world-view and societal structure. But Britishers also hindered Brazilian development, and it is historically important to perceive the ambiguity of their role on the Brazilian stage. Brazil's development—and lack of development—is a complex story and neither a 'devil theory' nor a panegyric will satisfy its exigencies.

Scholars of many disciplines are today concerned with the kind of change which I here describe in Brazil, and it is not my purpose to add to the extant literature on the theory of modernization. I only say what so many already know: that this process is not an easy one to foster. If, on the contrary, I seem optimistic about the achievements of the nineteenth century, it is only to point out that the roots of modern change run deep in the Brazilian past even though present results are still unsatisfactory. I do not believe, as is sometimes argued, that the transformation of Brazil began only in 1930, or in 1914, or even in 1889. True, it did not originate precisely in 1850, but I think this date is closer to the truth.

To convey some idea of the importance of subsequent changes, I begin by briefly contrasting Britain and Brazil as they stood in 1850. In Chapter 1 I survey the transformation through which Brazil passed during the period from 1850 to 1914. Chapters 2, 3 and 5 discuss the role of the British in the economic development of Brazil, while Chapter 4 introduces a respite by discussing the accompanying changes in the style of urban life. Chapter 6 is concerned with that part of the British impact which has heretofore received most attention: efforts to end the slave trade and curtail slavery. Chapters 7, 8 and 9 are concerned with Brazilian innovators, mostly businessmen, and the ideas which impelled them: industrial capitalism, the gospel of work, *laissez faire*, the joint-stock company idea, the belief in progress, and a vague trust in science. The next two chapters explore the relevance to modernization of the belief in the individual as expressed in political and religious beliefs. Finally, I examine the ambiguities of the British role in view of the growing impact of other countries and the increasing momentum of change within Brazil itself.

This study was made possible by the generous support of various agencies. Research was begun in Brazil in 1959–60 under the terms of a Research Training Fellowship from the Social Science Research Council. This Fellowship was renewed in 1960–1 and the Council revealed its tenacity through a Faculty Research Grant in 1964–5, renewed in 1966–7. The Rockefeller Foundation, through its International Relations Program, provided the major support for a year's research in Brazil during 1964–5. The American Philosophical Society aided my research in Britain during the summer of 1962, and Cornell University, through its History Department, its Latin American Studies Program, and its Faculty Research Grants Committee also supplied funds for expenses connected with the preparation of this book.

Librarians and archivists make the work of the historian possible.

Preface

In addition to the staffs of the archives listed at the end of this volume and of the libraries attached to some of them, I wish to thank the personnel of the following institutions: the Library of the University of Texas and especially the Latin American Collection there; the Olin Research Library of Cornell University; the Library of Congress in Washington; the Biblioteca Nacional in Rio de Janeiro; the Biblioteca do Ministério da Educação e Cultura, the Biblioteca Demonstrativa Castro Alves, and the library of the Sociedade de Cultura Inglêsa, all in the same city; the Biblioteca Municipal de São Paulo; the library of the Faculdade de Direito in São Paulo; the library of the British Chamber of Commerce of São Paulo and Southern Brazil; the British Museum; and the Institute of Historical Research at the University of London. Some of the back files of the *Estado de São Paulo* and the *Jornal do comércio* were made available by the managers of these respective newspapers.

Those who grant access to private papers are especially to be commended and are, therefore, acknowledged in specific footnotes. Establishing contact with the persons who have this power often depends upon the good will of others and it is in this connexion that I wish to thank Mr Charles H. Wrigley once of the British consulate in São Paulo and Mr J. C. Hunt of the Luso-Brazilian Council (Canning House) in London.

The author's task is made lighter by individuals so numerous that it is impossible to list here all those who helped. Unnamed, but especially remembered are those who eased me around those problems that arise in connexion with life and work abroad. Here I can only acknowledge the debt I owe to a few who were of extraordinary help in advancing the research and writing itself. Thus in Rio de Janeiro I owe special thanks to José Honório Rodrigues, Américo Jacobina Lacombe, Eulália Lahmayer de Lobo, Raimundo Magalhães Júnior, Hélio Vianna, Zilda Araújo, and Maria de Lourdes Claro de Oliveira. In São Paulo I am especially obliged to Sérgio Buarque de Holanda, João Cruz Costa,

Preface

Alice Cannabrava, Nícia Villela Luz, Myriam Ellis, Roque Spencer Maciel de Barros, Rubens Borba de Morais, and Adelpha Figueiredo. Francisco Marques dos Santos made possible my work in Petrópolis. In Recife my efforts were greatly aided by José Antônio Gonsalves de Mello (Neto) and Lúcia Nele da Fonseca. In London I was helped by Robin Humphreys and Mary Coates and in Ithaca, New York, by David B. Davis, Walter LaFeber, Frederick G. Marcham, Eleanor Parker, Virginia Valiela, and William Lofstrom. I would never have initiated this study if it had not been for Lewis Hanke, who by encouragement and guidance gave another expression to his constant effort to advance Brazilian studies. And most of all do I owe thanks to my wife, Ann, whose labor, critiques, patience, and love made this book possible.

R.G.

Dryden, N.Y.
15 March 1968.

ABBREVIATIONS USED IN
THE FOOTNOTES

AHI	Arquivo Histórico do Ministério de Relações Exteriores, Itamaratí.
AIHGB	Arquivo do Instituto Histórico e Geográfico Brasileiro.
AMIP	Arquivo do Museu Imperial de Petrópolis.
AN	Arquivo Nacional.
APEP	Arquivo Público Estadual de Pernambuco.
ARFM	Archives of Rio de Janeiro Flour Mills and Granaries, Ltd.
BT	Public Record Office: Board of Trade.
Cia.	Companhia.
FO	Public Record Office: Foreign Office.
GPL	Edward Greene Papers: Letterpress Books.
Imp.	Imprensa.
JNP	Joaquim Nabuco Papers.
NA/DS	National Archives: Department of State.
PWL	Papers of Wilson Sons & Co., Ltd: Letterpress Book.
RIHGB	*Revista do Instituto Histórico e Geográfico Brasileiro.*
Rio	Rio de Janeiro.
SAJ	*South American Journal and River Plate Mail.*
Tip.	Tipografia.
Typ.	Typographia.
Univ.	University.

A NOTE ON SPELLING

Changes in Brazilian orthography may cause some confusion. When using names or words in Portuguese within the text, I have here adopted modern spellings, e.g. Rui Barbosa and *Jornal do comércio*; but in the footnotes I have cited authors and titles as they appeared in the work used, as, Ruy Barbosa and *Jornal do commercio*.

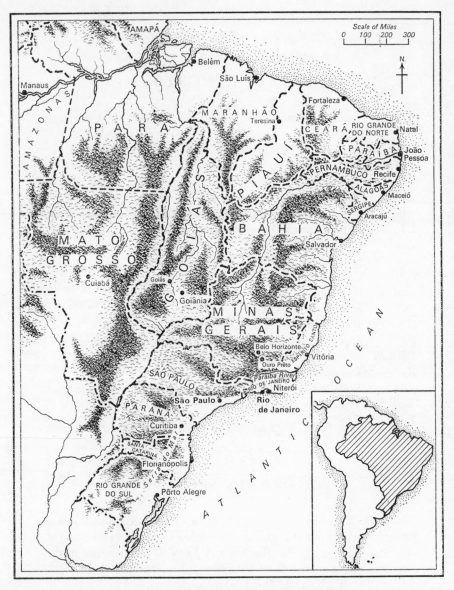

Brazil: physical features and state capitals

Note. The state capital Goiás was replaced by Goiânia in the 1930s; and
Ouro Prêto by Belo Horizonte in 1895.

INTRODUCTION

CONTRASTING SOCIETIES:
BRITAIN AND BRAZIL

Brazil was a backward country in 1850. To make this point, it is worthwhile to contrast it with a society which was modernizing at that time. There has sometimes been a tendency to draw precise lines to separate those nations that are modern from those that are not. Whether these measurements are based on the degree of urbanization or on per capita income or on the number of automobiles, they are all misleading in that they focus attention on secondary factors. It is the direction and rate of change that must be examined and not the establishment of particular benchmarks. Therefore, a look at Britain in 1850, no matter how brief, and perforce superficial, will here be useful; for it is not only by contrast with modern nations of the twentieth century that Brazil's condition at that time must be evaluated. In addition, even a hasty glance at Britain will make clear that the British presence in Brazil was not an isolated instance of British expansion, but part of a larger trend in that nation's history.

The steadily increasing flow of innovation—which goes hand-in-hand with rapid economic growth and the steady process of capital formation—is an identifying mark of modern economies. It is especially by this standard that Britain may be considered modernizing over a hundred years ago.[1] Thus, although by 1850 the adoption of mechanical means of production had not yet become common in any but a small number of industries, the goal of mechanization had been accepted and rapid strides toward it were being taken. The ever-accelerating stream of technological improvement had begun, and the dynamic quality of English economic and social life in 1850 clearly requires the label 'modernizing'.

[1] The contrast between Brazil and Great Britain has not disappeared even today, as can be seen from the wealth of secondary literature on British history and the relative dearth of historical writing for this period in Brazil. Boldness verging on recklessness is required in both cases if summaries are to be made, but it seems worthwhile, for the reasons mentioned, to take the risk.

Introduction

At least a century of ever more rapid industrial growth, based upon the accumulated wealth of the old merchant capitalists, lay behind the Britain of 1850.[1] By the mid-nineteenth century cotton manufacture had been completely transformed by the use of mechanized processes, and the industry was experiencing an especially productive period. World economic prosperity, stimulated by the increased supply of gold mined in California and, later, in Australia, spurred on the export of British products, especially textiles. In the early 1850s over 60 per cent of Britain's export earnings were derived from this item. Six-tenths of the cotton fabrics produced in the United Kingdom were being exported, and the total value of cotton manufactures had risen 43 per cent in the preceding twenty years. Textile and apparel industries occupied one in every five gainfully employed persons.

Iron, steel, and coal were to be the basis of further economic growth, and Britain excelled at the production of all three. The annual average output of iron during 1850–54 was 2·8 million tons. Twenty years earlier it had been only a quarter of that figure and in the following twenty years it would more than double. The growth of the industry culminated in the invention of the Bessemer process for making steel in 1855, and by 1883 the production of steel was over two million tons. Coal production had risen from 17·4 million tons in 1820 to 49·4 million in 1850 and would reach 110·4 million in 1870.

Technological improvement was also having a marked effect on transportation. By 1850, only some twenty-five years after the building of the first railway, 5000 miles of track stretched across the small nation. In the face of the technical and financial obstacles to this entirely new type of enterprise, it was an astonishing achievement, and, in the sheer size and rapidity of the job, an

[1] This summary of economic aspects is based on John Harold Clapham, *An Economic History of Modern Britain*, 2nd ed., 3 vols. (Cambridge University Press, 1930–8). Other valuable surveys are by G. P. Jones and A. G. Pool, *A Hundred Years of Economic Development in Great Britain (1840–1940)* (London: Duckworth, 1940); William Ashworth, *An Economic History of England, 1870–1939* (London & New York: Methuen & Barnes & Noble, 1960); and Charles R. Fay, *Great Britain from Adam Smith to the Present Day. An Economic and Social Survey* (London: Longmans, Green, 1928). A summary of the growth of various sectors of the economy is presented in Arthur D. Gayer, *et al.*, *The Growth and Fluctuation of the British Economy, 1790–1850*, 2 vols. (Oxford: Clarendon Press, 1953), I, 406–55.

unprecedented one. The death of George Stephenson in 1848 marked the end of this initial period but the beginning of an era of even more rapid expansion. In the next twenty years rails were not only to link together every important British center, but also to stretch across vast areas of other lands that now became easily available to the salesmen of British manufactured goods.

Finally, the radical improvement of the machine-tool industry in the 1850s and the application to technical problems of such scientific theories as those of thermodynamics cleared away the last obstacles to the continuous flow of technological change. And so it is not surprising to note that the years following 1850 were years of rapid economic expansion. The average annual increase of the national product from 1851 to 1891 was 3·2 per cent. Even in per capita terms, the growth rate during these four decades was 1·9 per cent per year.[1]

Meanwhile, great accumulations of capital were taking place. The legislation regarding joint stock companies was finally settled in 1862 with a consequent and immediate increase in the number of companies with limited liability for their shareholders. By 1880 the London *Economist* demonstrated that the annual new capital subscriptions had almost doubled just in the preceding three years. Because of the rapidity of its accumulation, this capital was frequently directed toward investments abroad.[2]

Britain at this time was rapidly extending its economic interests over the entire underdeveloped world. Even at the end of the eighteenth century it had become impatient with the restraints imposed on its expanding international trade by the closed-door policies of the Spanish and Portuguese colonial empires and

---

[1] Statistical information has been drawn from J. R. T. Hughes, *Fluctuations in Trade, Industry, and Finance, A Study of British Economic Development, 1850–1860* (Oxford: Clarendon Press, 1960), pp. 72, 74; Phyllis Deane and W. A. Cole, *British Economic Growth, 1688–1959*, Cambridge University Department of Applied Economics, Monograph 8 (Cambridge University Press, 1962), pp. 187, 211, 216, 225, 232, 253; and Clapham, *Economic History*, II, 53–8.

[2] Bishop Carleton Hunt, *The Development of the Business Corporation in England, 1800–1867* (Cambridge, Mass.: Harvard Univ. Press, 1936); Clapham, *Economic History*, III, 201; *The Economist*, XXXVIII (1880), 1510; *The Bankers' Magazine, Journal of the Money Market, and Commercial Digest*, XXXVIII (London, 1878), 191. Also see A. K. Cairncross, *Home and Foreign Investment, 1870–1913. Studies in Capital Accumulation* (Cambridge University Press, 1953).

so exerted pressure to bring about the independence of Latin America. As the country's vigor increased, the sphere of its economic life reached further and further into non-modern areas. With the transformation of techniques of ocean and land transport, more and more of the world became a part of one economic system, a system dominated by Britain. The nineteenth century was an era characterized by a rapid migration of British peoples, the spread of British governmental ideals, the growing export of British goods, and the increasing overseas investment of British money.[1]

Technological improvements in shipping were one key to this development. Not only was steam applied to mail and passenger service, but notable modifications in sailing vessels were also being undertaken. The better design of these ships induced by reforms in the reckoning of tonnage for tax purposes, plus the publication in 1850 of the statistical compilations of winds and currents made by Mathew F. Maury, U.S.N., greatly cheapened sea-going transport as did the later application to sailing vessels of mechanical labor-saving devices, iron and steel hulls, and steel rigging. Finally, with improvements in steel, it was possible to build high-pressure steam engines which not only raised the speed of steamships but reduced by 90 per cent the amount of coal that had to be carried in otherwise good cargo space. Already by 1865 more tonnage was being built in steamships than in sailing vessels.[2]

[1] Charles K. Webster, ed., *Britain and the Independence of Latin America, 1812–1830. Select Documents from the Foreign Office Archives*, 2 vols. (London and New York: Oxford Univ. Press for the Ibero-American Institute of Great Britain, 1938), pp. 3–81; William W. Kaufmann, *British Policy and the Independence of Latin America, 1804–1828*, Yale Historical Publications Miscellany, 52 (New Haven: Yale Univ. Press, 1951); Robin A. Humphreys, 'The Fall of the Spanish American Empire', *History: the Journal of the Historical Association*, n.s. XXXVII (1952), 220–7; Caio de Freitas, *George Canning e o Brasil, influência da diplomacia inglêsa na formação brasileira*, Brasiliana, 298–298A, 2 vols. (São Paulo: Editôra Nacional, 1958); John Gallagher and Ronald Robinson, 'The Imperialism of Free Trade', *Economic History Review*, 2nd series, VI (1953), 5, 8–10; Carl Johannes Fuchs, *The Trade Policy of Great Britain and Her Colonies Since 1860*, transl. Constance H. M. Archibald (London: Macmillan, 1905), 109–77; S. B. Saul, *Studies in British Overseas Trade, 1870–1914* (Liverpool: Liverpool Univ. Press, 1960); Sanford A. Mosk, 'Latin America and the World Economy, 1850–1914', *Inter-American Economic Affairs*, II, no. 3 (Winter, 1948), pp. 53–82.

[2] Gerald S. Graham, 'The Ascendancy of the Sailing Ship, 1850–1885', *Economic History Review*, n.s. IX (1956–7), 74–88.

The repeal of the last export tax in 1850 symbolized the initiation of a period of rapidly rising exports. The declared value of British goods exported in 1848 was £53 million, a rise of only about £1 million since 1815; but in 1858 this figure was £117 million, and two years later £136 million. Yet these exports were not enough to pay for increasingly large food and raw material imports. Only the earnings derived from shipping and the returns on foreign investment could compensate for the unfavorable balance of trade.[1]

Foreign and, especially, Latin American investments increased rapidly in the latter half of the nineteenth century. Whereas the amount of British capital in Latin America in 1850 was still small, it increased steadily during the 1850s and 1860s. Even though investments slowed down during the years 1873–9, by 1880 the nominal value of British capital invested in Latin America totaled £179 million. Of this amount, £38·8 million were applied to Brazil. British foreign investments as a whole increased rapidly during the 1880s, declined during the depression of the 1890s, and then shot up during the first decade of this century. The same trends were reflected in their Latin American investments. By 1913 the nominal value of British capital in this area was estimated at £999·3 million, of which £223·9 million were invested in Brazil.[2]

Britain in 1850, then, was caught up in a process of steadily accelerating change. Technological improvements in textile manufacture, metallurgy, and transport followed each other with increasing speed. Capital was mobilized for investment at home and overseas. Sail and steam vessels swiftly carried ever larger shipments of British manufactured goods into the underdeveloped world, bringing in return raw materials and foodstuffs. Change had become normal.

[1] Hughes, *Fluctuations in Trade*, pp. 4–5, 7; Ashworth, *Economic History of England*, pp. 10, 11.

[2] J. Fred Rippy, *British Investments in Latin America, 1822–1949. A Case Study in the Operations of Private Enterprise in Retarded Regions* (Minneapolis: Univ. of Minnesota Press, 1959), esp. pp. 25, 28, 32, 36–46, 66, 67, 150; cf. W. W. Rostow, *British Economy of the Nineteenth Century* (Oxford: Clarendon Press, 1948), pp. 191–201; Charles K. Hobson, *The Export of Capital*, Studies in Economic and Political Science, 38 (London: Constable, 1914), esp. p. 218.

Social transformations also identify Britain as modernizing at this time. The population was rapidly increasing, and, more important, it was also shifting. Even in the eighteenth century the spread of scientific farming had led to an enclosure movement in the rural areas, driving thousands to the cities. By 1851 Great Britain was a half-rural, half-urban nation, and only 21·7 per cent of the total occupied population was engaged in agriculture, forestry and fishing, as compared with 42·9 per cent employed in manufacturing, mining and other industry. The rapid growth of the cities led to wretched living conditions, marked by over-crowding, lack of sewerage or fresh water, and poor ventilation. Although the availability of inexpensive labor during this century may have aided economic growth and ultimately increased the well-being of the population as a whole, modernization was not a pleasant experience.[1]

In an urban setting it became increasingly easier for persons of non-aristocratic origins to rise within the social structure. The social mobility of nineteenth-century British society should not be exaggerated, since, by the standards of present-day America, it was certainly restricted. Nevertheless, moneyed wealth became not only respectable but increasingly the primary criterion by which a man's worth was measured. The rise of a new class to political power as reflected in the Reform Act of 1832 had been a sign of this change. A succession of educational reforms in the latter half of the century made it possible for wider and wider segments of the population to have the tools for self-advancement. And conflicts between and within individuals on the way up or down the social scale formed the material for the many English novelists whose works were read aloud in the drawing-rooms of the new middle class.

One clear expression of the upward push of the individual was the full development of the idea of capitalism and its application

---

[1] Clapham, *Economic History*, I, 536; II, 489; Deane and Cole, *British Economic Growth*, p. 142; Leon S. Marshall, 'The Emergence of the First Industrial City: Manchester, 1780–1850', in Caroline Ware, ed., *The Cultural Approach to History* (New York: Columbia Univ. Press, 1940), pp. 140–61; Neil J. Smelser, *Social Change in the Industrial Revolution: an Application of Theory to the British Cotton Industry* (Chicago: Univ. of Chicago Press, 1959), pp. 265–312.

to industry. Perhaps no factor was of larger importance in Britain's rapid economic growth than the willingness to take risks which characterized the 1850s. Concerted action tending toward monopoly had not yet become the rule, and the investor in iron, coal, railways, shipbuilding, or textile industry was boldly daring in his practices.[1]

Of course, some of the characteristics of this modernizing society far antedated the rise of industry. The industrial and technological developments of the era were based on scientific principles of mechanics developed in the seventeenth century; these, in turn, would have been unthinkable in an age of mysticism and otherworldliness. The belief in the individual and in his potential mobility could be dated back at least to the sixteenth century.[2] Britain had really been modernizing for centuries.

There is perhaps no better symbol of the exuberant attitudes of the modern society of constant technological improvement and unquestioned mastery over nature than the Great Exhibition of the Works of Industry of All Nations held in the Crystal Palace in 1851. The Palace itself—conceived by Joseph Paxton, a large-scale gardener and entrepreneur—was a result of innovation, applying as it did the new industry of iron work to the old profession of architecture. It was essentially a huge greenhouse and it had this distinct advantage over the exhibits within it: it was entirely functional. The absence of guidelines for the design of new products led to blatant expressions of bad taste on the part of the new middle class, devoid as it was of the traditions of aristocratic life. Leafing through the illustrated publications of this first world's fair, one notes what today would be called a Babbittish love of 'gadgetry' and gimcracks, a glorification of the latest practical achievements of science. And here we have one of the most important aspects of the exhibition: it was considered irrefutable proof of man's progress. A weekly publication concerning the exhibition opened with these words: 'The Great

---

[1] Hughes, *Fluctuations in Trade*, pp. 288–9; Ashworth, *Economic History of England*, p. 19.

[2] See the provocative study by F. S. C. Northrop, *The Meeting of East and West: an Inquiry Concerning World Understanding* (New York: Macmillan, 1947), esp. pp. 66–192.

Industrial Exhibition of 1851...is an achievement, the beneficial effects of which are not for our own day only, but "for all time".'¹ It was this spirit—innovative, practical, a bit crass, scientific, and optimistic—that Englishmen were to carry to Brazil during the next seventy years. As one British engineer there put it, 'the introduction of machinery refines labor and links it to art', and he urged Brazil to move in this direction.² This same admiration for the wonders of modern technology inspired struggling industrial entrepreneurs in Brazil, one of whom referred to the steam engine as 'the sublime invention whose practical application honors the century in which we live'.³ The 'English ornamentation which is today [1887] dominant in industrial art', evoked ohs and ahs from Eduardo Prado because of its blending of 'the classic, the modern, the exotic, the archaic, the Japanese and the Byzantine'.⁴ The memory of 1851 dominated the similar London Exposition of 1862 where young Brazilians received inspiration to begin the transformation of their own country. But to the Crystal Palace in 1851 no official Brazilian representation had been sent. Those who held power then were not interested.⁵

¹ *The Crystal Palace and Its Contents: Being an Illustrated Cyclopaedia of the Great Exhibition of the Industry of All Nations, 1851...* (London: W. M. Clark, 1852); *The Art Journal Illustrated Catalogue: The Industry of All Nations, 1851* (London: Virtus, 1851); London, Great Exhibition of the Works of Industry of All Nations, *Official Catalogue*, 2nd ed. (London: Spicer & Clowes, 1851); Society of Arts, Manufactures and Commerce, *Lectures on the Results of the Exhibition* (London: Bogue, 1852); Christopher Hobhouse, *1851 and the Crystal Palace; Being an Account of the Great Exhibition and its Contents*, 2nd ed. (London: Murray, 1950); Yvonne Ffrench, *The Great Exhibition, 1851* (London: Harvill, 1951); Charles R. Fay, *Palace of Industry, 1851. A Study of the Great Exhibition and its Fruits* (Cambridge University Press, 1951); Asa Briggs, *1851*, Historical Association General Series, 18 (London: Historical Association, 1951).

² J. J. Aubertin, 'Communicado. Ilms. amigos e snrs. fazendeiros de S. Paulo', *Correio paulistano*, 3 Jan. 1867, p. 2; J. J. Aubertin, 'O algodão [carta a Fidelis Preta]', *Correio paulistano*, 21 July 1864, p. 3.

³ Irineo Evangelista de Souza, *visconde* de Mauá, *Autobiografia* ('*Exposição aos credores e ao público*') *seguida de 'O meio circulante no Brasil'*, 2nd ed. (Rio: Valverde, 1942), p. 146.

⁴ Eduardo Prado, *Collectaneas*, 4 vols. (São Paulo: Escola Typographica Salesiana, 1904–5), I, 263.

⁵ Francisco Carvalho Moreira, *barão* do Penedo, *Relatorio sobre a exposição internacional de 1862* (London: Brettell, 1863), pp. xxxiii, lxiv; André Rebouças, *Agricultura nacional, estudos economicos; propaganda abolicionista e democratica* (Rio: Lamoureux, 1883), p. 88; Agostinho Victor de Borja Castro, 'Relatorio do 2º grupo', in Antonio José de Souza Rego, comp., *Relatorio da segunda exposição nacional de 1866* (Rio: Typ. Nacional, 1869), p. 55; Joaquim Thomas de Amaral (Brazilian chargé d'affaires in London) to Paulino José Soares de Sousa (Brazilian foreign minister), London, 6 May 1851, AHI, 216/2/215, no. 22.

Brazil in 1850 presented a sharp contrast to Britain. True, its backwardness must not be exaggerated. It is impossible to maintain that any part of the American continent was alien to the broad changes initiated in Europe by the Renaissance and even the Reformation, except for certain areas with ancient indigenous civilizations. Portugal at one time had been characterized by a rather dynamic merchant capitalism and a secular state. Brazil had had its early colonial economic life dominated by the development of sugar plantations, and these plantations had been founded for profit by capitalists, many of whom borrowed heavily from merchants who remained in Portugal. The Negro slaves imported from Africa were considered merchandise, and the capital invested in them was one of the carefully considered factors of production. Indeed, the idea of the worker, not as a serf bound to the lord by the deepest ties of tradition and religion, but as property to be bought and sold, was in keeping with an early but essentially modern view of society. Furthermore, as a colony in a mercantilist era, Brazil was not a self-sufficient entity, but a recipient of manufactured goods from the metropolis, a subject of its political control, and a recipient of its intellectual direction. It will not do to suggest that the traditional society of Brazil in the mid-nineteenth century was equivalent to that of, say, medieval Europe.

Nevertheless, the steady stream of technological innovations that are basic to a modern society had not yet become a part of Brazilian life in 1850, and it may be questioned whether Brazil has even now entered this stage. Why Brazil, despite its earlier connexions with the modern world, had not yielded to more of its impulse lies outside the scope of this work. After a certain point in the sixteenth century the Iberian peninsula and the colonies of Spain and Portugal were more or less cut off from the mainstream of European development for some two hundred years. For all the early signs of change, the scientific world-view and the modern concept of the individual's place in society did not become a part of the Brazilian's mental equipment during the colonial period. The legal and social system emphasized the prestige and power of the large landowner. Even the relations between the masters and the slaves often became personal ties of loyalty and protection more characteristic of lord and serf than employer and employee. Little effort was made to keep up with innovations in the technique of sugar production, and Brazil lost the technological superiority that had once guaranteed its place in the world market.

In the eighteenth century there was a slow beginning of change. But, although the forces of the Enlightenment affected Portugal, Brazil still lagged behind. The predominantly rural nature of its life dampened the forces of change. The absence of any printing presses or universities is just one evidence of Brazil's backward agrarian society. There were, of course, a few persons acquainted with the ideas of the Enlightenment, and some changes did begin to take place, principally as a result of the sharply modified personal relationships created by the new mining economy and resulting urban clusters of south-central Brazil. In the 1820s and 1830s some of the leaders of the newly independent country were men formed in the context of the European Enlightenment who had completely absorbed the modern spirit.[1]

Yet, Brazil remained basically traditional. By the middle of the nineteenth century it was a sparsely settled country of 3 million square miles and only 7 million inhabitants. Most of them were concentrated on the eastern seaboard, but, even so, the cities accounted for only a small proportion of the population. Towns were sleepy and provincial, made up of packed-mud (*taipa*) houses along muddy and unilluminated streets where pack mules and slaves stumbled over pigs and chickens.[2]

Economic life was extremely backward. No one who has traveled in the more remote parts of Brazil today will doubt the words of one foreign observer at that time who wrote that

[1] Celso Lafer, 'O problema dos valores n'Os lusiadas', *Revista camoniana*, II (1965), 9–44; Antônio Cândido de Mello e Souza, *Formação da literatura brasileira (momentos decisivos)*, 2 vols. (São Paulo: Martins, 1959), pp. 236–65; Charles R. Boxer, *The Golden Age of Brazil* (Berkeley: Univ. of California Press, 1962); Octavio Tarqüínio de Sousa, *História dos fundadores do império do Brasil*, 2nd ed., 10 vols. (Rio: José Olympio, 1957), I, V, VI and VII, as well as IX, 9–25; Carlos Rizzini, *Hipólito da Costa e o 'Correio braziliense'*, Brasiliana, Grande Formato, 13 (São Paulo: Editôra Nacional, 1957); Lídia Besouchet, *Mauá e seu tempo* (São Paulo: Anchieta, 1942), 74–5.

[2] For a perceptive and concise treatment of mid-nineteenth-century Brazil see Gilberto Freyre, 'Social Life in Brazil in the Middle of the Nineteenth Century', *Hispanic American Historical Review*, V (1922), 597–630.

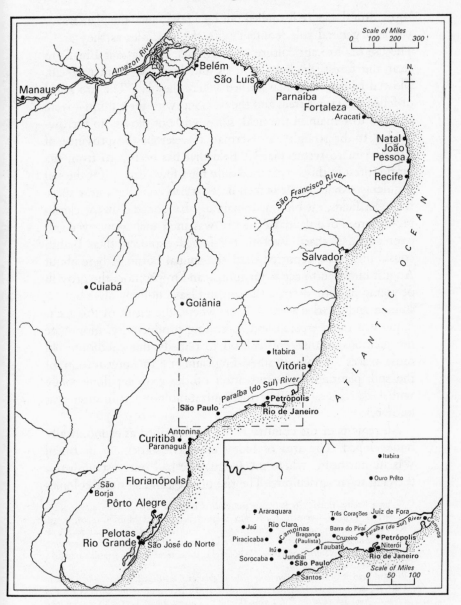

Brazil, showing towns referred to in the text

'agricultural science is studied but by a few', and 'the planters...
are, as a general rule, content with the processes as they are'.[1]
The use of 'fire agriculture' was the rule throughout Brazil: to
clear the forest the smaller trees and brush were merely cut,
allowed to dry, and then burned where they lay. The fire killed
or felled the larger trees and they—along with the stumps—were
allowed to remain in the field, since, without plows, no furrows
needed to be straight. A German traveler in the province of
Rio de Janeiro wrote that 'A field that has been torn from the
virgin forest in this way is used only for a few years...for the soil
is quickly exhausted. It is then necessary to conquer a new space
for other fields, the old one remaining abandoned'.[2] In the cattle-
raising areas of inland Brazil fire was used each year over and
over again. Richard Burton, the famed explorer, then British
consul in Santos, reported that 'the annual burnings here about
August intended to act as manure...and to promote the growth
of young pasture, destroy the soil and leave nothing alive but...
stunted and gnarled trees'.[3] Everywhere, the result of this technique was rapid erosion and decreasing productivity. Nor were
the methods of tillage calculated to remedy this condition. 'In
most places', wrote another Englishman, 'the preparation of
the soil, planting, and cultivation of the crop are done solely
with heavy hoes.' Neither mechanization nor fertilization was
known.[4]

All regions of the country could be described as economically
undeveloped. The area of oldest extensive settlement in Brazil
was its northeast, where the Portuguese had once established a
thriving sugar agriculture. The rise of West Indian sugar colonies

[1] William Scully, *Brazil: Its Provinces and Chief Cities; the Manners and Customs of the People; Agricultural, Commercial and Other Statistics*... (London: Murray, 1866), p. 19.
[2] Karl Hermann Konrad Burmeister, *Viagem ao Brasil através das províncias do Rio de Janeiro e Minas Gerais, visando especialmente a história natural dos distritos auridiamantíferos*, transl. Manoel Salvaterra and Hubert Schoenfeldt, Biblioteca Histórica Brasileira, 19 (São Paulo: Martins, 1952), p. 76.
[3] Richard Francis Burton, *Explorations of the Highlands of the Brazil; with a Full Account of the Gold and Diamond Mines. Also, Canoeing Down 1500 Miles of the Great River São Francisco from Sabará to the Sea*, 2 vols. (London: Tinsley, 1869), I, 75; also see Adolphe d'Assier, *Le Brésil contemporain: races, mœurs, institutions, paysage* (Paris: Durand et Lauriel, 1867), p. 127.
[4] Scully, *Brazil*, p. 18.

in the seventeenth century had undercut its prosperity and only
the disruption of Caribbean life by political strife and the end of
slavery at the end of the next century had temporarily rejuvenated
the sugar economy of Brazil.[1] The techniques of production were
still those of the seventeenth century, however. One observer
commented that the cultivation of sugar 'is in general carried on
in the most primitive manner', and he was struck by 'the rude-
ness of the machinery and the want of knowledge of the latest
and most improved processes of manufacture'. Another traveler
in the 1840s described a sugar mill where 'under a slight shed,
four oxen yoked to long poles, and walking round and round in
a ring, turned a simple wheel, which put in motion three upright,
iron plated rollers or cylinders...On one of these poles sat a
negro boy who directed the beasts with a long stick. Two other
blacks were busied in drawing the cane, with their hands, through
the two spaces of different sizes between the rollers—first the
larger and afterwards the smaller'. These same techniques were
in use in the province of Rio de Janeiro where sugar was also the
established crop along the narrow strip of low-lying land between
sea and mountains and in the delta at the mouth of the Paraíba river.[2]

But along the banks of the middle Paraíba river sugar was
being displaced by a new crop: coffee. Prices were rising and
production increasing rapidly. Although this development was
eventually to be of the greatest significance, the source of this
new prosperity was not the use of new techniques, but the use of
new lands. The methods of clearing, planting, and cultivating
remained unscientific. Harvesting was done by hand and the
cherry-like fruit transported to the plantation house on an oxcart.
Even the processing of the coffee for shipment left much to be
desired. It was most commonly spread on a beaten-earth patio to
dry, and then separated from the blackened shell in a slow-moving
water-powered wooden mortar called a *monjolo*. Only the largest

[1] Celso Furtado, *The Economic Growth of Brazil: a Survey from Colonial to Modern Times*,
transl. Ricardo W. de Aguiar and Eric Charles Drysdale (Berkeley and Los Angeles:
Univ. of California Press, 1963), p. 99.
[2] Scully, *Brazil*, p. 23; Adalbert, Prince of Prussia, *Travels in the South of Europe and in
Brazil; with a Voyage up the Amazon and its Tributary the Xingú, Now First Explored*,
transl. R. H. Schomburgk and J. E. Taylor, 2 vols. (London: Bogue, 1849), II, 72.

Introduction

and most prosperous planters had begun to introduce more sophisticated machinery to carry out this process. On the average, a coffee bush yielded only two pounds of finished coffee beans per year, and it required one slave just to harvest and care for every 3000 bushes, not counting the workers involved in transporting and processing the harvest. With the exhaustion of the soil, productivity decreased. On one plantation a 74 per cent increase in the number of bushes over a ten-year period led to an increased yield of only 25 per cent. Either new techniques would have to be adopted, or fresh soil brought into cultivation. But the possibilities of the latter course were limited by the distance which separated suitable new lands from the coast and the high cost of mule-back transportation.[1]

Methods of transportation were everywhere rudimentary. The oxcart and the mule train were practically the only means used for the shipment of merchandise overland. As one critical writer put it, 'The things called roads, by which the produce leaves the farms, are absolutely impassable to wheel carriages.' Characteristically, the first roadway prepared for horse-drawn vehicles was one to link steaming Rio de Janeiro with the emperor's summer palace in Petrópolis.[2] Most internal commerce was, therefore, limited to coastal shipments by sea, and yet even here the provinces had more trade with foreign countries than with each other, as can be seen from Table 1.

Manufacturing industries were practically non-existent. Such capital as was available was in the hands of merchants who concentrated on the export of plantation produce, the importation of slaves and manufactures, and the maintenance of local food monopolies. From 1838 to 1850 only four corporations were established, all of them small and insignificant.[3]

[1] Thomas Ewbank, *Life in Brazil; or, a Journal of a Visit to the Land of the Cocoa and the Palm* ...(New York: Harper, 1856), pp. 308–9; Johann Jacob von Tschudi, *Viagem às províncias do Rio de Janeiro e São Paulo* (São Paulo: Martins, 1953), pp. 36, 39, 42, 43, 46–7.

[2] Charles Blackford Mansfield, *Paraguay, Brazil and the Plate; Letters Written in 1852–1853* ...(Cambridge, England: Macmillan, 1856), p. 48; Daniel Parish Kidder and James Cooley Fletcher, *Brazil and the Brazilians Portrayed in Historical and Descriptive Sketches* (Philadelphia: Childs & Peterson, 1857), p. 300.

[3] Stanley J. Stein, *The Brazilian Cotton Manufacture; Textile Enterprise in an Underdeveloped Area, 1850–1950* (Cambridge, Mass.: Harvard Univ. Press, 1957), pp. 5–6;

Contrasting Societies

Table 1. *Value of Goods Shipped from Various Ports, 1848–1849*[a] *(in contos)*[b]

Port	Shipped to ports outside the empire	Shipped to ports within the empire
Rio de Janeiro	27,329	717
Salvador	8,547	208
Recife	9,638	360
São Luís	1,644	82
Belém	1,312	76
Rio Grande, S. José do Norte, Pôrto Alegre, and S. Borja	3,056	1,381
Santos and Paranaguá	1,852	68
João Pessoa	1,226	—
Fortaleza, Aracati	167	178
Florianópolis	92	14
Alagoas	1,171	146
Sergipe	226	303
Vitória	—	25
Natal	—	24
Parnaíba	—	39
Other ports	—	636
Total	56,259	4,142

[a] Source: Quadro G, 'Recapitulação da exportação para dentro e para fóra do imperio, por provincia', in Brazil, Commissão Encarregada da Revisão da Tarifa, *Documentos estatisticos sobre o commercio do imperio do Brasil nos annos de 1845 a 1849 que acompanhão o relatorio da commissão*...(Rio: Typ. Nacional, 1853).

[b] The *milreis* was the unit of Brazilian currency and could be theoretically divided into one thousand *reis*. One *conto* was worth one thousand *milreis*.

The general lack of technological progress among artisans may be judged by the remarks of an American, who, with pretentious

Antonio de Barros Ramalho Ortigão, 'Surto de cooperativismo', *RIHGB, Tomo especial: Contribuições para a biographia de D. Pedro II* (Rio: Imp. Nacional, 1925), p. 290; *Annuario politico, historico e estatistico do Brazil: 1846* (Rio: Firmin Didot, [1846?]), pp. 28–34; Élisée Reclus, 'Le Brésil et la colonisation, II. Les provinces du littoral, les noirs, et les colonies allemandes', *Revue des deux mondes* (July–Aug. 1862), p. 394.

erudition, remarked in 1856 that, among the building trades, 'hammers, trowels, hoes for mixing and lifting mortar, and round baskets for carrying it on the head, are precisely such as we see in illustrated works of the fifteenth and illuminated MSS. of preceding centuries'. And he continued: 'The first tool I took up I recognized at once as Roman and Egyptian. There was no resisting the striking resemblance between it and those...portrayed in Theban sculptures.'[1]

Trading and industrial activity were regarded with contempt. One traveler reported that Brazilians would 'starve rather than become mechanics'. The urban artisanry, that in some traditional societies has prepared the way for industrial activity, was in Brazil monopolized, on the one hand, by Portuguese immigrants and, on the other, by the slaves. 'I have seen slaves working as carpenters, masons, pavers, printers, sign and ornamental painters, carriage and cabinet makers, fabricators of military ornaments, lamp-makers, silversmiths, jewelers and lithographers... *All* kinds of trades are carried on by black journeymen and boys.'[2] The ambition of the immigrant's son was naturally to dissociate himself from an activity that only his ill-adjusted father would share with slaves.

The social structure of Brazil in 1850 was, first of all, rigidly stratified. A Frenchman, familiar with the country, observed that a person's class was immediately ascertainable even in the middle of the forest, and an Englishman noted that 'Brazilians pay great regard to distinction and rank, and perhaps in no other language are these so precisely determined'. This rigidity is also reflected by the shock felt by a Brazilian diplomat working in London when he was confronted with an occasional disregard for decorum and proper dress displayed by the British foreign minister.[3]

---

[1] Ewbank, *Life in Brazil*, pp. 188–9.

[2] *Ibid.* pp. 184, 185, 186, 195; the last phrase suggests that Nelson Werneck Sodré, *História da burguesia brasileira*, Retratos do Brasil, 22 (Rio: Civilização Brasileira, 1964), pp. 49–50, is correct in suggesting that there was a more fully developed artisanry than is generally thought.

[3] Adolphe d'Assier, *Le Brésil contemporain: races, mœurs, institutions, paysage* (Paris: Durand et Lauriel, 1867), p. 137; Scully, *Brazil*, p. 11; José Marques Lisboa (Brazilian minister in England) to Paulino de Sousa, London, 8 Nov. 1851, AHI, 216/2/15, no 62.

Class origins pre-determined position. A critic of the system later said the civil service was a 'refuge for the heirs of ancient, wealthy and noble families that had thrown away their fortunes'. If a man was not himself entitled to position, then personal connexion was the only other way to gain advancement. One Brazilian referred to this as 'the influence of proper names'; others complained of men raised to high position by family or personal connexions, 'so common in this sorry country where the English precept "to put the right man in the right place" is entirely unknown'.[1] Occasionally, men of low position would accidentally win favor with the emperor and, fairy-tale like, be showered with royal attention. Otherwise, there was little hope of social mobility.

Education was the prerogative of those entitled by birth or position to the benefits which it could bring. As late as 1877 it was estimated that only 1,563,000 free persons knew how to read and write while 5,580,000 free persons over five years of age did not. Only 170,000 children were in any school. Secondary schools were rare and poorly run with the exception of a model institution in Rio de Janeiro. Prepared by private tutors and helped on by the 'pull' which they commanded, the sons of the landed elite could easily pass the entrance examination to the two law schools and two medical schools then in the country. Although some learned and able Brazilians were trained here, it seems clear that in general these schools made a farce of education. The professors did little to advance the learning of the young, having won their position by personal favor as well. It was said at that time that 'men who have always been known as zeros in the republic of letters are now occupying the most important places as professors in the Brazilian law schools'. Their teaching method was to repeat by rote the texts and compendiums prepared by Europeans. Continued use of one's connexions made graduation from these institutions almost automatic. Technical education in 1850

[1] Joaquim Nabuco, *O abolicionismo*, [2nd ed.?] (Rio & São Paulo: Civilização Brasileira & Editôra Nacional, 1938), p. 179; São Paulo (state), Assembléia Legislativa, *Anais*, 1867, p. 82; Antonio Augusto da Costa Aguiar, 'A continuação da confissão dos meus intimos pensamentos', 28 Sept. 1862, AMIP, cxxi, 6422, p. 2.

was limited to the army officers' school which prepared some army engineers. Vocational schools were unknown.[1]

A pre-scientific world-view was characteristic of most Brazilians at mid-century. Among the lower classes fetishism mixed with badly digested Catholicism was the rule. Among the elite the progress of modernity had gone far enough to make them skeptical of revealed religion, but their interest in science was limited to after-dinner conversation. The conviction that the problems that beset their country could and must be solved by the systematic application of scientific principles was not theirs. God might not be blamed for everything, but reality was still shrouded in mystery, neither understood nor controlled.

But if the leaders of Brazil cared little for religion, they cared a great deal about the religious orthodoxy of social institutions. Catholicism was the official religion of the state, and the constitution, the laws, the formulas for every act—birth, marriage, death—were Roman Catholic. Roque Spencer Maciel de Barros, the Brazilian historian of ideas, has pointed out how orthodoxy was to prove the chief weapon used by the defenders of the old order against the attacks of the modernizers and rationalists. Those who would defend the *status quo* regarded society as divinely ordained. No act expressed more clearly the religious underpinning of the social structure than the request for the blessing from one's betters. Standing higher in the scale that led to God, they were entitled to reply 'God bless you'.[2]

[1] Roque Spencer Maciel de Barros, *A ilustração brasileira e a idéia de universidade*, Universidade de São Paulo, Cadeira de História e Filosofia da Educação, Boletim, 241 (2) (São Paulo: Universidade de São Paulo, 1959), pp. 200–4, 207–11; *The Statesman's Year-Book*, (London: Macmillan, 1870), p. 495; Miguel do Sacramento Lopes Gama quoted by Renato Mendonça, *Um diplomata na côrte de Inglaterra; o barão do Penedo e sua época*, Brasiliana, 219 (São Paulo: Editôra Nacional, 1942), p. 22. Also see Júlio Ribeiro, *Cartas sertanejas*, [? ed.], Coleção Nacionalista, 3 (São Paulo: Brasil Editôra, 1945), pp. 105–7.

[2] See Ewbank, *Life in Brazil*, for a critical view of Brazilian religious practices and beliefs; similarly, see the remark by Raimundo Teixeira Mendes, the Positivist leader, that 'in the great majority...rules a fetishism one could call Catholic', quoted by Barros, *A ilustração brasileira*, p. 31 n.; on orthodox institutions see pp. 38–40 and cf. Morris Ginsberg, *The Idea of Progress, a Revaluation* (Boston, Mass.: Beacon, 1953), p. 7; on the blessing see Stanley J. Stein, *Vassouras, A Brazilian Coffee County, 1850–1900*, Harvard Historical Studies, 69 (Cambridge, Mass.: Harvard Univ. Press, 1957), p. 147; Ewbank, *Life in Brazil*, p. 400 n.; as a child in the backlands of Brazil, I found that children of lower class, my age and older, would be told to ask my blessing.

It was precisely in the early 1850s that the law schools—from which sprang the governing elite—were reorganized so as to emphasize still further the values of the traditional society. Natural law, 'prescribed to us by the Creator in the nature with which he has endowed us', was the basis of the curriculum. The belief in authority and hierarchy were emphasized by its study, and the idea of 'social contract' was ruled out. The necessity of State–Church union for the sake of social stability was deeply inculcated. One critic maintained the professors 'fled from science as the devil from the cross'.[1]

Appearances have led to many misconceptions as to how far governmental institutions had moved along the road to modernity. Brazil was unique in the western hemisphere at that time in that it retained a monarchical form of government. When Napoleon's forces invaded Portugal in 1807 the queen, the prince regent, and the court fled to Brazil as a government in exile. Brazil was raised to the position of kingdom in 1815 and in some ways Brazil may mark its independence from that date. However, when the king was forced to return to Portugal in 1820 as a result of revolutionary disturbances there, Brazil was threatened with a return to colonial status. Left in Brazil by his father, the young and impetuous prince Pedro saw the direction in which developments were moving and decided to sacrifice allegiance to Portugal and his father in exchange for an immediate crown. He declared Brazil independent in 1822, and became its first emperor as Pedro I.

The Brazilian landed aristocracy soon began to chafe under the supercilious Portuguese courtiers and advisers with whom the young emperor surrounded himself. Finally, in 1831, he was driven from Brazil, abdicating in favor of his five-year-old son, Pedro II. A regency was then set up and it guided Brazil through its most turbulent days, days in which Brazil flirted with repub-

[1] Afonso Arinos de Melo Franco, *Um estadista da república* (*Afrânio de Melo Franco e seu tempo*), Documentos Brasileiros, 85, 3 vols. (Rio: José Olympio, 1955), I, 132, 151; James J. Fox, 'Natural Law', *The Catholic Encyclopedia*, IX (1910), 76–9; André Rebouças, *Diário e notas autobiográficas*, ed. Ana Flora and Inácio José Veríssimo, Documentos Brasileiros, 12 (Rio: José Olympio, 1938), p. 38; Ribeiro, *Cartas sertanejas*, pp. 22, 104–12, esp. III.

licanism but never entirely lost its loyalty to the young monarch-to-be. When the boy was fifteen years old such a crisis had developed in the nation, especially with the growth of centrifugal forces in the outlying areas, that he was declared of age and hastily crowned. During the first years of his reign from 1840 to 1849, major effort was directed toward crushing the various smoldering and active rebellions. A period of internal peace then ensued, lasting until 1889.

The trappings of a modern state were boldly flaunted. Brazil was a constitutional monarchy. The French Bourbon charter of 1814, some ideas of Benjamin Constant, and aspects of British experience had been combined in the constitution granted by Pedro I in 1824. With certain modifications this was the form of government still in use in 1850. Besides the emperor and his Council of State, there was a Senate whose members were appointed for life by the emperor from lists submitted to him by the provincial legislatures; an indirectly elected Chamber of Deputies whose procedures were consciously modeled on the British House of Commons; a supposedly independent judiciary; and provinces organized on roughly the same pattern.

But realities of government did not correspond to this gleaming exterior. The emperor's 'moderative power' gave him the right and the responsibility to balance the various branches of government; one of the ways in which he did this was to alternate the parties in power. As a result, for all the Chamber of Deputies might mimic the House of Commons, a new ministry could be named at the wish of the emperor. Indeed, only such intervention could preserve the apparent similarity to the mid-nineteenth-century British model, since as a result of electoral procedures, whoever controlled the government would win the elections. It is further suggestive that in 1869 over half the Deputies were public employees and another twenty-eight were close relatives of important public functionaries. The 'crown interest' was well protected.[1]

---

[1] José Ignácio Silveira da Motta, *Degeneração do sistema representativo [discurso na Conferência Radical, 25.4.1869]* (Rio: Typ. Americana, 1869), p. 13; João Camillo de Oliveira Tôrres, *A democracia coroada: teoria política do império do Brasil*, 2nd ed. (Petrópolis, R. J.: Editôra Vozes, 1964), pp. 95–9.

The emperor exercised such power because it pleased the landed aristocracy so to allow. The electorate was almost entirely limited to the members of this class and a small number of their dependents in the villages and towns. It is said that after an electoral reform in 1881 which extended the suffrage, only 142,000 persons were qualified to vote out of a population of 15 million. Since the extended family characterized Brazilian society, politics consisted primarily in advancing the interests of one's clan. The stability of the regime was partly won by ignoring the feuds that raged for decades on end at the local level, sometimes with not inconsiderable bloodshed.[1] Although local self-government was practically non-existent according to the formal structures of government, the landed chief of the area made almost all decisions affecting the locality, and only in those places closest to the seat of power could the will of the central government be effectively applied. A Brazilian novelist and reformer later compared the plantation to a medieval manor, pointing out that the planter 'had there a private jail, enjoyed effective jurisdiction, and was very much judge over life and death. To rule his liege subjects he was guided by one code—his sovereign will. In fact, he was outside the reach of justice: the written law did not touch him'. A foreign traveler seconded his report: 'Society is patriarchal rather than civil. The proprietor of a sugar or cattle estate is, practically, an absolute lord. The community that lives in the shadow of so great a man is his feudal retinue; and...a few such men...are thus able to bring scores of lieges and partisans into the field.'[2]

The throne—as distinct from the emperor—strengthened the hierarchical structure and lent its cohesive force to an outdated society. The loyalty the crown commanded not only prevented Brazil from breaking up into various and separate nations as was the case in the Spanish-speaking republics of the hemisphere, but

[1] Alan K. Manchester, 'Dom Pedro Segundo, the Democratic Emperor', in Lawrence F. Hill, ed., *Brazil* (Berkeley and Los Angeles: Univ. of California Press, 1947), p. 43; Arthur Quadros Collares Moreira, *A Câmara e o regimen eleitoral no império e na república* (Rio: J. Leite, n.d.), p. 58; Ulysses Lins de Albuquerque, *Um sertanejo e o sertão* (Rio: José Olympio, 1957), pp. 321–45.
[2] Julio Ribeiro, *A carne* (São Paulo: Teixeira, 1888), p. 169; Kidder and Fletcher, *Brazil and the Brazilians* (1857), p. 522.

also rescued it from the chaos of *caudillismo* caused by the displacement of traditional structures and the free play of modern, struggling, personalistic individualism. Even the liberal leaders of the first half of the century had been frightened by the implications of their ideology and, turning their back on the future, had bent their efforts to strengthening the institutions of the traditional society. Brazilians later accepted the monarchy as chiefly responsible for stabilizing the social order and maintaining the ancient hierarchies.[1] Because of the tendency among historians to be more interested in change and progress than in those who opposed it, little has been done to examine and understand the conservative ideology. This study is no exception, and it is the beginning of modern change that is the focus of attention.

[1] Richard M. Morse, 'Toward a Theory of Spanish American Government', *Journal of the History of Ideas*, xv (1954), 71–93; José Maria dos Santos, *Os republicanos paulistas e a abolição* (São Paulo: Martins, 1942), p. 10; Antonio Augusto da Costa Aguiar, 'Copia de um memorial dirigido por mim ao Exmo. Presidente désta provincia, o Conselheiro Vicente Pires da Motta, no dia 3 de fevereiro de 1883', AMIP, cxxxII, 6484.

I

THE ONSET OF MODERNIZATION
IN BRAZIL

Brazil has been modernizing for at least a century, despite the survival today of some characteristics of a traditional society. If the pace of change has been slow, it is because so many of the economic, social, and psychological prerequisites for a modern system were not present in 1850. The pre-conditions cannot be formed overnight, and the steps taken to establish them, be they ever so small, are as significant as later changes that are more easily measured. These early changes are what interest us here. Brazil began to move closer to the modern world during the period from 1850 to the First World War.

This period may be sub-divided at two points: 1865–70 and 1888–90. The pace of change was initially so sluggish that the modifications of the established order during the first fifteen or twenty years after 1850 were not easily perceived. But they were very real, nevertheless, and, working in subterranean ways, these changes softened the foundations of the old regime to such an extent that only a major crisis was needed to send cracks up along the exterior walls and spread alarm among the guardians of the ancient structure. Such a crisis was the war with Paraguay which began in 1865 and lasted for five frustrating years. At its end, Brazil entered a period in its life characterized by increasingly virulent attacks upon the traditional society. Slowly, the aging edifice began to crumble, and, in twenty years, some of the staunchest pillars of conservatism had given way. After 1890 the work proceeded more briskly as energies turned to preparing the open field upon which would play the forces of an industrial economy, a secular state, and a more flexible social structure. But many elements of the old order had not been completely destroyed by 1914, remaining as stumbling blocks to the forces of innovation. Brazil has not yet succeeded in completely eliminating these obstacles to steady acceleration.[1] But the original structure has been destroyed and cannot be restored.

During the first fifteen years after 1850, Brazil was decisively swept into the vortex of the international economy. The increasing momentum of the industrial revolution in Europe and the United States led to the production there of more goods by fewer workers and the corresponding need to seek markets more actively than ever. As noted in the Introduction, it also meant a rising urban population, a growing demand for raw materials, and an increasing leisure with which to enjoy luxury items such as coffee. An expanded supply of international currency stimulated world trade. And the application of new technology to sea and land transport meant a drastic cheapening in the cost of commodities shipped to and from Brazil. In 1851 a regular steam packet service was established between Brazil and England, as if to signal the closer ties between two continents.

During the 1850s the amount of sugar exported from Brazil remained relatively steady while exports of coffee experienced a dizzying rise. Yet, since south-central Brazil concentrated almost all its attention on coffee and the production of sugar now centered exclusively in the northeast, this old sugar region enjoyed an ephemeral prosperity which obscured the meaning of these developments. Even in the 1840s there had been a sharp rise in the average annual value of sugar exported from Bahia and Pernambuco. The continuing trend in the 1850s was noted by William Scully, an English commercial observer, who stated that the average number of *arrobas* (15 kilos) exported from Pernambuco in the 1840s was 2·7 million, while in 1853 this province exported 3·7 million *arrobas*, and, by 1858, the amount reached 4·5 million. Sugar exports from the northeast then declined. The competition of the sugar beet in Europe and of Cuban exports in North America spelled the end of this prosperity and the decadence of this region.

But with regard to coffee Brazil consistently enjoyed sharply increasing exports. Even in the latter half of the 1840s the average

---

[1] There is, of course, no inevitability implied here: it may never do so.

annual value of coffee exports reached 22,488 *contos* in comparison with sugar which only accounted for 15,136. Whereas in the decade of the 1830s Brazil had exported only 9·7 million uniform sacks of coffee and in the 1840s 17·1 million sacks, in the 1850s this figure was 26·2 million. During the same period the value of coffee exports went from £21·5 million and £22·7 million to £48·7 million. The bulk of this production centered in the valley of the Paraíba river, and coffee exports from the province of Rio de Janeiro far outstripped sugar both in quantity and value.[1]

Increasing export trade stimulated commercial growth and the rise of new urban groups. The Commercial Code of 1850, by standardizing the rules regarding bankruptcy, contracts, mortgages, and like matters, made it much easier and less risky to engage in commercial activity. The end of the slave trade that same year is said to have drawn into other enterprises a good deal of capital once lent to slave traders. The 1850s saw the rapid increase of new companies, especially banking establishments. Difficult as it still was under this Code to create corporations, eleven of them were granted permission to organize in 1851 and during the years 1852–9 another 135 companies received their patents, in contrast to the total of 4 during the period 1838–50. These corporations were designed to serve the rising demands of an export economy. In 1866, of the 69 foreign and Brazilian companies excluding banks that were then in existence, only 3 were engaged in manufacture, one operating a textile mill, one a tannery, and one a factory for candles and soap. What had been established were 27 transport companies (fluvial, marine, rail, and highway), 22 insurance companies, 13 companies to provide urban services, and 4 mining companies.[2] It was the multiplying needs

---

[1] Brazil, Commissão Encarregada da Revisão da Tarifa, *Documentos estatisticos sobre o commercio do imperio do Brasil nos annos de 1845 a 1849 que acompanhão o relatorio da commissão*...(Rio: Typ. Nacional, 1853), first section, pp. 12, 14 (Brazilian statistics are subject to considerable error, but are useful for showing relative change); William Scully, *Brazil: Its Provinces and Chief Cities; the Manners and Customs of the People; Agricultural, Commercial, and Other Statistics*... (London: Murray, 1866), pp. 197, 326–30; Affonso d'Escragnolle Taunay, *Pequena história do café no Brasil (1727–1937)* (Rio: Departamento Nacional do Café, 1945), pp. 547–8. Until 1871 a 'sack' of coffee weighed 165 lbs.; subsequently, 132 lbs.

[2] Antonio de Barros Ramalho Ortigão, 'Surto de cooperativismo', *RIHGB, Tomo especial: Contribuições para a biographia de D. Pedro II* (Rio: Imp. Nacional, 1925), pp. 290–1; Brazil, Ministerio da Agricultura, Commercio e Obras Publicas, *Relatorio*, 1866, Anexo T.

of export trade that impelled these modifications of the traditional society.

Commercial activity was primarily in the hands of foreigners— Portuguese retailers and British, French, and American international merchants—but Brazil's increasing prosperity gradually reduced the antipathy towards outsiders. One concrete evidence of this change was the repeal in 1855 of the law that every alien must carry a special license issued by the government; this requirement, it was said, had been 'founded on the suspicion of the foreigner'. There were as yet few competitors to encourage strident nationalism.[1]

A small but increasingly important group of modernizers— including many foreigners or Brazilians closely linked to foreigners—concentrated their attention on the establishment of roads and railways. In the 1850s a stagecoach company, using the best techniques of the day, constructed a macadamized highway with way-stations, warehouses, stables, and pastures, which made it possible to travel by stagecoach from Petrópolis to Juiz de Fora across the Paraíba river and into the province of Minas Gerais, covering the distance in twelve hours instead of the four days previously required. Much of the initial cost was met by a loan of £700,000 raised in London.[2] But a new development in transportation was soon to eclipse the significance of this engineering feat. In 1852 a general railway law was passed which guaranteed 5 per cent interest to investors in approved railway lines. This amount was soon raised to 7 per cent by the addition of a supplemental guarantee by the provinces. Within the next four years

---

[1] Stanley J. Stein, *The Brazilian Cotton Manufacture: Textile Enterprise in an Underdeveloped Area, 1850–1950* (Cambridge, Mass.: Harvard Univ. Press, 1957), p. 211, n. 31; José Thomaz Nabuco de Araujo quoted by Joaquim Nabuco, *Um estadista do imperio, Nabuco de Araujo. Sua vida, suas opiniões, sua época*, [2nd ed. ?], 2 vols. (Rio & São Paulo: Civilização Brasileira & Editôra Nacional, 1936), I, 200; Antonio Augusto da Costa Aguiar, *O Brazil e os brazileiros* (Santos: Typ. Commercial, 1862), p. 76; on the role of foreigners in traditional societies, see William Arthur Lewis, *The Theory of Economic Growth* (London: Allen & Unwin, 1955), p. 180.

[2] Richard P. Momsen, Jr., *Routes Over the Serra do Mar: the Evolution of Transportation in the Highlands of Rio de Janeiro and São Paulo* (Rio: [Privately printed?], 1964), pp. 45–70, 73–5; Louis Agassiz and Elizabeth Cabot Cary Agassiz, *A Journey in Brazil*, 2nd ed. (Boston, Mass.: Ticknor and Fields, 1868), pp. 63–4; Irineo Evangelista de Souza, visconde de Mauá, *Autobiografia* ('*Exposição aos credores e ao público*') seguida de '*O meio circulante no Brasil*', ed. Claudio Ganns, 2nd ed. (Rio: Valverde, 1942), p. 137 n.

The Onset of Modernization

concessions were granted for the construction of railroads inland from Rio de Janeiro, Salvador, Recife, and Santos. In 1864 the railway from Rio de Janeiro reached the Paraíba valley, giving a new boost to coffee production there, and in 1868 a rail link was established between the new coffee lands of the province of São Paulo and the port of Santos. This latter step, as we shall see, was perhaps even more important than the Paraguayan War in eventually bringing down the empire and its institutions, but no observer at that time would have thought it.

The most noticeable feature of the fifteen years from 1850 to 1865 was the political stability of the regime. The constant succession of regional revolts characteristic of the preceding years had ended. The leaders of these protest movements either retired from the political scene or, lured by titles and portfolios, adhered to the coalition government known as the *conciliação*.[1] By avoiding men of exalted party spirit on either side, Pedro II and his advisers managed to tone down the political struggle to the point where it practically ceased. The *conciliação* was a victory for the old order and for those who wished to maintain the political *status quo*. One liberal later spoke of the 'sweet and gentle absolutism' that dominated them at this time.[2] Aside from an electoral reform that, while lessening the direct control of the government over elections, lowered the prestige of those elected and thus strengthened the executive branch, the 1850s were barren of political reform.[3]

In a larger context, however, we can see that this conservatism was the price paid for weakening regional loyalties. Whereas up to that point the landed aristocrats had viewed the central govern-

[1] Theophilo Benedicto Ottoni, *Circular dedicada aos srs. eleitores pela provincia de Minas-Geraes no quatriennio actual e especialmente dirigida aos srs. eleitores de deputados pelo 2º districto eleitoral da mesma provincia para a proxima legislatura*, 2nd ed. (Rio: Typ. do Correio Mercantil, 1860), p. 139; Raimundo Magalhães Júnior, ed., *Três panfletários do segundo reinado: Francisco de Sales Torres Homem e o 'Líbelo do povo'; Justiniano José da Rocha e 'Ação; reação; transação'; Antônio Ferreira Vianna e 'A conferência dos divinos'*, Brasiliana, 286 (São Paulo: Editôra Nacional, 1956), pp. 3–43.

[2] Francisco de Paula Ferreira de Rezende, *Minhas recordações*, Documentos Brasileiros, 45 (Rio: José Olympio, 1944), p. 228.

[3] *Ibid.* pp. 313–14; Euclydes da Cunha, *A margem da história*, 6th ed. (Pôrto: Lello, 1946), p. 280; Nabuco, *Um estadista do imperio*, I, 127–30, 156–8, 279–92; José Wanderley Pinho, *Cotegipe e seu tempo: primeira phase, 1815–1867*, Brasiliana, 85 (São Paulo: Editôra Nacional, 1937), pp. 551–2; Lídia Besouchet, *Mauá e seu tempo* (São Paulo: Anchieta, 1942), pp. 70–2.

27

ment with suspicion—first as foreign and then as radical—they now saw it wedded to their own interests. They, therefore, submitted to the control of the central government and, by allowing the tradition of a centralized national administration to arise, unwittingly contributed to the weakening of their own position once the central government became more responsive to the pressures of rising urban groups.[1]

The war against Paraguay which began in 1865 strengthened the cities and put strains on the traditional Brazilian society which it was unable to ignore. The governing elite was greatly discredited because it took Brazil so long to be victorious. The technological backwardness of the country, the vastness of the sparsely settled western areas and the tenuous links which held those extremities to the Eastern spinal column, the antiquated nature of its labor system, the inefficiency of its bureaucracy filled through nepotism, and all the other qualities of a backward society were brought home not only to the young military officers drawn from the new and rising middle groups, but also to the other urban classes who bore the burden of financing the Brazilian armies. The war also stimulated those specific forces moving toward modernization. Many slaves were freed to fight in the war. Advocates of railroad building received funds to push studies for roads of strategic importance. The production of war materiel stimulated capital formation and industrial growth. And contact with republican institutions in other American countries fostered anti-monarchical sentiments among many Brazilian young men.[2]

---

[1] Americo Brasiliense de Almeida Mello, ed. *Os programas dos partidos e o 2º império. Primeira parte: exposição de principios* (São Paulo: Seckler, 1878), p. 27. This interpretation suggests the ambiguity of 'Federalism', in the name of which many regional revolts had been fought. I suggest that even some of those revolts led by 'Liberals' had been fought in defense of the old order. Later on, 'federalism' became the cry of those who would modernize society, yet when they successfully gained control of the central government, they ruefully found the federalism they had created used to weaken their effectiveness in spreading new ideas and new values. Cf. Nelson Werneck Sodré, *História da burguesia brasileira*, Retratos do Brasil, 22 (Rio: Civilização Brasileira, 1964), pp. 198, 222.

[2] José Maria dos Santos, *Os republicanos paulistas e a abolição* (São Paulo: Martins, 1942), pp. 27–9; José Ewbank da Camara, *Caminhos de ferro estratégicos do Rio Grande do Sul* (Rio: Typ. Americana, 1874), pp. 5, 21–5 and *passim*; Inácio José Veríssimo, *André Rebouças através de sua autobiografia*, Documentos Brasileiros, 20 (Rio: José Olympio, 1939), p. 130; speech of Domingos Andrade Figueira, 11 Oct. 1882, Brazil, Congresso, Câmara dos Deputados, *Anais*, 1882, v, 356; Nabuco, *Um estadista do imperio*, 1, 428.

The Onset of Modernization

In 1868 the political consensus began to give w
rubbed raw by the problems of prosecuting the w
impossible any longer to find the middle way in pt
The dismissal of a ministry led to the re-establishment of a
Liberal Party and the publication of a manifesto in May 1869,
demanding the responsibility of ministers, greater individual freedom, and *laissez faire* economic policies. In November of that
same year, a dissident group formed the Club Radical demanding
even more thoroughgoing reform of the political system. The
following year most of these men joined in issuing the Republican
Manifesto, a document that was to be the rallying cry of those who
opposed the monarchy until their final success in 1889. It is
curious to note how all these documents referred to the forced
recruitment of soldiers from the cities for the war in Paraguay
as one of the sources of their discontent. The landed and aristocratic society should have been able to see the rise of urban power
written on the wall of their mansion of privilege.[1]

It was not only political life that was transformed after the end
of the war. The economic changes initiated before it began now
became more widespread, and fledgling industries began to
emerge. Brazil felt the impact of larger and more important
groups of modernizers who rushed toward what they believed
would be a new era of individual freedom and economic growth.

Railway building was the first area of accelerating change. As
can be seen from Table 2, there was a marked increase in the
mileage constructed in the 1870s, and the pace increased in the next
decade. The bulk of this construction was in the coffee provinces
of Brazil, especially in São Paulo. Once the escarpment had been
conquered by the railway from Santos to Jundiaí (completed in
1868), few barriers presented themselves to those who would
throw their net of steel across the new coffee regions of west-
central and western São Paulo.

With the railroads went the spread of a new crop: coffee.
Pushed by fear of the draft during the Paraguayan War, many

[1] Brasiliense, *Os programas dos partidos*, pp. 29–31, 37–9, 43, 68, 69; João Camillo de Oliveira Tôrres, *A democracia coroada: teoria política do império do Brasil*, 2nd ed. (Petró-polis, R. J.: Editôra Vozes, 1964), pp. 303–9.

The Onset of Modernization

Table 2. *Brazilian Railway Construction, 1851–1920*[a]

Years	New Construction (in Km.)	Total constructed through this period (in Km.)
1851–5	15	15
1856–60	208	223
1861–5	276	499
1866–70	246	745
1871–5	1,056	1,801
1876–80	1,597	3,398
1881–5	3,532	6,930
1886–90	3,007	9,937
1891–5	3,030	12,967
1896–1900	2,349	15,316
1901–5	1,465	16,781
1906–10	4,686	21,467
1911–15	5,280	26,747
1916–20	1,906	28,653

[a] Source: J. Palhano de Jesus, 'Rapida noticia da viação ferrea do Brasil', in Instituto Historico e Geographico Brasileiro, *Diccionario historico, geographico e ethnographico do Brasil* (*commemorativo do primeiro centenario da independencia*), 2 vols. (Rio: Imp. Nacional, 1922), I, 736–7.

pioneers had already fled more settled areas to begin small plantations. Now, where the railroads went, there went the large, modern coffee plantations: straight rows of glistening bushes up and down the rolling countryside where disorderly patches of subsistence crops had once been scattered in the virgin forest. No longer dependent on the mule trains to carry their produce to the waiting ships in Santos, the planters could now move to better lands. Similarly new areas in the province of Minas Gerais were brought into cultivation. Meanwhile, the Paraíba valley entered a period of decline with decaying mansions bespeaking a grander past. Just as coffee had by now eliminated sugar as an important export item, so now coffee of São Paulo displaced the coffee of Rio de Janeiro.[1]

[1] J. P. Wileman, comp., *The Brazilian Year Book, 1908–1909*, 2 vols. (Rio: Brazilian Year Book and London: McCorquodale, n.d.), II, 612; Pierre Monbeig, *Pionniers et planteurs de São Paulo*, Collection des Cahiers de la Fondation Nationale des Sciences Politiques,

30

The Onset of Modernization

The prosperity of the new coffee era brought to the fore a new group of men. The great coffee planters here were not dominated by the traditions of a seignorial past but were drawn from a relatively unfavored group of small landowners and merchants. With the enthusiasm of men on the way up they threw themselves at the land, driving their insufficient slaves, borrowing money, engaging in battles over land, acquiring more, pushing ever westward. They looked upon their land as capital rather than as a guarantee of position. They acquired it in order to produce wealth and, if old solutions did not work, they would try new ones. Their counterparts in Rio province were scandalized because 'the São Paulo planter blindly adopts the newest fad'.[1] These planters were landed entrepreneurs and they demonstrated their innovating spirit by adopting a new crop, using novel techniques to process it, demanding a more plentiful and flexible source of labor than could be provided by slavery, and enthusiastically welcoming the railroads, which they often built themselves. Eventually, they also invested in industry. Many of them were to be among the most vocal elements to demand political change in the late 1880s.[2]

Yet, at first, the existing government was strengthened by the rise of coffee. Brazil now enjoyed an era of general prosperity marked by favorable balances of trade, balanced budgets, and rising governmental revenues. Whereas imports exceeded exports during eleven of the fifteen years ending in 1865, in the following fifteen years the balance of trade was never unfavorable.[3] Nevertheless, inexorable forces were at work to weaken the old regime.

28 (Paris: Colin, 1952), p. 116; Afonso Arinos de Melo Franco, *Um estadista da república* (*Afrânio de Melo Franco e seu tempo*), Documentos Brasileiros, 85, 3 vols. (Rio: José Olympio, 1955), I, 230–1; Sodré, *História da burguesia*, pp. 182, 185.

[1] *Novidades*, 28 Feb. 1888, quoted by Stanley J. Stein, *Vassouras, a Brazilian Coffee County, 1850–1900*, Harvard Historical Studies, 69 (Cambridge, Mass.: Harvard Univ. Press, 1957), p. 252.

[2] Monbeig, *Pionniers et planteurs*, pp. 121–5, 128–9; Celso Furtado, *The Economic Growth of Brazil: a Survey from Colonial to Modern Times*, transl. Ricardo W. de Aguiar and Eric Charles Drysdale (Berkeley and Los Angeles: Univ. of California Press, 1963), p. 126; Fernando Henrique Cardoso, 'Condições sociais da industrialização de São Paulo', *Revista brasiliense*, no. 28 (Mar.–Apr. 1960), pp. 34–7; Sérgio Buarque de Holanda, *Raízes do Brasil*, 2nd ed., Documentos Brasileiros, 1 (Rio: José Olympio, 1948), pp. 258–61; Santos, *Os republicanos paulistas*, pp. 236–58.

[3] Sodré, *História da burguesia*, p. 118.

The Onset of Modernization

Increasing export trade encouraged the rise of new urban interests. Many Brazilians now became merchants, and a growing number of city dwellers administered the additional banks, transport companies, and insurance corporations which continued to be organized to serve the rising demands of coffee commerce. The expanding revenues derived from coffee also financed a proliferating bureaucracy in the capitals to deal with the increasingly complex problems of administering a prosperous country. Smaller towns, such as Itú, Sorocaba, and Campinas, became more important as distributing centers for foodstuffs and supplies in a monocultural area that had previously been self-sufficient.[1] Smaller port cities like Santos and Niterói shared in the new prosperity. Urban growth became characteristic, as can be seen in Table 3.

Three types of city dwellers deserve special mention: military officers, engineers, and industrialists. The officers had not been drawn from the landed aristocracy but from the cities, and during

Table 3. *Population of Selected Brazilian Municipalities, 1872–1920*[a]

Municipality	1872	1890	1900	1920
Federal District	274,972	522,651	746,749	1,157,873
São Paulo	27,557	64,934	239,820	579,033
Salvador	112,641	174,412	205,813	283,422
Recife	101,535	111,536	113,106	238,843
Belém	53,150	50,046	96,560	236,402
Pôrto Alegre	35,843	52,421	73,674	179,263
Curitiba	11,730	24,553	49,755	78,986

[a] Source: J. P. Wileman, comp., *The Brazilian Year Book, 1909* (n.p., n.d.), p. 35; Instituto Historico e Geographico Brasileiro, *Diccionario historico, geographico e ethnographico do Brasil (commemorativo do primeiro centenario da independencia)*, 2 vols. (Rio: Imp. Nacional, 1922), i, facing 247; cf. J. F. Normano, *Brazil, a Study of Economic Types* (Chapel Hill: Univ. of North Carolina Press, 1935), p. 111.

[1] Nícia Villela Luz, 'O papel das classes médias brasileiras no movimento republicano', *Revista de história*, xxviii, no. 57 (Jan.–Mar. 1964), p. 21; Johann Jacob von Tschudi, *Viagem às províncias do Rio de Janeiro e São Paulo* (São Paulo: Martins, 1953), pp. 48–9.

the Paraguayan War they had developed contempt for the *bacharéis* produced by the traditional educational institutions. They were dissatisfied with their status and looked to the future with hope of a better era. Closely linked to them were a new group of engineers, civilians who had either begun their careers as military engineers or had been trained at the Escola Central created in 1858 and renamed Escola Politécnica in 1874. The engineers were also in close contact with another new-fledged group formed by the industrialists. The Paraguayan War had stimulated a great deal of consumer manufacturing and, after the end of the war, the upstart capitalists had turned their attention to the civilian market. By the mid-1870s iron foundries, textile mills, breweries, shoe factories, and the hat industry had all attained significant importance. Textile manufacturing shifted away from the decadent northern areas of Bahia and invaded the prospering south-central region where the industrial tradition really got its start. To these three clusters must be added the professional men who, despite their education in the traditional law and medical colleges, were impelled by their contact with urban society to adopt the new values of the city and the new ideas imported from Europe.[1]

The new interests were divorced from the land and skeptical of aristocratic values. The complete dominance of personal relations began to weaken in the cities and nostalgic words were soon being uttered about the good old days in contrast to what Joaquim Nabuco, in his autobiography, called the 'mercenary instinct of our time'. The idea that men should be placed according to their ability began to receive wider acceptance.[2] The growth of an export economy created a distinctive culture, oriented towards

---

[1] Francisco Clementino de San Tiago Dantas, *Dois momentos de Rui Barbosa: conferências* (Rio: Casa de Rui Barbosa, 1951), pp. 18–19; Percy Alvin Martin, 'Causes of the Collapse of the Brazilian Empire', *Hispanic American Historical Review*, IV (1921), 25; *Revista de engenharia*, IV (1882), 1; *SAJ*, XII, no. 11 (8 June 1875), p. 8; Nícia Villela Luz, 'O industrialismo e o desenvolvimento econômico do Brasil', *Revista de história*, XXVII, no. 56 (Oct.–Dec. 1963), p. 276; Sodré, *História da burguesia*, p. 151; Stein, *Brazilian Cotton Manufacture*, p. 21.

[2] Deposition of Maxwell, Wright, and Co. quoted by Nabuco, *Um estadista do imperio*, I, 188–9; Joaquim Nabuco, *Minha formação*, [? ed.], Documentos Brasileiros, 90 (Rio: José Olympio, 1957), p. 188; Brasiliense, *Os programas dos partidos*, p. 32; Péricles Madureira do Pinho, *Luís Tarqüínio, pioneiro da justiça social no Brasil* (Salvador: Imp. Vitória, 1944), pp. 71, 73.

Europe, as can be seen in the changes in fashions, the modification of eating habits, the use of novel architectural styles, and the adoption of urban improvements. European opinions came to be highly valued by these urban classes. This new sector of the population believed in change and 'progress'. Despite occasional despair in the face of deep pools of stagnation—'Oh, good God, it is impossible to make this country move!' exclaimed André Rebouças—they pushed steadily toward development. They were the modernizers. Their view of man's relation to his environment was summed up by José Maria da Silva Paranhos (first), *visconde* do Rio Branco: 'In the nineteenth century the sciences predominate...and their discoveries...are variously applied to extend the dominion of man over the external world...In a word, it is the century of industry.'[1] The century of industry, and of many other novel ways applauded by this set. This rising group of 'changers' would restructure the country.

And ideas were the weapons with which they struggled against the established order. Pushed by broad forces of economic and social change—coffee exports and urbanization—these individuals found themselves in new situations for which the old concepts were no longer suitable. Faced with new economic opportunities and new places in society, they tended to discard those attitudes and values that stood in their way. It was with positive eagerness that they sought out new ideas more in keeping with their bourgeois position.[2]

[1] André Rebouças, *Diário e notas autobiográficas*, ed. Ana Flora and Inácio José Verissimo, Documentos Brasileiros, 12 (Rio: José Olympio, 1938), p. 172; *visconde* do Rio Branco quoted by Roque Spencer Maciel de Barros, *A ilustração brasileira e a idéia de universidade*, Universidade de São Paulo, Cadeira de História e Filosofia da Educação, Boletim, 241 (2) (São Paulo: Universidade de São Paulo, 1959), p. 192; on his modernizing role see Lídia Besouchet, *José Ma. Paranhos, visconde do Rio Branco. Ensaio histórico-biográfico* (Rio: Valverde, 1945), pp. 213–16; José Maria da Silva Paranhos 2º, *barão* do Rio Branco, *O visconde do Rio Branco*, ed. Renato Mendonça, [? ed.] (Rio: A Noite Editôra, n.d.), pp. 216–22.

[2] One Brazilian insisted in 1879 that 'What brings progress is not moral laws, but... ideas', Sílvio Romero quoted by Barros, *A ilustração brasileira*, p. 23. Cf. Leon Festinger, *A Theory of Cognitive Dissonance* (Evanston, Ill. and White Plains, N.Y.: Row, Peterson, 1957), pp. 273–5; T. S. Epstein, *Economic Development and Social Change in South India* (Manchester, England: Manchester Univ. Press, 1948), pp. 326–35; see esp. foreword by Arthur Lewis, p. ix; it does not follow, as implied by Lewis, that economic opportunities can be as quickly seized or as fully utilized in societies that must change their ideas or attitudes in this way as in those that begin from such a base.

These concepts came from abroad. To be swept up in the currents of European thought was not to betray Brazilian values, but to reassert the proper place of Brazil within Western civilization. They wished to Europeanize or Westernize their country: 'Our evils are many; but the truly fundamental one is our spirit of timidity—Chinese, lazy, late, inimical to newness, passive and accommodating. We must change our customs...And I know of no better way than to open freely the doors of the Empire to the foreigner.'[1] Foreigners and their ideas were more welcome than they had ever been before.

But Brazilians accepted only those ideas that suited their needs and not just any notion cast up upon their shores. Philosophies of history which suggested that all societies move along the same path to a common end suited the modernizers who could then believe that Brazil was not really different, but only younger, and that its future was the modern, industrialized society of Europe. Modernizing intellectuals typically believe that steady progress indefinitely stretched out into the future is the normal state of affairs for societies that do their part by constant striving. The suggestion that progress was inevitable strengthened the determination of these Brazilians despite the pessimism created by a realistic analysis of their country.[2]

The ideals of European liberalism were especially attractive since they had been similarly employed by the European middle class. The emphasis upon the rights and freedom of the individual would serve to weaken the paralyzing hold upon him which society now exercised and release his energies for progress. The belief in equality insofar as it meant the end of special privilege and the breakdown of those distinctions that prevented mobility from one class to another—but not that equality that suggested an end to classes—was seized upon as an effective weapon against the *status quo*. The Republican Manifesto of 1870 spoke for all the critics of the old order when it pointed to 'privilege' as the

---

[1] Aureliano Cândido Tavares Bastos, *Cartas do Solitário*, 3rd ed., Brasiliana, 115 (São Paulo: Editôra Nacional, 1938), p. 414; also see Barros, *A ilustração brasileira*, p. 165.

[2] Barros, *A ilustração brasileira*, pp. 25–6, 193–4, 196; John Friedman, 'Intellectuals in Developing Societies', *Kyklos...International Review for Social Sciences*, XIII (1960), 526.

'social and political formula of our country—religious privilege, race privilege, educational privilege, and privilege of position'. It went on to defend the individual against the state, decrying the condition

where the will of the citizen and his individual liberty are dependent on the agents of the government...Liberty of conscience nullified by a privileged Church, economic liberty stifled by a restrictive legislation, liberty of the press subordinated to the jurisdiction of Government functionaries, freedom of education suppressed by the arbitrary inspection of the government and the official monopoly, individual liberty subject to preventive imprisonment, to the draft, to the discipline of the National Guard, deprived even of the guarantee of *habeas corpus*... such are in practice the real conditions of the present system of government.[1]

Other Brazilians preferred the precepts of Auguste Comte to those of liberalism. French Positivism was in vogue after the Paraguayan War. The adoption of this philosophy was both an attempt to take on a scientific outlook toward the world and a direct attack upon the traditional order. Beginning in 1850 young military engineers began to find in Positivism an organizing principle for their budding scientific knowledge which, while not requiring deep philosophic perceptions, could strengthen the prestige of science in a pre-scientific society. A book on slavery published in 1865 first applied the principles of Auguste Comte to the Brazilian social situation. Two years later Benjamin Constant Botelho de Magalhães presented before the military engineering school a thesis on mathematics impregnated with Comtian philosophy. He later argued that, instead of sterile 'metaphysics', the government should administer 'a good system of scientific education' oriented toward Positivism.[2] He soon became a teacher at the military academy and exerted a preponderant

---

[1] Brasiliense, *Os programas dos partidos*, pp. 62, 68–9; the Liberal Party also saw the individual standing against the corporate society, p. 29; Rui Barbosa agreed the republic was a direct attack on special privileges, quoted by Nícia Villela Luz, *Aspectos do nacionalismo econômico brasileiro. Os esforços em prol da industrialização*, Coleção da 'Revista de história', 16 (São Paulo: 'Revista de história', 1959), p. 83.

[2] Benjamin Constant Botelho de Magalhães quoted by Barros, *A ilustração brasileira*, pp. 122–3.

influence on the education of a whole generation of engineers and military officers. He was instrumental in the conversion in the mid-1870s of Miguel Lemos and Raimundo Teixeira Mendes, who were later to be the leaders of the Positivistic inner core. Although the number of orthodox Positivists remained small and their direct influence on affairs negligible, wide were the effects of the doctrine in weakening the hold of tradition among bureaucrats, merchants, engineers and professional men.[1]

Many, of course, chose to oppose change, and they found in religion the surest ground for the defense of a hierarchical society and a stable political order. Whereas one cannot speak of Brazil as being earlier dominated by devout Catholicism, the very inertia of the regime had meant the dominance of a Catholic viewpoint, restricting religious liberty and dampening the belief in the individual. Now, faced with these threatening new ideas, those who sought an effective defense against change dusted off their Catholic heritage and brought it up to date. The amoral nature of modern society expressed in a secular state, secular education, secular mores, ideas, or economic activity menaced the settled order of things, and a return to religion could perhaps still save it. To fight off the secular waves that threatened to engulf the system, it was considered necessary, as P.ᵉ Júlio Maria put it, to 'Catholicize Brazil'.

One result of these sharpening distinctions was a struggle over Church–State relations. The ancient right of the Portuguese dynasty to grant or withhold permission for the reading of papal bulls was brought into question, and precipitous government action led two bishops to jail. Despite much ambiguity, the modernizers generally sided with the regalists. The ultramontanist Soriano de Souza saw the cleavage: 'Only two opinions could be held, opinions that were diametrically opposed. On the one side were the incredulous, sectarians, rationalists, demagogues, in a word, all those for whom there does not exist either supernatural

---

[1] Ivan Monteiro de Barros Lins, *História do positivismo no Brasil*, Brasiliana, 322 (São Paulo: Editôra Nacional, 1964), pp. 233–99; João Cruz Costa, *Contribuição à história das idéias no Brasil (O desenvolvimento da filosofia no Brasil e a evolução histórica nacional)*, Documentos Brasileiros, 86 (Rio: José Olympio, 1956), pp. 142, 146, 161–7; Barros, *A ilustração brasileira*, pp. 117–19, 121–2.

order, or real religion, or Church, but only a God-state personified in Caesar, with his laws and his sanctions of punishments and prizes...On the other were all the Catholics.' Yet a leading churchman was also right when he pointed out that to destroy the prestige of the Church was to threaten the throne. 'The monarchy must choose: either collaborate with the Church in the great work...of a Catholic reconstruction of Brazil; or drown itself in the wave of anarchic skepticism that rises all the way from the hut to the palace. It is no longer possible to hide the dangers that threaten royalty.' It would never be possible, he added, to link 'Catholic, monarchical majesty with the anarchical doctrines of free inquiry, freedom of worship, secularization of education, independence of the civil power, etc.'. He knew that the modernizers were foes of both the Church and the Crown.[1]

The enemies of the monarchy were to drive home the validity of this claim. 'First of all,' said the republican Anibal Falcão, 'the establishment of the Republic is equivalent to the declaration of complete spiritual liberty.' The Republican Manifesto had made clear in 1870 that 'God has nothing to do with the life of the State, which is a community apart from and foreign to any spiritual interest'. The republicans, once they were in power, separated Church and State, instituted civil marriage, secularized the cemeteries, and established freedom of religion. They also revamped the curriculum of the law schools in order to conform with the new values.[2]

Whether the complex of religion-monarchy-privilege-slavery were logically linked to each other or not, they were so linked in the minds of those who lived at that time, and this is, perhaps, the only meaningful reality for the historian. A literary critic later recalled, no doubt with some exaggeration, that

---

[1] Júlio Maria, Soriano de Souza, and D. Vital, quoted by Barros, *A ilustração brasileira*, pp. 39, 45n., 52n., respectively.
[2] Anibal Falcão quoted by Barros, *A ilustração brasileira*, p. 174; cf. statement by Silva Jardim (another republican) on p. 169; 'Manifesto Republicano', in Brasiliense, *Os programas dos partidos*, p. 82; João Camillo de Oliveira Tôrres, *A formação do federalismo no Brasil*, Brasiliana, 308 (São Paulo: Editôra Nacional, 1961), p. 37; Franco, *Um estadista da república*, I, 133; it is ironic that the defenders of the old order also appealed to Europe, i.e. to the Vatican Council and European Catholic writers, Cruz Costa, *Contribuição à história das idéias*, pp. 120–9.

Until 1868 the reigning Catholicism had not suffered in these parts the least tremor; the spiritual, Catholic, and ecclesiastical philosophy not the most insignificant opposition; the authority of monarchical institutions not the smallest serious attack from any sector of the population; slavery and the traditional rights of the practically feudal large landowners not the most indirect opposition...Everything slept beneath the mantle of the monarch...Suddenly, the instability of all things was made clear by a subterranean movement long in preparation ...A flock of new ideas fluttered its wings over our heads.[1]

One of these ornithological specimens was republicanism, and the republicans played the principal role in bringing down a major bastion of the traditional society. Like the orthodox Positivists, they formed a small but closely knit group. Unlike the Positivists, they were able to take advantage of temporary liaisons, and, through disciplined action, exercise what power they had at precisely the most effective moments. One of their techniques was to lure into their ranks some of the opponents of modern change. When slavery was abolished in 1888 bitter planters, intent on revenge, filled out the ranks of the Republican Party. Even earlier, groups displaced from privileged positions had misguidedly looked upon the republic as a way of restoring traditional values.[2]

But the movement's greatest strength was derived from those interests that demanded new structures to deal with new situations. The entrepreneurially minded planters of São Paulo were dissatisfied with the slowness with which the imperial government reacted to new conditions and, perhaps most important, the continued predominance in government of men drawn either from the decadent northeastern sugar areas or the declining coffee regions of the Paraíba valley. The coffee planters of Minas Gerais favored a republic as a means of wiping out the hegemony of the mining region within that state. The rising new sector of urban industrialists were also dissatisfied with the policies of the empire. Even those who admired the emperor were disgusted by

---

[1] Sílvio Romero quoted by Barros, *A ilustração brasileira*, p. 30.
[2] Evaristo de Moraes, *A campanha abolicionista (1879–1888)* (Rio: Leite Ribeiro, Freitas Bastos, Spicer, 1924), pp. 393–5; Luz, 'O papel das classes médias', pp. 13–27; José Maria dos Santos, *Os republicanos paulistas*, *passim*.

his insistence that Brazilian capitalists should concentrate, as in the past, on advancing funds to the profligate planters. The abolition of slavery meant an expanded money economy and an increase in consumption; the failure of the old regime to expand the currency despite these growing needs added to the dissatisfaction of both manufacturers and planters. The stock-market bubble which succeeded the overthrow of the empire resulted, at least in part, from long pent-up desires for easy money and investment opportunities.[1]

So, many of those who desired change saw the republic as their hope. Although the republicans did not acknowledge until 1889 that revolution was the end toward which they moved, most of them were agreed that the traditional society must be destroyed.[2] Their position within the ranks of the modernizers is clearly reflected in the 1870s by the support given by *A republica* to those who advocated

administrative decentralization, free navigation of our rivers, open coasting trade, development of commercial relations with the American peoples, the acquisition of electric telegraph, the expansion of commercial freedom, the establishment of a vast system of railroads; freedom of worship, the encouragement of immigration; electoral reform based on direct suffrage...reform of our Parliament based on regularly elected Senate and proportional representation, and, finally, the democratization of all our governing formulas.[3]

When the forces of reform and change had isolated the monarchy as the chief obstacle to continued change, it was only logical that the republicans should spearhead the movement to overthrow the empire. By skillful manipulation of military officers long dis-

---

[1] J. F. Normano, *Brazil, a Study of Economic Types* (Chapel Hill, N.C.: Univ. of North Carolina Press, 1935), pp. 116–17; Franco, *Um estadista da república*, p. 231; Anfriso Fialho, *Um terço de seculo (1852–1885): recordações* (Rio: Typ. da 'Constituinte', 1885), *passim*; Rebouças, *Diário*, p. 189; Roberto Simonsen, 'As consequências econômicas da abolição', *Revista do Arquivo Municipal de São Paulo*, XLVII (1938), 260–8; Sodré, *História da burguesia*, p. 198.

[2] George C. A. Boehrer, *Da monarquia à república; história do Partido Republicano do Brasil (1870–1889)*, transl. Berenice Xavier (Rio: Ministério da Educação e Cultura, Serviço de Documentação, 1954), pp. 237–9.

[3] *A republica*, 7 Aug. 1873, quoted by Carlos Pontes, *Tavares Bastos (Aureliano Candido), 1839–1875*, Brasiliana, 136 (São Paulo: Editôra Nacional, 1939), pp. 338–9.

satisfied with their place in the imperial sun, they deposed the emperor without forceful opposition in 1889.

Yet, paradoxically, the emperor himself was not the least of the modernizers. The man Pedro II cannot be confused with his position. He had been raised on the ideals of the Enlightenment, and he unquestionably believed in individual freedom, social mobility, and economic growth. He had been to Europe and the United States and had seen and admired industrialized societies. He was probably the best educated man in Brazil, certainly the one with the broadest knowledge of his country within the world context. He may even have been ashamed of the pomp and ceremony surrounding his office. At least he publicly bemoaned his fate at finding himself emperor and expressed a desire for a republic and, for himself, the position of a teacher. Privately, he urged the liberalization of the laws regarding the religion of the state, the attraction of immigrants, the reform of the land tenure system through a land tax, the spread of education and the establishment of agricultural schools, the adoption of scientific farming, the extension of the transport system, the reduction and final abolition of Negro slavery, the appointment of public servants through demonstrated merit, and the extension of the suffrage.[1]

But the position was more powerful than the man who occupied it. The Crown was the heart of the traditional society. As its bearer Pedro II was responsible for maintaining stability, perpetuating the empire, and safeguarding society against the forces of disintegration. As suggested earlier, the enthroning of a powerful and dynastically legitimate monarch was really a step backward, a step away from the chaotic transition to modernity. This preserving task was not only a divine charge upon the emperor, but Pedro II could not afford, politically, to abandon that role

[1] Mary Wilhelmine Williams, *Dom Pedro the Magnanimous, Second Emperor of Brazil* (Chapel Hill, N.C.: Univ. of North Carolina Press, 1937), pp. 214, 294–7; Hélio Vianna, 'Programa de governo, por D. Pedro II, dado ao visconde de Paraná (1853)', *Jornal do comércio*, 16 Oct. 1964; Hélio Vianna, 'Relações do Poder Moderador com o Poder Executivo, conforme D. Pedro II', *Jornal do comércio*, 31 May 1964; Hélio Vianna, 'Instruções de D. Pedro II ao presidente do conselho, marquês de Olinda', *Jornal do comércio*, 22 May 1964. These and subsequently cited articles by Hélio Vianna have been gathered in his *D. Pedro I e D. Pedro II: acréscimos às suas biografias*, Brasiliana, 330 (São Paulo: Editôra Nacional, 1966).

and undercut his regime. His failure to push through reform did not derive from an alleged absence of good men, but, rather, from the realization that he would be failing his calling and sacrificing his throne if he ceased to count on those who opposed change and began to rely on those who proposed it. Before the urban public he appeared invariably as the symbol of rigidity. He accepted this necessity, and, when the government was being attacked, he proposed the creation of an official newspaper to 'defend the immutable principle of authority'.[1] His policies were vacillating when it came to pushing through significant reforms, and his support of change was almost always secretive except when it was either innocuous or ambiguous, as in the Church–State controversy. In the end he had to yield to the innovators anyway. It might have been better if he had imitated his father by placing himself at the head of the insurgents, becoming first *caudillo* of a republican Brazil. Pedro II did not do this, and, given his personality, it is hard to conceive of his having done so.[2] So he was swept aside by the rising forces of modernization.

The emperor's ambivalent position is made clear by the issue of slavery. The modernizers demanded the end of this institution. There were not enough slaves to satisfy the demands of rising agricultural entrepreneurship, and industrial capitalists apparently found slavery unsuitable to their needs. The spread of European attitudes in the cities cast a pall over such a 'barbarous' device for organizing labor. But the emperor could not make up his mind. He encouraged the initial consideration of measures regarding the emancipation of the slaves, then, in 1868, dismissed the boldly imaginative ministry that was moving in that direction. A compromise solution that freed the children of all slaves born after 1871 seemed to him to combine the best of both traditional and modern worlds. The emperor did not become interested in the question again until the 1880s, when young abolitionists began a virulent campaign in behalf of abolition. But even then he continued to blow hot and cold, until finally, during his absence in

[1] Hélio Vianna, 'Instruções de D.Pedro II ao marquês de Olinda e ao visconde de Abaeté', *Jornal do comércio*, 5 June 1964.
[2] Richard M. Morse, 'Some Themes of Brazilian History', *The South Atlantic Quarterly*, LXI (1962), 171–82.

1888, his daughter bowed to the inevitable and signed an abolition law. On being informed of the measure he expressed doubt about the wisdom of such a *hasty* move.[1]

And he was right, for it signaled the end of his reign and the beginning of a new era. Men devoid of traditional values soon replaced him. Free from the sanctions of the old order, secular, amoral, striving to rise, they were ruthless in their struggle to do so and did not hesitate to depose the moribund ruler in November 1889. Coffee planters now struggled for power with the urban-based military officers, finally winning out in 1894. New values and attitudes were now more widely accepted. Fortunes were made and lost on the stock market overnight. Monetary wealth was now partially accepted as a mark of status. Immorality and corruption seemed to increase. A shocked British missionary wrote that 'The people are more given over to wickedness than they were in the old days of the empire', and the rapidity of the change created a nostalgia for the old regime of honorable men.[2]

The conflict of old and new was clearly expressed in the fanatic, mystical folk movement led by Antônio 'Conselheiro' in the backlands of Bahia. The people of this area, cut off from the Western world and untouched by modernity, were alienated by the new regime. Refusing to disperse, this community successfully fought off the forces of the republic for some time, and were, therefore, falsely accused of receiving aid from monarchists. Urban dwellers considered their medieval spirit an affront to the modern vision of reality; so they destroyed this uncomfortable node of tradition in 1897.[3]

---

[1] Santos, *Os republicanos paulistas*, pp. 45–57; Osorio Duque Estrada, *A abolição (esboço histórico—1831–1888)* (Rio: Leite Ribeiro e Maurillo, 1918), pp. 299–315. A contrary viewpoint on the emperor's role in the abolition of slavery is presented by Heitor Lyra, *História de D. Pedro II, 1825–1891*, Brasiliana, 133, 3 vols. (São Paulo: Editôra Nacional, 1938–40), III, 3–37 (but see p. 12n.), and Moraes, *Campanha abolicionista*, pp. 85–7; it is largely a matter of judgement regarding imponderables and I believe Duque Estrada essentially correct.

[2] *Help for Brazil: Occasional Papers*, no. 2 (July 1893), p. 2; cf. Ronald E. Wraith and Edgar Simpkins, *Corruption in Developing Countries Including Britain until 1880* (London: Allen & Unwin, 1962), pp. 11–53; Luís Martins, *O patriarca e o bacharel* (São Paulo: Martins, 1953), *passim*.

[3] Euclides da Cunha, *Os sertões (Campanha de Canudos)*, 23rd ed. (Rio: Francisco Alves, 1954); José Maria Bello, *A History of Modern Brazil, 1889–1964*, transl. James L. Taylor (Stanford, California: Stanford Univ. Press, 1966), pp. 150–1; Arthur Silveira da Motta,

ernizers, in their uncompromising drive toward
supported by the immigrants, alien to the attitudes
ing order and anxious to make Brazil over in the
ir own European experience. As slavery approached
its end, coffee planters satisfied their demands for labor with the
Italians, Spaniards, and others that began to pour into the country.
Whereas for the period 1855–84 the average annual number of
immigrants to São Paulo was only 1,135, during the next thirty
years the average was 46,492. The immigrant, however, was
often not satisfied to remain on the land without its possession,
and, in addition to those who returned home or re-migrated to
Argentina, thousands flocked to the cities. They carried with
them their entrepreneurial skills, competing with the relatives
of the plantation owners for whom they had worked, and
frequently exceeding them in ability and success. Much of
Brazil's industrial growth has been the result of immigrant effort,
although movement in this direction had started before their
arrival.[1]

Industry became steadily more important after 1889. Whereas
only 626 of the industrial enterprises responding to a 1920 census
had been created before 1889, 6,946 more were established between 1890 and 1914. Most of these factories were for the production of small consumer goods, but some of them attained
significant proportions and had moved far from handicraft. The
most important industries were textile mills, tanneries, shoe and
hat factories, breweries, and cereal mills, but the production of
paper, glass, cigarettes, soap, and matches was also significant.
In addition, there were several noteworthy foundries and iron-
works that produced hardware, agricultural machinery, and railway cars and wagons. Hydro-electric power plants were then

---

barão de Jaceguay, *De aspirante a almirante*, [*Vol. IV:*] *1860–1902; minha fé de officio documentada, 1893–1900* (Mendes, R. J.: Typ. Cia. Industrial Santa Rita, 1906), p. 170; the
transitional character of Brazilian society at this time and subsequently is reflected in the
strange mixture of fetishism and atheism found in central Brazil by Arnold Henry Savage
Landor, *Across Unknown South America*, 2 vols. (London and New York: Hodder &
Stoughton, 1913), I, 48, 92, 110–11.

[1] Alfredo Ellis Júnior, *Populações paulistas*, Brasiliana, 27 (São Paulo: Editôra Nacional,
1934), p. 70; cf. the perceptive comedy by Jorge Andrade, 'Os ossos do barão', in '*A
escada' e 'Os ossos do barão*' (São Paulo: Brasiliense, 1964).

established to relieve industries of the necessity to import coal. In 1890 Brazil had a total output of 10,350 horsepower in electricity; by 1915 this figure had risen to 396,580.[1]

Still, there were obstacles to the continued growth of manufacturing enterprises. Although the extension of railways greatly aided the development of industry by expanding consumer markets, many areas remained untouched. A French observer noted that outside Rio de Janeiro and São Paulo industry was very dispersed. 'One finds tiny factories in small straggling villages which one would never guess beforehand to be industrial centers.' Because of the size of the country and the persistently high cost of transport, each factory controlled 'a kind of protected zone within which it enjoys an absolute monopoly...having its own circle of consumers upon whose forced fidelity it may rely'.[2] Economies of scale were precluded and Brazil still had far to go before it could be considered industrial. But the point is that Brazil had embarked upon a course of industrialization.

The production of agricultural machinery is especially suggestive of the larger changes within this society. The building of thrashing machines, coffee hullers, and sugar mills had become an important part of the country's industrial output.[3] The application of modern technology to agricultural production is a basic aim of modernizing countries and, slow as it may have been, the movement in this direction serves to differentiate Brazil at this time from what it had been in 1850.

The 'whir and din of the factory' now characterized the large coffee plantations, in sharp contrast to the universally backward

---

[1] Normano, *Brazil*, pp. 99, 103–5 (given the short-lived nature of enterprises in developing economies, these industrial census figures must be used with caution), 108; T. Oscar Marcondes de Souza, *O estado de São Paulo: physico, politico, economico e administrativo* (São Paulo: Universal, 1915), pp. 146–67; Reginald Lloyd, *et al.*, eds., *Twentieth Century Impressions of Brazil: Its History, People, Commerce, Industries and Resources* (London: Lloyd's Greater Britain Publishing Co., 1913), p. 645; Ernani Silva Bruno, *História e tradições da cidade de São Paulo*, Documentos Brasileiros, 80, 3 vols. (Rio: José Olympio, 1954), III, 1163–4, 1169–70, 1173, 1174, 1176, 1179, 1182, 1185; Arthur de Barros Alves Dias, *The Brazil of Today; a Book of Commercial, Political and Geographical Information on Brazil...*(Nivelles, Belgium: Lanneau & Despret, 1907), pp. 452, 464–5; Clayton Sedgwick Cooper, *The Brazilians and Their Country* (New York: Stokes, 1917), p. 197; *São Paulo de ontem, de hoje, e de amanhã*, VII, no. 25 (Aug. 1947), p. 47.
[2] Pierre Denis, *Brazil...*(London: Unwin, 1911), p. 132.
[3] Souza, *O estado de São Paulo*, pp. 165–6.

techniques of that earlier era.[1] Elaborate equipment was installed for processing the coffee, although not for its cultivation since land was still cheap and fertile. Smaller planters sent their coffee to the towns to be processed mechanically. The coffee was now carried to the center of the large plantation by railroad instead of oxcart, and one estate had more than forty miles of track in its privately owned system.[2] The harvest converted a large *fazenda* 'into a hive of industry': the coffee was first run through a pulping machine, and then fermented in tanks to remove the saccharine matter. After drying on terraces where they were constantly turned for several weeks, the stripped berries were successively placed in a purifier, a thrasher, and a polishing machine. The beans were then ready for sacking and shipping.[3] On a well-run plantation 500 sacks of 32 pounds each could be prepared every twelve hours.[4]

The existence in 1914 of several agricultural schools is an especially sharp departure from conditions in Brazil as they had been in 1850. The best-known of these schools at that time was maintained by the state of São Paulo in the town of Piracicaba. The curriculum included soils analysis, stock raising, botany, physics, and agricultural engineering, and every student was required to work on the experimental farm for two hours each day. This work included 'handling a plow, rigging a harrow, managing a mower or reaper', as well as the repair of such machinery.[5] This description of the school suggests new attitudes in an agricultural society; but it may also explain why enrollment remained small.

[1] (Mrs) Marie Robinson Wright, *The New Brazil: Its Resources and Attractions, Historical, Descriptive, and Industrial*, 2nd ed. (Philadelphia: Barrie, 1907), p. 260.

[2] Denis, *Brazil*, p. 223; Monbeig, *Pionniers et planteurs*, p. 87; but on use of machinery for coffee cultivation see illustration in J. C. Oakenfull, *Brazil (1913)* (Frome, England: Butler & Tanner, 1914), facing p. 232; Nevin Otto Winter, *Brazil and Her People of To-Day: an Account of the Customs, Characteristics, Amusements, History and Advancement of the Brazilians, and the Development and Resources of Their Country* (Boston, Mass.: Page, 1910), pp. 132, 268.

[3] Wright, *The New Brazil*, pp. 262–3; Landor, *Across Unknown South America*, I, 30; Winter, *Brazil and Her People of To-Day*, pp. 268–70.

[4] Wright, *The New Brazil*, p. 257 (on similar transformations on a much lesser scale in sugar agriculture see p. 448); Monbeig, *Pionniers et planteurs*, pp. 87–8.

[5] Winter, *Brazil and Her People of To-Day*, p. 226; Souza, *O estado de São Paulo*, p. 390.

Other kinds of technical education were also available. The engineering school in São Paulo opened in 1893 and Mackenzie Institute in the same city began to offer an engineering degree in 1896. Along with the similar school in Rio de Janeiro and the School of Mines in Ouro Prêto, both organized in the 1870s, these institutions inevitably inculcated new attitudes toward the natural world and a new awareness of the possibility of human progress.[1] But the modernizers now discovered that they could not agree on the next steps to be taken. While engineers and entrepreneurs had once cooperated with coffee planters in bringing down the empire, they soon found themselves in opposing camps. Coffee interests had been the principal beneficiaries of the changes so far, and the American ambassador reported in 1907 that 'never before has the country and especially everyone connected with the Government been so much under the influence of the coffee planters as at the present'.[2] The industrialists, even those who were brothers or cousins of the planters, soon realized that those who relied on commodity exports could not be counted on to help foster industrialization. As in political revolutions, some leaders were satisfied with moderate measures, while others were anxious to push on still further toward an entirely new order. Some hint of this struggle may be gathered from the intense debates over tariffs in the years before and after the First World War.[3] The industrialists wished to use the techniques of the developed world in competition with it and clearly believed industrialization to be a national goal. Only the artificial barrier of war was available to them as yet, but they were developing their arguments and their power.

It is evident that Brazil by 1914 had begun to move along the path toward a modern society.[4] Some of the changes that had

[1] Fernando de Azevedo, *A cultura brasileira: introdução ao estudo de cultura no Brasil*, 4th ed., Obras completas de Fernando de Azevedo, 13 (São Paulo: Melhoramentos, 1964), p. 622.
[2] G. L. Lorillard quoted by E. Bradford Burns, *The Unwritten Alliance: Rio Branco and Brazilian–American Relations* (New York: Columbia Univ. Press, 1966), p. 5.
[3] Luz, *Aspectos do nacionalismo econômico*, pp. 45–151.
[4] It is not argued that Brazil was more developed at this time than Spanish American countries. In fact, the backwardness of Brazil in 1850 as described in the Introduction may suggest that even at that time Spanish America was 'ahead' of Brazil in some subtle but very important ways.

taken place cannot be measured and others still were so small as to be insignificant when measured; but the importance of first steps cannot be ignored even when they are stumbling ones. Brazil was far more industrialized at this time than it had been sixty or seventy years before. Simply by definition, more manufacturing activity means that Brazilians were less dependent on human and animal power and that, since 1850, productivity had correspondingly increased. It also suggests that Brazilians were more aware of the importance of industrial growth, less contemptuous of industrial activity, more willing to value hard work, more anxious to invest in industrial enterprises and raise capital for this end, and readier to apply scientific knowledge to the solution of human problems. One foreign observer referred in 1907 to the 'development of an essentially modern spirit of progress and enterprise... which...dominates the national life at the present moment'.[1] The traditional society was disappearing.

Brazil was also a more urban society as attested not only by the census figures but also by the increased use of national funds for the improvement of the cities. In the first years of this century Rio de Janeiro was transformed by the installation of new sewage and water systems, the opening up of broad tree-lined avenues in place of slum-buildings dating from colonial days, and the construction of public buildings in a *fin de siècle* style. Especially important were campaigns to eradicate mosquitoes. The possibility of controlling the environment was brought home by the consequent cessation of the yellow-fever epidemics that had been an annual occurrence since 1850. Similar steps were undertaken in São Paulo and in the other capitals. The cities were now becoming the focus of national attention as traditional rural structures were breaking down.[2]

The growth of cities meant that an urban style of life was becoming that of an increasing number of Brazilians. More and more people flooded into the towns breaking their ancient ties to

---

[1] Wright, *The New Brazil*, p. 13.
[2] *Ibid.* pp. 129–148; Alured Gray Bell, *The Beautiful Rio de Janeiro* (London: Heinemann, 1914), pp. 21–33, 97–100; Winter, *Brazil and Her People of To-Day*, pp. 53–8, 68–70; Bruno, *História e tradições da cidade de São Paulo*, III, 970, 1016–21, 1086, 1106–9, 1122–8; Lloyd, *Twentieth Century Impressions*, p. 645.

the land. Social mobility is more characteristic of cities than of plantations, and in an increasingly urban society relationships are likely to be based upon other than face-to-face contacts. The sleepy tempo of life in 1850 had given way to bustling activity. Some idea of the change may be gathered from this badly translated description of São Paulo written in 1904 by Arthur Dias: 'A forest of chimneys throw [*sic*] from sunrise to sunset spirals of smoke into the air crossed in all directions by electrical wires. In the streets is a confusion of vehicles, and men running here and there. There is the noise of human voices, the rattling of the wagon-wheels upon the pavement of the streets, the whistles of the factories.' Another traveler, Arnold Savage Landor, not usually so subtle in his criticisms, contrasted São Paulo with Rio de Janeiro, saying that in the former 'people walked along fast as if they had something to do, and numerous factory chimneys ejected clouds of smoke, puffing away in great white balls'. He could find no higher praise than to say that 'It seemed almost as if we had suddenly dropped into an active, commercial, European city'. It was not a pretty sight, but it was a modern one.[1]

Still, many of the sand castles of modernity had been washed away by the constant tides of conservatism. Furthermore, some steps toward a modern society had not even been attempted, and these are the same moves that are causing difficulty today. Education was still the privilege of the few—one planter feared more schools would help spread 'insidious ideas'—and most teaching was not concerned with technical and scientific questions.[2] Agricultural techniques had been improved in only a small area of the country. The wider distribution of land holdings which could have done so much to break down the rigid stratification of society had not been tackled. Rural values were sometimes carried to the city, where they died out very slowly. Politics remained in the hands of rural clans. Many of the traits of a traditional society remained present, although hidden by modern trappings, like

---

[1] Dias, *The Brazil of Today*, p. 452; Landor, *Across Unknown South America*, p. 14.
[2] Quoted by Warren K. Dean, 'São Paulo's Industrial Elite, 1890–1960', unpub. Ph.D. diss., Univ. of Florida, 1964, p. 122n.

The Onset of Modernization

the old colonial *taipa* houses of the cities that were given European façades.[1]

The northeastern part of Brazil was not as much transformed as the coffee regions, and, indeed, it still maintains more characteristics of the traditional society than most of the country. This sluggishness may be partly explained by the initial strength of the old structures, it being a more heavily populated area for a much longer time than, say, São Paulo; but principally, it was because its products did not enjoy the advantages of a burgeoning export market as did those of the south. Nevertheless, during the late nineteenth century even this traditional society suffered blows powerful enough to knock the old structures askew if not to destroy them. The abolition of slavery and the creation of central sugar factories undermined the old patriarchal relationships, leaving the region in the grip of a cruel transition that seems to have no end.

But in the country as a whole enough change had been effected to lay the basis for striking progress later on. The 1920s were a period of continuing though hesitant growth, and in 1930 a British commercial mission reported with some surprise that the value of Brazilian industrial products exceeded that of its agricultural ones.[2] Getúlio Vargas, who took power by revolution in 1930, made it his task—sometimes as president, sometimes as dictator—to push Brazil toward further industrialization during the next twenty-four years. The administration (1955–60) of Juscelino Kubitschek was also marked by forced-draft manufacturing expansion through foreign capital importation and state investment, and development-minded young men were given a free hand both in research and administration. None of this would have been possible if the Brazil of 1914 had been like the Brazil of 1850. Modernization had begun, and an examination of the British role in this process will provide a more specific knowledge of its nature.

[1] Oakenfull, *Brazil (1913)*, pp. 323–4, 338–9; Santos, *Os republicanos paulistas*, p. 82. Some nineteenth-century modernizers had urged land reform, including Joaquim Nabuco and André Rebouças.
[2] *Report of the Sheffield Industrial Mission to South America* quoted by Normano, *Brazil*, p. 112.

2

COFFEE AND RAILS

Coffee exports provided the fuel for the steadily accelerating thrust of economic and social change in Brazil during the latter half of the nineteenth century. And the increase of coffee production to meet world demand, that is, the cultivation of coffee on lands ever further from the coast, was made possible by the railways. As already noted, coffee and rails spread together and were partners in the conquest of a new frontier, an economic frontier, from which were to spring the pioneers not only of coffee but of industry.[1] Therefore, the role of the British in fostering the railway system which served the coffee region is central to this study.

Brazilians early caught the fever for stretching rails of steel across the land, and the carrier of the infection was the British engineer and promoter. A Britisher even inspired Brazil's basic railroad law. Thomas Cochrane—a second cousin of the Admiral Cochrane who gained fame in the wars of Latin American independence—prepared a glowing prospectus as early as 1839 for a railroad which, he said, by linking São Paulo and Rio de Janeiro would do for Brazil what the Stockton and Darlington had done for Britain. Although the project had to be abandoned after he had managed to organize a company to build it, his efforts were not without fruit. His experiences and the pressure he exerted led at last to the acceptance of the idea that railroads would not be built in Brazil without government aid: he urged the government to guarantee interest of 5 per cent on approved railroad projects, and after much debate the government finally accepted this suggestion. It became law in 1852.[2]

---

[1] Brazilian railroad mileage was overwhelmingly concentrated in the coffee regions, Affonso d'Escragnolle Taunay, *Pequena história do café no Brasil (1727–1937)* (Rio: Departamento Nacional do Café, 1945), pp. 103, 179.

[2] Thomas Cochrane, 'Esboço historico sobre o primitivo projecto da Estrada de Ferro D. Pedro II', in Aroldo de Azevedo, *Cochranes do Brasil. A vida e a obra de Thomas Cochrane*

Coffee and Rails

But even the guarantee of interest was not enough to attract direct British investment to Brazil's most important project, a railroad to connect Rio de Janeiro with the middle Paraíba valley and the other regions beyond the coastal escarpment or *serra*. The Brazilian government attempted to interest British capitalists, but they were reluctant to invest, partly because of the uncertainty within the London financial market caused by the Crimean War.[1] Therefore, in 1855, a Brazilian company was formed in which the government owned most of the stock. It was named the Estrada de Ferro Dom Pedro Segundo and, after 1889, is known as the Estrada de Ferro Central do Brasil.

Despite the original lack of enthusiasm, the British contributed substantially to its establishment. Almost as soon as it was organized, the company raised a loan in Great Britain of over £1·5 million guaranteed by the Brazilian government. The first president of the company, Cristiano Benedito Otoni—generally a critic of the British—was forced to admit that 'without this loan the railroad would not have crossed the *cordilheira*'. In 1871 and 1875, after the line became outright government property, large loans were raised in London for further construction.[2]

The British technical contribution, on the other hand, may be considered more a drawback than a help. The company hired an

e *Ignacio Cochrane*, Brasiliana, 327 (São Paulo: Editôra Nacional, 1965), pp. 285–99; Stanley J. Stein, *Vassouras, a Brazilian Coffee County, 1850–1900*, Harvard Historical Studies, 69 (Cambridge, Mass.: Harvard Univ. Press, 1957), pp. 101–2; Thomas Cochrane to Camara dos Srs. Deputados, 10 Apr. 1848, AN, C585, P1, D1; Clodomiro Pereira da Silva, *A evolução do transporte mundial (enciclopédia dos transportes)*, 6 vols. (São Paulo: Imp. Oficial do Estado, 1940–6), v, 406–8; José do Nascimento Brito, 'Bernardo Pereira de Vasconcelos e a verdadeira origem das estradas de ferro no Brasil', *Engenharia*, VIII (1950), 557–9; José do Nascimento Brito, *Meio século de estradas de ferro* (Rio: Livraria São José, 1961), pp. 21–7, 32; Law no. 641 of 26 June 1852, in Pereira da Silva, *Evolução do transporte*, VI, 545–7; British interest at this time in Brazilian railroad building is reflected in José Marques Lisboa (Brazilian minister to the court of St James) to Paulino José Soares de Sousa (Brazilian foreign minister), London, 6 Sept. 1851, AHI, 216/2/15, no. 44; cf. contemporary use of land-grant incentives in the United States, Paul W. Gates, *The Illinois Central Railroad and its Colonization Work*, Harvard Economic Studies, 42 (Cambridge, Mass.: Harvard Univ. Press, 1934), esp. pp. 21–43; on English control of this railway see p. 76.
[1] Felisberto Caldeira Brant, *visconde* de Barbacena, to Francisco Gonçalves Martins, *barão* de São Lourenço (Minister of Empire), London, 26 July 1853, AMIP, CXIX, 5906.
[2] Pereira da Silva, *Evolução do transporte*, v, 413, 415; Valentin F. Bouças, *História da dívida externa*, 2nd ed. (Rio: Edições Financeiras, 1950), pp. 92, 109–10; Christiano Benedicto Ottoni, *Autobiografia...Maio, 1870* (Rio: Typ. Leuzinger, 1908), p. 117.

Coffee and Rails

Englishman, Edward Price, as contractor for the first section of the line. The Brazilian minister in London arranged the terms, acting on behalf of the company, and Price was given the freedom to build the road as he saw fit, since the Brazilians frankly admitted that they did not know the first thing about the special problems involved in crossing the *serra*.[1] Price soon had a falling out with the management of the company. The government had hired another Britisher, Christopher B. Lane, as consulting engineer to inspect Price's work. Lane claimed that it was because of his efforts that Price agreed to reduce the maximum grade and to build iron bridges instead of wooden ones. But the president of the company became convinced that Lane and Price were in collusion to defraud the company, and so replaced them with Americans as soon as the first section of the railroad was completed in 1858.[2] Those first forty-eight kilometers cost £625,991, and it is not surprising that the company went bankrupt. In 1865 the government took over the line to operate it directly.[3]

Thus, the British played an important role in the initiation of one of Brazil's most important coffee railways. The effect of this line on the economy of the Paraíba valley was not long-lasting because the valley had almost reached its peak productivity by the time the rails wandered into it. But it served to prolong its prosperity by lessening the cost of transport. It also contributed to the intensification of coffee production in the upper Paraíba

[1] Christiano Benedicto Ottoni, 'Estrada de ferro do Parahyba', *Jornal do commercio*, 7 June 1855, p. 2; also see 10, 14, 17, and 22 June 1855, p. 2; Ottoni, *Autobiografia*, pp. 103, 107, 115; the Brazilian minister in London was removed for overstepping his authority on this matter, Renato Mendonça, *Um diplomata na côrte de Inglaterra; o barão do Penedo e sua época*, Brasiliana, 219 (São Paulo: Editôra Nacional, 1942), p. 146.

[2] C. B. Lane to Pedro de Araújo Lima, marquês de Olinda (Minister of Empire), [Rio], 19 Nov. 1858, copy, AMIP, cxxvi, 6265 (Lane was suggesting that a new contract for his services should pay at least £4,000 a year); Ottoni, *Autobiografia*, pp. 107, 108, 112, 114; Ottoni said Lane 'dominated by jealousies of nationality' systematically opposed all the work of the American Garnett, Christiano Benedicto Ottoni, *Esboço historico das estradas de ferro do Brazil* (Rio: Villeneuve, 1866), p. 6; on this controversy see Charles I. M. Garnett to Christiano Benedicto Ottoni, Rio, 21 Oct 1857, AMIP, cxxiv, 6222.

[3] Irineo Evangelista de Souza, *visconde* de Mauá, *Autobiografia* ('*Exposição aos credores e ao público*') seguida de '*O meio circulante no Brasil*', ed. Claudio Ganns, 2nd ed., Depoimentos Históricos (Rio: Valverde, 1942), pp. 180, 182; Pereira da Silva, *Evolução do transporte*, v, 411, 413; Julian Smith Duncan, *Public and Private Operation of Railways in Brazil*, Studies in History, Economics and Public Law, 367 (New York: Columbia Univ. Press, 1932), p. 29.

valley in the province of São Paulo. Later on, by virtue of connexions to the capital of this province, it sometimes helped to drain off the massive crops of west-central São Paulo itself. It also linked Rio de Janeiro with a line serving southern Minas which was built in the 1880s, thus indirectly contributing to the prosperity of still another coffee region. In all, it accelerated the growth of the export economy, and its effect upon specific localities was electrifying. Tiny Barra do Piraí, for example, was the center of Paraíba commerce as long as it remained the railhead. Other cities were to be similarly transformed as they were touched by the magic wands of steel.[1] The building of the lines was commenced by a British contractor in the absence of alternatives, and for this contribution the Brazilians paid dearly. More important, British capitalists had lent their money to the company and this loan enabled it to cross the escarpment.

The British also made loans to private Brazilian companies. One such railway was the Estrada de Ferro São Paulo e Rio, which linked the city of São Paulo to the Estrada de Ferro Dom Pedro Segundo in 1877. It borrowed £600,000 in London in 1874 and another £164,200 five years later. In 1890 the federal government bought the railroad from the company in order to make it a part of the government's line, and the British loan became part of the national debt.[2] Two roads of the Minas Gerais coffee district also raised loan capital in London. The Estrada de Ferro do Sapucaí borrowed £1,100,000 in England in 1889, a year after it was organized. A loan of £3,700,000 was raised there in 1893 by the Estrada de Ferro do Oeste de Minas.[3]

Almost all the Brazilian lines serving the coffee region of São Paulo were also connected to the British financial market at one

---

[1] Escragnolle Taunay, *Pequena história do café*, p. 102; Richard P. Momsen, Jr., *Routes over the Serra do Mar: the Evolution of Transportation in the Highlands of Rio de Janeiro and São Paulo* (Rio: [privately printed?], 1964), p. 79; Stein, *Vassouras*, p. 109; Alberto Ribeiro Lamego Filho, *O homem e a serra*, 2nd ed., Biblioteca Geográfica Brasileira, A–8: Setores da Evolução Fluminense, 4 (Lucas, GB: Conselho Nacional de Geografia, 1963), pp. 178–84; cf. effect of a twentieth-century railway built in Mato Grosso, Fernando de Azevedo, *Um trem corre para o oeste; estudo sôbre a Noroeste e seu papel no sistema de viação nacional*, 2nd ed., Obras completas, 12 (São Paulo: Melhoramentos, 1959), pp. 87–107.
[2] *SAJ*, XXXIX (1890), 634; Pereira da Silva, *Evolução do transporte*, v, 565–6.
[3] Joseph R. West, 'The Foreigner in Brazilian Technology, 1808–1900', unpub. Ph.D. diss., Univ. of Chicago, 1950, pp. 581, 584.

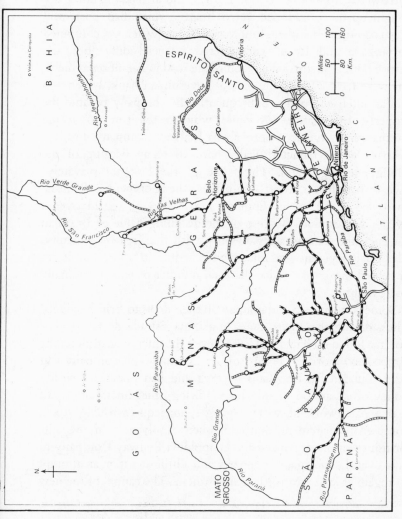

Railways of south-central Brazil by 1918

———— Lines which were at one time directly owned by the British.

▬▬▬▬ Lines owned by companies that borrowed funds in Britain.

▭▭▭▭ Lines which were not connected with the British.

time or another. British capitalists loaned £483,700 to the Companhia Mogyana, for instance, in the late 1880s. The Sorocabana borrowed £230,000 in London in 1877, and in 1892 this company bought up the Estrada de Ferro Ituana, which had borrowed £150,000 from Britishers four years earlier. When the combined Sorocabana and Ituana encountered financial difficulties, the British bondholders tried to acquire the road in lieu of repayment, but were frustrated by the federal government bank, which was also an interested party. Subsequently the company became the property of the state of São Paulo, which leased it in 1907 to the internationally financed Sorocabana Railway Company, Ltd.[1]

Loans were characteristically hard to repay because of the falling exchange rates. Thus, one of the best-run privately-owned Brazilian railway companies, the Companhia Paulista, borrowed £150,000 in England in 1878 to be repaid over a twenty-year period. Because of the declining value of Brazilian currency the loan was repaid only with the greatest difficulty. The final payment was made on schedule in 1898, but it represented more than twice the total number of *milreis* originally borrowed.[2]

Some companies could not pay off their debts to British lenders. Thus, during the 1890s, the Companhia Estrada de Ferro Leopoldina found itself unable to meet even the interest charges on the £7,000,000 worth of bonds sold in London. This company had been founded by Brazilians in 1872 and had pursued a steady policy of expansion mainly by acquiring other lines. The result was a patchwork of various gauges, inadequate rolling stock, confused management, and consequent insolvency. In 1897 the British creditors organized the Leopoldina Railway Company to take over the mortgaged property and administer it, in an attempt to regain at least part of their investment. The capital of the new

---

[1] West, *op. cit.* pp. 608, 610, 611, 613; Charles A. Gauld, *The Last Titan: Percival Farquhar, American Entrepreneur in Latin America* [Special issue of the *Hispanic American Report*], (Stanford, California: Institute of Hispanic American and Luso-Brazilian Studies, Stanford University, 1964), pp. 172–4.

[2] Adolpho Augusto Pinto, *Historia da viação publica de São Paulo (Brasil)* (São Paulo: Vanorden, 1903), p. 46. Cf. Odilon Nogueira Matos, 'A evolução ferroviária de São Paulo', in IX Congresso Brasileiro de Geografia, *Anais*, 5 vols. (Rio: Conselho Nacional de Geografia, 1941–4), IV, 559.

company was £5,500,000, and an additional £1,100,000 was raised by issuing debentures to pay immediate claims. The company never became a very prosperous one; but, in view of its precarious base upon property that had once failed, it was fairly successful. The average dividend during the first thirteen years was 3·17 per cent, the lowest being 1·5 percent in 1899 and 1900 and the highest being 4·5 per cent in 1907. By 1912 the Leopoldina had a total of 2,660 kilometers under its administration, either as owner or lessee, making it the largest privately-owned network in Brazil.[1]

It was in the field of direct investment, rather than loans, that the British exerted their greatest influence on the Brazilian transportation system. By the end of 1880 there were eleven British-connected railways in Brazil and ten years later there were twenty-five such companies. Aside from government bonds, almost half of all British investments in Brazil before the First World War were in railroad enterprises.[2] Many of these companies represented investments of doubtful value. Usually a Brazilian would secure a concession from the government and then offer it for sale in England. Promoters, or 'professional directors' as they were called by the *Rio News*, hastily organized the companies to buy up these concessions:

They have floated schemes which they must have known to be visionary and unpromising, and they have flattered and wheedled Brazilian officials into the belief that scores of these wretched enterprises could be made remunerative, and that the 'natural resources' of the country are incalculably great, but can be developed properly only through these so-called improvements... Then they have turned

[1] Edmundo Siqueira, *Resumo historico de The Leopoldina Railway Company, Limited* (Rio: Gráfica Editora Carioca, 1938), 11–33; Reginald Lloyd et al., eds. *Twentieth Century Impressions of Brazil: Its History, People, Commerce, Industries, and Resources* (London: Lloyd's Greater Britain Publishing Co., 1913), pp. 210–13; Brazil, Directoria Geral de Estatistica (Ministerio da Agricultura, Industria e Commercio), *Annuario estatistico do Brazil. Annuaire statistique du Brésil. 1º anno. 1ère année. (1908–1912)*, 2 vols. (Rio: Typ. de Estatistica, 1917), II, 33; Pereira da Silva, *Evolução do transporte*, V, 408–10, 471–95, 506–8, 516–18, 611–38, 671, 672; Centre Industriel du Brésil, Rio de Janeiro, *Le Brésil. Ses richesses naturelles, ses industries. Extrait de l'ouvrage: 'O Brazil, suas riquezas naturaes, suas industrias'*, 2 vols. (Paris: Aillaud, 1909–10), II, 229–35.

[2] J. Fred Rippy, *British Investments in Latin America, 1822–1949. A Case Study in the Operations of Private Enterprise in Retarded Regions* (Minneapolis: Univ. of Minnesota Press [1959]), pp. 34–5, 68, 151.

to the confiding investor and have made him believe Brazil to be the long sought El Dorado, and that for every shilling planted there, nothing less than a sovereign could be produced. They have traded upon the amiability and rectitude of the Emperor, the peaceableness of the Brazilian people, the fertility of the soil, the wide expanse of territory, the product of a few gold and diamond mines, and the 'splendid future' in store for the country. They have baited their hooks with many a glittering generality and have never failed to catch their fish with them.[1]

These accusations, however, did not fully apply to the coffee region, where an El Dorado had really been found. Three lines deserve mention here: the moderately profitable Minas and Rio Railway, the short-lived but successfully speculative Rio Claro São Paulo Railway, and the truly golden São Paulo Railway.

The Minas and Rio Railway Company, Ltd, was a minor British-owned line serving a relatively small coffee region in south-western Minas Gerais. It was founded in 1880 to buy up concessions granted five years earlier to a Brazilian concern in which the Anglophile *visconde* de Mauá had been interested. Waring Brothers, British contractors, secured these concessions, promoted the company in Britain, and then built and equipped the line. The company was formed with a capital of £1,000,000 on which the Brazilian government guaranteed dividends of 7 per cent. It borrowed an additional £750,000 in 6 per cent debenture bonds in 1881–2. There was early speculation in its shares and they sold well above par even before the company began operation. Perhaps this was because its name suggested some sort of rival to the Pedro Segundo railway, whereas in reality it was only a small feeder to that line. Construction began in 1881 and was completed three years later, linking Cruzeiro (province of São Paulo) to Três Corações (Minas Gerais), a distance of 170 kilometers over difficult terrain.

At first its chief business was as a substitute for the cattle drive

---

[1] *Rio News*, 24 Apr. 1887, pp. 2–3; similar criticisms had become common by then, Joaquim Nabuco, 'Correspondencia', *Jornal do commercio*, 4 Mar. 1882, p. 3, although some still spoke of profitably opening up 'a new country', *SAJ*, XXIII (1886), 109.

from a sparsely settled area. But the railroad broke down the region's isolation and transformed its economic base. Coffee began to spread throughout the area. In 1888 and 1889 concessions were secured for the extension of the railway into what *The Times* called 'the best coffee districts'. But, because of the overthrow of the empire in 1889, the company was unable to raise the necessary capital in Europe and these concessions were withdrawn, falling into the hands of Brazilian companies.

The installation of the republican regime marked the beginning of the company's decline. Its ordinary shares sold below par for the first time in 1890. Its position of dependence upon the Estrada de Ferro Central now became an evident weakness since, with the increasing traffic on that line and the decreasing efficiency of its administration, the Rio and Minas sometimes lacked sufficient fuel for its locomotives at the very time it was paying storage costs for large amounts of coal in the city of Rio de Janeiro. The new government, finding itself burdened with the interest guarantees to foreign companies, began to search for an escape from its predicament. In 1893 it changed accounting procedures so as to prevent the companies from charging to 'losses' amounts resulting from a falling off in the exchange rate. Although the company had always had a net profit, this was never enough to pay the 7 per cent dividend, and the government had had to make up the difference. Now the actual dividend fell from 7 to 5 per cent. In 1898 the government went even further and began to pay the guaranteed dividend in bonds instead of cash. The stock market value of the company's shares plummeted with this announcement. The company, however, optimistically continued to invest in new rolling stock and other equipment.

The end was near. At first, the company turned a deaf ear to government offers to buy up the railway, but changed its mind when faced with the carrot of a good price and the stick of threatened confiscation. The shareholders received Brazilian government 4 per cent sixty-year bonds whose face value was 20 per cent higher than the par value of the shares. Since these shares were selling earlier in the year for as little as half their par value, the shareholders seem to have come out well ahead. The company was wound up in January 1902, never having paid less than a 5 per cent dividend.[1]

Another road that belonged briefly to the British was the Rio Claro São Paulo Railway Company, Ltd. A Brazilian firm had built the road from the town of Rio Claro to Araraquara and Jaú during the period 1881–7. British financial interests, led by the English Bank of Rio de Janeiro, perceived that this line was the key to the further expansion of the vigorous Estrada de Ferro Paulista. They organized a company with a capital of £600,000—soon increased to £850,000—and encountered no difficulty in purchasing the line in 1889, perhaps because of rumors of the impending revolution to overthrow the empire. In 1892, after some small expansion, the line was sold to the Paulista railroad in exchange for £2,750,000 worth of preferred shares of the latter company. Coffee railroads could evidently make a fortune for the quick-witted.[2]

The most important British railway in Brazil was one that tapped the heart of the coffee district. The San [*sic*] Paulo (Brazilian) Railway Company, Limited, as it was officially named in England, built and operated the line running from the port of Santos into the coffee districts of the province of São Paulo. When completed it measured only 139 kilometers, but its key role in the monocultural economy of Brazil made it the wealthiest and most powerful railway of the country. It served as a funnel, gathering with the help of connecting lines the agricultural pro-

[1] Mauá, *Autobiografia*, pp. 211–14; *SAJ*, XVIII, no. 11 (26 May 1881), p. 13; XXIX (1890), 634; *Investor's Monthly Manual, a Newspaper for Investors*, n.s. XV (1885), 602; n.s. XVII (1887), 568; n.s. XXII (1892), 557; n.s. XXIII (1893), 608; n.s. XXVII (1897), 661; n.s. XXVIII (1898), 665; n.s. XXX (1900), 667; Pereira da Silva, *Evolução do transporte*, V, 641–2; London *Times*, 31 Jan. 1885, p. 11; 29 Nov. 1886, p. 10; 16 Nov. 1887, p. 12; 3 Nov. 1890, p. 11; 4 Nov. 1892, p. 11; 31 Oct. 1893, p. 11; 11 Nov. 1893, p. 11; 6 Nov. 1897, p. 5; 12 Nov. 1897, p. 12; 6 Nov. 1901, p. 13; 13 Nov. 1901, p. 3; 25 Dec. 1901, p. 11; 16 Jan. 1902, p. 4; government policy is described by José Carlos Rodrigues, *Resgate das estradas de ferro do Recife a S. Francisco e de outras que gozavam da garantia de juros: relatorio*... (Rio: Imp. Nacional, 1902); see Appendix A for figures on stock prices, profits and dividends.

[2] Pereira da Silva, *Evolução do transporte*, V, 536; David Joslin, *A Century of Banking in Latin America; to Commemorate the Centenary in 1962 of the Bank of London and South America, Limited* (London: Oxford Univ. Press, 1963), p. 169; Warren K. Dean, 'São Paulo's Industrial Elite, 1890–1960', unpub. Ph.D. diss., Univ. of Florida, 1964, pp. 148–9; West, 'Foreigner in Brazilian Technology', pp. 606–7; Nogueira Matos, 'A evolução ferroviária de São Paulo', pp. 560–1.

ducts of a vast region and pouring them into the British ships gathered in the harbor. It deserves more detailed attention than the other lines examined so far.

It was once again the *visconde* de Mauá, a Brazilian entrepreneur deeply influenced by the British and closely connected with England, who brought the investors and the project together. He persuaded the owner of some plans drawn up many years earlier to join him and another Anglophile, José Antônio Pimenta Bueno, *marquês* de São Vicente, in securing a new concession. He also hired the British engineer Robert Milligan to make further studies and then contracted the London engineering firm of James Brunlees to prepare detailed plans and make cost estimates. Brunlees sent out Daniel Makinson Fox—later chief engineer and superintendent of the railway—to undertake the surveys and supply the data for Brunlees' work, and the plans drawn up and presented by Brunlees were accepted by the Brazilian government in March of 1858, after slight changes made by C. B. Lane.[1]

The next step was to organize a British company, and this was done in December 1859. In order to persuade British capitalists to invest, the provincial assembly of São Paulo passed a law

[1] Requerimento do visconde de Mauá, Marquez de Monte Alegre, e José Antonio Pimenta Bueno, 21 Dec. 1854. AN, C585, P1, D14. On this railroad see Manuel Ferreira Garcia Redondo, 'A primeira concessão de estrada de ferro dada no Brasil', *Revista do Instituto Historico e Geographico de São Paulo*, VI (1900–1), 1–11; Carlos W. Stevenson, 'Os bandeirantes das ferrovias', in Instituto de Engenharia de São Paulo, *1º Centenario da locomotiva, Commemoração 1825–1925* (São Paulo: Gordinho Braune, [1925?]), p. 43; Decree no. 1759, 26 Apr. 1856, in Pereira da Silva, *Evolução do transporte*, VI, 552; Mauá, *Autobiografia*, p. 117; Claudio Ganns, 'Introdução', *ibid.* p. 65; Nascimento Brito, 'Bernardo Pereira de Vasconcelos', p. 559; Anyda Marchant, *Viscount Mauá and the Empire of Brazil: a Biography of Irineu Evangelista de Sousa (1813–1889)* (Berkeley and Los Angeles: Univ. of California Press, 1965), pp. 76–7; Edgard de Cerqueira Falcão, 'A primeira maquina a vapor introduzida no Brasil e o primeiro barco a vapor que sulcou aguas brasileiras', *Revista do Arquivo Municipal de São Paulo*, Ano I, vol. VI (1934), 63–8, who says a German first thought of the idea, citing Miranda Azevedo, *Frederico Fomm, apontamentos biographicos* (São Paulo, 1879); Daniel Makinson Fox, *Description of the Line and Works of the São Paulo Railway in the Empire of Brazil... with an Abstract of the Discussion upon the Paper*, ed. James Forrest (London: Clowes, 1870), pp. 3–5, calls this man Fred Forum, 'an English merchant residing in Santos' (p. 3); on Brunlees' interest in other Anglo-Brazilian railways, e.g. the Minas and Rio Railway Company and the New Hamburg Railway in southern Brazil, see *SAJ*, XVIII, no. 11 (26 May 1881), p. 12; Joaquim Nabuco, 'Correspondencia', *Jornal do commercio*, 28 July 1882, p. 3; Michael George Mulhall, *The English in South America* (Buenos Aires: 'Standard' Office, 1878), p. 350; Hastings Charles Dent, *A Year in Brazil, with Notes on the Abolition of Slavery...* (London: Kegan Paul, Trench, 1886), p. 270.

guaranteeing an additional 2 per cent annual interest on the capital so invested, and the Brazilian minister in London took a hand in promoting the company, thus throwing the weight of the imperial government behind the enterprise. Mauá and his partners subscribed for almost a tenth of the capital. The company immediately paid Mauá £45,000 for the plans and concession. Its officials were later to point to this large sum in an effort to discredit him, but he claimed that he had spent £25,000 for the preliminary studies drawn up by Brunlees and Fox and that the remaining £20,000 went to N. M. Rothschild & Sons for allowing their name to be used in the prospectus.[1]

It is quite possible that the company would have failed and the line remained unfinished if it had not been for Mauá's continued enthusiasm and gullibility. The railway company contracted with Robert Sharpe & Sons to acquire the land, execute the works, and supply all rolling stock and plant. The major financial backer of the contractor was the Mauá bank. According to Mauá, he had been led by the company into advancing large sums to the contractor upon assurance that works being done in addition to the original contract would be paid for. What he did not know was that the company had signed a secret additional contract with Sharpe to the effect that he would carry out all these extra works for a piddling sum. When Sharpe went bankrupt, the Mauá bank found that it could not collect from the company the £340,000 to which, it claimed, Sharpe was entitled. Mauá charged 'fraud' and was upheld by the lower courts in Brazil. But the Supreme Court, reversing an earlier decision, ruled that the case could be tried only in London, where the company officially had its seat. By the time Mauá could take the case to England, the statute of limitations made it impossible for it to be examined there.[2]

In his autobiography, Mauá later stated that his only consolation

[1] Letter to Carvalho Moreira, draft, unsigned, undated, AN C585, P1, D-; Companies Registration Office, London, File no. 45390; Mauá, *Autobiografia*, pp. 168-9.

[2] Mauá, *Autobiografia*, pp. 169 n., 170-3, 175-6, 176 n.; Alberto de Faria, *Mauá—Ireneo Evangelista de Souza, barão e visconde de Mauá, 1813-1889*, 2nd ed., Brasiliana, 20 (São Paulo: Editôra Nacional, 1933), pp. 508, 518-20, 523; Marchant, *Viscount Mauá*, pp. 236-7; *Investor's Monthly Manual*, n.s. III (26 Apr. 1873), 148; n.s. v (1875), 781-2; n.s. VI (1876), 401, 506; n.s. VII (1877), 33, 312; London *Times*, 2 Sept. 1875, p. 7; Mendonça, *Um diplomata na côrte de Inglaterra*, pp. 463-4.

for his losses was the fact that the results of his actions were 'transcendant'. The company was on the point of failure, having used up all its capital and being unable to borrow money. No road would have been built except for his effort. And indeed, when, at the time, a partner in his banking firm protested the large amounts being advanced to the contractors, Mauá replied 'What do you want me to do? No doubt there is risk...but it is not possible that the works should cease. With the heavy rains the cuts will suffer and the earthworks will be lost. In spite of the risk, it's necessary to go on; [and] no one except us will furnish the means.' But it was also true that Mauá was interested in protecting his considerable investment in the company, the future profits of which he rightly considered a sure thing.[1]

Even if Mauá is allowed due credit for making the railway possible, the fact remains that it was the British themselves who were chiefly responsible for providing the capital, managerial skill, technical ability, and equipment for the construction of this railway, a monument to nineteenth-century engineering.

The technical difficulties involved in building the São Paulo Railway were substantial. The first obstacle was the need to rise 2530 feet in 5 miles. The topography of this region may be described as a plateau originating at a sharp escarpment or *serra* in the east and gently inclined to the west. Whoever conquered the *serra* was master of the hinterland, and the British railway did it by building a series of inclined planes. Cars were drawn up by means of steel cables and towed short distances between inclines by standard locomotives. Braking engines were attached to each set of cars to operate clamps acting upon the rails when needed, as well as to hook onto the steel cables for the ascent or descent.[2]

The second problem was the torrential rains which characterize the escarpment during the rainy season. The average annual rainfall on the *serra* is 147 inches, as compared with 54 inches only a

[1] Mauá, *Autobiografia*, pp. 172, 176; Mauá to Ricardo Ribeiro, quoted by Faria, *Mauá*, p. 194. Mauá's confidence in the railway was shared by a penniless contemporary, Antonio Augusto da Costa Aguiar to San Paulo Railway Company, São Paulo, 14 Sept. 1861, AMIP, cxxx, 6398.

[2] The basic features of the system are still in use today although it is being abandoned. For a fuller description of it as it operated in 1911 see Lloyd, *Twentieth Century Impressions*, p. 235.

few miles away in the city of São Paulo. The effect of these rains was compounded by the loose character of the soil, causing frequent washouts.[1] The chief engineer wrote that in the construction of the São Paulo Railway 'earthworks...were subject to extensive and sudden slips...and embankment after embankment was carried away during construction'. The reports to the stockholders made frequent references to these same factors. In 1868 it was said that 'violent rains had seriously impeded progress toward the completion of minor works'. In 1869 the line was closed for twenty-three days as a result of a 'slip' and ten years later flash floods washed away an entire inclined plane.[2] The only solution to these problems was an extensive drainage system, the pitching of slopes to prevent water penetration, and even the building of Inca-like stone walls along embankments.

The experience gained was later put to good use when the line was doubled in 1898–9 using the same basic system. Soon after that it purchased for £115,000 the Estrada de Ferro Bragantina, linking the original line with Bragança Paulista and other towns near the border of Minas Gerais. In general, however, the company was content to profit from its strategic position without bothering to expand.[3]

Investments which played an integral part in fostering initial but rapid steps toward the modernization of Brazil were not unprofitable. The conquest of the *serra* was fully rewarded and the financial record of the São Paulo Railway Company became one

---

[1] Duncan, *Public and Private Operation of Railways*, pp. 7–8; British Chamber of Commerce of São Paulo and Southern Brazil, *Facts About the State of São Paulo* (São Paulo: British Chamber of Commerce of São Paulo and Southern Brazil, 1950), p. 51; John Casper Branner, *The Railways of Brazil, a Statistical Article. Reprinted from the 'Railway Age' with Notes and Additions* (Chicago: Railway Age Publishing Co., 1887), p. 10.

[2] Fox, *Description of the Line and Works*, p. 11; *Investor's Monthly Manual*, IV (1868), 148; VI (1870), 124; n.s. X (1880), 111.

[3] Pereira da Silva, *Evolução do transporte*, V, 568 n.; *Investor's Monthly Manual*, n.s. XXXIII (1903), 222; São Paulo Railway Company, *São Paulo Railway Company como successora da Companhia Bragantina: documentos relativos ao prolongamento de Bragança a Socorro* (São Paulo: São Paulo Railway Company, 1904); Gauld, *The Last Titan*, pp. 172–4 on the company's lack of dynamic expansionism; in its early days, apparently discouraged by the difficulty of settling controversies with the government over capital expended, the company turned its back on concessions which fell into the hands of the Estrada de Ferro Paulista, Manuel da Cunha Galvão, *Relatorio apresentado...sobre os trabalhos de sua commissão em Londres* (Rio: Typ. Nacional, 1871), p. 126.

of continuing prosperity, whether seen in terms of capital formation, gross receipts, net profits, returns on capital invested, or
stock market quotations. The initial authorized capital of the
company was £2,000,000 in £20 shares. By 1865 it had all been
subscribed. That same year the company set about raising additional capital through 7 per cent debentures. Although at first
there were few takers, by 1870 the total issue of debentures had
risen to £750,000. They were later converted to $5\frac{1}{2}$ per cent
debenture stock. By 1946 when the ninety-year privilege was at
an end and the government bought out the company, the
called-up capital was £4,000,000, one-fourth of which was in
5 per cent preferred stock. Outstanding debentures were worth
some £2,400,000.[1]

The railroad prospered from the start. The very first month of
operation it carried more than half and the next month over
three-quarters of the coffee shipped to Santos, rapidly asserting
its superiority over mule-back transportation. By the end of the
fourth month of operation the railway had carried 25,000 persons
and freight weighing 15,000,000 kilograms. Receipts at that time
stood at £45,478 while expenses were only £11,216.

With such receipts the profit record of the company was
naturally very favorable. By the end of the first four months of
operation the divisible profit was over £24,000. Profits for the
second half of 1867 reached £29,000, and a year later the half-
year profits were roughly £67,000. In 1871 this figure stood at
almost £82,000, although profits suffered a decline in the next
two years and only approached this amount again in 1873. After
that the company's prosperity steadily increased.

The investor in the company received a steady return of more
than 6 per cent on his capital. In the first half of 1874, only seven
years after the line was opened, profits were enough to pay
dividends of 7 per cent without government aid. After that and

[1] *Investor's Monthly Manual*, I (1865), 54, 358, 374; II (1866), 33, 188; III (1867), 110, 153;
v (1869), 315; n.s. III (1873), 369; in 1865 the company actually borrowed funds in
order to pay dividends on its share capital while the line was still in construction, Robert
A. Heath (chairman of the board) to *barão* do Penedo (Brazilian minister to England),
London, 13 Apr. 1866, AMIP, CXXIII, 6127; British Chamber of Commerce of São
Paulo, *Facts about the State of São Paulo*, p. 50.

until the last years of the empire, the returns never fell below 8 per cent; after 1877 they never went below 9 per cent, and after 1880, never below 10 per cent. The fluctuations increased in the 1890s, a period of political disturbance and economic instability. Thus, while the dividend and bonus for the year 1893/4 was only 6 per cent, it was 14 per cent each of the following two years. Starting in 1902 this figure remained at 12 per cent or better until the outbreak of the First World War.

Purchasers of stock in the railway at the time of its creation not only got a high return every year from dividends, but were able to make a considerable profit on re-sale of their shares. The cost of each share had been £20 at the beginning of the company's history, yet by 1875 they might have been sold for £30. 10s. and in 1882 for £40. 10s. Seven years later they were selling for £50. 10s., after which they suffered a decline in value. By 1905 they were again selling for more than twice their par value, a condition that remained true until the First World War. In all, the São Paulo Railway was the most profitable British railway enterprise anywhere in Latin America and its owners were proud of it.[1] A Brazilian spokesman for the coffee interests shared their viewpoint that 'the millions of sterling pounds applied to our land deserve the just reward for the improvements they bequeathed us'.[2]

But this prosperity depended upon one crop. All the railways in south-central Brazil were wedded to coffee. An American explorer commented that the Estrada de Ferro Dom Pedro Segundo 'was built to carry away the coffee; that is its main business,

[1] J. J. Aubertin, *A estrada de ferro e a provincia de S. Paulo. Carta ao illmo. snr. dr. Antonio da Silva Prado* (São Paulo: Typ. Americana, 1867), pp. 8 and 17; *Investor's Monthly Manual*, III (1867), 374; n.s. IV (1874), 395; Lloyd, *Twentieth Century Impressions*, p. 239; Rippy, *British Investments*, pp. 73, 154; figures on profits, dividends, and stock prices are drawn from Appendix B; note that they are not congruent with those presented by Rippy, *British Investments*, p. 175, who says the period of highest return was from 1896 to 1900.

[2] Tobias do Rego Monteiro, *O presidente Campos Salles na Europa*, 2nd ed. (Rio: F. Briguiet, 1928), p. 111; William Speers, comp., *Companhia São Paulo Railway e o governo imperial. Reproducção dos artigos sob essa epigraphe publicados no jornal pelo dr. Engenheiro Fiscal d'esta estrada de ferro com as respostas dadas aos ditos artigos pela respectiva superintendencia e os documentos a que os mesmos se referem* (São Paulo: Typ. a vapor de Jorge Seckler, 1889), p. 9; also see Julio Ribeiro, *A carne* (São Paulo: Teixeira, 1888), p. 137.

almost its only income'. Similarly, in the very first two months of operation of the São Paulo Railway Company over half the freight it carried was coffee. And when, the next year, the traffic on the line increased by 36 per cent, the explanation was to be found in the 'rapid development' of coffee production. When coffee exports rose profits increased and when they declined profits dwindled.[1] It was, then, the demands of an international market that made coffee important, and it was the pursuit of this newly valued product that drew the railways inland.

It is enlightening to contrast the role of coffee with the role of cotton. J. J. Aubertin, superintendent of the São Paulo Railway from 1860 to 1869 and later consultant to the railway, was a great enthusiast of Brazilian cotton culture during and after the American Civil War. In 1861 he noticed by accident that abandoned cotton plants still produced excellent cotton in some of the valleys near the city of São Paulo. He wrote to his directors and they passed on this information to the Cotton Supply Association of Manchester, which was then conducting an intensive campaign to find new areas of supply. That same year he received seeds and distributed them among his planter friends. He sent samples of the resulting cotton to Manchester and they were received with enthusiasm. In 1866 he was still 'in direct communication' with the Cotton Supply Association and offered to get any quantity of seeds at the most reasonable prices for any Brazilian who wanted them. He carried on an active campaign to teach the landowners how to plant cotton and the value of planting it.[2] An American traveler reported in 1865 that a Brazilian in Sorocaba

[1] Herbert Huntington Smith, *Brazil, the Amazons and the Coast* (New York: Scribner's, 1879), p. 531; Aubertin, *A estrada de ferro e a provincia de S. Paulo*, pp. 16–17; *Investor's Monthly Manual*, V (1869), 315; n.s. XXVII (1897), 220; n.s. XLI (1911), 180.
[2] J. J. Aubertin, 'O algodão [Carta a Fidelis Preta]', *Correio paulistano*, 21 July 1864, pp. 2–3; J. J. Aubertin, *O norte da provincia de S. Paulo (1866). Carta dirigida ao illm. snr. João Ribeiro dos Santos Camargo* (São Paulo: Typ. Schroeder, 1866), pp. 11, 12–13; J. J. Aubertin, *Eleven Days Journey in the Province of São Paulo with the Americans, Drs Gaston and Shaw, and Major Mereweather. Letter Addressed to His Excellency the Baron of Piracicaba. Translated from... Portuguese by the Author* (London: Bates, Hendy, 1868), pp. 5, 7, 11; James McFadden Gaston, *Hunting a Home in Brazil. The Agricultural Resources and Other Characteristics of the Country; also, the Manners and Customs of the Inhabitants* (Philadelphia: King & Baird, 1867), pp. 277–8; Alice P. Cannabrava, *Desenvolvimento da cultura do algodão na provincia de São Paulo (1861–1875)* (São Paulo: Siqueira, 1951), p. 9.

felt under 'special obligation' to Aubertin for having introduced the man's cotton 'to favorable notice in England'.[1] Even after Aubertin's return to England, he continued to urge cotton cultivation in Brazil. In 1869 he received from the Manchester Cotton Supply Association a gold medal for services rendered in creating a source of supply in Brazil.[2]

At the time some Brazilians called into question the reasons for Aubertin's interest in cotton culture. They said that too much praise was being heaped upon him for publicizing cotton, since 'it is certain that the motive for... [it] was [only] indirectly the prosperity of the province, but directly the industrial interest of cotton manufacturers of Manchester. This was the end; the cotton prosperity of São Paulo was the means'.[3] We may go a step further and suggest that Aubertin was not so much interested in the cotton manufacturers as in the prosperity of the São Paulo Railway, because he realized that a well-balanced and prosperous agricultural economy would help the railway.[4] An American traveler in Brazil observed in 1865 that 'it is important for the railroad interest that cotton shall be successfully cultivated in this region of the country'.[5] In 1869 Aubertin wrote from England that the interest there in the coming cotton crop was great 'as much within the cotton trade as among the stockholders of our presently well-known railroad'.[6]

[1] Gaston, *Hunting a Home in Brazil*, p. 285.
[2] 'Noticiario. Plantação do algodão', *Correio paulistano*, 14 Oct. 1868, p. 1; Cannabrava, *Desenvolvimento da cultura do algodão*, p. 14. Aubertin advocated use of British-made cotton gins, Aubertin, *Eleven Days Journey*, p. 12; J. J. Aubertin, *Carta dirigida aos srs. habitantes da provincia de S. Paulo por... superintendente da estrada de ferro da mesma provincia* (São Paulo: Typ. Litteraria, 1862), p. 28; as did the Brazilian minister to England, Francisco Carvalho Moreira, *barão do Penedo*, *Relatorio sobre a exposição internacional de 1862* (London: Brettell, 1863), pp. xxiv–xxv; the board of the São Paulo Railway sent Aubertin a gin along with a ton of seed, Aubertin, 'O algodão', p. 2. Cf. the similar role of the Cotton Supply Association in India, Frederick Clairmonte, *Economic Liberalism and Underdevelopment: Studies in the Disintegration of an Idea* (London: Asia Publishing House, 1960), p. 122.
[3] 'Noticiario. O sr. Aubertin e a producção do algodão em S. Paulo', *Correio paulistano*, 6 May 1869, p. 1.
[4] William Scully, *Brazil: Its Provinces and Chief Cities; the Manners and Customs of the People: Agricultural, Commercial, and Other Statistics...* (London: Murray, 1866), p. 312.
[5] Gaston, *Hunting a Home in Brazil*, p. 277.
[6] J. J. Aubertin, 'Carta do Sr. Aubertin, Londres, 21/12/1869', *Correio paulistano*, 30 Jan. 1870, p. 1.

Yet cotton did not become a major source of revenue for the railway nor a major crop of São Paulo. This failure resulted from the recovery of the United States productive capacity, against which the Brazilians could not compete. Despite the best efforts of the railway, São Paulo remained monocultural. The conclusion may be drawn that these railways depended for success upon the demands of the international market—for which the British were not particularly responsible. The British played a role in a major change in Brazilian economic life but cannot be considered its cause.

The same point may be made by reference to British railways built in the Brazilian sugar zone. There were several of these, most of them unprofitable, and they led to no significant economic development because the conditions of international trade were unfavorable. Aside from their partial responsibility for replacing the traditional sugar mills with central sugar factories, they did not transform this most traditional area of Brazil.[1]

The very first British railroad in the country had been built by the Recife and São Francisco Railway Company, Ltd. It ran southwest from the capital of Pernambuco with the intention— not fulfilled for many decades—of connecting this city with the navigable portion of the São Francisco river. Mauá—who had invested substantial amounts in the enterprise—later pointed out an initial source of difficulty: the plans had been based on a foreign engineer's 'gallop across the terrain', rather than upon deliberate and systematic study by those long acquainted with the area. Furthermore, traffic was not heavy enough to make the enterprise pay. The line proved a financial loss and the guaranteed interest was a constant drain on the government treasury.[2]

Other British lines of the northeast included the Nova Cruz

---

[1] Manuel Diégues Júnior, 'O banguê em Pernambuco no século XIX', *Revista do Arquivo Público [Estadual de Pernambuco]*, Anos VII–X (1952–6), nos. 9–11, p. 22; Manuel Diégues Júnior, *O engenho de açucar no nordeste*, Documentário da Vida Rural, 1 (Rio: Serviço de Informação Agrícola, Ministério da Agricultura, 1952), pp. 46–7.

[2] Estevão Pinto, *História de uma estrada-de-ferro do nordeste (contribuição para o estudo da formação e desenvolvimento da empresa 'The Great Western of Brazil Railway Company Limited' e das suas relações com a economia do nordeste brasileiro)*, Documentos Brasileiros, 61 (Rio: José Olympio, 1949), pp. 59–60, 63; Mauá, *Autobiografia*, pp. 152–4.

in Rio Grande do Norte; the Conde d'Eu in Paraíba; the Alagoas and the Alagoas Brazilian Central; and the Great Western of Brazil. Only the latter proved moderately successful. Grandiloquently named after the Great Western Railway in England, it was organized in 1872, began construction in 1879, and was completed three years later just in time to take advantage of the renewed optimism caused by establishment of the first central sugar factories. The line was only 83 kilometers long, but the area it traversed northwest of Recife was richer than that of the Recife and São Francisco, the company's adminstration was wiser, and the line made a small profit. Despite the fact that it was unable altogether to dispense with the official subsidy to bolster its dividends, the government did not buy it out as it did the other British railroads of the area. When, in 1902, the government leased its newly acquired lines in the northeast to private operators, the Great Western was lowest bidder and thus came to operate most of the railroads in the area with a total of more than 1,000 kilometers. But its influence upon the modernization of the area remained limited.[1]

In the province of Bahia the story was much the same. The Bahia and São Francisco Railway was organized—as were the Estrada de Ferro Dom Pedro II and the Recife and São Francisco Railway— during the rush stimulated by provincial rivalries at the time of passage of the basic railroad law in 1852. The first section of this line was opened to traffic in 1860, but its rails did not reach the São Francisco river until 1896. The venture proved an unrelieved financial failure.[2]

The small-gauge Paraguassú Steam Tram-Road avoided the high initial investment of these railways. Its purpose was to tap the diamond district of central Bahia after traversing a wide expanse of arid and sparsely populated terrain. The prospectus published in 1866 described in glowing terms the 'great traffic that... has sprung up by the discovery of diamonds in the interior of Bahia'. It also predicted that the production of other minerals

[1] Pinto, *História de uma estrada-de-ferro*, pp. 78–9, 83–4, 91–2, 97, 128.
[2] José Wanderley Pinho, *Cotegipe e seu tempo; primeira phase, 1815–1867*, Brasiliana, 85 (São Paulo: Editôra Nacional, 1937), pp. 295–327; Pereira da Silva, *Evolução do transporte*, v, 418, 461.

such as gold, silver, lead, copper, iron, nitrate, alum, and limestone, as well as agricultural products, principally cotton, would yield an enormous profit to the investors. But the company failed in 1869 before operation of any portion had begun, and the concession was taken over by the Brazilian Imperial Central Bahia Railway organized in London by the contractor Hugh Wilson. This time, a guarantee of interest was secured and construction finally began in the 1880s. By then the diamond rush had subsided and the line never reached its initial goal.[1] But toy-like trains, belching clouds of black wood-smoke, today still creep across the seared land on the narrow rails laid without ballast directly on dirt. The area languishes in backwardness. Without a profitable crop like coffee to feed a growing international demand, no railroad could transform this region.

But the importance of British railroads in, the coffee states is striking even if larger forces were primarily responsible for their establishment. The major railways serving the coffee area were either British-owned or British-financed. In 1898, a year of marked productivity in the coffee zones, the São Paulo Railway carried 328,000 tons of coffee, the Estrada de Ferro Central carried 102,000, and the Leopoldina 54,000. Except for lines that fed into the São Paulo Railway, all other lines together carried only 30,000 tons.[2] The railroad made the continued increase of coffee production possible. Given the productive techniques then current, the very survival of coffee as a major Brazilian export would have been threatened if there had been no opportunity for the geographical spread of the crop. Before the construction of the São Paulo Railway it had been axiomatic that, regardless of soil productivity, coffee could not be planted west of Rio Claro because freight costs ate up the profits. Now, overcoming immense technical difficulties that no one else had been prepared to tackle, Britishers had laid the track from the port of Santos to the edge

[1] John Morgan, *The Paraguassú Steam Tram-Road, in the Province of Bahia, Empire of Brazil*... (London: Smith, Elder, 1866); Pereira da Silva, *Evolução do transporte*, v, 458–9.

[2] Brazil, Ministerio da Industria, Viação e Obras Publicas, Directoria Geral de Obras e Viação, *Estatística das estradas de ferro da união e concedidas pela união em 31 de dezembro de 1898* (Rio: Imp. Nacional, 1900), Table 15.

of the coffee district, and had made it possible for other railroads to stretch out across the plateau into the producing region. The region's prosperity was thus assured. Direct ownership by the British of this major Brazilian railway clearly indicates the importance of the British role in advancing Brazil's initial moves toward a modern economy.

3

THE EXPORT–IMPORT COMPLEX

If the exports which moved to the coast on British-owned railways initially stoked the engine of Brazilian modernization, the resulting complex of British export–import interests acted as a brake. When the economy began to pulse with its own life and some energies began to turn to industrialization, they found the forces that had given birth to growth now seeking to smother it. The British were directly connected with almost every aspect of this export-oriented system. The grip which the British held upon the railroad, the exporting firm, the import business, the shipping company, the insurance agency, the financial bank, and even the government treasury now tended to choke off any efforts to reduce the reliance on British imports. So did the wide currency of free trade doctrines coined in Britain. The Brazilian minister in London noted as early as 1854 that 'the commerce between the two countries is carried on with English capital, on English ships, by English companies. The profits,...the interest on capital,...the payments for insurance, the commissions, and the dividends from the business, everything goes into the pockets of Englishmen'.[1]

On the other hand, the very fact that Brazil did begin to industrialize suggests that that grip was not a stranglehold. There were significant areas of productive activity which the British did not dominate, and there were some points at which, as will be made clear in later chapters, they even fostered industrialization. But here emphasis is placed on the way in which they slowed it down by controlling and channeling one current of Brazilian economic life after another.

[1] Sérgio Teixeira de Macedo (Brazilian minister to Great Britain) to Lord Clarendon, London, 16 May 1854, copy encl. in Macedo to Antonio Paulino Limpo de Abreu (Brazilian Foreign Minister), London, 30 May 1854, AHI, 217/3/8, no. 21; Stanley J. Stein, *The Brazilian Cotton Manufacture: Textile Enterprise in an Underdeveloped Area, 1850–1950* (Cambridge, Mass.: Harvard Univ. Press, 1957), p. 211, n. 29.

The Export–Import Complex

The control of the export business was the most immediate contact the British had with the export economy. The most firmly established British export houses in 1850 were those in the northeast that handled sugar, for, since it was exported to Great Britain in large amounts, they could dominate both ends of the business. Sugar exports from the northeast increased during the period 1850–75, and, encouraged by the removal of British sugar duties, they were largely being shipped to Great Britain. According to the reminiscences of an old Recife resident, A. J. Watts, the major shipping house was Saunders Brothers, whose local agent was Philip Needham, a popular member of the business community, three times elected president of the local Chamber of Commerce. Another major sugar exporter, John Harvey Boxwell, also dealt in raw cotton, having set up a hydraulic baling press. In the late 1870s Britain continued to be the major customer for the products of that region, but, as can be seen from Table 4, Brazilian sugar exports to Britain declined both absolutely and relatively thereafter.[1]

As sugar declined and coffee increased in importance the British share of Brazilian exports was sharply curtailed. In 1850 the United States received 47·3 per cent of Brazil's coffee, and one incensed Brazilian diplomat, with justifiable hyperbole, said that Great Britain imported only £9 worth of Brazilian coffee while sending out in return £3,000,000 of manufactured goods.[2] In the early 1870s coffee consumption in Britain began to decrease, and by 1875 the port of Rio de Janeiro, where coffee then predominated, exported over five times as much to the United States as to tea-drinking Great Britain. After that, Brazilian shipments to England

[1] Alan K. Manchester, *British Preëminence in Brazil; Its Rise and Decline: A Study in European Expansion* (Chapel Hill, N.C.: Univ. of North Carolina Press, 1933), p. 325; William Scully, *Brazil: Its Provinces and Chief Cities; the Manners and Customs of the People, Agricultural, Commercial and Other Statistics...* (London: Murray, 1866), p. 83; Nelson Werneck Sodré, *História da burguesia brasileira*, Retratos do Brasil, 22 (Rio: Civilização Brasileira, 1964), p. 121; Alfredo J. Watts, 'A colônia inglêsa em Pernambuco', *Revista do Instituto Arqueológico e Geográfico de Pernambuco*, XXXIX (1944), 164; Cone to Department of State, Recife, 6 Feb. 1879, NA/DS, Despatches Consuls, Pernambuco, no. 16.

[2] *The Rio Mercantile Journal*, 24 Jan. 1851, p. 5; Macedo to Clarendon, London, 16 May 1854, copy encl. in Macedo to Limpo de Abreu, London, 30 May 1854, AHI, 217/3/8, no. 21.

Table 4. *Value of Imports (in £) from Brazil into Great Britain, 1855–1909* [a]

Year[b]	Cotton	Coffee	Sugar	Cocoa	Hides	Rubber	Other	Total
1855–9	3,618,415	759,486	4,943,558	89,455	848,003	613,528	2,237,013	13,109,458
1860–4	9,386,271	1,359,861	5,161,348	131,346	1,976,996	1,340,497	1,470,649	20,826,968
1865–9	21,098,631	1,825,213	6,266,430	55,143	1,800,443	2,122,994	1,536,481	34,705,335
1870–4	16,117,228	2,943,466	8,978,617	122,288	2,390,478	4,343,919	1,778,232	36,674,228
1875–9	6,271,202	4,261,606	9,152,871	219,819	1,791,223	4,844,851	1,800,681	28,342,253
1880–4	5,557,913	4,049,278	8,396,807	177,810	1,251,854	7,350,565	2,138,965	28,923,192
1885–9	4,977,123	4,037,228	3,609,638	190,924	721,894	7,551,773	2,114,214	23,202,854
1890–4	3,634,474	2,916,827	1,348,127	336,758	354,067	9,453,535	2,644,908	20,688,696
1895–9	949,492	1,122,315	894,643	381,264	243,437	14,558,376	1,816,337	19,965,864
1900–4	3,586,601	1,553,399	465,767	543,502	287,618	20,772,189	2,876,997	30,086,073
1905–9	4,509,291	2,090,438	1,080,116	723,879	424,179	32,133,313	4,195,094	45,156,310

[a] Based on Great Britain, Board of Trade, Customs and Excise Department, Statistical Office, *Annual Statement of the Trade of the United Kingdom with Foreign Countries and British Possessions* (London: H.M. Stationery Office, 1855–1910).

[b] No data are available for the early years on amount re-exported, so, for the sake of consistency, this factor is ignored.

declined even more sharply. From £4·3 million during 1875–9 British imports of Brazilian coffee fell to £1·1 million twenty years later. Both sugar and coffee remained relatively small items after 1895, but British imports from Brazil did enjoy a spectacular though ephemeral increase during the first years of the twentieth century as a result of the rubber boom (Table 4). Nevertheless, in 1900 Britain bought only 18 per cent of Brazil's exports while the United States bought 43 per cent. The relative positions with regard to Brazil's major crop remained lopsided and became spectacularly disproportionate during the First World War: in 1918 Brazil exported only 1000 bags of coffee to Great Britain as contrasted with 4,562,000 bags to the United States.[1]

But the British made up for meager imports from Brazil by controlling the trade between it and other countries. Almost half the Brazilian exports of sugar, half the coffee, and over half the cotton were being exported by British firms in the 1840s. The difference between the vast imports from Great Britain and the small exports to that country was made up by the credits accruing to the British exporters of Brazilian commodities to the United States, to Germany and to the rest of the European continent. The same conditions prevailed after 1850 and, despite the competition of a few American merchants, the British firmly held on to the export trade. One of the largest British export houses was that of Phipps Brothers & Co., which increased its volume from 94,000 bags of coffee in 1850 to half a million bags—valued at £2,000,000—by the mid-1870s.[2]

At that time E. Johnston & Co. was the second most important British export firm. Edward Johnston, a Londoner who had

---

[1] E. Constantine W. Phipps, 'Report...on the Trade and Commercial Relations of Brazil and on Finance (24 June 1872)', C636, in Grea. Britain, Parliament, House of Commons, *Sessional Papers*, Readex Microprint Edition, ed. Edgar L. Erickson, 1872, LIX, 644, 646; Agostinho Victor de Borja Castro, *Descripção do porto do Rio de Janeiro e das obras da doca d'alfandega* (Rio: Imperial Instituto Artistico, 1877), p. 50; Sodré, *História da burguesia*, p. 185; E. Lloyd Rolfe, *Report on Brazil's Trade & Industry in 1918 with Special Reference to the State of São Paulo. Hints, Information for Manufacturers & Merchants* (São Paulo: British Chamber of Commerce of São Paulo and Southern Brazil, 1919), p. 16.

[2] Manchester, *British Preëminence*, p. 315; Michael George Mulhall, *The English in South America* (Buenos Aires: 'Standard' Office, 1878), p. 349; Reports on Business Houses, Rio de Janeiro, 1852, Baring Papers, House Correspondence, HC 16.

arrived in Rio de Janeiro in 1821 and married the daughter of a Dutch plantation owner in the vicinity, had founded this firm in 1842. Three years after its establishment, he moved to Liverpool in order to widen the sphere of his activities. He established partnerships with a British house in Bahia and a mercantile firm in Liverpool and his business grew rapidly, shipping only 9,000 bags of coffee in 1848, but 39,000 the next year and 59,000 in 1850. This was still a small amount, however, compared to the volume handled by the American firm of Maxwell, Wright and Co., so in the early 1850s Johnston established partnerships in New York and New Orleans, where most Brazilian coffee was being sold.[1]

In 1853 Edward Johnston took his eldest son into the partnership, and the founder of the firm thus continued to dominate it until his death in 1876, not only as senior partner, but as father of all the other ones, Francis, Charles, Reginald and Cyril. Two of them were placed in charge of the Santos branch when it opened in 1881 and this town gradually became the center of the Brazilian end of the business. A landmark in the firm's development was the appointment of Edward Greene to the Santos branch in 1891. His cool mind and nerves of steel soon brought him to the attention of the Johnstons and he was included in the partnership in 1895. He eventually became the driving force behind the firm's activities in Brazil and he later moved to London to direct the entire operation. By 1924 E. Johnston and Co. was described in a Chamber of Commerce publication as 'the largest British export firm in the country'.[2]

---

[1] Mulhall, *The English in South America*, p. 349; E. Johnston & Co., *One Hundred Years of Coffee* (London: E. Johnston & Co., 1942), pp. 7, 13–15; *Rio Mercantile Journal*, 24 Jan. 1851, p. 5; Joseph R. West, 'The Foreigner in Brazilian Technology, 1808–1900', unpub. Ph.D. diss., Univ. of Chicago, 1950, p. 713 n.; Reports on Business Houses, Rio de Janeiro, 1852, Baring Papers, House Correspondence, HC 16.

[2] E. Johnston & Co., *One Hundred Years*, pp. 14, 16, 20, 22; Edward Greene to Charles Johnston, Santos, 25 July 1895, GPL, I, 33; British and Latin American Chamber of Commerce, *Commercial Encyclopedia Comprising a Series of Standard Publications on the Actual and Potential Markets of the World, Compiled and Issued by Sections: Fourth Sectional Issue: South America*, ed. W. H. Morton-Cameron, 2nd ed. (London: Globe Encyclopedia Co., 1924), p. 367. Johnston's most serious competitor in the first years of this century was another British firm with the not so English name of Naumann, Gepp & Co., Greene to Alexander, Santos, 12 May 1896, GPL, I, 92; Werner Haas, et al., *Os investimentos estrangeiros no Brasil* (Rio: privately mimeographed, 1958), Section II, no. 167. On foreign exporters cf. Caio Prado Júnior, *História econômica do Brasil* (São Paulo:

There were two distinct participants in the coffee business: the *comissário* or coffee broker, who handled the planters' coffee as it arrived in the city; and the exporter, who shipped it to the importing firms in Europe and the United States with which he was associated. The *comissário* was usually a Brazilian, although isolated Englishmen were sometimes coffee brokers. He was a powerful figure since he usually lent money to the planters at very high interest and often ended up as the owner of plantations himself. On the other hand, he sold to the British export house and was, in turn, frequently in debt to it.[1]

At the turn of the century, E. Johnston & Co. still did most of its business with *comissários* in Santos. But the firm was also beginning to send agents, usually Englishmen, into the interior to buy directly from the planters, or, what was then more likely, from the 'millers' who shelled the coffee of the smaller planters. Traveling in jolting wooden railway cars, burned by flying sparks, and staying at mean pensions, they skillfully searched for business opportunities, probing the export economy in search of weaker spots to be controlled. Other 'rich and foreign' exporters pursued similar policies to eliminate the Brazilian middle man, said the governor of the state of Rio de Janeiro. This tendency to take over all aspects of the business was matched in England by Greene's ambitious proposal that E. Johnston & Co. should enter the retail business.[2]

Outright ownership of coffee *fazendas* was also undertaken by some Britishers, especially after many Brazilian planters were ruined in the coffee crisis of 1897. By 1909 one British company with an authorized capital of £800,000 operated the second

Brasiliense, 1945), pp. 234, 242, with Gilberto Freyre, *Introdução à história da sociedade patriarcal no Brasil, III: Ordem e progresso*...2 vols. (Rio: José Olympio, 1959), II, 441–2. Mr Edward Greene (II) of the Brazilian Commodities Trading Co., Ltd, kindly made available his father's letters.

[1] William D. Christie, *Notes on Brazilian Questions* (London & Cambridge: Macmillan, 1865), pp. xxxiiin., 74n.; J. C. Oakenfull, *Brazil (1913)* (Frome, England: Butler & Tanner, 1914), p. 315; J. F. Normano, *Brazil, a Study of Economic Types* (Chapel Hill, N.C.: Univ. of North Carolina Press, 1935), p. 42; Julio Ribeiro, *A carne* (São Paulo: Teixeira, 1888), p. 82; Sodré, *História da burguesia*, pp. 144, 148, 181–2.

[2] Greene to Reginald Johnston, Santos, 17 Apr. 1896; 12 Nov. 1896; 27 Mar. 1899; Greene to Charles Johnston, Santos, 24 Oct. 1898, GPL, I, 76, 148, 188, 219–20; Rio de Janeiro (State), Governador, *Mensagem*, 1897, p. 78; Sodré, *História da burguesia*, p. 189.

largest coffee plantation in Brazil with almost five million trees.[1] But this was not common, and British control of the business more often ended with the itinerant buying agent. This was fortunate for the cause of Brazilian development. For the Brazilian coffee planters continued to secure a healthy share of the profits and were thus able to build up the necessary capital for industrialization. It is doubtful that the British—had they owned most of the plantations themselves—would have followed the same course. They would surely have remitted their profits to Britain to be invested there or in whatever area of the world offered the greatest reward. The large share of export earnings accruing to Brazilians sets this country off from many other export economies where the foreigner found either primitive peoples or ancient civilizations whose contacts with the modern world were even more tenuous than Brazil's.[2]

One of the most urgent drives felt by the coffee exporter was the reduction of risk. The large fluctuation in prices, the long period between orders and deliveries, the vagaries of ocean and overland transport, all combined to make his operations extremely dangerous. Greene reported that he had developed the practice of selling to buyers in New York before buying from the *comissários*; if he could not supply the quality sold he shipped what he could get and New York arbitrators decided on proper grading, his firm paying the difference. The same process operated for the European market to which the Santos branch also sold, in contrast to Rio de Janeiro, which dealt almost exclusively with New York. Evidently he found this procedure preferable to facing the risk that the price would have drastically declined between the time he bought in Santos and the date of delivery in the United States or Europe. His firm also acquired an interest in a shipping line and in the Leopoldina Railway in order to have

[1] Nevin Otto Winter, *Brazil and Her People of To-Day: an Account of the Customs, Characteristics, Amusements, History and Advancement of the Brazilians, and the Development and Resources of Their Country* (Boston, Mass.: Page, 1910), pp. 132–3; Arnold Henry Savage Landor, *Across Unknown South America*, 2 vols. (London and New York: Hodder & Stoughton, 1913), I, 30–2; Greene to Charles Johnston, Santos, 3 Jan. 1898; 1 Aug. 1898; Greene to Reginald Johnston, Santos, 15 Mar. 1904, GPL, I, 168, 181; II, 471.
[2] Jonathan Levin, *The Export Economies, Their Pattern of Development in Historical Perspective* (Cambridge, Mass.: Harvard Univ. Press, 1960), pp. 4–15.

some say in transportation matters that could so deeply affect its operations. Another attempt to lessen the dangers of operating in a commercial environment which lacked adequate supporting institutions was Greene's creation in 1906 of the Companhia Paulista de Armazens Geraes, a general warehousing company. At this time 85 per cent of the crop flowed to Santos in a six-month period, so the ownership of storage facilities provided the exporter with still greater leverage.[1]

When Greene returned to England in 1910, one of his first interests was the creation of the Brazilian Warrant Co., Ltd, whose purpose was to control the warehousing company and provide loans to coffee suppliers. The Board was an international one, including British, French, German and Brazilian members, and one of these was the son of São Paulo's leading planter, Antônio Prado. The *comissários* boycotted it at first since its ultimate purpose was to bypass them completely, but they were overcome. During the First World War the company was expanded and the original trading partnership (E. Johnston & Co.) was transformed into a limited liability corporation with the majority of shares held by the Brazilian Warrant Company. The paid-up capital of the latter was £600,000 in 1912 and £1,500,000 in 1924.[2]

The tendency of the export business to concentrate in the hands of a few British firms was natural but not constructive. In view of the risks involved, the smaller businessmen were gradually eliminated. British exporters came to play a dominant role in the exportation of Brazilian coffee mainly because of their ability to hedge or minimize their risks, and they especially did this by extending their control over the entire export economy. The

[1] Greene to Ford, Santos, 20 Apr. 1896; Greene to Reginald Johnston, Santos, 10 Apr. 1899, GPL, I, 64, 229–35; E. Johnston & Co., *One Hundred Years*, p. 23; British Chamber of Commerce of São Paulo and Southern Brazil, *Facts about the State of São Paulo* (São Paulo: British Chamber of Commerce of São Paulo and Southern Brazil, 1950), p. 157a; Clarence F. Jones, 'The Evolution of Brazilian Commerce', *Economic Geography*, II (1926), 556.

[2] E. Johnston & Co., *One Hundred Years*, pp. 24, 26; Oakenfull, *Brazil (1913)*, p. 316; Lillian Elwyn (Elliot) Joyce, *Brazil, Today and Tomorrow* (New York: Macmillan, 1917), p. 179; British and Latin American Chamber of Commerce, *Commercial Encyclopedia*, p. 367; J. Fred Rippy, *British Investments in Latin America, 1822–1949. A Case Study in the Operations of Private Enterprise in Retarded Regions* (Minneapolis: Univ. of Minnesota Press, 1959), p. 155.

basic element of Brazilian economic life was in the hands of these large British companies and the continuance of the export system was their constant interest. Not only did they fail to be concerned with the newer manufacturing sectors of the economy, but by easing the international transfer of coffee they aided the process of over-concentration and monoculture still characteristic of Brazil. In addition, although their action served to develop these local products, they left the human resources relatively unaffected. If it had not been for the coffee planters themselves, aided by the immigrants whom they brought in, capital would not have been transferred to more productive enterprises and the mass of Brazilians would have remained totally unskilled and undeveloped. The bigger the British exporter and the less risk he faced, the more profitable was his business and smaller his contribution to Brazilian modernization.[1]

Exports required imports and Britain was more than ready to do its part in supplying the latter. The relationship between these two trades was not merely the familiar economic fact that exports cannot increase unless there is an accompanying rise in imports. For one thing, the exporters were themselves importers so their earnings were directly converted from one sector to the other. For another, there were many import categories that specifically contributed to increasing exports: in addition to the railway equipment suggested by the previous chapter, much of the agricultural machinery that was increasingly used in Brazil was imported, as were the clothes worn by plantation workers and the tools they handled. Finally, as will become clear in the next chapter, the export economy focused attention abroad and converted the cities into outposts of Europe, outposts that could be adequately supplied only by importing European goods. Thus, every member of society, from the slave wielding an iron hoe to the planter

[1] P. T. Bauer, 'Concentration in Tropical Trade: Some Aspects and Implications of Oligopoly', *Economica*, n.s. xx (1953), 302–21; Frederick Clairmonte, *Economic Liberalism and Underdevelopment: Studies in the Disintegration of an Idea* (London: Asia Publishing House, 1960), pp. 258, 278. Edward Greene was later (1925) connected with a land development company in Paraná which opened up the northern part of that state to coffee production, Arthur H. M. Thomas and Hermann Moraes Barros, 'Cia. Melhoramentos do Paraná formerly Cia. de Terras Norte do Paraná' (mimeographed), part i, p. 1.

installing new coffee-hulling equipment, from the city worker who bought cheap cottons to the gentlewoman who used fine soaps, all were touched by English imports. In no other way was Brazil's dependence upon the British economy more marked. The importance of British goods among Brazilian imports dates at least as far back as the Methuen treaty between Great Britain and Portugal in 1702. Direct British imports to Brazil began in 1808, at the time of the transfer of the Portuguese court to Brazil. In that year the ports were thrown open to international trade, and two years later a commercial treaty was signed that gave the British merchant a more favorable position than even that held by the Portuguese themselves. This state of affairs continued and British commercial advantages increased after Brazilian independence. British goods flooded the Brazilian market and British merchant houses were set up in Brazil to handle them. Protected by a mild form of extraterritoriality, the group prospered. Although this era of unencumbered action in the field of importation came to an end in 1844 when the old treaty expired, the British found that they continued to hold their own as a result of their enterprise, their entrenched position, the industrial superiority of their home country, and their control of Brazilian shipping.[1]

So Great Britain remained the chief supplier of Brazil's imports. Statistics are scant, but it is clear from available data that no other nation was even a close competitor in this respect. During 1845–9 the average annual imports by country were the following:

[1] Manchester, *British Preëminence*, pp. 1–53, 69–98, 206–10, 262, 285–306, 316–17, 320; Armando Marques Guedes, *A aliança inglêsa (notas de história diplomática), 1383–1943* (Lisbon: Enciclopédia, 1943); Bentley Duncan, 'Uneasy Allies: Anglo-Portuguese Commercial, Diplomatic and Maritime Relations, 1642–1662', unpub. Ph.D. diss., Univ. of Chicago, 1967; Francisco Sierra y Mariscal, 'Idéas geraes sobre a revolução do Brazil e suas consequencias [Lisbon, 10 Nov. 1823]', in Biblioteca Nacional do Rio de Janeiro, *Anais*, XLIII–XLIV (1920–1), 56–7; Pinto de Aguiar, *A abertura dos portos do Brasil: Cairú e os inglêses*, Marajoara, 30 (Salvador: Progresso, 1960); Nícia Villela Luz, *Aspectos do nacionalismo econômico brasileiro. Os esforços em prol da industrialização*, Coleção da 'Revista de história', 16 (São Paulo: 'Revista de história', 1959), 9–11; Horace Émile Say, *Histoire des relations commerciales entre la France et le Brésil et con sidérations générales sur les monnaies, les changes, les banques, et le commerce extérieur* (Paris: Guillaumin, 1839), p. 260; Bento da Silva Lisboa and J. D. de Attaide Moncorvo, 'Juizo sobre a obra intitulada "Histoire des rélations [sic] commerciales entre la France et le Brésil"', par Horace Say', *RIHGB*, I (1839), 325; R. G. Albion, 'British Shipping and Latin America', *Journal of Economic History*, XI (1951), 361–2, 369.

Country	Value of imports in *contos*
Great Britain	27,540
United States	6,016
France	5,781
Portugal	5,309
Río de la Plata	2,821
Hanseatic Cities	2,798
Spain	1,237
Others	5,219
Total	56,721

In 1875 Great Britain supplied 43,200 *contos* of the roughly 97,700 *contos* of imports entering Rio de Janeiro. By that time the nearest rival was France with only 18,400 *contos*, which was almost three times as much as that of the next runner-up, Portugal.[1]

Most of the goods imported from Great Britain in the mid-nineteenth century were received on British accounts. Thus, the ships' manifests published in a Rio de Janeiro newspaper during January 1850 show that the bales and bundles arriving from England went to sixty-three merchants, forty-one of whom were British.[2] This was probably also true at all the other Brazilian ports. An 'old Brazil hand' later recalled that 'When I first arrived in this country in 1859 English import houses were established throughout all the principal sea-coast towns'.[3] At least many of those at the capital sold not only to Brazilian wholesalers but directly to retailers in Rio de Janeiro and in the interior, so that the products of British factories were distributed by a well-oiled machine controlled by British hands.[4]

---

[1] Brazil, Commissão Encarregada da Revisão da Tarifa, *Documentos estatisticos sobre o commercio do imperio do Brasil nos annos de 1845 a 1849 que acompanhão o relatorio da commissão...* (Rio: Typ. Nacional, 1853), Quadro H, p. 83; Borja Castro, *Descripção do porto*, p. 49.

[2] 'Importação—Manifestos', *Jornal do commercio*, 1 Jan. p. 2; 3 Jan. p. 3; 5 Jan. p. 3; 8 Jan. p. 7; 11 Jan. p. 3; 17 Jan. p. 3; 23 Jan. p. 3; 24 Jan. p. 3; 25 Jan. p. 3; 28 Jan. p. 3, 1850; list of British merchants, *Almanak administrativo, mercantil e industrial do Rio de Janeiro e indicador para 1850. Obra estatistica e de consulta* (Rio: Laemmert, 1850), Supplemento, p. 97.

[3] London *Times*, 3 Mar. 1897, p. 15.

[4] *The Rio Mercantile Journal*, 12 Jan. 1852, p. 1; Stanley J. Stein, 'The Brazilian Cotton Textile Industry 1850–1950', in Simon Kuznets et al., eds., *Economic Growth: Brazil, India, Japan* (Durham, N.C.: Duke Univ. Press, 1955), p. 434.

The close connexion of exports and imports is reflected by the fact that most of the British commercial houses in Brazil engaged in both kinds of business. E. Johnston & Co., for instance, was the biggest Rio de Janeiro importer of cotton goods in early 1850. The firm later handled 'engines' for milling coffee, cement, flour, lard, mineral water, champagne, and similar items. But by the end of the century this linkage was not so characteristic. Even while the exporters were getting bigger, Portuguese and Germans were displacing the British as importers despite the fact the bulk of their goods continued to come from Britain. Furthermore, with the installation of submarine cables to Britain, the British importers were bypassed by traveling British salesmen representing specific manufacturers. The orders they placed were then wired direct to the supplier and, in this case, it was the British middle man who was eased out.[1]

Most of the importing firms in the 1850s had no field of specialization, but imported a wide variety of goods. The example of Nathan Brothers can be drawn from the manifests to show the diversity of their interests. Although this firm was a bigger importer than most, the heterogeneity of its wares was not atypical. Among foodstuffs and beverages, it received, during one month in 1850, 105 barrels of butter, 4 drums of preserved foods, 2 kegs of special sugar, 200 kegs of beer, 12 boxes of cinnamon, and 16 barrels of herring. Of other types of imports, it had carted off from the customs house 16 small barrels of white lead, 490 of paints, 6 quarts of linseed oil, 20 barrels of pitch, 30 of tar, 400 of gunpowder, 50 small barrels of saltpeter, 25 casks of gypsum, 10 small barrels of chalk, 12 boxes and one barrel of copper, one package of general hardware, 4 bundles of twine, 5 bundles of canvas or sailcloth, 20 boxes of candles, 2 packages of woolen goods, and 793 tons of coal.[2]

Within this great variety, dry goods were unquestionably the single most important item unloaded in Brazil. Out of total imports from Great Britain in 1850 valued at £2·5 million, textiles took up almost £2 million, and, of this, £1·5 million represented

[1] GPL, *passim*; Stein, *Brazilian Cotton Manufacture*, p. 71.
[2] 'Importação—Manifestos', *Jornal do commercio*, Jan. 1850.

cotton goods. As can be seen from Appendix C, almost three-quarters of all imports during the five-year period 1850–4 were in textiles and textile manufactures, and until 1870, these items consistently represented over 65 per cent of Brazilian imports from Great Britain. With a rising domestic manufacture cotton imports began to decline, but the value of dry goods continued to be more than half of British-made imports until 1890.

The diversity within this general classification is illustrated by the advertisement appearing in an 1855 paper for an auction in behalf of J. Dalglish, Thompson, & Co. for 'white cotton cloth, prints...handkerchiefs...linen duck...worsted cloth, Merino fabric...white tulle...cloaks...ornaments...cotton lace, stockings...and various tailor's cloths'. This importing house was something of a specialist in dry goods, and in 1871 similar auctions were still one of its methods for moving large quantities of merchandise. Another large importer of cottons in early 1850 was Bradshaw, Wanklin & Co., described by the correspondent for the House of Baring as a 'large importing house—in very good credit'.[1]

Modernization includes the painful process of eliminating handcraft industries with their wasteful processes, and building up a market for mass-produced industrial products. The large-scale importation of cheap British-made cottons contributed substantially to that process. It might have been done in a much less socially disorganizing fashion if the unemployed workers could have immediately found employment in Brazilian textile plants, but the exact repetition of the British industrial revolution has never been possible elsewhere. The effects of industrial production, though, were repeated: the Brazilian cotton-goods craft industry rapidly dwindled under the impact of British-made fabrics. As early as 1853 a tariff commission reported that 'the English have tried to imitate the different qualities of our textiles; as to the

[1] Great Britain, Board of Trade, Customs and Excise Department, Statistical Office, *Annual Statement of the Trade of the United Kingdom with Foreign Countries and British Possessions* (London: H. M. Stationery Office, 1854), p. 237; *Jornal do commercio*, 1 May 1855, p. 2; 1 Jan. 1871, p. 7; 'Importação—Manifestos', Jan. 1850; Reports on Business Houses, Rio de Janeiro, 1852, Baring Papers, House Correspondence, HC 16; Stein, *Brazilian Cotton Manufacture*, p. 70.

The Export–Import Complex

coarse, they have done this entirely'. By 1862 hand-loomed cloth had suffered a severe decline.[1] This is the only positive connexion between British textile imports and the process of modern change, except for the fact that, by reducing the cost to the planters of clothing their workers, they contributed to the growth of the export economy. But the importers of British-made cotton goods understandably did little to aid Brazilian textile mills: a Brazilian cotton magnate later recalled 'the terrible war of competition to which I was subject at the beginning on the part of foreign merchants in Rio, representatives of English manufacturers, who always tried to smother and demoralize national industry'.[2]

In contrast, one of the indications of the modern spirit of some Brazilian planters was their use of agricultural machinery, and much of it came from Britain. At the 1866 national exposition held in Rio de Janeiro, Ransomes and Simms of Ipswich and London displayed plows which, along with those made by Howard, were recommended by the judges as being 'the best turn-plows built in England'. The plows of Henry Rogers Sons & Co. enjoyed a continuous popularity in the coffee regions of São Paulo. Plows were later even used on sugar plantations, and in 1882 plows imported from Britain for sale in Recife were described as 'very much suited to preparing and planting cane'.[3]

The British also made machinery to process raw materials for export. In 1850 advertisements were placed in the Rio de Janeiro

---

[1] Brazil, Commissão Encarregada da Revisão da Tarifa em Vigor, *Relatorio...que acompanhou o projecto de tarifa apresentado pela mesma commissão ao governo imperial* (Rio: Empreza Typ. 'Dous de Dezembro' de Paula Brito, 1853), p. 334; Stein, *Brazilian Cotton Manufacture*, p. 5.

[2] Bernardo Mascarenhas to *visconde* de Figueiredo, 16 Nov. 1888, in Nelson Lage Mascarenhas, *Bernardo Mascarenhas. O surto industrial de Minas Gerais* (Rio: Gráfica Editôra Aurora, [1955?]), p. 56.

[3] Giacomo Raja Gabaglia, 'Relatorio do 3º grupo', in Antonio José de Souza Rego, comp., *Relatorio da segunda exposição nacional de 1866* (Rio: Typ. Nacional, 1869), pp. 102–4; Alice P. Cannabrava, 'Máquinas agrícolas', *O estado de São Paulo*, 6 July 1949, p. 2; *A provincia de São Paulo*, 9 Mar. 1884, p. 3; *Jornal do Commercio*, 3 May 1891, p. 8; John Smith, 'Memoria...por parte dos herdeiros Bowman, sobre melhoramentos introduzidos na producção do assucar desta provincia', in Sociedade Auxiliadora d'Agricultura de Pernambuco, *Acta da sessão solemne da Assembléa Geral de 28 de setembro de 1882 e relatorio annual do gerente Ignacio de Barros Barreto* (Recife: Typ. Central, 1882), p. 111; cf. C. Reginald Enock, *The Republics of Central and South America, Their Resources, Industries, Sociology, and Future* (London & New York: Dent & Scribners, 1913), p. 92.

newspapers for sugar-processing equipment made at 'the well-known iron foundry of Low-Moor'. As the technical requirements for this equipment became more complex and adequate protection for Brazilian manufacturers remained absent, British-owned foundries in Recife that had once manufactured this type of equipment turned almost entirely to its importation from Britain. They imported not only portable track systems for conveying cane to the mills, but also grinders, steam engines, cauldrons, and distilling equipment. Machinery for de-hulling coffee and preparing it for export was also handled by the British, especially by Henry Rogers Sons & Co., but the most important supplier of this machinery was an American with manufacturing plants in England and Brazil. Finally, the British led the way in supplying cotton gins during the American Civil War.[1]

General hardware was imported from Great Britain and every plantation slave probably worked with some British-made product during his life-long labor to produce more exports. The average five-year value of imports in this category was over a million pounds sterling throughout the entire period 1850 to 1910. A typical list of the items included under this heading appeared in an 1850 advertisement for an auction by an English import house:

Iron hoes, steel-reinforced hoes, locks for boxes and doors, machined hinges, wrought hinges, hinge pins, spades, pointed knives, corkscrew penknives, pointed penknives, hunting knives, razors, carpenter's plane irons, tin-coated spoons and forks, metal soup and teaspoons, bridle bits, spurs, padlocks, files, nails of various qualities, English spikes, anvils, vises, various paints, paper...pistols, rifles, caps, and iron pins.[2]

Another merchant announced he had just received 200 dozen iron spades from Liverpool. During one month alone in 1850, one importer received from Great Britain 71 kegs of nails, 50 dozen plus 100 bundles of spades, 115 stoves, 4,192 iron pots and

[1] *Jornal do commercio*, 18 Jan. 1850, p. 3; 1 Jan. 1871, p. 4; 2 Feb. 1882, p. 6; 1 Nov. 1891, p. 9; Smith, 'Memoria', pp. 111–17; Tobias do Rego Monteiro, *O presidente Campos Salles na Europa*, 2nd ed. (Rio: Briguiet, 1928), pp. 88, 95; West, 'Foreigner in Brazilian Technology', pp. 262–3; Alice P. Cannabrava, *Desenvolvimento da cultura do algodão na província de São Paulo (1861–1875)* (São Paulo: Siqueira, 1951), pp. 185, 188, 191, 192, 205 n., 208; Cannabrava, 'Máquinas agrícolas', p. 2.

[2] *Jornal do commercio*, 10 Jan. 1850, p. 3.

pans, 50 bellows, 10 barrels of tin, and 3 boxes of lead pipes, in addition to 76 packages and 14 barrels of other unspecified hardware. Thus few plantations would have been without British manufactured goods. There they facilitated the production of foodstuffs to be sold to British exporters and shipped on British bottoms.[1]

Great Britain's control of the world's largest shipping trade gave it one more stake in Brazil's export–import economy. Brazilians in government, being convinced that theirs was an agricultural country, encouraged foreign navigation. So British ships carried Brazil's exports to the world and brought manufactured goods from England in return. During January 1850, all the ships arriving in Rio de Janeiro from Great Britain were British, as were a large number of those from other ports. Nearly half the steamers entering Rio de Janeiro from foreign ports in selected years during the rest of the nineteenth century were British, while the next nearest competitors, the French, owned only 15 per cent. British importers were the agents for British shipping lines, and British exporters relied on British ships to carry their goods. In 1913 British vessels handled by far the largest part of Brazil's coffee exports, with over 5,000,000 bags out of a total of 13,000,000. Only 9,000 bags were handled by American companies even though the bulk of Brazilian coffee went to the United States.[2]

The Royal Mail Steam Packet Company was the first line to provide regular steamship services between Britain and Brazil. In 1840, at the time of its first contract to carry the British mails to the West Indies, its founder, James McQueen—convinced that the 'possession of all the channels of communication' could secure for Britain 'the principal political influence' of any given area—had

---

[1] *Jornal do commercio*, 4 Jan. 1850, p. 3; 'Importação—Manifestos', *ibid.*, Jan. 1850.

[2] José Mauricio Fernandes Pereira de Barros, *Apontamentos de direito financeiro brasileiro* (Rio: Laemmert, 1855), p. 167; 'Importação—Manifestos', *Jornal do commercio*, Jan. 1850; West, 'Foreigner in Brazilian Technology', pp. 793, 1165; Albion, 'British Shipping and Latin America', p. 373; *Jornal do commercio*, 1 Jan. 1871, p. 7; 2 Jan. 1871, p. 3; *A provincia de São Paulo*, 14 Mar. 1884, p. 3; Brazil, Serviço de Estatística Econômica e Financeira, *Commercio exterior do Brasil. Foreign Trade of Brazil. Commerce extérieur du Brésil. Importação...Exportação...Annos 1913–1915–1916–1917–1918*, 2 vols. (Rio: Monotypado nas officinas da Estatistica Commercial, 1921–3), II, 240–1.

vainly urged the government to grant him an additional contract
for mail service to Brazil. In the late 1840s he approached the
Brazilian government and secured from it the necessary privileges. The British mail contract was finally granted in mid-1850
and the first regular service was established in January of the next
year. Its principal purpose was to wrest from the American
clippers their place in Brazilian shipping. There was an almost
immediate increase in traffic to England. In 1871 the government
subsidy was given up and the main interest of the company
became cargo and passengers. The terminal point of the line in
the early years was Rio de Janeiro, but, because of French competition, the line was extended to Montevideo and Buenos Aires
in 1869. By 1878 it included Santos in its itinerary. The line was
exceedingly prosperous at least until competition drove it from
its privileged position. In 1913 its ships still represented more
than twice the tonnage of any other line arriving in Brazilian
ports.[1]

It had been after considerable study that the Royal Mail had
chosen Southampton as its home port, presumably to fulfill more
easily its mail contract. This choice alarmed the merchants of
Liverpool, who had already experimented with steam navigation
to Brazil on a sporadic basis. Their response was the foundation of
a rival line. Liverpool was the port for the cotton district, but
it was not only the British exporters who were interested. It was
argued at the time that such a line 'would render Liverpool a
depot for the coffee and other Brazilian produce consumed in
the north of Europe...and would enable the English capitalists
who supply the funds with which the greater part of the Brazilian
trade with the Continent is carried on to keep their property

[1] McQueen quoted by Thomas Alexander Bushell, '*Royal Mail*', *a Centenary History of the Royal Mail Line, 1839–1939* (London: Trade and Travel Publications, 1939), p. 6; also see pp. 5, 19, 56, 59, 124, 131; Paulino José Soares de Sousa (Brazilian foreign minister) to Joaquim Thomas de Amaral (Brazilian chargé d'affaires in London), Rio, 9 Sept. 1850; 21 Oct. 1850; and José Marques Lisboa (Brazilian minister to Great Britain) to Paulino de Sousa, London, 8 Nov. 1851, AHI, 218/4/6, nos. 41 and 44 and 216/2/15, no. 61; London *Times*, 6 May 1850, p. 5; British Chamber of Commerce of São Paulo and Southern Brazil, *Grã Bretanha: seu commercio e industria* (São Paulo: Camara de Commercio Britannica de São Paulo & Sul do Brasil, 1927), p. 37; West, 'Foreigner in Brazilian Technology', p. 799; Brazil, Serviço de Estatística Econômica e Financeira, *Commercio exterior do Brasil...1913–1918*, II, 337–8.

under their own eyes'. The reference to Liverpool merchants like Edward Johnston is unmistakable.[1] This line proved unsuccessful and had to be abandoned in 1855, but in the early 1860s the merchant house of Lamport & Holt of Liverpool began a regular shipping service to and from Brazil, and in 1865 founded the Liverpool, Brazil, and River Plate Steamship Company, often referred to simply as Lamport & Holt. In view of the coffee interests of the Liverpool merchants, it was only natural that it should be the first steamship line to begin calling at Santos, and that it eventually established services from Brazil to New Orleans and New York. In 1876 it owned 13 steamers and by 1894 it had doubled this number. Although it trailed well behind the Royal Mail line in tonnage arriving in Brazilian ports in 1913, it was the major handler of coffee exports, carrying six times more coffee than the older line.

Other British companies serving Brazil included the Anglo-Brazilian Steam Navigation Company, the Pacific Steam Navigation Company, the London, Belgium, Brazil and River Plate Steam Packet Company, the Real Companhia Anglo-Luso-Brazileira, the Merchant Steam Ship Company Ltd, whose Rio de Janeiro agent in the 1880s was Edward Johnston, the Blue Star Line, the Maranham Steamship Company, the Nelson Line owned by Hugh & William Nelson, Ltd, the Booth Steamship Company which served northern Brazil, the Harrison Line, the Prince Line, and the White Star Line. In addition, much of the coasting trade during the period 1866–89 was also in the hands of the British; and even after its re-nationalization, British masters were in charge of many Brazilian ships. Several lighterage companies were also owned by the British, the best-known of which was the Rio de Janeiro Lighterage Company Ltd, founded in 1902 and reorganized in 1911 by Reginald and Charles Johnston.[2]

[1] Bushell, *Royal Mail*, pp. 21–2, 61; West, 'Foreigner in Brazilian Technology', p. 800; unlabeled newspaper clipping encl. in Lisboa to Paulino de Sousa, London, 2 Oct. 1851, AHI, 216/2/15, no. 51.

[2] West, 'Foreigner in Brazilian Technology', pp. 711, 712, 717, 720–2, 727, 753, 800–4, 833, 836; J. J. Aubertin, *O norte da provincia de S. Paulo* (1866). *Carta dirigida ao illm. snr. João Ribeiro dos Santos Camargo* (São Paulo: Typ. Schroeder, 1866), p. 33; *Jornal do commercio*, 1 Sept. 1860, p. 2; 1 June 1882, p. 3; 7 Jan. 1895, p. 7; Brazil, Serviço de Estatística Econômica e Financeira, *Commercio exterior do Brasil…1913–1918*, II, 241,

The control of Brazilian shipping was clearly British, and in this way Brazil was still more deeply enmeshed in the net of these foreign interests. The dangers of having so much of the country's shipping in the hands of another became apparent during the First World War when, long before Brazil became a belligerent, its shipping connexions with the outside world were drastically curtailed.[1]

Another tie that the British maintained with the export trade was in the field of insurance. The ships that carried Brazilian coffee and brought in the British goods were generally insured in London, frequently by Lloyd's. Shippers could also buy insurance in Rio de Janeiro from British companies such as the Marine Insurance Company, Ltd, or the Home and Colonial Marine Insurance Company, Ltd. The Royal Insurance Company emphasized that it insured coffee and even the plantations themselves, presumably against fire. Whether insuring plantations or ships, these companies were tied to coffee. Thus Reginald Johnston was a director of the Guardian Assurance Company of London, and his export firm was the agent for this company in Rio de Janeiro and Santos. By 1910 a number of Brazilian insurance companies had been created, but the British still sold over a quarter of all insurance and considerably more than was handled by all other foreign companies put together.[2]

337–8; Macedo to Paulino de Sousa, London, 8 Apr. 1852, AHI, 216/2/15, no. 9; Manchester, *British Preëminence*, p. 325 n.; Centro Industrial do Brasil, *O Brasil. Suas riquezas naturaes, suas industrias*, 3 vols. (Rio: Orosco, 1907–8), I, 315; A. H. John, *A Liverpool Merchant House: Being the History of Alfred Booth and Company, 1863–1958* (London: Allen & Unwin, 1959), pp. 34, 53–70; British Chamber of Commerce of São Paulo and Southern Brazil, *Grã Bretanha*, pp. 37, 61; Watts, 'Colônia inglêsa', p. 166; Antonio Felicio dos Santos, *et al.*, 'Auxilios á industria', *Jornal do commercio*, 6 July 1892, p. 2; E. Johnston & Co., *One Hundred Years*, p. 17; Rio de Janeiro Lighterage Company Limited, *Memorandum and Articles of Association; Date of Incorporation, the 28th day of December, 1911* (London: privately printed, 1911), pp. 6, 8, 22, 37.

[1] H. W. Leslie, ' *The Royal Mail* ' *War Book, Being an Account of the Operations of the Ships of the Royal Mail Steam Packet Co.*, *1914–1919* (London: Heinemann, 1920); Otto Schoenrich, *Former Senator Burton's Trip to South America, 1915*, Carnegie Endowment for International Peace, Division of Intercourse and Education, Publication 9 (Washington, D.C.: Carnegie Endowment for International Peace, 1915), p. 27.

[2] *Jornal do commercio*, 2 Sept. 1860, p. 2; 4 Sept. 1860, p. 2; 2 Jan. 1871, p. 2; 4 Feb. 1882, p. 3; 5 Feb. 1882, p. 3; 3 May 1891, p. 4; 6 Jan. 1895, p. 8; Aviso de 23 de setembro de 1876, Pareceres do Conselho do Estado, AN, 783, I, 15, pp. 122–5; André Rebouças, *Diário e notas autobiográficas*, ed. Ana Flora and Inácio José Veríssimo, Documentos

The exporters, the importers, and the shipping companies demanded better port facilities, and the British took a particular interest in this part of the Brazilian economic 'infrastructure'. In 1851 the Brazilian government decided to improve the port of Rio de Janeiro and contracted a British engineer, Charles Neate, to make studies and plans and carry out the works. Although a part of them collapsed in 1863 and he was subsequently dismissed, the works he started were carried on—with hydraulic winches and other machinery mostly imported from England— by his friend André Rebouças, and they remained Rio de Janeiro's major port facility until the twentieth century.

The British were also connected with plans for port works elsewhere, most of which proved abortive. After his failure in Rio de Janeiro Neate was hired by the Bahia Docks Company of London—promoted by the *visconde* de Mauá—to study plans for the port of Salvador. But the enterprise failed and these plans were never put into effect, the port being built by others during the First World War. In 1874 the Brazilian government asked Sir John Hawkshaw, a leading British engineer, to study the principal ports of the empire, particularly in the provinces of Maranhão, Ceará, Pernambuco, Rio de Janeiro (Campos), and Rio Grande do Sul. His plans for the port of Fortaleza formed the basis of those used in 1884 by the Ceará Harbour Corporation, a firm which was mostly British and borrowed large sums in Britain. These works were actually built, and the Brazilian government bought out the company in 1900.[1]

The sugar port of Recife was not improved before the First World War, but it was not for lack of interest on the part of the British. As early as 1856 the Englishmen Henry Law and John

Brasileiros, 12 (Rio: José Olympio, 1938), p. 28; E. Johnston & Co., *One Hundred Years*, p. 24; Greene to Charles Johnston, Santos, 27 Mar. 1899; Greene to Reginald Johnston, Santos, 15 Mar. 1904, GPL, I, 273–4; II, 471; Brazil, Directoria Geral de Estatistica, *Annuario estatistico do Brazil. Annuaire statistique du Brésil. 1º anno. 1ère année.* (1908–1912), 2 vols. (Rio: Typ. de Estatistica, 1917), II, 215.

[1] Borja Castro, *Descripção do porto*, pp. 20, 44; Rebouças, *Diário*, pp. 136–7; Pedro II, 'Diario', entry for 7 Jan. 1863, AMIP, XXXV, 1055; James William Wells, *Exploring and Travelling Three Thousand Miles Through Brazil from Rio de Janeiro to Maranhão...* (London: Low, Searle & Rivington, 1886), I, 21–2; West, 'Foreigner in Brazilian Technology', pp. 839–40, 846, 848, 850–2, 864, 866, 867; John Hawkshaw, *Melhoramento dos portos do Brasil; relatorios* (Rio: Leuzinger, 1875).

Blount had advocated its improvement, appealing to urban ambitions by saying it would make Recife equal to the other great cities of the world. Charles Neate criticized their plans and opposed favorable action on the part of the government. Nevertheless, the Pernambuco Dock and Harbour Company was organized in London in 1868, although it failed to raise the necessary capital and was finally dissolved. Meanwhile the *visconde* de Mauá and others had submitted plans for port works based on a design drawn up by the indefatigable Charles Neate and Christopher B. Lane. Hawkshaw gave a favorable opinion of these plans, but later, after visiting the port, presented his own as an alternative. Nothing was done, however, to implement these dreams.[1]

The first really modern port in Brazil was built in Santos in the last decade of the nineteenth century. The São Paulo Railway had long taken an active interest in the matter: in 1878 it had built a pier that could accommodate seven steamers for direct loading and unloading into railway cars; and it bid for the construction of modern docks in 1888. But the concession was granted, instead, to Brazilian entrepreneurs of French descent. Friction soon developed between the railway and the dock company, but they eventually came to cooperate closely, as was necessary for companies that worked in relays to export Brazilian coffee.

Rio de Janeiro was the next port to be modernized. The contract was given without open bidding to the British firm of C. H. Walker & Co., Ltd, largely because of the friendships struck up by the persistent Joseph R. Walker, one of the directors. The firm, created in the 1850s, had earlier built Swansea Dock, the Manchester Ship Canal, and the Buenos Aires Docks. The Rio de Janeiro job, lasting from 1904 to 1911, represented a £4,500,000 contract, and the company regularly employed over 2,000 men. An extensive sea-wall was built, the area behind it filled in, a long

---

[1] Alberto de Faria, *Mauá—Ireneo Evangelista de Souza, barão e visconde de Mauá, 1813–1889*, 2nd ed., Brasiliana, 20 (São Paulo: Editôra Nacional, 1933), p. 530; 'Report of Charles Neate...July, 1856'; Charles Neate, 'Port of Pernambuco, Observations...Westminster, 20 April 1871', AMIP, cxxiii, 6139; clx, 7408; File on Pernambuco Dock and Harbour Co., BT 31/1428/4175; Rebouças, *Diário*, p. 172; Hawkshaw, *Melhoramento*, pp. 11–53.

line of warehouses constructed upon it, and modern British-made cranes installed to load freight directly from the ships onto railroad cars or into the warehouses.

These port works and the others the British constructed served to link Brazil more closely to Europe while facilitating the concentration of more resources on the export economy. On the other hand, like the railways, harbor construction also strengthened other sectors of the developing economy. There is no doubt that the manufacturing growth of Rio de Janeiro was aided by the modern port.[1]

Credit facilities were an important aspect of the export–import complex and the British were soon offering them to the trade. Both the counting houses themselves and the British banks lent the funds that made the commerce possible. In 1850 the English importers in Rio de Janeiro signed a convention to restrict credit terms, limiting the repayment period to eight months and refusing to participate in other practices of the local merchants which they considered unbusinesslike. But they were not successful in maintaining this aloof position, and in 1878 an American reported that some import houses had up to a half million dollars tied up in credits to purchasers.[2] Thirty years later the terms they offered were considered unfairly generous by Brazilian manufacturers. The coffee exporters in their turn, especially as they began to buy directly from the producers, would make small advances to the planters or to the 'millers' in the interior towns. Thus both ends of the import–export shuttle were lubricated with British credit.[3]

[1] West, 'Foreigner in Brazilian Technology', pp. 853–6; Helio Lobo, *Docas de Santos, suas origens, lutas e realizações* (Rio: Typ. do 'Jornal do Commercio', Rodrigues, 1936;) Alured Gray Bell, *The Beautiful Rio de Janeiro* (London: Heinemann, 1914), pp. 54–9; Richard Graham, 'A British Industry in Brazil: Rio Flour Mills, 1886–1920', *Business History*, VIII (1966), 30; British Chamber of Commerce of São Paulo and Southern Brazil, *Grã Bretanha*, p. 37; Reginald Lloyd et al. eds., *Twentieth Century Impressions of Brazil: Its History, People, Commerce, Industries, and Resources* (London: Lloyd's Greater Britain Publishing Company, 1913), p. 259; Alfredo Lisboa, 'Portos do Brasil', in Instituto Historico e Geographico Brasileiro, *Diccionario historico, geographico e ethnographico do Brasil (commemorativo do primeiro centenario da independencia)*, 2 vols. (Rio: Imp. Nacional, 1922), I, 560–710.

[2] *Almanak administrativo* (Laemmert), 1850, Supplemento, p. 96; Thomas Adamson, 'Report of Consul-General Adamson...', in *Commercial Relations of the United States with Foreign Countries, 1878* (Washington, D.C.: Government Printing Office, 1879), p. 196.

[3] Stein, *Brazilian Cotton Manufacture*, p. 70; Greene to Charles Johnston, Santos, 24 Oct. 1898, GPL, I, 188; Caio Prado Júnior, *História econômica*, p. 221.

The merchant houses drew their funds not only from their own capital but from the British banks in Brazil with which they were closely connected. Charles Johnston, for instance, was one of the founders and first directors of the London and Brazilian Bank, and helped manage it as well as bolster its financial position at times of crisis. One of the oldest firms trading in Brazilian commodities was Knowles & Foster of London. Members of the firm were among the creators of the English Bank of Rio de Janeiro and also acted as directors of the London and River Plate Bank.[1]

Most Anglo-Brazilian banks were founded during the early 1860s when a new company law in England facilitated their creation. The London and Brazilian Bank was started in 1862 to cope with what was then recognized as the 'rapid increase of the commercial relations between Brazil and Great Britain'. Beginning with a paid-up capital of £450,000, it soon absorbed the Anglo-Portuguese Bank founded the same year. It did over £2,000,000 worth of business during its first year of operation. After surviving a period of hard times in the later 1860s it went on to solid prosperity, and established branches in Pernambuco, Bahia, Paraná, and Rio Grande do Sul in addition to Rio de Janeiro. It opened a branch in Santos in 1881, the very year E. Johnston & Co. began operations there. The sagacity of its directors and the flow of coffee wealth from Brazil paid off handsomely, and from 1873 to 1923 this bank paid a nominal annual average return of 12·8 per cent, and during the five years 1910–14 this figure was 19·2 per cent. In 1923 it joined the London and River Plate Bank, then owned by Lloyds Bank, to become the Bank of London and South America.[2]

---

[1] E. Johnston & Co., *One Hundred Years*, pp. 23–4; David Joslin, *A Century of Banking in Latin America; to Commemorate the Centenary in 1962 of the Bank of London and South America Limited* (London: Oxford Univ. Press, 1963), pp. 65, 66, 71, 74, 80–1, 83–4; Knowles & Foster, *The History of Knowles & Foster, 1828–1948* (London: Knowles & Foster, 1948), pp. 46, 49.

[2] Joslin, *A Century of Banking*, pp. 27, 66, 75, 162, 244, and 'Resolution', quoted on p. 65; Antonio de Barros Ramalho Ortigão, 'Surto de cooperativismo', *Revista do Instituto Historico e Geographico Brasileiro, tomo especial: Contribuições para a biographia de D. Pedro II* (Rio: Imp. Nacional, 1925), p. 293; Bank of London and South America, Ltd, *A Short Account of the Bank's Growth and Formation* (London: privately printed, 1954), pp. 10, 11; Manchester, *British Preëminence*, p. 327; Rippy, *British Investments*, p. 175; Scully, *Brazil*, pp. 68–9, 161.

Another British bank in Brazil was the English Bank of Rio de Janeiro. It was organized in 1863 as the Brazilian and Portuguese Bank with a nominal paid-in capital of £500,000. Its name was changed three years later and it enjoyed a boisterous prosperity in its early years. It returned an annual average dividend of nearly 9·5 per cent from 1874 to 1892. It was the first foreign bank to open a branch in Santos to tap the coffee trade there, and established itself in the city of São Paulo in 1886. By 1884 its Santos branch had outstanding loans of nearly £1 million. In 1891 the bank was sold for a very generous price to one of the Brazilian banks created during a stock-market craze, and then, with capital derived from the sale, its directors opened the British Bank of South America that same year. The newly named bank, however, was to prove relatively unsuccessful. Although prosperous during the First World War, it was bought up by the Anglo-South American Bank in 1920.[1]

The London and River Plate Bank was still a third large British bank operating in Brazil. Having established itself successfully in Buenos Aires thirty years before, it entered the Brazilian field in early 1892. After 1899, when it opened offices in São Paulo and Santos, it dealt with coffee exporters, railroad companies, and import firms. It also began to play a role as agent for government loans and as financial backer of railroad enterprises.[2]

The major interest of the British banks was the export–import business, although the financing of imports—which increasingly meant capital goods—led eventually to industrial loans. They probably had a hand in every part of the economy, especially considering their relative size. It has been calculated that by 1913 British banks held 30 per cent of the total assets of all banks and 57 per cent of those of all foreign banks in Brazil. Only a small part of their resources represented British capital; the bulk of their funds was drawn from local depositors, for whose money they competed with Brazilian banks. Even some of their capital was invested by Brazilian shareholders. But their overseas con-

---

[1] Rippy, *British Investments*, p. 154; Joslin, *A Century of Banking*, pp. 82, 168, 170, 259; *A provincia de São Paulo*, 12 Mar. 1884, p. 2.
[2] Joslin, *A Century of Banking*, pp. 139–40, 144, 146–7, 156–7; Brazil, Serviço de Estatística Econômica e Financeira, *Commercio exterior do Brasil...1913–1918*, II, 390–419.

tacts gave them a crucial advantage over Brazilian banks. Since their home offices were in the 'City' of London they knew of large loans, impending investments, or declining markets sooner than most of their competitors in Brazil. Furthermore, their conservative business practices insured their continuity. Possibly Brazilian banking 'know-how' was increased by their long presence; books on banking practices written by Britishers were paternalistically translated and advertised for sale at the time of the financial collapse of several Brazilian banking firms in 1864. In any case, the British banks were a powerful force within the Brazilian economy.[1]

The banks functioned smoothly by keeping their eyes on every operation. The exporter shipped his coffee or other produce, prepared the bills, and presented them, sometimes along with the shipping documents or bills of lading, at the banking officer's desk. The bank lent the exporter the funds for purchasing imports or additional coffee, while collecting for the produce through agents in New York or on the Continent. The same transaction was carried out in London for the shipper of manufactured goods, and paper was usually all that need be moved from Brazil to London and back again. Only occasionally, at moments of crisis, was it necessary to ship bullion from London to maintain the banks' position. The establishment of branches in the various regional centers of the country made it possible to match imports in one port with exports at another, according to the season. This practice eventually led them to finance internal trade as well as exports and imports.

The British banks made it a practice to avoid lending to planters on the security of their land or of future crops, although once in a while they fell heir to land when mortgages had been foreclosed by merchants who in turn became insolvent. They also avoided the *comissários* if they could, considering them much too

[1] Manchester, *British Preëminence*, p. 327; Joslin, *A Century of Banking*, pp. 19–20, 23, 26, 165; Brazil, Ministerio da Fazenda, *Relatorio*, 1872 (Rio: Typ. Nacional, 1872), p. 100; *Jornal do commercio*, 3 Jan. 1871, p. 2; 4 Jan. 1871, p. 7; 3 May 1891, p. 6; 1 Nov. 1891, p. 8; 6 Jan. 1895, p. 7; *A provincia de São Paulo*, 10 Feb. 1884, p. 2; 12 Mar. 1884, p. 2; advertisement for book by James William Gilbart in Pedro Antonio Ferreira Vianna, *A crise commercial do Rio de Janeiro em 1864* (Rio: Garnier, 1864), inside front cover.

unstable a risk. In addition to the import–export houses, accounts were kept in the British banks by British railway companies, urban service enterprises, and dock company contractors. From them they drew funds for payments of local bills and wages; into them they paid receipts; and through them they remitted profits as they had earlier transferred capital. The banks were essential to the maintenance of this 'informal British empire'.[1]

The British banks were not popular. The competition they offered Brazilian merchant bankers helped set off the panic of 1864, and their exchange speculation triggered the ruin of several weak Brazilian banks in 1900. Indeed, the most frequent charge brought against the British banks was that they manipulated the exchange rate. Their home offices were dead set against exchange speculation, but the local managers sometimes indulged in this heady game. To their defense came the Rio de Janeiro Chamber of Commerce, whose members were probably clients of the British banks; in 1883 it spoke out vehemently to deny they contributed to the lowering exchange rate. It was argued that, on the contrary, the British banks had several times been forced to use their reserve funds to reconstitute the capital account of their Brazilian branches depleted by exchange losses. But that the banks might speculate on the exchange rate was admitted, this being considered a legitimate banking activity. Nor was it denied that the banks might effect short-term oscillations in the exchange which would be to their benefit.[2]

In view of their close connexions to the coffee trade one may suspect that they were sometimes inclined to foster a decline in the exchange if they could. Those who received hard currency and made payments in local currency were naturally interested in lowering the value of Brazilian money, since domestic costs then rose more slowly than their income. A Frenchman observed at the turn of the century that the coffee planter felt this way. Edward Greene, the Santos partner of E. Johnston & Co., complained that 'however good for the country at large a steady

[1] Joslin, *A Century of Banking*, pp. 21, 25, 67, 76, 82, 140, 141, 159–60, 162–4.
[2] *Rio News*, 24 Feb. 1887, p. 3; Joslin, *A Century of Banking*, pp. 68–9, 142–8, 161; Sodré, *História da burguesia*, p. 155; Associação Commercial do Rio de Janeiro, *Resposta... aos quesitos da Commissão Parlamentar de Inquerito* (Rio: Typ. Montenegro, 1883), p. 18.

exchange may be, it makes business for coffee exporters very difficult', although he doubtless preferred it to a rising exchange.[1] If powerful interests with whom the banks had intimate relations wished to make exchange transactions, the banks may well have momentarily manipulated the market in their behalf. By this operation, the intangible psychological factors that affect exchange may have been adversely touched.

On the other hand, the importers—and they were often the same men as the exporters—disliked falling exchange since they were forced to raise their prices, temporarily limiting sales. And the banks would also be pulled by the long view, recognizing that declining exchange curtailed foreign investment, which in turn, as they thought, would dampen national growth and the banks' eventual prosperity. There is no doubt that the banks speculated on exchange, but—despite the fact they sometimes concentrated more on exchange business than on anything else— there is little concrete evidence to suggest they drove it only in one direction. Furthermore, they profited relatively little from the foreign loans which a falling exchange forced Brazil to make.[2]

By far the bulk of the revenues of the Brazilian government was derived from import duties. Whenever the value of exports declined, whether for internal or external reasons, imports also fell off and the government was hard pressed for funds. It then resorted either to printing additional currency or borrowing abroad. If it printed currency its income lessened even further since the duties were collected in local currency and were some-times fixed, not *ad valorem*. So foreign loans became an integral part of the financial system, although expansion of the currency was also used, especially after 1889. When the exchange rate fell off, repayment of these foreign loans became truly onerous. One historian claims that servicing the foreign debt ate up between 50 and 99 per cent of what was otherwise a favorable balance of trade between 1870 and 1900. The willingness of the British to

---

[1] Pierre Denis, *Brazil...* (London: Unwin, 1911), pp. 151–2; Greene to Reginald Johnston, 24 Apr. 1899, GPL, I, 246.
[2] Joaquim Nabuco to João Artur de Souza Corrêa, Rio, 2 Mar. 1898, in Joaquim Nabuco, *Obras completas*, 14 vols. (São Paulo: Instituto Progresso Editorial, 1949), XIII, 277; Joslin, *A Century of Banking*, pp. 83, 143–5.

The Export–Import Complex

continue to apply their funds in this manner was one of the distinctive features of the relationship between these two countries before the First World War.[1]

During all the period of the empire and much of the republican era, the only foreign loans made by Brazil were made in London —'the credit reservoir of the entire world' as one Brazilian called it.[2] Their size and frequency are impressive evidence of Brazil's dependence on Great Britain. Table 5 will give some idea of this condition. The import–export economy would have faced much rougher sledding if it had not been for these loans.

Table 5. *Brazilian Public Loans Raised in England before 1918*[a]

Year	£[b]	Year	£[b]
1824/25	1,333,300	1888	6,297,300
1825	1,400,000	1889	19,837,000
1829	769,200	1893	3,710,000
1839	411,200	1895	7,442,000
1843	732,600	1898	8,613,717
1852	1,040,600	1901	16,619,320
1858	1,526,500	1903	8,500,000
1859	459,500	1906	1,100,000
1860	1,360,100	1908	4,000,000
1863	3,855,300	1910	11,000,000
1865	6,963,600	1911	4,500,000
1871	3,459,600	1911/12	2,400,000
1875	5,301,200	1913	11,000,000
1883	4,599,600	1914	14,502,396
1886	6,431,000		

[a] Source: Valentin F. Bouças, *História da dívida externa*, 2nd ed. (Rio: Edições Financeiras, 1950), tables inserted following pp. 61, 76, 138, 202, 262.
[b] Loans frequently included the consolidation of previous debts.

[1] Cf. Sodré, *História da burguesia*, p. 186 with Celso Furtado, *The Economic Growth of Brazil: a Survey from Colonial to Modern Times*, transl. Ricardo W. de Aguiar and Eric Charles Drysdale (Berkeley and Los Angeles: Univ. of California Press, 1963), p. 175 n.
[2] Rui Barbosa, *Mocidade e exilio. Cartas ao conselheiro Albino José Barbosa de Oliveira e ao dr. Antônio d'Araújo Ferreira Jacobina*, ed. Américo Jacobina Lacombe, Brasiliana, 38 (São Paulo: Editôra Nacional, 1934), p. 305.

In addition to borrowing by the federal government, there were also state and municipal loans. The city of Rio de Janeiro borrowed over £500,000 in London in 1889. The state of São Paulo negotiated various loans including one in 1888 to be used for the development of immigration and colonization. Another loan which included the same purpose along with sanitation of the cities of Santos and São Paulo was arranged for in 1904 with the London and Brazilian Bank. This bank also made loans to the states of Amazonas and Bahia. In 1906 the state of São Paulo borrowed £3,000,000 from J. H. Schroeder & Co. of London and the First National City Bank of New York in connexion with a price support program for coffee.[1]

But all the loans negotiated in Britain by the central government were handled by the house of Rothschild. It was named sole financial agent for Brazil in 1855. According to the contract, these bankers were to handle all funds sent by Brazil for payment of dividends, salaries or other expenses; do all the buying for the government; and pay all the dividends on Brazilian debts. The British investor in Brazilian government bonds bought them from Rothschild's and accepted their recommendations.

The 1855 agreement was signed by Francisco Inácio de Carvalho Moreira, later *barão* do Penedo (1815–1906), who, like the other Brazilian ministers to London, was always on very good terms with this banking family. A great friend of the British— he had once been the lawyer for Britishers in Brazil—Penedo was minister in London from 1855 until 1889 with the exception of a five-year period beginning in 1867. Even when Brazil broke off diplomatic relations with England in 1863 and he ostensibly lived in Paris, Penedo was frequently in London to discuss Brazil's foreign loans with the Rothschilds. Despite the fact that his predecessor had been dismissed for allegedly being more loyal to these bankers than to Brazil, Penedo did not keep his distance from them. Baron Lionel de Rothschild frequented Penedo's house and advised him not only on Brazil's foreign loans but also

---

[1] Francisco Agenor de Noronha Santos, *Indice alphabetico do livro 'Contractos e concessões'*, *Prefeitura do Distrito Federal* (Rio: Typ. do Instituto Profissional, 1902), p. 46; Brazil, Directoria Geral de Estatistica, *Annuario...* (*1908–1912*), II, 260–1, 264–5.

on his private investment policy, which was characterized by successful speculation. As was the practice in that day, the negotiator of foreign loans was given presents by the agents, and Penedo admitted receiving some £200,000 in this way over the years. There were naturally occasions when Penedo was charged with favoritism in dealing only with Rothschild's in raising foreign loans. But his Anglophile successor, João Artur de Souza Corrêa, followed in his footsteps. The Marquis of Salisbury is supposed to have asked maliciously whether it was true that Souza Corrêa did not know how to speak Portuguese, and Alfred de Rothschild referred to this Brazilian diplomat as 'a good and affectionate friend'. So Brazilian loans continued to be handled by Rothschild's.[1]

The position of this banking house made its opinions worth considering, and it was not in favor of bold measures to encourage industrialization. The Brazilian government in 1892, faced with the crashing end of a speculative boom, prepared to issue industrial development loans. But Rothschild's telegraphed the Minister of the Treasury criticizing this plan, and this opposition was used as an argument in the Senate against the bill. Some writers accused Rothschild's of combating this measure because it would tend to reduce imports of manufactured goods from England. Although the measure was passed and implemented, Brazil's position became weaker in the London bond market.[2]

One of the most controversial loans in Brazilian history was the 'funding loan' of 1898. In the early days of the republic Rothschild's had denied the possibility of raising a Brazilian loan,

---

[1] Contract between Rothschild's and Brazilian government quoted by Gustavo Barroso, *Brasil, colonia de banqueiros (história dos emprestimos de 1824 a 1934)*, 6th ed. (Rio: Civilização Brasileira, 1937), pp. 234–5; Sodré, *História da burguesia*, p. 86; Renato Mendonça, *Um diplomata na côrte de Inglaterra; o barão do Penedo e sua época*, Brasiliana, 219 (São Paulo: Editôra Nacional, 1942), pp. 76, 99, 158–9, 161–7, 292, 315, 414, but cf. p. 33; Honório Hermeto Carneiro Leão, *marquês* do Paraná, quoted *ibid.* p. 148; Manoel de Oliveira Lima, *Memorias (estas minhas reminiscências)* (Rio: José Olympio, 1937), p. 197; Francisco Ignacio de Carvalho Moreira, *barão do Penedo, O empréstimo brasileiro contraido em Londres em 1863* (Paris: n.p., 1864); Brazil, Ministerio da Fazenda, *Correspondencia entre o Ministerio da Fazenda e a Legação em Londres concernante ao empréstimo contraido em 1865* (Rio: Typ. Nacional, 1866); Monteiro, *O presidente Campos Salles*, pp. 57, 65.

[2] *Jornal do commercio*, 19 June 1892, p. 4; 23 June 1892, p. 1; Luz, *Aspectos do nacionalismo econômico*, pp. 80–2; Stein, *Brazilian Cotton Manufacture*, p. 93.

but had finally agreed to handle one in 1895. The bankers may have regretted it, since Brazil's financial house continued in disorder. Deficit financing, surplus coffee crops, and lack of foreign confidence caused the Brazilian exchange rate to fall from $27\frac{1}{2}d$. to the *milreis* in November 1889 to $7\frac{3}{16}d$. in 1898. Rothschild's, in fact, was accused of fostering this decline. One of its results was that payments on the foreign debt were crushing the breath out of Brazil's government finances. Over 240,000 *contos* had to be paid for servicing the debt out of a total revenue of only 300,000 *contos*. The Press suggested defaulting on the foreign debt, but it was rumored that this would lead to intervention.[1]

At the beginning of 1898 Manuel Ferraz de Campos Sales (1841–1913), a large coffee planter, was the president-elect of Brazil. Surveying the state of affairs in the country over which he was about to preside, he determined to bring order out of financial chaos by appealing to European bankers for a large loan to consolidate the nation's debts while at the same time securing a moratorium on their repayment. This would give him a breathing spell in which to reorganize the country's financial apparatus. In his campaign speeches he had said that the question of government finances was the most important one to be resolved. So he now made it his major goal. The outgoing president and minister of finance agreed to appoint him as government representative before the European bankers. Upon arrival in Europe he discovered to his dismay that there was very little interest in his plans. Even Rothschild's, whom Campos Sales had warmly defended at the time of the industrial loan controversy in 1892, turned him down. He then turned his attention to Continental bankers without much greater success.

[1] José Carlos Rodrigues to Rui Barbosa, 10 June 1895, in Raimundo Magalhães Júnior, *Rui, o homem e o mito*, Retratos do Brasil, 27 (Rio: Civilização Brasileira, 1964), p. 159; Luís Viana Filho, *A vida de Rui Barbosa* (centenary edition) [6th ed.?] (São Paulo: Editôra Nacional, 1952), pp. 220–2; Joslin, *A Century of Banking*, p. 142; Barbosa, *Mocidade e exilio*, pp. 290–2; Alcindo Guanabara, *A presidencia Campos Salles: politica e finanças, 1898–1902* (Rio: Laemmert, 1902), pp. 27, 281, 310; Bernardino de Campos to Rothschild's, 25 Jan. 1898, in Bernardino de Campos, ed., *Funding Loan: o accôrdo do Brasil com os credores externos realisado pelo governo do dr. Prudente de Moraes em 15 de junho de 1898; documentos inéditos; varias apreciações* (São Paulo: Duprat, 1909), p. 19; Manuel Ferraz de Campos Salles, *Da propaganda á presidencia* (São Paulo: Typ. 'A Editora', 1908), pp. 184, 186.

Meanwhile in Rio de Janeiro, the London and River Plate Bank, now anxious to steady the exchange, offered to spearhead a move on the part of Brazil's bondholders and the owners of railroad companies receiving guaranteed interest to provide a solution. According to their plan, these groups would agree to a consolidation of the debt, a postponement of its amortization, and a moratorium on the payment of interest, in exchange for a rigid austerity program and a new mortgage on Brazilian assets, especially the customs revenues. Arrangements for reducing the amount of national currency were to be inspected by the London and River Plate Bank itself. Rothschild's then agreed to act as agent after all, and the deal was accepted. Brazilian bonds began to rise in value. A banquet was given in London in honor of Campos Sales by Alfred de Rothschild. The keynote speech was made by Charles Johnston, as vice-president of the London and Brazilian Bank, and Reginald Johnston was also present. So were Edward Greene and a representative of Rio Flour Mills, the major British manufacturing establishment in Brazil.[1]

Alfred de Rothschild then made warm and rosy remarks about Brazil's future. But a few days after the banquet he wrote Campos Sales to say that in order to recommend to the bondholders that they should accept the plan after all he would need a letter from Brazil's future president personally committing himself to the austerity program called for in the agreement. What seems now to have been an unnecessary insult may have been a way of reminding Campos Sales that other banks or not, the final word on any arrangement would have to be given by Rothschild's. In any case, Campos Sales complied with the request on the recommendation of Souza Corrêa. One of the Rothschilds later complained plaintively that the London and Brazilian Bank and the directors of the railways receiving guaranteed interest

---

[1] Guanabara, *A presidencia Campos Salles*, pp. 47, 50, 61; Campos Salles, *Da propaganda á presidencia*, pp. 170–1, 179, 184, 187–91, 194; Campos Salles to Luiz Piza, Paris, 1 May 1893, in Manuel Ferraz de Campos Salles, *Cartas da Europa* (Rio: Leuzinger, 1894), pp. 155–6; Nabuco to Souza Corrêa, Rio, 2 March 1898, in Nabuco, *Obras completas*, XIII, 277; Campos, *Funding Loan*, pp. 24, 26–7; Joslin, *A Century of Banking*, pp. 143, 156; Caio Prado Júnior, *Historia econômica*, p. 235; Monteiro, *O presidente Campos Salles*, p. 104; Greene to Reginald Johnston, Santos, 4 July 1898, GPL, I, 174; minutes General Meeting, 20 Dec. 1898, ARFM.

had blamed him for the 'imposition' of the moratorium upon them.[1]

Nor were the arrangements accepted without protest in Brazil. Even a year later the political reformer Rui Barbosa suggested that the contract be broken unilaterally. A spokesman for the industrialists regretted the terms of the loan, but argued that it must now be carried out. Another believer in industrialization attacked Campos Sales for being interested only in the affairs of the coffee planters and his English friends. The president was labeled a puppet of the British bankers.[2]

Still, the program had the desired result. The *milreis* increased in value to $12\frac{1}{2}d$. Payments on the debt were resumed on schedule, and the improvement in the exchange rate made it much easier to meet the interest charges. But the austerity program also caused a severe crisis for the economy and slowed down the government's efforts to build up the country's economic base.[3]

On the whole, most of the foreign loans did little to advance modernization, although, with rare exceptions, one must blame the Brazilian government rather than the British bankers. Some railroad construction and the building of the port of Rio de Janeiro were directly tied to loans raised through Rothschild's. But the bulk of their proceeds were used to ease the government around the temporary crises of the export–import economy. None of them were directed, so to speak, toward the hard task of digging the tunnels in the entirely different direction of industrialization.

Still another way in which the British contributed to the export–import economy while slowing down moves toward a manufacturing system was through the supply of free trade arguments to Brazilian policy-makers and the application of official

---

[1] Campos Salles, *Da propaganda á presidencia*, pp. 195–6; Guanabara, *A presidencia Campos Salles*, pp. 69–71, 73; Monteiro, *O presidente Campos Salles*, p. 112n.; José Carlos Rodrigues, *Resgate das estradas de ferro do Recife a S. Francisco e de outras que gozavam da garantia de juros: Relatorio*...(Rio: Imp. Nacional, 1902), p. 5.

[2] Guanabara, *A presidencia Campos Salles*, p. 397; speech of Serzedello Corrêa, 8 Dec. 1898, *ibid.* pp. 369–70; *Cartas de Londres* (São Paulo: Duprat, 1902), pp. 16, 18; Campos, *Funding Loan*, p. 39.

[3] Guanabara, *A presidencia Campos Salles*, pp. 360, 448, 457; Caio Prado Júnior, *História econômica*, p. 235.

pressure against the erection of tariff barriers. But one must be careful to adopt the proper historical perspective. It is tempting to tie Brazilian free traders to the pillory and castigate them for defending the traditional society. This may be a fair judgement with regard to those who still held on to free trade ideas in the last few years of the nineteenth century, and it is certainly justifiable to criticize those who continued to advocate free trade well into the present era. But it is a mistake not to differentiate the advocates of free trade before, say, 1875, from those who stuck to this doctrine after Brazil had begun to industrialize. In the earlier period, Brazil was still shaking off the restrictions on trade which stood in direct opposition to the modern economic state, interfering with the free exchange of goods. It was only after these shackles had been weakened and the wealth produced by growing exports had pumped new life into the Brazilian economy and new strains into the Brazilian society, that industrialization became a serious possibility and free trade a drag rather than a boost. Even then, it is not uncommon to find members of the new entrepreneurial, anti-latifundiary groups mistakenly advocating free trade because they still associated it with progress. The meaning of free trade thought must be carefully assessed within the context of its time.

The same thing is true of the British. Adam Smith, when he said the commerce of the world should flow according to natural law, had obviously been arguing for an entirely 'modern' system of economic organization. Subsequently, the free-trade principle became the battle cry of a crusade; the last infidel stronghold in England collapsed with the repeal of the corn laws in 1846, but the banners were then hoisted in other parts of the world and the struggle continued. When Englishmen urged Brazil to adopt free-trade policies in the 1850s they were not consciously attacking Brazilian industrialization, which in any case was a very distant threat. They were convinced free trade would benefit all peoples by bringing them into the modern world.

Thus, free trade in Brazil during those years was not the slogan of the traditional elements, but, rather, of the modernizers. What low tariffs Brazil had previously adopted were due to political

The Export–Import Complex

necessity: the British held the upper hand in the early nineteenth century and could secure what they wished. The presence in Brazil of a few free traders formed by the Enlightenment would not have been enough alone to alter ancient policies. And the moderately protective tariff of 1844 was primarily used not to defend modern manufacture, but to shield a waning craft industry.[1]

By the middle of the century, with the increasing strength of the coffee areas of the Paraíba valley and the new power of this dynamic export trade, government commissions carefully defended free trade. The one charged in 1853 with revising the tariff law devoted almost all of its 400-page report to urging a reduction. Adam Smith's *Wealth of Nations* was frequently cited, and a spot check of economic theorists referred to in the report indicates that they were mostly British and their works were cited in English. Furthermore, the commission presented a list of free-trade thinkers in which appear the names of twenty-eight Englishmen, including Thomas Malthus, David Ricardo, Jeremy Bentham, John Stuart Mill, Robert Peel, and, of course, Richard Cobden. It concluded that protective tariffs were 'a denial...of justice, a denial of liberty, and a denial of the right of property'. The recommendations of the commission were adopted, and, by 1855, a Brazilian lawyer wrote that his country had now begun to feel the 'beneficent influx of free-trade theories'.[2]

The British now tried to get Brazil to renew the commercial treaty that had expired in 1844. But Brazilians consistently turned a deaf ear to proposals regarding such an international agreement, although not failing to claim credit for the liberal tariffs of 1853, even planting articles in *The Economist* applauding their own actions. But the reform of 1853 was not enough to satisfy the

[1] An example of a modernizer who advocated free trade is André Rebouças, *Agricultura nacional, estudos economicos; propaganda abolicionista e democratica* (Rio: Lamoureux, 1883), p. 44; on the meaning of free trade in Britain see William D. Grampp, *The Manchester School of Economics* (Stanford, California, & London: Stanford Univ. Press & Oxford Univ. Press, 1960), pp. 1–38; on an early free trader in Brazil see Alcides Bezerra, 'Visconde de Cayrú: vida e obra', in Brazil, Arquivo Nacional, *Publicações*, xxxiv (1937), 339–54.
[2] Brazil, Commissão...Tarifa, *Relatorio*, pp. 249, 287, 305, 307, 309, and esp. 298; Fernandes Pereira de Barros, *Apontamentos*, p. 119.

The Export–Import Complex

Foreign Office. In 1854 the British minister in Rio de Janeiro translated and printed up a memorandum he had received from his government in which the advantages that were accruing to Brazil from British free-trade policies were pointed out and Brazil was urged to move in the same direction by signing a commercial treaty. The pressure continued for nearly a decade until, finally, Brazil made it clear in no uncertain terms that it would under no circumstances sign such a document. There is no evidence to suggest that the reprisals against Brazil which were undertaken shortly thereafter (1863) had any connexion with this stand, but we may presume that if Brazil had not come out of that incident in as favorable a position as it did, a treaty might well have been the result.[1]

Brazilians who were influenced by the British were at the fore-front of those who, excited by the prospects opened up by coffee prosperity, called for the free international exchange of goods. At the very time when Britain was forcing down the doors of China and suggesting to Brazil that it sign a commercial treaty, the Brazilian minister in London expressed the belief that one of the great achievements of the epoch was the commercial penetration of all points of the globe 'over the wreckage of artificial obstacles created by governments'.[2]

The three-way connexion between the coffee export economy, the British, and the Brazilian belief in free trade is to be seen in the thought of Aureliano Cândido Tavares Bastos (1839–75). Although the son of a political leader in Alagoas, he was sent to the São Paulo law school and became a spokesman for coffee interests when he entered the Chamber of Deputies almost immediately upon graduation. His first concern was for the prosperity of the coffee trade. The thesis he presented to the law

[1] Macedo to Paulino de Sousa, London, 23 Sept. 1853; Taques to Carvalho Moreira (Penedo), Rio, 8 Aug. 1862, AHI, 217/3/7, no. 21; 410/5/93, no. 10; The Economist, XII (19 Feb. 1854), 170–1; Memoria sobre o commercio entre a Grãa Bretanha e o Brazil (Rio: Typ. da Viuva Vianna Junior, 1854), encl. in British minister to Luiz Pedreira do Couto Ferraz, Rio, 28 May 1854, AMIP, cxx, 5970; Richard Graham, 'Os fundamentos da ruptura de relações diplomáticas entre o Brasil e a Grã-Bretanha em 1863:"A questão Christie"', Revista de história, XXIV (Jan.–June 1962), 117–38, 379–402.
[2] Francisco Carvalho Moreira, barão do Penedo, Relatorio sobre a exposição internacional de 1862 (London: Brettell, 1863), p. xxxi.

school in 1859 revealed his solicitude in studying export and import taxes. Thereafter he consistently defended the interests of coffee exporters, urging the government to foster the expansion of agriculture. He wanted it to undertake only those public works that would lead to expanded exports, and not accept foreign loans unless they were used in such projects. He especially demanded the institution of direct maritime communications with Brazil's chief coffee market—the United States—through the subsidization of a shipping line.

For him, development meant the exchange of goods with the rest of the world; progress was to be measured by a nation's foreign commerce. He was successful in his campaign to have the Brazilian coasting trade and the Amazon river thrown open to the ships of all nations. He felt Brazil had no right to keep the wealth of the Amazon from being developed and he defended the rights of Western commerce in China. He also opposed protective tariffs in Brazil. Yet he was clearly a critic of the traditional structures of society. His advocacy of free and compulsory education, immigration, gradual emancipation of the slaves, decentralization and federalism, liberalization of the political system, the end of the emperor's moderating power, and the improvement of Brazil's internal communications, clearly identify him as a modernizer.[1]

He has often been mistakenly identified solely with the United States because of his interest in an American shipping line and his American friendships. But his belief in free trade makes him less of an emulator of the Americans than is usually thought. He had traveled to England in 1867, visiting Parliament, the Bank of England, and industrial establishments. He was much impressed. He spoke of 'glorious Albion', and called himself a 'raving en-

[1] Carlos Pontes, *Tavares Bastos (Aureliano Candido), 1839–1875*, Brasiliana, 136 (São Paulo: Editôra Nacional, 1939), pp. 92–8, 105, 169–70, 172, 205, 260–1, 293–5, 327–8, 338–9, 348; Aureliano Cândido Tavares Bastos, *Cartas do Solitário*, 3rd ed., Brasiliana, 115 (São Paulo: Editôra Nacional, 1938), pp. 222–411, esp. 237, 357; Aureliano Cândido Tavares Bastos, *Os males do presente e as esperanças do futuro*, 2nd ed., Brasiliana, 151 (São Paulo: Editôra Nacional, 1939), p. 50; Aureliano Cândido Tavares Bastos, *O valle do Amazonas: a livre navegação do Amazonas...* 2nd ed., Brasiliana, 106 (São Paulo: Editôra Nacional, 1937); Percy Alvin Martin, 'The Influence of the United States on the Opening of the Amazon to the World's Commerce', *Hispanic American Historical Review*, I (1918), 153–6.

thusiast of England'. When he was only 19 years old he spoke of England as 'the *palladium* of modern liberties', subsequently pointing with admiration to the heroes of British history.[1] He was the perfect example of the Brazilian committed to modern change, who, influenced by the British, believed in free trade without question. And he helped gain for this doctrine an acceptance among the new generation that made it almost impossible to shake off free-trade policies in later years.

Eventually, the belief in free trade slowed the effort to industrialize Brazil. When Brazilian industrialists began forcefully to raise the issue of tariff protection in the 1880s they were defeated. Although upon occasion enjoying moderately protective duties after 1889, the vacillating policies of the government tended more often toward lower tariffs. In 1898 the presidential candidate Campos Sales, intimately linked to the coffee business, promised to avoid 'inopportune protectionism'. His friend Tobias do Rego Monteiro (1866–1952), a journalist with considerable political influence during the years before the First World War, hailed all free-trade policies, saying Brazil must welcome any contact with 'more advanced civilizations'. And the Chamber of Commerce, largely made up of importers, long maintained that 'direct trade with other countries will be one of the best means of achieving development and progress'.[2] Thus, the continued prestige of the British, built up in so many other ways, led to the defense of free trade in Brazil even after confidence in such a policy was waning in Britain. The adoption of a frankly protectionist tariff was too long delayed.

In this, as in all those actions which continued to place primary emphasis on exports and imports after the conditions for industrialization had been created, the British were a drag upon the forces of modernization. The funding loan of 1898 helped cause a depression and the other public loans were rarely earmarked for projects that would build up the country's economic potential.

[1] Mendonça, *Um diplomata na côrte de Inglaterra*, pp. 232, 237, 330; Tavares Bastos, *Cartas do Solitário*, p. 415; Pontes, *Tavares Bastos*, pp. 87–8, 99.
[2] Guanabara, *A presidencia Campos Salles*, p. 48; Monteiro, *O presidente Campos Salles*, pp. 108–9; Associação Commercial do Rio de Janeiro, *Resposta*, p. 9; Greene belonged to the similar chamber of commerce in Santos, Receipt, GPL, I, 183.

The Export–Import Complex

The British banks were primarily tied into the export sector rather
than the industrial one, and, through exchange speculations, may
occasionally have taken advantage of Brazil's weakness to further
damage the country's financial position. The shipping companies
and insurance firms facilitated the concentration on export commodities, although, of course, they were not causative factors in
restricting industrialization. British imports cheapened the cost
of coffee production and emphasized the monocultural nature of
the Brazilian economy. The houses which handled the bulk of
the coffee exports from Brazil and thus controlled the trade were
also British. Of activities discussed thus far, only in the case of
port facilities and railroads may the British role be considered
potentially neutral, benefiting both planters and industrialists.
Although urban classes, depending on both one and the other
activity, found the British eminently helpful in making Brazilian
cities over in the image of the modern world, the complex of
British interests in the export–import economy tended to slow
down the process of modern change.

4

THE URBAN STYLE

In Brazil cities were the beachheads of the modern world. Urban groups wished to approximate the models created in Europe in their economic organization, social structure, attitudes, and style of life. Brazilians must now eat imported foods, cure their sickness with patent medicines, perfume themselves with new scents, fill their homes with strange furniture and novel sanitary devices, light their houses without oil, go into town with greater speed and return to garden suburbs, dress in the foreign mode, and adopt new forms of recreation, all because Europeans were doing it.[1] And even when Paris was the ideal, it was the British who supplied the wherewithal to imitate it. Aspiring to enter the ranks of modernity, the Brazilian urban classes proudly adopted a new way of life as if holding up a coat of arms largely designed by the British and emblazoned with British devices.

One of the most striking aspects of the Brazilian import structure was the degree to which these urban groups, formed by the beginning processes of modernization, demanded in their cities the products that were available overseas. Few things are more intimately a part of one's culture than one's diet; yet urban, mobile Brazilians were led by their fascination with modernity to use imported foodstuffs. British foods were a common item on the shelves of the nineteenth-century merchant in Rio de Janeiro. At first, dairy products headed the list. One importer received 500 barrels of butter from England during one month in 1850, and English butter continued to be advertised in the Rio de Janeiro papers until the 1870s. The total value of imported butter reached a peak of more than £700,000 during the period

---

[1] This general theme and related aspects, especially for the first half of the nineteenth century, are explored by Gilberto Freyre, *Inglêses no Brasil: aspectos da influência britânica sôbre a vida, a paisagem e a cultura do Brasil*, Documentos Brasileiros, 58 (Rio: José Olympio, 1948); see esp. pp. 55–61.

1855–9, but declined sharply after 1875, and butter subsequently disappeared from the 'for sale' column of the newspapers. Cheese was also imported from Great Britain, and *queijos londrinos* were being advertised not only in Rio de Janeiro, but also in São Paulo. Other foodstuffs imported from England included potatoes from Jersey, Huntley and Palmers' biscuits, English sauces and mustard, and English hams. Of course, some of these foods were imported especially for the foreign colony, as is evident from the following advertisement printed in English, or what passed for English: 'Hams, Gheese [*sic*], & Bacon fresh arrived al [at] n. 125 rua Direita.'

English beer and ale were also imported. All that one merchant house received during January 1850 was 200 kegs of beer and 100 barrels of butter. The firm of George Harvey & Silva in São Paulo advertised its English Bass beer in 1875, while a few years later in Rio de Janeiro an auction of household goods included 31 bottles of English beer. Between 1850–4 and 1865–9 the value of beer and ale exported from Great Britain to Brazil grew from £111,000 to £480,500. Subsequently, probably because of competition from breweries built by German immigrants, this item dwindled in importance, so that in 1885–9 it was worth only £91,000.[1]

Other items of importation that bespeak the 'Europeanization' of city life include medicine and beauty aids. A typical advertisement was for Halloway's unguent made in London. It was sup-

---

[1] 'Importação—Manifestos', *Jornal do commercio*, 1 Jan. p. 2; 3 Jan. p. 3; 5 Jan. p. 3; 8 Jan. p. 7; 11 Jan. p. 3; 17 Jan. p. 3; 23 Jan. p. 3; 24 Jan. p. 3; 25 Jan. p. 3; 28 Jan. p. 3, 1850; *Jornal do commercio*, 15 Jan. 1850, p. 3; 3 May 1850, p. 4; 7 May 1850, p. 4; 5 May 1855, p. 4; 1 Sept. 1855, p. 4; 1 Sept. 1860, p. 3; 5 Sept. 1860, p. 3; 7 Sept. 1860, p. 2; 1 Jan. 1871, p. 3; 4 Feb. 1882, p. 4; 4 June 1882, p. 4; *A provincia de São Paulo*, 10 Jan. 1875, p. 4; 23 Apr. 1875, p. 3; 4 Mar. 1884, p. 4; T. Oscar Marcondes de Souza, *O estado de São Paulo: physico, politico, economico e administrativo* (São Paulo: Universal, 1915), p. 161; Aroldo de Azevedo, *Cochranes do Brasil: A vida e a obra de Thomas Cochrane e Ignacio Cochrane*, Brasiliana, 327 (São Paulo: Editôra Nacional, 1965), p. 95; Great Britain, Board of Trade, Customs and Excise Department, Statistical Office, *Annual Statement of the Trade of the United Kingdom with Foreign Countries and British Possessions* (London: H.M. Stationery Office, 1853–1910); Gilberto Freyre, *Introdução à história da sociedade patriarcal no Brasil, III: Ordem e progresso*...2 vols. (Rio: José Olympio, 1959), i, cxxx; see Jonathan Levin, *The Export Economies, Their Pattern of Development in Historical Perspective* (Cambridge, Mass.: Harvard Univ. Press, 1960), p. 7.

posed to cure 'scrofula, cramps, calluses, chancre, skin diseases, liver diseases, circulation disorders, scorbutic eruptions, fistulas, frigidity or lack of warmth at the extremities, internal and external inflammations, gout, chilblain, leg, breast, and eye disorders, burns, rheumatism, putrid suppurations, ringworm, and mouth ulcers'. In 1882 the African Elixir of Dr Hobarts of London was advertised as a cure for an equally impressive variety of ailments including malaria, yellow fever, typhus, plague, difficult menstruation, digestive irregularity, and anemia. Something of the manner in which the Victorian British businessman had to make adjustments in keeping with the Brazilian social environment is shown in the screamingly large type with which in 1850 the Pharmacia Ingleza urged the use of Sanford's Divine Mixture to cure gonorrhea and leuchorrhea.[1]

Brazilian ladies were meanwhile told to use the perfumes of 'the most famous London manufacturers', or the 'English perfumeries of the well-known manufacturers, John Gornell and others'. Other beauty aids included Rowland's Macassar oil for the hair and Odonto for whitening the teeth, both of which could be obtained from London or through George Janson, 52 Rua do Rosario. Fine English soap was also available, especially the 'Transparent Crystal Soap' of William Rieger.[2]

The lady's escort was more than likely dressed in the British fashion. The social historian Gilberto Freyre has drawn attention to this aspect of the British influence with regard to straw hats, monocles, umbrellas, and canes.[3] Trouser cuffs were copied from the British and it is said one Brazilian, sporting the latest fad on a blazing afternoon and taunted for having rolled up his trousers, retorted, 'Well, it may be raining in London.'[4]

The list of luxury goods imported from Great Britain goes on and on. References can be found to English watches and chronometers, pianos, dishes, china and crockery, saddles and riding equipment, parasols, straw hats, raincoats, 'London segars', fire-

---

[1] *Jornal do commercio*, 2 Jan. 1850, p. 4; 7 May 1855, p. 3; 5 Feb. 1882, p. 6.
[2] *Ibid.*, 1 Jan. 1871, p. 4; 6 Jan. 1871, p. 7; 3 Feb. 1882, p. 5; 5 Feb. 1882, p. 6; 4 June 1882, p. 4. See similar notice in *A provincia de São Paulo*, 10 Jan. 1875, p. 4.
[3] Freyre, *Ordem e progresso*, I, cxx, 278; II, 656, 667, 671, 674, 678.
[4] João Afonso, *Três séculos de modas* (Belém: Tavares Cardoso, 1923), p. 101.

arms, iron safes of Chubb and Sons, burial caskets, writing ink, silver-cleaning powder, bicycles, sewing scissors, and empty bottles.[1]

Home furnishings sharply distinguish cultures, and, next to foodstuffs, probably nothing was as significant as this class of imports in indicating changing styles of life. The typical Brazilian home had been bare and austere with high ceilings and wide board flooring. The only comfortable place was the hammock. The contrast was sharply felt by a young woman just arrived from Britain, who remarked with shock that 'the houses...are certainly not what the English people would call home-like, for there are no fireplaces, very seldom any carpets, and very little furniture !' But the British importing house stood ready to correct this deficiency, and the increasingly prosperous Brazilian city residents were ready to buy its goods, often selling to the acquisitive British merchant their massive but perfectly wrought colonial pieces. Dealers were sometimes hard put to find Portuguese words for the British-made furniture they had for sale, thus further indicating the degree to which these items were foreign to the culture. One advertiser used the words *aparador inglez* (*sideboard*), while another advertised his dish cabinet as a *bom 'étagère' inglez*. Other furniture for sale included an 'English desk' and a 'solid English washstand of mahogany with marble and mirror'.

[1] *Jornal do commercio*, 1 Jan. 1850, p. 4; 3 Jan. 1850, p. 4; 8 Jan. 1850, p. 3; 11 Jan. 1850, p. 4; 16 Jan. 1850, p. 3; 23 Jan. 1850, p. 3; 26 Jan. 1850, p. 4; 2 May 1850, p. 4; 4 May 1850, p. 4; 6 May 1850, p. 4; 1 Sept. 1850, p. 3; 2 Sept. 1850, p. 3; 1 Jan. 1855, p. 4; 3 Jan. 1855, p. 4; 4 Jan. 1855, p. 3; 2 May 1855, p. 2; 3 May 1855, p. 3; 1 Sept. 1855, pp. 3, 4; 2 Sept. 1855, pp. 2, 3; 2 Sept. 1860, p. 4; 5 Sept. 1860, p. 3; 7 Sept. 1860, p. 2; 1 Jan. 1871, p. 5; 3 Jan. 1871, p. 2; 2 Feb. 1882, p. 5; 4 Feb. 1882, p. 4; 5 Feb. 1882, p. 5; 3 May 1891, p. 7; 1 Nov. 1891, p. 8; 6 Jan. 1895, p. 10; Giacomo Raja Gabaglia, 'Relatorio do 3⁰ grupo', and Agostinho Victor de Borja Castro, 'Relatorio do 2⁰ grupo', in Antonio José de Souza Rego, comp., *Relatorio da segunda exposição nacional de 1866* (Rio: Typ. Nacional, 1869), pp. 71–2, 81, 112; Brazil, Ministerio da Fazenda, Commissão de Inquerito Industrial, *Relatorio* (Rio: Typ. Nacional, 1882), p. 126; *A provincia de São Paulo*, 11 Jan. 1875, p. 4; 23 Mar. 1875, p. 4; 23 Mar. 1884, p. 4; Julio Ribeiro, *A carne* (São Paulo: Teixeira, 1888), pp. 45, 173, 176; Appendix C; Caio Prado Júnior, *História econômica do Brasil* (São Paulo: Brasiliense, 1945), p. 143; Ina von Binzer (pseud. for Ulla von Eck?), *Alegrias e tristezas de uma educadora alemã no Brasil*, transl. Alice Rossi and Luisita da Gama Cerqueira (São Paulo: Anhembi, 1956), p. 90; 'Importação—Manifestos', *Jornal do commercio*, Jan. 1850; Richard M. Morse, *From Community to Metropolis: a Biography of São Paulo, Brazil* (Gainesville, Fla.: Univ. of Florida Press, 1958), pp. 130–1.

Other strange devices were also imported from Britain and advertisements appeared for English 'patent and ordinary latrines, grates, washstands, kitchen sinks, porcelain bathtubs, and glazed pipes for drinking-water and sewage'.[1]

'Cleanliness is next to godliness' would seem to have been a Brazilian motto, to hear the way Brazilians roundly castigated themselves for the slovenliness of their cities, the lack of modern sewage facilities, the absence of garbage removal companies, and the scarcity of plumbing. It was generally to the British that Brazilians turned to install these accouterments, and it was now thought necessary for any 'civilized' person to have such facilities. In the 1850s the Brazilian sewage system was still described as 'a portable instead of an underground affair', and in 1855 an Englishman advertised his private company for the removal of 'fecal matter'.[2] But that same year a Brazilian doctor submitted a report on the sewage system of London, urging the adoption of the same techniques in Rio de Janeiro. The year before an Englishman had proposed to install a system like the one used in Rugby, Leicester, Worcester, Chester, Coventry, and Birmingham. The sewage and drainage contract was finally let to the Rio de Janeiro City Improvements Company, Ltd, organized in London in 1862. The company also installed and operated a water system, and nearly £2 million were invested in the total project by 1895.[3]

Other cities soon followed Rio de Janeiro's example. In 1870 Thomas Cochrane, the railway entrepreneur, founded a company

[1] Alice V. Hurford, 'First Impressions of São Paulo', *South America, the Magazine of the Evangelical Union of South America*, III (1914–15), 202; Freyre, *Ordem e progresso*, I, lxi; *Jornal do commercio*, 6 Jan. 1855, p. 2; 2 Sept. 1860, p. 4; 4 Feb. 1882, p. 4; 5 Feb. 1882, p. 7.

[2] Daniel Parish Kidder and James Cooley Fletcher, *Brazil and the Brazilians Portrayed in Historical and Descriptive Sketches* (Philadelphia: Childs and Peterson, 1857), p. 25; *Jornal do commercio*, 2 May 1855, p. 2.

[3] *Jornal do commercio*, 4 May 1855, p. 3; Joaquim Pereira Vianna de Lima Junior (partner of John Frederick Russell), letter of 9 Oct. 1854, AMIP, CXX, 6009; Joseph R. West, 'The Foreigner in Brazilian Technology, 1808–1900', unpub. Ph.D. diss., Univ. of Chicago, 1950, p. 1023; Alan K. Manchester, *British Preëminence in Brazil; Its Rise and Decline: A Study in European Expansion* (Chapel Hill, N.C.: Univ. of North Carolina Press, 1933), p. 326; Michael George Mulhall, *The English in South America* (Buenos Aires: 'Standard' Office, 1878), p. 347; J. Fred Rippy, *British Investments in Latin America, 1822–1949. A Case Study in the Operations of Private Enterprise in Retarded Regions* (Minneapolis: Univ. of Minnesota Press, 1959), p. 43.

to supply water and gas to Santos. Ten years later the growth of that city, stimulated by coffee exports, made it necessary to expand the system, and the City of Santos Improvements Company, Ltd, was founded in London to buy out Cochrane's enterprise. In São Paulo the Companhia Cantareira de Aguas e Esgôtos was built by British engineers mostly with British loan capital, was operated by Englishmen, and borrowed from the English Bank of Rio de Janeiro for later expansion. The state of São Paulo bought the company from its Brazilian owners in 1892. Twenty years later the state of Rio de Janeiro borrowed £3 million in London to be used for the 'sanitation' of three of its smaller cities, and other loans were made for similar improvements in Manaus and Salvador.[1]

In Recife the water company was managed by Englishmen and it frequently borrowed funds in England. It worked in tandem with the Recife Drainage Company, Ltd, which, with a subsidy from the provincial government, was organized in London in 1868. Its capital was only £50,000 and it faced immediate financial difficulties. After much controversy in Recife over allegedly forged or altered contracts, the company was transferred to a new group of British stockholders in 1878, who immediately issued £100,000 in debentures, paid off in 1908.[2] The company encountered special difficulties because Recife was a more traditional city than Rio de Janeiro or São Paulo and it was only the elite who there shared

[1] Rippy, *British Investments*, p. 73; 'Album Estrada de Ferro Santos a Jundiaí: história de uma ferrovia', *Magazine das nações*, edição especial, Ano 10 (Oct. 1957), p. 5; West, 'Foreigner in Brazilian Technology', pp. 1017–19, 1028; Randolpho Homem de Mello, 'A agua em S. Paulo', *Revista do Arquivo Municipal de São Paulo*, XIV (1935), 165, 166; Morse, *From Community to Metropolis*, p. 179; *A provincia de São Paulo*, 13 Jan. 1884, p. 4; Brazil, Directoria Geral de Estatistica, *Annuario estatistico do Brazil. Annuaire statistique du Brésil. 1º anno. 1ère année (1908–1912)*, 2 vols. (Rio: Typ. de Estatistica, 1917), II, 260–5.

[2] West, 'Foreigner in Brazilian Technology', p. 1009; Alfredo J. Watts, 'A colônia inglêsa em Pernambuco', *Revista do Instituto Arqueológico e Geográfico de Pernambuco*, XXXIX (1944), 166; *Investor's Monthly Manual, a Newspaper for Investors*, n.s. VIII (1878), 514; file on Recife Drainage Company, Ltd, BT 31/1427/4171; Henry Law, *Exposição das questões entre o presidente da provincia de Pernambuco, o...dr. Henrique Pereira de Lucena, e a Companhia Recife Drainage* (Rio: Winter, 1873); Law & Blount (agents Recife Drainage Company) to Manoel do Nascimento Machado Portella (provincial president), Recife, 17 Aug. 1871, APEP; Pernambuco, Presidente, *Relatorio*, 1874, pp. 44–6; 'Report of Consul Lennon Hunt, 18 Aug. 1864', in Great Britain, *Commercial Reports Received at the Foreign Office from Her Majesty's Consuls*, 1865, p. 55.

the foreigners' belief in plumbing. Whereas the British consul referred to the 'great and beneficent enterprise of the English Drainage Company, whose operations will, it is trusted, tend to induce cleanly habits into the houses of the inhabitants', the provincial president had to confess that 'there are 400 homes or hearths which must have contrivances, but the company has not been able to place them because of the opposition of the owners or renters'.[1]

Other symbols of modernity were streetcars and gas lights. The *barão* de Mauá, heavily influenced by the British example, created a gas company in Rio de Janeiro which he later sold to the British. The similar companies in Recife and Salvador were built by the same contractors who organized the Recife Drainage Company. In this activity they were more successful, as was the San [*sic*] Paulo Gas Company, Ltd, organized in 1869, which paid an average dividend of nearly 9 per cent from 1882 to 1913. By 1876 there were British-owned gas companies in Rio de Janeiro, São Paulo, Santos, Salvador, Fortaleza, Belém, and Rio Grande do Sul. As towns grew larger, the need for urban transport companies increased. At first depending on mules, British-owned streetcar lines were later electrified. In 1912 there were nine British-owned urban transport companies in Brazil, one in every major city of the country. Counting all types of utility companies, the British were connected with twelve of them by the end of 1890, with a nominal capital of £3·3 million; in 1927 there were 33 such British companies with a capital of £94·7 million.[2]

Urban change was also accelerated by British railroads. It was because of the railway that São Paulo began to be transformed from a sleepy academic town into a major city, and it was because

---

[1] 'Report of Consul Doyle, 31 Mar. 1872', in Great Britain, *Reports from Her Majesty's Consuls on the Manufactures, Commerce, etc., of Their Consular Districts*, 1872, Part 2, p. 635; Pernambuco, Presidente, *Relatorio*, 1878, p. 41.

[2] Irineo Evangelista de Souza, *visconde* de Mauá, *Autobiografia* ('*Exposição aos credores e ao público*') *seguida de 'O meio circulante no Brasil'*, ed. Claudio Ganns, 2nd ed. (Rio: Valverde, 1942), pp. 115–20; West, 'Foreigner in Brazilian Technology', pp. 966–9, 972, 977; Rippy, *British Investments*, pp. 39, 155, 240; Brazil, Directoria Geral de Estatistica, *Annuario . . . (1908–1912)*, II, 58–61; British Chamber of Commerce of São Paulo and Southern Brazil, *Grã Bretanha: seu commercio e industria* (São Paulo: Camara de Commercio Britannica de São Paulo & Sul do Brasil, 1927), p. 37.

of it that Santos did away with the constant presence of dirty mule trains in the streets. The modern urban life represented by the opera companies that entertained São Paulo would surely have been missing if the singers had had to brave the *serra* on horseback. The railroad also tended to create a mass society. Regardless of the presence of first-, second-, and third-class carriages, a railway station thronged by persons of all conditions—workmen and governors, immigrants and planters, fine ladies and prostitutes—was a monument to the impersonal relationships and social mobility of the modern world. And the trains were literally vehicles for contact between the modern and traditional societies. Thus, the Brazilian 'sisters of charity' which the railroad was required to carry free of charge traveled in the same cars as the British Protestant Bible salesman. The landowner trekking to the capital to beg a title of nobility met the British engineer *en route*. These aspects of mass travel had not been a part of mule-back transportation, and the cities where the trains stopped were inevitably affected.[1]

The British influence was also felt in urban planning and development. Narrow and crooked streets with houses built flush with the sidewalk had been characteristic of Brazilian cities up to that point. But now, as Richard Morse has put it, the rise of a 'traditionless, industrial-commercial elite' was reflected in the adoption of 'the ideals of an energetic, Anglo-Saxonized plutocracy dedicated to "home", sports, and comfort, an image popularized by the work of English urbanists'. The first section of town to follow the ideal of 'cottage squares' was called Higienópolis as if to suggest the germ-free world of plumbing and modern science. In 1911 the City of San [*sic*] Paulo Improvements & Freehold Land Company, Ltd, was organized in London to develop land purchased from a Belgian promoter. It owned some 3,000 acres on which it built streets and sewers, installing water

---

[1] Joaquim Antonio Pinto Junior, *Santos e S. Vicente de 1868 a 1876* (Rio: Santos, 1877), p. 6; over half a million mules had entered Santos in 1865, William Scully, *Brazil: Its Provinces and Chief Cities; the Manners and Customs of the People; Agricultural, Commercial and Other Statistics* (London: Murray, 1866), p. 311; Morse, *From Community to Metropolis*, p. 190; Decree no. 1759, 26 Apr. 1856, in Clodomiro Pereira da Silva, *A evolução do transporte mundial (enciclopédia dos transportes)*, 6 vols. (São Paulo: Imp. Oficial do Estado, 1940–6), VI, 556; 'Bible Work in Brazil', *South America*, I (1912–13), pp. 15–17.

and gas piping and a streetcar line. It also landscaped the area and sold the lots at a substantial profit. Barry Parker, the British architect and urban planner, famous for creating garden cities and villages in England, drew up the over-all scheme. He said his belief was that one's first impression on entering a house should be 'How exquisitely comfortable!' and Brazilians must now share this reaction. The far-off modern world was also recalled by streets named after European countries.[1]

The urban middle classes were also fascinated with the English model of how one should live and play. The upper-class Brazilians who traveled to Europe and mixed with European high society were not likely to have had high regard for the British merchants and engineers who found their way to Rio de Janeiro. But the influence of the Britishers who lived there—estimated at 400 in 1850 and enumerated as 1344 in 1890—was much greater on less well placed Brazilians who were nevertheless rising and ambitious, anxious to identify with these ambassadors of the modern world.[2]

Although not men of wealth at home, Englishmen and Scots often represented wealthy and powerful firms in Brazil and were much better off than most of the Brazilians with whom they dealt. In the twentieth century one traveler noted for Latin America as a whole that 'The lower-class Briton is rarely encountered'.[3] At an earlier date railroad companies had imported skilled workmen while English millers and machinists were employed at other industries.[4] But most Britishers in Brazil always had a standard

---

[1] Morse, *From Community to Metropolis*, pp. 272–3, 279–280; Plínio Barreto, *Uma temerária aventura forense* (*a questão entre D. Amalia de Moreira Keating Fontaine de Lavaleye e a City of San Paulo Improvements & Freehold Land Company, Limited*). *Allegações finaes do advogado desta ultima* (São Paulo: Revista dos Tribunaes, 1933), pp. 7, 19, 40, 139, 219; Barry Parker and Raymond Unwin, *The Art of building a home: a collection of lectures and illustrations*, 2nd. ed. (London, etc.: Longmans, Green, 1901), p. 5; Barry Parker, 'Two Years in Brazil', *Garden Cities and Town Planning*, n.s. IX (1919), 143–51; Barry Parker, 'Town-planning experiences in Brazil', *Architects Journal*, II (1920), 48–52.

[2] On size of British colony see Hesketh to Lord Palmerston, Rio, 13 May 1850; Telegram Wyndham to Foreign Office, Rio, 31 Oct. 1893, FO 13/276; 13/708, no. 52.

[3] C. Reginald Enock, *The Republics of Central and South America, Their Resources, Industries, Sociology and Future* (London & New York: Dent & Scribners, 1913), p. 497.

[4] Daniel Makinson Fox, *Description of the Line and Works of the São Paulo Railway in the Empire of Brazil...with an Abstract of the Discussion upon the Paper*, ed. James Forrest (London: Clowes & Sons, 1870), pp. 20–2; Richard Graham, 'A British Industry in Brazil: Rio Flour Mills, 1886–1920', *Business History*, VIII (1966), 25; Kidder and Fletcher, *Brazil and the Brazilians* (1857), pp. 202–3, 318.

of living which attracted immediate attention. One young man who was merely 'employed in commerce' advertised for a room saying that 'price is no object'. English families could live in Rio de Janeiro on a scale to which they were unaccustomed, with large houses, stables, and many more servants than they could have had in London or Manchester. Their habits were markedly different from those of Brazilians, and, if a woman wished to be employed as a domestic by one of them, she must make clear that she 'knows the customs of Europe'.[1]

It was also important to learn English if one expected to do business with the British. Whereas French had once been the only foreign language worth knowing—and it remained the 'polite language'—English became steadily more important. English teachers, to judge by the frequency of advertisements in the Rio de Janeiro newspapers, had long been easy to find. One promised the student his money back if he did nót learn 'English in 20 days'. Thomas Gosling, who claimed to have studied at 'one of the principal universities of England', was less specific, but said he could make 'the great difficulties of the English language disappear entirely in a very short while'. Others drew the attention of the business community to the fact they offered classes in the evening for 'those who work during the day'. Of course, not all Britishers remained unable to speak the language and advertisements also appeared in English announcing Portuguese classes, Portuguese grammars, or Portuguese–English dictionaries. Still, the ambitious Brazilian learned English. As one traveler noted in the early years of the twentieth century, 'As commerce has developed, the desire to know English has increased.'[2]

So had the desire to engage in British sports. Victorian England was known for its interest in outdoor games. The rising British middle class, emancipated from older restraints but denied the

---

[1] *Jornal do commercio*, 5 Sept. 1860, p. 4; 6 Jan. 1871, p. 8; 1 Feb. 1882, p. 6.

[2] *Jornal do commercio*, 2 Jan. 1850, p. 4; 5 Jan. 1850, p. 4; 8 Jan. 1850, p. 4; 10 Jan. 1850, p. 4; 2 May 1850, p. 4; 1 Sept. 1850, p. 3; 1 Jan. 1855, p. 4; 3 Jan. 1855, p. 3; 4 Jan. 1855, p. 4; 1 Sept. 1855, p. 3; 2 Sept. 1855, p. 3; 2 Sept. 1860, p. 3; 3 Sept. 1860, p. 4; 1 Jan. 1871, p. 8; 3 Jan. 1871, p. 3; 4 Jan. 1871, pp. 3, 4; 3 Feb. 1882, p. 6; 1 Nov. 1891, p. 9. Nevin Otto Winter, *Brazil and Her People of To-Day: an Account of the Customs, Characteristics, Amusements, History and Advancement of the Brazilians, and the Development and Resources of their Country* (Boston, Mass.: Page, 1910), p. 222.

entertainments of the aristocracy, had turned its attention to in-expensive team sports or athletic activities like tennis that could be set up at home. Nothing could be more foreign in Brazil. One traveler had noted in 1865 that 'a great want in Brazil is the out-door games' as well as 'the debating clubs, the cheap concerts, the lectures', all of which 'the European at home has at his command to strengthen and improve both mind and body'.[1] Before 1880 or 1890 the young man of good breeding in Brazil paid no attention to sports and physical exercise, being either more inclined to poetry and politics, or to amorous adventures with visiting actresses. But in the last twenty years of the nine-teenth century various British sports were introduced, the most popular of which proved to be soccer. It was first played by Englishmen in São Paulo around 1886 and teams were organized by Charles Miller, the agent for the Royal Mail Lines. A square near the São Paulo stadium was named for him, and teams strove to win the Charles Miller Cup. The Corinthians Football Club of São Paulo imitated its famous British namesake, and most of the terms used in the game in Brazil were of English derivation. Although soccer caught on and became a national sport played by all classes, sports remained in general the preserve of the middle groups. These diversions perhaps contributed to their health and energy, and were surely a means of identifying with modernity.[2]

New forms of literary expression accompanied the rise of an urban life-style. The novels of Walter Scott were widely read by literate Brazilian city dwellers. The great Brazilian novelist Joaquim Maria Machado de Assis (1839–1908), who was probably

---

[1] Scully, *Brazil*, p. 7.
[2] Carolina Nabuco, *The Life of Joaquim Nabuco*, transl. and ed. Ronald Hilton (Stanford, California: Stanford Univ. Press, 1950), p. 12; Gilberto Freyre, 'Social Life in Brazil in the Middle of the Nineteenth Century', *Hispanic American Historical Review*, v (1922), 621; Morse, *From Community to Metropolis*, p. 203 n.; golf, tennis and even cricket were also introduced by the British, Reginald Lloyd *et al.*, eds., *Twentieth Century Impressions of Brazil: Its History, People, Commerce, Industries, and Resources* (London: Lloyd's Greater Britain Publishing Co., 1913), p. 156; Freyre, *Ordem e progresso*, I, lxii; interview with Mr Darling, British Consulate, São Paulo, 26 Nov. 1959; cf. Ronald E. Wraith and Edgar Simpkins, *Corruption in Developing Countries, Including Britain until 1880* (London: Allen & Unwin, 1962), p. 169. It is suggestive that a twentieth-century modernizer, Getúlio Vargas, emphasized the importance of sports, Getúlio Vargas, *A nova política do Brasil*, 11 vols (Rio: José Olympio, 1938–47), VII, 267, 311–12.

influenced by British authors, depended as they did on the increasing number of leisured persons present in a prospering, urban society. Perhaps he depended as well on the increasing ability of readers to imagine themselves as others; social scientists have pointed out how people in traditional societies are relatively unable to perform this feat. Previous Brazilian writers had excelled at self-expression in poetry and essays, but now a new form could provide a field for real distinction. In addition, the increasing fluidity of class lines combined with their simultaneous persistence to give Machado de Assis the subject matter for his novels, reflecting as they do the ambitions of an urban group struggling for recognition within an aristocratic society.[1]

It was the export-oriented economy that drove Brazil into the modern world, and the first areas to enter it were the cities created by the increased commercial life that accompanied larger exports. It is worth noting that among the directors of the City of San Paulo Improvements & Freehold Land Company, Ltd, were a director of the São Paulo Railway and Manuel Ferraz de Campos Sales, coffee planter and ex-president.[2] The British were the cause of these urban transformations only insofar as they played a role in fostering the dynamic export-oriented economy itself.

But as modern change went on, an anxiety to look like Europe swept through the urban classes. Water systems, sewage facilities, urban transport companies, gas works, and electric plants were all necessary if urban Brazilians were to hold up their heads. Here the British aided the Brazilians in satisfying these ambitions and heightened these aspirations by their salesmanship and by their presence. Although it may be that British capital invested in urban services was being spent to meet 'social overhead' charges

---

[1] Freyre, *Ordem e progresso*, I, 143, 273, 275, 278; Afrânio Coutinho, ed., *A literatura no Brasil*, 3 vols. (Rio: Editorial Sul Americana, 1955–9), II, 77–106; Lúcia Miguel Pereira, *Machado de Assis (estudo crítico e biográfico)*, 5th ed., Documentos Brasileiros, 82 (Rio: José Olympio, 1955); Eugênio Gomes, *Influências inglêsas em Machado de Assis (estudo)* (Bahia: Regina, 1939); Daniel Lerner and Lucille W. Pevsner, *The Passing of Traditional Society: Modernizing the Middle East* (Glencoe, Ill.: Free Press, 1958), p. 52; Lionel Trilling, *The Liberal Imagination, Essays on Literature and Society* (Garden City, N.Y.: Doubleday, 1953), pp. 200–15. I do not mean to suggest that there had been no earlier Brazilian novelists of note.

[2] Barreto, *Uma temerária aventura forense*, p. 19.

by improving the country's health and in increasing the efficiency of the urban population—as is argued for foreign aid funds today—it seems more defensible to say that the real significance of these enterprises was simply the way they enabled Brazilian cities to approximate the appearance of the European models.

The importation of British-made consumer goods cannot be considered especially constructive assistance toward modernization, but it was also part of that larger process which brought Brazil out of its sleepy colonial past into a world characterized by steadily growing wants, status seeking, and conspicuous consumption. The eventual rise of certain industries would not have been so rapid if the urban classes had not been speedily accustomed to using goods relatively foreign to the traditions of the old society. Importation probably helped pave the way for Brazilian manufacturing, as is suggested by the sharp decline, after about 1880 or 1885, in the import figures of many items, such as foodstuffs, furnishings, and luxury goods. With today's hindsight one may see that more essential industries might have been created instead. But putting heavy industry before consumer goods would have required a social and intellectual revolution that at that time had not yet been successful even in Europe. It has been precisely because of the growth of Brazilian cities and their participation in modern currents that it is possible to consider such alternatives today.

The British role was important as a reflection of the fact that with the urban setting went a new style of life. Plumbing and soccer, beer and pianos, umbrellas and streetcars were the ritual dress and sacred instruments in the rites of passage from traditional to modern.

5

BRITAIN AND THE
INDUSTRIALIZATION OF BRAZIL

The British contributed substantially to Brazilian industrial development. Despite the strength of the British-controlled export–import complex which was indifferent to manufacturing, Britishers helped directly and indirectly to begin the transformation of Brazil from an agrarian to an industrializing economy. First, they built the major part of the transport system on which industry was to depend for the receipt of raw material and access to markets. Second, much of the industrial machinery and supplies which were used by Brazilian factories were produced in Britain and sold through a distributive system created by the British. Third, they advanced not only the credits to finance these sales but often provided the loan capital that enabled Brazilians to invest in manufacturing enterprises. Fourth, the technicians who installed the equipment, directed its operation, and taught the workers to operate it were frequently British. And, finally, they invested directly in textile plants, shoe industries, sugar factories, and flour mills. The idea that the struggle for Brazilian industrialization was simply a conflict between Brazilians and foreigners is so patently erroneous that it would require no comment were it not so widespread. Although it cannot be said that their actions were the chief cause of industrialization, the British shared significantly in that task, and in so doing helped begin the modernization of Brazil.

Economic development requires certain physical facilities—e.g. roads, railroads, power plants, and port facilities—which economists have labeled the 'infrastructure'. The fact that the British built railways and harbor works primarily to serve an export economy did not prevent these facilities from being used by industrialists. True, they were not ideally located for industrial

125

needs. But they were placed well enough to perform a useful function. If the Brazilian consuming markets were being supplied by foreign goods transported by rail and distributed through certain cities, perspicacious Brazilian manufacturers established in those places could use the same railroads and tap the same markets. For instance, the railways of the coffee area which were built with British capital or British equipment made the city of São Paulo the center of a state-wide market for industrial goods. Brazilian entrepreneurs were not slow to seize this opportunity and choose that site for their plants.

The role of the railroads in distributing Brazilian manufactured goods can also be judged by their importance in marketing flour made in Rio de Janeiro. One flour mill there specifically differentiated its various markets according to the railroads serving each area. Every traveling salesman was assigned one line along which he moved to sell the flour shipped by rail. Southern Minas Gerais was an area of direct conflict between the products of Rio de Janeiro and São Paulo precisely because there were railways in that region which served both industrial centers. Generally, the growth of the rail system meant an immediate growth in markets. The manager of the flour mill expressed jubilation when the Leopoldina Railway built a line linking Rio de Janeiro to Vitória, the capital of the state of Espírito Santo, thus making it possible to compete there with foreign flour brought in by sea. On another occasion he commented that 'as the Central Ry. has continued to extend further into the state of Minas we look for a steady improvement in our business'.[1]

These railways could also be used for the transport of raw materials either from the interior or from the ports: it was the São Paulo Railway that made it possible for the industrialist Francisco de Matarazzo (1854–1937) to bring Argentine wheat to São Paulo for his flour mill created in 1899. And cotton grown in the Sorocaba area was delivered to mills in Petrópolis by rail. So the railroads which had depended on the British for engineering

[1] Reports of the General Manager, first half of 1904, p. 2; 1904, p. 6; 1907, p. 12, ARFM. Mr John Hansard and Mr Lawrence W. Lowe of Rio Flour (Holdings) kindly made available the records of the company.

skill, loan capital, and direct investment provided emerging Brazilian industries with the transport essential to their existence.[1]

Modern ports performed a similar function, and the construction of the Rio de Janeiro harbor works in 1910 greatly aided the process of industrialization. Raw cotton from the northeast had once been unloaded into lighters there, then placed in warehouses, and finally carted to the railway station. Now all this delay and risk of loss was avoided. A flour mill in Rio had originally been forced to invest a large amount of its initial, hard-to-get capital in a pier for unloading wheat. With the new quay this could all be handled automatically and capacity doubled. Out through the same port went the manufactured products to be sold in those areas of Brazil that were not yet linked by direct rail connexions to the capital. It was an immense advantage to industrialists no longer to depend on lighters for loading and unloading goods in Rio de Janeiro.[2]

Brazilian manufacturing plants, as was true with railroads and docks, depended upon the British to furnish machinery and industrial supplies. Coal, for instance, came at first almost entirely from the British Isles. The importance of this origin does not lie, of course, in that the coals were 'British', but in the human resources that had been mobilized to supply and distribute them. These efforts served Brazilian modernization, although it would be foolish to argue that British miners braved chokedamp with such high purposes. It is also true that, next to steamships, railroads were the chief consumers of coal; thus coal, in the first instance, served the export economy. But just as railways did not discriminate against Brazilian-made goods, neither did the coal they burned.

Furthermore, the importation of coal increased significantly as a result of increasing Brazilian industrial growth. In 1850 Brazil imported so little coal from Britain—only £20,320 worth—that

[1] Stanley J. Stein, *The Brazilian Cotton Manufacture; Textile Enterprise in an Underdeveloped Area, 1850–1950* (Cambridge, Mass.: Harvard Univ. Press, 1957), p. 46. Also see J. N. Thadani, 'Transport and Location of Industries in India', *Indian Economic Review*, I, no. 2 (Aug. 1952), pp. 19–42.

[2] Minutes of the General Meeting, 17 Jan. 1911, ARFM; Stein, *Brazilian Cotton Manufacture*, p. 46.

importers could not afford to specialize in it. The chief firms receiving coal in January 1850 were Nathan Brothers and E. Johnston & Co., which received only 793 tons and 238 tons, respectively. But industrialization meant larger amounts of coal were needed. For instance, coal-burning steam engines powered a textile mill set up in 1871. Central sugar factories initially burned coal, and flour mills depended upon it until the advent of reasonably priced electricity. While in 1850–4 coal represented only 4·13 per cent of all Brazilian imports from Great Britain, this figure rose to 13·91 per cent in 1900–4. The periods of greatest increase were 1870–4, 1890–4 and 1900–4, periods of rapid growth.[1]

In time, Britishers set up importing houses which specialized in the importation of coal. Wilson Sons & Company, Ltd, was one of the most important of these. Organized in 1877, it took over a private firm which had been engaged in construction and general trading in Brazil for forty years. Warehouses and local managers were located in Recife, Salvador, Rio de Janeiro, Santos, São Paulo, as well as in the Canary Islands, Montevideo, and Buenos Aires. It owned lighters and tugboats, a small sawmill, and a foundry. In 1902 it founded the Rio de Janeiro Lighterage Company, later sold to E. Johnston & Co., and by 1913 Wilson Sons also dealt in stevedoring and shipyards. But its chief interest became increasingly the importation of coal. It was allied with the Ocean Coal Company, Ltd. The company placed storage facilities for 30,000 tons on one of the islands of the bay of Guanabara, and it held lucrative contracts for supplying coal on a large scale to the British Admiralty, the Pacific Steam Navigation Company, and the British-owned Western Telegraph Company. At the other extreme it delivered coal door-to-door by mule cart to small consumers in São Paulo. The constant worry about having enough coal at the proper place at the right moment

---

[1] Joseph R. West, 'The Foreigner in Brazilian Technology, 1808–1900', unpub. Ph.D. diss., Univ. of Chicago, 1950, p. 800n.; 'Importação—Manifestos', *Jornal do commercio*, 1 Jan. p. 2; 3 Jan. p. 3; 5 Jan. p. 3; 8 Jan. p. 7; 11 Jan. p. 3; 17 Jan. p. 3; 23 Jan. p. 3; 24 Jan. p. 3; 25 Jan. p. 3; 28 Jan. p. 3, 1850; Brazil, Ministerio da Fazenda, Commissão de Inquerito Industrial, *Relatorio* (Rio: Typ. Nacional, 1882), p. 30; Pernambuco, Presidente, *Relatorio*, 1886, p. 51; figures are based on Appendix C. The Ince Hall Coal Company shipped coal to Brazil in 1850, *Jornal do commercio*, 24 Jan. 1850, p. 3.

at competitive prices is a poignant motif in the company correspondence.[1]

The lack of a Brazilian source of coal was recognized as an obstacle to rapid industrialization in that era, and some Britishers of mediocre talents helped in the vain search for coalfields to remove this bottleneck. In 1853 James Johnson, a Lancashire coal man, began to exploit deposits in Rio Grande do Sul with the aid of Welsh and Irish miners. It was not a successful venture and two years later he examined other fields with the encouragement of the authorities. Having found what he thought were promising indications, he wrote the provincial president reminding him of the promise 'that when I had found coals your Excy. would procure some good results for myself'. The long-awaited reward turned out to be the concession for working these deposits. Johnson's one stroke of genius was to sell it for £30,000 to the Imperial Brazilian Collieries, Ltd, organized in England in 1870 with a capital of £100,000. Charles Neate was named consulting engineer and Johnson was made superintendent. Fifty British miners were sent out to work the coal mine. But Johnson was so incompetent he was afraid to enter the mine he himself had constructed. The company was liquidated in 1876 and the mine was sold to a local German importer and a Brazilian company he organized to operate it. It was relatively successful, but only because of the difficulty encountered by ocean-going ships in crossing the bar at Rio Grande. In most of the country coal continued to come from Britain.[2]

British iron was also imported to Brazil, and the increasing demand for it was an important reflection of Brazil's industrial growth while simultaneously an indication of its continued position as a market for British goods. Of course, with increasing use

---

[1] Wilson Sons & Co., Ltd, *Wilson Sons & Co., Ltd, 1837–1946: an Historical and Descriptive Account of the Organization Built Up in One Hundred and Ten Years' Happy Trading* (London: Wilson Sons & Co., 1946), p. 1; Lillian Elwyn (Elliot) Joyce, *Brazil, Today and Tomorrow* (New York: Macmillan, 1917), p. 290; Board Minutes, 1878–1913, *passim*, Papers of Wilson Sons & Co., Ltd; F. M. Farrell to R. A. Mather, London, 16 Jan. 1900, PWL, p. 228 and *passim*. Mr T. H. Noot of Wilson Sons & Co., Ltd, kindly made available the papers of his company.

[2] West, 'Foreigner in Brazilian Technology', pp. 458–63; James Johnson to president of the province of Rio Grande do Sul, São Jeronymo, 25 June 1855, AMIP, cxxi, 6074.

of iron in construction, not necessarily all British iron represented a productive investment. But the old agrarian society would not have had much need for iron. In the first month of 1850 the largest importer of this metal received only 196 tons, and the total value of iron imported from Great Britain during the period 1850–4 was merely £534,000. By 1875–9 this figure had risen to £3,329,000, and in 1905–9 it was £4,494,000. From 3·32 per cent of all British exports to Brazil in 1850–4, iron came to represent 10·92 per cent in 1905–9. Despite all this, demand was not large enough or concentrated enough to encourage serious effort at iron mining and manufacturing, even though large deposits of iron ore were known at the time to exist in Brazil. Finally, in 1911, the internationally financed Itabira Iron Ore Co. was organized with the participation of British capital. But little if anything was done by the company to produce Brazilian iron during the period we are discussing, and much less to manufacture steel. If industrial supplies were needed they would come from Britain.[1]

Growth toward an industrial nation was not possible without large importation of machinery of all sorts. Much of it came from the United Kingdom. British machinery had long enjoyed great fame in Brazil, where it was said in 1839 that it could be used to produce goods with a 'uniformity and perfection which a man's hands could never equal, even in a country with the lowest possible labor costs'.[2] Industrialization, with its accompanying standardization, was carried out with British capital goods.

[1] 'Importação—Manifestos', *Jornal do commercio*, Jan. 1850; Nícia Villela Luz, *Aspectos do nacionalismo econômico brasileiro. Os esforços em prol da industrialização*, Coleção 'Revista de História', 16 (São Paulo: 'Revista de História', 1959), p. 151n.; J. Fred Rippy, *British Investments in Latin America, 1822–1949. A Case Study in the Operations of Private Enterprise in Retarded Regions* (Minneapolis: Univ. of Minnesota Press, 1959), p. 52; Caio Prado Júnior, *História econômica do Brasil* (São Paulo: Brasiliense, 1945), p. 279; Charles A. Gauld, *The Last Titan: Percival Farquhar, American Entrepreneur in Latin America* [Special Issue of the *Hispanic American Report*] (Stanford, California: Institute of Hispanic American and Luso-Brazilian Studies, Stanford University, 1964), pp. 319–20; cf. Frederick Clairmonte, *Economic Liberalism and Underdevelopment. Studies in the Disintegration of an Idea* (London: Asia Publishing House, 1960), p. 124. Note use of iron from England in such things as the construction of a government warehouse, Brazil, Ministerio da Fazenda, *Relatorio*, 1872, p. 78.
[2] Bento da Silva Lisboa and J. D. de Attaide Moncorvo, 'Juizo sobre a obra intitulada "Histoire des rélations commerciales entre la France et le Brésil", par Horace Say', *RIHGB*, I (1839), 325.

The new cotton mills were especially apt to be equipped by the British, who had been pioneers in the field. In 1853 a government commission reported that a cotton mill had recently received a new steam engine and other machinery from England. Four years later a short-lived cotton textile plant was set up in Sorocaba with English machinery run by English-made steam engines. Two mills built in the province of São Paulo during the more prosperous 1870s used fuses, cards, and looms manufactured by Platt Brothers of Manchester.[1] In that same decade Brazilians organized one of the most important cotton textile companies, the Companhia Brasil Industrial. Its initial prospects were clouded, and it was in the face of considerable risk that the British manufacturers Gregson and Monk accepted the contract for supplying its equipment, including 24,000 spindles and 400 looms. In 1882 John Edington's small factory hummed and clattered busily with an all-English plant made by Curtis & Sons, including 336 fuses and 52 looms, plus mule-jennies, warpers, stretchers, and other machinery driven by a 25-horsepower steam engine.[2] A much larger company placed orders for British textile machinery during the 1880s, and another one, organized in 1889, bought its entire equipment from a British manufacturer. In 1913 spinning and weaving machinery was still the principal item under the heading 'machines' on the import list.[3]

Competition from other nations in the production of Brazil's cotton manufacturing equipment was intense. Generally, wherever Britishers were the owners or directly responsible for the

---

[1] Brazil, Commissão Encarregada da Revisão da Tarifa em Vigor, *Relatorio...que acompanhou o projecto de tarifa apresentado pela mesma commissão ao governo imperial* (Rio: Empreza Typographica 'Dous de Dezembro' de Paula Brito, 1853), p. 339; Alice P. Cannabrava, *Desenvolvimento da cultura do algodão na província de São Paulo (1861–1875)* (São Paulo: Siqueira, 1951), pp. 278, 283; Stein, *Brazilian Cotton Manufacture*, p. 35; Brazil, Ministerio da Fazenda, Commissão de Inquerito Industrial, *Relatorio*, p. 26.

[2] Stein, *Brazilian Cotton Manufacture*, pp. 36–8, 219n. 49; Companhia Brazil Industrial, *Petição ao corpo legislativo* (Rio: Maximino, 1875), p. 7; Brazil, Ministerio da Fazenda, Commissão de Inquerito Industrial, *Relatorio*, p. 30.

[3] 'Exposição industrial', *Jornal do commercio*, 29 Nov. 1895, p. 1; Nelson Lage Mascarenhas, *Bernardo Mascarenhas. O surto industrial de Minas Gerais* (Rio: Gráfica Editôra Aurora, [1955?]), p. 125; Brazil, Serviço de Estatística Econômica e Financeira, *Commercio exterior do Brasil. Foreign Trade of Brazil. Commerce extérieur du Brésil. Importação... Exportação...Annos 1913–1915–1916–1917–1918*, 2 vols. (Rio: Monotypado nas officinas da Estatistica Commercial, 1921–3), I, 216, 218.

installations, English machinery was used. The same was probably true of other nationalities; thus a company founded by a Frenchman was reported in 1866 to have used only French equipment. When the mills were in Brazilian hands, equipment was bought here and there depending on quality and price. Nevertheless, the British held their own, and Platt Brothers and Co., Ltd, of Lancashire was always one of the chief suppliers of textile machinery. This old firm, started in 1821 by Henry Platt, today still has direct interests in supplying Brazilian textile machinery. There were some British importers that made the importation of these machines their chief interest. The Brazilian agency of Henry Rogers Sons & Company of Wolverhampton, for instance, concentrated on spinning and weaving apparatus made by British manufacturers.[1]

Flour mills were also equipped by the British. The first flour mill in Brazil—a British concern usually referred to as Rio Flour Mills—was filled with machinery built by Henry Simon, milling equipment manufacturer. He had been one of the strongest advocates in England of radically new techniques perfected in America. When they finally caught on, practically all British mills used Simon's designs. To accompany the prospectus for the Rio de Janeiro mill he prepared plans he claimed were 'better than in any automatic mill I have yet known in this or any other country'. The large automatic flour mill built for Matarazzo at the turn of the century was also equipped entirely by Simon, as were the next two mills this Italian-born industrialist constructed in São Paulo as well as the one he built in Antonina, Paraná. English machinery was also used in the Moinho Fluminense—built in 1886 and re-

---

[1] Brazil, Commissão...Tarifa, *Relatorio*, p. 338; Agostinho Victor de Borja Castro, 'Relatorio do 2º grupo' in Antonio José de Souza Rego, comp., *Relatorio da segunda exposição nacional de 1866* (Rio: Typ. Nacional, 1869), pp. 36, 44; Stein, *Brazilian Cotton Manufacture*, pp. 36–7, 41, 147–8, 221 n. 76; John Harold Clapham, *An Economic History of Modern Britain*, 2nd ed., 3 vols. (Cambridge University Press, 1930–8), I, 447; Werner Haas, *et al.*, *Os investimentos estrangeiros no Brasil* (Rio: privately mimeographed, 1958), items no. II, 1005, 1087; III, 162; Richard M. Morse, *From Community to Metropolis: a Biography of São Paulo, Brazil* (Gainesville, Fla.: Univ. of Florida Press, 1958), p. 172; *Jornal do commercio*, 3 May 1891, p. 8; 'Exposição industrial', *ibid.*, 29 Nov. 1895, p. 1; Brazil, Ministerio da Fazenda, Commissão de Inquerito Industrial, *Relatorio*, p. 26; Cannabrava, *Desenvolvimento da cultura do algodão*, p. 283; Mascarenhas, *Bernardo Mascarenhas*, pp. 62–5, 70, 74.

modeled in 1911—and in the Moinho Riograndense in Pôrto Alegre constructed during the First World War. Thus, despite the predominance of the United States in the development of modern flour milling, it was to the British that entrepreneurs turned when they began this industry in Brazil.[1]

The smaller nascent industries also depended upon British manufacturers for their machinery. A government study made in 1882 referred in passing to a lead pipe factory which used an English engine, boiler, and hydraulic press; a bronze foundry with an English engine; and another foundry (unspecified) also employing English machinery. One of the most persistent promoters of the use of steam engines, fixed and on wheels, was Ruston Proctor & Co. of Lincoln. The iron foundry of Low-Moor in England made boilers and other gear which it sold through an agent in Rio de Janeiro. In 1895 William Reid & Co. advertised their services as 'engineers and importers': they sold gas or gasoline motors and English-made leather and canvas belts for industrial use, maintaining half- to five-horsepower engines in stock to meet immediate needs. 'Genuine English' leather drive-belts were also sold by Arens Irmãos, while similar cotton belts made by F. Reddaway & Co. were handled by Crashley & Co.[2]

Thus the increasing pace of industrialization in Brazil meant a radical alteration in the nature of imports arriving from Great Britain. It was no longer cottons, butter, and pianos that lined Brazilian wharves and filled the warehouses of the international merchants in Rio de Janeiro. Machinery imported during 1850–4 had represented only 0·85 per cent of the value of all British imports. Thirty years later this proportion had risen to 6·52 per cent and by 1905–9 it was 9·96 per cent. Imports of all capital

---

[1] 'Report of Henry Simon, 8 December 1886', printed circular; minutes General Meeting, 25 Oct. 1888; Reports General Manager, first half of 1904, p. 3; 1911, p. 4, ARFM; John Storck and Walter Dorwin Teague, *Flour for Man's Bread: a History of Milling* (Minneapolis: Univ. of Minnesota Press, 1952), pp. 243–5, 272, 364; *The Northwestern Miller*, XLVIII (1889), 299; A. E. Humphries, 'Modern Developments in Flour Milling', Royal Society of Arts, *Journal*, LV (1906–7), 109–26; *In Memoriam. Conde Francisco Matarazzo* (São Paulo: Orlandi, 1937), p. 51; interview with Artur Coimbra Ferros, Rio, 19 May 1965.

[2] Brazil, Ministerio da Fazenda, Commissão de Inquerito Industrial, *Relatorio*, p. 136;. *Jornal do commercio*, 4 June 1882, p. 7; 3 May 1891, pp. 7, 8; 1 Nov. 1891, p. 10; 6 Jan. 1895, p. 10; 18 Jan. 1895, p. 3.

goods, including coal, chemicals, railway and telegraph equipment, hardware and tools, seed oil, machinery, and metals, had accounted for only 14 per cent of British exports to Brazil in 1850–4. But, as can be seen in Table 6, during the five-year period beginning in 1905 this figure reached 42 per cent. If we take into account that in 1904 British goods arriving in Brazil were worth twice as much as those from Britain's next best competitor, the importance of British materials in equipping and supplying Brazil's industrial plant becomes evident. The change in the nature of imports is shown by the fact that by 1913 coal imports alone were worth one and a half times as much as British cotton goods. Furthermore, both the categories of 'iron and steel', and 'machines and tools' were by that time each close competitors with cottons. Brazil had begun a transformation and the British had provided the instruments of change.[1]

As with coal, it was not the mere origin of these products that was important. The active work of developing sales systems, shipping lines, insurance businesses, and procedures for transacting financial operations, all backed up by a long-established industrial leadership, made the British effort decisive in Brazil's struggle to industrialize—but then only once the other motivating conditions had been developed. A broad spectrum of changes in Brazil made possible the destruction of traditional values, the accumulation of capital, the supply of qualified labor, and the expansion of markets, all of which worked together to impel Brazil toward an industrial economy. And Britishers, possessing both the needed equipment and the institutions to place it on Brazilian shores, were ready to supply it when it was needed.

Every sale of machinery meant at least short-term and often long-term loans. It has already been noted that the typical importing firm allowed a long line of credit to Brazilian purchasers. The same rule applied to buyers of industrial equipment and supplies. Wilson Sons & Co., for instance, extended £10,000 to £15,000 worth of credit just to one customer. In turn, the

[1] Centro Industrial do Brasil, *O Brasil. Suas riquezas naturaes, suas industrias*, 3 vols. (Rio: Orosco, 1907–8), I, 293–4, 301; Brazil, Serviço de Estatística Econômica e Financeira, *Commercio exterior do Brazil . . . Foreign Trade . . . 1913–1918*, II, 98–9; see also Appendix C.

Table 6. *Capital Goods Imports from Britain 1850–1909: Percentage of Total Imports*[a]

	1850–4	1855–9	1860–4	1865–9	1870–4	1875–9	1880–4	1885–9	1890–4	1895–9	1900–4	1905–9
Coal	4·13	3·49	1·94	2·35	4·48	3·65	3·49	5·25	7·02	9·39	13·91	9·88
Chemicals	0·32	0·35	0·35	0·32	0·39	0·37	0·31	0·35	0·85	1·12	1·67	1·85
Machinery	0·85	1·99	1·80	1·28	3·20	3·43	6·52	7·62	9·96	7·49	6·98	9·96
Railway & telegraph equipment					4·23	0·99	0·74	0·95	2·44	3·20	2·80	1·67
Cement							0·58	0·52	0·51	0·44	0·23	0·61
Seed oil	0·33	0·42	0·47	0·35	0·41	0·49	0·53	0·61	0·60	1·00	1·27	0·82
Hardware: tools, etc.	3·46	3·84	2·86	6·22	3·77	4·12	3·61	3·77	3·47	3·52	3·69	4·17
Iron, wrought and unwrought	3·32	5·48	5·51	3·77	8·28	9·19	9·99	8·26	10·34	10·83	8·77	10·92
Metals, other than iron	1·82	2·47	1·97	1·48	1·25	1·32	1·16	1·03	1·60	1·97	2·28	1·91
Total	14·23	18·04	14·90	15·77	26·01	23·56	26·93	28·36	36·79	38·96	41·60	41·79

[a] Derived from Appendix C.

British manufacturer granted generous accommodations to the importing firm in Brazil that bought from him, and banks in Britain lent money there to industrial concerns awaiting payment. British banks in Brazil collected on manufacturer's bills with interest, sometimes demanding their full pound of flesh.

Of more direct importance, British banks in Brazil lent both to railways and industries. Half the discounts and advances of the São Paulo branch of the London and Brazilian Bank went to the Mogyana railroad company, while the São Paulo Railway depended heavily on the English Bank of Rio de Janeiro. The London and Brazilian Bank also lent large sums to the textile industry during the early years of the twentieth century, and one of the main businesses of the branch at São Paulo was to provide loans to promising manufacturing firms in that burgeoning industrial setting. The English Bank of Rio de Janeiro, now called the British Bank of South America, also financed the equipment of textile mills. One of its especially important transactions was a loan to Francisco Matarazzo. Having arrived in Brazil as an immigrant of modest means, he had gradually acquired an impressive reputation as a merchant, first in lard, and then in cereals and other foodstuffs. Primarily with money borrowed from this British bank he organized a modern flour mill in 1899 and shifted into manufacturing. With this as his base he built up an imposing industrial empire.[1]

Besides industrial equipment and industrial credit, the British contributed 'know-how' to the Brazilian developmental process. An underdeveloped country cannot hope to have the trained personnel necessary for rapid development, and Brazil naturally turned to Great Britain, the industrial capital of the world. The charges for this technical expertise were often inflated, as they still

[1] Farrell to Mather, London, 19 July 1900, PWL, p. 459; J. R. T. Hughes, *Fluctuations in Trade, Industry, and Finance. A Study of British Economic Development, 1850–1860* (Oxford: Clarendon Press, 1960), p. 38; Edward N. Hurley, *Banking and Credit in Argentina, Brazil, Chile and Peru*, U.S. Bureau of Manufacturers Special Agents Series, 90 (Washington, D.C.: Government Printing Office, 1914), pp. 69–70; Stein, *Brazilian Cotton Manufacture*, p. 220n. 59; David Joslin, *A Century of Banking in Latin America; to Commemorate the Centenary in 1962 of the Bank of London and South America, Limited* (London: Oxford Univ. Press, 1963), pp. 165, 166, 171; Warren K. Dean, 'São Paulo's Industrial Elite, 1890–1960', unpub. Ph.D. diss., Univ. of Florida, 1964, pp. 56, 69; *In Memoriam . . . Matarazzo*, pp. 14, 351.

are today; but at least at that time it was hard to argue that it could be dispensed with. The first area where the British contributed technical knowledge was in civil engineering. As knowledgeable Brazilians frequently confessed at the time, they were often overwhelmed by the technical problems they faced. The first Brazilian engineering school was not created until 1858 and it was not until the end of the empire that Brazil could begin to rely almost entirely on its own engineers to carry out the works of public and private construction. In contrast, the British had long excelled at producing daring but meticulous civil engineers who had built the canals, roads, railways, and docks to make England and Scotland one economic whole. There were so many British engineers in Brazil that the Brazilian image of an Englishman came to be that of an engineer. Often, as in the cases of Charles Neate and Henry Law, they remained a lifetime. Some engineers came out to Brazil for an adventure as young men and had chances to court the local girls, while others arrived already with their fame established. In either case they helped train Brazilians by giving them field experience: British engineers advertised for assistants in the Rio de Janeiro papers and Brazilian engineers worked under the direction of famous professionals like Sir John Hawkshaw. One British engineer in Brazil introduced accounting methods which were generally adopted for engineering works throughout the country.[1]

The spread of industrial processes also required technical knowledge. Brazilian cotton mills were heavily dependent upon British talents. First of all, British engineers supervised the installation of British machinery, and, even when the equipment was American, British mechanics were often used to mount it. Then, several Brazilian-owned mills were managed by Britishers, including the two most successful mills in Rio de Janeiro during the 1890s. The skilled workers who operated the mills were also brought from

[1] William Ashworth, *An Economic History of England, 1870-1939* (London & New York: Methuen & Barnes & Noble, 1960), p. 9; Ina von Binzer [pseud. for Ulla von Eck?], *Alegrias e tristezas de um educadora alemã no Brasil*, transl. Alice Rossi and Luisita da Gama Cerqueira (São Paulo: Anhembi, 1956), pp. 77, 79, 91, 94, 95, 130-2, 137; *Jornal do commercio*, 2 Jan. 1871, p. 4; André Rebouças, *Diário e notas autobiográficas*, ed. Ana Flora and Inácio José Veríssimo, Documentos Brasileiros, 12 (Rio: José Olympio, 1938), pp. 137, 244.

Britain. British master mechanics had long held an enviable reputation in Brazil, and one company in 1875 hired five of them at once; in 1898 Lancashire mechanics were still being employed there, and British master spinners and weavers were prominent in almost every fledgling textile mill in Brazil.[1]

Railroads and flour mills also found their skilled workers in Britain. The railway companies used British men as foremen on the more complicated jobs such as plate-laying and as engine drivers and fitters. English and Irish workers helped build the most difficult section of the Estrada de Ferro Dom Pedro Segundo. Rio Flour Mills brought its first millers from England and as late as 1907 it still had to fall back upon this source upon occasion. Nor was it alone: Matarazzo traveled personally to England to hire men with knowledge of flour milling. In both railroading and flour manufacturing it was evident that the skills needed were not to be found in a traditional society.[2]

But the foreign companies, contrary to occasional allegations still heard today, were not satisfied to hire only European skilled workers. Although it is true some British firms relied exclusively on British personnel, even for carpenters, in general the cost of such practices encouraged British companies to hire Brazilians. Rio Flour Mills, for example, was alarmed to discover how much it cost to bring workers from England. European workers were also unsatisfactory because they had difficulty adjusting to the country. English workmen were usually engaged for three years with passage home at the end of that time or earlier if sick; but tropical disease often felled them immediately upon arrival. Furthermore, the social environment, or 'the climate' as Fox, the railroad engineer, would have it, caused them to become 'wild'

[1] Stein, *Brazilian Cotton Manufacture*, pp. 35, 38, 43, 57, 218 n.46, 219 n.52; Mascarenhas, *Bernardo Mascarenhas*, p. 41; Borja Castro, 'Relatorio do segundo grupo', in Souza Rego, *Relatorio*, pp. 39, 41; *Rio News*, 5 Apr. 1892, p. 3; Lisboa and Moncorvo, 'Juizo sobre a obra', p. 325.

[2] Daniel Makinson Fox, *Description of the Line and Works of the São Paulo Railway in the Empire of Brazil...with an Abstract of the Discussion upon the Paper*, ed. James Forrest (London: Clowes, 1870), pp. 20–2; Daniel Parish Kidder and James Cooley Fletcher, *Brazil and the Brazilians Portrayed in Historical and Descriptive Sketches* (Philadelphia: Childs and Peterson, 1857), p. 318; Board Minutes, 10 July 1883; 19 June 1888; Reports General Manager, 1907, p. 20, ARFM; *In Memoriam...Matarazzo*, p. 14.

and insubordinate.[1] One company convinced by these hard facts was the British-owned St John d'El Rey Mining Company, not otherwise known for enlightened labor policies. In 1884 the instructions for the manager said that 'European labour is most expensive—many men earning, with overtime, about £20 per month—and if there be even one European whose work can be done equally well by a native, the former's service should be dispensed with'.[2]

So the training of Brazilian operatives was a constant concern. Textile workers were often contracted with the specific purpose of preparing Brazilians for these tasks. Sometimes they were reluctant to perform this function once they were in Brazil, since it would lead to their replacement, but, nevertheless, towards the end of the century the prevalence of British laborers in the textile mills became less marked because of increasing numbers of skilled Brazilians. When a British cotton mill opened in 1912 it was able to 'find sufficient skilled labor on the spot and so avoid the necessity of maintaining a large and expensive European staff'. Effort was also made to teach the skills of flour milling. The president of Rio Flour Mills reported in 1900 that through a training program many Brazilians had learned the trade so that 'all our millers, engineers, and other skilled workmen, with the exception of less than half a dozen, and all our ordinary workmen to the number of about 250, are natives of, or permanently settled in the country'. In 1909 it was reported that only fourteen of its 400 regular employees in Brazil were British subjects, and Brazilians were said to 'assist ably in the milling and mechanical business of the mill'. Similarly, in 1913 only one per cent of those working in the locomotive department of the Great Western of Brazil Railway were Britishers. The industrial growth of the

---

[1] Wilson Sons & Co. showed definite preferences for Englishmen, Farrell to Mather, London, 16 Jan. 1900; 29 June 1900, PWL, pp. 226, 432; other companies did not, Reports General Manager, 1903, p. 21, ARFM; Fox, *Description of the Line and Works*, pp. 22, 27. Wages for English smiths, carpenters, bricklayers, and masons were reported to run from £12 to £14 per month and for foremen, platelayers, and engine drivers, £14 to £16, 'Report of Consul Lennon Hunt, 18 Aug. 1864' in Great Britain, *Commercial Reports Received at the Foreign Office from Her Majesty's Consuls*, July–Dec. 1864, p. 55.

[2] Bernard Hollowood, *The Story of Morro Velho* (London: St John d'El Rey Mining Company, Ltd, 1955), p. 53.

country as a whole depended on the development of skilled labor and the British were working to this end.[1] Development would also depend on a widely shared belief in industrialization. The British who invested in manufacturing joined forces with those Brazilians committed to modernization to advocate policies which would contribute to this end. The manager of a British flour mill in Rio noted the decline of imported flour with satisfaction since it 'materially strengthens not only our position, but also that of the milling industry in general in Brazil'. When new Brazilian mills were established he admitted that 'this, of course, means more competition, but the idea is to expel from the various markets all foreign flours'. And the fact that a flour importer was British did not lessen the miller's animosity toward him one whit.[2] Furthermore, if the British firm—by definition—believed in foreign investments in Brazil, so did contemporary Brazilian industrialists; there was no cause for divergence there. The common interest of the British manufacturer and the Brazilian one is shown by the support given by some Britishers to tariff legislation. The British flour mill, for example, contributed fully to efforts to erect a tariff barrier against the imported article. Other Britishers had joined Brazilian industrialists in 1882 to demand protective tariffs against foreign imports generally.[3]

The British, then, were not uniformly linked to non-industrial interests, and this fact is brought home once more by the fact that even British importers sometimes became industrialists. Noting the same factors that encouraged Brazilian merchants to

---

[1] Stein, *Brazilian Cotton Manufacture*, pp. 51, 52, 62, 63; Mascarenhas, *Bernardo Mascarenhas*, p. 66; Minutes of the General Meetings, 18 Dec. 1900; 19 Jan. 1909; 14 Jan. 1913, ARFM; Reginald Lloyd et al., eds., *Twentieth Century Impressions of Brazil: Its History, People, Commerce, Industries, and Resources* (London: Lloyd's Greater Britain Publishing Co., 1913), p. 251.

[2] Reports General Manager, 1903, p. 3; 1907, p. 2; 1912, p. 4, ARFM.

[3] Francisco de Paula Mayrink, *O cambio, a producção, o governo; artigos publicados na imprensa da corte em maio de 1881* (Rio: Typ. do Cruzeiro, 1881), p. 31; *Rio News*, 10 Feb. p. 5; 17 Feb. p. 3; 10 Mar. p. 3; 17 Mar. p. 3; 24 Mar. p. 3; 31 Mar. p. 3, 1891; 'Memorial sobre a organização, producção e futuro da industria dos moinhos de farinhas de trigo na Republica dos Estados Unidos do Brasil, 1/3/1903' and 'Os efeitos que causa a redução dos direitos concedidos sobre as farinhas americanas contra as importadas da Republica Argentina e a industria da moagem nacional [undated, 1904]', MSS. enclosed in Reports General Manager, 1903 and 1904, ARFM; Antonio Felicio dos Santos, 'Discurso na Camara dos Deputados', *Diario official*, 25 Apr. 1882, p. 4.

begin manufacturing—especially growing markets, availability of raw materials, and rising tariffs—it was only natural that men of ideas and capital should turn to industry. In addition to a shoe company to be discussed below, there were several importing houses that made this transition. Edward Ashworth & Co., a British counting house with a branch in Rio de Janeiro dating back to the 1840s, was active in founding a canvas and canvas-goods factory in São Paulo, a woolens factory in Petrópolis, and a textile mill in Taubaté. A British importer of jute bagging in Recife decided to take advantage of the tariff legislation of 1891 to install a bag factory. The venture was successful and in 1904, with the participation of large sugar interests, he organized a joint-stock company to operate it called the Companhia Fabrica de Juta. The Hargreaves brothers, Henry and Charles, sons and heirs of a British merchant who had dealt predominantly in textiles, were, perhaps, the most important examples of importers-turned-manufacturers. They first built coffee-processing machinery and other metal products. In 1877 they established a textile factory, and subsequently installed machinery for other cotton manufacturers. They also took an interest in railroad building, river transport companies, and other entrepreneurial ventures, some of which involved them in government affairs and public loans. It was most unlikely that these Britishers would maintain the same viewpoint as their compatriots who remained importers.[1] National origins did not affect attitudes as much as financial interest.

[1] *Almanak administrativo, mercantil e industrial do Rio de Janeiro e indicador para 1850. Obra estatistica e de consulta. Supplemento* (Rio: Laemmert, 1850), p. 97; *Jornal do commercio*, 1 Jan. 1871, p. 7; British and Latin American Chamber of Commerce, *Commercial Encyclopedia Comprising a Series of Standard Publications on the Actual and Potential Markets of the World, Compiled and Issued by Sections: Fourth Sectional Issue: South America*, ed. W. H. Morton-Cameron, 2nd ed. (London: Globe Encyclopedia Co., 1924), pp. 457, 581; Alfredo J. Watts, 'A colônia inglêsa em Pernambuco', *Revista do Instituto Arqueológico e Geográfico de Pernambuco*, XXXIX (1944), 168; 'Importação—Manifestos', *Jornal do commercio*, Jan. 1850; André Rebouças, 'Noticia sobre a organização da Companhia das Docas de D. Pedro II', *Revista de engenharia*, IV (1882), 42; West, 'Foreigner in Brazilian Technology', pp. 263, 610, 749; Brazil, Ministerio da Fazenda, Commissão de Inquerito Industrial, *Relatorio*, p. 30; Stein, *Brazilian Cotton Manufacture*, p. 218 n. 42; Rebouças, *Diário*, pp. 244, 268; Dean, 'São Paulo's Industrial Elite', pp. 69, 71; Rui Barbosa, *Mocidade e exilio. Cartas ao conselheiro Albino José Barbosa de Oliveira e ao dr. Antônio d'Araújo Ferreira Jacobina*, ed. Américo Jacobina Lacombe, Brasiliana, 38 (São Paulo: Editôra Nacional, 1934), pp. 262–3.

Direct British investment in Brazilian manufacturing grew with Brazil's over-all industrial power. In this way the British actively participated in the transformation of the relationship between man and his environment and between man and man, so essential to modernization. The nature of British interests varied with the course of Brazilian economic growth. The production of processing machinery for exportable products was their earliest concern, as it was for Brazilians. Then, it was textile mills, and British ones were among the first to be founded in Brazil. Shoe manufacturing plants benefited from the same tariff legislation and the same expanding urban markets that made Brazilian-owned factories possible. The first modern flour mill in Brazil was founded by Britishers to be succeeded by many Brazilian establishments. And finally, in the vain effort to modernize the most traditional economic activity of Brazil, the British struggled to create central sugar factories. The British were not the cause of Brazilian industrialization. As we have seen, the activities of some of them tended to hinder that process. But others worked shoulder-to-shoulder with Brazilians to bring it about.

The first British manufacturing establishments to be created in Brazil were iron foundries that made the machinery for processing raw materials for export. One of the most famous of these was the Fundição Aurora in Recife owned by the Britisher Christopher Starr. It was established as early as 1829 and made not only parts with which to fix broken equipment, but also complete steam-operated mills. The lack of adequate tariff protection and the consequent importation of similar equipment from abroad forced him out of business in 1876. Similar establishments, such as that of David William Bowman (founded 1840), were simultaneously reduced to mere importers. Later on, however, this firm re-entered manufacturing, as the Pernambuco Engineering Works. In Salvador the emperor Pedro II visited a foundry run by two Englishmen, a loquacious Mr Cameron and a taciturn Mr Smith. Cameron had come to Brazil at first to work for the *barão* de Mauá. Their establishment made grinding wheels, steam engines, and complete sugar mills with British-made machine-tools. In 1859 it employed 84 master workmen, and 28 apprentices. British people also created a similar foundry in Campos to serve the sugar district of the state of Rio de Janeiro.[1] Textile manufacturing was of greater significance. It is often one of the first steps toward industrialization taken by developing countries. By the First World War Brazil had established a substantial cotton industry. Before 1865 efforts had been sporadic and generally unsuccessful, but after that, the process of modernization accelerated and mills began to multiply. Simultaneously, as coffee concentrated more and more people in the south-central regions, the mills moved closer to the consuming centers and away from the northeastern sources of raw material. In 1884 cotton manufacturers in São Paulo were advertising that their goods were 'better than the English', and many were convinced: by the beginning of the twentieth century domestic production exceeded imports by a healthy margin.[2]

The British were interested from the beginning. Shrewdly noting the increasing exports of Brazil, they were first attracted to the production of bagging. In 1852 a Scot proposed to move to Brazil and establish a factory to make 'coarse material... for coffee sacks'. But other textile products did not escape their attention. As early as 1846 or 1847 an Englishman had founded a mill in Minas Gerais that was said to make cottons as good as those imported from England. Like most of those founded in that era, it was unsuccessful, largely because of inadequate transport and scarcity of skilled labor.[3]

---

[1] Manuel Diégues Júnior, *O engenho de açucar no nordeste*, Documentário da Vida Rural, 1 (Rio: Serviço de Informação Agrícola, Ministério da Agricultura, 1952), p. 28; *Diario de Pernambuco*, 3 Jan. 1850, p. 2; 4 July 1860, pp. 5, 7; 18 Jan. 1870, p. 4; Brazil, Commissão ...Tarifa, *Relatorio*, pp. 345, 346; John Smith, 'Memoria...por parte dos herdeiros Bowman, sobre melhoramentos introduzidos na producção do assucar desta provincia', in Sociedade Auxiliadora d'Agricultura de Pernambuco, *Acta da sessão solemne da Assembléa Geral de 28 de setembro de 1882 e relatorio annual do gerente*...(Recife: Typ. Central, 1882), pp. 110–12; Michael George Mulhall, *The English in South America* (Buenos Aires: 'Standard' Office, 1878), p. 349; Watts, 'Colônia inglêsa', p. 167; British and Latin American Chamber of Commerce, *Commercial Encyclopedia*, p. 749; Pedro II, *Diário da viagem ao Norte do Brasil*, ed. Lourenço Luiz Lacombe (Bahia: Univ. da Bahia, 1959), p. 150.

[2] *A provincia de São Paulo*, 13 Jan. 1884, p. 4; Heitor Ferreira Lima, *Mauá e Roberto Simonsen: dois pioneiros do desenvolvimento* (São Paulo: Editôra Edaglit, 1963), p. 48.

[3] Sérgio Teixeira de Macedo to Paulino José Soares de Sousa, London, 4 Feb. 1852, AHI, 216/2/15, no. 3; Brazil, Commissão...Tarifa, *Relatorio*, p. 338; Mascarenhas, *Bernardo Mascarenhas*, pp. 31–2.

The British were more active after the Paraguayan War. John Edington, an Englishman, established a cotton factory in Bahia in 1875. That same year a Manchester industrial concern bought property in the province of São Paulo for the establishment of a cotton mill. It was later sold to Brazilians. Two Britishers established the Fabrica Santa Rita in Rio de Janeiro in that same period, and, as already noted, Edward Ashworth & Co. later operated a wool factory in Petrópolis and a cotton cloth factory in Taubaté. The latter employed 600 workers by 1913. Englishmen owned still another factory, located in Juiz de Fora. And a British manufacturer of drive belts invested almost 43 per cent of the original capital in the company which purchased and modernized the Carioba textile mill in the state of São Paulo.[1] Another mill was built by British flour interests in 1910, at first to manufacture flour sacks, and then to make 'coarse greys for sugar bags'. The company later bleached some material and decided eventually 'to go in for finer cloths'. In 1914 it operated 437 looms and doubled its plant in 1920.[2]

In addition to these textile mills the British were the owners of the São Paulo thread factory established during 1906–8 by J. & P. Coats (Machine Cottons, Ltd). Thirty Scottish workers were brought over to train the Brazilian workers. It completely monopolized the sewing-thread market before the First World War, a position it maintained by giving no quarter to its commercial foes.[3]

Another industry frequently established in newly industrializing economies is the manufacture of shoes. Footwear had long

---

[1] Brazil, Ministerio da Fazenda, Commissão de Inquerito Industrial, *Relatorio*, pp. 26, 30; 'Communicado. Desenvolvimento industrial em Itú', *Correio paulistano*, 16 Feb. 1875, p. 1; Cannabrava, *Desenvolvimento da cultura do algodão*, p. 286; Stein, *Brazilian Cotton Manufacture*, pp. 26, 218 n. 42; Santos, 'Discurso na camara', p. 4; British and Latin American Chamber of Commerce, *Commercial Encyclopedia*, pp. 457, 581; T. Oscar Marcondes de Souza, *O estado de São Paulo: physico, politico, economico e administrativo* (São Paulo: Universal, 1915), pp. 148–9; Mascarenhas, *Bernardo Mascarenhas*, p. 123; Dean, 'São Paulo's Industrial Elite', pp. 53 n., 68–9, 71, 98 n.

[2] Minutes General Meetings, 16 Jan. 1914; 14 Jan. 1915; 26 Jan. 1920; Reports General Manager, 1917, p. 21, ARFM.

[3] 'Linhas Para Coser—Empire of Thread', *Brazilian Business*, XXXIX, no. 7 (July 1959), pp. 34–5; Haas, *Investimentos Estrangeiros*, item no. II, 260; Stein, *Brazilian Cotton Manufacture*, pp. 144–5, 253.

been a large item of importation from Great Britain, especially shoes for men. The Clark Shoe Company of Kilmarnock, Scotland, had been shipping shoes to Brazil since before 1840, and the business was so successful that members of the Clark family had personally handled the Brazilian end of the business. In 1850 the firm advertised their receipt in Rio de Janeiro of 'a new selection' including ladies' shoes of fabric, and men's three-soled shoes, patent-leather shoes, and rain shoes. In the 1880s Clark shoes were also being advertised in São Paulo, and by the end of the nineteenth century thirty family-owned outlets were scattered all the way from the Amazon to Rio Grande do Sul. Clark shoes became *de rigueur* for the well-dressed Brazilian male.

Eventually the company began manufacturing in Brazil. Already in 1891, just two years after the declaration of the republic and the initiation of its emphasis on manufacturing goals, the Companhia Industrial advertised Brazilian-made shoes 'for men and women made on Clark forms'; it is not clear whether this meant pirating or a licensing agreement. But in 1898 the senior member of the Clark shoe family went to Rio de Janeiro to supervise personally the establishment of a shoe factory, and by 1908 the company had 300 workers in another plant in São Paulo. Although it was not the largest employer among shoe factories there, it utilized almost twice the horsepower of any other establishment and was thus able to produce a greater value of shoes than any competitor. Another concern which manufactured footwear was the São Paulo Alpargatas Company established in 1907 by a British importing firm. The increasing domestic production of such items as shoes is reflected in the decline in the value of wearing apparel imported from Great Britain from over £590,000 during the period 1865–9 to £240,000 thirty years later and only £80,000 in 1905–9. By 1920 the footwear industry employed nearly 15,000 workers in Brazil.[1]

[1] Brazil, Ministerio da Fazenda, Commissão de Inquerito Industrial, *Relatorio*, p. 114; Borja Castro, 'Relatorio do 2º grupo', in Souza Rego, *Relatorio*, p. 65; George Clark to the author, Kilmarnock, 16 Aug. 1962; João Gomes da Rocha, *Lembranças do passado. Ensaio histórico do início e desenvolvimento do trabalho evangélico no Brasil, do qual resultou a fundação da 'Igreja Evangélica Fluminense' pelo dr. Robert Reid Kalley*, 4 vols. (Rio: Centro Brasileiro de Publicidade [vols. I–III] and 'O Cristão', [vol. IV], 1941–57), II, 55;

After textiles and apparel industries, food-processing plants are always among early industrial ventures. And by far the most successful investment of the British in Brazilian manufacturing was the Rio de Janeiro Flour Mills and Granaries, Ltd, usually referred to as Rio Flour Mills. Modern flour milling is a sophisticated industry involving large capital investment, complicated automatic machinery, mass production processes, a high proportion of skilled workers, and considerable organizational ability. The problems it posed were so great that, until the mid-1880s, all Brazilian flour with minimal exceptions was imported either from Hungary and Italy or from the United States. Risking a great deal to overcome the problems inherent in an underdeveloped country, Rio Flour Mills pioneered the way for this industry in Brazil. Although its example was immediately followed by an indifferently profitable Brazilian mill, it was not until it had been shown that these difficulties could be successfully overcome that others entered the field.

The company was organized in 1886 with £250,000 as capital. Early reverses threatened its existence, chiefly because of the mill's location in an underdeveloped, tropical country. Although it was initially maintained that 'a very large margin' had been 'allowed for such items as may be affected by the fact of the company's mill being established at Rio de Janeiro', this margin was not large enough. The lack of machine shops made it hard to secure spare parts, and the company had to acquire an extra set of engines to be used in case of breakdown. Brazilian industrialists had similarly complained about this deficiency in the supporting institutions necessary for manufacturing operations. Because of backward harbor facilities it was impossible for ships to pull up alongside the mill and it was difficult to discharge wheat

Jornal do commercio, 1 Jan. 1850, p. 3; 3 May 1891, p. 7; *A provincia de São Paulo*, 8 Mar. 1884, p. 4; Gilberto Freyre, *Introdução à história da sociedade patriarcal no Brasil, III: Ordem e progresso...*, 2 vols. (Rio: José Olympio, 1959), I, cxxx; II, 674, 676; Julio Ribeiro, *A carne* (São Paulo: Teixeira, 1888), pp. 27, 265; Centro Industrial do Brasil, *Le Brésil. Ses richesses naturelles, ses industries (édition pour l'étranger)*, 3 vols. (Rio: Orosco, 1908–9), III, 118; Marcondes de Souza, *O estado de São Paulo*, p. 154; British and Latin American Chamber of Commerce, *Commercial Encyclopedia*, p. 457; Appendix C; J. F. Normano, *Brazil, a Study of Economic Types* (Chapel Hill, N.C.: Univ. of North Carolina Press, 1935), p. 107.

efficiently. Then, due to the prevalence of yellow fever, there were frequent occasions when the wheat ships were not allowed even to touch the pier which the company had built, and it was necessary to revert to lighters. Fixed capital expenditures alone soon exceeded the company's total share capital. The result was what a director called an 'important crisis of the Company's existence', and even the sale of the property was considered. The possibility of closing the mill was placed before the shareholders, but it was decided to carry on. The company eventually solved its problems one by one and emerged from its time of troubles.[1]

The shareholders were amply rewarded for their perseverance. By 1893 the company issued its first dividend and never again did it fail to do so. In 1900 dividends reached 10 per cent and the next year they touched 17·8 per cent. In 1902 the dividend represented 21·4 per cent of the capital and the company decided on a '10 for 7 stock split', and a doubling of the capital. After that the dividends were never less than 15 per cent until after the First World War, and there were numerous bonuses. The quotations of Rio Flour Mills' shares on the stock market reflected.this increasing prosperity. From a low of £2 per £10 share in 1891 their value rose steadily so that in 1900 they were selling at par and in 1902, just before the stock split, they shot up to £24. 8s. 9d. By 1912 it was again possible to sell a £1 share for £4.

It was only through an intelligent effort to overcome the obstacles presented by the mill's location that the company was able to win out. As the chairman pointed out in 1895, 'Rio is not a favorite place for investors...It is recognized that commercial undertakings in Brazil are liable to fluctuations, and are attended with a certain amount of risk.' It was this risk that Rio Flour Mills was ready to run in order to establish the first modern flour mill in Brazil.[2]

[1] Richard Graham, 'A British Industry in Brazil: Rio Flour Mills, 1886–1920', *Business History*, VIII (1966), 13–38; 'Report of Henry Simon, 8 December 1886', printed circular; Minutes General Meeting, 29 Sept. 1891, ARFM; Henri Raffard, ed., *O centro da Industria e Commercio de Assucar do Rio de Janeiro* (Rio: Cia. Typ. do Brazil, 1892), p. 115.
[2] Minutes General Meeting, 13 Dec. 1895; 16 Jan. 1903; 20 Feb. 1903; Board Minutes, 9 June 1903; 1 Sept. 1903, ARFM; Graham, 'A British Industry', p. 38.

On the other hand, it was the larger over-all changes in Brazil that made the company's existence and prosperity possible. The use of wheat flour had not been customary in Brazil, where rice, corn, and manioc were widely used instead. It was only the increasing penetration of European ways during the nineteenth century and the growth of European-oriented city populations that made the mill conceivable. André Rebouças, a Brazilian modernizer, writing at a time when the rise and fall of civilizations was sometimes attributed to their diets, had decried the backward eating habits of his countrymen and urged the establishment of flour mills so that 'the use of bread would advance into the interior, carried by the railways, and would give our agricultural workers more energy-producing and healthier food than flour of *mandioca* and corn'.[1] For many years it could still be said by the manager of the mill that in most of the country 'wheat flour is...looked upon as a luxury', and in 1905 he wrote with some disgust that in certain areas maize and manioc flours were still 'largely used as human food by the natives'. Even at the time of the First World War it was reported that, although by then the population of the cities had 'become used to bread made with wheat flour and will no doubt continue to use it no matter what it costs', in rural areas and small towns 'this is not so, and, as real distress prevails, they will be unable to find the money to pay the relatively high currency price of wheat flour'. The future of an industrial enterprise depended on making the country over in the image of the modern world.

The company was also benefited by the rising standards of the lower classes. In good times the freed slaves were said to 'use nothing but wheaten bread'. And the vast numbers of immigrants that arrived during these years meant that another large segment of the lower strata of the population would 'not eat the *farinha de mendioca* [*sic*] formerly almost the universal food of the working

---

[1] Gilberto Freyre, *The Masters and the Slaves (Casa-Grande & Senzala): a Study in the Development of Brazilian Civilization*, transl. Samuel Putnam (New York: Knopf, 1956), pp. 21, 46; Gilberto Freyre, *The Mansions and the Shanties (Sobrados e Mucambos): the Making of Modern Brazil*, transl. Harriet de Onís (New York: Knopf, 1963), p. 46n.; André Rebouças, *Agricultura nacional, estudos economicos; propaganda abolicionista e democratica* (Rio: Lamoureux, 1883), pp. 39–40.

classes'. Thus, just as the urban middle groups were growing, the lower classes were improving their condition and changing their tastes. These changes contributed toward a larger market for manufactured goods, including wheat flour.[1]

After Rio Flour Mills had scouted the terrain and built the forts, other settlers entered the flour milling frontier. By 1918 mills had been built in São Paulo, Santos, Niterói, Curitiba, Florianópolis, Pôrto Alegre, and Recife, and flour milling had become an important Brazilian industry. As a pioneer the British company had contributed directly to the initiation of modern change in Brazil.

Another area of food processing in which the English invested considerable sums was the manufacture of sugar. In building central sugar factories the British lost much more than they made in flour mills, and it was precisely their position as innovators inadequately dealing with a hostile environment that made this so. Sugar manufacturing processes in Brazil were described by one Brazilian in 1878 as 'the same as those used for over 200 years'. Small and primitive wooden grinding cylinders driven by water-wheels or oxen were trying to compete on the world market not only with European beet sugar but also with highly mechanized processes in the Caribbean. Exportation was declining rapidly in the 1870s and the sugar economy was in crisis. Frantic efforts were made to find a solution, the president of the province of Pernambuco clearly perceiving that 'Our sugar will only be able to compete, when the same instruments and machinery are used in its manufacture as are adopted in more advanced countries'.[2]

Brazilians believed the establishment of sugar centrals would be a big step toward the modernization of their country and especially of the backward northeast. Vast economic and social changes were foreseen as the result. The separation of the manufacture of sugar from the production of cane would 'bring about the complete and indispensable division of labor as the future requires'. The factories, by eliminating waste in personnel, fuel, and power,

[1] Reports General Manager, 1905, p. 11; Minutes General Meetings, 13 Dec. 1895; 14 Jan. 1915, ARFM.
[2] Pernambuco, Presidente, *Relatorio*, 1874, p. 61; 1878, p. 59.

would produce enormous earnings: in the Caribbean these factories returned annual profits of 16 to 48 per cent. It was further believed that by reducing the capital requirements of cane growing the road would then be open for the small planter and family-sized farm. André Rebouças, a Brazilian committed to modern change and the abolition of slavery, imagined central sugar factories owned by cooperatives of small planters. The official organ of the abolitionists hailed this innovation as a step toward land reform and a blow to the institution of slavery. The minister of agriculture in 1880 similarly pointed to economic necessity and social need as impelling the government to encourage central sugar factories.[1] These arguments were later to prove indeed ironic.

It soon became apparent that special stimuli would be needed if these factories were to be created. Rebouças urged passage of a law guaranteeing interest on capital so invested. The newspapers supported him, arguing that such a guarantee would make English capital flow into the country for this purpose. And such a law was finally enacted in 1875.[2]

It was primarily to Britain that Brazil looked for the financing and equipping of sugar factories, although a Brazilian landed family in the sugar zone of the province of Rio de Janeiro founded the first sugar factory in Brazil and equipped it with French machinery. French equipment was also used in two other factories which opened in Bahia in 1880. But after that the British monopolized the market for sugar machinery and supplied the bulk of the capital for several years. The Brazilian minister in London was put in charge of stimulating the creation of such companies there and, working through Rothschild's, he was fairly successful.[3]

---

[1] Pernambuco, Presidente, *Relatorio*, 1878, p. 60; Rebouças, *Agricultura nacional*, pp. 65, 160, 196; *O abolicionista: orgão da Sociedade Brasileira Contra a Escravidão*, no. 11, 1 Sept. 1881, p. 8; Manuel Buarque de Macedo quoted *ibid.*, no. 12, 28 Sept. 1881, p. 5; João Maurício Wanderley, *barão* de Cotegipe, quoted by Renato Mendonça, *Um diplomata na côrte de Inglaterra; o barão do Penedo e sua época*, Brasiliana, 219 (São Paulo: Editôra Nacional, 1942), p. 302.

[2] Rebouças, *Agricultura nacional*, pp. 147ff., 195, 270; *Jornal do commercio, retrospecto commercial* (Rio: Villeneuve, 1874), p. 14; Lei n. 2.687 de 6/11/1875, quoted in *Jornal do commercio*, 18 Jan. 1882, p. 1.

[3] Luiz Monteiro Caminhoá, *Engenhos centraes. Relatorio publicado por ordem do snr. cons. João Ferreira de Moura* (Rio: Imp. Nacional, 1885), p. 81; West, 'Foreigner in Brazilian Technology', pp. 67–8; Mendonça, *Um diplomata na côrte de Inglaterra*, p. 302. Plans were

There were five principal British companies, almost all organized in 1882, and they received concessions to build thirty-two factories in the states of São Paulo, Rio de Janeiro, Espírito Santo, Bahia, Alagoas, Sergipe, Pernambuco, Rio Grande do Norte, and Ceará.

The Rio de Janeiro Central Sugar Factories, Ltd, was organized to operate two factories but delayed so long in getting machinery for one of them to Brazil that the terms of the second concession were violated and it was cancelled. The factory in operation was said to be poorly managed. Its directorate was identical with that of the San [*sic*] Paulo Central Sugar Factory of Brazil, Ltd, whose plant was built in 1884. Its machinery was inadequate and the company went bankrupt while waiting for replacements; it was liquidated in 1886–9.[1]

The Bahia Central Sugar Factories, Ltd, was organized to purchase concessions held by the Englishmen Frank Dennis and James Edward Blair to build eight such factories. Some £315,000 were invested by the shareholders, but by 1887 the capital had been reduced to £138,240 because of losses. The British firm of Hugh Wilson & Son contracted to build the mills and had completed two of them by 1886 when further construction was halted. Despite financial difficulties, the company held on to these two mills at least until 1902.[2]

A firm of Anglo-Brazilian railroad contractors promoted the North Brazilian Sugar Factories, Ltd. British investors placed £300,000 into this venture, lured on by the prospectus, which claimed the company would make profits of more than 14 per cent per year. The company bought up some concessions and properties previously acquired by the never-functioning Brazilian Sugar Factories Company, Ltd, and secured additional concessions

also made to use French equipment in some mills in Pernambuco which were never built, Pernambuco, Presidente, *Relatorio*, 1876, pp. 9, 100; 1877, p. 79; 1879, Anexo 1, p. 38; 1881, p. 94.

[1] Caminhoá, *Engenhos centraes*, pp. 78–80; West, 'Foreigner in Brazilian Technology', pp. 78, 80; Joaquim Nabuco, 'Correspondencia', *Jornal do commercio*, 5 Dec. 1882, p. 3; *A provincia de São Paulo*, 1 Mar. 1884, p. 2; file on Rio de Janeiro Central Sugar Factories, Ltd, BT 31/3030/14148.

[2] File on Bahia Central Sugar Factories, Ltd, BT 31/2955/16554; West, 'Foreigner in Brazilian Technology', p. 77.

bringing the total number of proposed plants to fifteen. One hundred planters were persuaded to sign contracts for the supply of sugar cane, but only one of the factories was ever completed. The company limped along, despite financial difficulties, until the First World War.[1]

The Central Sugar Factories of Brazil, Ltd, with a capital of £600,000, was promoted by Anfriso Fialho, a scheming Brazilian lawyer, and Theodor Christiansen, the son-in-law of the owner of seven sugar plantations in Pernambuco. Fialho and Christiansen were initially given remunerative positions in the company administration in Brazil. Six concessions were acquired by this company, but only four mills were ever completed, and they never worked satisfactorily. Despite its non-compliance with the terms of its concession, it continued to receive guaranteed interest, some said because the house of Rothschild—through which most of the company shares had been sold—put pressure on the Brazilian government in its behalf. Finally, in 1886, the government cancelled payment on guaranteed interest to all companies that had not fulfilled the terms of their concessions, and this one was forced into liquidation.[2]

These companies were universally a failure and the British adventure in sugar factories short-lived. Whereas in 1886 Englishmen held four out of every five concessions calling for guaranteed interest, by 1889 almost 90 per cent were held by Brazilians.[3] The principal cause of the difficulty for the British companies

[1] Prospectus of the North Brazilian Sugar Factories, Ltd, enclosed in Atherton to Department of State, Recife, 10 Aug. 1883, NA/DS, Despatches Consuls, Pernambuco, 1883, no. 115; Francisco do Rego Barros to Ignacio Joaquim de Sousa Leão, Recife, 11 June 1886, APEP, EC 1; Watts, 'Colônia inglêsa', p. 167; West, 'Foreigner in Brazilian Technology', pp. 75–6.

[2] Rodolpho Smith de Vasconcellos and Jayme Luiz Smith de Vasconcellos, 1º e 2º *barões* Smith de Vasconcellos, *Archivo nobiliarchico brasileiro* (Lausanne, Switzerland: La Concorde, 1918), p. 103; Joaquim Nabuco to *barão* do Penedo, Rio, 31 May 1884, in Joaquim Nabuco, *Obras completas* (São Paulo: Instituto Progresso Editorial, 1949), XIII, 116; Francisco do Rego Barros to Sancho de Barros Pimentel, Recife, 19 Dec. 1884, APEP, EC 1; Anfriso Fialho, *Um terço de seculo (1852–1885): recordações* (Rio: Typ. da 'Constituinte', 1885), pp. 176–9; Richard Kidner, Secretary, Central Sugar Factories, Ltd, to Nabuco, London, 9 Feb. 1883, JNP, Lata 7; Pernambuco, Presidente, *Relatorio*, 1885, p. 37; 1886, pp. 50, 56; Pernambuco, Presidente, *Falla*, Dec. 1886, p. 78; West, 'Foreigner in Brazilian Technology', pp. 79–80. Sr. Maurício Nabuco kindly made available the papers of his father Joaquim Nabuco.

[3] West, 'Foreigner in Brazilian Technology', p. 66.

was the gross mismanagement of their affairs by the directors and local managers. The complexity of the problems with which they had to deal demanded men of unusual talent rather than the mediocrities who occupied these positions. In their defense it should be said that the distance that separated the home offices from the scene of operations made it practically impossible to become intimately familiar with local conditions and hard to root out incompetent employees. But Rio Flour Mills, faced with the same problem, had managed to survive. True, the basic divergence between traditional and modern interests was greater here, making the relationships between the foreign entrepreneurs and the local economy especially difficult. But the simultaneous financial success of some Brazilian sugar factories and the subsequent survival of many planter-owned ones would indicate that it was not impossible to run them successfully.

Contemporary opinion was unanimous in regarding the direction of these companies as deplorable. Both the American consul in Recife and the presidents of the province were appalled. One of the latter noted the 'maladministration of the factories by persons who are completely ignorant of the Portuguese language', and the American reported that the poor showing of one company was 'the result of the worst sort of management, and even worse is said by outside parties'. He was referring to charges made by Fialho, who, after promoting the Central Sugar Factories of Brazil and being dismissed from his self-established position as local manager, now claimed that the directors had deliberately defrauded the shareholders and the Brazilian government by conniving with the contractors. If their relationship with the latter was not dishonest, it was certainly bad business, for 80 per cent of the contract price had been paid before construction had even begun. When the construction firm went bankrupt, the company could recover nothing. Additional weight is given to Fialho's charge by the company's apprehensions about the contractor's difficulties as early as 1882.[1]

---

[1] Pernambuco, Presidente, *Falla*, 1888, p. 38; Pernambuco, Presidente, *Relatorio*, 1885, p. 38; Atherton to Dept. of State, Recife, 28 Apr. 1885; 26 Aug. 1887, NA/DS, Despatches Consuls, Pernambuco, 1885, no. 199; 1887, no. 273; Fialho, *Um terço de seculo*, pp. 174–5; I. Morris to Nabuco, London, 11 Dec. 1882, JNP, Lata 7.

But bankruptcies by contractors were characteristic, as the mere problems of acquiring the site, constructing the plant, and importing and mounting the machinery seem to have sapped the strength of the most experienced firms. Several British companies had to terminate their plants themselves. Furthermore, the Brazilian government did nothing to inspect their construction, despite the payment of guaranteed interest and in the face of unhappy previous experiences with the railways.

The typical factory began operations with works that had been inadequately equipped or badly built. The most disastrous example of this condition was the collapse of a mill building as soon as the machinery began to set up vibrations. The tramway system to bring the cane to the mill from the surrounding fields was a basic element in its smooth functioning, yet it was always left to last and was either never installed or too hastily built. Much of the machinery was old and outdated. Four complete mill systems were brought over from Egypt after many years of service there. As soon as one of them began operation it was paralysed by a burst centrifugal. Nor did the machinery that worked perform the task for which it was installed: it was incapable of recovering from the cane much more sugar than the old primitive systems. It also tended to consume too much coal, running up the cost; so the factories turned to wood, thus hastening deforestation. Belatedly locking the barn door, the Brazilian government refused after 1885 to allow the machinery to enter under the free-of-duty clause of the concessions unless it had been previously approved by government officials in Europe.[1]

Another cause of the financial difficulties encountered by the sugar factories was the high cost of cane in relationship to the

[1] Pernambuco, Presidente, *Relatorio*, 1885, p. 38; 1886, p. 51; Pernambuco, Presidente, *Falla*, 1886, p. 56; 1886 (2nd), p. 78; West, 'Foreigner in Brazilian Technology', pp. 75–6, 77; Atherton to Dept of State, Recife, 9 Jan. 1884; 25 Feb. 1884, NA/DS, Despatches Consuls, Pernambuco, 1884, nos. 134, 138; José Bernardo Galvão Álcofarado Junior, *Discursos proferidos nas sessões de 27 de julho e 20 de agosto de 1886* (Rio: Imp. Nacional, 1886), p. 27; Manuel Diégues Júnior, 'O banguê em Pernambuco no século xix', *Revista do Arquivo Público [Estadual de Pernambuco]*, Anos vii–x, nos. 9–11 (1952–6), p. 23; Francisco do Rego Barros to Luiz Correia de Queiroz Barros, Recife, 16 Sept. 1885, APEP, EC 1. Ironically, Egypt had once been the model of the central sugar factory system, Rebouças, *Agricultura nacional*, pp. 160, 225.

price of sugar. The Brazilian government had insisted from the first that no concessions would be granted unless the companies could show that they had persuaded the plantation owners to supply the raw material. In 1878 complaints were heard that the planters lacked confidence in the central factory system and were reluctant to sign contracts for delivery of cane to a mill that was yet to be built. The same attitude could still be discerned four years later. But eventually contracts were signed, usually for a period of ten years. When the plants did not commence operation on schedule, the company's first concern was to get out of this obligation, and they usually had their way. But when they began functioning the tables were turned, and they were obliged to pay at the rate originally agreed upon even though the price of sugar had drastically declined. The American consul reported that 'They are paying double price for the cane over its market value'.[1]

Friction continued between the producers and the sugar companies. The factories attempted to circumvent the planters and buy cane directly from the share-croppers and tenants, only to find that their original contracts with the planters precluded such procedures, a prohibition enforced by the planters.[2] Other misunderstandings revolved around the factories' inefficiency. When the Central Sugar Factories of Brazil advertised in the local Press for additional suppliers of cane, an anonymous letter writer warned the planters to beware. He alleged that, due to constant stoppages caused by breakdowns, the company's plants were not even prepared to handle the cane for which contracts were already signed. Furthermore, at one of its factories the tramway system had no relationship to its needs, having been built to carry bricks for the building, and all its cane had to be carried by the public

---

[1] Engenheiro fiscal to vice-presidente da provincia, Recife, 11 June 1886, APEP, EC 1; Anfriso Fialho, *Processo da monarquia brasileira; necessidade da convocação de nova constituinte* (Rio: Typ. da 'Constituinte', 1886), p. 89; Sociedade Auxiliadora d'Agricultura de Pernambuco, *Acta da sessão...1878* (Recife: Typ. Central, 1878), p. 31; Sociedade Auxiliadora d'Agricultura de Pernambuco, *Boletim*, Sept. 1882, p. 21; Nabuco to Penedo, London, 26 Mar. 1884, in Nabuco, *Obras completas*, XIII, 111; Kidner to Nabuco, London, 14 Feb. 1883; 31 Mar. 1883; 24 Mar. 1884, JNP, Lata 7; Pernambuco, Presidente, *Falla*, 1886 (2nd), p. 78; 1888, p. 38; Atherton to Dept of State, Recife, 18 Oct. 1886, NA/DS, Despatches Consuls, Pernambuco, 1886, no. 251.

[2] Nabuco to Penedo, London, 26 Mar. 1884, in Nabuco, *Obras completas*, XIII, 111.

railway. The latter, also owned by the British, carelessly lost cane on the way to the factory and did not keep its schedules, thus causing each planter to leave idle workers at the stations awaiting the arrival of the trains for loading. Moreover, after being delivered to the factory, the cane was allowed to dry out while awaiting milling although the planter was paid only according to final weight; and the cane was often eaten by stray cattle since no fence had yet been built around the property.[1]

Other clashes punctuated the history of these companies. The municipal councils, dominated by the more traditional forces, insisted on levying taxes on the central sugar factories despite their tax-exempt status. There were also unverified but believable charges that the factories were polluting the rivers with toxic wastes, and police forces had to be summoned to protect the factories.[2]

Yet the British-owned central sugar factories made substantial contributions toward the modification of the northeast, despite their obsolete equipment, their failure to bring about the democratization of land tenure, their stripping of the landscape for firewood, their original and misguided concentration on the export market, their bad management, and their unrelieved financial failure. First of all, the physical facilities, inadequate as they were, remained in the hands of Brazilians. Many planters, for instance, left in the lurch when the Central Sugar Factories stopped operations at mid-harvest, secured through judicial means the right to lease the mill and run it themselves until the liquidation of the company was complete. Subsequently, large planters sometimes organized themselves into cooperatives to operate the sugar factories. At other times Brazilian entrepreneurs purchased the properties for a song and were able to make the factories profitable because of their small investment.

Furthermore, the lessons learned by the British were carefully observed by Brazilians who then started entirely new factories. In 1888 the correspondence of the provincial president began to reflect rapid growth in the number of such Brazilian-owned enter-

[1] *Jornal do Recife*, 28 Jan. 1886, p. 2.
[2] Pernambuco, Presidente, *Relatorio*, 1889, p. 37; APEP, EC 1, *passim*.

prises. They received an additional boost in 1891 when they were granted a large number of government loans. Soon many tall chimneys began to appear like exclamation marks within the agrarian setting. By 1907 there were 200 central sugar factories operating in Brazil, and they employed thirteen thousand workers. Of course, neither the separation of agricultural from industrial activities nor the stimulus to small landowners was thus achieved. But, although the methods were often still backward in comparison with those being used in other countries—and only 35 per cent of Brazilian sugar was produced in central sugar factories in 1920— there had been a considerable change since the days when all sugar was produced in old-fashioned mills. The transformation of both economy and society was significant.[1]

Perhaps the most important change brought about by the central sugar factories was the altered relationships of employer and employee. The worker in a central sugar factory received a money-wage, could be easily fired, was unrelated to the employer by ties of kinship or loyalty, and was essentially an atom adrift in a non-traditional and unkind world. The ties between the laborer and the landowner began to loosen as the sugar region became more money-oriented and more production-conscious. As the planter began to receive according to 'sugar content' and 'weight delivered', he began to think of his operation in more measured terms. No longer did he loll on the veranda of the big-house watching unnumbered oxcarts roll to the sprawling mill shed. Now he received monthly written reports and grim statements of his account at the central sugar factory. Often what he read there meant his land became the factory's. In any case he had neither time nor resources to care for the worker.

A laborer later reminisced with heavily tinted nostalgia that in the old days 'there was a lot of happiness; there was much satis-faction between the planter and the Negro worker'. He could take cane syrup and sugar home at will, and, besides his money wage, he had enjoyed the right to graze animals and plant manioc,

---

[1] Raffard, *O Centro da Industria*, p. 114; Engenheiro fiscal to presidente da provincia, Recife, 18 July 1888, APEP, EC 1; Pernambuco, Governador, *Mensagem*, 1891, pp. 44–6; Normano, *Brazil*, p. 25; J. C. Oakenfull, *Brazil (1913)* (Frome, England: Butler & Tanner, 1914), p. 323.

corn, and beans on the master's land. 'But after the arrival of the central sugar factory all things changed and misery was the lot of the Negro worker.' The factory manager watched every penny and nothing could be taken home. Nor would the plantation owner let the hands plant foodstuffs for fear it would ruin the soil. The security of the corporate society with every man happily in his place had been destroyed forever.[1]

These changes, although more sharply discerned in the case of sugar factories, were not unlike those that occurred wherever industrialization took place. To work for a wage, to have only impersonal relationships with one's employer, to run the risk of being dismissed, to be brought together with other workers simply as a factor of economic necessity, to be (relatively) free to seek other employment, are all concomitants of an industrial way of life radically different from the rural, almost manorial organization of society which had been characteristic of all Brazil in 1850. The best evidence of changing relationships is the appearance of labor discontent and the occurrence of the first tentative strikes.[2]

The nature of the shift is reflected in the difficulties encountered by earlier industrial employers in what had been an entirely agrarian setting. Brazilian industrialists had complained of the 'inconstancy of the Brazilian worker...who does not fear being fired from the factory'. The same problems had been encountered on the British railroads. The chief engineer of the São Paulo Railway concluded that 'the native Brazilian has an indisposition to work', since those who because of 'good wages regularly paid [were] induced to leave their cabins and little plantations' always returned home at the planting season.[3]

These were the pre-industrial workers, and one may well

---

[1] Júlio Bello, *Memórias de um senhor de engenho*, 2nd ed., Documentos Brasileiros, 11 (Rio: José Olympio, 1948), p. 186; Jovino da Raiz, 'O trabalhador negro no tempo do banguê comparado com o trabalhador negro no tempo das uzinas de assucar', in *Estudos afro-brasileiros. Trabalhos apresentados ao 1º Congresso Afro-brasileiro reunido em Recife em 1934* (Rio: Ariel Editôra, 1935), 191–3; Diégues, 'O banguê em Pernambuco', pp. 29–30.

[2] Everardo Dias, *História das lutas sociais no Brasil*, Temas Brasileiros, 8 (São Paulo: Editôra Edaglit, 1962), pp. 243–304.

[3] Raffard, *O Centro da Industria*, p. 115; Mascarenhas, *Bernardo Mascarenhas*, p. 74; Fox, *Description of the Line and Works*, pp. 21–2.

imagine the contrasting experience of steady work in a factory. The hours were fixed, the work monotonous, the pace unchanging. Man-and-machine replaced man-and-land. A placid, seasonally variable existence now became mechanical. Crowded quarters about the factory, jarring noises of machinery, and cold, momentary relationships replaced the open spaces, the idyllic lowing of the cattle, the ages-long familiarity with every creature. But the usable cash, the exciting mobility, the sense of freedom even if illusory, and the vague promise of equal opportunity were welcome substitutes for the money-less economy, the limited horizons, the increasingly evident oppression, and the constant dependency of the traditional society.

Industrialization meant all these transformations, and the British had a hand in almost every aspect of the process. They built transport facilities, they provided machinery and supplies, they advanced industrial credits, they volunteered technicians, they trained workers, and they risked their capital in central sugar companies, flour mills, shoe factories, and textile plants. Although not the predominant investors in manufacturing—their share of the total was relatively small—their over-all material contribution was impressive. Furthermore, as will be made clear in the next two chapters, it was accompanied by major influences upon the labor system and the entrepreneurial mentality. The British were intimately involved in the process of modernization.

6

CHANGING PATTERNS OF LABOR: SLAVE TRADE AND SLAVERY

One of the most significant early landmarks on the road toward a modern society in Brazil was the end of Negro slavery in 1888. Although, seen in the context of world history, slavery may be considered a part of the mercantile expansion of Europe characteristic of the modern era, in Brazil few institutions were more clearly a part of the traditional order. It was the most eloquent manifestation of the belief in a man's immutable social position and it was the antithesis of individualism. It frustrated attempts to encourage immigration and acted as a brake on economic development. On the other hand, the abolition of slavery strengthened the modernizing, European-oriented cities that had worked for it and weakened the backward countryside. It was the *coup de grâce* for the sugar zone of the northeast and the old coffee regions of the Paraíba valley, and served to shift power definitely into the hands of those who controlled the new coffee area of São Paulo state.[1] It seriously weakened the monarchy, which until then had been staunchly defended by the slave-owners: the abolitionists had pointedly referred to 'the slave quarter barons...the buttress of throne and pillory'.[2] Abolition contributed powerfully to economic, social, and political change in Brazil.

It was also the product of beginning change. The two sources of abolitionist sentiment were to be the coffee planters of São

[1] José Maria dos Santos, *Os republicanos paulistas e a abolição* (São Paulo: Martins, 1942), p. 53; Roberto Simonsen, 'As consequências econômicas da abolição', *Revista do Arquivo Municipal de São Paulo*, XLVII (1938), 261–3, 265; Stanley J. Stein, *Vassouras, a Brazilian Coffee County, 1850–1900*, Harvard Historical Studies, 69 (Cambridge, Mass.: Harvard Univ. Press, 1957), pp. 250–76; cf. Joaquim Nabuco's perceptive comment that since São Paulo had not yet been destroyed by slavery (i.e. was not traditional), it would survive the crisis of abolition, *O abolicionismo*, [2nd ed.?] (Rio & São Paulo: Civilização Brasileira, Editôra Nacional, 1938), p. 151.
[2] *O abolicionista: orgão da Sociedade Brasileira Contra a Escravidão*, no. 12, 28 Sept. 1881, p. 8.

Paulo, dissatisfied with the dwindling supply of slaves, and the new groups on the rise within the cities that saw slavery as a threat to their world-view. The planters had to bring under cultivation ever vaster stretches of good coffee land. But, although 68 per cent of the slaves were concentrated in the southern region of Brazil in 1888, they were not nearly enough to satisfy the demands of a burgeoning export economy. Furthermore, the number of slaves was decreasing even in absolute terms. Whereas it is estimated that in 1850 there were over two million slaves for a population of seven and a half million, by 1885, when the population of the country was approximately thirteen million, there were only a little over one million slaves left. The very high proportion of males to females among those imported from Africa and the increasingly widespread practice of manumission, combined with the harsh realities of slave life—especially for the pregnant and recently delivered woman—prevented a natural increase. In addition, slavery had been doomed by two legal measures: the end of the slave trade in 1850 and the freeing of the children born after September 1871. The entrepreneurially minded coffee planters of São Paulo looked, therefore, to European immigration to fill the gap, only to find that immigrants were reluctant to come because slavery debased the worker and gave Brazil a bad name. The more advanced planters could not help but chafe under these conditions. Urban abolitionists played upon these dissatisfactions, and André Rebouças wrote that '*human freedom* must be applied to the production of coffee, for it is the first and most powerful agent of progress'.[1]

The new urban interests created by the process of modernization were also important in bringing about the end of slavery. As we have seen, the cities were filled not only with an expanding number of merchants and bureaucrats directly related to the export economy, but also with industrial entrepreneurs, engineers, military officers, and the sons of the older aristocracy, who absorbed

---

[1] Simonsen, 'As consequências econômicas', p. 261; André Rebouças, *Agricultura nacional, estudos economicos; propaganda abolicionista e democratica* (Rio: Lamoureux, 1883), p. 76; cf. the support for those sugar planters who used free labor in the mills expressed by the Sociedade Auxiliadora d'Agricultura de Pernambuco, *Acta da sessão da assembléia geral ...1877* (Recife: Typ. Central, 1877), p. 7.

the values of these new groups. They were almost invariably opposed to slavery. Although no thorough study of this issue has yet been made, it appears from available evidence that those men associated with industry were especially committed to ending slavery. Not only did they oppose tying up capital in labor which could not be dismissed in bad times, but their whole way of life demanded the freedom of all men, units to be freely contracted, freely fired, freely sold to, freely moved; units to be joined and disjoined where and how economic imperatives should dictate. Brazilian entrepreneurs were generally willing to support the abolition of slavery. They complained that slavery slowed down capital formation, and Luís Tarqüínio, an industrialist in Bahia, said that the best protection government could give industry would be to end slavery. André Rebouças, dock company promoter, insisted that 'without freedom there is no industry. Freedom is the mother, the guardian angel of all industry'.[1] The nascent equivalent of a manufacturers' association joined the two major abolitionist societies as early as 1881 in advocating the end of slavery. The students and professors at the engineering school—the seedbed of the new progressive and industrial-minded elite—formed an abolitionist society all their own. It was 'in the name of Brazilian engineering' that one of them hailed the final passage of the abolition law.[2] Industrialists believed that the substitution of a free work force for the slave one was the solution to Brazil's labor problem, and it is worth noting that the leading São Paulo coffee-planters-turned-railroad-builders were active in the importation of European laborers to take the place of the slave.[3]

[1] Luiz Tarqüínio, *Direitos de importação em ouro. Cartas dirigidas ao Ministro da Fazenda, cons. Ruy Barbosa, e ao dr. Aristides Galvão de Queiroz, seguidas de considerações sobre as tarifas do Brazil e da União americana* (Salvador: Imp. Popular, 1890), p. 32; André Rebouças, *Agricultura nacional*, pp. 10, 78.

[2] *O abolicionista*, no. 8, 1 June 1881, p. 8 and no. 1, 1 Nov. 1880, p. 8; André Rebouças, *Diário e notas autobiográficas*, ed. Ana Flora and Inácio José Verissimo, Documentos Brasileiros, 12 (Rio: José Olympio, 1938), pp. 299, 302; Francisco Picanço, 'Estradas de ferro', *Imprensa fluminense* (Rio), 20 May 1888, p. 2.

[3] Irineo Evangelista de Souza, *visconde de Mauá, Autobiografia* ('*Exposição aos credores e ao público*') *seguida de* '*O meio circulante no Brasil*', ed. Claudio Ganns, 2nd ed. (Rio: Valverde, 1942), p. 222; Anyda Marchant, *Viscount Mauá and the Empire of Brazil: a Biography of Irineu Evangelista de Sousa (1813–1889)* (Berkeley and Los Angeles: Univ. of California Press, 1965), p. 37; Adelino R. Ricciardi, 'Parnaíba, o pioneiro da imigração', *Revista do*

Within the context of these broad changes which impelled the abolitionist cause, the British played two important roles. First, through diplomacy and force, Her Majesty's government made sure the institution of slavery could not survive indefinitely in Brazil. This was done not only by cutting off the supply of fresh slaves from Africa, but by prevailing upon Brazil to decree the freedom of all children born after 1871. Second, the British supplied inspiration and encouragement for the abolitionists who were indirectly to effect the final end of slavery in Brazil.

The first step toward this goal was to dry up the source of supply in Africa and to it the British contributed heavily. They had ended all slave trading connected with their own empire during the years 1806–7 and by 1833 slavery itself had been abolished there. Meanwhile, interest turned to the slave trade outside England.

Brazil was the biggest importer of Africans, and British attention soon began to concentrate on this tropical empire. In exchange for the recognition of its independence by Great Britain, Brazil signed a treaty in 1826 which included an agreement to end the slave trade within three years. In 1831 the Brazilian government belatedly and under continuing British pressure put through a law declaring free all Africans brought in thenceforward. But it was impossible to enforce this restriction at that time, and thousands of slaves continued to be bought from the slave traders. When the treaty expired, Brazil refused to renew it. In retaliation, George Gordon, Lord Aberdeen, had a bill introduced in Parliament in 1845 giving the British Admiralty the power to treat all Brazilian slave ships as pirate ships. The bill became law and was known as the Aberdeen Act. During the next few years, despite the capture of many ships on the high seas, the importation of slaves to Brazil steadily increased, partly because these seizures presaged the end of the trade and stimulated feverish activity by the traders, partly because the spreading cultivation of coffee near

Arquivo Municipal de São Paulo, IV, no. 44 (1938), pp. 137–84; Nazareth Prado, ed., *Antonio Prado no imperio e na republica: seus discursos e actos colligidos e apresentados por sua filha* (Rio: Briguiet, 1929), p. 30; Carolina Nabuco, *The Life of Joaquim Nabuco*, transl. and ed. Ronald Hilton (Stanford, California: Stanford Univ. Press, 1950), p. 80.

Rio de Janeiro demanded large drafts of slave labor. While less than twenty thousand were imported in 1845, fifty thousand entered the following year, and sixty thousand in 1848. In 1850, however, British ships entered Brazilian ports and rivers and seized any ships they found fitted out for the slave trade. From 54,000 Africans imported in 1849, the number dropped to 23,000 in 1850, a little over 3,000 the next year, and to barely 700 in 1852.[1]

But whether the British can be considered primarily responsible for this result was immediately the subject of much controversy and continues to be a moot point. In September 1850 the Brazilian Parliament put through a new law to forbid the slave trade which included an all-important enabling clause. It was the application of this law that brought the slave trade to an end. But the British minister reported that its terms were the result of the forceful naval actions and his own skillful diplomacy. Lord Palmerston became nearly apoplectic when the Brazilian govern-

[1] Frank J. Klingberg, *The Anti-Slavery Movement in England* (London & New Haven: Milford and Oxford & Yale Univ. Press, 1926); Alan K. Manchester, *British Preëminence in Brazil; Its Rise and Decline: A Study in European Expansion* (Chapel Hill, N.C.: Univ. of North Carolina Press, 1933), pp. 211, 214–17, 246–63, 265 and 265 n.; Alfredo Gomes, 'Achegas para a história do tráfico africano no Brasil—aspectos numéricos', in Instituto Histórico e Geográfico Brasileiro, *Anais do IV Congresso de História Nacional (1949)*, v (1950), 34. For further examination of the slave trade issue see William Law Mathieson, *Great Britain and the Slave Trade, 1839–1865* (London: Longmans, Green, 1929); Christopher Lloyd, *The Navy and the Slave Trade; the Suppression of the African Slave Trade in the Nineteenth Century* (London: Longmans, Green, 1949); Jane Elizabeth Adams, 'The Abolition of the Brazilian Slave Trade', *Journal of Negro History*, x (1925), 607–37; Lawrence F. Hill, 'The Abolition of the African Slave Trade to Brazil', *Hispanic American Historical Review*, xi (1931), 169–97; Wilbur Devereux Jones, 'The Origins and Passage of Lord Aberdeen's Act', *Hispanic American Historical Review*, xlii (1962), 502–20; Leslie M. Bethell, 'Britain, Portugal and the Suppression of the Brazilian Slave Trade: the Origins of Lord Palmerston's Act of 1839', *English Historical Review*, lxxx (1965), 761–84; Maurício Goulart, *Escravidão africana no Brasil (das origens à extinção do tráfico)* (São Paulo: Martins, 1949), pp. 219–63; Evaristo de Moraes, *A escravidão africana no Brasil (das origens a extinção)*, Brasiliana, 23 (São Paulo: Editôra Nacional, 1933), pp. 65–99; Maurílio Gouveia, *História da escravidão* (Rio: Gráfica Tupy, 1955), pp. 115–35; Manoel Alvaro Sousa Sá Vianna, 'O tráfico e a diplomacia brasileira', *RIHGB, tomo especial consagrado ao primeiro Congresso de Historia Nacional (1914)*, v (1917), 539–84; Affonso d'Escragnolle Taunay, 'Subsídios para a história do tráfico africano no Brasil', *Anais do Museu Paulista*, x, 2.ª parte (1941), pp. 257–72; and, on legislative aspects, João Luiz Alves, 'A questão do elemento servil. A extincção do tráfico e a lei de repressão de 1850. Liberdade dos nascituros', *RIHGB, tomo especial...primeiro Congresso de Historia Nacional*, iv (1916), 187–258; Luís Henrique Dias Tavares, 'As soluções brasileiras na extinção do tráfico negreiro', *Journal of Inter-American Studies*, ix (1967), 367–82.

ment tried to 'divide with him the glory' of ending the trade.[1]
His reply was that

during the 24 years which elapsed between 1826 and 1850, the British
government...exhausted in vain all its powers of persuasion to induce
the Brazilian government to fulfill its treaty engagements and to put
the slave trade down...But in 1850 the British government changed
its system and extended with vigor and energy to the coast of Brazil
its operations against the slave trade; and no sooner was this done, than
the Brazilian government and legislature were awakened to a sense of
their duties and obligations and...began, for the first time, to take
active steps for the purpose of cooperation with the British government.[2]

The Brazilians argued with convincing evidence that all the
details of the law had been worked out and were about to be
presented to Parliament when the British cruisers began their
work. The cruisers, they maintained, only made the government's task that much harder. They argued, furthermore, that it
was precisely the large importation of slaves stimulated by the
Aberdeen Act that prompted the Brazilian planter class itself to
accept the end of the slave trade, since the large number of new
imports not only posed the threat of insurrection but had also
burdened the planters with heavy debts to the slave traders who
would be, according to the terms of the law, deported from the
country. The British, it was said, merely made it more difficult
to act by giving the slave traders the opportunity to charge the
government with kowtowing to foreigners. The Brazilian point
of view, disguised as the opinion of the *Daily News*, was that
'in a strain of congratulation and adulation that are perfectly
British, the credit for what Brazil is doing is claimed for England'.
The Brazilians were especially fond of pointing out that the British

[1] James Hudson to Lord Palmerston, Rio, 27 July 1850, extract, Slave Trade Correspondence Class B, no. 88, in Great Britain, Parliament, House of Commons, *Sessional
Papers*, Readex Microprint Edition, ed. Edgar L. Erickson, 1851 [1424-II], LVI, Pt II,
230–1; José Marques Lisboa to Paulino José Soares de Sousa, London, 8 Sept. 1851,
AHI, 217/3/6, no. 16.

[2] Palmerston to Lisboa, London, 10 Oct. 1851, encl. in Lisboa to Paulino de Sousa,
London, 27 Oct. 1851, AHI, 216/2/15, no. 56; Palmerston's argument was echoed
fifteen years later by William D. Christie, *Notes on Brazilian Questions* (London and
Cambridge, England: Macmillan, 1865), pp. xxxv, lv, 88.

had not suppressed the slave trade in spite of hundreds of seizures both before and after the Aberdeen Act: they had not been able to do in many years what the Brazilians had done in a few months.[1] Credit must be ascribed to both nations. For the first time in its independent history Brazil had a strong government anxious to establish its prestige in Europe. Without its cooperation all the British efforts would surely have failed. In addition, the argument that many planters were alarmed by the proportions of the slave trade has some weight. But it was surely to escape the sheer humiliation of having the nation's ports invaded with impunity, that both the government and the Parliament were moved to pass and enforce the law. The invasion of the ports, if continued, could well discredit the government and reverse the gains in central power of which the leaders were so proud. Furthermore, the success of the government in borrowing in the British financial market depended on maintaining a favorable image in Britain. And, in view of the impending difficulties with Argentina over spheres of influence in Uruguay, the Brazilian government had special reason to come to a settlement with Britain. Finally, there is no doubt that in the next few years the British diplomatic and consular service and Admiralty gave valuable aid in the effort against slave traders, acting virtually as an intelligence system against them and bringing to the attention of the Brazilian government even the slightest suspicion of trading activity. On the whole, we may conclude that British activity was an essential factor in ending the slave trade. Hard as it is at this time to see how they could have considered it any of their concern, the fact is that they did, and that the slave trade to Brazil was ended because of the energetic actions of the British government, combined with a propitious set of circumstances in Brazil itself.[2]

[1] The *locus classicus* for the Brazilian point of view is Eusébio de Queiroz Coutinho Matôso da Câmara, speech of 16 July 1852, Brazil, Congresso, Câmara dos Deputados, *Anais*, 1852, II, 244–53; *Daily News*, 13 Mar. 1851, encl. in Joaquim Thomas de Amaral to Paulino de Sousa, London, 18 Mar. 1851, AHI, 216/2/15 (this article was inspired by the Brazilian minister in London); Lisboa to Palmerston, London, 27 Sept. 1851, encl. in Lisboa to Paulino de Sousa, London, 30 Sept. 1851, AHI, 216/2/15, no. 49; Paulino de Sousa to Amaral, Rio, 22 July 1850, AHI, 218/4/6, Reservado, no. 10.

[2] Note opposition of some planters to measures ending slave trade, Sérgio Teixeira de Macedo to Paulino de Sousa, London, 22 Aug. 1853, AHI, 217/3/7, no. 19; in 1852 Brazil borrowed over a million pounds sterling in England, the first loan of any size

Slave Trade and Slavery

The end of the slave trade did not mark the end of British interest in ending Brazilian slavery. It was not until Brazil gave evidence of a firm commitment to end the institution itself that Great Britain ceased to exert pressure. Whereas the law freeing those children of slaves born after 28 September 1871 is usually considered the first evidence of an abolitionist campaign, it was really the conclusion of the British phase of the story which had begun forty years earlier. After the end of the slave trade, British moves to attack slavery revolved around three issues. First, there were the thousands of Africans who had entered the country since 1831 in violation of laws and treaties. Another question turned about those Negroes who had been found aboard slave-ships and freed by the Mixed Commission Court which sat in Rio de Janeiro, but who had been deprived of their liberty nevertheless. Finally, and most important, was the issue of slavery itself.

To raise the problem of slaves illegally imported was to threaten the entire institution, because they represented such a large proportion of the slave population and because it was obviously impossible to know which ones had been smuggled in. But this did not restrain the British from making precisely this suggestion. As early as 1850, William Gladstone, although arguing the absurdity of such a course of action, admitted that, before international law, 'We have now a perfect right to go to Brazil and call upon her to emancipate every slave imported since 1830, and, upon refusal, to make war with them [sic] even to extermination.'[1] And so the Brazilians naturally feared any references

since 1843 and the largest since 1825, Valentin F. Bouças, *História da dívida externa*, 2nd ed. (Rio: Edições Financeiras, 1950), p. 86; on British help in enforcing the law see Joaquim Nabuco, *Um estadista do imperio, Nabuco de Araujo. Sua vida, suas opiniões, sua época*, [2nd ed.?], 2 vols. (Rio & São Paulo: Civilização Brasileira & Editôra Nacional, 1936), I, 165, 168; Nabuco is much fairer than some earlier emancipationists, for instance, Affonso d'Albuquerque Mello, *A liberdade no Brasil: seu nascimento, vida, morte e sepultura* (Recife: Typ. Figueroa de Faria, 1864), p. 138, who gave all the credit to England; the debate was also carried on in the British House of Commons, Great Britain, Parliament, *Hansard's Parliamentary Debates*, 3rd series, CXIV (Feb.–Mar. 1851), 1196, 1202, 1217–21; finally, see Manchester, *British Preëminence*, pp. 265 and 265n.; and Antonio Ferreira Cesarino Júnior, 'A intervenção da Inglaterra na suppressão do tráfico de escravos africanos para o Brasil', *Revista do Instituto Histórico e Geográfico de São Paulo*, XXXIV (1938), 145–66, esp. 164.

[1] Speech of Gladstone, 19 Mar. 1850, Great Britain, Parliament, *Hansard's Parliamentary Debates*, 3rd series, CIX (Mar. 1850), 1170.

to this matter. When, in 1852, the Brazilian minister in London was asked by a member of the British cabinet what Brazil intended to do about those slaves, he answered that they numbered 'tens of thousands, and that in slavery *they shall remain*; that England does not have any right to intervene in their respect; that the question is one of life or death for Brazil for it would produce general revolution to touch on this point;...that Brazil would not hesitate to fight a war even if it meant complete destruction'.[1]

The Brazilian government fully supported this position, but the British continued to press the point officially and unofficially. The British and Foreign Anti-Slavery Society, for instance, demanded that Brazil be forced to free all slaves illegally imported after 1831.[2] In 1857 the British minister in Rio de Janeiro asked the government to make a census of all slaves in order to 'avoid that free persons of colour should be reduced to slavery'. The Council of State refused to sanction such a step, saying that it would serve no useful function and would only be an encouragement to the British to make further demands.[3] In 1861 another minister, William D. Christie, wrote to Earl Russell that 'Advertisements continually appear in the Rio journals for the sale of slaves, African-born, with a declaration of age, which, if true, renders obvious or probable their importation since 1831.' He was further delighted to discover that when he had presented this evidence to the Brazilian foreign minister, the latter 'did not seek to deny the responsibility of the Brazilian government as to slaves imported since 1831'.[4]

Another question revolved about those Negroes who had been found aboard slave-ships and freed by the Mixed Commission Court which sat in Rio de Janeiro from 1827 to 1845. They had been turned over to the Brazilian government for a period of apprenticeship, and it could either use them in public works or let

[1] Macedo to Paulino de Sousa, London, 8 Oct. 1852, AHI, 217/3/7, no. 18.
[2] Paulino de Sousa to Macedo, Rio, 13 Nov. 1852, AHI, 218/4/7, Reservado, no. 30; London *Times*, 20 Oct. 1852, p. 7.
[3] Consulta do Conselho de Estado, 2 Mar. 1857, in Nabuco, *Um estadista do imperio*, II, 438–9.
[4] Christie, *Notes on Brazilian Questions*, pp. 83–4.

them out to private individuals. They were called *emancipados*. As early as 1833 the British minister in Rio had complained about their treatment, and the way in which fraud was practiced so as to deprive them permanently of their liberty. Twenty years later the English diplomatic representative was protesting in the same vein against Brazilian policies.[1] During Christie's stay as British minister in Brazil, 1861–3, there were constant demands on his part for a list of all the *emancipados* and their whereabouts; but no answers were forthcoming. As Christie explained it, 'the object of the list which has been asked for is the complete emancipation of all those free Africans now serving the Brazilian government or private individuals.' Some ten thousand Africans were estimated to be in this group, and the British government felt bound to protect them, as they had been 'liberated under British auspices'.[2]

But the larger aim in mind was the end of Negro slavery altogether. As early as 1856 the British minister was suggesting to the Brazilians that they must lessen their ties to this institution.[3] It was Christie again who thrust at the vitals of the country to which he was accredited. In 1862 he wrote Lord Russell: 'I have, on various occasions, suggested to your lordship the importance of endeavouring if possible, to...persuade the Brazilian government to measures leading to the ultimate extinction of slavery, and in the meantime mitigating its evils.'[4]

His methods of persuasion were effective: in January 1863 Christie ordered reprisals against Brazilian shipping, and a break in diplomatic relations was the result. Minor and patently insignificant incidents were the pretext for this action; the real issues at stake were the uncounted Africans imported since 1831, the thousands of *emancipados*, and Brazilian slavery itself. Christie later claimed especial credit for the definitive freeing of the *eman-*

---

[1] Manchester, *British Preëminence*, pp. 230–3; Evaristo de Moraes, *A campanha abolicionista (1879–1888)* (Rio: Leite Ribeiro, Freitas Bastos, Spicer, 1924), p. 190.

[2] Christie, *Notes on Brazilian Questions*, p. 13, and Christie's letters to Lord John Russell quoted on pp. xxxvii–xxxviii, 11, 47; on the number of *emancipados* see p. xxxiv.

[3] Speech of José Maria da Silva Paranhos (1º), 7 June 1864, Brazil, Congresso, Senado, *Anais*, 1864, II, 56.

[4] Quoted in Christie, *Notes on Brazilian Questions*, p. 66.

Slave Trade and Slavery

cipados in 1864. But Brazilians believed—probably with reason—
that his actions were part of a broader push by the British to secure
the end of the entire slave system.[1]

Just one year after the reprisals were initiated and at a time when
the British response to the ensuing rupture of diplomatic relations
was still uncertain, the emperor urged the cabinet to begin
thinking about the future of slavery 'so that the same thing will
not happen to us as with respect to the slave trade'. A similar fear
of 'force' was then expressed in the Senate. Pointing also to the
unhappy news arriving in 1864 from the United States, the emperor urged passage of a law to free the children of slave mothers
born after a specified date.[2] During 1865 a law along these lines
was drafted at the emperor's request, and eventually it was carefully studied by the Council of State. It is abundantly clear that
arguments in favor were two: fear of eventual slave insurrection
and fear of foreign intervention. 'The slaves desire freedom and
by the natural order of things this desire will increase steadily, and
there is no way to stop it. It follows that we must prevent external
pressure from increasing this danger, and, if we do not take
measures of this sort, it will come.'[3] Perhaps this 'external pressure'
included moral condemnation by world opinion, and, in fact, the
government seized upon one of the innumerable memorials which
regularly arrived from Europe to announce that Brazil was considering steps toward ending slavery. In May 1867 the emperor
for the first time publicly referred to the slavery issue in the Speech

[1] Richard Graham, 'Os fundamentos da ruptura de relações diplomáticas entre o Brasil e a
Grã-Bretanha em 1863: "A questão Christie"', *Revista de história*, xxiv (Jan.–June 1962),
122–3, 397; Christie, *Notes on Brazilian Questions*, pp. xlv, 79; Brazilian sentiment on
behalf of the *emancipados* was also inspired by the British, Aureliano Cândido Tavares
Bastos, *Cartas do Solitário*, 3rd ed., Brasiliana, 115 (São Paulo: Editôra Nacional, 1938),
pp. 138n.–145n., 463–5; on Brazilian opinion on the purpose of the reprisals see Carlos
Americo Sampaio Vianna to João Maurício Wanderley, *barão* de Cotegipe, Rio, 8 Jan.
1863, in José Wanderley Pinho, *Cotegipe e seu tempo: primeira phase, 1815–1867*, Brasiliana,
85 (São Paulo: Editôra Nacional, 1937), p. 677.
[2] Pedro II, 'Apontamentos', 14 Jan. 1864, in Hélio Vianna, 'Instruções de D. Pedro II aos
presidentes do conselho, Zacarias e Furtado', *Jornal do comércio*, 3 July 1964; Heitor Lyra,
História de D. Pedro II, 1825–1891, Brasiliana, 133, 3 vols. (São Paulo: Editôra Nacional,
1938–40), ii, 236; speech of Ângelo Muniz da Silva Ferraz, 6 June 1864, Brazil,
Congresso, Senado, *Anais*, 1864, ii, 49.
[3] Brazil, Conselho de Estado [José Antonio Pimenta Bueno, *marquês* de São Vicente, *et al.*],
Trabalho sobre a extincção da escravatura no Brasil (Rio: Typ. Nacional, 1868), p. 89; also
pp. 6, 62–3, 93.

from the Throne.[1] But his earlier concern with the threat of British action was surely still present. And when the government thus committed itself to the gradual end of slavery, Britain became ready to repeal the arbitrary anti-slave-trade legislation, reasoning that if the end of slavery was approaching the slave trade could no longer be a danger.[2] The eventual result in Brazil was the law of 1871: it freed the slaves born thenceforward, although they were to work for their mother's master until the age of 21 by way of compensation. Although nothing was said at this time about freeing adult slaves, it was clear that, sooner or later, slavery in Brazil was doomed to extinction. British pressure had clearly contributed to this result.[3]

With the eventual end of slavery a certainty because of British pressure, the forces within Brazil that were emerging to urge its abolition became stronger. The coffee planters of São Paulo were less adamant in the defense of this institution and the new urban groups were increasingly convinced it must end. Abolitionist leaders soon arose to take advantage of these forces, and Britain, of course, was one of the places to which they turned for inspiration, ideas, and organizational models. But the importance of this fact rests, first of all, upon an evaluation of the role played by these men in ending Brazilian slavery. The conventional view is that the Brazilian Parliament issued the law in 1888 which freed the slaves in response to humanitarian sentiments and the pressure of public opinion aroused by a propaganda campaign ably directed by a handful of crusading reformers. But it is hard to believe that the representatives of the slave-owners—in many cases slave-owners themselves—abandoned their clearest and most vital economic interests as a result of brilliant speeches and the outcry of the Press. The ideas propagated by the abolitionists did in fact

---

[1] 'Falla do throno...22 de maio de 1867', in Brazil, Sovereigns, etc., *Fallas do throno desde o anno de 1823 até o anno de 1889 acompanhados* [sic] *dos respectivos votos de graças* (Rio: Imp. Nacional, 1889), p. 627.

[2] Joaquim Saldanha Marinho (i), *A Monarchia; ou, a politica do rei* (Rio, 1885), p. 53; the Aberdeen Act was repealed in 1869, Manchester, *British Preëminence*, p. 264n.; on the official British attitude see Great Britain, Parliament, *Hansard's Parliamentary Debates*, 3rd series, CCLXVII (Mar. 1882), 877–8.

[3] For the story of this law's elaboration see especially Santos, *Os republicanos paulistas*, pp. 30, 49–50, 56; and Nabuco, *Um estadista do imperio*, I, 565–70, II, 15–54.

play a decisive role in bringing about the end of slavery, but not in this way. What they did do was to stimulate the new urban interests to encourage and abet the virtual revolt of the slaves. The planters, faced with a *fait accompli*, preferred to legalize their freedom in order to prevent the further decay of their own position. The more realistic and progressive coffee planters—already aware of the perplexing problem created by expanding labor needs and declining slave supply—propelled the final legislation through Parliament. Since this is not the usual view and since the importance of the British role relies on it, some attention must be given to this interpretation. Its key lies in the months and years immediately preceding the end of slavery.

The most important immediate cause of abolition was the flight of the slaves from the coffee plantations of São Paulo and Rio de Janeiro. In the two years before the law of abolition was passed in May 1888, the number of slaves who revolted against authority with their feet, departing the plantations, at first secretly, one by one, and later in mass and almost publicly, was simply enormous. It was a form of direct action against which the planters could do nothing by themselves, and the dichotomy of city and country now became clearly evident. For in the system of escape the cities played an essential part, agents as they were of the forces of modern change. Rio de Janeiro, Niterói, Petrópolis, Campos, Santos, São Paulo, and minor cities of the coffee region were all part of the network and were considered virtually free cities by the slaves. There measures were adopted to help the escaped slaves on to the state of Ceará, where slavery had been abolished in 1884; or legal action was undertaken on their behalf to prove they were illegally held as slaves; or permanent asylum was assured until abolition became a fact.[1]

---

[1] Joaquim Nabuco, *Minha formação*, [? ed.], Documentos Brasileiros, 90 (Rio: José Olympio, 1957), pp. 120, 196; Moraes, *Campanha abolicionista*, pp. 223–34; Clarence H. Haring, *Empire in Brazil: a New World Experiment with Monarchy* (Cambridge, Mass.: Harvard Univ. Press, 1958), p. 102; Florestan Fernandes, 'Do escravo ao cidadão', in Roger Bastide and Florestan Fernandes, *Relações raciais entre negros e brancos em São Paulo* (São Paulo: Anhembi, 1955), p. 46; even Ouro Prêto played this role, Oiliam José, *A abolição em Minas* (Belo Horizonte: Itatiaia, 1962), p. 95; Raimundo Girão, *A abolição no Ceará* (Fortaleza: Fentenele, 1956); on role of the cities generally see *O abolicionista*, no. 1, 1 Nov. 1880, p. 8, and Associação Commercial do Rio de Janeiro, *Resposta da Associação*

The organizer of the program of mass flights in São Paulo was Antônio Bento de Souza e Castro, who supervised the system by which slaves were lured away from the plantations, put on trains or shepherded on foot to Santos, and installed in shanty-towns. He also had the temerity to offer runaway slaves to plantation owners as hired hands during the peak harvest season. The very railways that had made the extension of coffee agriculture possible now served the slaves. As José Maria dos Santos, the historian, put it, 'There was not a passenger or freight train on which a runaway slave might not find means of hiding himself, and there was not a station where someone would not discreetly receive him and help him.' Almost all the railroad employees were said to be abolitionists, and not the least enthusiastic were the managers. In Santos, where all local slaves had been freed in 1886 by funds raised by public subscription, the slaves who arrived via the 'underground railroad' were immediately sheltered in the outskirts of the city, where 10,000 of them were sometimes gathered.[1]

In other cities the story was much the same. In the city of Rio de Janeiro, center of the abolitionist campaign movement, there was no difficulty in finding temporary asylum in the houses of interested persons, whence they were hustled to the outlying area of Leblón. Petrópolis also became a haven for escapees. In Campos direct action took an even more overt form. Luís Carlos de Lacerda urged slave revolts and was blamed for the burning of cane fields.[2]

Commercial do Rio de Janeiro aos quesitos da Commissão Parlamentar de Inquerito (Rio: Typ. Montenegro, 1883), p. 20. On this and on other matters discussed in this chapter see Emília Viotti da Costa, *Da senzala à colônia*, Corpo e Alma do Brasil, 19 (São Paulo: Difusão Européia do Livro, 1966).

[1] Santos, *Os republicanos paulistas*, pp. 170–1, 179, 181–2; Francisco Martins dos Santos, *Historia de Santos...1532–1936*, 2 vols. (São Paulo: Gráfica 'Revista dos Tribunaes', 1937), II, 27, 33; Moraes, *Campanha abolicionista*, pp. 261–6; Osvaldo Orico, *O tigre da abolição*, Edição Comemorativa do Centenário de José do Patrocínio (Rio: Gráfica Olímpica, 1953), pp. 84–5; also see attitude toward slavery of railway manager J. J. Aubertin, 'Communicado. Ilms. amigos e snrs. fazendeiros de S. Paulo', *Correio paulistano*, 3 Jan. 1867, p. 2.

[2] Moraes, *Campanha abolicionista*, pp. 155–6, 238–50; Rebouças, *Diário*, p. 312; *Rio News*, 24 Feb. 1887, p. 3; cf. Octavio Ianni, *As metamorphoses do escravo. Apogeu e crise da escravatura no Brasil meridional*, Corpo e Alma do Brasil, 7 (São Paulo: Difusão Européia do Livro, 1962), pp. 228–9; no mention of these events is made by Clovis Moura, *Rebeliões da senzala (quilombos, insurreições, guerrilhas)* (São Paulo: Zumbi, 1959).

Why did the government not stop the mass flights of the slaves? Although both the provincial and central governments took action from time to time, it soon became clear that their agents—many of whom were second-generation bureaucrats with urban backgrounds—did not have their hearts in the attempt to repress slave flights. It was in the cities that the government was located, and efforts to destroy the escape system there met civilian opposition at every turn. But especially significant is the fact that it was from the cities that the armed forces were recruited, especially the officers of the army. The military schools had for years been the site of abolitionist societies. Many are the proofs of the reluctance of the military to act as slave hunters; finally, in October 1887, the Club Militar, made up of the leading elements of the army, issued a petition to the princess-regent to be exonerated from chasing slaves. This was an era of growing timidity on the part of the landed aristocracy before the demands of the increasingly self-assertive officers, and the latter had their way. It has even been suggested that, if the legislature had not passed the law of abolition in 1888, the cities would have risen in revolt and the military would not have defended the regime.[1]

The cooperation of urban classes can be seen in a humorous incident that took place in Santos. The government of the province had sent a trainload of troops to capture runaway slaves there. When the train pulled into the station, the soldiers found it filled by the leading matrons of the town, who jammed the doors of the cars, preventing the troops from alighting. The superintendent of the São Paulo Railway persuaded the half-hearted commandant of the expedition to give up and surrender before the superior force of the buxom females, returning to the provincial capital. Neither the soldiers nor these representatives of the new

[1] Rebouças, *Diário*, p. 309; Osorio Duque Estrada, *A abolição (esboço histórico—1831–1888)* (Rio: Leite Ribeiro & Maurillo, 1918), pp. 96–101; Maria Stella Novaes, *A escravidão e a abolição no Espírito Santo: história e folclore* (Vitória: Departamento de Imprensa Oficial, 1963), p. 134; Moraes, *Campanha abolicionista*, pp. 33, 167, 248, 312–14, 322–3; June Edith Hahner, 'The Role of the Military in Brazil, 1889–1894', unpub. M.A. thesis, Cornell Univ., 1963, pp. 4–13; the rank and file of the army was considered untrustworthy, being generally Negroes or mulattoes, Hastings Charles Dent, *A Year in Brazil, with Notes on the Abolition of Slavery*...(London: Kegan Paul, Trench, 1886), p. 287

urban groups were interested in protecting the human property of the landowners.¹

Finally, during the first months of 1888, the planters began to free their own slaves right and left in order to prevent them from leaving the plantations. By May it was estimated that half the slaves that had been in the Campos area six months earlier were free; and one-third of the São Paulo plantations were being worked by recently freed slaves. Thus the law abolishing slavery was merely a formality since the process then in full swing would have ended slavery to all intents and purposes within a few months.² The *barão* de Cotegipe, an anti-abolitionist, asked 'For what, an abolition law? In fact it is done already—and revolutionarily. The terrified masters seek to stem the exodus by giving immediate freedom to their slaves'.³

What role did the abolitionists play in all this? Evidently, a very large one. The slaves themselves were persuaded to leave the plantations by dint of hard work. The Confederação Abolicionista in Rio de Janeiro hired Italian peddlers to persuade the slaves to leave the plantations. They were also given leaflets to distribute throughout the interior, and presumably these were read to the illiterate slaves. Some of the peddlers were murdered by slave foremen, but the news continued to spread. The abolitionists took pains to convey their message to those slaves who passed through the city with their masters. On their return home these bondsmen carried with them the idea of escape and the knowledge that they and their fellows would be helped and protected.⁴

It was also because of the force and effectiveness of the abolitionist crusade that large segments of the urban population were persuaded to acquiesce or contribute to the success of the movement. If it had not been for their constant effort to drive home the anachronism of slavery in the age of 'progress' it is doubtful that the military officers would have refused to cooperate in pre-

¹ Santos, *Os republicanos paulistas*, p. 184.
² Moraes, *Campanha abolicionista*, pp. 304–9, 321–5, 339; Fernandes, 'Do escravo ao cidadão', pp. 49–50; Stein, *Vassouras*, pp. 253–5.
³ Cotegipe to Francisco Ignácio de Carvalho Moreira, *barão* do Penedo, Petrópolis, 8 Apr. 1888, in Renato Mendonça, *Um diplomata na côrte de Inglaterra; o barão do Penedo e sua época*, Brasiliana, 219 (São Paulo: Editôra Nacional, 1942), p. 397.
⁴ Duque Estrada, *A abolição*, p. 102; Dent, *Year in Brazil*, pp. 285–7.

serving the *status quo*. And the participation of other urban groups was a marked feature of the successful escape of the slaves. Without their enthusiastic cooperation this effort would have failed.

The movement in the provinces of São Paulo, Minas Gerais, and Rio de Janeiro was of first importance. In other parts of Brazil similar sentiments were probably prevalent in the cities, but the majority of the slaves were already concentrated in the south-central region, and political power was fast slipping from the hands of the sugar planters of the northeast. To be sure, Ceará offered a haven for escaped slaves; but the campaign to liberate the slaves of that arid state in 1884 was relatively simple since, at that time, there were so few slaves to free.[1] The abolitionist movement in the national capital and in the coffee states may be given the credit for bringing about this modification of Brazilian social and economic life.

So the use of British ideas and organizational models by abolitionists there assumes real importance. Early publicists for this cause were influenced by the British, and one of the most important abolitionist leaders, Joaquim Nabuco (1849–1910), inspired by the earlier British crusade, created a propaganda organization modeled on the British and Foreign Anti-Slavery Society. Furthermore, he relied, as did his confederates, on arguments against slaveholders devised by the British Foreign Office.

One of the precursors of the abolitionist movement had already made use of these bellicose debating points. Aureliano Cândido Tavares Bastos, the advocate of free trade, maintained that Brazilians should feel nothing but gratitude toward Britain for putting an end to the trafficking in slaves and thus opening up the way for immigration and the end of slavery itself. At the very time that Christie was preparing reprisals against Brazil, Tavares Bastos had defended the British minister, and quoted from the British Blue Books and the publications of British enemies of slavery. He attacked the exploitation of the *emancipados* and gave wide publicity to Lord John Russell's letter following Christie's actions, a letter which linked the reprisals with the fate

[1] Girão, *A abolição no Ceará*.

of these unfortunates. Tavares Bastos came to be a symbol of general innovation, and, had he lived longer, he would surely have been among the front ranks of the abolitionists, along with Joaquim Nabuco.[1]

In the hectic abolitionist campaign that began in 1879 there were many leaders impelled by diverse motives and conditioned by various backgrounds and experiences. One thinks especially of the fiery Negro leader, José do Patrocínio. But Joaquim Nabuco, whose contacts with the British were intimate and extensive, was among the most important of these campaigners. Born into a northeastern sugar family of moderate means but excellent connexions, Nabuco was dominated by the nearly overpowering image of his father Nabuco de Araújo, elder statesman of the old regime. Ripped at the age of seven from the loving arms of his godmother, in whose care he had been since babyhood, he was thrown into the highly demanding atmosphere created by an exacting father. For many years his energy and ability seemed without direction, as if in no way could he excel where his father had not done it better. Despite the best legal training then available in Brazil, Joaquim Nabuco was content to merely dabble in law, literature, and journalism for nearly ten years after graduation. While thrashing about in this futile manner in search of self-fulfilment, he traveled widely, sometimes on his own and sometimes as Brazilian legation secretary in the United States and Great Britain, positions secured for him by his father. He soon acquired a reputation as a dandy, occupied as he was with the limited perspectives open to his father's son. But, when Nabuco de Araújo died in 1879, Joaquim suddenly discovered a meaning for himself, and it was to be in destroying one of the mainstays of the regime to which his father had been such a great credit. Yet, after the end of the empire Joaquim remorsefully devoted the bulk of his time for another ten years writing a massive biography of his father, a 'life and times' treatment that still

[1] *Correio mercantil*, 13 July, p. 1; 15 July, p. 1; 17 July, p. 1, 1862; Tavares Bastos, *Cartas do Solitário*, pp. 119–80 (esp. pp. 153, 156–8, 161, 180), 461–5. Christie used Tavares Bastos' position as support for his attack on Brazil, *Notes on Brazilian Questions*, p. xx; Carlos Pontes, *Tavares Bastos (Aureliano Candido), 1839–1875*, Brasiliana, 136 (São Paulo: Editôra Nacional, 1939), pp. 338–9.

remains a classic. Only then did he feel able to live with the republican regime he had done so much to bring about, becoming one of its leading diplomats.

It was immediately upon his election to the Chamber of Deputies in 1879—an election arranged by his father's friends as a sort of posthumous tribute—that Joaquim Nabuco launched the abolitionist campaign for which he has become chiefly famous. He was practically the first to introduce emancipationist bills into that legislative body, and he there delivered powerful verbal attacks on slavery and the slave-owners. Defeated for re-election in 1881 because of these views, he left for London the next year, where he strengthened the ties of the Brazilian abolitionists with their British counterparts and wrote his brilliant polemic against slavery entitled *O abolicionismo*. He returned to Brazil in 1884 and was both titular and effective leader of the movement until its success in 1888.[1]

The British influence upon his development was very large. Although given the characteristic French-oriented education of his time, he read British books on politics while still in law school.[2] His first trip abroad included only one month in England, but he left it, as he put it, 'fascinated by London, touched with a beginning of Anglomania'.[3] He eventually learned English so well that an English abolitionist was condescendingly led to comment, 'Your English is very nearly as good as an Englishman's: in fact, it is a great deal better than many of us can write.'[4] Referring later to his appointment as legation secretary in Britain in 1877, he stated that 'I loved London above all the other cities and places I visited'.[5] 'If I had been born an Englishman,' he wrote to a friend, 'perhaps I would detest England; but as I was born a Brazilian, I adore it.'[6] Looking back on his intellectual develop-

---

[1] Nabuco, *Minha formação*, pp. 16, 163, 169, 171–3; Carolina Nabuco, *Life of Joaquim Nabuco, passim*; Nabuco, *Um estadista do imperio*; cf. Luís Martins, *O patriarca e o bacharel* (São Paulo: Martins, 1953).

[2] Carolina Nabuco, *Life of Joaquim Nabuco*, p. 216; Nabuco, *Minha formação*, p. 68, but cf. pp. 245, 248.

[3] Nabuco, *Minha formação*, p. 54.

[4] Charles H. Allen to Nabuco, London, 21 May 1886, JNP, Lata 7.

[5] Nabuco, *Minha formação*, p. 96.

[6] Quoted by Carolina Nabuco, *Life of Joaquim Nabuco*, p. 82.

ment he later wrote that the 'English influence was the strongest and most lasting of those upon me'.[1] So it was not surprising that he chose London for his self-imposed exile in 1882–4 when he said it was 'to me the paradise of Europe'.[2]

True, the chief British intellectual influence upon him was not with regard to slavery but in his ideas about political structure. His views on slavery sprang from the liberal orientation of his French education and the increasing European influence that permeated the cities in which Nabuco lived. Although he was later to point especially to his childhood observations of the cruelty of slavery as the source of his concern, these would not have been meaningful in another temporal or intellectual context.

It was inevitable, however, that a traveled Brazilian concerned about slavery from whatever cause should have looked to Britain and British experience for well-honed arguments and tested methods; how much surer it was to be in the case of Nabuco. He had become acquainted with British abolitionist thought when, as a student, he translated articles from the *Anti-Slavery Reporter* for his father to use in the Liberal Party organ which Nabuco de Araújo had founded. It was at this time that Joaquim wrote a small book which still remains unpublished, entitled 'A escravidão', in which he quoted extensively from the British abolitionist leaders, Sir Thomas Buxton, William Wilberforce and Henry Peter, Lord Brougham, whom he called the 'courageous defender of human liberty'. The very first bill he introduced for the complete emancipation of the slaves was written with the British experience in mind.[3]

His bill suffered such a swift and resounding defeat that he realized that only a long and intensive propaganda campaign would mobilize public opinion and force the entrenched interests

---

[1] Nabuco, *Minha formação*, p. 89; also see Eugênio Gomes, *Prata de casa (ensaios de literatura brasileira)* (Rio: Editora 'A Noite', [1953?]), pp. 109–10.

[2] Carolina Nabuco, *Life of Joaquim Nabuco*, pp. 83, 197.

[3] Nabuco, *Minha formação*, pp. 34, 120; Nabuco, *Um estadista do imperio*, II, 82; Joaquim Nabuco, 'A escravidão', MS., 1870, Part I, pp. 83, 85, AIHGB, L135, MS2346; Carolina Nabuco, *Life of Joaquim Nabuco*, p. 17; his initial bill, on the British example, called for indemnities for slave-owners, but at more critical moments later on it was they who appealed to this example, see speech of Benedicto Valladares, Brazil, Congresso, Camara dos Deputados, *Anais*, 1885, III, 283.

to give way. Looking again to the British model, he founded in 1880 the Sociedade Brasileira Contra a Escravidão. He immediately sent the society's manifesto off to its namesake, the Anti-Slavery Society in London, and its leaders later asserted that 'the abolitionists of Brazil...have the support of the British public and of this society'. Nabuco founded an abolitionist periodical in which he welcomed evidence of this support in England, and it was with somewhat exaggerated pride that he printed a letter from the Ladies' Negros' Friend Society of Birmingham.[1]

Nabuco soon decided to make a personal appeal for British support, a move especially indicated at that time since he had lost his seat in Parliament and with it the most efficacious way to gain public attention for the cause. He later explained that 'World opinion seemed to me a legitimate weapon to be used in a question which belonged to all humanity and not only to us', but one may wonder, given his knowledge of earlier British diplomatic pressure on Brazil, whether he did not hope to bestir more than world opinion.[2] It was, for instance, to London that he went, since he could 'do more for the cause' there than in Italy, where he would have liked to visit friends.[3] He conferred with the surviving leaders of the British movement, and made speeches in praise of Wilberforce and Buxton before the British and Foreign Anti-Slavery Society. He made frequent trips to London in later years to cultivate these contacts and, although probably disappointed in the political leverage which they wielded, he gladly accepted their financial contributions toward his travel and other expenses in his effort to awaken European sentiment. It was also in England, at the British Museum and in Richard Cobden's private library—in which most books had not yet had their pages cut—that he settled down to work on his book *O abolicionismo*, a convincingly argued and thoroughly researched book on slavery and its drawbacks.[4]

---

[1] *O abolicionista*, no. 1, 1 Nov. 1880, pp. 2–3; no. 2, 1 Dec. 1880, pp. 3–4; Allen to Nabuco, London, 22 June 1885, JNP, Lata 7; on the influence of the British campaign as a model see Rebouças to Nabuco, Funchal, 7 Apr. 1895, in Rebouças, *Diário*, p. 427.

[2] Nabuco, *Minha formação*, p. 224.

[3] Carolina Nabuco, *Life of Joaquim Nabuco*, p. 84.

[4] Joseph Cooper to Nabuco, Walthamstow, 15 Apr. 1881; Allen to Nabuco, London, 9 Feb. 1881; Joseph G. Alexander to Nabuco, London, 28 July and 4 Aug. 1883, JNP,

Meanwhile, a number of abolitionist societies began to be formed in Brazil, and the abolitionist crusade gained momentum. In 1883 the Confederação Abolicionista was founded to join all the clubs of this nature of the Rio de Janeiro–Niterói area. For the next five years the member clubs presented a series of lectures, one almost every week, and on the flimsiest excuse would stage a demonstration, with parades, banners, and speeches. Several newspapers were published, and all possible means of bringing their cause to the public were given a try. Parliament was taken up with the slavery question almost constantly from 1884 to 1888, and it was the publicists and the flight of the slaves taken together that were blamed for this new interest.[1]

One argument that the Brazilian abolitionists took up almost verbatim from the British diplomatists of twenty years before was the point that a large segment of the slave population was so held illegally, having been imported after 1831 or being descendants of such slaves. Nabuco was especially given to playing on this point. 'The simple examination of the titles to slave property would be enough to end it', he said in the initial manifesto of his society in 1880. The next year he surveyed the achievements of the first few months of the abolitionist campaign and concluded that nothing was more significant than 'the declaration made many times by our adversaries that to enforce the law of 1831 is equivalent to immediate emancipation:...we forced slavery to admit its illegality'. Using the same methods as those adopted by Christie, the abolitionists began to examine the advertisements placed in the newspapers for slaves for sale and found many evidences of slaves reputedly born in Africa and of such an age as to have been imported after 1831. If the emperor could do nothing against the 'slave barons', they wrote, at least he should put an end to these 'revolting advertisements'.[2]

Lata 7; *O abolicionista*, no. 6, 1 Apr. 1881, p. 3; no. 7, 1 May 1881, p. 5; Nabuco to Penedo, Brighton, 4 Oct. 1882, in Joaquim Nabuco, *Obras completas*, 14 vols. (São Paulo: Instituto Progresso Editorial, 1949), XIII, 73; Nabuco, *O abolicionismo*, which is full of citations denoting British influence, e.g. pp. 28, 88, 94n., 96, 230, 239, and most chapter headings.

[1] Moraes, *Campanha abolicionista*, pp. 21, 24–5, 33–4, 45–171 (esp. 58), 321–53.

[2] Joaquim Nabuco, 'Manifesto da Sociedade Contra a Escravidão, 1880', in Osvaldo Melo Braga, *Bibliografia de Joaquim Nabuco*, Instituto Nacional do Livro, Coleção B–1,

Other abolitionists, such as Luís Gama (1830–82), began to elaborate the legal argument on behalf of these slaves, referring without rancor to the British role in creating the law of 1831 and British protests against Brazilian attempts to modify it.[1] Eventually they forced the question into court, despite the establishment's fear of this issue. When, in 1854, a minor judge had threatened to declare it illegal to hold a slave imported after 1831, it was Nabuco's father who had written that the government was determined not to touch on this matter, basing itself on 'the principles of public order' and acting with 'the general approval of the whole country'. 'It would not be right', he added, 'to have a judgement against law, but it is obviously right to avoid [altogether] a judgement which would endanger these principles and cause the proprietors alarm and exasperation.' Now, however, the courts could not avoid making judgements since the abolitionists were pressing the cases of hundreds of slaves on this basis. In 1881 the abolitionists could still say, referring to the law and the years that had passed since its passage, that 'the judges of this country either can't read or can't count'.[2] But soon some judges, moved by the very force of the abolitionist campaign, began to hand down favorable decisions. After about 1883, few courts would deny freedom to the slave who could prove that he or his parents had been brought in after 1831. One lawyer on one single occasion secured the freedom of 716 slaves on this basis.[3]

Bibliografia, 8 (Rio: Imp. Nacional, 1952), p. 21; *O abolicionista*, no. 3, 1 Jan. 1881, p. 5. See other references to law of 1831 in Nabuco, *O abolicionismo*, pp. 60, 102–3; Carlos Arthur Busch Varella, *Conferencia sobre a lei de 7 de novembro de 1831 realisada no dia 9 de março de 1884 a convite do Club Abolicionista Sete de Novembro* (Rio: Typ. Central de Evaristo Rodrigues da Costa for the Confederação Abolicionista, 1884). Christie had not been the last Englishman to urge abolition in Brazil on this ground, British and Foreign Anti-Slavery Society to Prince Louis of Orléans, *comte* d'Eu, London, 24 Oct. 1870, AMIP, CLVII, 7363; cf. this stand with that in *O abolicionista*, no. 1, 1 Nov. 1880, p. 1; no. 3, 1 Jan. 1881, p. 3.

[1] Luiz Gama, 'Questão juridica: subsistem os effeitos manumissores da lei de 26 de janeiro de 1818, depois da de 7 de novembro de 1831 e 4 de outubro de 1850?', *A provincia de São Paulo*, 18 Dec. 1880, p. 5; this article can also be found in serialized form in *O abolicionista*, no. 2, 1 Dec. 1880, p. 6; no. 6, 1 Apr. 1881, pp. 2–4; no. 8, 1 June 1881, p. 8; and in Sud Menucci, *O precursor do abolicionismo no Brasil (Luiz Gama)* (São Paulo: n.p., 1938), pp. 165–86.

[2] Nabuco de Araujo to José Antonio Saraiva, 22 Sept. 1854, in Nabuco, *Um estadista do imperio*, I, 177; *O abolicionista*, no. 12, 28 Sept. 1881, p. 8.

[3] Moraes, *Campanha abolicionista*, pp. 182ff., 203n.

Slave Trade and Slavery

The use of Great Britain as a model of humanitarian action presented certain difficulties to publicists acting at a time of increasing national self-consciousness. The insulting deeds perpetrated by Christie had by no means been forgotten. The abolitionists sometimes ignored the problem, but on other occasions they faced it squarely and defended the British actions. Nabuco, for instance, had already devoted a large section of his little book composed in student days to the British efforts to eradicate the slave trade. Although he referred to the Aberdeen Act as 'an insult to our dignity as an independent people', he maintained that 'In this question Brazil was for a long time on the side of the slave trade, leaving to England the role of defender of humanity'. He recognized that the extinction of the slave trade to Brazil was equally due to British action and to Brazilian cooperation, neither country being able to do anything on this question alone. As he later put it, 'the issue should never have been Brazil against England, but rather Brazil and England against the trade.'[1]

Naturally, the opportunity to accuse him of being a vile creature of the British, a traitor to his country, was not lost by his opponents. If they had known that he not only owned both of Christie's books on Brazil but that he lent them to his friends, they would have been even louder in their diatribes.[2] He defended himself by saying that 'those who wish to see Brazil linked to the progress of our century... are always pointed to as foreign agents', and added: 'nothing offends the patriotism of the defenders of slavery more than the appeal to world opinion. No one may do it without being accused of connexions with England. They have not yet forgiven her for ending the slave trade!'[3]

Ironically, in view of his delicate position here, Englishmen themselves managed to stay out of the limelight in the abolitionist campaign. What the British residents in Brazil were doing on

[1] Nabuco, 'A escravidão', Part I, pp. 36, 38; Nabuco, O abolicionismo, p. 94. Nabuco's views about the English role did not change with age, Nabuco, Um estadista do império, I, 165. Also see Nabuco, O abolicionismo, pp. 89, 90, 96; Rebouças, Diario, p. 400.

[2] Braga, Bibliografia de Joaquim Nabuco, p. 245; Francis Clare Ford to Nabuco, Petrópolis, 11 Dec. 1880, JNP, Lata 7.

[3] Nabuco, 'Manifesto da Sociedade Contra a Escravidão, 1880', pp. 15, 18.

behalf of abolition appears only through occasional references. An American southerner wrote critically in 1867 that 'the English element of the population in this country is antagonistic to slavery, and is quietly instilling this principle, not simply by the expression of opinions, but in some instances by aiding in the liberation of slaves through contributions of funds'.[1] At least one British engineer in Rio de Janeiro championed the cause of emancipation. The *Anglo-Brazilian Times*, published by the Englishman William Scully, also lent heavy support to the abolitionists. Other Britishers supported emancipation in Rio Grande do Sul.[2] And it seems probable that being urban residents, part of the very commercial community that spearheaded manumission drives, the British in Brazil could not help but be involved. If they had not contributed we may guess the campaigners would not have hesitated to point them out as friends of slavery much as Christie had once done.

On the other hand, we may also presume that, like most businessmen, they were afraid of any change which might endanger their position. Large-scale importers were more likely to see the dependence of the country on slave-produced coffee than were the retail merchants that made up the bulk of the commercial community. Nor can we be sure that those who had invested in Brazil felt differently. The famous St John d'El Rey Mining Co., founded in 1830, was notorious for its use of slaves in the pits. Nabuco denounced the company in the Brazilian Parliament, and a copy of his speech was sent to the Foreign Office. The British Anti-Slavery Society took up the case and pushed it before the House of Commons.[3] But little could be done about it. Nabuco

[1] James McFadden Gaston, *Hunting a Home in Brazil. The Agricultural Resources and Other Characteristics of the Country; also, the Manners and Customs of the Inhabitants* (Philadelphia: King & Baird, 1867), p. 228.

[2] Rebouças, *Diário*, pp. 283, 302; João Frick, *Abolição da escravatura. Breve noticia sobre a primeira sociedade de emancipação no Brazil (Fundada na cidade do Rio Grande do Sul em março de 1869)* (Lisbon: Lallemant Frères, 1885), *passim* and esp. pp. 8, 12, 13, 18, 26, 29.

[3] David Joslin, *A Century of Banking in Latin America; to Commemorate the Centenary in 1962 of the Bank of London and South America Limited* (Oxford Univ. Press, 1963), p. 153; speech of Joaquim Nabuco, Brazil, Congresso, Camara dos Deputados, *Anais*, 1879, IV, 182–5; Ford to Nabuco, Rio, 3 Oct. 1879; Allen to Nabuco, London, 22 Nov. 1881, and 21 June 1883; David Cornfoot to Nabuco, London, 29 March 1881, JNP, Lata 7; Great Britain, Parliament, *Hansard's Parliamentary Debates*, 3rd series, CCLXXII (July 1882), 1685–6; CCLXXIII (July–Aug. 1882), 581–2, 744; Joaquim Nabuco, 'Correspondencia', *Jornal do commercio*, 13 Aug. 1882, p. 2; 26 Aug. 1882, p. 2; Carolina Nabuco,

summed up the situation in 1882 when he wrote that, although the cause of abolition had been won before Europe, it had not been won before 'the Europeans established in the country who in large part either own slaves or do not believe in Brazil without slaves and fear for their interests'.[1] But, as it turned out, British interests suffered only momentarily when slavery was finally abolished.[2]

The law ending slavery in Brazil without compensation was signed by the princess-regent on 13 May 1888. Month-long celebrations were the rule in the urban centers of Brazil, with fireworks and speeches and parades. In the countryside, however, there was little celebration. The slaves themselves were disoriented, knowing not what to do with their freedom. Many flocked into the cities to find their fellows who had earlier fled the plantations, contributing to the social problems of the towns and cities. The masters, even those who had acquiesced or cooperated in the final stages of the movement, cannot help but have been dazed by the rapidity of the transformation. Economic depression in the countryside was the initial result of the law of abolition.

And it was to the British that Brazil turned to soften the blow. In the latter half of 1888 the government decided to aid the coffee planters now faced with an enormous payroll both by lending money to banks who would in turn lend to planters and by allowing the banks to issue currency on their own. To finance this move the government borrowed over six million pounds sterling in London, an operation that was repeated with a similar purpose the next year. But the only effect of all this was to initiate a giant investment bubble which was blown up even further in the next few years in behalf of the urban-based entrepreneurial class, the very elements who had done most in the long run to overthrow slavery. The more progressive Brazilian planters were saved by the continuing demand for coffee on the world market,

Life of Joaquim Nabuco, p. 57; London *Times*, 27 Oct. 1883, p. 13; 3 Nov. 1890, p. 11; Rebouças, *Diário*, p. 297. Cf. Bernard Hollowood, *The Story of Morro Velho* (London: St John d'El Rey Mining Company, Ltd, 1955), pp. 31, 34, 38.

[1] Nabuco, *O abolicionismo*, p. 42; in 1850 an English family in Rio advertised for a mammy, and this was surely typical, *Jornal do commercio*, 11 Jan. 1850, p. 4.

[2] Joslin, *A Century of Banking*, p. 153; minimal effects of abolition on a British railway serving a coffee district can be seen in London *Times*, 27 Oct. 1888, p. 13; 3 Nov. 1890, p. 11.

a demand they were equipped to meet because of British actions in other areas of Brazilian life.[1]

The British had played a substantial part in ending Negro slavery in Brazil. Despite the friction between the British and Brazilians over the slave trade issue, the two countries had effectively combined to end that trade, drying up the source of supply of new slaves, thus spelling out the eventual end of the institution. By constant pressure, the British government had suggested the need to end slavery altogether. By forcing the Brazilians to pass the earlier law of 1831 they provided the abolitionists half a century later with a devastating legal argument against the slave-owners. And it was a man deeply influenced by the British who made the cause of abolition his consuming passion, and it was to Britain that he appealed both for his campaign model and for his arguments.

On the other hand, the conclusive causative factor was the larger change taking place within Brazil. It was the very process of modernization that made the end of slavery necessary. It became impossible for anyone in the 1880s, literate, in touch with the outside world and committed to the new values—as more and more Brazilians were, because of modern change—to be blind to the backwardness of slavery or immune to what the Western world considered its revolting aspects. To be the one country in the 'civilized' world still to have that institution was considered a blight and a shame. Increasingly vocal and cohesive urban groups responded eagerly to the appeal of the abolitionists and lent their vital support to the slave flights from the plantations. Coffee planters newly established on the lands of west-central São Paulo willingly sought alternatives to slavery. The real British contribution toward the end of slavery in Brazil is to be found in all those actions of whatever sort that tended to transform the economic and social structure of the country and bring Brazil into closer touch with the outside world. Their direct aid to the cause of abolition was only part of this larger effort.

[1] Simonsen, 'As consequências econômicas', pp. 263–5; ruined planters also fled to the cities, where they snapped up sinecures and desperately tried to maintain appearances, Francisco José de Oliveira Vianna, 'O povo brasileiro e sua evolução', in Brazil, Directoria Geral de Estatistica, *Recenseamento do Brazil, 1920, Vol. 1: Introducção* (Rio: Typ. da Estatistica, 1922), pp. 305–6; Bouças, *História da divida externa*, pp. 119, 121.

7

BRITAIN AND THE ENTREPRENEURS

The spread of entrepreneurial attitudes and ideas is a basic aspect of modernization, and it is the purpose of this chapter to examine some Brazilian entrepreneurs who were in close contact with the British. Not only is our understanding of some of the problems they faced at this early stage of development enhanced by a consideration of their business activities, but their experience also suggests that businessmen often sought out foreign images to reinforce a position they had already assumed within Brazil. Thus the presence of the foreigner contributed to their success but was not its initial cause, which is not to say that they were not deeply affected by the British. Special attention will be paid to these four: Irineu Evangelista de Souza, *barão* and later *visconde* de Mauá (1813–89); the Rebouças brothers, André (1838–98) and Antônio (1839–74); and Luís Tarqüínio (1844–1903). In addition, reference will be made to several other businessmen who were in contact with the British to a lesser extent.

Mauá was a representative of an older generation already in their thirties by 1850. Although not alone, he was widely recognized as the leading industrial capitalist during the period before the Paraguayan War. At the age of thirteen he had begun working for Richard Carruthers, head of a large English importing firm. This was the turning point in his life: seven years later he became a partner in the firm. And the next year Carruthers retired to England, leaving the future *visconde* de Mauá, aged twenty-four, as manager of the Brazilian house, a position through which he amassed a large fortune.[1]

---

[1] The chief biographers of Mauá are Anyda Marchant, *Viscount Mauá and the Empire of Brazil: a Biography of Irineu Evangelista de Sousa (1813–1889)* (Berkeley and Los Angeles: Univ. of California Press, 1965) and Alberto de Faria, *Mauá—Ireneo Evangelista de Souza, barão e visconde de Mauá, 1813–1889*, 2nd ed., Brasiliana, 20 (São Paulo: Editôra Nacional, 1933); the latter's panegyrist tendencies are sharply corrected by E. de Castro Rebello,

He then became involved in a wide variety of enterprises, most important of which were a foundry-shipyard, railways, and banks. The initial impetus that led him to broaden his interests and eventually break away from the importing business altogether was a visit to England in 1840. The industrial might of Great Britain greatly excited him and he dreamed of creating a similarly powerful and industrialized Brazil. Of particular importance was Mauá's visit to an iron foundry in Bristol. He later wrote that 'I was deeply impressed by what I saw and observed, and right there the idea of founding in my country an identical establishment was born in my spirit'.[1]

Encouraged by a protective tariff adopted in 1844 and assured in advance that he would be given the government contract for the metal pipes to be used in draining a swampy section of Rio de Janeiro, he bought a small iron foundry and shipyard in 1846. It prospered from the first. By 1850 he was advertising that his establishment could handle 'all the necessities of the country'. He had 300 employees including a number of skilled workers from 'the most famous shops of England and Scotland'.[2]

During its days of prosperity, this establishment was the basis of a business empire. The firm built 72 ships, most of them steam. Among these vessels were those bought by a shipping company which Mauá created in the Amazon and also the ship he used to begin a tug-boat service in Rio Grande do Sul. He also made the pipes and lamps to be employed in the Mauá-owned gas company in Rio de Janeiro. By the time the firm began to decline in prosperity during the later 1850s, Mauá had moved on to other concerns.[3]

Railroads were one of Mauá's greatest enthusiasms. The very

Mauá, restaurando a verdade (Rio: Universo, 1932); a balanced view is presented by Claudio Ganns, 'Introdução', in Irineo Evangelista de Souza, *visconde* de Mauá, *Autobiografia* ('*Exposição aos credores e ao público*') *seguida de 'O meio circulante no Brasil'*, 2nd ed. Claudio Ganns (Rio: Valverde, 1942). Other studies include Lídia Besouchet, *Mauá e seu tempo* (São Paulo: Anchieta, 1942); and Ennor de Almeida Carneiro, *Mauá (Irineo Evangelista de Souza)*, Pequenos Estudos Sôbre Grandes Administradores do Brasil, 8 (Rio: Serviço de Documentação do DASP, 1956).
[1] Mauá, *Autobiografia*, p. 108.
[2] *Jornal do commercio*, 2 May 1850, p. 4.
[3] Mauá, *Autobiografia*, pp. 110–11, 114; Ganns, 'Introdução', *ibid.* pp. 37, 45–6; Castro Rebello, *Mauá, restaurando a verdade*, p. 39.

first railroad in Brazil was his creation. The Petrópolis railway, inaugurated in 1854, was only some fourteen kilometers long, but Mauá liked to say that it served as a 'sample cloth' to the nation of what railroads were and what they could do.[1] But Mauá was also interested in many other railroads. He tried desperately to conciliate the interests of the Estrada de Ferro Dom Pedro Segundo and those of the British contractor, Edward Price. His advances for the construction of the São Paulo Railway were among his most serious financial mistakes. In addition, his firm was a large investor in the Recife and São Francisco Railway Company, Ltd, and, as company agent in Brazil, he lobbied vigorously in its behalf. Mauá also had minor interests in the Bahia and São Francisco Railway Company, Ltd, the Minas and Rio Railway Company, Ltd, the railway that ran inland from the coast to Curitiba, and the proposed railway to run from Paraná across Mato Grosso to the western border of the country.[2]

Mauá visualized banks as the partners of railways in pushing the country toward economic development. In 1860 he wrote: 'When the masses understand the immense advantage of drawing credit from their money, what great sums may accumulate in our branches to be newly employed with advantage, aiding labor and industry, producing conditions of prosperity in different localities.'[3] When in England in 1840, he became a partner in the Manchester banking firm of Carruthers, de Castro and Company, with financial connexions in London, New York, and Buenos Aires. With the knowledge he had thus acquired, Mauá created, in 1851, the Banco Mauá e Companhia, which was merged into a semi-governmental bank two years later. He then organized the banking house Mauá, MacGregor, & Cia.

[1] Mauá quoted by Faria, *Mauá*, p. 165; Clodomiro Pereira da Silva, *A evolução do transporte mundial (enciclopédia dos transportes)*, 6 vols. (São Paulo: Imp. Oficial do Estado, 1940–1946), V, 410; the Petrópolis railway did not impress Christiano Benedicto Ottoni, *Esboço historico das estradas de ferro do Brazil* (Rio: Villeneuve, 1866), p. 13.

[2] Mauá, *Autobiografia*, pp. 156–8, 178, 191–207, 214–18; William Lloyd, *Caminho de ferro de d. Isabel da provincia do Paraná a de Matto Grosso. Considerações geraes sobre a empresa pelo visconde de Mauá; relatorio por William Lloyd* (Rio: Leuzinger, 1875).

[3] Mauá quoted by Marchant, *Viscount Mauá*, p. 133.

with branches in Buenos Aires, Montevideo, Rio Grande do Sul, Pelotas, Pôrto Alegre, Santos, São Paulo, Campinas, and Belém.[1]

But banks were also to prove his undoing. By 1865 he was facing serious business difficulties brought on partly by the Brazilian financial crash of 1864 and partly by the over-extension of credit to the São Paulo Railway; he now also encountered problems in the Río de la Plata. Although he still managed to organize the banking house of Mauá & Cia., which experienced an initially rapid growth, its involvement in the politics of Uruguay was responsible for his ultimate downfall. Having lent large sums of money to the losing factions, his firm faced financial ruin.[2] In 1875 he received a moratorium for three years during which he tried to reorganize his finances. But, finding this impossible, he went into bankruptcy in 1878. In the final years of his life, he worked steadily to rehabilitate his name, paying off his creditors one by one. He died in 1889 leaving a heritage of courageous entrepreneurship. André Rebouças once referred to him as 'undoubtedly the most intelligent and the most patriotic of the capitalists with whom I have dealt'.[3]

André and Antônio Rebouças belong to a generation of innovators that came to maturity during the 1860s. Mulattoes descended from several generations of free men and sons of a lawyer and politician, the Rebouças went everywhere and did everything together well into manhood. Since André kept a diary we know

---

[1] Marchant, *Viscount Mauá*, pp. 117–131; Anyda Marchant, 'A New Portrait of Mauá the Banker: a Man of Business in Nineteenth-Century Brazil', *Hispanic American Historical Review*, xxx (1950), 413, 424, 426; Mauá, *Autobiografia*, pp. 237n., 273n.; Faria, *Mauá*, p. 221.

[2] Mauá's position as an agent of Brazilian economic imperialism in Uruguay is apparent in the *Autobiografia*, pp. 247–62, and in his letter dated 20 Apr. 1864, to the *Jornal do commercio*, 22 Apr. 1864, given in full by Ganns in *ibid.* pp. 252n.–257n.; also see Irineo Evangelista de Souza, *visconde de Mauá, Correspondência política de Mauá no Rio da Prata (1850–1885)*, ed. Lídia Besouchet, 2nd ed., Brasiliana, 227 (São Paulo: Editôra Nacional, 1943), *passim*. His role in the Río de la Plata region has been studied by Lídia Besouchet, *Mauá e seu tempo*; by Álvaro Teixeira Soares, 'Mauá, o Uruguai e o Brasil (1851–1875)', *RIHGB*, ccix (1950), 3–213; and by the same author in his *O gigante e o rio. Ação de Mauá no Uruguai e Argentina, 1851–1878* (Rio: Cia. Brasileira de Artes Gráficas, 1957).

[3] André Rebouças, *Diário e notas autobiográficas*, ed. Ana Flora and Inácio José Verissimo, Documentos Brasileiros, 12 (Rio: José Olympio, 1938), p. 193.

much more about his activities than about those of his brother, but one may presume a harmony of views most of the time. They attended the military academy together and were students there when it was transformed into a sort of engineering school in 1858. They then traveled to Europe to complete their professional training. There they examined bridges, canals, tunnels, railroads, dockworks, and factory buildings, and sought out the leading engineers of their day. A visit to the International Exposition in London in 1862 was decisive in awakening their zeal for developmental enterprises. At the invitation of the Brazilian minister to Britain, the *barão* do Penedo, they prepared reports on the Exposition's most relevant aspects.[1]

As were so many of their contemporaries, the Rebouças brothers were excited by the promise of railroads. Antônio studied railway equipment at the Exposition, and stated that railroads were 'identified with the moral and material progress of all nations'. He believed their construction would solve Brazil's economic problems.[2]

Antônio then became interested in a railway in southern Brazil. In 1868 he was charged by the government with making preliminary studies for a line to run over a difficult mountain range and link the capital of the province of Paraná to the coast. When the project had to be abandoned for lack of funds, André and Antônio decided to organize a private company to carry on this idea. In 1871 they approached various financiers, but only Mauá showed any interest. Through his effort they were brought into contact with a team of engineers sent to Brazil by 'English capitalists' to look for solid investment opportunities.[3] Although Antônio exclaimed that the resulting plans would 'assure me my fortune', their euphoria was shortlived.[4] The London financiers changed their minds, and the leading landowning family of

[1] Inácio José Veríssimo, *André Rebouças através de sua auto-biografia*, Documentos Brasileiros, 20 (Rio: José Olympio, 1939), pp. 5–10; on the continuing influence of the Exposition see Rebouças, *Diário*, pp. 16, 17, 31, 128, 150, 197, 240.

[2] Antônio Rebouças in Francisco Carvalho Moreira, *barão* do Penedo, ed., *Relatorio sobre a exposição internacional de 1862* (London: Brettell, 1863), pp. 197, 198.

[3] Veríssimo, *André Rebouças*, pp. 133, 135, 139–40; Rebouças, *Diário*, pp. 192–3.

[4] Antônio Rebouças quoted by Veríssimo, *André Rebouças*, p. 141.

Paraná demanded that the track should be laid from a different port. Faced with the political power of this competing group Mauá and his young friends had to give up.[1] But this experience did not dim the brothers' interest in railroads. Antônio was next contracted by the Brazilian-owned Paulista railway company to direct the construction of the first stretch beyond Campinas. He drew up the definitive plans, but died in 1874 before their execution. André had meanwhile traveled to Europe in the company of Henry Edward Hargreaves, who had been Antônio's aid in the Paraná scheme, and in London they proposed the construction of a railroad in the Brazilian northeastern province of Paraíba. On their return to Brazil in 1874 Hargreaves and André Rebouças once again approached Mauá and persuaded him to underwrite the contractors for the company. But the British capital market continued sluggish and only in 1880 was the company finally organized as the Conde d'Eu Railway Company, Limited. By this time Rebouças had had to give up his financial interest in this enterprise. It was not successful and was bought up by the government in 1901.[2]

At the International Exposition in London in 1862 André had paid particular attention to harbor works and dry docks. The hydraulic system used in the English ports, especially at the 'great commercial establishment' of Victoria Docks, and the repair services used along the Thames had already attracted his special attention. And the new system of dry docks devised by the engineer Edwin Clark was the one he considered best of all the systems demonstrated at the Exposition.[3]

At this time he was also impressed by the use of private companies to construct these establishments, to which he attributed the superiority in this regard of England and the United States over other countries. Liverpool, which he visited after the Exposition, had 29 dry docks while Marseilles, with 50 per cent more commercial traffic, had not a single one. In the Anglo-Saxon

---

[1] Veríssimo, *André Rebouças*, pp. 141, 143; Rebouças, *Diário*, pp. 199, 261, 265, 270–3; Mauá, *Autobiografia*, pp. 185–8.
[2] Rebouças, *Diário*, pp. 212, 229, 232, 267, 268, 289; Veríssimo, *André Rebouças*, p. 131; Pereira da Silva, *Evolução do transporte*, v, 442.
[3] André Rebouças in Penedo, *Relatorio sobre a exposição*, pp. 244–5, 361, 378.

countries, wrote André, these and other harbor works were almost always constructed by private companies. 'This example, to which we might add a great number of others based on quays, inland communications, transatlantic navigation, etc., shows very clearly how defective is the old system of leaving works of public utility solely to governments.' After making these observations, he was always a staunch defender of the principle that free enterprise should be responsible for the construction of harbor works.[1]

Five years later Rebouças was gratified to see a plan for which he had campaigned approved by the Brazilian parliament and a law passed which authorized the government to make concessions to private companies for the construction of harbor works. A senator commented that Rebouças' ideas at this time were a 'veritable pill of liberalism administered to the Conservative government'. André recorded in his diary that he hoped the law 'produces the beneficent results that I expect from it: the construction and financing of Dock Companies in every port of the empire'.[2]

He was ready to do his part. In October 1867 he showed the emperor his plans for a dry dock and wharf to be built and administered by a new company, the Companhia das Docas de D. Pedro II. It was directly inspired by the Victoria Docks in London and, although greatly simplified from that model, included the use of the Edwin Clark dry docks he had examined there. He then persuaded the owners of a British import–export house to invest in the proposed company. The prime minister, on whom the concession partly depended, was much impressed by this sign of international backing, but the petition had to be examined by several government agencies, including the municipal council, and, with frequent changes in governments, there were many delays. It was not until 1870 that the concession was granted, and by then the English investors had cooled off; Rebouças was forced to appeal to Brazilian capitalists for the necessary funds. Although construction finally began in Septem-

---

[1] André Rebouças in Penedo, *Relatorio sobre a exposição*, p. 380; Rebouças, *Diário*, p. 164.
[2] Rebouças, *Diário*, pp. 174 and 154 respectively. On the legislation on harbor works see Veríssimo, *André Rebouças*, p. 75; and Joseph R. West, 'The Foreigner in Brazilian Technology, 1808–1900', unpub. Ph.D. diss., Univ. of Chicago, 1950, p. 839.

ber 1871, the stockholders still lacked confidence in Rebouças and he was unable to marshall their full support for his enterprise. Despite his later success at raising a loan of 6000 *contos* (say £700,000) in London with the help of a guarantee of interest offered by the Brazilian government, under another cabinet his company was soon prohibited from loading or unloading coffee, that is, the major item of local commerce. Finally in 1877 the company leased its works to the government.[1] André sighed and wrote: 'One word characterizes the story of the Companhia das Docas de D. Pedro II—betrayal.'[2]

The London Exposition of 1862 was also the beginning of the Rebouças brothers' interest in exploiting the timberlands of southern Brazil. In their reports both of them suggested places where Brazilian lumber should be used in place of the imported supply. Later on, as director of works at the government-owned wharf in Rio de Janeiro, André Rebouças returned to this idea saying he could not understand why Brazil should buy timber abroad when good pine was available in the southern province of Paraná. He eventually got the government to accept bids made by interested merchants to supply Paraná pine, but by 1868 he was forced to admit that his work in this direction had come to naught. He would have to organize the supply himself. In mid-1871 he wrote in his diary that he had begun to elaborate plans for the organization of a company to be called the Companhia Florestal Paranaense, whose purpose would be to develop the 'rich pine forests' of Paraná. The company was organized a year later with all the capital being subscribed by Mauá—British investors having been wary of the project—and Antônio was placed in charge of the operation. By 1877, however, André confessed that the opposition of the major landowning family which had defeated his brother's railroad project was also an insuperable

---

[1] Veríssimo, *André Rebouças*, pp. 76, 78–81, 83, 89–91; Rebouças, *Diário*, pp. 157, 159, 160, 163, 172, 195–6; André Rebouças, *Melhoramento do porto do Rio de Janeiro. Organização da Companhia das Docas de D. Pedro II (nas enseadas da Saude e Gamboa): colleção de artigos publicados* (Rio: Typ. Nacional, 1869), pp. 3, 9, 11, 14, 17, 23; the proposed contract for the company's concession even used English words in parentheses for all technical references, *ibid.* p. 12.

[2] Rebouças, *Diário*, p. 197.

obstacle to the success of his lumbering company, and he abandoned the enterprise.[1]

Luís Tarqüínio was much more successful in his business activities than were the Rebouças brothers, and his early career in some ways resembles that of Mauá. Born into a poverty-stricken family which the father abandoned, Luís was clerking by the age of ten. He was recommended to the British import–export firm of Bruderer & Co. and rose rapidly in position. Within four years he was given a percentage of profits. He then began to travel to Europe to deal with the suppliers—principally British—of textiles for the Bahian market. He became a full partner of Bruderer & Co. in 1877. In 1891, stimulated by the republican zeal for industrialization and the new tariff laws, Luís Tarqüínio abandoned the importing business and founded a textile factory, the Companhia Empório Industrial do Norte. He organized it with a capital of roughly £250,000 and rapidly expanded the operation, setting up one of the biggest weaving mills in Brazil in 1893. By 1910 Tarqüínio controlled one of the nation's largest cotton mills with 31,000 spindles, 1,288 looms, and 1,600 workers. Unfortunately, less is known about his business activities than about those of Mauá or the Rebouças.[2]

Three men whose interests centered on railroads were also connected with the British to some degree: Antônio da Silva Prado (1840–1928), his brother Eduardo (1860–1901), and Francisco Pereira Passos (1836–1913). When Antônio Prado made a tour of Europe as a young man just out of law school, few things made as deep an impression upon him as the London Exposition of 1862. Witness the ecstatic letters he wrote home about the power of industry to transform society and satisfy man's needs.

[1] Antônio Rebouças in Penedo, *Relatorio sobre a exposição*, pp. 197–8, 214, 218; André Rebouças in *ibid.* p. 379; Rebouças, *Diário*, pp. 140, 159–60, 168, 194–5, 270; Thomas Plantagenet Bigg-Wither, *Pioneering in South Brazil: Three Years of Forest and Prairie Life in the Province of Paraná*, 2 vols. (London: Murray, 1878), I, 73–4; Veríssimo, *André Rebouças*, pp. 156–7. Note André Rebouças' authorship, along with his brother José Rebouças, of *Ensaio de indice geral das madeiras do Brazil* (Rio: Typ. Nacional, 1877).

[2] Péricles Madureira do Pinho, *Luís Tarqüínio, pioneiro da justiça social no Brasil* (Salvador: Imp. Vitória, 1944), pp. 3–4, 38, 48, 76; Stanley J. Stein, *The Brazilian Cotton Manufacture; Textile Enterprise in an Underdeveloped Area, 1850–1950* (Cambridge, Mass.: Harvard Univ. Press, 1957), pp. 40, 104.

A few years later, while sitting in the provincial assembly, he revealed through his speeches a close familiarity with British institutions and economic history.[1] These influences, combined with many other factors, were doubtless of some importance in impelling him to become the chief founder of the Companhia Estrada de Ferro Paulista. It was one of the most important Brazilian railways, and from this base he went on to build Brazil's first modern slaughterhouse, first glass factory, and the Banco do Comércio e Industria, one of the principal banks of the era.[2]

Eduardo Prado is usually thought of as a foppish intellectual, but his library was full of stock guides, interest or exchange-rate tables, texts on company law, directories, and other books typical of a businessman. His fast and intelligent action as agent for his brother Antônio enabled the Paulista railroad to buy up the Rio Claro Railway Company, Ltd, thus opening the way for Antônio's line to expand beyond Campinas into the coffee area. When the province of São Paulo, prodded by Antônio Prado, raised a loan in London in 1888, Eduardo handled the negotiations.[3] It would seem logical that Eduardo passed on to his brother his deep admiration for the British. 'The English people', he wrote, are 'the freest people on earth and have risen the highest in the human scale.' British educators, scientists, philosophers, poets, statesmen, and artists, he continued, 'have made English life the most worthy of being lived'.[4]

Another innovator who shared their business interests was Francisco Pereira Passos. Like the Prado brothers, he was the son of large coffee planters, but in the less prosperous province of Rio de Janeiro. Perhaps this explains why he took the engineering course at the military school, along with many who were less well placed, instead of entering the law school or medical faculty.

[1] Nazareth Prado, ed., *Antonio Prado no imperio e na republica: seus discursos e actos colligidos e apresentados por sua filha* (Rio: Briguiet, 1929), p. 18; speeches of Antônio Prado in São Paulo (state), Assembléia Legislativa, *Anais*, 1866, pp. 233, 234, 358, 367.
[2] José Honório Rodrigues, *Notícia de vária história* (Rio: Livraria São José, 1951), pp. 86–91.
[3] Eduardo Prado, *Catalogue de la bibliothèque Eduardo Prado* (São Paulo: Typ. Brasil de Rothschild, 1916); Nazareth Prado, ed., *Antonio Prado*, p. 351; Renato Mendonça, *Um diplomata na côrte de Inglaterra; o barão do Penedo e sua época*, Brasiliana, 219 (São Paulo: Editôra Nacional, 1942), pp. 413–14.
[4] Eduardo Prado, *Collectaneas*, 4 vols. (São Paulo: Escola Typographica Salesiana, 1904–5), I, 255–6.

After graduation he went to France to complete his studies, but, despite this fact, his biographer describes him as 'an Englishman magnificently adapted to Brazil'. He dressed in London styles, traveled frequently to England, and had frequent and close relationships with Englishmen in Brazil. He read widely and was especially familiar, we are told, with the works of Adam Smith, John Stuart Mill, Charles Darwin, and Herbert Spencer.[1]

Railroads were his chief concern when he first returned from Europe. He was soon awarded a post as engineer for the Estrada de Ferro Dom Pedro Segundo. He was later named government inspector for the São Paulo Railway Company, Ltd, and got along so well with its manager that the government chose him in 1871 to go to England to settle all outstanding questions between the government and this railway. He spent two years in London at that time with occasional trips to Europe to study inclined planes at the request of Mauá. On return he sold these technical studies to Mauá for use in the ascent of the mountain range toward Petrópolis, and accepted the job of directing the Ponta d'Areia foundry, where he urged Mauá to start building railroad cars. In 1877 he was named managing director of the Estrada de Ferro D. Pedro II. He remained in that post for three years and returned to it in 1896 for an equal period. Among his other enterprises was the very profitable, tourist-oriented Corcovado railway, in which he used the techniques he had earlier suggested to Mauá.

Urban improvements were another of his interests. He not only created an urban transport company in Rio de Janeiro, but was also named city engineer there, eventually became prefect, and carried out an extensive program to remodel the city. Curiously, Antônio Prado was also prefect in São Paulo at a time of impressive urban improvements.[2]

Shipping companies, just as railways and urban improvements, were of interest to others besides Mauá. José Antônio Pimenta Bueno, *marquês* de São Vicente (1803–78), had not only been Mauá's partner in the enterprise which led to the creation of the

[1] Raymundo Austregesilo de Athayde, *Pereira Passos, o reformador do Rio de Janeiro; biografia e historia* (Rio: Editôra 'A Noite', [1944?]), pp. 76, 108.

[2] *Ibid.* pp. 168–9 and *passim*; Mauá, *Autobiografia*, p. 186; Ernani Silva Bruno, *História e tradições da cidade de São Paulo*, 3 vols. (Rio: José Olympio, 1954), III, 1001–8.

São Paulo Railway, but was also connected with the Amazon Steam Navigation Company. In 1877 he defended the latter company in the Senate, urging a larger subsidy on the ingenuous ground that 'the management in London is made up of honorable men... We must believe in the published balance sheets'.[1] Five years later the company offered him twenty *contos* (over £2,000) in recognition of his 'important services'.[2] Shipping also interested one of the intimates at the *barão* do Penedo's residence in London, a young naval officer named Artur Silveira da Mota, later *barão* de Jaceguai (1843–1914). His strong attachment to Britain perhaps led him to dream of creating a Brazilian transatlantic steamship line to imitate the example set by the Royal Mail Steamship Line or Lamport & Holt. In any case, in 1890 he organized the Lloyd Brasileiro company, which combined four pre-existing smaller lines, a shipyard, and a foundry. It began operations with 64 steamers and soon secured a virtual monopoly of all coastwise traffic when this trade was restricted to Brazilian companies.[3]

Credit facilities are basic to a modernizing economy. As we have noted, Mauá was deeply involved in banking activities and Prado made the Banco do Comércio e Indústria one of São Paulo's major financial institutions. Francisco de Figueiredo, *visconde* and later *conde* de Figueiredo, was another innovator known for the banking ventures he launched. He learned from the British some of the less admirable qualities of the capitalistic system.

---

[1] José Antonio Pimenta Bueno, *marquês* de São Vicente, *Companhia de Navegacão do Amazonas. Discurso proferido no Senado na sessão de 8 de outubro de 1877* (n.p., n.d.), p. 7; also note his *Memoria justificativa dos planos apresentados ao governo imperial para o prolongamento da Estrada de Ferro de S. Paulo* (Rio: Imp. Nacional, 1876).

[2] Joaquim Nabuco, 'Correspondencia', *Jornal do commercio*, 28 July 1882, p. 3.

[3] Mendonça, *Um diplomata na côrte de Inglaterra*, p. 334; Alexandre José Barbosa Lima Sobrinho, *Artur Jaceguai, ensaio bio-bibliográfico*, Coleção Afrânio Peixoto, 3 (Rio: Publicações da Academia Brasileira de Letras, 1955), pp. 69, 78; West, 'Foreigner in Brazilian Technology', pp. 724–7; Herculano Marques Inglez de Souza, 'O commercio e as leis commerciais do Brasil', *Jornal do commercio*, 2 Oct. 1915, p. 3. On Jaceguai's attachment to Britain see Arthur Silveira da Motta, *barão* de Jaceguay, *De aspirante a almirante*, [*Vol. IV:*] *1860–1902. Minha fé de officio documentada, 1893–1900* (Mendes, R.J.: Typ. Cia. Industrial Santa Rita, 1906), pp. 7, 25, 82–103 *passim*, 169; his father, José Ignacio Silveira da Motta, was a liberal politician fond of citing the British example, as in his *Degeneração do sistema representativo* [*discurso na Conferência Radical, 25.4.1869*] (Rio: Typ. Americana, 1869), pp. 3, 8, 19, 20, 23. On Jaceguai also see Raul Tavares, 'Almirante Arthur Jaceguay', in Arthur Silveira da Motta, *barão* de Jaceguay, *Reminiscencias da guerra do Paraguay* (Rio: 'A Noite', 1935), pp. 5–80.

Born in 1843, he had become manager of his father's merchant house at the age of eighteen. In 1871 the Rebouças brothers vainly hoped he would back their first railway enterprise, since he was 'the richest capitalist that deals with Paraná'. Figueiredo dreamed up instead a fantastic railway scheme to link Pernambuco with Chile. He was one of the major promoters, along with William Henry Holman, manager of the Rio Gas Company, of the Rio de Janeiro Flour Mills and Granaries, Ltd, and the two of them invested enough in it to secure for themselves the right to choose the contractor for the flour mill, a choice that brought them a 'kick-back' from the latter. Besides being an officer in a shipping company, Figueiredo later organized the Companhia de Obras Hydraulicas no Brasil to operate wharves and dock works in Rio de Janeiro, Pernambuco, and elsewhere. But it was as a banker that he truly prospered. He became a director of the Banco do Brasil in 1879, founded another bank in 1886, and became best known for the Banco Nacional do Brasil founded in 1889 and immediately the subject of bitter controversy. Along with it he tried unsuccessfully to organize a bank in London with interlocking directorates to be called the National Bank of Brazil, Ltd. His various activities—whether scrupulous or not —link him both to the British and to Brazil's developmental efforts.[1]

The British influence upon all these men is notable. In the case of Mauá, it is fair to say that his early contact with Richard Carruthers was of paramount importance. In 1861 he wrote to Carruthers to say that 'all that is good in me' was 'inspired into my youthful mind thirty years ago by you'.[2] He believed that his vision of an industrialized, modern society was derived from his early visit to England. In all his entrepreneurial activity he

---

[1] Rebouças, *Diário*, p. 192; Borstel to Department of State, Recife, 15 Nov. 1888, NA/DS, Despatches Consuls, Pernambuco, 1888, enclosure in no. 59; Richard Graham, 'A British Industry in Brazil: Rio Flour Mills, 1886–1920', *Business History*, VIII (1966), 14, 21; Augusto Victorino Alves Sacramento Blake, *Diccionario bibliographico brazileiro*, 7 vols. (Rio: Typ. Nacional, 1883–1902), II, 446; West, 'Foreigner in Brazilian Technology', pp. 844, 847; Raimundo Magalhães Júnior, *Rui, o homem e o mito*, Retratos do Brasil, 27 (Rio: Civilização Brasileira, 1964), 50–1, 60–1, 70, 77.

[2] Mauá quoted by Marchant, 'A New Portrait of Mauá the Banker', p. 420; also see Mauá, *Autobiografia*, p. 101.

was in close contact with the British. He depended almost exclusively upon Englishmen for technical advice and managerial ability.[1]

The visit of the Rebouças brothers to the International Exposition in 1862, is, in its effects, reminiscent of Mauá's inspection of the Bristol foundry in 1840. The Exposition was the seedbed for all their important new departures: there Antônio studied railroad equipment, André inspected harbor works and dry docks and they both revealed an interest in developing Brazilian lumber resources.

One of the most important influences upon André Rebouças was exercised by the British engineer Charles Neate. In 1866 André was appointed to take Neate's place as chief engineer in charge of constructing a government-financed quay. Neate had proved none too successful in his efforts up to that point, for the foundations had crumbled beneath his work. André conducted himself with the greatest tact and the Britisher deeply appreciated this consideration. Rebouças asked Neate to remain on until he became familiar with the works, and he recorded in his diary that Neate expressed his pleasure at being succeeded by 'an engineer like me, saying I was truly the ablest engineer he had met in Brazil'. Neate went out of his way to warn Rebouças of intrigues going on behind the scenes, and Rebouças returned the favor by praising this foreigner before the prime minister. After Neate left, Rebouças kept up a steady correspondence with him, and Neate acted as the London agent for Rebouças' proposed northeastern railway enterprise. When Rebouças went to London in 1873, Neate arranged valuable professional contacts, and nine years later when Rebouças temporarily moved to London, it was in Neate's office that he began work elaborating plans for Brazilian port improvements. The British engineer took care to introduce him to other businessmen in London, and this led to consulting fees even after Rebouças returned home in 1883. When Neate visited Rio de Janeiro again he made sure to call

[1] Mauá, *Autobiografia*, pp. 130n., 212. For further evidence of the British influence upon him see Ganns, 'Introdução', *ibid*. p. 43; Faria, *Mauá*, pp. 52, 66, 68, 72, 74; Besouchet, *Mauá e seu tempo*, p. 92; Marchant, 'A New Portrait of Mauá the Banker', p. 412n.; J. J. Aubertin, 'O algodão [Carta a Fidelis Preta]', *Correio paulistano*, 21 July 1864, p. 3.

on Rebouças and enhanced the Brazilian's prestige by publicly praising his work.[1]

Luís Tarqüínio's attachment to John Gasper Bruderer was not unlike Mauá's admiration for Richard Carruthers. In 1893 he wrote the Englishman that 'without you no one would speak of poor Luís Tarqüínio...I am obliged to thank you for everything which you have done for me, taking me out of nowhere and placing me where everyone pays me respect'.[2] He repeatedly cited the English example in other connexions and evidently remained closely linked to Britain for many years. As his biographer put it, England was for him 'the great teacher', as it was to a lesser degree for other innovators like Antônio and Eduardo Prado and Pereira Passos.[3]

Though others have portrayed Mauá as Brazil's first economic nationalist bravely fighting off the foreigner, an unbiased reading of the record clearly reveals Mauá as a willing instrument in the extension of British economic power in Brazil. He tried unsuccessfully to get his most important industrial undertaking, the foundry and shipyard, transferred to British hands. His two most prosperous enterprises—the gas works and the Companhia de Navegação do Amazonas—were both sold to British companies he had promoted for this purpose. In the case of the Amazon company, the deal included almost a million acres of Brazilian lands. Mauá was also instrumental in organizing the Brazilian Submarine Telegraph Company, Ltd, to which he made a gift of the concession which he held for linking Brazil to Portugal by cable. Furthermore, he attempted unsuccessfully in 1864–5 to amalgamate his bank with the London and Brazilian Bank. He fully believed in the value of English capital for Brazil, and his support of the Recife and São Francisco railway was a direct result of his desire to stimulate British investments.[4] He defended

---

[1] Rebouças, *Diário*, pp. 136–9, 149, 152, 162, 190, 273, 279, 295, 295n., 296, 297, 298, 301; W. T. Youle, his partner in the dock company, and Henry Edward Hargreaves, the importer-industrialist, were also among André's personal friends, pp. 194, 201, 244, 268; Rebouças to José Americo dos Santos, 17 Jan. 1897, in *ibid.* p. 440; Rebouças, *Melhoramento do porto*, p. 10.

[2] Tarqüínio quoted by Madureira do Pinho, *Luís Tarqüínio*, p. 6. [3] *Ibid.* p. 4.

[4] Nelson Werneck Sodré, *História da burguesia brasileira*, Retratos do Brasil, 22 (Rio: Civilização Brasileira, 1964), p. 140; Joel Rufino dos Santos, *et al.*, *Da independência à*

Englishmen in their relations with Brazilian companies even when he knew the former were wrong, simply to preserve the 'credit of Brazil in London'.[1] Only isolated phrases taken out of context from his autobiography can suggest any concern for keeping the Brazilian economy in the hands of Brazilians. What he was interested in was the modernization of the country, and the means to that end was the capitalist system in the hands of businessmen of any nationality.

Tarqüínio and the Rebouças brothers similarly believed in the value of British investment for Brazil. Tarqüínio opposed measures which he feared would frighten foreign capital away, since he believed that Brazil's progress depended upon it. André probably spoke also for his brother when he wrote that 'it is not possible to render greater service to Brazil than unceasingly to promote the importation and fixation of foreign capital', especially for 'the great enterprises of public interest'. By foreign capital he meant 'capital which comes principally from London, which, thanks to the wisdom of the Anglo-Saxon race, is the treasury of the whole world'. On the other hand, he was not blind to some of the unfavorable aspects of foreign investment. He complained about the large cost of administration charged by the English companies that received guaranteed interest, especially the premiums and commissions paid in London to consultants, brokers, and promoters. What he thought best was British capital with Brazilian administration and technical direction. In any case, these men all felt that nationality was of less importance than the entrepreneurial mentality.[2]

Contacts with the British did not produce this mentality in

república, Coleção História Nova, 7 (Rio: Campanha de Assistência ao Estudante, Ministério da Educação e Cultura, 1964), pp. 41–5; Mauá, *Autobiografia*, pp. 112n., 116, 143–5, 148, 148n., 151n., 152–3, 208–11, 269; Ganns, 'Introdução', *ibid.* p. 77; Faria, *Mauá*, p. 143; files on Rio de Janeiro Gas Company, Ltd, and Amazon Steam Navigation Company, Ltd, BT 31/1064/1912C and BT 31/14438/6238; Pareceres do Conselho de Estado, Nov. 1876, AN, Cod. 783, 1, 17, pp. 135–47; David Joslin, *A Century of Banking in Latin America: to Commemorate the Centenary in 1962 of the Bank of London and South America, Limited* (London: Oxford Univ. Press, 1963), pp. 69–74, 79.

[1] Mauá, *Autobiografia*, p. 182.

[2] Luiz Tarquinio, *A solução da crise; artigos publicados na imprensa da capital federal* (Salvador: Imp. Popular, 1892), p. 27; André Rebouças, *Agricultura nacional, estudos economicos; propaganda abolicionista e democratica* (Rio: Lamoureux, 1883), pp. 277–8, 283, 338; Rebouças, *Diário*, p. 172.

these men. The myriad influences sweeping over Brazil from abroad, the rapid creation of business opportunities by the burgeoning export business, and the complex nature of human personality, all combined to lead them to this end. As economic conditions were altered, innovators—abnormal in the earlier traditional society—were rewarded and encouraged and, because of their success, began to influence others. But the unusual personalities that were impelled toward entrepreneurial activity were in special need of encouragement from abroad since they were still faced with many traits of the traditional society at home. So they turned to Britain, the industrial giant of the era, for their models and their beliefs. Naturally, others who were similarly engaged in opening up new avenues to business success were in closer contact with the French or the Germans; if I have selected those influenced by the British, it is to pursue my technique of exploring one theme within a larger process, much as a biographer sheds light on an era while examining the life of one man.

The personality of the entrepreneur is a subject much too vast for examination here.[1] But it is evident that it is of basic importance in explaining why Mauá, the Prados, Pereira Passos, the Rebouças, and Tarqüínio were driven toward entrepreneurship. The case of the Rebouças brothers is illustrative of the complexity

---

[1] The literature on entrepreneurship is extensive. See especially Bert F. Hoselitz, *Sociological Aspects of Economic Growth* (Glencoe, Ill.: Free Press, 1960), pp. 151–2; and Albert O. Hirschman, *The Strategy of Economic Development* (New Haven: Yale Univ. Press, 1958), pp. 3, 36; also see Albert Lauterbach, *Enterprise in Latin America: Business Attitudes in a Developing Economy* (Ithaca, N.Y.: Cornell Univ. Press, 1966), pp. x–xii, 156–9; Alec P. Alexander, 'Industrial Entrepreneurship in Turkey: Origins and Growth', *Economic Development and Cultural Change*, VIII (July 1960), 349–65; Henry G. Aubrey, 'Industrial Investment Decisions: a Comparative Analysis', *Journal of Economic History*, XV (1955), pp. 337–9, 343–6; cf. comment by James Baster, *ibid.* pp. 354–5; Alexander Gerschenkron, 'Social Attitudes, Entrepreneurship and Economic Development', *International Social Science Bulletin*, VI (1954), 252–8; Thomas C. Cochran, '"Social Attitudes, Entrepreneurship, and Economic Development": Some Comments'; David S. Landes, '"Social Attitudes, Entrepreneurship, and Economic Development": a Comment'; John E. Sawyer, 'In Defense of an Approach: A comment on Professor Gerschenkron's "Social Attitudes, Entrepreneurship, and Economic Development"', *Explorations in Entrepreneurial History*, VI (1954), 181–3, 245–72, 273–86; Bert F. Hoselitz, 'Entrepreneurship and Capital Formation in France and Britain since 1700', and Marion J. Levy, 'Some Social Obstacles to "Capital Formation" in "Underdeveloped Areas"', in Universities—National Bureau Committee for Economic Research, *Capital Formation and Economic Growth, a Conference* (Princeton, N.J.: Princeton Univ. Press, 1955), pp. 291–337, 441–501.

of the problem and the danger of ascribing too much importance to their contacts with the British. To begin with, their race sometimes led to discrimination, and one can easily imagine the emotional effects this would have had upon sons of a national legislator who would otherwise be automatically entitled to deference. André, at least, seems to have compensated for this by over-valuing himself. As a young lieutenant during the conflict with Paraguay he considered it his place to advise the generals on the prosecution of the war. Whenever he failed to achieve his aspirations, he attributed it to persecution, writing that Brazil was 'the sad battlefield for the basest passions and vilest interests'. Both brothers seem to have been unusually attached to their father, deferring to his every wish, sentimentally depending upon him to advise them on all decisions. Although Antônio did get married, André occasionally expressed a great repugnance toward sex. It was with great admiration that he regarded the mother of one of his closest friends as 'the most manly woman I know'. The brothers were not ordinary nor conventionally minded. It is, therefore, difficult to know to what extent their affinity for the British was cause or effect of their innovative qualities.[1]

Nor can we blame the British influence if some of these men failed. And failures were frequent. Not only did Mauá finally fail in business, but his whole career was marked by a series of business defeats and large amounts written off to capital loss.[2] The Rebouças brothers were never successful in an enterprise, and supported themselves primarily from their salaries as engineers.

The opposition of the traditional society to their efforts was evidently one cause of failure. Despite the titles given Mauá and despite the position of emperor's protégé enjoyed by André Rebouças, it is evident that the aristocracy did not cooperate enthusiastically in their attempts at modernization. Large landed interests in Paraná frustrated not only the Rebouças brothers' efforts to construct a railway there, but also André's attempt to found a lumber company that would exploit for the first time one

---

[1] Rebouças, *Diário*, pp. 131, 196, 204; Veríssimo, *André Rebouças*, pp. 8, 12, 19–21, 29, 34–51, 56, 83; Rebouças, *Agricultura nacional*, pp. 220, 222n.

[2] Mauá, *Autobiografia*, pp. 184–7, 189.

of the natural resources of the region. Mauá was made constantly aware of the low esteem in which he was held by the traditional upper class.[1] The best evidence of this opposition to change is to be found in the policies of the government, dominated as it was by plantation interests. As André Rebouças complained, government officials were 'absolutist, restrictive, and routine-minded to the marrow of their bones! Poor Brazil that still has such men deciding its destiny'.[2] The failure of the government consistently to maintain protective tariffs was one of the most difficult problems posed for the industrialists. Its refusal to extend credit was what finally brought down Mauá. The constant battle with government officials in a country where company law still required their approval for practically all economic activities was a further deterrent to success. This was especially exasperating in view of the dilatory nature of governmental affairs combined with the rapid turnover in the upper echelons of bureaucracy.

But their own mistakes must not be overlooked. The tendency toward over-extension so natural for innovators in a society where better ways to do things are evident everywhere presented a dangerous temptation to Mauá and the Rebouças. In addition to those enterprises already mentioned, Mauá was connected with a drayage company, a floating dock, a waterworks, a candle factory, a gold mine, a tannery, and a tramway. Antônio Rebouças dreamed of a plank-road company in the heart of the Amazon, and, along with his brother, planned a company to supply water for Rio de Janeiro.[3] André possessed a special notebook in which to list 'various projects designed to accelerate the progress of the empire'.[4] The construction of telegraph lines,

---

[1] Albino José Barbosa de Oliveira, *Memórias de um magistrado do império*, ed. Américo Jacobina Lacombe, Brasiliana, 231 (São Paulo: Editôra Nacional, 1943), pp. 260-1, 283-5; Besouchet, 'Introdução', in Mauá, *Correspondência política*, p. 13; Besouchet, *Mauá e seu tempo*, p. 77; Faria, *Mauá*, p. 52. His problems were typical of the emerging entrepreneur in underdeveloped areas, see Max F. Millikan and Donald L. M. Blackmer, eds., *The Emerging Nations, Their Growth and United States Policy* (Boston: Little, Brown, 1961), p. 38.

[2] Rebouças, *Diário*, p. 164.

[3] Antonio Rebouças, *Apontamentos sobre a via de communicação do Rio Madeira* (Rio: Typ. Nacional, 1870); Antonio Rebouças, *Relatorio da commissão de estudos do abastecimento d'agua desta capital* (Rio: Typ. Nacional, 1871); Veríssimo, *André Rebouças*, pp. 99-110.

[4] Rebouças, *Diário*, p. 181.

canals, bridges and other urban improvements, all received his attention, and he was involved to a greater or lesser degree in plans for harbor works in Maranhão, Pernambuco, Bahia, and Rio Grande do Sul. André also planned a river-boat enterprise, a woolens factory, a gas company, and a coal mine.[1] It was probably with reason that he was criticized in the Senate for being a man of 'many enterprises'. In view of what he himself called 'the immense effort that it takes to promote enterprises in Brazil', it would have been better had he concentrated more of his effort on making one or two companies successful.[2] Tarqüínio provides a sharp contrast, for, by limiting himself to the textile business, he died a highly successful man.

In addition, there was the difficulty of matching capital resources with technical competence and administrative ability, that is, of really being an entrepreneur. Mauá seems to have always encountered difficulty in recruiting suitable personnel either in terms of business sense and commercial integrity, or with reference to adequate technical education. The first managers of his foundry and shipyard were British, although in the 1870s he placed Pereira Passos in charge. Most of his firms were directed by foreigners. He never worked in an industrial enterprise himself, much preferring the role of financier and over-all administrator to that of technician. The Rebouças, on the other hand, had the technical knowledge and were directly engaged in the operation of their enterprises, but lacked adequate capital. To secure it they were constantly in a dither. Thus, when major stockholders in the dock company began heavy selling of their partially paid-up stock, Rebouças had to look frantically for new investors.[3] Again in contrast, Tarqüínio both had capital and provided personal direction to his enterprise. The Prado family could count on the tremendous capital resources provided by one of the biggest coffee plantations in Brazil, and Pereira Passos, although less wealthy, could compensate for this fact by the excellent con-

[1] Rebouças, *Agricultura nacional*, p. 321; Rebouças, *Diário*, pp. 201, 221; Veríssimo, *André Rebouças, passim*.
[2] Rebouças, *Diário*, pp. 195, 265.
[3] Mauá, *Autobiografia*, pp. 125, 160, 163–4, 165; Rebouças, *Diário*, p. 197; Rebouças to Rangel da Costa, 11 Aug. 1894, in *ibid.* p. 417; Veríssimo, *André Rebouças*, p. 84.

nexions established through his old family and by his own technical knowledge. It is clear that contacts with the British are not the most important consideration in evaluating the success or failure of these businessmen, just as British influence was not solely responsible for impelling them toward entrepreneurial activity. But the British impact upon them was very large nevertheless.

The ideas and attitudes of these British-influenced entrepreneurs are a final aspect of this inquiry. They were caught up by the idea of capitalism, by the belief in industrialization, and by a faith in work and practicality. Once again, it is not suggested here that Britain was the only place to which entrepreneurs could turn for these concepts. Rather, the point is that these men, whom we have chosen to examine because of their British connexions, were dominated by these beliefs. Having said this, the fact remains that they often did turn to Britain for reinforcement of their guiding principles.

Attitudes regarding 'risk-taking' and 'profit-making' are evidently of key importance to development. We have noted how the willingness to risk money for the sake of possible profits lay at the root of the dynamic and creative aspects of the Victorian age. This spirit stood in direct opposition to the static agrarian life of Brazil, where profits were still considered akin to usury. As Mauá complained, it was generally thought that the state would be defrauded if the recipient of a government contract did not lose on his venture. He believed that, on the contrary, profit was the driving force of all progress: 'The powerful cooperation of labor and capital for the creation of wealth can only be obtained with the indispensable condition of finding corresponding remuneration.'[1]

Industrialization was the goal toward which capitalism would impel the nation. Few things made André Rebouças angrier than the oft-repeated statement that Brazil must not industrialize because it was an 'essentially agricultural' nation. If there were any really agricultural country, he said, it was England, 'where they

---

[1] Mauá, *Autobiografia*, pp. 115, 202; cf. Everett E. Hagen, *On the Theory of Social Change: How Economic Growth Begins* (Homewood, Ill.: Dorsey, 1962), p. 37n.

love rural life above everything else'. Since real agricultural development was obviously unlikely in Brazil under the then existing system, it was ridiculous to oppose industry.[1] Similarly, the *barão* do Penedo, despite his connexions with the more traditional sectors in Brazil, was sufficiently influenced by his long residence in London as Brazilian minister and his close connexions with the British financial and business community to believe in industrialization and oppose the idea that Brazil was 'destined to have an exclusively agricultural setup'. He maintained that 'nothing can deny' Brazil's 'legitimate ambitions to enter the area of manufacturing'. Industry, he felt, was the road to perfection: it was the 'agent of man's productive power' and would link Brazil to 'the immense chain of civilization's achievements'. It was for this reason that he insisted that his country should take a full part in the International Exposition of 1862, for he maintained the Brazilian government should imitate England by taking a more direct interest in the nation's industrial development.[2]

The best evidence of their belief in industrialization and capitalism, of course, was precisely the fact that these men were entrepreneurs. Mauá, as we have seen, adopted the basic principles of capitalistic economic organization. He used money to make profits and he understood the nature of credit. He saw the superiority of industry as an economic activity both for the investor and for the nation. He welcomed the use of new technological processes, casting traditional methods aside. Finally, he took risks where necessary and undertook projects without assurance of success. As Joaquim Nabuco later said, his 'great breadth of interests and industrial courage' made him 'a powerful factor in the opening up and progress of our country'.[3]

André and Antônio Rebouças also felt that the nation would be better served by profit-making entrepreneurs than by publicly owned establishments. Furthermore, although they concentrated

---

[1] Rebouças, *Agricultura nacional*, p. 357.
[2] Penedo, *Relatorio sobre a exposição*, pp. v, xvi, xxxi, xxxvi, lxxvii.
[3] Joaquim Nabuco, *Um estadista do imperio, Nabuco de Araujo. Sua vida, suas opiniões, sua época*, [2nd ed.?], 2 vols. (Rio & São Paulo: Civilização Brasileira & Editôra Nacional, 1936), II, 306n.

on railroads, dock companies, and timberlands development, a belief in industrialization was implicit in most of their activities. André campaigned for the creation of central sugar factories as a move in this direction: his ideal was for Brazil to export nothing but manufactured goods, and the first step toward this goal, he argued, would be domestic processing of Brazil's raw materials, whether refined sugar, woven cloth, finished cigars and cigarettes, or chocolate. Furthermore, he actively considered organizing a company to reopen an abandoned iron works, thus laying the basis for further industrial growth.[1] As a teacher at the engineering school from the 1860s until the end of the empire—a position through which he influenced a whole generation of young 'doers' with whom he kept in touch for years afterwards—he was recognized as the 'representative of new ideas' and a spokesman for the belief in capitalism and industrialism.[2]

Tarqüínio also promoted the belief in industry and those policies which would encourage private investment. He urged that the national internal debt be converted to a lower interest rate so that capitalists would prefer industrial investments, and he pointed to England as an example of a country where this had been done successfully. He opposed rural credit banks because, he said, they enabled large landowners to continue their conspicuous consumption, while neglecting the needs of industry. If he did not support high tariffs it was not because he did not believe in industrialization, but because he was beguiled by the association of free trade and industry in England.[3]

Another quality which characterized these entrepreneurs was their belief in the value of work. The traditional society which they sought to destroy had not inculcated the value of constant toil. In the slave society of mid-nineteenth-century Brazil, work was equated with demeaned status, and not even poverty could drive respectable people to it. To suggest to them the possibility

[1] Rebouças, *Agricultura nacional*, pp. 6, 65, 147ff., 159–60, 195–6, 225, 270; Rebouças, *Diário*, pp. 169, 269; *O abolicionista; orgão da Sociedade Brasileira Contra a Escravidão*, no. 11, 1 Sept. 1881, p. 8.

[2] Rebouças, *Diário*, pp. 159, 323, and correspondence in *ibid.* pp. 383–452.

[3] Madureira do Pinho, *Luís Tarqüínio*, pp. 24, 26; Stein, *Brazilian Cotton Manufacture*, p. 92.

of employment in commerce or industry was to insult them, and one foreign observer noted that 'Labor is [considered] degrading and...custom, instead of honoring useful toil, withholds all stimulus to exertion'. The society as a whole considered inner dignity, social pleasure, intellectual exercise, or spiritual rewards a greater good than hard, disciplined work.[1] Although a cynical observer on Copacabana beach may today object that the ideal of work has still made little progress in Brazil, the fact is that the urban–industrial complexes there would have been impossible if the attitudes of the planter and slave had not been significantly altered in the last one hundred years.

The elevation of work into a positive good is one of the distinctive qualities of modernizing groups: there is so much to do, and still so few ready to do it.[2] And not only does work contribute to modernization, but, with the increasing mobility modernization brings on, it can now lead to tangible rewards on earth. The belief in the virtue of work thus acquires a peculiarly middle-class ring. Those who hope for further upward movement or fear slippage downward must engage in unrelieved effort; yet, to assert their distinctive position and justify their single-minded concentration, the means becomes the end and it is work itself that seems to make life worth living. Simultaneously, no idea can be more conveniently preached to their employees than that the latter should toil hard and constantly. Entrepreneurs believed industrious qualities would help forge a modern nation, and the British served them as a model. André Rebouças recorded with great pride that a British engineer had said he 'works like an Englishman'.[3]

[1] Thomas Ewbank, *Life in Brazil; or a Journal of a Visit to the Land of the Cocoa and the Palm* ...(New York: Harper, 1856), pp. 184, 405; also see William Scully, *Brazil: Its Provinces and Chief Cities; the Manners and Customs of the People; Agricultural, Commercial, and Other Statistics*...(London: Murray, 1866), p. 9. Cf. Felice Battaglia, *Filosofia del lavoro* (Bologna: Zuffi, 1951), pp. 41–2, 60, 68–9; John P. Gillin, 'Some Signposts for Policy', in Richard N. Adams *et al.*, *Social Change in Latin America Today* (New York: Harper for the Council on Foreign Relations, 1960), pp. 28–47; William F. Whyte and Allan R. Holmberg, 'Human Problems of U.S. Enterprise in Latin America', *Human Organization*, xv, no. 3 (fall 1956), pp. 1–40.

[2] John Friedman, 'Intellectuals in Developing Societies', *Kyklos...International Review for Social Sciences*, XIII (1960), 526, 533.

[3] Rebouças, *Diário*, p. 274.

The gospel of work was a characteristic theme of the Victorian era. It was said in England that 'the duty of work is universal... No man on God's earth has a right to be idle'. Diligence was linked to the idea of Christian vocation, the love of neighbor, and the workmanship of God.[1] Typical were the books of Samuel Smiles, who extolled the virtue of work and urged its adoption by everyone as a guiding principle of life. His most famous work, published in 1859, was entitled *Self-Help*, and its 'chief object', he wrote, was 'to stimulate youths to apply themselves diligently to right pursuits'. He told them that 'fortune is usually on the side of the industrious', and that great results were to be expected from 'sheer industry and perseverance'. He saw that 'the men who have most moved the world have not been so much men of genius, strictly so called, as men of...untiring perseverance; not so often the gifted...as those who have applied themselves diligently to their work...It is indeed marvellous what continuous application will effect in the commonest of things.' Besides other titles such as *Character* (1871), *Thrift* (1875), and *Duty* (1880), there was one significantly entitled *Life and Labour* (1887). It began with the statement that 'Every man worth calling a man should be willing and able to work'.[2]

In Brazil Smiles and his countrymen filled the same pulpit. J. J. Aubertin, the popular superintendent of the São Paulo Railway, announced that 'the man who has too much pride to work, should also be too proud to live', adding that 'he who works enjoys happiness and health; poverty and misfortune are the natural attribute of the lazy man'. The books of Samuel Smiles were translated into Portuguese and were being sold in Rio de Janeiro in the 1880s. A questionnaire sent out by a Brazilian writer to persons who grew up during the last quarter of the nineteenth century turned up several who had read Smiles in that era. One of them stated that as a boy he had read 'all the books

[1] William Cunningham, *The Gospel of Work: Four Lectures on Christian Ethics* (Cambridge Univ. Press, 1902), pp. 29, 39, 53, and esp. 42.
[2] Samuel Smiles, *Self-Help with Illustrations of Conduct & Perseverance* (London: Murray, 1958), pp. 33, 115, 116, 117–18, and 'Introduction' by Asa Briggs, pp. 11–14; Samuel Smiles, *Life and Labour, or Characteristics of Men of Industry, Culture and Genius* (London: Murray, 1916), p. 1; Aileen Smiles, *Samuel Smiles and His Surroundings* (London: Hale, 1956).

of Samuel Smiles' and another said he had even been taught to admire Smiles in school.[1]

Brazilian entrepreneurs and innovators—especially those influenced by the British—continued the task of proselytizing. Mauá asserted that '*work* is the perennial fountain of public prosperity, and is not only worthy of...protection, but even of high honor'. His coat of arms expressed his idea by the legend, *Labor improbus omnia vincis*. Tavares Bastos criticized the first settlers in Brazil because they were 'anxious for wealth earned without the hallowed sweat of toil', and a merchant insisted that 'labor is ennobling' and the basis of all manly independence. André Rebouças put it this way: 'When God created the world He said to the world: move; when God created man He said to him: work.'[2]

These entrepreneurs saw that one of the obstacles to the success of their vision was the concept of work as degrading. The lower classes must learn that work was a privilege to be performed joyfully—no belief could be more helpful to the industrialist. Luís Tarqüínio leveled his guns at those 'unfortunates, ignorant of the true meaning of labor, who prefer to suffer the greatest deprivations...rather than engage in work which they consider proper only for Negroes...They forget that only ability entitles a person to choose his work'. Another Anglophile felt São Paulo was a land of promise, since the poor there did not hesitate to encourage their children toward the mechanical arts, 'thus instilling in their spirit a love of honest work'. Work, he said, was good for the poor and contributed to their moral improvement. Even the victims of a drought in Brazil's northeast needed not alms, but work, said André Rebouças. Another writer held up the end-of-century British

[1] J. J. Aubertin, *Carta dirigida aos srs. habitantes da provincia de S. Paulo por...superintendente da estrada de ferro da mesma provincia* (São Paulo: Typ. Litteraria, 1862), pp. 29, 30; *Jornal do commercio*, 2 Feb. 1882, p. 6; Gilberto Freyre, *Introdução à história da sociedade patriarcal no Brasil, III: Ordem e progresso...* 2 vols. (Rio: José Olympio, 1959), I, 178, 272; Gilberto Freyre, *Inglêses no Brasil: aspectos da influência británica sôbre a vida, a paisagem e a cultura do Brasil* (Rio: José Olympio, 1948), p. 51.

[2] Mauá, *Autobiografia*, p. 133; Besouchet, *Mauá e seu tempo*, p. 97; Aureliano Cândido Tavares Bastos, *Os males do presente e as esperanças do futuro*, 2nd ed., Brasiliana, 151 (São Paulo: Editôra Nacional, 1939), p. 30; Malvino da Silva Reis quoted in *Jornal do commercio*, 20 Jan. 1882, p. 4; Rebouças, *Agricultura nacional*, p. 15.

poor laws as an example for post-abolition Brazil: 'Who would be helped must work'; therefore, England had 'work houses' instead of 'poor houses'.[1] The gospel of work served the same needs in Brazil as it had in Britain. The importance of practical, technical education was a direct corollary of the gospel of work. The aversion to manual labor had been reinforced by the purely literary and classical nature of colonial education and the similar alienation of the nineteenth-century law academies from the practical necessities of the country. André Rebouças put forward the idea that 'We must educate the growing generation... for work... Up to now education has been merely political: from the academy of law to the electoral colleges... to national parliament. Therefore [we have] this general repugnance for productive work'. He attacked the law schools and their rhetorical training, which robbed Brazil of its best elements, teaching the planters' sons nothing of value. Another industrialist, Antônio Felício dos Santos, echoed this view saying that 'Brazil's plight is to have been always governed by the Academies, from which one goes to the Privy Council without any interval spent in the practice and experience of business'.[2]

In contrast, André Rebouças pointed to the 'eminently practical and industrious quality which constitutes the incontestable superiority of the Anglo-Saxon race'. The *barão* de Jaceguai pointed with approval to the useful instruction given British naval officers. Having spent some time as naval attaché in London, he observed 'the traditional English system of trusting more in practice than in theory' and felt that this was 'one more proof of the incomparable practical sense of the English'. He eventually became

---

[1] Tarqüínio quoted by Madureira do Pinho, *Luís Tarqüínio*, p. 73; Antonio Augusto da Costa Aguiar, 'A continuação da confissão dos meus intimos pensamentos', MS. dated 28 Sept. 1862, AMIP, cxxxi, 6422, p. 8; André Rebouças, *Soccorros publicos; a sêcca nas provincias do norte* (Rio: Leuzinger, 1877), pp. 46–7; João Fernandes Lopes, *Colonias industriaes destinadas á disciplina, correção e educação dos vagabundos regenerados pela hospitalidade e trabalho* (Recife: Typ. d'A Provincia, 1890), pp. 26–30, esp. 27; see p. 129 for connexion with abolition.

[2] Rebouças, *Agricultura*, pp. 323, 356–7; Antonio Felicio dos Santos, 'Discurso na Camara dos Deputados', Brazil, *Diário official*, 25 Apr. 1882, p. 3; also see Carlos Pontes, *Tavares Bastos (Aureliano Candido), 1839–1875*, Brasiliana, 136 (São Paulo: Editôra Nacional, 1939), p. 105.

director of the Brazilian naval academy and tried to modify its curriculum in this direction.[1]

The essentially pragmatic spirit of the British—which Nabuco described as the 'realistic, practical, positive attitude' impelling their 'spirit of progress'—was also felt through the various English secondary schools set up in Brazil. Although many of them were for girls, others were for boys and exercised a great influence. One of them was the Ginásio Anglo-Brasileiro founded in 1899 in São Paulo by Charles W. Armstrong. By 1910 the school had opened a branch in Rio de Janeiro which advertised that it followed 'the example of the best schools of England'. Although one does not usually think of nineteenth-century British education in this light, within the Brazilian context these schools exerted a strong influence toward solid practicality. The generation educated at the Anglo-Brasileiro came to maturity only after the end of the period being studied here, but it is worth noting that within a list of the leading men of Brazil in 1933, over fifty of them were its graduates, including seven engineers and six industrialists. Among the latter was Roberto Cochrane Simonsen, today considered the man chiefly responsible for launching São Paulo's industrial program after the First World War.[2]

Entrepreneurs believed in concrete results and measurable effectiveness, and the English schools in São Paulo and Rio worked to develop these qualities. These men preached the gospel of work to themselves and to their employees and so were led not only to read Samuel Smiles but to sound like him. They believed in industrial-capitalism by definition, and close contact with the British strengthened their conviction that this was the way to progress. Although this contact cannot explain why they were entrepreneurs nor be considered the cause of their failure or success, the British exerted a large influence upon these Brazilians.

[1] Rebouças, *Agricultura*, p. 13; Jaceguay, *De aspirante a almirante*, pp. 85, 98; Lima Sobrinho, *Artur Jaceguai*, pp. 127–38.

[2] Joaquim Nabuco, *Minha formação*, [?ed.], Documentos Brasileiros, 90 (Rio: José Olympio, 1957), p. 118; *Jornal do commercio*, 29 June 1910, p. 8; *Anglo-Brazilian Chronicle* (São Paulo), Mar. 1931, p. 103; British Chamber of Commerce of São Paulo and Southern Brazil, *Personalidades no Brasil; Men of Affairs in Brazil* (São Paulo: British Chamber of Commerce of São Paulo and Southern Brazil, 1933). On practical education cf. Friedman, 'Intellectuals in Developing Societies', p. 526.

Britain and the Entrepreneurs

Whether their principal interest was in railway lines, shipping companies, harbor works, iron foundries, food processing, timberlands, urban improvements, or banking institutions, their contact with the British helped shape the direction of their work. The British impact upon these restless and creative innovators may be considered one of the most intriguing aspects of the British role within the process of modernization in Brazil.

8

FREEDOM AND ASSOCIATION

The belief that government should refrain from meddling in business was one of the most important ideas adopted by the emerging innovators of Brazil in their attack upon the traditional society. The old regime had been characterized by concessions, monopolies, general prohibitions, special privileges, and chartered companies. Government agencies set prices, especially for staple foods. Business activity required a license, and its retention depended on compliance with numerous regulations and no offense to official sensibilities. The transport of goods was slowed at frequent inspection stations where lesser bureaucrats filled their time by demanding to see all requisite papers, duly notarized. Petty taxes caused inconvenience while producing little revenue. All these factors added weight to the other characteristics of a traditional society in discouraging private initiative, slowing the drive for profits, and making all businessmen the clients of the administration, that is, of the landed gentry that controlled the governmental machinery.

The modernizers in Brazil were outraged by this state of affairs and looked abroad for alternatives. The British middle class, probably because they had once been faced by similar problems, had already elaborated an ideology to combat the rigidity of that system. They had derived from Adam Smith, Jeremy Bentham, and other political economists the conviction that every individual should be free in his economic life to do as he pleased; for, it was said, society would only benefit if each man sought to do what was best for himself. Britain had made great strides while preaching this doctrine, and many young Brazilian leaders believed it was the key to British success. Just as they had derived from Britain their ideas of industrial capitalism, so they found useful principles there regarding economic freedom and financial association.

Freedom and Association

The conditions that these innovators considered essential to material change in Brazil were expressed in three closely related principles: that individual initiative must be fostered; that this aim required, first of all, government policies of *laissez faire*, especially regarding industrial activity; and that individuals could achieve their greatest success through the free-will pooling of private resources and the adoption of the 'spirit of association', that is, the joint-stock company.

The importance of individual initiative as a means toward economic growth was widely recognized among those committed to change. Mauá, in his typically awkward style, referred to 'individual liberty which so powerfully works for the creation of wealth that is the keystone of modern civilization'. Antônio Prado advocated private enterprise as the best way to overcome the barriers to economic development.[1] Lawmakers cited the British example in urging the government to encourage 'private initiative'. But others, although accepting the principle, questioned whether all of Brazil was far enough along the road towards modernity to take advantage of it. As one national legislator said, 'Pernambuco is not like [São Paulo]...where private initiative performs miracles and riches pile up. In the north, in those inhospitable regions, there is only one force, only one initiative: the government's.'[2] Others became pessimistic as they grew older. Tavares Bastos in one of his earliest works had urged that the state 'foster the free spirit of private enterprise'. Although ten years later he was still insisting on the need of 'guaranteeing the right and promoting the exercise of individual initiative', he had to admit that the problem was more complex than he had originally foreseen: 'No one doubts the superiority of individual initiative—it is preferable to anything—but what to do when it does not exist? What to do where laws, institutions,

---

[1] Irineo Evangelista de Souza, *visconde* de Mauá, *Autobiografia* (*'Exposição aos credores e ao publico'*) *seguida de 'O meio circulante no Brasil'*, ed. Claudio Ganns, 2nd ed. (Rio: Valverde, 1942), p. 239; speech by Antônio Prado, São Paulo (state), Assembléia Legislativa, *Anais*, 1866, p. 234.
[2] Francisco Octaviano Almeida Rosa quoted by Nazareth Prado, ed., *Antonio Prado no imperio e na republica: seus discursos e actos colligidos e apresentados por sua filha* (Rio: Briguiet, 1929), pp. 127–8; José Bernardo Galvão Alcofarado, *Discursos proferidos nas sessões de 27 de julho e 20 de agosto de 1886* (Rio: Imp. Nacional, 1886), p. 24.

the habits of the people, the system of government weaken or forbid it?'¹ The solution was to change the laws, the institutions, the system of government. The administration must adopt a hands-off policy. As early as 1810 the *Correio braziliense*, published in London by an émigré, had said 'the less government the better'. By the early 1850s it was not uncommon to defend the principle of *laissez faire*, and an official government commission reported that every industry should have 'the liberty... to dispose of its products and manage its own transactions and business'.² But little had really been done to put these ideals into practice. As Mauá saw it, 'A grave error has been committed by the political parties, to whom has been given the government of the state, in decreeing and maintaining restrictive laws contrary to liberty and to the true principles upon which is based the work of society.' Rebouças still found it necessary in the 1870s to urge that 'governmental action [be] circumscribed to the limits of the indispensable'. He quoted John Stuart Mill and complained that there was 'one liberty that only the Anglo-Saxon race knows in practice: *Industrial Liberty*'. For him, 'the best formula is always this simple one: maximum of individual liberty, minimum of government interference.'³

On the other hand, some progress was being made during this period, and, when Antônio Prado through private Brazilian initiative succeeded in building railroads, a young lawyer in the coffee region hailed it as an 'eloquent proof that the people no

¹ Aureliano Cândido Tavares Bastos, *Os males do presente e as esperanças do futuro*, 2nd ed., Brasiliana, 151 (São Paulo: Editôra Nacional, 1939), p. 50; Aureliano Cândido Tavares Bastos, *A provincia: estudo sobre a descentralização no Brasil*, 2nd ed., Brasiliana, 105 (São Paulo: Editôra Nacional, 1937), pp. 264, 272. Cf. Frederick Clairmonte, *Economic Liberalism and Underdevelopment: Studies in the Disintegration of an Idea* (London: Asia Publishing House, 1960), esp. pp. 20, 23.

² *Correio braziliense ou armazem literario*, IV (Feb. 1810), 188; Brazil, Commissão Encarregada da Revisão da Tarifa em Vigor, *Relatorio... que acompanhou o projecto de tarifa apresentado pela mesma commissão ao governo imperial* (Rio: Empreza Typ. 'Dous de Dezembro' de Paula Brito, 1853), p. 298. Also see Alan K. Manchester, *British Preëminence in Brazil; Its Rise and Decline: A Study in European Expansion* (Chapel Hill, N.C.: Univ. of North Carolina Press, 1933), p. 93.

³ Mauá, *Autobiografia*, p. 239 (also see p. 235); André Rebouças, *Agricultura nacional, estudos economicos; propaganda abolicionista e democratica* (Rio: Lamoureux, 1883), pp. 12, 14, 274. Also see André Rebouças, *Ao Itatiaya* (Rio: Lombaerts, 1878), p. 15.

longer need the tutelage of the government in the promotion of the country's progress'.[1] The end of the empire in 1889 meant to some at least that the era of *laissez faire* had arrived.

Joaquim Murtinho, minister of the treasury from 1898 to 1902, having forgotten an earlier statement that 'the American and English system of liberty presupposes a certain spirit of individual initiative which is dead in the greater part of our country', now asserted that it was necessary to

implant in our spirit the ideal of individualism, the ideal of energy, the ideal of work, the ideal of independence to which the English people owe all their greatness . . . Each of us must have confidence and faith in himself, work and struggle against all competitors through effort, through perseverance, and through competence. These are the principles of liberalism.

He concluded that these doctrines should be high state policy: 'To consolidate the republic is. . .principally to impregnate not only our politics but our administration and our customs in the principles of liberty. It is necessary, Mr President, to *republicanize the republic.*'[2]

Not all the members of the elite were astute enough, as was Mauá, to note that the theory of *laissez faire* must not be carried too far. He relied on government tariffs, government contracts, government concessions, government credit, and government diplomatic support for his successes.[3] A few others understood this very well, and it was said in 1853 that the government must interfere to some extent in economic life, so as to 'guarantee the free

---

[1] Martin Francisco Ribeiro de Andrada paraphrased by José Maria dos Santos, *Os republicanos paulistas e a abolição* (São Paulo: Martins, 1942), p. 136.

[2] Joaquim Murtinho quoted by Virgílio Corrêa Filho, *Joaquim Murtinho* (Rio: Imp. Nacional, 1951), p. 41; Joaquim Murtinho, *Introducções aos relatorios do dr. Joaquim Murtinho* [probably ed. José Carlos Rodrigues] (n.d., n.p. [probably Rio, 1901 or 1902]), 1897, pp. xxxii, xxxiv, italics added. Cf. Roque Spencer Maciel de Barros, *A ilustração brasileira e a idéia de universidade*, Universidade de São Paulo, Cadeira de História e Filosofia da Educação, Boletim, 241 (2) (São Paulo: Universidade de São Paulo, 1959), p. 169.

[3] Mauá's seemingly contradictory stance is discussed by E. de Castro Rebello, *Mauá, restaurando a verdade* (Rio: Universo, 1932), pp. 39–41; Mauá defended himself on the ground it could not be done otherwise in such a society, *Autobiografia*, pp. 223–4; on his use of dollar diplomacy see Renato Mendonça, *Um diplomata na côrte de Inglaterra; o barão do Penedo e sua época*, Brasiliana, 219 (São Paulo: Editôra Nacional, 1942), pp. 370–1.

and unhindered growth of industry, the right of property, technical education, and the betterment of industrial techniques'.[1]

A real controversy later developed between those who advocated government credit facilities, protective tariffs, and guaranteed interest to new industries, and those who argued that the best protection for industry was to let each enterprise sink or swim on the strength of its ability to survive in a competitive market. Some of these even confused the idea of *laissez faire* policies toward industries with the principle of free trade, thus revealing the extent to which they derived inspiration from Britain, where there had been no contradiction between these two guidelines. It is a mistake to suggest, as some have done, that the difference between those who desired government protection and those who opposed it was that the former were the modernizers, while the others were defenders of a traditional order. While it is true that some of those who advocated absolute *laissez faire* as a benefit to industry did so tongue-in-cheek because they feared change, many of them were sincerely committed to a belief in the need to industrialize.[2] Thus Luís Tarqüínio, the entrepreneur, said that 'the industrial progress of a nation, if it be real, must undergo the struggles of liberty, the incentive for the betterment of the product'. He and those who agreed with him had not understood the subtleties of the British middle class in this matter, who, like Mauá, attacked government interference but gladly accepted government support. In both Brazilian groups were those who opposed the traditional structure of economic life and what the Liberal Party called its 'privileges and monopolies'.[3]

[1] Brazil, Commissão...Tarifa, *Relatorio*, p. 249; however, the main burden of this report is to urge the lowering of tariffs; see the curiously ambiguous statement, apparently by a Brazilian, in *The Economist*, xii (1854), 170–1. Also see Cezar Augusto Vianna de Lima, *Estudo sobre o ensino primario no Reino Unido da Grã-Bretanha e Irlanda* (Rio: Imp. Nacional, 1885), p. 23.

[2] Nícia Villela Luz, *Aspectos do nacionalismo econômico brasileiro. Os esforços em prol da industrialização*, Coleção 'Revista de história', 16 (São Paulo: 'Revista de História', 1959), pp. 30, 33; Nelson Werneck Sodré, *História da burguesia brasileira*, Retratos do Brasil, 22 (Rio: Civilização Brasileira, 1964), p. 202; Rebouças, *Agricultura nacional*, pp. 43–4.

[3] Luiz Tarquinio, *Direitos de importação em ouro. Cartas dirigidas ao ministro da fazenda cons. Ruy Barbosa e ao dr. Aristides Galvão de Queiroz seguidas de considerações sobre as tarifas do*

Freedom and Association

The third condition considered basic by the economic innovators of that era was the freedom to associate their capital in limited liability companies without prior governmental authorization. If one remembers that ordinarily one who contracts a debt is responsible for its repayment to the full extent of his property, it is not surprising that governments long regarded with much caution a system where, as in a modern company, the shareholders lose only their investment if the enterprise fails. In England, for instance, companies of this sort were chartered by special act of parliament until the nineteenth century. The rise of the middle class to power in 1832 meant the political success of capitalists anxious to make limited liability no longer a special privilege but the right of all. A series of company laws were passed culminating in the Companies Registration Act of 1862 which made it possible to have all these advantages simply by registering the company, that is, by depositing at the designated office a few papers regarding the nature, purpose, organizers, and capital of the company.[1]

Brazilians were much impressed. Precisely in 1862 Antônio Rebouças explained that in advanced countries of that day, 'private persons associate and unite their capital, in order to make it bear fruit for themselves and for the progress of their country. It was the spirit of association that raised England to the degree of wealth and prosperity that it now reveals, and that a long time ago placed the English nation as a leader of Europe in the industrial movement.' Mauá had elaborated the same theme ten years earlier:

The spirit of association, gentlemen, is one of the strongest factors of prosperity of any country, and is, so to speak, the soul of progress... The spirit of association is responsible for the greatness and prosperity

Brazil e da União americana (Salvador: Imp. Popular, 1890), *passim* (the quoted statement is on p. 32); Péricles Madureira do Pinho, *Luís Tarqüínio, pioneiro da justiça social no Brasil* (Salvador: Imp. Vitória, 1944), pp. 64–7; Liberal Party Manifesto in Americo Brasiliense de Almeida Mello, ed., *Os programas dos partidos e o 2º império. Primeira parte: exposição de principios* (São Paulo: Seckler, 1878), p. 38.

[1] Bishop Carleton Hunt, *The Development of the Business Corporation in England, 1800–1867* (Cambridge, Mass.: Harvard Univ. Press, 1936); Geoffrey Todd, 'Some Aspects of Joint Stock Companies, 1844–1900', *Economic History Review*, IV (Oct. 1932), 46–71; Sylvio Marcondes Machado, *Ensaio sôbre a sociedade de responsabilidade limitada* (São Paulo: n.p., 1940), pp. 23–30.

of England, for it furnishes the means of carrying out those gigantic enterprises which increase the value of every corner of the country... The spirit of association provided that country in twenty years with 1600 leagues of railroads which, crossing the country in all directions, take abundance and cheapness to all parts.[1]

But whereas France had copied major aspects of the English legislation of 1862 the very next year and Belgium soon followed, Brazil long retained the provisions of the Brazilian commercial code of 1850—actually drafted in 1835—which required previous authorization from the government for the organization of any limited liability company.[2]

The new elite saw that code as a red flag, challenging them to gore the restrictive spirit that produced it. André Rebouças complained that whereas the government's task was to protect 'individual initiative, the spirit of association, in short, Liberty', instead it acted in ignorance of the 'holy principles of Economic Science, killing off individual initiative in its cradle and smothering the spirit of association even in its most tenuous manifestations'. For him the task ahead was clear: 'Open room for individual initiative and the spirit of association: cast down the barriers that still impede free movement on the road of progress.'[3] Other reformers of the era joined the chorus, linking 'freedom of industry' and 'freedom of association, all incompatible with restrictions and privileges, monopolies and prohibitions'.[4]

In the 1850s Mauá had tried to get around the restrictions of the code by organizing a banking firm with silent partners and then dividing up its 'dormant' capital into shares. As he said, he noted the insufficiency of Brazil's banking structure and was 'over-

---

[1] Antônio Rebouças in Francisco Carvalho Moreira, *barão do Penedo, Relatorio sobre a exposição internacional de 1862* (London: Brettell, 1863), p. 198; Mauá quoted by *Jornal do commercio*, 3 Mar. 1851, in Mauá, *Autobiografia*, p. 127n.

[2] Art. 295, Lei n. 556 de 25 de junho de 1850, Brazil, Laws, statutes, etc., *Colleção das leis do imperio do Brasil* (Rio: Imp. Nacional, 1850 [reprinted 1909]), p. 80; British merchants were satisfied with the code, for it protected commercial interests, *The Rio Mercantile Journal*, 19 Feb. 1850, p. 12; Joaquim Thomas de Amaral to Paulino José Soares de Sousa, London, 8 Apr. 1851, AHI, 216/2/15, no. 22. On the history of the code see Herculano Marques Inglez de Souza, 'O commercio e as leis commerciais do Brasil', *Jornal do commercio*, 2 Oct. 1915, p. 3.

[3] Rebouças, *Agricultura nacional*, pp. 3, 9, 11, 69.

[4] *O abolicionista; orgão da Sociedade Brasileira Contra a Escravidão*, no. 10, 1 Aug. 1881, p. 1.

come by a desire to put at the service of our progress a new instrument which, away from the guidance of the government, would be able to have the necessary development free of any *government interference*; in other words, *individual initiative*.[1] No sooner had the government got wind of this move than it issued a decree forbidding silent partnerships from dividing their capital into shares. It feared that Mauá's action would abuse 'public credulity' and make it impossible for creditors to collect their due.[2] Mauá then played his trump, arguing that this policy would hamper the flow of foreign capital to Brazil; he himself, he said, was in correspondence with 'moneyed men of England' who were prepared to invest huge sums in his firm if their responsibility were limited to their investment.[3] His arguments were nonetheless ignored, and he later attributed the ultimate downfall of his banking empire to his inability to strengthen its capital through this means.[4]

The government itself was thus to blame, he argued, if development did not take place:

They complain that in Brazil everything is expected from the *government* and that individual initiative *does not exist*! How can it be otherwise when everything that depends upon the action of *capital* organized for any purpose of public or private usefulness in which the liberty of contract should be the *regulating principle*, soon runs up against the terrible preventive laws and [when], if these are not enough, the *undue* intervention of the government appears as a tutor? The fact, therefore ...that everything is expected from the government, is the *necessary* result of the legal system under which the country has been placed.[5]

All his effort was still in vain. Indeed, out of the debate on currency and banking policy of the late 1850s and the economic

---

[1] Mauá, *Autobiografia*, p. 235.
[2] Joaquim Nabuco, *Um estadista do imperio, Nabuco de Araujo. Sua vida, suas opiniões, sua época*, [2nd ? ed.] (Rio & São Paulo: Civilização Brasileira & Editôra Nacional, 1936), pp. 191–2; Britishers in Rio supported Mauá, *The Rio Mercantile Journal*, 15 Jan. 1855, p. 1.
[3] Mauá to Nabuco de Araujo, Rio, 5 Aug. 1856, AIHGB, Lata 381, Doc. 4.
[4] Mauá, *Autobiografia*, pp. 240, 287; Anyda Marchant, 'A New Portrait of Mauá the Banker: A Man of Business in Nineteenth-Century Brazil', *Hispanic American Historical Review*, xxx (1950), 431n.; Inglez de Souza, 'O commercio e as leis commerciais', p. 3.
[5] Mauá, *Autobiografia*, pp. 223–4.

crisis of 1857 emerged the retrograde Brazilian company law of 1860 which remained in force for over twenty years. The law, drawn up to stipulate the penalties for violation of the existing code, was largely inspired by Ângelo Moniz da Silva Ferraz, later *barão* de Uruguaiana (1812–67), the then Minister of the Treasury, acting with the encouragement of the emperor.[1] According to it and the decree which regulated its application, the Council of State had to give its authorization before any limited liability company could operate in Brazil. The Council would examine the proposed company to see whether it would serve the public interest; whether the purpose of the company was not 'contrary to good custom' or tending toward monopoly of staple goods; whether the proposed capital was sufficient; whether it would 'probably succeed'; whether, if part of the capital consisted of real property, its worth had been correctly valued; whether the shareholders would be able to adequately protect their interests in the company according to its statutes; and whether the promoters of the company offered 'moral guarantees indispensable to the credit of the enterprise and the security of the shareholders and the public'.[2] Tavares Bastos, citing Bentham, denounced it as 'a fearful law' designed to 'undermine public liberties'.[3] Other innovators shared his view.

When the Conservative Party was defeated in the elections of 1861 Mauá wrote his partner in England that 'the Conservatives have lost their ground completely in consequence of their restrictive views and the meddling in every man's right to act and work according to his own idea instead of having all his actions and doings regulated by government and the law'. That same

[1] Brazil, Ministerio da Fazenda, *Relatorio*, 1860, pp. 64–5; Pedro II in Helio Vianna, 'Instruções de D. Pedro II ao visconde de Abaeté e Silva Ferraz', *Jornal do comércio*, 12 June 1964; Pedro II, Speech from the Throne, 11 May 1860, in Brazil, Sovereigns, etc., *Fallas do throno desde o anno de 1823 até o anno de 1889 acompanhados [sic] dos respectivos votos de graças* (Rio: Imp. Nacional, 1889), pp. 549–50; Notes [apparently prepared by Joaquim Nabuco] in AIHGB, Lata 381, Doc. 4; Inglez de Souza, 'O commercio e as leis commerciais', p. 3; Luiz Gastão d'Escragnolle Doria, 'Cousas do passado', *RIHGB*, LXXI, Part 2 (1908), pp. 364–7.

[2] Art. 1 and 2, Lei n. 1.083 de 22 de agôsto de 1860, Brazil, Laws, statutes, etc., *Collecção das leis do imperio do Brasil*, p. 31; Decreto n. 2.711 de 19 de dezembro de 1860, *ibid.* 2.ª parte, pp. 1128, 1133.

[3] Aureliano Cândido Tavares Bastos, *Cartas do Solitário*, 3rd ed., Brasiliana, 115 (São Paulo: Editôra Nacional, 1938), p. 46.

year he wrote to Carruthers, his old friend and mentor, saying that the Conservatives had lost because of their 'anxiety to govern *too much*... On the other hand, the Liberals have entirely changed their ideas... and, as they promise to meddle but little with the working of industry and trade, their attainment of power is hail'd with hope'.[1] Such hope was misplaced, however, as Liberals like senator Nabuco de Araújo were able to do very little to change the situation.

In 1865, inspired by the British and French laws of 1862 and 1863, he decided to take some steps in his capacity as Minister of Justice to free limited liability companies from the requirement of prior authorization, despite the fact that he had once been the instrument for quashing Mauá's plans. Felisberto Caldeira Brant Pontes, second *visconde* de Barbacena (1802–1906), a diplomat and businessman for many years intimately linked to Great Britain, wrote to the senator in mid-1865 from London saying that he was sending 'the latest publication on limited liability: you cannot imagine the growth that has taken place in this new kind of business'.[2] Using the British law as a model, Nabuco de Araújo then drafted a bill in which the first article began, 'there may be established without previous approval or authorization' companies with limited liability.[3]

He then submitted it to various institutions for their opinion. The Bar Association of Recife, among others, studied it carefully, referring at length to the history of company law in England, repeating the arguments used in the British parliament, and quoting the *Westminster Review*, *The Economist*, and *The Banker's Magazine*. It concluded in favor of the liberalization of company law, but suggested that the government should move cautiously and impose some restrictions as had the French. A separate opinion was rendered by José Antonio de Figueiredo, father of the *visconde* de Figueiredo and one of the largest merchants of the empire.

[1] Mauá in Anyda Marchant, 'A sorte não o permitiu', *RIHGB*, CXCII (1946), 46; Mauá in Marchant, 'A New Portrait of Mauá the Banker', p. 421.

[2] Barbacena to Nabuco de Araujo, London, 22 June 1865, AIHGB, Lata 381, Doc. 4; Nabuco, *Um estadista do imperio*, p. 557; Machado, *Ensaio sôbre a sociedade de responsabilidade limitada*, pp. 27–8.

[3] [Nabuco de Araujo], 'Projecto para se estudar' (MS.), AIHGB, Lata 381, Doc. 4.

He preferred the English system of complete freedom rather than the French one. He wrote:

In a free country, the right of property, the freedom of work, and the freedom of association are ideas which go together...It will be in the spirit of association—which cannot exist without liberty—that Brazil will find the most fertile means of production and wealth...It will be to this powerful instrument that the country will one day owe the success and conclusion of enterprises beyond the means of isolated men, for example, canals, railroads, vast and expensive constructions, bridges, roads, ports, etc.[1]

The Council of State, however, vetoed any change in the Brazilian legislation on the subject. It insisted that the proposed new law was 'in keeping with the conditions of the English people, with its *self government*, with the sober character of the British citizen, the cautious, pensive man who respects his own dignity and knows how to maintain untouched his political liberty and therefore will not abuse this commercial freedom...It is our painful but necessary duty to note the condition of Brazil, which is truly deplorable'. The population, it said, was made up of adventurers, without traditions, 'without the independence that characterizes the Englishman', inexperienced, as if asleep. Could Brazil 'be considered perchance in identical circumstances with these other countries'? If, in spite of the control of the government, companies in Brazil were characterized by fraud and mismanagement, how much worse would it not be without the old requirements? It, therefore, decided to postpone any changes until 'better times', and so killed the proposal of Nabuco de Araújo.[2] But his ideas lived on and, through them, the British influence. It was to his proposal that all the debate referred ten years later when the subject was once again brought up.

[1] Brazil, *Diario official*, 13 June 1866, pp. 2–4; 14 June 1866, pp. 1–3. Cf. Figueiredo's statement with the following one by British men in 1825: 'The freedom which under our government every man has to use his capital, his labour and his talents, in the manner most conducive to his interests, are inestimable advantages; canals are cut and railroads constructed by the voluntary association of persons whose local knowledge enables them to unite in the most desirable situations, and these great advantages cannot exist under less free government'. Quoted by Clairmonte, *Economic Liberalism and Underdevelopment*, p. 17.

[2] Parecer das secções de justiça e fazenda do Conselho de Estado, 9 July 1866, AIHGB, Lata 381, Doc. 4.

Meanwhile, the issue was kept alive only by an occasional reference. In 1869 there were organized in Rio de Janeiro a series of lectures by the Radical Liberal Party, and two of them dealt with the need for reform of company law. The father of the *barão* de Jaceguai, senator José Inácio Silveira da Mota (1807–1893), with frequent appeals to the shining example of England, referred to the contrastingly 'unbearable tutelage of the government over our industries... The law of 22 August 1860 killed off individual initiative and the spirit of association. Since everything depends on the government, it has become the custom to undertake nothing without soliciting permission, privilege, subvention, and authorization'.[1] Another speaker said the country needed roads and railroads, 'but the legislation of 1860 has imposed shackles on all this'. He then asked, 'Where among us is the spirit of association? When will companies be created to carry out any large enterprises? If anyone thinks of doing it, he immediately must struggle with the Council of State, with the ill humor of the ministers, with the political partiality of the nation's representatives.'[2] The next year Tavares Bastos took up the refrain. 'Fear of companies', he said, 'is an anachronistic tradition of despotism' denied by 'the modern spirit of liberty... Capital, like the individual, must be free to unite in any form; the state... does not have the right to regulate the form and the life of companies.'[3] Again, in 1875, a writer published a second edition of his earlier attack upon 'the dire legislation of 1860 that today throws up invincible obstacles to the spirit of association and even individual activity'. About the same time André Rebouças, stung by his difficulties in organizing a dock company, pointed to the British Companies Act of 1862, the proposal of Nabuco de Araújo of 1865, and the 'really unforgivable' lack of progress in Brazil since that date.[4]

[1] José Ignácio Silveira da Motta, *Degeneração do sistema representativo* [*discurso na Conferência Radical, 25. 4. 1869*] (Rio: Typ. Americana, 1869), pp. 21–2.
[2] Joaquim Antonio Pinto Junior, *Liberdade do commercio* (Rio: Typ. Imperial Instituto Artistico, 1869), pp. 4, 14, 16.
[3] Tavares Bastos, *A província*, pp. 264, 286.
[4] Henrique Augusto Milet, *O meio circulante e a questão bancária*, 2nd ed. (Recife: Typ. do Jornal do Recife, 1875), p. 6; Rebouças, *Agricultura nacional*, p. 322. Restrictive company law was partly blamed for the crisis of 1864, Pedro Antonio Ferreira Vianna, *A crise commercial do Rio de Janeiro em 1864* (Rio: Garnier, 1864), p. 11.

Finally, Nabuco de Araújo's plan began to bear fruit. The issue was brought to the fore by a scandal in which one of the leading politicians of the day was convicted as criminally responsible for the failure of a company. It was widely held that only an outmoded legal system could make such a conviction possible and that its effect would be to discourage respectable men from assuming the direction of limited liability companies. New legislation was proposed in 1877, and, after many detours, the bill was referred to a committee which reported in 1879 by first outlining the history of company law: 'The start came in England...To remedy a situation which tended to deprive industry and commerce of the capital which is their necessary food', the English government ceased to require previous authorization. It then described the various British laws that led to the one of 1862, and pointed to the effects of this law: 'The result of the new order of things was really magnificent. The spirit of association...grew prodigiously. The number of companies organized rose to an elevated figure and the capital represented by them to an almost fabulous sum.' The idea spread and 'liberty of association is today...almost universally accepted'. The committee then proposed a new law.[1]

Once again the debate in the Chamber of Deputies stressed the crying need for liberalization and the deleterious effects of restriction. One by one the old objections were argued down. There was no need to protect the shareholders, since 'individual self-interest, when protected only by the zeal and diligence of the individual instead of the illusory protection which is said to come from official guidance or legal regulations, is certainly the best of guarantees'.[2] The new Liberal Minister of Justice, a close associate of Mauá, repeated that 'the prosperity of the United States and of England is, in large part, due to individual initiative in the form of the limited liability company'.[3] Although the Belgian company law was now held up as the latest foreign example of

---

[1] Committee Report, Session of 3 Mar. 1879, Brazil, Congresso, Câmara dos Deputados, *Anais*, 1878 [1879], III, 157, 158. On legislative background see 1872, I, 20; 1878, I, 223–5. On the incident that raised the issue at this time see Inglez de Souza, 'O commercio e as leis commerciais', p. 3.

[2] Speech of Tavares Belfort, 26 Mar. 1879, Brazil, Congresso, Câmara dos Deputados, *Anais*, 1878 [1879], IV, 188–9.

[3] Speech of Lafayette Rodrigues Pereira, 27 Mar. 1879. *Ibid.* IV, 220.

good legislation, continued references to the English experience were common, and heated arguments took place about what actually was the British practice.[1] The Chamber was also reminded that 'the project of Counselor Nabuco [de Araújo], presented in 1866, consecrated the core of the English legislation'.[2] The success of the British in fostering economic growth through a liberal law finally proved a convincing argument, and the bill was passed on to the Senate in 1879.[3]

But opposition to the measure was by no means overcome. The bill remained in the Senate until 1882, and even old Liberals there were heard to cite John Stuart Mill in support of some degree of regulation.[4] When the bill was finally returned (slightly amended) to the lower house, voices were once again raised against it. One Conservative said 'A favorite argument in favor of the project is that its basic idea is generally accepted in the civilized nations and that the Brazilian system is absolutist, antiquated, and does not correspond to the necessities of modern societies...There is no doubt that England, prepared by her system of limited liability companies which she has had for many years, was ready to establish this freedom'; but in other countries, the experience had not been a happy one. He concluded that Brazil did not have the experience to make it work.[5]

But others continued to insist that the legislator must 'identify himself with the ideas of his time, abandon routine, and listen to the heralds of progress'.[6] These arguments prevailed and the law was finally passed in October 1882. Its first article, like that of Nabuco de Araújo's proposed law, read 'Companies...may be established without government authorization.'[7]

[1] *Ibid.* IV, 303, 305, 307, 308, 340, 341–2, 363 and *ibid.*, 1879, II, 232, 244, and III, 59.
[2] *Ibid.* 1878 [1879], IV, 362; for other references to his inspiration see *ibid.* 341, and *ibid.* 1878, I, 223–4, III, 160.   [3] *Ibid.* 1879, III, 64.
[4] Speech of Zacarias de Góes e Vasconcellos, 29 Sept. 1877, *Diário do Rio de Janeiro*, 6 Oct. 1877, p. 4. Cf. opposite use of Mill in session of 3 Mar. 1879, Brazil, Congresso, Câmara dos Deputados, *Anais*, 1878 [1879], III, 158.
[5] Speech of Domingos Andrade Figueira, 11 Oct. 1882, Brazil, Congresso, Câmara dos Deputados, *Anais*, 1882, V, 358.
[6] Speech of Affonso Celso Junior, 12 Oct. 1882, *ibid.* V, 374.
[7] Art. 1, Lei n. 3.150 de 4 de novembro de 1882, Brazil, Laws, statutes, etc., *Collecção das leis do imperio do Brazil*, p. 139. On the legislative course of this bill see Brazil, Congresso, Câmara dos Deputados, *Anais*, 1882, V, 317, 356–62, 417–23.

Thus at last Brazil shook off one of the symbols of its traditionalism. When the empire was overthrown six years later, an
early move of the new regime was to pass an even more liberal
company law, a law which was instrumental in stimulating the
stock market boom of the early 1890s known as *o encilhamento*.
Of course, changing the law was not enough. The investors themselves must be willing to participate. André Rebouças had long
noted 'the lack of the spirit of association in this country, the
ignorance of the capitalists, and the miserable spirit of routine'.[1]
Furthermore, as is typical in a traditional society, the investors
mistrusted distant and impersonal management. It was for this
reason that in 1912 it was proposed that Brazil adopt the German
practice, which combined the advantages of partnerships (direct
control of the enterprise) with that of corporations (large amount
of capital). This became the law in 1919, and the nature of
Brazilian *sociedades anônimas* remains basically unchanged today.[2]

During the latter half of the nineteenth century the men who
dreamed of a modern Brazil singled out for special attack the
laws and customs which hampered private economic activity.
Convinced that the monopolies and privileges characteristic of
the old regime were a brake upon economic development, they
insisted that the initiative of the individual should be encouraged
in every instance. The government must abstain from controlling,
regulating, and interfering with business activity. Some even went
so far as to shun government support altogether; but other, wiser
men applauded tariffs and credits when properly administered. If
it were argued that only the government could manage the large
investments required as a basis for economic growth, the innovators of that day retorted that joint-stock companies could be as
large as necessary and were the solution for Brazil's developmental

---

[1] André Rebouças, *Diário e notas autobiográficas*, ed. Ana Flora and Inácio Veríssimo,
Documentos Brasileiros, 12 (Rio: José Olympio, 1938), p. 173.
[2] Inglez de Souza, 'O commercio e as leis commerciais', p. 3; Stanley J. Stein, *The
Brazilian Cotton Manufacture; Textile Enterprise in an Underdeveloped Area 1850–1950*,
(Cambridge, Mass.: Harvard Univ. Press, 1957), pp. 7–8; Machado, *Ensaio sôbre a
sociedade de responsabilidade limitada*, pp. 34, 42, 44. For a summary of the provisions of
the 1919 law see *Brazilian Bulletin*, Nov. 1966, p. 4. The example of speculative 'bubbles'
in England was used to justify the excesses of the *encilhamento*, Ruy Barbosa, *Finanças e
política da republica: discursos e escriptos* (Rio: Cia. Impressora, 1892), p. 91.

problems. But, first, the government must cease to require prior authorization for their creation.

In defending these tenets Brazilians appealed to Britain for models of success and examples of specific measures. The British were recognized as economic individualists who had shaken off governmental control of business activity. British company law provided the pattern for the Brazilian one. Thus the economic liberalism of the British, like their belief in progress, was adopted by those Brazilians committed to changing their society.

9

PROGRESS AND SPENCER

Modernizers within Brazil's traditional society were in desperate
need of intellectual reinforcement for their position. A new ideology which would reorganize and re-explain the nature of their
social and institutional environment and which would logically
link their work to a meaningful goal could be emotionally satisfying while simultaneously advancing the effort to win over converts. Not surprisingly, this group scoured the resources of Europe
in search of useful ideas for this purpose. It is a mistake to consider
them, as is sometimes done, as alienated intellectuals agape before
Europeans and merely swept along by the prestige of an idea's
source. It is also only partially correct to say they failed to understand the full meaning of the ideas they found there, for as they
understood them, these concepts were exactly what they were
searching for. If they sometimes devoured their intellectual fare
without reference to context or logical affinity, as if having red
wine with fish, this was because they craved only certain kinds of
sustenance and could well afford to forget the niceties of consistency, thorough understanding, and intellectual rigor. Indeed,
they exerted surprising though unconscious creativity in establishing the criteria of selection: for they adopted primarily those
ideas that served a function within the process of modernization
in Brazil.

Ideas which could relate progress, science, and industry to each
other had a special appeal for those who were working to destroy
the traditional society. The thought of Herbert Spencer did this
admirably well, for they understood him to be saying that progress was inevitable, that it led to an industrial future, and that
science proved the validity of both assertions. In addition, Spencerianism provided a grand synthesis which could be easily understood by the middle-class Brazilian while free of some drawbacks

present in the philosophy of Auguste Comte. Furthermore, Spencer lent credence to the belief in *laissez faire* government policies and provided well-reasoned arguments against social welfare legislation, thus advancing the hopes and quelling the fears of many members of the new urban groups. All in all, it was a system of thought well-suited to the task at hand in Brazil, and these Brazilians could well afford to play down those aspects of the Englishman's work which could be adopted in Brazil only at the cost of sacrificing their ambitions. For instance, conservatism and opposition to change could also be found within the tenets of Spencerianism. Spencer lent support to those who suggested Brazil was doomed not to progress but to decay because of its imperfect 'racial stock'. And his ideas could be used to argue that weak nations must yield to the strong, and in that age of outright imperialism Brazilians knew their country was not a major power. But although these viewpoints received some attention, they were usually forgotten as soon as decency would allow.

The belief in progress is characteristic of modern societies. That tomorrow will be better than today has been a growing conviction of Western man ever since the Renaissance. He has gradually abandoned the idea of a static society and accepted the inevitability of change. At times he has come to feel that this change would certainly be for the better and so concluded that progress was also inevitable. In Britain by 1850 such a view of things was generalized throughout all segments of society. Although the idea of progress was not new, it may be considered the trademark of that era. Materially, intellectually, and spiritually, progress was irresistible.[1] Thomas Babington Macaulay, the historian, was convinced that all classes were better off in his day than in previous times and that the trend must continue: 'We too shall, in our turn, be outstripped.' J. J. Aubertin, the British manager of the São Paulo Railway, carried these optimistic attitudes to Brazil, telling friends

---

[1] John Bagnell Bury, *The Idea of Progress; an Inquiry into its Origin and Growth* (London: Macmillan, 1920); William Ralph Inge, *The Idea of Progress*, The Romanes Lecture (Oxford: Clarendon, 1920); Francis Sydney Marvin, ed., *Progress and History* (London & New York: Milford and Oxford Univ. Press, 1916), pp. 8–16, 23; Morris Ginsberg, *The Idea of Progress, a Revaluation* (Boston: Beacon, 1953); Esmé Cecil Wingfield-Stratford, *Those Earnest Victorians* (New York: Morrow, 1930), pp. 111–21.

there that 'all things were made to progress and become better', and that 'progress is the essence of world survival'.[1]

But in Brazil there was no such widely held belief in progress: the conditions of today were the same as those of yesterday and it was assumed they would remain the same tomorrow. It was only as small groups representing novel economic activities and new urban agglomerations became restless with this traditionalism that European attitudes on this score began to be accepted in Brazil. For this minority, science and progress went together. Progress would depend upon the spread of a scientific outlook; and the inevitability of progress was defended by elaborate appeals to the 'strong medicine' of science. Thus, for example, both the orthodox followers of Auguste Comte and the wider circles that felt the indirect impact of his thought believed that all civilizations moved through fixed stages to a scientifically organized ideal society. Evolutionary theory also contributed to their certainty of progress.[2] Joaquim Nabuco, who read Charles Darwin's *Origin of the Species* in the original, understood the English scientist to be saying that 'In every century the species becomes better;...if our remote ancestors were monkeys, the remote descendants of our species will be demigods'. Darwin 'makes us move slowly toward perfection'.[3] It was an exhilarating perspective for the modernizers.

The adaptation of the theory of evolution to human society had a wide impact upon Brazil. Spencer was unmistakably the most imaginative nineteenth-century thinker thus to apply this theory, and Spencer was widely read and quoted in Brazil, specially after 1889, that is, after the traditional society had been seriously shaken by the abolition of slavery and the end of the empire. João Cruz Costa, the Brazilian historian of ideas, has already pointed out that Spencer appealed to the emerging middle

[1] Macaulay quoted by George M. Trevelyan, 'Macaulay and the Sense of Optimism', in Harman Grisewood, *et al.*, *Ideas and Beliefs of the Victorians: an Historical Revaluation of the Victorian Age* (London: Sylvan, 1949), p. 49; J. J. Aubertin, *Carta dirigida aos srs. habitantes da provincia de S. Paulo por...superintendente da estrada de ferro da mesma provincia* (São Paulo: Typ. Litteraria, 1862), p. 14.

[2] Roque Spencer Maciel de Barros, *A ilustração brasileira e a idéia de universidade*, Universidade de São Paulo, Cadeira de Historia e Filosofia da Educação, Boletim 241 (2) (São Paulo: Universidade de São Paulo, 1959), pp. 26–7, 166.

[3] Joaquim Nabuco, 'Um darwinista alemão', *O Globo*, 15 Aug. 1875, p. 1.

class, especially to professional people. They enthusiastically embraced the belief in progress that formed such an essential part of Spencer's thought; and they wanted a synthesis which they could grasp, but which had scientific overtones.[1] Although Spencer never became as commanding an influence in Brazil as did Comte, his importance cannot be ignored.

His popularity was determined in some ways by the reluctance of many Brazilians to accept the rigid and illiberal political system proposed by Comte. Spencer's emphasis on voluntary cooperation formed a welcome alternative to the authoritarian overtones of the Positivist philosophy. Although those who created the republic in 1889 have often been taxed with adherence to Comte, one of the participants in those events strongly denied it, saying the majority of the Republican Party was 'dominated by ideas of democratic liberalism, American federalism, and Spencerianism'.[2] Francisco Rangel Pestana, founder and editor of the leading republican newspaper in the country, registered his preference when he agreed to write a book entitled *The Theory of Selection Applied to Society*. The *Catecismo republicano* prepared by Alberto Sales, a leading ideologue of the party, was described by one critic as 'a vast teratological museum of premature Spencerian fetuses'.[3] Whether or not this grisly image was appropriate, the political implications of Spencer's thought were in keeping with the liberal spirit of these reformers.[4]

Furthermore, his ideas were immediately useful, for he clearly defined the nature of progress and suggested its inevitability. Even before Darwin's publication of the *Origin of the Species*, Spencer

[1] João Cruz Costa, *Contribuição à história das idéias no Brasil. (O desenvolvimento da filosofia no Brasil e a evolução histórica nacional)*, Documentos Brasileiros, 86 (Rio: José Olympio, 1956), pp. 301, 353, 355.

[2] Felisbello Firmo de Oliveira Freire, *Historia constitucional da republica dos Estados Unidos do Brasil*, 2nd ed., 3 vols. (Rio: Typs. Aldina & Moreira Maximino Chagas, 1894–5), II, 65.

[3] Júlio Ribeiro, *Cartas sertanejas*, [? ed.], Coleção Nacionalista, 3 (São Paulo: Brasil Editôra, 1945), p. 125.

[4] Herbert Spencer, 'Reasons for Dissenting from the Philosophy of M. Comte', in *Essays, Scientific, Political and Speculative*, 3 vols. (New York: Appleton, 1891), II, 118–44; Cruz Costa, *Contribuição à história das idéias*, p. 301; Barros, *A ilustração brasileira*, pp. 146, 159, 165, 167; on the republicanism of Pestana see Edith Sabóia, 'Francisco Rangel Pestana (notas biográficas por ocasião do centenário do seu nascimento, 1839–1939)', *Revista do Arquivo Municipal de São Paulo*, Ano VI, Vol. LXI (Sept.–Oct. 1939), 23, 31, 36, 39, 40.

had said that 'Always toward perfection is the mighty movement'. He later wrote that 'evolution can end only in the establishment of the greatest perfection and the most complete happiness'. And in his essay entitled 'Progress: Its Law and Cause' he summarized his views on the qualities of this onward march. He asserted that societies develop according to the same rules of differentiation and organization as do living organisms. 'It is settled beyond dispute that organic progress consists in a change from the homogeneous to the heterogeneous'; by the same token, society 'undergoes continuous growth. As it grows, its parts become unlike: it exhibits increase of structure'. In fact, 'Every organism of appreciable size is a society.' Furthermore, 'The change from the homogeneous to the heterogeneous is displayed in the progress of civilization as a whole, as well as in the progress of every nation; and is still going on with increasing rapidity.' All human institutions, even art, could be similarly reduced to a pattern characteristic of natural organisms. In economic life this 'progress' led from tribal handicrafts to medieval guilds and finally to the 'industrial organization of society'. Bettering communications meant both greater differentiation and closer organic unity. 'Progress has been, and still is, towards an economic aggregation of the whole human race.'[1] Evidently, the industrialized, individualistic society was the highest product of human progress, as had been recognized by those who participated in the Exhibition of 1851.[2]

While Spencer was still writing, his ideas were going out of style not only in England but also in the United States, where they had had a far greater impact.[3] Yet where they served to discredit a relatively undifferentiated, non-industrial order—as in

[1] Herbert Spencer, *Social Statics: or, the Conditions Essential to Human Happiness Specified, and the First of Them Developed* (London: Chapman, 1851), p. 293; Herbert Spencer, *First Principles* [? ed.] (New York: Appleton, 1898), p. 530; Herbert Spencer, 'Progress: Its Law and Cause', in *Essays, Scientific, Political and Speculative*, I, 10, 19, 22, 23; Herbert Spencer, *The Principles of Sociology*, System of Synthetic Philosophy, 6–8, 3 vols. (New York: Appleton, 1889), I, 462.

[2] Bury, *The Idea of Progress*, p. 330; on Spencer, generally, see Frederick Copleston, S. J., 'Herbert Spencer—Progress and Freedom', in Grisewood, *et al. Ideas and Beliefs of the Victorians*, pp. 86–93; Crane Brinton, *English Political Thought in the Nineteenth Century* (London: Benn, 1933), pp. 226–39.

[3] Richard Hofstadter, *Social Darwinism in American Thought*, 2nd ed. (Boston: Beacon, 1955), pp. 123–69.

Brazil—his influence remained strong. Euclides da Cunha (1866–1909), an engineer and influential newspaper correspondent, reflected the well-known Spencerian influence upon him when he insisted in 1902 that 'either we progress or we disappear: this is certain'. A few years earlier the historian João Capistrano de Abreu (1853–1927) said that, in fact, Brazil had already moved in this direction. He contrasted his time with that of the first settlements in these terms: 'This is what history tells us about the sixteenth century: a slight organism, of rudimentary structure, in which each organ carried out more than one function and in which there was not a special organ for each function...In the nineteenth century we have a thicker population, greater division of labor, better performance of the organs, more specialized functions, integrated action.' Francisco José de Oliveira Vianna (1885–1951), a social historian who has exerted considerable influence upon Brazilian thought in the twentieth century, spoke as late as 1922 of the political institutions of colonial Brazil as evolving and becoming 'differentiated' through the division of older 'organs' or the creation of new ones. With the increase in population, Brazil was becoming ever less 'gangliated and dispersed'.[1]

It was often those Brazilians determined to bring about economic development that were most influenced by Spencer. André Gustavo Paulo de Frontin (1860–1933), for instance, was reported by one of his friends to have been an ardent follower of the British thinker. His biographer has written that 'Frontin took Spencer for teacher and counselor...on questions of [national] well-being and social progress'. A graduate of the engineering school, he became a teacher at the prestigious Colégio D. Pedro II after submitting a thesis based on John Stuart Mill and Spencer. He became known principally as a railway engineer, and in 1896

---

[1] Euclides da Cunha, *Os sertões (Campanha de Canudos)*, 23rd ed. (Rio: Francisco Alves, 1954), p. 62; João Capistrano de Abreu, *O descobrimento do Brasil* (Rio: Annuario do Brasil for the Sociedade Capistrano de Abreu, 1929), pp. 133–4; Francisco José de Oliveira Vianna, 'O povo brazileiro e sua evolução', in Brazil, Directoria Geral de Estatistica, *Recenseamento do Brazil, 1920, Vol. I: Introducção* (Rio: Typ. da Estatistica, 1922), pp. 349, 399; cf. the review of later editions of this last work by Emílio Willems, *Hispanic American Historical Review*, XXXVII (1957), 499–500. It is not suggested here that these writers and the others mentioned in this chapter were not also influenced by other currents of European thought. An intellectual history that would weigh the relative importance of each influence is outside the scope of this study.

he was named director of the Estrada de Ferro Central. His term of office was short, but in 1910 he was once again placed in this post, where he remained until the beginning of the First World War. He later became an active congressional spokesman for Brazilian industrialists.[1]

Another convinced Spencerian was Joaquim Duarte Murtinho (1848–1911), a controversial figure, who besides being an active businessman rose under the republican regime to a highly influential government post from which he shaped the course of Brazilian economic life. Born the son of an army doctor in the western province of Mato Grosso, he maintained family contacts there despite having left the area as a boy. A graduate of both the engineering and medical schools, he practiced medicine and taught engineering courses for some years before entering public life. In 1890 he took advantage of the *encilhamento* or investment fever then current in Brazil to create companies to function in Mato Grosso. As he wrote to a friend at the time, 'We must take advantage of the good will of capital here to enrich our state.'[2] Ironically, he was later to criticize the measures that led to the *encilhamento* pointing to that good will of capital as evidence of policy failure. His enterprises included railroads, colonization and real-estate companies, banking firms, and a company to cultivate, process, and export maté. This last venture later became so prosperous that its income exceeded the entire revenue of the state of Mato Grosso.

A republican of long standing, Murtinho was elected to the Senate soon after the republican revolution and was named Minister of Industry, Transportation, and Public Works in 1896. His report in the next year—in which the Spencerian influence is clearly apparent—was the most important factor in winning him appointment as Minister of the Treasury in the administration (1898–1902) of Manuel Ferraz de Campos Sales. From that position Murtinho hailed the funding loan of 1898 as a measure of national salvation and supervised the austerity program that fol-

[1] Raymundo Austregésilo de Atayde, *Paulo de Frontin, sua vida e sua obra*, Coleção Cidade do Rio de Janeiro, II (Rio: Estado de Guanabara, Secretaria Geral de Educação e Cultura, 1961); the quotation is from p. 37. Also see Luiz Dodsworth Martins, *Presença de Paulo de Frontin* (Rio and São Paulo: Freitas Bastos, 1966).

[2] Quoted by Virgílio Corrêa Filho, *Joaquim Murtinho* (Rio: Imp. Nacional, 1951), p. 51.

lowed. His prestige was so high and presidential support so strong that he became a virtual prime minister; the Chamber of Deputies gave him a vote of confidence in 1901 in which only one vote was cast against him. Two years later he re-entered the Senate as a sort of elder statesman, sought out for advice on all government policies.[1]

Murtinho was a social Darwinist. He is supposed to have read every publication of Herbert Spencer and has been described as a 'fervent admirer' of the English thinker.[2] He had long been advocating Spencerian ideas among his students at the engineering school. Miguel Lemos (1854–1917), co-founder of the Positivist Church in Brazil, was first led to break out of the traces of traditionalism by Murtinho. As he wrote in his later reminiscences, during his first year at the engineering school one of his teachers had been Joaquim Murtinho: 'Remembering that he was an admirer of Herbert Spencer...I decided to read that sophist.' He attributed to that experience the final ruin of his theological beliefs. Lemos, of course, soon discarded Spencer along with the Gospels, but one may presume that Spencer's influence was felt by other students who were not ready to go so far.[3]

One reason for Spencer's appeal was the curious emphasis he had placed on railways as part of the organic system of a modern society. As Oliveira Vianna put it for Brazil, the development of railroads and other means of communications was bringing the 'social nodules' ever closer, facilitating 'the development of the general circulatory system'. Furthermore, the variety of tasks associated with these complex enterprises meant greater division of labor. Spencer said that because of 'the invention of the locomotive engine' the 'social organism had been rendered more

[1] Corrêa Filho, *Joaquim Murtinho*, pp. 50–2, 97, 122, 144, 180, and *passim*; on his relations with Campos Sales see pp. 80–1, and Alcindo Guanabara, *A presidencia Campos Salles: politica e finanças, 1898–1902* (Rio: Laemmert, 1902), p. 48; on his later views of the *encilhamento* see Joaquim Murtinho, *Introducções aos relatorios do dr. Joaquim Murtinho* [probably ed. José Carlos Rodrigues] (n.d., n.p. [probably Rio, 1901 or 1902]), 1897, p. vi; on some of his business ventures see Raimundo Magalhães Júnior, *Rui, o homem e o mito*, Retratos do Brasil, 27 (Rio: Civilização Brasileira, 1964), pp. 71–2.

[2] Corrêa Filho, *Joaquim Murtinho*, p. 60; also see pp. 44, 174.

[3] Miguel Lemos and Raimundo Teixeira Mendes, *Nóssa inissiassão no pozitivismo. Nóta retificativa ao 'Rezumo istórico do movimento pozitivista no Brazil' publicado en 1882* (Rio: Apostolado Pozitivista do Brazil, 1889), pp. 18–19.

heterogeneous'. Júlio Ribeiro, a Brazilian novelist deeply affected by evolutionary theory, had shared this fascination and described the equipment of the São Paulo Railway as 'clean, shiny, well-oiled, working like a healthy organism'. The men who, like Frontin, were associated with the construction of railroads were enabled by the Spencerian perspective to consider their work a large step toward universal progress.[1]

Another reason that generation of Brazilians was attracted to Spencer was his ability to synthesize all knowledge and bring it to heel behind natural science. Spencer had applied evolutionary theory to all phenomena from the sun and stars to painting and music. This ability to systematize a vast amount of data and present it in non-technical language attracted those who needed another *Summa theologica* for the new understanding of reality required by the modern world. It provided a single handle by which they could grasp and dominate it all.

Spencer's drawing power in this respect is reflected by the essayists and critics who popularized his viewpoint or praised his work. The Brazilian writer who most fully adopted Spencerianism was Sílvio Romero (1851–1914), a caustic literary critic who spent much of his effort pondering the identity of Brazil. Although considered a disciple of the Brazilian Germanophile Tobias Barreto (1839–89), Romero differed from the latter in many ways, especially in his predilection for Spencer. He wrote that 'after searching for a sure path, I chose Herbert Spencer. Tobias did not admire this remarkable genius'.[2] Romero had entered law school in 1868, at the very moment when the old structures were beginning to crack. His student thesis presented five years later held Spencer up as a model of clear thinking, and by 1876 he judged Spencer's work more profound and important than that of either Comte or Émile Littré, the schismatic Positivist.[3] In his book *Doutrina contra doutrina: o evolucionismo e o positivismo no*

---

[1] Oliveira Vianna, 'O povo brazileiro', p. 399; Spencer, 'Progress: Its Law and Cause', pp. 57–8; Julio Ribeiro, *A carne* (São Paulo: Teixeira, 1888), pp. 129, 136.

[2] Quoted by Cruz Costa, *Contribuição à história das idéias*, p. 315n.; also see Barros, *A ilustração brasileira*, pp. 135–6, 146.

[3] Carlos Sussekind de Mendonça, *Sílvio Romero, sua formação intelectual, 1851–1880; com uma indicação bibliográfica*, Brasiliana, 114 (São Paulo: Editôra Nacional, 1938), pp. 103, 121, 141–2.

Brasil, Romero discussed the differences between Spencer and Comte and concluded in favor of the Englishman. He included long quotations taken directly from Spencer's works, some of which had not yet been translated into French and were consequently, as he said, 'almost entirely unknown in Brazil'. He was especially impressed by Spencer's synthesizing ability. After referring to Spencer's 'philosophic structure' as based on a long list of nineteenth-century philosophers and scientists, he concluded that Spencer's thought was founded upon 'all these immortal discoveries which are the glory of our century', whereas Comte 'ceased to read in 1822'. Romero considered Spencer 'one of the leading minds of our time', and urged Spencerianism upon Brazilians as a philosophy 'more serious and more invigorating for our people' than that of Comte.[1]

In São Paulo the Spencerian approach was popularized by the 'sociologist' Paulo Egydio. He had begun this work in the pages of the *Correio paulistano* as early as the 1870s.[2] In a fifty-page survey of the history of sociology, published in 1899, he emphasized the applicability of scientific principles to the study of society, and referred to Spencer enthusiastically. The previous year he had published a study in which he revealed a special liking for Spencer's *Synthetic Philosophy* saying that 'this magnificent idea of the complete unification of knowledge...belongs to Herbert Spencer'. Since Spencer was also responsible for the admirable 'organic theory of society', Egydio concluded that Spencer 'should be read continuously'.[3]

Raimundo de Farias Brito (1863–1917) was a sort of Will

---

[1] Sylvio Romero, *Doutrina contra doutrina: o evolucionismo e o positivismo no Brasil* (Rio and São Paulo: Livraria Classica de Alves, 1895), pp. 98, 100, 103, 104–21; the comparison with Comte goes to p. 199. There was apparently no translation of Spencer into Portuguese, see Paulo Egydio de Oliveira Carvalho, *Do conceito scientifico das leis sociologicas;...introducção. Volume primeiro* (São Paulo: Ribeiro, 1898), p. 29n.; Sílvio Romero, *História da literatura brasileira*, 6th ed., 5 vols. (Rio: José Olympio, 1960), v, 1692.

[2] Richard M. Morse, *From Community to Metropolis: A Biography of São Paulo, Brazil* (Gainesville, Fla.: Univ. of Florida Press, 1958), p. 157n.; Cruz Costa, *Contribuição à história das idéias*, p. 389n.

[3] Paulo Egydio de Oliveira Carvalho, *Contribuição para a historia philosophica da sociologia*, (São Paulo: Ribeiro, 1899), pp. 10, 13, 14, 15, 40; Egydio de Oliveira Carvalho, *Do conceito scientifico das leis sociologicas*, pp. 32, 29n., 55n., 124; on a comparison with Comte see pp. 48–58.

Durant of philosophy in Brazil. Summary and explanation were his virtues and superficiality his major weakness. In general, he was critical of Comte and Spencer, yet, as João Cruz Costa has pointed out, he accepted many of their basic tenets, especially those of Spencer. In one of his books, for instance, he placed Spencer along with Kant, Hegel, and Comte as founders of modern thought, but gave Spencer more attention than he paid to any other thinker.[1]

The Spencerian influence is also seen in the massive four-volume work of J. Augusto Coelho on a suggested educational plan for Brazil. He said his ideas had their origin in Spencer's *Education: Intellectual, Moral, and Physical*, first published in 1861. Spencer's views, said Coelho, emphasized individualism, the growing specialization of each child, and a heavy emphasis on scientific education. Not wishing to appear slavish, he maintained that Spencer's educational work was merely a collection of commonplaces taken from Pestalozzi, Rousseau, and others; 'as a work, however, which condenses the guiding principles of modern education, that demonstrates them with admirable logical vigor, that seeks to popularize them with this concise and clear style so characteristic of the English philosopher, his pedagogic work has a great value.' Spencer's key idea, as Coelho saw it, was that 'only the educational evolution of the race can be a guide for the phases through which must pass the educational life of the individual'. Primary was divided from secondary education by the arrival at the age when specialization begins. He gave special attention to the teaching of 'sociology', for the student must come to realize that societies evolve through integration and differentiation.[2] If his proposal had been turned into reality the Spencerian influence in Brazil would now be a commonplace. This was not the case, however, and the significance of this work is rather that

---

[1] Cruz Costa, *Contribuição à história das idéias*, pp. 321, 326; Raimundo de Farias Brito, *A base physica do espirito; historia summaria do problema da mentalidade como preparação para o estudo da philosophia do espirito* (Rio: Francisco Alves, 1912), pp. 210–25.

[2] J. Augusto Coelho, *Principios de pedagogia*, 4 vols. (São Paulo: Teixeira, 1891–3), I, vii, 94, 95, 343, 377; IV, 57, 517; cf. Herbert Spencer, *Education: Intellectual, Moral, and Physical* (New York and London: Appleton, 1920), esp. pp. 102–6, 117–20. For a list of other Spencerians in Brazil see Cruz Costa, *Contribuição à história das idéias*, p. 117n.

it gave additional currency to the Spencerian synthesis of knowledge and emphasized once again the importance of science. Those
who believed in man's control of his environment were strengthened in their position.

Despite the glorification of science which made Spencer so
appealing, there was little scientific inquiry going on in Brazil.
Darwin's strictly scientific ideas, for instance, received relatively
little attention since there were virtually no scientists to read him.
Brazilians were more apt to write poetry about their butterflies
than to be struck as was Darwin by their variety. And what there
was of Darwinian thought in Brazil was generally absorbed
through Ernst Heinrich Haeckel, Darwin's German popularizer.
But in this tendency toward the acceptance of popularizations
these urban Brazilians were not unlike their middle-class counterparts in Victorian England. It was not necessary to be a scientist
in order to appreciate Darwin's importance or be influenced by
scientific viewpoints on man and the world.[1] And a few paren-
thetical remarks on the influence of Darwin may, therefore, be
appropriate here.

An openness to a new understanding of man's nature was in
fact characteristic of those who would recast their society. The
old religious beliefs were suited only to an outworn world-system,
and one of the instruments the reformers used against it was the
idea of evolution. The chief criticism leveled against Spencer by
Farias Brito had been that his philosophy did 'not recognize the
deepest reality: the spirit'. Although the more cosmopolitan
Nabuco failed to see any conflict between science and religion,
evolutionary theory surely meant that the Biblical account
of the creation was less than the whole story.[2] The new perspective on the nature of man would shatter the older world-

---

[1] Cruz Costa, *Contribuição à história das idéias*, pp. 352n.–354n., 443; Gilberto Freyre,
Inglêses no Brasil; aspectos da influência britânica sôbre a vida, a paisagem e a cultura do Brasil,
Documentos Brasileiros, 58 (Rio: José Olympio, 1948), p. 63; Barros, *A ilustração
brasileira*, pp. 145–6, 167–9; Morse, *From Community to Metropolis*, p. 157n.; note fleeting
reference to Darwin in Egydio, *Contribuição para a historia philosophica da sociologia*, p. 46;
cf. Charles Darwin, *Journal of Researches into the Natural History and Geology of the
Countries Visited during the Voyage of 'H.M.S. Beagle' Round the World under the Command
of Capt. Fitz Roy, R.N.* (New York: Appleton, 1896), pp. 33–4.
[2] Farias Brito, *A base physica do espirito*, p. 213; Nabuco, 'Um darwinista alemão', is a
review of Haeckel in translation.

view, and the long-run import of this theory would thus be very large.

One writer who took it seriously was Júlio César Ribeiro [Vaughan] (1845–90). Unmistakably a member of the innovating groups characteristic of the cities, this son of an American father and a Brazilian mother (from whom he took his name) studied in the engineering school, participated in the abolitionist campaign, supported the republican movement, and composed poetry in praise of railways. He earned his living by teaching Latin, publishing Portuguese grammars, translating books from English, and writing novels.[1] In one of these entitled *A carne* (1888), he has his hero study with Darwin in England and fall in love during a conversation about evolution. The main point of the novel is that man is just an animal, struggling for survival like any one of them; his only advantage is that he has more cunning. The heroine of the story, educated at the best schools, of an intelligence almost without equal in the country, 'in spite of her powerful mind, with all her science, was nothing more in the species than a mere female, and what she felt was desire, the organic need for a male'.[2] The novel was not great literature, but it was certainly Darwinian and served—like Spencerianism—to discredit the traditional religion.

Another way in which Spencer's ideas served the needs of the new entrepreneurially minded urban interests was in the encouragement he gave to those who opposed social welfare legislation. Spencer had said in 1851 that 'Pervading all nature we may see at work a stern discipline which is a little cruel that it may be very kind'. It was much better for aged deer to be killed by carnivorous animals than that they 'should linger out a life made painful by infirmities'. Beasts of prey also 'weed out the sickly, the mal-

---

[1] Evaristo de Moraes, *A campanha abolicionista (1879–1888)* (Rio: Leite Ribeiro, Freitas Bastos, & Spicer, 1924), p. 263; João Gualberto de Oliveira, *Conselheiro Francisco de Paula Mayrink; as ferrovias paulistas, a vila Mayrink, seu fundador, pioneiros...* (São Paulo: Bentivegna, 1958), p. 11; Augusto Victorino Alves Sacramento Blake, *Diccionario bibliographico brazileiro*, 7 vols. (Rio: Typ. Nacional, 1883–1902), v, 254.

[2] Ribeiro, *A carne*, pp. 18, 36, 73, 183; also see Ribeiro, *Cartas sertanejas*, pp. 19–21, 41, 51, 61, 95. Ribeiro's more personal challenge to the traditional religion was his temporary conversion to Protestantism in 1870, Henriqueta Rosa Fernandes Braga, *Música sacra evangélica no Brasil (contribuição à sua história)* (Rio: Kosmos, 1961), p. 327.

formed, and the least fleet or powerful'. Thus 'all vitiation of the race through the multiplication of its inferior samples is prevented'. Similarly, 'the well-being of existing humanity, and the unfolding of it into this ultimate perfection, are both secured by the same beneficent, though severe discipline'. 'The poverty of the incapable, the distresses that come upon the imprudent, the starvation of the idle...are the decrees of a large, far-seeing benevolence.' He said he felt sorry for the unskilled worker, the unemployed because of sickness, the widows, and the orphans, but he saw 'these harsh fatalities...to be full of the highest beneficence'. 'The whole effort of nature', he said, 'is to get rid of such, to clear the world of them, and make room for better.'[1]

As Minister of the Treasury, Joaquim Murtinho reflected these views. 'Improvidence, the love of laziness, and dissipation are vices which can only be cured by the evils and suffering which they bring on. To try and remove this suffering...is to perpetuate those vices and destroy the only natural and efficient agent of regeneration...It would be against the principles of justice to defend the inept, the improvident, the addicts, with the sacrifice of those who struggle, who try, and who win through their own individual energy.' He was against a pension system since each person should be left to take care of his own future. Any other course robs man of his 'will, courage, initiative, and moral energy for the struggle'. Echoing Spencer's essay entitled 'From Freedom to Bondage', he described socialism as a 'return of society to primitive slavery'. So any threat that might be posed to the new entrepreneurial groups by the rise of a proletariat was already being warded off by an appeal to Spencer.[2]

As we have seen, the innovators were also deeply engaged in a struggle to break the hold of the traditional society upon economic activity. Fortunately for them, the belief in *laissez faire* was reinforced by Herbert Spencer. He had maintained that in a developed society there must be, as in advanced natural organisms, 'a function to each organ and each organ to its function'. The

---

[1] Spencer, *Social Statics*, pp. 322, 323; Spencer quoted by Hofstadter, *Social Darwinism*, p. 41.
[2] Murtinho, *Introducções aos relatorios*, 1897, pp. xii–xiii, xvii, xxv, xxviii; cf. Herbert Spencer, 'From Freedom to Bondage', in *Essays*, III, 445–70.

State's function was to defend the freedom of each man, and any effort to perform other functions would lead to disaster.[1] Spencer's *laissez faire* attitudes did not appeal equally to all his followers in Brazil. Joaquim Murtinho concluded that 'we must hand over all enterprises to individual activity' and translated this view into action by leasing out government-owned railways to private operators. Like Spencer he was even against government management of the post office, although here he was unable to put his ideas into practice. When the country faced a serious crisis because of the declining price of coffee, Murtinho opposed any government interference in market processes. The solution to the crisis, he maintained, was to be found through free competition, 'leading through business failures to natural selection, revealed by the disappearance of the inferior and the permanence of the superior'.[2] On the other hand, Frontin pursued a seemingly inconsistent course. In early 1890 he attacked the financial policies of Rui Barbosa on the ground that they tended to 'limit the liberty of industry' and curtail 'individual initiative'. Yet in 1892 he signed a petition drawn up by industrialists which managed to cite Spencer while demanding government subsidies for industries then in distress because of a financial crash. And in 1897 he was fired from his position as director of the Estrada de Ferro Central for opposing Murtinho's policy of leasing that railway to a private company.[3] Finally, Rangel Pestana had opposed the subsidies in 1892, not by appealing to Spencer but on the ground that the opposition of British bankers on whom Brazil depended would be disastrous.[4] On this question Brazilian Spencerians were in a quandary. They wished to industrialize, and Spencer supported their belief in industrialization; he said industry would be best served by *laissez faire*, but they were not all sure. Some of them

---

[1] Spencer, *Social Statics*, pp. 274, 275.
[2] Murtinho quoted by Corrêa Filho, *Joaquim Murtinho*, p. 59; Murtinho, *Introduções aos relatorios*, 1897, p. xxiii; 1899, p. xxvi.
[3] Frontin quoted by Magalhães Júnior, *Rui, o homem e o mito*, p. 59; also see p. 58; Antonio Felicio dos Santos, *et al.* 'Auxilios á industria', *Jornal do commercio*, 6 July 1892, p. 2; Corrêa Filho, *Joaquim Murtinho*, pp. 82–3.
[4] Nícia Villela Luz, *Aspectos do nacionalismo econômico brasileiro. Os esforços em prol da industrialização*, Coleção 'Revista de história', 16 (São Paulo: 'Revista de história', 1959), pp. 80–2.

rightly questioned whether the policies that served industrial interests in Britain would do equally well in Brazil.

It has been argued that through his *laissez faire* policies Murtinho favored a 'feudal' society over a modern one. It is true that Murtinho seemed partial to agriculture rather than industry. He felt that only 'natural' industries should be encouraged and, like Spencer, strongly believed in free trade. He advocated a reduction of the export tax on coffee and, of course, it was as part of the coffee-magnate Campos Sales' government that he worked. But it is important to note that he made no effort in defense of the decadent planters who had ruled Brazil before 1889. His refusal to defend the coffee trade at a time of crisis may have strengthened the large landowners, but this is not evidence that he represented the traditional society; the old aristocracy would have much preferred to maintain unprofitable properties as symbols of their status. It was only the more dynamic and entrepreneurially spirited plantation owners that could profit from this policy. Furthermore, his attack on protectionism was principally based on a deep aversion to all special privileges characteristic of a traditional society. 'The state', he said, 'neither can nor should protect individuals or classes, but only the rights of each one.' In historical perspective he cannot be considered retrograde: the new groups— São Paulo coffee planters and urban industrialists—were just beginning to divide and many of them were still closely related by family ties. As an entrepreneur himself, he could not have been alien to the ambitions of the industrial groups. The most likely explanation for his position is that, like Spencer, he sincerely believed *laissez faire* and the struggle for survival would lead to industrialization.[1]

Yet there is no doubt that Spencerianism included some really perplexing paradoxes for the Brazilian modernizers. First of all, the logical implication of evolutionary change is that it comes about very, very slowly. A monarchist, for instance, used Spencer to argue that the evolution of Brazilian society had not yet reached

[1] Murtinho, *Introducções aos relatorios*, 1897, pp. v, vii, x, xiv, xxiii; 1899, p. xv. For a contrary point of view see Nelson Werneck Sodré, *História da burguesia brasileira*, Retratos do Brasil, 22 (Rio: Civilização Brasileira, 1964), pp. 226, 233.

the stage for republican government. Murtinho was also aware of this implication. In his report of 1897 he said 'The growth of each nation is subject to natural laws; like all living beings, nations need a certain fixed time...for their growth. When any people seek to violate these laws, instead of absorbing and growing they are absorbed'.[1] Such a view would not suit most of those committed to rapid change in Brazil, and they, as so often happens with those who speak of an 'inevitable' future, shunned its logical implications and strove to bring about evolution through speedy reform.

There were even greater puzzles posed by social Darwinism. For one thing, the evolutionists placed considerable emphasis on race as a major factor in development. Now Brazil was not noted for the purity of its racial background nor for the predominance of northern Europeans. Murtinho, for instance, argued that the United States could not be used as 'a model for our industrial development, because we do not have the superior aptitudes of her race, the principal cause of the industrial progress of that great country'. Euclides da Cunha had noted that 'in this admirable competition of nations, all evolving through struggle without quarter in which selection makes use of qualities preserved by heredity, the mestizo is an outsider'. Some Brazilians concluded that the solution was to foster immigration. Romero went so far as to suggest that it was through miscegenation that the white race would win in its struggle for existence. But most of those committed to change preferred to ignore the question.[2]

[1] Antonio Luiz dos Santos Werneck, *O positivismo republicano na Academia* (São Paulo: Seckler, 1880), pp. 125, 126; Murtinho, *Introducções aos relatorios*, 1897, p. xvii.

[2] Murtinho, *Introducções aos relatorios*, 1897, p. ix; Euclides da Cunha, *Os sertões*, p. 97; on immigration see Anfriso Fialho, *Processo da monarquia brasileira; necessidade da convocação de nova constituinte* (Rio: Typ. da 'Constituinte', 1886), p. 47; on Romero see Antônio Cândido de Mello e Souza, *O método crítico de Sílvio Romero*, 2nd ed., Universidade de São Paulo, Cadeira de Teoria Literária e Literatura Comparada (1), Boletim 266 (São Paulo: Universidade de São Paulo, 1963), p. 45. Cf. the ambiguous attitude of João Baptista de Lacerda, 'The *Metis*, or Half-breeds, of Brazil', in *Papers on Inter-racial Problems Communicated to the First Universal Races Congress Held at the University of London, July 26–29, 1911*, ed. G. Spiller (London & Boston: King & World's Peace Foundation, 1911); despite Joseph Arthur, *comte* de Gobineau's presence in Brazil as French consul, there are relatively few references to race in his private correspondence with the emperor, *D. Pedro II e o conde de Gobineau (correspondências inéditas)*, ed. and transl. George Raeders, Brasiliana, 109 (São Paulo: Editôra Nacional, 1938).

Only the abolitionists could not ignore it. Their opponents denied the possibility of 'an inferior race unschooled in the precepts of civilization and the social state of other races' ever adapting to freedom. Yet those influenced by Spencer were nevertheless abolitionists, and, of course, Spencer himself had not defended Negro slavery. Frontin and Júlio Ribeiro were both abolitionists, and Sílvio Romero was against slavery, although he wanted it to end without state action.[1] The degree of their perplexity can be seen in the pages of the abolitionists' official organ. In 1881 it said 'It interests us very little to know whether the Negro is biologically or sociologically inferior to the white. Inferior or superior, there is no reason for two, three, and four hundred Negroes to work for one white man...Fortunately...the chief...of the evolutionists, Mr Darwin...[is] on the side of the abolitionists'. In an interesting reversal of arguments heard today in the southern United States, it added, 'this [racist] point of view is perhaps scientific, but our Constitution enshrined the equality of man and it is not for us to carry out sociological experiments'.[2] Joaquim Nabuco later refined the abolitionist argument. Many of the characteristics of slavery 'may be attributed to the Negro race, to its retarded mental development, to its barbarous instincts, to its crude superstitions...but even so...if they had been brought to Brazil at a time when slavery did not exist...the mixture of whites and Negroes would not have been accompanied by the mongrelization of the advanced by the backward race, but by the gradual elevation of the latter'. Brazil, he argued, would have been a 'much more robust nation' if it had been developed by free Africans working under Portuguese leadership. In short, 'The bad element in the population has not been the Negro race but this race reduced to captivity.'[3]

Social Darwinists also maintained that to the victor belong the

[1] Associação Commercial do Rio de Janeiro, *Elemento servil;...representação da commissão especial...1884* (Rio: Villeneuve, 1884), p. 10; Moraes, *Campanha abolicionista*, pp. 28–30; Ribeiro actually reflected a racist point of view in *A carne*, pp. 39–40, 44, 170.

[2] *O abolicionista: orgão da Sociedade Brasileira Contra a Escravidão*, no. 10, 1 Aug. 1881, pp. 3, 4.

[3] Joaquim Nabuco, *O abolicionismo* [2nd ed.?] (Rio & São Paulo: Civilização Brasileira & Editôra Nacional, 1938), pp. 138–41; Nabuco thus foreshadowed viewpoints that made Gilberto Freyre famous after 1930.

spoils and that the weak must give way. Natural selection and the survival of the fittest must be the guiding principles of society. Despite Spencer's preference for peaceful international relations he was forced to the conclusion that just as 'the struggle for existence has been an indispensable means to evolution' in the 'animate world at large', so 'similarly with social organisms. We must recognize the truth that the struggles for existence between societies have been instrumental to their evolution'. None of the developments of human society 'would have been possible without inter-tribal and international conflicts'.[1] Oliveira Vianna had similarly spoken of natural selection, and Júlio Ribeiro had reiterated that 'in the battle of existence, no matter what weapon is used, what matters is not to be vanquished: the victor is always right'.[2]

In a world of conflict, Brazil lay relatively defenseless. Europeans took no pains to hide this opinion. As one British missionary put it, 'this land awaits its master, a race that will "clear the land of evil, drive the road and bridge the ford"'.[3] Some Brazilians rejected such ideas out of hand. Murtinho took it as a warning to avoid the Europeans until the Brazilian 'race' was better equipped for the struggle. One of his contemporaries, a novelist, preferred to laugh at the whole idea. But on the whole, these urban groups took it to mean that in order to compete Brazil must modernize.[4]

Those who were pledged to modern change could evidently find encouragement even in threatening ideas. They could also afford to overlook the pessimistic though logical conclusions to be drawn from these new concepts if they could gain, in compensation, a massive synthesis of human knowledge in which the core was science and a reassurance that industrialization was the

---

[1] Spencer, *Principles of Sociology*, II, 240, 241. Also see Jacques Barzun, *Darwin, Marx, Wagner: Critique of a Heritage* (Boston: Little, Brown, 1941), pp. 100–6; Hofstadter, *Social Darwinism*, pp. 170–200.

[2] Oliveira Vianna, 'O povo brasileiro', p. 286; Ribeiro, *A carne*, p. 183.

[3] A. Stuart McNairn, *Three Republics; A Study in Contrasts* (London: Evangelical Union of South America, n.d.), p. 11.

[4] Eduardo Prado, *Collectaneas*, 4 vols. (São Paulo: Escola Typographica Salesiana, 1904–5), II, 162, 171–4; Salvador de Menezes Drummond Furtado de Mendonça, *A situação internacional do Brazil* (Rio: Garnier, 1913), p. 43; Murtinho, *Introducções aos relatorios*, 1897, p. xvii; Joaquim Maria Machado de Assis, *Quincas Borba* (n.p.: Instituto de Divulgação Cultural, n.d.), p. 19; Barros, *A ilustração brasileira*, p. 166.

goal of an inevitable progress. If man was merely an animal, then he could not be bound by divinely sanctioned but outworn traditions; reason could be brought to bear on all his problems. *Laissez faire* and competition without quarter were the most rational policies, so let them be. Nothing but the highest accolades could thus be given Herbert Spencer: in the commencement address delivered at the Rio de Janeiro medical school in 1899 the speaker referred to him as 'the greatest thinker of our times, the modern Aristotle, the thinker in honor of whom this century should be called the century of Spencer'.[1]

[1] According to Corrêa Filho, *Joaquim Murtinho*, p. 174.

10

MIDDLE-CLASS BRITAIN AND
THE BRAZILIAN LIBERALS

Nineteenth-century Brazilians who took an interest in English developments recognized the Reform Bill of 1832 as one of the most important events in British history. Indeed, it had meant a transformation in the texture of British politics and was the result of new patterns in the economic and social fabric of the nation. Napoleon is supposed to have said that England was a nation of shopkeepers; but it was only through the Act of 1832 that the shopkeepers secured political power to match their pre-eminent position in the economy. And throughout the first half of the nineteenth century the British middle class sought to strengthen this newly acquired power by propagating ideas which would clear away the vestiges of the old aristocratic order or protect its position from any threat posed by the lower classes. Nineteenth-century political liberalism served these purposes abundantly. Although intellectuals heaped a growing pile of criticism upon these concepts, the *bourgeoisie* continued to accept most of them without question at least until the First World War. Their example was not lost on similarly motivated groups in Brazil.

Four ideas of this social class in Britain were to prove most important in Brazil. First, the privileges of special groups or individuals must all be ended as relics of an outworn system. Instead, all members of society, even the sovereign, should be subject to the rule of a uniform law. Second, British industrialists and businessmen placed their faith in results. They believed laws should be formulated for the rational solution of problems even if this were to mean radical departures from past tradition. Third, the most important legal objective was to make the individual free to fulfill himself. Society's only duty was to protect his freedom and thus give him the opportunity for this self-realization. The struggles in Britain on behalf of civil liberties, the abolition of slavery, the poor laws, intellectual and religious freedom, were all reflections of this concept. Finally, although not as clearly defined, the belief was current that only those members of society who were making a genuine contribution should be represented in government. These were primarily the capitalists, the entrepreneurs, those who by becoming rich themselves were enriching the nation.

The core of their ideology was the belief in the freedom of the individual. John Stuart Mill was much quoted in Brazil. His famous essay, *On Liberty*, proved especially appealing, for in it he had developed the argument that the only cause the state has to restrict an individual is to keep him from infringing upon the liberty of another: 'Human beings should be free to form opinions, and to express their opinions without reserve... [And] men should be free to act upon their opinions—to carry these out in their lives, without hindrance...from their fellow-men, so long as it is at their own risk and peril.' For Mill, the individual was all-important. Society was not greater than the sum of its parts, but rather 'The worth of a State, in the long run, is the worth of the individuals composing it.'[1]

The British middle class was anxious to justify its hegemony over the working classes, and egalitarian democracy was not a part of its scheme of things. Mill pointed out that '"the tyranny of the majority" is now generally included among the evils against which society requires to be on its guard'.[2] The equalization of economic power was even further from the *bourgeois* concept of the social good. The Combination Acts of 1824 and 1825 had assured the freedom of the individual to sign onerous contracts. Thomas Robert Malthus led his readers to believe that since population tended to increase faster than food-supply, human misery was the natural and unavoidable result. David Ricardo argued that an increase in wages would merely lead to an increase in numbers eventually causing even greater misery. In addition, according to his 'wage-fund' theory, there was only so much to be paid in wages and any increase in the wages earned by one group

[1] John Stuart Mill, *On Liberty*, 3rd ed. (London: Longman, Green, Longman, Roberts & Green, 1864), pp. 100, 207. Also see pp. 21–2, 26, 102, 168, 190.
[2] *Ibid.* p. 13.

of workers would result in the loss of wages by another group. The logical conclusion was that labor unions and social legislation were to be avoided in the interest of the laborers themselves. The 'classical economists' were said to have created a dismal science; but it was dismal only for the workers, not for the *bourgeoisie*.[1]

The same gusty winds that drove political liberalism in England impelled it in Brazil: the restlessness of a new class anxious to destroy the traditional system, establish its own position, and defend it against any later menace. In a traditional society the individual is unimportant and his rights are determined by his unchanging place in a static social structure. It was the ambition of the Brazilian liberals to smash this system and release the individual from its binding force. When this class had been small, as in the period before 1850, the liberals enjoyed very limited success. Even in the fifteen years preceding the outbreak of the Paraguayan War most of this set remained quiescent. But subsequently, with the developing strength of the new interests, their voice was increasingly heard in political life.

It is not commonly recognized that the liberals had been generally ineffective before the process of modern change began to affect Brazilian society. They had habitually avoided social and economic issues, and even the end of the slave trade had not been particularly theirs. Their political ideas had made progress only haltingly despite the efforts of a few vigorous exponents. The

[1] British political thought is discussed by the following writers: Walter Edwards Houghton, *The Victorian Frame of Mind, 1830–1870* (New Haven: Wellesley College and Yale Univ. Press, 1957); Jerome Hamilton Buckley, *Victorian Temper: a Study in Literary Culture* (Cambridge, Mass.: Harvard Univ. Press, 1951); Harman Grisewood, *et al. Ideas and Beliefs of the Victorians: an Historical Revaluation of the Victorian Age* (London: Sylvan, 1949); Crane Brinton, *English Political Thought in the Nineteenth Century* (London: Benn, 1933); John Bowle, *Politics and Opinion in the Nineteenth Century. An Historical Introduction* (London: Cape, 1954); Ernest L. Woodward, *The Age of Reform, 1815–1870*, Oxford History of England (Oxford: Clarendon, 1946); Guido de Ruggiero, *The History of European Liberalism*, transl. R. G. Collingwood (Boston: Beacon, 1959), pp. 93–157; Albert Venn Dicey, *Lectures on the Relation between Law and Public Opinion in England during the Nineteenth Century* (London: Macmillan, 1905), pp. 64, 125–209. Note lengthy references to Mill in Paulo Egydio de Oliveira Carvalho, *Do conceito scientifico das leis sociologicas;...introducção. Volume primeiro* (São Paulo: Ribeiro, 1898), pp. 69–93; Raimundo de Farias Brito, *A base physica do espirito; historia summaria do problema da mentalidade como preparação para o estudo da philosophia do espirito* (Rio: Francisco Alves, 1912), pp. 196–209.

Constitution of 1824 had not been a 'liberal' document and, especially in view of its promulgation by the king himself and its faulty implementation, it had done little to upset the traditional dominance of the landed aristocrats. Occasional liberal victories—not to be confused with the political success of the Liberal Party—were more apparent than real and, in any case, quickly reversed by the forces of conservatism, as happened with the home-rule provisions of the Additional Act of 1834. Their most brilliant political maneuvers, for instance the declaration of the emperor's majority in 1840, had invariably backfired. And when they turned to revolution they had been regularly defeated, not so much by the military might of the central government as by the general apathy of the population. Finally, the liberals seem to have conceded defeat, and throughout the 1850s and into the 1860s they had either abandoned politics or joined in a coalition government where liberal demands were pretty much ignored.

But a new era was being engendered in Brazil by the very tranquility that this arrangement made possible. With the economic growth of that period there arose more powerful groups of city dwellers interested in political change. They now came to believe that, as long as the government was the private preserve of a landed oligarchy, was directed by an aging and unimaginative monarch, and was unresponsive to the growing tide of discontent, nothing would or could be done to create the progressive society they envisioned. They became steadily more dissatisfied with the spirit of political conciliation of the 1850s, with the middle-of-the-road Liberal Progressive Party created in 1862, with the Constitution, and with the emperor himself. Some members of the old Liberal Party—since extinguished—strained at the leash and demanded thoroughgoing reform instead of coalition with conservatives. In 1868 and 1869 they joined a new group of liberals to form the Club da Reforma, create a new Liberal Party, and issue a program known by the bravado of its last words as 'Reform or Revolution'. Still more radical elements drew up the Republican Manifesto in 1870 and eventually did choose revolution.[1]

[1] João Camillo de Oliveira Tôrres, *A democracia coroada: teoria política do império do Brasil*, 2nd ed. (Petrópolis, R.J.: Editôra Vozes, 1964), pp. 303–9; Americo Brasiliense de

In both cases the liberals had as principal function, as one of them put it somewhat wistfully, 'the development and realization of the modern and civilizing aspirations which are held by the more intellectual and progressive part of the nation'.[1]

The Brazilian liberals echoed the demands of the British middle class with a fidelity which would be surprising if their common purposes were not clear. Thus, the most important and steadily recurring call was for individual freedom. Whether this idea was directed toward the insistence on civil liberties through reform of the criminal code, or whether it was expressed in the abolitionist crusade, it was central to their liberalism. The right to use 'words freely, written or spoken, at meetings or in the newspapers', said one influential Anglophile, 'never harmed free institutions but only oppressive ones'.[2] Keeping education free from state control was another evidence of liberal feeling, and England was used as an example of the achievements that were possible through private initiative in education. Liberty of conscience was still another demand regularly voiced by Brazilian liberals.

They also insisted on the rule of law equally applicable to all and the end of special privileges, prerogatives, and exemptions derived from one's social 'condition'. They denounced the privilege of the large landowner over the merchant and industrialist, of the well-born over the *nouveau riche*, and of the courtier over the entrepreneur. The Republican Manifesto pushed the liberal point to its ultimate conclusion, decrying 'the arbitrary and hateful distinctions which create...the monstrous superiority of one over all or of a few over many'.[3]

Almeida Mello, ed., *Os programas dos partidos e o 2º império. Primeira parte: exposição de principios* (São Paulo: Seckler, 1878), p. 42; only in 1889 did the republicans acknowledge the revolutionary conclusion to which their argument led, George C. A. Boehrer, *Da monarquia à república; história do Partido Republicano do Brasil (1870–1889)*, transl. Berenice Xavier (Rio: Ministério da Educação e Cultura, Serviço de Documentação, 1954), pp. 237–9. On class origins of the movement cf. Ruggiero, *History of European Liberalism*, pp. 94–8.

[1] Joaquim Nabuco, 'Manifesto da Sociedade Contra a Escravidão, 1880', in Osvaldo Melo Braga, *Bibliografia de Joaquim Nabuco*, Instituto Nacional do Livro, Coleção B–1: Bibliografia, 8 (Rio: Imp. Nacional, 1952), p. 17.

[2] Ruy Barbosa, *Liberdade commercial. O partido liberal bahiano. Discurso proferido...na Assembléa Provincial da Bahia na sessão de 27 de junho de 1878* (Bahia: Typ. do 'Diario da Bahia', 1878), p. 19.

[3] Brasiliense de Almeida Mello, *Os programas dos partidos*, p. 62.

Some of the proposals voiced by the liberals were particular to the Brazilian situation, but even here the basic inspiration was much the same. Thus, as the above remark by the republicans makes clear, the Brazilian liberals believed that the freedom of the individual required that the might of the emperor be weakened and the power of the 'people' increased. The means to such an end, agreed most liberals, would be to end the life tenure of Senators, provide for their direct election instead of appointment by the crown, put through electoral reforms to lessen corruption and widen the suffrage, and institute a ministry responsible to the representatives of the people rather than to the arbitrary wishes of the emperor. In his 'personal power', that is, the alleged abuse of the Moderative Power ascribed to him by the constitution, they quarried rhetorical stones to hurl at the outgoing order.

On one point the liberals preferred the example of the United States to that of Great Britain. They felt that in a country as large as Brazil only federalism could adequately protect the individual from the State. The central government must be weakened; not only should the municipalities have greater powers, but the provinces must be erected into virtual states instead of being merely administrative districts.

Democracy, as in early-nineteenth-century Britain, was not part of the liberal program. Universal manhood suffrage was not considered either a realistic or desirable goal. Extension of the franchise consisted in lowering but not abolishing property qualifications. And it would have been indeed surprising if, at a time when they were still battling so backward a structure of society, they had taken up the demands for economic equality then beginning to be heard in industrial Europe. When they took a position with regard to social justice it was to declare that justice did not mean equality, but rather, that each man should have as much freedom as the next. Tavares Bastos advocated those reforms in the electoral system which would allow Protestants, naturalized citizens, freedmen, and even ex-convicts to vote, but agreed to exclude wage-earners, apprentices, and servants. Besides reflecting his desire to encourage immigration, his ideas suggest that qualities of birth and even an occasional lapse from the straight-and-narrow should not deprive a person of political rights; but the failure to achieve financial success raised serious questions about one's fitness. He was scandalized by the fact that the law regarding property qualifications was then being applied so as to allow 'vagabonds...indigents...and even servants' to vote.[1]

A curious aspect of Brazilian liberalism at that time was its marked concentration on particular demands and relatively little concern with abstract considerations on liberty or the sovereignty of the people. The experience of France, or of some of the Spanish American republics, or perhaps of their own country in the period before 1850 seems to have discouraged any speculation of this sort. In general, it was not the search for Liberty, but for 'liberties', only theoretically to be exercised by all men, that impelled these Brazilian liberals. In this sense they were closer to what Guido de Ruggiero has called 'English liberalism' than to the French liberal ideology.[2]

Brazilian liberalism naturally derived its inspiration from many sources. Some families passed on their liberal leanings generation after generation dating back to the days of struggle between the colonials and Portuguese administrators. Iberian individualism itself made some Brazilians particularly open to the liberal

---

[1] Quoted by Oliveira Tôrres, *A democracia coroada*, p. 310; note that, relying on property qualifications, they had little need for literacy tests, José Honório Rodrigues, *Conciliação e reforma no Brasil. Um desafio histórico-político*, Retratos do Brasil, 32 (Rio: Civilização Brasileira, 1965), pp. 135-63. The liberal program is summarized by Theophilo Benedicto Ottoni, *Circular dedicada aos srs. eleitores pela provincia de Minas-Geraes no quatriennio actual e especialmente dirigida aos srs. eleitores de deputados pelo 2º districto eleitoral da mesma provincia para a proxima legislatura*, 2nd ed. (Rio: Typ. do Correio Mercantil, 1860); Brasiliense de Almeida Mello, *Os programas dos partidos*, pp. 25-6, 29-30, 37-9, 43; Oliveira Tôrres, *Democracia coroada*, pp. 295-320; and José Maria dos Santos, *A politica geral do Brasil* (São Paulo: Magalhães, 1930) pp. 50, 122-7. (On pp. 5-8 and 113-14 he denies the grounds of their complaint against the 'personal power'.) On 'freedom of education' see Cezar Augusto Vianna de Lima, *Estudo sobre o ensino primario no Reino Unido da Grã-Bretanha e Irlanda* (Rio: Imp. Nacional, 1885), p. v; Roque Spencer Maciel de Barros, *A ilustração brasileira e a idéia de universidade*, Universidade de São Paulo, Cadeira de História e Filosofia da Educação, Boletim, 241 (2) (São Paulo: Universidade de São Paulo, 1959), pp. 87, 107; and cf. Mill, *On Liberty*, p. 191. On the federal idea see João Camillo de Oliveira Tôrres, *A formação do federalismo no Brasil*, Brasiliana, 308 (São Paulo: Editôra Nacional, 1961), pp. 17-41, 82-151.

[2] Ruggiero, *History of European Liberalism*, pp. 347-50; this treatment has profited from discussions with Professor Charles Hale.

doctrine. And of course, the French literary-cultural tradition was necessarily a vehicle for the transmission of a certain liberalism.[1]

Nevertheless, it is noteworthy that the British influence was one of the canals through which coursed the liberal stream. For one thing, Britishers in Brazil sought out and became identified with the liberals, and no doubt the importance of these contacts in fostering liberalism goes far beyond the written records.[2] Even more widespread was the acquaintance of educated persons with British history and British authors. In the attack upon the 'personal power' of the emperor, appeal was made to British eighteenth-century efforts against the royal prerogative and even to the seventeenth-century English revolutions. Tito Franco de Almeida, one of the angriest writers against the emperor's arbitrary use of power, made effective use of the British experience to defend his case in 1867. Pointing to the Stuarts, he alleged that death or dethronement was the inevitable fate of kings who 'thirsted for absolute power in a free country'.[3] Nabuco de Araújo, who had been somewhat influenced by English writers, helped frame the liberal program, denouncing 'irresponsible power' and hailing the importance of 'individual liberty as a practical reality'.[4] Some republicans, finding that the monarchists gleefully pointed to the liberalism of monarchical England, resorted to the Irish as their model.[5]

[1] See e.g. Afonso Arinos de Melo Franco, *Um estadista da república (Afrânio de Melo Franco e seu tempo)*, Documentos Brasileiros, 85, 3 vols. (Rio: José Olympio, 1955), I, 98; Vianna de Lima, *Estudo sobre o ensino primario*, p. 38.

[2] Luís Viana Filho, *A vida de Rui Barbosa* (centenary edition) [6th ed.?] (São Paulo: Editôra Nacional, 1952), p. 91; Antonio Augusto da Costa Aguiar to D. Pedro II, São Paulo, 26 June 1862; and Antonio Augusto da Costa Aguiar, 'Copia de um memorial dirigido por mim ao Exmo. Presidente désta provincia, o Conselheiro Vicente Pires da Motta, no dia 3 de fevereiro de 1863' (MS.), AMIP, CXXXII, 6422 and 6484.

[3] Tito Franco de Almeida, *Conselheiro Francisco José Furtado. Biografia e estudo da história política contemporânea*, 2nd ed., Brasiliana, 245 (São Paulo: Editôra Nacional, 1944), pp. 12–14, 357–61, esp. p. 13; also see *A provincia de São Paulo*, 20 Jan. 1875, p. 2.

[4] Joaquim Nabuco, *Um estadista do imperio, Nabuco de Araujo. Sua vida, suas opiniões, sua época*, [2nd ed. ?], 2 vols. (Rio & São Paulo: Civilização Brasileira & Editôra Nacional, 1936), II, 77–83, 400n.–401n., esp. 81 and 82n.; note appeal to English example in speech of Rodolpho Dantas, 17 June 1879, Brazil, Congresso, Câmara dos Deputados, *Anais*, 1879, II, 122; and copying of British political tactics, Brasiliense de Almeida Mello, *Os programas dos partidos*, p. 41.

[5] Mauro Ivan, 'Fenianos nasceram na luta pela república', *Jornal do Brasil*, 27 Jan. 1965, Caderno B, p. 3.

Four liberal leaders who were particularly influenced by the British deserve special mention. Francisco Otaviano de Almeida Rosa and Zacarias de Góes e Vasconcelos were older men—educated before 1850—who played important roles in the formation of the new Liberal Party in 1868–9. Joaquim Nabuco and Rui Barbosa, both born in 1849, were leading critics of the old regime during the last decade of the empire and, in consequence, had to face the problems posed to later liberals by the democratic emphasis on equality. The ideals of the British middle class were accepted by both generations.

Francisco Otaviano de Almeida Rosa (1826–89) had a hand in almost every liberal advance of this period. A mulatto, son of a Rio de Janeiro physician, he was a graduate of the São Paulo law school. His first legal practice was in the offices of Francisco Inácio de Carvalho Moreira, later *barão* do Penedo, and a prominent friend of the British. In 1848 he became secretary to the governor of the province of Rio de Janeiro and five years later was elected to the Chamber of Deputies. In 1862 he was the mouthpiece for the protest movement that began the destruction of the era of conciliation. For several years he used as a vehicle for his ideas the liberal *Correio mercantil*, of which he was editor. In 1867 he was chosen for the Senate, where he actively defended liberal ideals. Having contributed powerfully to the passage in 1871 of the law freeing the children of slave mothers, he later became an outright abolitionist.[1]

By the time he was eight years old Otaviano was studying English, and in law school he became an admirer of Lord Byron. He didn't live his Byronism as did some of his fellow students who delighted in staging midnight parties in taverns, locking themselves up for week-long orgies with prostitutes, or engaging in macabre festivals of necromancy. But he translated a great number of the Englishman's poems, and absorbed from him a romantic love of liberty. In 1867 he traveled to Europe via England, where, along with his good friend Tavares Bastos, he 'did'

---

[1] Phocion Serpa, *Francisco Otaviano; ensaio biográfico* (Rio: Publicações da Academia Brasileira, 1952); Santos, *Politica geral*, p. 51; Nabuco, *Um estadista do império*, II, 144, 151–2.

all the tourist spots no doubt including some scenes of Byron's indiscretions.[1]

On his return, he immediately launched an attack on the emperor and on the 'despotic laws' of the empire. He signed the Liberal Manifesto of 1869, and it was he who put into it the maxim 'the king reigns but does not govern', with which he meant to refer to the English model.[2]

His middle-class connexions are emphasized by the fact that he was Mauá's friend and lawyer. When in England he took pains to visit the Bank of England and spent some time in the 'City' with the *barão* do Penedo, participating in financial discussions. There he must have found the same attitudes toward the state that he injected into his liberalism in Brazil. It was, for instance, to England that he pointed when he argued on behalf of free enterprise.[3] As a leading force within the body politic, he greatly advanced the cause of liberalism, and the English influence upon him was a notable aspect in the development of his ideology.

One of the most important liberal leaders of Brazil was the fiery Zacarias de Góes e Vasconcelos (1815–77). Born in Bahia, he studied law at the Recife academy, where he became a teacher

[1] Serpa, *Francisco Otaviano*, pp. 27, 35, 49, 158, 161, 165; Xavier Pinheiro, ed., *Francisco Octaviano, carioca illustre nas letras, no jornalismo, na politica, na tribuna, e na diplomacia* (Rio: Edição da Revista de Lingua Portuguesa, 1925), pp. 105, 112, 115, 175, 183, 188, 189, 193, 197, 241–8; on his professional use of English see Otaviano to José Carlos de Almeida Arêas, *visconde* de Ourém, Rio, 6 July 1848, in Max Fleuiss, ed., 'Francisco Octaviano inedito', *ibid.* p. 382; Renato Mendonça, *Um diplomata na côrte de Inglaterra; o barão do Penedo e sua época*, Brasiliana, 219 (São Paulo: Editôra Nacional, 1942), pp. 329–30. On Byron's influence at the law academy see Pires de Almeida, 'A escola byroniana no Brazil (suas origens, evolução, decadencia e desapparecimento)', *Jornal do commercio*, 17 July 1904, p. 2; 5 Feb. p. 4; 26 Feb. pp. 3–4; 22 Mar. p. 3; 8 June p. 4; 13 July p. 3; 20 Nov. pp. 3–4, 1905; Jamil Alamansur Haddad, *O romanticismo brasileiro e as sociedades secretas do tempo* (São Paulo: Siqueira, 1945), pp. 81–3; Samuel Putnam, *Marvelous Journey: A Survey of Four Centuries of Brazilian Writing* (New York: Knopf, 1948), p. 116; Brazil's great poet, Manuel Antonio Alvares de Azevedo (1831–52), was almost Otaviano's contemporary in law school and closely modeled his work on that of Byron, Vera Pacheco Jordão, *Maneco, o byroniano* (Rio: Ministério da Educação e Cultura, 1955).

[2] Otaviano quoted by Mendonça, *Um diplomata na côrte de Inglaterra*, p. 238; also see pp. 240–1; Brasiliense de Almeida Mello, *Os programas dos partidos*, pp. 37, 54.

[3] Serpa, *Francisco Otaviano*, p. 140; Mendonça, *Um diplomata na côrte de Inglaterra*, pp. 302, 330, 370; Nazareth Prado, ed., *Antonio Prado no imperio e na republica: seus discursos e actos colligidos e apresentados por sua filha* (Rio: Briguiet, 1929), pp. 127–8.

not long after graduation. At that time Jeremy Bentham was much read there and John Stuart Mill was being published in Portuguese translation by a local printer. After having served terms as president of various provinces, Zacarias was elected to the Chamber of Deputies in 1850, where he remained until 1864. He was then named a Senator, was included in several cabinets, and presided over three of them, most notably in 1866–8. He had begun as a Conservative, but in the 1850s he joined the coalition government, and his liberalism gradually increased in all but his attitudes toward the Church. His programs as prime minister included opening the Amazon to the trade of all nations and emancipation for the slaves. Although especially gifted at making enemies, at times he wielded great political force and, therefore, he played a significant role in advancing the liberal cause in Brazil. Indeed, his dismissal from power in 1868 led to the foundation of the new Liberal Party.[1] In praise of liberalism he was always fond of comparing Brazilian and British legislative practice to the disadvantage of the former.[2]

Zacarias' most famous contribution to the liberal ideology was his book *Da natureza e limites do poder moderador* published as early as 1860. Its principal demand was that the cabinet should be responsible to Parliament for the acts of the Moderative Power. He cited British history as principal defense for his case and quoted Thomas Babington Macaulay extensively, sometimes in English, as, for example: 'If this prerogative were without limit the English government could scarcely be distinguished from a pure despotism.' In other places his discussion of English constitutional history was based on Henry Peter, Lord Brougham's *The British Constitution: Its History, Structure and Working*. But the chief inspiration for this Brazilian writer was John Stuart Mill, and he quoted *On Liberty* even on the title page of his book. His acquaintance with Mill in the original English and his dependence

---

[1] José Maria dos Santos, *Os republicanos paulistas e a abolição* (São Paulo: Martins, 1942), pp. 46–7; Barros, *A ilustração brasileira*, p. 96n.; Nabuco, *Um estadista do império*, 1, 11–12; Gilberto Freyre, *Ingléses no Brasil; aspectos da influência britânica sôbre a vida, a paisagem e a cultura do Brasil*, Documentos Brasileiros, 58 (Rio: José Olympio, 1948), p. 65.

[2] Speech of Zacarias, Senado, 29 Sept. 1877, *Diario do Rio de Janeiro*, 6 Oct. 1877, p. 3.

upon him as a source of his political ideas is altogether evident.[1] Brazilian liberals thus found sustenance in Britain for their struggle against the restraining forces laid on the individual by a traditional society. The abolitionist Joaquim Nabuco was also a liberal in his political views. As a student in the São Paulo law school he participated in the protest of 1868 caused by the dismissal of Zacarias, thirty-five years his senior.[2] Although he later campaigned for political office primarily as an abolitionist, he never failed to point to his other liberal beliefs. His maiden speech in 1879 outlined his ambitions: 'direct election, religious freedom, the emancipation of the slaves.'[3] Two years later he promised 'to continue the fight for liberal principles from which I have never once strayed', especially for a government that would not be 'autocratic'.[4] He battled forcefully for measures tending toward separation of Church and State, and in 1885 he proposed the creation of a federal system within the monarchy.[5] The English influence upon his liberalism was as great as upon his abolitionism. 'When I enter the Chamber [of Deputies] I am entirely under the influence of English liberalism, as if I were working under the orders of Gladstone. This is really a result of my political education: I am an English liberal... in the Brazilian Parliament.'[6]

Why did this proponent of change not join so many of his friends and colleagues in becoming a republican? Because of the influence upon him of the British middle class. He explained that as a law student he had fluctuated between republicanism and monarchism until he read Walter Bagehot's *The English Consti-*

[1] Zacarias de Góes e Vasconcellos, *Da natureza e limites do poder moderador*, 2nd ed. (Rio: Laemmert, 1862), pp. vii, 49, 61–2, 105, 202, 214–37, 248–50; Daniel Parish Kidder and James Cooley Fletcher, *Brazil and the Brazilians Portrayed in Historical and Descriptive Sketches*, 9th ed. (Boston: Little, Brown, 1879), p. 602.

[2] Joaquim Nabuco, *Minha formação*, [? ed.], Documentos Brasileiros, 90 (Rio: José Olympio, 1957), pp. 16–18; Carolina Nabuco, *The Life of Joaquim Nabuco*, transl. & ed. Ronald Hilton (Stanford, California: Stanford Univ. Press, 1950), p. 15.

[3] Quoted by Carolina Nabuco, *Life of Joaquim Nabuco*, p. 41.

[4] *O abolicionista; orgão da Sociedade Brasileira Contra a Escravidão*, no. 10, 1 Aug. 1881, p. 1.

[5] Joaquim Nabuco, speech of 16 July 1880, in *Obras completas*, 14 vols. (São Paulo: Instituto Progresso Editorial, 1949), XI, 102–18; note number of speeches on Church and State listed by Braga, *Bibliografia de Joaquim Nabuco*, pp. 43–52; Tôrres, *A formação do federalismo*, pp. 28–31.

[6] Nabuco, *Minha formação*, p. 182. Also see pp. 112, 119.

tution (published 1867). Bagehot, a leading social Darwinist, had been highly influential as editor of *The Economist* in forming the British businessman's mentality. In this book of summary and popularization he explained the British political system. Nabuco wrote that 'I owe to this little book...my unalterable monarchical fixation'. It was from Bagehot that he derived his understanding of the importance of royalty, aristocracy, pomp, and ceremony in keeping the people happy and in their place. These institutions were 'one of the artifices necessary to govern and satisfy the imagination of the masses'. As he later admitted, republicanism was just too democratic, for there was in it a certain illiberal lack of tolerance. 'French republicanism, which was and is our republicanism, has a ferment of hate, an egalitarian predisposition which leads logically to demagoguery.' He was horrified by the thought of the 'inevitable evils of democracy', that is, the vices of the lower classes brought to bear on the process of government. His anti-republicanism had derived from the English writer: without his guidance 'I would have been irresistibly swept into the republican movement which was then beginning'. Instead, he was a confirmed monarchist by 1873 and was to remain one until long after 1889.[1]

It is easy to understand how Nabuco could have been a monarchist in London, but it is more difficult to sympathize with that view when held in nineteenth-century Rio de Janeiro. From Bagehot he had discovered 'that a centuries-old monarchy of feudal origins, bounded by aristocratic forms and traditions, as is the English one, could be a government more directly and immediately of the people than a republic'.[2] In 1882 he confirmed through observation that 'the English constitution in the present reign has become the most liberal, open, and progressive of all political constitutions, without exception, past and present'.[3] But as he himself said in 1885, only the forms of parliamentary government were observed in Brazil: the Brazilian structure of government had as 'its sole purpose to conceal from the eyes of the

---

[1] Nabuco, *Minha formação*, pp. 20, 30, 33, 39, 51, 146, 200. On Bagehot see W. W. Rostow, *British Economy of the Nineteenth Century* (Oxford: Clarendon Press, 1948), pp. 162–3.
[2] Nabuco, *Minha formação*, p. 31; also see pp. 25–30.
[3] Joaquim Nabuco, 'Correspondencia', *Jornal do commercio*, 1 Apr. 1882, p. 3.

country the real government of the Lord's Anointed behind an appearance of popular authority'. Three years later he wrote to a friend to say that 'Although I have no faith in a Brazilian republic, I have no desire to support the monarchy against democracy in our present phase of feudalism'. Yet he felt there was more hope of remaking the monarchy into a liberal government than of creating a liberal government through republicanism: 'All my efforts are bent toward making the monarchy the creator and the protector of the only democracy that we can have in Brazil, that of the people themselves.'[1]

The 'people' to whom he referred were not the lower classes, for Nabuco had absorbed from his British contacts contempt for and hostility toward the workers. 'All that is superior has, in effect, the stamp of individuality and involves, therefore, contempt for the masses', he wrote. The thought of labor movements horrified him. They would hurt the worker more than anyone; the lower classes should rather entrust the success of their demands 'to the moral progress of laws'. He held that when these groups were militant, their leadership was always in the hands of opportunists. Finally, it was impossible for him 'to imagine a human society organized upon the negation of private property', and direct action by the workers, he thought, would lead only to tragedy.[2]

Yet his concern for the abolition of slavery elicited from him some sympathy for the plight of unprivileged groups, a recognition of the value of certain kinds of direct action, and an admission of some doubt about the sacredness of private property. He approved of old age security plans even though Herbert Spencer had said they would kill man's ability to struggle. Nabuco suggested that all progress had diminished this bestial ability. He half fearfully foresaw that inevitably the twentieth century would bring about the 'political predominance of the workers, not as clients of political parties that administer the nation with the ideas of the *bourgeoisie*, but as the governing class' itself.[3]

[1] Nabuco quoted by Carolina Nabuco, *Life of Joaquim Nabuco*, pp. 141, 182.
[2] Nabuco, *Minha formação*, p. 154 (also see p. 160); Joaquim Nabuco, 'O 1º de Maio', *Jornal do Brasil*, 10 June 1891, p. 1.
[3] Nabuco, 'O 1º de Maio'.

Despite these comments, the general thrust of Nabuco's thought as it related to the problems of his own day was precisely that of a *bourgeois*. He campaigned for the abolition of slavery not because he believed the slaves should have an equal share of political power, but because slavery was contrary to middle-class values. Slavery 'prevented the rise of regular family life...; robbed them of their savings and never paid their salaries;...made it impossible for them to have habits of...voluntary work, of responsibility, of personal dignity'. It was a contradiction of the individualism for which he fought.[1]

His political and social attitudes are not surprising in view of his close ties to the British business community which he greatly admired. In 1882, in 1883, and again in 1886-7, Nabuco lived in London chiefly dependent upon income earned as a corporation lawyer for British companies interested in Brazil. In 1883, for instance, he earned £52 per month from the Central Sugar Factories of Brazil, Ltd, and an average of £10 from miscellaneous legal cases. The *barão* do Penedo, Brazilian minister in London, helped him considerably by referring to him those businesses that inquired for legal advice at the Brazilian legation. Although they sometimes complained that he charged too much, Nabuco found the experience satisfactory and wished to repeat it in 1898.[2]

One of his most frequent business contacts was with Frederick Youle, a brother of one of André Rebouças' partners in promoting the D. Pedro II dock company. In 1892 Nabuco wrote Youle saying that 'with my sympathy and affinities for English life I could never cure myself of the wish to live in England and from that probably came the persistent hope that I would succeed in obtaining a position of trust, private not official, in which I could serve the interests of my own country and those of the British

[1] Joaquim Nabuco, *O abolicionismo*, [2nd ed. ?] (Rio & São Paulo: Civilização Brasileira & Editôra Nacional, 1938), pp. 29, 35, 142; cf. Nabuco, *Um estadista do império*, I, 75. However, Nabuco viewed sympathetically those members of the British parliament who spoke for the workers, Nabuco, 'Correspondencia', *Jornal do commercio*, 8 Mar. 1882, p. 2.

[2] Nabuco to *barão* do Penedo, Rio, 8 June, 31 July, 1881; 17 May 1885; London, 23 Jan. 1882; Nabuco to José Maria da Silva Paranhos, 2nd *barão* do Rio Branco, Rio, 3 Apr. 1886; Nabuco to João Arthur de Souza Correia, Rio, 20 Apr. 1898, in Nabuco, *Obras completas*, XIII, 47, 52, 66, 137, 143, 280; Linklater & Co. to Nabuco, London, 18 Apr. 1887; Field Roscoe & Co. to Nabuco, London, 18 July, 27 July, 29 July, 1887, JNP, Lata 7; Nabuco, *Minha formação*, pp. 91-3; Carolina Nabuco, *Life of Joaquim Nabuco*, pp. 91-2, 96.

capital seeker in her'. Sometimes Youle lent Nabuco considerable sums of money, yet they remained good friends. In 1894 he wished Youle would find him a sinecure working for a British company, as he had done for another Brazilian lawyer, but this good fortune was never to be his. In the 1890s he found his position as a monarchist made it inadvisable to continue the legal work he had occasionally carried out for the São Paulo Railway. Through Penedo he became acquainted with the Rothschilds and in 1881 was invited to a soirée at Alfred de Rothschild's. He later became an intimate of the financier's household and the latter even introduced him to the Prince of Wales. Nabuco was unable to parlay this friendship into employment, but when he had become Brazilian ambassador to the United States, Alfred de Rothschild referred to himself as one of 'your intimate and personal friends'.[1]

His close connexions with the British business community make it easy to understand why Nabuco's liberalism had a peculiarly middle-class quality. He distrusted the workers, found democracy alarming, and believed that against its threat only a monarchy would be successful. But his belief in the freedom of the individual impelled him to share many intellectual positions with the republicans, and his commitment to the abolition of slavery was to place him, like Rui Barbosa, among those who contributed heavily to the overthrow of the empire.

Probably the most important Brazilian liberal was Rui Barbosa (1849–1923). An expert on law and a spellbinding public speaker, he had a brilliant mind and a deep commitment to liberal ideals. He spoke several languages, owned a huge private library, and gained wide admiration for his erudition. His thought was largely influenced by the British, and it was the political liberalism of the middle class that made the deepest impression upon him.

[1] Nabuco to Youle, copy in Nabuco, 'Diário' (MS.), entry for 5 Oct. 1892, and entries for 19 Feb., 23 Mar., 1891; 16 May 1892; 14 Apr. 1893, JNP, Unclassified; Nabuco to Penedo, Rio, 29 Jan. 1885; 17 May 1885; 29 Sept. 1890; 6 Oct. 1892; 22 May 1894; 11 June, 9 Aug., 1894; London, 26 Feb. 1881; Nabuco to Rodolpho Dantas, London, 8 Jan. 1891; Nabuco to Correia, Rio, 20 Apr. 1898: in Nabuco, *Obras completas*, XIII, 44, 129, 137, 191, 197, 218, 235–6, 237, 239, 280; San Paulo (Brazilian) Railway Co., Ltd, to Nabuco, London, 9 June 1887, JNP, Lata 7; Alfred de Rothschild to Nabuco, London, 23 Feb. 1906, *ibid.* Lata 10; Carolina Nabuco, *Life of Joaquim Nabuco*, p. 253.

As a child he was taught English by his Anglophile father and when at law school in São Paulo he read English history avidly and acquired a thorough knowledge of the English language, although much of his reading at that time was still done in French. Even then he always identified himself with William Gladstone and the English liberals.

Barbosa began his political career in 1878 when he became a member of the provincial legislature of Bahia. The next year he went to Rio de Janeiro as a deputy and became linked to the Liberal Party by demanding greater local self-government and more protection for the rights of the individual. It was a short step from this position to a passive acceptance of republicanism, and, in 1889, after the *coup d'état* that toppled the empire, he was made a member of the governing junta. As Minister of the Treasury he revolutionized the country's currency structure, and he was largely responsible for the adoption of a constitution which closely followed the North American model.

When a military dictatorship was installed soon afterwards under Floriano Peixoto, Barbosa found himself at odds with the regime. His attacks upon it became so notorious that he had to flee for his life, first to Argentina and then to England in 1894. As a means of livelihood there he set up a law practice to serve British merchants and investors in Brazil. He also invested in the stock market. As he said, he had caught the 'good English disease'.[1]

In 1895 Barbosa returned to Brazil. His subsequent life was characterized by famous legal cases, classic opinions on judicial questions, participation in international conferences, and vigorous political campaigns. In 1907 he was sent to the Second Hague Peace Conference as head of the Brazilian mission. There, speaking in defense of small nations, he attracted great attention because of his erudition, ability to handle languages, and exaggerated sense of self-importance. In 1910 he waged a famous but abortive campaign for the presidency in which his opposition to mili-

---

[1] Barbosa to Jacobina, [London], 29 Jan. 1895, in Ruy Barbosa, *Mocidade e exilio. Cartas ao conselheiro Albino José Barbosa de Oliveira e ao dr. Antônio d'Araújo Ferreira Jacobina*, ed. Américo Jacobina Lacombe, Brasiliana, 38 (São Paulo: Editôra Nacional, 1934), p. 308.

tarism became a slogan against the military candidate, Hermes da Fonseca. Nine years later he ran again for the same office, certain of defeat, yet determined to make his views known to the public.[1] Barbosa's exile in 1894 provides an excellent opportunity to know something about his admiration for England, because not only did he write numerous private letters, but the *Jornal do comércio* asked him to write a series of articles dealing with the English scene.[2] These articles were received in Brazil with great interest and considerable controversy. He was accused of writing panegyrics of England. He did not apologize for this attitude, retorting that 'the tone of these studies does not vary the least bit from that with which I have invariably referred to this country of which I have always been one of the warmest defenders. My collection of English books is, I suppose, the biggest that there is among us. No one has studied English things more than I in our country. In the press, in parliament, on the speaker's platform, England has always been the great teacher for my liberal principles'.[3] Now he was drunk with England. 'Here I am,' he wrote to a friend, 'in this land...where I feel so wretched at being a Brazilian and so proud of being a man.'[4]

[1] Biographical information has been drawn from the following: Viana Filho, *A vida de Rui Barbosa*, esp. pp. 11, 15, 36, 37, 52, 287n.; Fernando Nery, *Rui Barbosa, ensaio biográfico*, 2nd ed. (Rio: Casa de Rui Barbosa, 1955); João Mangabeira, *Rui, o estadista da república*, Documentos Brasileiros, 40 (Rio: José Olympio, 1943); Floresta de Miranda, *Ruy Barbosa and England. A Short Talk at the Brazilian Society of English Culture on 5th November, Ruy Barbosa's Birthday*, reprint from Casa de Rui Barbosa, *Conferências*, IV (Rio: Casa de Rui Barbosa, 1954); Homero Pires, *Anglo-American Political Influences on Rui Barbosa*, transl. Sylvia Medrado Clinton (Rio: Casa de Rui Barbosa, 1949); Constancio Alves, 'Ruy Barbosa e os livros', *Revista da Academia Brasileira de Letras*, XVII (Mar. 1925), 242–3; Rui Barbosa, *Finanças e politica da republica* (Rio: Cia. Impressora, 1892); Aliomar Baleeiro, *Rui, um estadista no ministério da fazenda* (Rio: Casa de Rui Barbosa, 1952); Américo Jacobina Lacombe, *Rui Barbosa e a primeira constituição da república* (Rio: Casa de Rui Barbosa, 1949); Rubem Nogueira, *O advogado Rui Barbosa: momentos culminantes de sua vida profissional* (Rio: Gráfica Olímpica, 1949); Barbosa to Jacobina [London], 3 Sept. 1894, in Barbosa, *Mocidade e exilio*, pp. 252–3; Ruy Barbosa, *Cartas de Inglaterra* (Rio: Leuzinger, 1896), pp. 209, 210.

[2] Selected private letters are found in Barbosa, *Mocidade e exilio*, and his articles for the *Jornal do comércio* were gathered in *Cartas de Inglaterra*.

[3] Barbosa, *Cartas de Inglaterra*, pp. 402–3.

[4] Barbosa to Jacobina, Teddington, 20 Aug. 1894, in Barbosa, *Mocidade e exilio*, pp. 245, 246 and esp. 240; for other evidence of British influence see *ibid.* pp. 245, 246; Barbosa, *Cartas de Inglaterra*, pp. 33, 44n., 45, 45n., 48–9, 339; Raimundo Magalhães Júnior, *Rui, o homem e o mito*, Retratos do Brasil, 27 (Rio: Civilização Brasileira, 1964), pp. 120, 211.

Could a person of such attitudes have had much influence in Brazil? An enemy he met in London said to him in an ironic tone, 'Now you are among your people: you must be very happy.'[1] The criticism was natural but apparently not convincing: most of his contemporaries did not believe him to have betrayed his country. His description of Brazilians as a people 'who lack fiber, who are untempered, who want will power, who do not have a collective conscience', was a common one among Brazilian urban groups at that time.[2] In their struggle for modernization they found the qualities of their fellow countrymen one of the major obstacles to progress. Not having yet understood the socio-economic causes for these characteristics, they were satisfied to marvel at the foreigner. Barbosa had not been reared outside the Brazilian milieu, nor was he an unimportant sycophant of aliens, factors that might have lessened the importance of his thorough acceptance of British values. His sanguine temperament contrasted sharply with what the Brazilians called the 'English phlegm', making him a more effective channel for British influence than the British themselves. His eloquence and love of public speaking—at the Hague Peace Conference he was nicknamed 'Mr Verbosa'—endeared him to Brazilians. His prostrate admiration for the British is best explained by a reference to the growing acceptability of a foreign example as a model of the good society. Accidental factors of birth and education tell why Barbosa should have been the one who was so affected by British ideas; but it was the changing nature of his country that made him a hero even in his own day. He was a prominent *pensador*, and, if his ideas were sometimes rejected as those of a prophet in his own land, his statements received wide currency nevertheless.[3]

Barbosa has properly been considered a spokesman for the Brazilian urban groups. He was closely linked to Brazilian bankers and industrialists, and translated their ambitions into public policy.

---

[1] Barbosa, *Cartas de Inglaterra*, p. 212.

[2] *Ibid.* p. xviii; cf. tone of pessimism in Paulo Prado, *Retrato do Brasil. Ensaio sôbre a tristeza brasileira*, 5th ed. (São Paulo: Brasiliense, 1944).

[3] Viana Filho, *A vida de Rui Barbosa*, p. 338. An example of the sycophant of foreigners, so characteristic of colonial or semi-colonial societies, is Antonio Augusto da Costa Aguiar; see his MSS. at AMIP, cxxx, 6398; cxxxi, 6422; cxxxii, 6484; clxii, 7555.

His most important service to this class was his ability to find intellectual justifications for their posture.[1] In so doing he chiefly relied on ideas previously elaborated in Britain. Barbosa's knowledge of British history and admiration for Anglo-Saxon institutions colored all his public utterances. A review of the struggle of the English liberal tradition against the forces of reaction was a common characteristic of his discourse, and he sprinkled references to Macaulay into almost all his speeches. Typical was a speech he delivered when only 25 years old. There he railed against the tyranny of the emperor and lengthily cited English history to the effect that 'the English constitutional system, which is the only one in which monarchy is compatible with liberty', was the result of a long struggle of the people against the presumptions of the Crown.[2] He felt that 'in matters of liberty, in political wisdom, in knowledge and practice of constitutional guarantees, England can be the teacher of France and the French liberals'.[3]

Barbosa was thoroughly read in British liberalism, and based his opinions on its axioms. Individual self-interest could be trusted to serve the best ends of the community: even 'justice...has the sanction of general utility'.[4] The rule of law and the rights of the individual were two facets of English life that he particularly admired. His *Cartas de Inglaterra* had as their unifying feature, as he himself pointed out, his belief in 'law and liberty'.[5]

He found the rule of law sadly missing from his own country, and described what he saw in England in these words: 'The law is the law, with all its insufficiencies, all its inequalities, all its unreasonableness, and the observation of it is the road to its reform, the only remedy for its evils.' He added that 'this habit of

---

[1] Francisco Clementino de San Tiago Dantas, *Dois momentos de Rui Barbosa: conferências* (Rio: Casa de Rui Barbosa, 1951), pp. 20–38, 41–5; Nelson Werneck Sodré, *História da burguesia brasileira*, Retratos do Brasil, 22 (Rio: Civilização Brasileira, 1964), p. 206; Barros, *A ilustração brasileira*, pp. 349–51, 363–4; Magalhães Júnior, *Rui, o homem e o mito*, pp. 52–66, 68, 71, 77–83, 88.

[2] Speech of 2 Aug. 1874, in Rui Barbosa, *Discursos e conferencias* (Pôrto: Cia. Portugueza Editora, 1921), p. 40; also see pp. 29, 30, 31–2, 36, 37, 41–3.

[3] Speech of 6 Mar. 1882, in Rui Barbosa, *Obras seletas*, 10 vols. (Rio: Casa de Rui Barbosa, 1952–61), I, 193; also see I, 179–80, 183, 191, 192.

[4] Barbosa, *Liberdade commercial*, p. 8; also see pp. 2, 9, 11.

[5] Barbosa, *Cartas de Inglaterra*, p. vi.

placing the permanent rights of justice on a level where it cannot be reached by the expediencies of government, the crises of politics, the clamor of popular storms, is the cardinal virtue of England'. In contrast, 'the tendency, I know not whether French or Latin, is to condemn because of impressions, to anticipate the sentence, to replace the judges, and to dictate the sentence to the courts'. In summary, he wrote that it was 'thanks to...the sovereignty of the legal principle, dominating all aspects of collective life, as the law to which all other laws are subordinate', that England had risen to its position of world power. He has quite properly been dubbed the 'apostle of law'.[1]

The rights of the individual were his major concern. His most famous legal cases depended upon the right to habeas corpus and jury trial. Religious liberty was a cause for which he worked in Brazil; he included separation of Church and State in the republican constitution and defended this principle even in Jesuit schools. He was a defender of the right to assemble and the freedom of the Press. All members of society had their liberties and he defended even the individual rights of prostitutes. He was also an advocate of the abolition of slavery, largely because of his belief in this central tenet of liberalism. In defense of the individual he supported direct elections, the spread of education, federalism, municipal autonomy, and the separation of judicial from policing functions. Even when he focused his attention on the international scene, as at The Hague, his position was dictated by his consideration of each nation as an individual whose rights must be protected.[2]

It is not surprising then to find him glorying in the individualism permitted by the British governmental system. It was the system

---

[1] Barbosa, *Cartas de Inglaterra*, pp. 17, 18, 30, 31. Also see Rui Barbosa, *Antologia*, ed. Luís Viana Filho (Rio: Casa de Rui Barbosa, 1953), p. 45. For his opinion of the Brazilian situation see p. 16; Maurílio Gouveia, *Rui—o apóstolo do direito (estudo biográfico)*, 2nd ed. (Rio: Gráfica Tupí, 1952).

[2] Nogueira, *O advogado Rui Barbosa*, pp. 91–168, 239–88; Pires, *Anglo-American Political Influences*, pp. 37–52; Viana Filho, *A vida de Rui Barbosa*, p. 301; speech of 21 June 1880, Barbosa, *Obras seletas*, I, 133–8; note quotation from J. S. Mill, *Emancipação dos escravos* in Rui Barbosa, *Obras completas* (Rio: Ministério da Educação e Cultura, 1942–), vol. XI (1884), Tomo I, p. 216; see also Barbosa's introduction to Johann Joseph Ignaz von Döllinger, *A questão religiosa. O papa e o concílio. Por Janus [pseud.]*, transl. and ed. Rui Barbosa (Rio: Brown and Evaristo, 1877), pp. i–cclxxxv; speech of 13 Mar. 1879, *Obras completas*, vol. VI (1879), Tomo I, pp. 153–4.

under which 'the individual, the human being, develops his powers to the greatest fullness'. The English people were the only free people on earth: 'the first impression of the liberal man upon stepping on English soil is that he is in the very bosom of liberty'.[1] It was the land 'where liberty is most perfect, where law is safest, where the individual is most independent, and where, for this very reason, man is happiest'.[2]

As for the workers, they too must be free and self-reliant. 'I see, among all the servile hopes that a people may have for the State, none perhaps so corrupting as that which sees in the administration the people's granary and looks to it for cheap bread... You will have to get your bread from your intelligence, your honesty, your work. In this matter count only upon yourself and on those who freely join you; and you will not be disillusioned.'[3]

He fully accepted the middle-class defenses against the labor movement. He opposed the extension of the suffrage to the workers and pointed to the Reform of 1832 as a model of wise restraint in this regard. Such a position was essential in this battle for survival against the barbarians. He wrote, for instance, that the United States was a society torn by social strife, where the 'healthy qualities of the primitive Saxon heritage struggle with difficulty against...the fierce passions of so many foreign elements...The Coxeys and the Debs find their hordes', among the 'sediment of European scum constantly seeping into the reservoirs from which that society in formation draws its life'.[4]

Did not the individualism which he glorified create scenes of

---

[1] Barbosa, *Cartas de Inglaterra*, pp. 44–5.
[2] Barbosa to Jacobina, Teddington, 20 Aug. 1894, in Barbosa, *Mocidade e exilio*, p. 240.
[3] Barbosa, *Liberdade commercial*, p. 10.
[4] Barbosa, *Cartas de Inglaterra*, pp. 346, 347–8; Magalhães Júnior, *Rui, o homem e o mito*, p. 27. His friendship with William T. Stead at the Hague Peace Conference in 1907 may have sprung from his familiarity with Stead's article on 'Incidents of the Labour War in America', which he cited in 1895, Barbosa, *Cartas de Inglaterra*, p. 348 n.; on this friendship see Viana Filho, *A vida de Rui Barbosa*, p. 339; and Magalhães Júnior, *Rui, o homem e o mito*, pp. 273–98; on Stead and the United States see Richard Heathcote Heindel, *The American Impact on Great Britain (1898–1914). A Study of the United States in World History* (Philadelphia: Univ. of Pennsylvania Press, 1940), pp. 21, 27, 138, 364. When he was finally forced to attack the right of property in slaves, he was careful to find British precedent in the land reform laws for Ireland, Barbosa, *Emancipação dos escravos*, in *Obras completas*, vol. XI (1884), Tomo I, pp. 113–18, 200–3; for other uses of British sources here see pp. 77, 81, 83, 107, 109, 119, 171, 216, 217, 227, 228.

misery within his beloved England? Were not wealth and poverty in violent disparity? His answer was that 'Her institutions are not responsible for this contrast. It develops in spite of them, I know not if I blaspheme in saying as a necessary evil, as an incurable result of the human sickness—our eternal insufficiency, our "original sin," to use the religious phrase, which is more expressive and perhaps the best name of this mystery perennially set over against the victories of our pride and the marvels of our progress'.[1]

Early-nineteenth-century liberalism included both egalitarianism and individualism as has been suggested by J. Salwyn Schapiro, the historian of modern European ideas. These two qualities went hand in hand for a time, and were often confused; but they were not equivalent, and ultimately tended toward separation. One segment of the liberal stream created a cult of the individual.[2]

It is startling to notice the Brazilian follower of English liberalism revealing this latter tendency. As early as 1878 Rui Barbosa had differentiated individualism from democracy. He said that 'tyranny, whether imposed by an autocrat on the people or exercised by democracy against the individual, is always tyranny'; but he felt that, of these 'two forms of the same abomination...the more hateful is that which crushes the sacred rights of a human entity, defenseless and unwilling, vanquished by the brute force of an extortionate majority'. The tyranny of a dictator, on the other hand, finds its 'guarantee of permanence...[and] almost justification...precisely...in the servile passivity, the moral pusillanimity, the corruption, the inertia, in short, the tacit consent of the oppressed and resigned majority to its own abasement'.[3]

During his stay in England in 1894–5, Rui Barbosa became a great admirer of Thomas Carlyle, whom Schapiro calls a 'herald of fascism'. With his own orientation toward individualism Rui Barbosa found in Carlyle a kindred spirit. The Brazilian was attracted by what he called the Englishman's 'enthusiasm for the heroic expressions of human individuality'. Given his view of his

---

[1] Barbosa to Jacobina, Teddington, 20 Aug. 1894, in Barbosa, *Mocidade e exilio*, pp. 240–1. Cf. Gilberto Freyre, *Inglêses* (Rio: José Olympio, 1942), p. 170.

[2] J. Salwyn Schapiro, *Liberalism and the Challenge of Fascism. Social Forces in England and France (1815–1870)* (New York: McGraw-Hill, 1949), esp. pp. 370–96.

[3] Barbosa, *Liberdade commercial*, p. 8.

own abilities, it is not surprising that he agreed that '"the greatest thing that a nation can do is to produce great men"'.[1]

In one of the articles Barbosa wrote for the *Jornal do comércio* he dealt especially with Carlyle. The Scottish writer had challenged, as Barbosa said, 'this century warbling with egalitarianism and demagoguery'. From Carlyle's essay on Chartism he quoted the statement that '"obedience is the first duty of man... Of all the *rights of man*, the most indisputable is the right of the ignorant man to be led, whether he like it or not, by the wise man"'. 'No one', wrote Barbosa with relish, 'has expressed in more cruel terms... his disdain for the multitude, his thesis of the incompetence of the majority. To the defenders of universal suffrage he would answer "Among any ten individuals, you will always find nine numbskulls"'.[2]

Barbosa was fascinated by this viewpoint. He saw past liberal writers in a new light: 'Even [J. S.] Mill, after all, the greatest political thinker of our time, the author of the best modern books on democracy and liberty, the wise man who was always temperate in his opinions,... even Mill shared the Carlylean belief in the essential mediocrity of the human multitudes... and the [Carlylean] disdain for the "present low level of society".' The link between liberalism and Carlyle was at least clear to Barbosa.[3]

Some writers have considered this entire article as sarcasm, and, since Barbosa was indeed often a sarcastic writer, it is difficult to know how far he accompanied Carlyle in the views here attributed to him. Yet, when taken in the context of his general liberalism, which was always individualistic and rarely egalitarian,

---

[1] Barbosa, *Cartas de Inglaterra*, pp. 214, 224. All quotations from Carlyle are here translated from the Portuguese as Barbosa generally did not give exact source indications; in his essay 'Duas glorias da humanidade', *Cartas de Inglaterra*, pp. 209–41, he cited or quoted from Carlyle, *The French Revolution: a History* (1837); *Chartism* (1840); *On Heroes, Hero-Worship & the Heroic in History* (1841); *Past and Present* (1843); *Latter-Day Pamphlets* (1850); *The Life of John Sterling* (1851); *History of Frederick II of Prussia, Called Frederick the Great* (1858); 'Dr Francia', *Foreign Quarterly Review*, XXXI (July 1843), 554–89; 'Shooting Niagara: and After?' *Macmillan's Magazine*, XVI (Aug. 1867), 319–36; 'The Nigger Question', in *Critical and Miscellaneous Essays*. Barbosa found them in this miscellany and in Carlyle's *Works*, but does not give the editions. He also cited John Nichol, *Thomas Carlyle*, and James Anthony Froude, *Thomas Carlyle: A History of His Life in London, 1834–1881*; cf. Isaac Watson Dyer, *A Bibliography of Thomas Carlyle's Writings and Ana* (Portland, Me.: Southworth Press, 1928).

[2] Barbosa, *Cartas de Inglaterra*, pp. 225–6.   [3] *Ibid.* p. 228.

it seems to reflect at least a flirtatious inclination toward these ideas. The fact that he occasionally found weaknesses in Carlyle's argument and pointed them out seems to indicate that he would have done the same at other points if he had disagreed. At least we must say that although possibly not convinced, he was certainly charmed by Carlylean viewpoints, toying with them if not adopting them.[1]

Middle-class Victorian England had succeeded in impregnating one of the most important Brazilian liberals. He studied British history, he read the liberal nineteenth-century writers, he visited England, and he fell in love with it. He expressed a belief in *laissez faire* principles. He shared the British middle-class suspicion of the working man. He believed strongly in individualism, even at the sacrifice of democratic theories of equality.

Brazilian liberals in the nineteenth century were elaborating the bases of a modern society. In a later age it is easy to sneer at their self-righteous disregard for social justice; but a modern society is impossible unless position is determined by achievement and each man is first considered a unit to be engaged at the most productive point. Whether Republicans, members of the Liberal Party, or even ostensibly Conservatives, whether old like Otaviano and Zacarias or young like Nabuco and Barbosa, whether lawyers or teachers, whether sons of politicians or physicians, these urban, Europeanized, modernizing Brazilians sought to free the individual for self-fulfillment. Although their success was limited and Brazil never established a tradition of liberalism, these men were struggling to the best of their ability toward a modern goal. They were searching for intellectual tools with which to file down the fetters of tradition and pry open the manacles of ancient custom. The instruments they chose had been forged in Britain but the result was a growing awareness of man's potential freedom in Brazil.

[1] Magalhães Júnior, *Rui, o homem e o mito*, p. 214; Nery, *Rui Barbosa*, p. 65; Barbosa, *Cartas de Inglaterra*, p. 231. It is possible, of course, to find quotations from Barbosa's work that would place him among egalitarians; but I believe the general tendency was to emphasize the individual. Note, for instance, the undercurrent of suspicion towards mass man placed alongside statements in defense of democracy in his speech of 21 June 1880, *Obras seletas*, I, 101–60.

II

INDIVIDUAL SALVATION

The idea of the mobile individual set free from the immutable ties of the traditional society was further strengthened by new religious doctrines. Roman Catholicism had been the social cement of the outgoing order, and the message of the Protestant missionary worked to loosen its bonds. As one observer noted in 1856, 'civil and social relationships would be broken up' if the missionary were successful.[1] Protestantism in Brazil did not particularly contribute, as it may have done in other times and places, to the growth of capitalism through new ideas on interest and usury, novel views of vocation, or the separation of business life from religious belief. But Protestantism, as it was preached in Brazil, emphasized individualism at the very time other currents were moving in the same direction. This was its major significance.

In addition, Protestantism contributed to the progressive secularization of society so essential to the process of modern change. The very presence of Protestants introduced an element into the social system which was not harmonious with the view of religion as the bulwark of the social order. The latter was seriously weakened once it could no longer rely on a universally shared belief in a faith which sanctioned that order. As we have noted, the idea of a secular state grew steadily in Brazil, culminating in the republic organized in 1889. Protestantism was a small but significant force toward this transformation.

Protestantism was spread in Brazil by missionaries of various nationalities. The most important numerically were the Americans, but not only were the British the first to begin missionary activity there, but they greatly influenced its direction and emphasis. A study of their activities will make possible a better

[1] Thomas Ewbank, *Life in Brazil; or, a Journal of a Visit to the Land of the Cocoa and the Palm* ... (New York: Harper, 1856), p. 239.

277

understanding of the Protestant element in initial moves toward modernization.

The influence of the British missionary was felt most directly by the workers and lower middle class. In this regard their work presents a sharp contrast to other British activities. The missionary helped prepare these less favored groups for urban and industrial life while protecting them from some of the devastating effects of their new setting. The Protestant chapel and the distinct mores which were attendant on Protestant belief protected these new urban residents from the complete anonymity of the city and the psychological shock of this condition, while simultaneously helping them to understand their newly individualistic and independent situation.

Before the middle of the nineteenth century no missionary activity had been undertaken in Brazil. Although the Anglican church had been present since 1810, it had not made any effort to convert Brazilians. A clause in the treaty of amity and commerce signed that year stipulated that merchants were to be allowed to worship God as they saw fit as long as they did it either in their own homes or in chapels which did not look like churches or have bells. No one would be persecuted for his religious beliefs if he did not engage in proselytizing. Although even this measure was vigorously opposed in some quarters, it was reported that the bishop had not objected, saying 'the English have really no religion but...if you oppose them, they will persist, and make it an affair of infinite importance;...if you concede to their wishes, the chapel will be built, and nobody will ever go near it!'[1]

At least, no one tried to bring Brazilians into it, for the Anglican church in Rio de Janeiro ministered almost solely to the English community. The chaplains published notices in the Brazilian papers in English, although occasional announcements appeared in Portuguese. The same limitations applied in the British churches subsequently placed in Recife and Salvador. In 1866 the first services of the Church of England in São Paulo were held in

[1] Robert Walsh, *Notices of Brazil in 1828 and 1829,* 2 vols. (Boston & New York: Richardson, Lord, and Holbrook & Carvill, 1831), I, 182; Alan K. Manchester, *British Preëminence in Brazil; Its Rise and Decline: A Study in European Expansion* (Chapel Hill, N.C.: Univ. of North Carolina Press, 1933), pp. 81, 83–6.

the office of the resident engineer of the São Paulo Railway. Workmen of the railroad later built a church on land given by the *visconde* de Mauá with bricks and roofing brought from England.[1] But the workmen were not expected to attend.

In contrast, the evangelical and nonconformist branches of British religious life took an active interest in converting Brazilians during the latter half of the nineteenth century, and organized societies for this purpose. The first British missionary was Robert Reid Kalley (1809–88). A physician from Glasgow with an independent income inherited from his merchant father, he had gone to Madeira for the sake of his wife's health in 1839 and there began propagating his religious views, at first to those who received from him free medical aid. This effort was successful to the point that over a thousand persons sometimes appeared to hear his sermons preached from the brow of a hill. Persecution very quickly developed and in 1845 he was forced to flee in disguise with a mob at his heels. Hundreds of his adherents soon followed him into exile to be widely scattered in the western hemisphere. Some went to Rio de Janeiro, where Kalley joined them in 1855.

There he found less hostile attitudes. The emperor visited Kalley at his home, and the Britisher converted some ladies of the court. With the help of his old friends from Madeira his work prospered and by 1858 he managed to organize a church in Rio de Janeiro with a congregational form of government. It was a vigorous, self-supporting institution with an extremely active calendar, and it was successively moved into better and better quarters. He later selected a young Brazilian to be his successor and sent him to England to be trained in theology and pastoral technique. Although his congregation was small by present standards—by 1871 it had only 150 members—it was a large achievement in that setting. One of his followers working under his direction made a number of converts in Recife, and in 1873 Kalley organized a church there. His friends founded another one in Niterói, and subsequently other churches were organized in the states of Rio

[1] *Jornal do commercio*, 5 May 1850, p. 3; *A provincia de São Paulo*, 1 Mar. 1884, p. 4; interview with Father Townsend, São Paulo, 25 Nov. 1959; George Upton Krischke, *História da Igreja Episcopal Brasileira* (Rio: Gráfica Tupy, 1949), p. 21; the missionary work within this religious tradition was done by Americans, p. 29.

Individual Salvation

de Janeiro, Minas Gerais, Paraná and São Paulo. The beginning of Protestant activity in Brazil dates from Kalley's arrival.[1] Being first, his work was also important in its influence upon later Protestants in Brazil. For instance, his wife, Sarah, was indefatigable in translating or composing hymns, and for many years the collection prepared under the auspices of the Kalleys remained the standard hymnal of Protestant groups in Brazil. These hymns were sung to music adopted from the hymnody of their own country and did not always sound at home in Brazil. As Kalley admitted, 'Our manner of singing is something new in divine worship in Portuguese due to the foreign form of the music chosen.' Nor was the versification always happy, and complaints were heard then and since. The couple subsequently began submitting their hymns to a friend for correction of the language. But the imagery sometimes remained foreign, and sweating congregations loudly intoned, 'Whiter than snow I shall become.'[2]

Sarah Kalley was also instrumental in building institutions to perpetuate missionary activity. After her husband's death in 1888

[1] Robert Reid Kalley quoted in *Esboço historico da escola dominical da Igreja Evangelica Fluminense, 1855–1932* (Rio: Igreja Evangelica Fluminense, 1932), p. 294; also see pp. 23–35, 293–300, 304, 316–33; João Gomes da Rocha, *Lembranças do passado. Ensaio histórico do início e desenvolvimento do trabalho evangélico no Brasil, do qual resultou a fundação da 'Igreja Evangélica Fluminense' pelo dr. Robert Reid Kalley*, 4 vols. (Rio: Centro Brasileiro de Publicidade [Vols. I–III] and 'O Cristão' [Vol. IV], 1941–57), I, 270, 378; III, 90–4, 221, 290; IV, 356–8; João Gomes da Rocha, 'Robert Reid Kalley', *Rio News*, 24 Feb. 1888, p. 3; Henriqueta Rosa Fernandes Braga, *Música sacra evangélica no Brasil (contribuição à sua história)* (Rio: Kosmos, 1961), pp. 319–23; John Baillie, *Memoir of the Rev. W. H. Hewitson, Late Minister of the Free Church of Scotland at Dirleton*, 2nd ed. (London: Nisbet, 1852), pp. 150–67, 216–22; Maxwell [no first name given], 'Robert Reid Kalley, the Founder of the "Help for Brazil" Mission', *South America. The Magazine of the Evangelical Union of South America*, II (1913–14), 207–8, 211, 226; Émile-G. Léonard, 'O protestantismo brasileiro. Estudo de eclesiologia e de história social', *Revista de história*, II (Jan.–June 1951), 137–42; José Carlos Rodrigues, 'Religiões acatholicas', in Associação do Quarto Centenario do Descobrimento do Brasil, *Livro do centenario (1500–1900)*, 3 vols. (Rio: Imprensa Nacional, 1900–2), II, section 3, p. 106; W. B. Forsyth, *A União Evangélica Sul-Americana* (São Paulo: União Evangélica Sul-Americana, 1960), p. 3. Only some sporadic and unproductive missionary activity had preceded Kalley's arrival. Many of the materials cited in this chapter were graciously made available by the Rev. Mr W. B. Forsyth of São Paulo and Sr. Remigio de Cerqueira Fernandes Braga of Rio de Janeiro, whose help is gratefully acknowledged.

[2] Rocha, *Lembranças do passado*, I, 194, 196, 256; II, 17; Synesio P. Lyra, 'Prefácio', in João Gomes da Rocha, et al. comps., *Salmos e hinos*, [? ed.] (São Paulo: Imp. Metodista, 1965), p. 4; João Gomes da Rocha, et al. comps., *Salmos e hinos com músicas sacras*, 5th ed. (Rio: Igreja Evangélica Fluminense, 1952), no. 51.

she turned her attention to the organization of a society for this purpose in England. In 1892, with the help of James Fanstone, whom her husband had recruited to the Brazilian scene in 1879, she successfully organized the Help for Brazil Missionary Society to sustain mission work and recruit missionaries. One new missionary was sent out with Fanstone in 1893, and four others followed the next year. By 1900 there were nine in all, despite some who had left the mission. The society had raised £330 in its first year of existence, and £651 the next; but by 1900 the amount had increased to only £847. In 1913 the Help for Brazil Missionary Society joined the Evangelical Union of South America, which had been organized the year before.[1] As Fanstone explained it, the 'work has not grown as we could have wished', and the support of a stronger society in Great Britain was greatly needed.[2]

The South American Evangelical Mission was another British organization working in Brazil that joined the Evangelical Union of South America. It had been founded in Toronto in 1895, but a subsidiary group in Liverpool became the real seat of the mission as activity in Canada dwindled away. Its work in Brazil began in 1898 with the Indians in the interior. In 1902 malaria forced the missionaries to retreat to the city of São Luís. Two years later Bryce Ranken, who had become its executive secretary in 1899, went to Brazil for the purpose of selecting a site for a central mission station from which to direct activities. He chose the city of São Paulo. There the mission fell heir to work started by some freelance missionaries and thus acquired an immediate and solid base of operations. With their help it rapidly extended its work far into the backlands of the country. Something of its activity can be judged by the fact that during the three years 1905–7 they held 4,177 meetings with an attendance of 120,217, sold 1,513 Bibles and 3,897 New Testaments, gave away 144,577 tracts, and

[1] Rocha, *Lembranças do passado*, IV, 228, 229, 250, 257–61, 272, 273; *Help for Brazil: Occasional Papers*, no. 1 (Apr. 1893), pp. 1, 2; no. 4 (Jan. 1894), p. 2; no. 8 (Jan. 1895), pp. 1, 2; no. 30 (Mar. 1901), pp. 2, 3; no. 51 (n.d. [1907]), p. 2; *South America*, II (1913–14), 152; Ismael da Silva Júnior, *Notas históricas sôbre a Missão Evangelizadora do Brasil e Portugal*, 3 vols. (Rio: Souza, 1960–1), I, 56–7.

[2] *South America*, II (1913–14), 154.

made 234 conversions 'eliminating those who have proved insincere'.[1]

This mission and the Help for Brazil Missionary Society made up the Brazilian segment of the Evangelical Union of South America, formed in Britain during the years 1911–13. The World Missionary Conference held in Edinburgh in 1910 would not consider Latin America as a legitimate field for missionary endeavor because it was already a Christian area. This stand brought protests from those who disagreed and, finding this common ground, several smaller missions working in the continent decided to unite. The South American Evangelical Mission and the Peruvian and Argentine sections of the Regions Beyond Missionary Union formed the Evangelical Union of South America in 1911. Other groups joined later, including the Help for Brazil Missionary Society.[2]

The new consolidated mission soon got under way. The Brazilian areas of missionary action included the coast between Rio de Janeiro and Santos, interior São Paulo, Minas Gerais, and Goiás. At the end of 1912 the missionary in São Paulo reported that a week's work included 'three preaching services, three prayer meetings, Sunday school, children's meeting, singing class, and four cottage meetings'.[3] But the number of converts remained small: by the end of 1912 the total number of those under the care of the Evangelical Union of South America in Brazil was only 511. This did not include the members of self-supporting churches such as those founded by Kalley.[4]

Another aspect of the British religious effort in Brazil was the work of the British and Foreign Bible Society and the Scottish

[1] South American Evangelical Mission, *Our Story, Being a Short Retrospect of the Work of the South American Evangelical Mission, with a Brief Reference to Our Field of Labor* (Liverpool: South American Evangelical Mission, 1908), pp. 3–5, 8–11; South American Evangelical Mission and Union of Prayer Circles, *Eighth Annual Report, 1904–1905* (Liverpool: South American Evangelical Mission, 1905), pp. 8, 15; *Illustrated Missionary News*, no. 154 (Oct. 1911), pp. 148–9; *South America*, III (1914–15), 127; XXVI (July–Sept. 1960), 109; Edward T. Reed, 'Off to the Putumayo', *South America*, I (1912–13), 209.

[2] *Illustrated Missionary News*, no. 154 (Oct. 1911), p. 146.

[3] *South America*, I (1912–13), 216.

[4] *Ibid.* I (1912–13), 78–80, 111, 112, 153–5, 156; II (1913–14), 12, 15. In 1942 Kalley's old churches joined those founded by the Evangelical Union of South America to form a denomination called União das Igrejas Evangélicas Congregacionais e Cristãs do Brasil, Silva Júnior, *Notas históricas*, I, 36.

Bible Society. These were non-profit organizations set up to translate, print, and distribute Bibles at cost or less than cost when
British philanthropy permitted. Their first agent arrived in Brazil
in 1856. The Bibles sold by the missionaries were generally published by these organizations, and by 1878 the British and Foreign
Bible Society maintained four salesmen in Brazil, selling in that
year 904 Bibles, 2,313 New Testaments, and 2,467 portions of the
scriptures.[1] The books' low cost was their most attractive feature,
since Roman Catholic Bibles were being sold at what one missionary called 'the exorbitant price of almost £2 10s.' In 1857 a
Brazilian wrote to a Rio de Janeiro newspaper complaining that

a great number of Bibles, printed in London...are being sold for a
low price, not only in stores, but also by these book peddlers that are
found in this city. One came into our hands for the minute amount of
only 3$500 [say 8s.] and in it we found ideas, which...are certainly
not what we have been taught in our Catholic catechism...It
isn't just, it isn't reasonable that in a Catholic country there should be
carried on this Protestant propaganda for which England has distinguished herself.

The Bible salesman was thus recognized as a foreign agent. One
Brazilian statesman similarly complained in 1864 about the English
who 'believe they know so much about religion that they would
teach all the world'.[2]

Other Brazilians recognized the connexion between these
efforts and the process of modernization even when they did not
fully understand the nature of this relationship. Rui Barbosa, for
instance, said that 'Where Protestantism exists, there is industrial
prosperity, vigorous and luxuriant as tropical vegetation', in contrast to the stagnation of Catholic countries. Another Brazilian
rushed to translate a book into Portuguese as soon as it was published in French (1875) because it argued that Protestant nations
would triumph over Catholic ones since Protestants believed in

---

[1] Rodrigues, 'Religiões acatholicas', pp. 105–6; *South America*, II (1913–14), 13; Rocha,
Lembranças do passado, I, 50; IV, 260.
[2] South American Evangelical Mission, *Our Story*, p. 15; *Correio mercantil*, 16 Dec. 1857,
quoted in *Esboço historico da escola dominical*, p. 58; Bernardo de Souza Franco quoted in
Rocha, *Lembranças do passado*, I, 320.

education, encouraged science, built up nationalism, and believed in individual freedom.[1]

The missionaries, of course, didn't doubt the social achievements of Protestantism. 'Where the Church of Rome's power predominates,' they said, 'ignorance and illiteracy are correspondingly great... Whenever the power of Rome wanes, enlightenment speedily manifests itself... As the people of South America leave the Roman Catholic church, the countries progress along all lines.' The claim of some Britishers in Brazil that all progress there—from railways to the abolition of slavery—derived entirely from the contribution of the British was not enough for the missionaries: they said all good things came from Protestant efforts. Even when it was reported that fanaticism was waning and religious liberty generally enforced, it was added that 'the tendencies to reform and progress, which one sees in the Roman Catholic church, can almost invariably be directly traced to the influence of the aggressive Protestant work'.[2] And few had been more zealously aggressive than the British missionary.

The principal contribution of the British missionaries to modernization—if one sets aside such sweeping claims—was the emphasis they placed upon the individual. Once people began to think of themselves as independent units rather than as parts of a larger whole in which their place was permanently fixed, the breakdown of the traditional society was imminent.

Certain Protestant sects were evidently more individualistic than others both in their theology and in their organization, and it is important to establish the position of the British missionaries. Whereas some Protestants believed that the goal of the salvation-experience was for the Church to be called as a people, as a group, as a New Israel, others considered the salvation of the individual as the end. Therefore, the latter insisted that baptism

[1] Rui Barbosa quoted by Homero Pires, *Anglo-American Political Influences on Rui Barbosa*, transl. Sylvia Medrado Clinton (Rio: Casa de Rui Barbosa, 1949), p. 41; Raimundo Magalhães Júnior, *Rui, o homem e o mito*, Retratos do Brasil, 27 (Rio: Civilização Brasileira, 1964), pp. 9–10; Roque Spencer Maciel de Barros, 'O germanismo nos fins do império', *O estado de São Paulo*, 12 Jan. 1958, p. 64.

[2] *South America*, III (1914–15), 71; J. G. Meen, 'Conditions in the Roman Catholic Church To-Day as Compared with Twenty-five Years Ago', *ibid.* p. 169n.

must be reserved for adults. Calvinists, because of their belief in predestination, considered the individual totally helpless, but some sects, following the sixteenth-century Jacobus Arminius, believed God wished all men to be saved and offered salvation to all; the individual could accept or reject this gift of his own free will. By the same token, salvation was not considered permanent and the individual must, therefore, be constantly on guard against 'backsliding'. Most American denominations in the nineteenth century, regardless of their theological roots, had been suffused with Arminian ideas because of their effective dissemination by John Wesley. In Britain as well, both the evangelical movement in the Anglican church and most nonconformists were swept along by this semi-romantic tendency. Individualism was especially enhanced among the Plymouth Brethren, a sect founded by John Nelson Darby in 1825. He carried the 'priesthood of all believers' to the logical conclusion that there should be no ministers, elders, or other church officers, salvation being a personal matter between the individual and his God.[1]

These ideas were reflected in Brazil by the British missionaries. Of course, they often made contradictory statements and accepted ideas from various sources without much critical examination of logical implications. Still, one may conclude that the main current of their thought was in a direction which would emphasize the individual.

Kalley himself had been brought up as a Scottish Presbyterian, but, after a youth of disbelief and atheism, was converted in his late twenties. He always insisted on his freedom from any denominational ties. He was adamantly opposed to the Anglican church because it was nearly Roman Catholic in its beliefs and practices. He described the Recife church as not belonging 'to any foreign denomination; it is not Presbyterian because this denomination

---

[1] Ernst Troeltsch, *The Social Teaching of the Christian Churches*, transl. Olive Wyon, Halley Stewart Publications, 1, 2 vols. (Glencoe and New York: Free Press & Macmillan, 1931), II, 477; Max Weber, *The Protestant Ethic and the Spirit of Capitalism*, transl. Talcott Parsons (New York: Scribner's, 1930), p. 145; Leonard E. Elliott-Binns, *Religion in the Victorian Era*, 2nd ed. (London: Lutterworth, 1946), pp. 55, 57; H. Richard Niebuhr, *The Social Sources of Denominationalism* (New York: Holt, 1929), pp. 38, 41, 65. My conversations with Dr John Lee Smith have been very helpful in connexion with this topic.

...practices infant baptism; it is closer to the Baptists, but prefers to admit to communion any believer who is faithful and obedient to the Lord'.[1] Kalley's successor was trained at a Baptist seminary in London, and Kalley later sent most of his helpers to the East End Training Institute run by H. Grattan Guinness of African missionary fame, a man closely connected to the Baptists. Yet Kalley was once on the verge of joining the Free Church of Scotland, an unequivocally Presbyterian denomination.[2] In 1907 a British missionary concluded that 'the Evangelical churches of Brazil...do not coincide with any particular sect in Britain, but have a character peculiarly their own. They stand for the old Puritan faith'.[3]

A better guide to their beliefs is found in sermons they preached and hymns they sang. Kalley emphasized that 'all who believe' would be saved, and his wife reflected her conviction that salvation was offered to everyone by leading her choir in singing, 'Come all! His vast compassion is limitless.'[4] It was up to the sinner to respond to this invitation. While still in Madeira Kalley translated a hymn which said '...thou bid'st me come to thee: O Lamb of God, I come, I come'.[5] In one of his sermons he further insisted that it was 'most rare' for a soul to be saved 'without making any effort'.[6] His wife translated a hymn that clearly spoke of the action of the individual: it was called 'O Jesus, thou art standing, outside the fast closed door'. Whereas the sinner would keep 'Him standing there', salvation was achieved when 'We open now the door'.[7] Kalley's doctrinal stand may be found in his twelve 'Articles of Faith', one of which defined the sinner as one who 'does not allow himself to be saved'.[8] If the individual could accept

[1] Rocha, *Lembranças do passado*, IV, 251.
[2] *Ibid.* III, 38, 174, 220–2, 225–6; IV, 39, 127, 183, 197; Silva Júnior, *Notas históricas*, I, 36, 39, 44–5; Braga, *Música sacra*, 331; Kenneth Scott Latourette, *A History of the Expansion of Christianity*, 7 vols. (New York and London: Harper, 1937–45), V, 111, 423.
[3] *Help for Brazil*, no. 51 (n.d. [1907]), p. 2.
[4] *Apud* Rocha, *Lembranças do passado*, 1,296, *Salmos e hinos com músicas*, no. 126.
[5] Rocha, *Salmos e hinos com músicas*, no. 39 (also see nos. 59, 73, 149, 158); William Garrett Horder, comp., *Worship-Song* (London: Elliot Stock, n.d. [before 1902]), no. 249; Rocha, *Lembranças do passado*, I, 87–8; Braga, *Música sacra*, p. 320.
[6] *Apud* Rocha, *Lembranças do passado*, II, 96.
[7] Rocha, *Salmos e hinos com músicas*, no. 135; Horder, *Worship-Song*, no. 525.
[8] 'Doze artigos de crença dos christãos que têm o dr. Kalley por seu ministro', in *Esboço historico da escola dominical*, p. 296.

Individual Salvation

or reject salvation initially, he could also change his fate afterwards. Kalley admonished his flock against the dangers of backsliding, and they sang hymns like this:

> I wish to serve my God
> and never sin again
> But I am close to a fall
> And may stumble after all.[1]

His was not a Church-oriented theology. One of his first actions in Brazil was to translate the highly individualistic *Pilgrim's Progress* and serialize it in a Rio de Janeiro newspaper. He did not care much about ordination of ministers by the churches, believing that ordination by the Holy Spirit was more important. It is true that in some hymns and doctrinal statements one may find suggestions that he believed the Church was important after all and that ministers and other officers were necessary to its good governance. But by 'Church' it seems he sometimes meant the particular congregation. Salvation was certainly not extended to the entire 'people of God', and baptism was not for the infant children of believers.[2]

The Plymouth Brethren had a special appeal in Brazil because of their individualism. Richard Holden, for several years Kalley's co-pastor in Rio de Janeiro, was a restless spirit who had gone from one belief to another. Born in England, as a young man he had been engaged in business in Brazil and had then gone to the United States to be trained as an Episcopalian missionary; he next abandoned the Anglican religion of his fathers to link himself with Kalley. At this time the relatives of Kalley's wife were taken up with the ideas of the Plymouth Brethren, and Kalley himself corresponded and debated with Darby and his followers. Holden eventually accepted their doctrines, especially after a visit to England in 1871, and this led to a violent break with Kalley. The younger man then persuaded several members of Kalley's

[1] Rocha, *Salmos e hinos com músicas*, no. 40; also see Rocha, *Lembranças do passado*, I, 73.
[2] Rocha, *Lembranças do passado*, I, 47, 50; IV, 33, 250–1; Igreja Evangélica Fluminense, *Artigos orgânicos da Igreja Evangélica Fluminense seguidos da breve exposição das doutrinas fundamentais do cristianismo recebida pela mesma igreja* (Rio: Estab. Gráfico 'Apollo', n.d.), pp. 19, 24; but cf. pp. 21, 23.

church to separate from it, although many of them were later prevailed upon to return. These churches always remained suspicious of clerical pretensions.[1]

Revivalism also had a considerable influence in Brazil through the British missionaries. The American revivalists Dwight L. Moody and Ira D. Sankey had had a large impact in Britain, and, when the Kalleys returned to Brazil after a sojourn there, Robert brought with him the news of this 'spiritual reawakening'. Sarah composed a special verse asking God to bring these blessings to Brazil. In 1878 Kalley received news of the promising Henry Maxwell Wright, son of a British merchant resident in Portugal. He had been converted by Moody when in London in 1875, and, with fluent Portuguese, had become an evangelist himself. On his first visit to Brazil in 1881, he preached to large audiences in theatres and public halls in Salvador, Rio de Janeiro, São Paulo, and other, smaller towns. Wright returned in 1890–1 as an interim pastor in Recife, his salary being paid by the church in Rio de Janeiro. He subsequently conducted evangelistic campaigns in Brazil during 1893 and 1914. He composed many hymns to be used at his meetings, one of which had as its constant refrain the less than social message: 'Christ for me! Christ for me!'[2]

One way in which Protestant belief strengthened individualism and social mobility was with regard to the *compadre* system. Nothing is more characteristic of the patron-dependent relationship so typical in Latin America than *compadresco*. A child's godfather is bound not only to the child but to its parents by sacred ties almost as strong as those that bind the family. In a society where personal and primary relationships were all-important and where the impersonal connexions of a money economy were not yet widespread, the choice of a *compadre* could make or break one's life. The large landowner or most prominent village citizen

[1] Rocha, *Lembranças do passado*, I, 226; II, 45–8, 174, 203, 330–1; III, 24–5, 170–1, 173, 184, 228–9, 248–50, 259; IV, 208–9, 210–11, 227, 248–9, 255, 317; *Esboço historico da escola dominical*, pp. 116–18.

[2] Rocha, *Lembranças do passado*, IV, 106, 254; Rocha, *Salmos e hinos com músicas*, nos. 139, 553; Braga, *Música sacra*, pp. 231–2, 329, 330; Silva Júnior, *Notas históricas*, I, 43; Elliott-Binns, *Religion in the Victorian Era*, pp. 212–21; K. S. Inglis, *Churches and the Working Classes in Victorian England* (London & Toronto: Routledge and Kegan Paul & University of Toronto Press, 1963), p. 65.

would be the first choice of all those further down the social scale, and, if he agreed to this relationship, he became their protector and guardian angel. The whole paternalistic structure was thereby strengthened since the worker did not depend on his own ability but relied instead on this personal tie, a connexion which was sustained and perpetuated by his loyalty and subservience. Richard Burton, writing in 1869, observed that '"compadre" and "comadre"...still form in Brazil a religious relationship...In small country places...all the inhabitants are connected by baptism if not by blood, and thus the ends of justice are carried out the clean contrary way'. Protestants in Brazil would not accept the idea of godfathers or godmothers. God was the only godfather. Every man was first of all an individual whose only or principal tie was a direct one to the deity.[1]

If social position is not unchanging but is the result of achievement, then the position of women will not be what it is in a traditional society. In nineteenth-century Brazil women lived a cloistered life, completely subordinate to their menfolk.[2] Roman Catholic writers there strongly opposed the emancipation of women because, they said, it would tend to destroy the family, that is, the most important of the divinely ordained groups which made up the social structure. They followed the lead of Pope Leo XIII, who stressed in 1880 that 'The husband is the ruler of the family and the head of the wife; the woman...is to be subordinate and obedient to the husband...' In Brazil it was said that 'The natural inequality of women and men should be reflected in private and public civil law and in the political order', and 'A moralized society should take away from women all public roles'.[3]

The modernizers would not agree with these statements. One said the Brazilian woman had unfortunately 'not yet taken the

[1] Richard Francis Burton, *Explorations of the Highlands of the Brazil; with a Full Account of the Gold and Diamond Mines. Also, Canoeing Down 1500 Miles of the Great River São Francisco from Sabará to the Sea*, 2 vols. (London: Tinsley, 1869), I, 80n.

[2] Charles Expilly, *Les femmes et les mœurs du Brésil* (Paris: Charlieu et Huillery, 1864), pp. 372–4.

[3] Augustine Rössler, 'Woman', *The Catholic Encyclopedia*, xv (1912), 688; José Maria Correia de Sá e Benevides quoted by Roque Spencer Maciel de Barros, *A ilustração brasileira e a idéia de universidade*, Universidade de São Paulo, Cadeira de História e Filosofia da Educação, Boletim 241(2) (São Paulo: Universidade de São Paulo, 1959), p. 56.

place which is rightfully hers as a powerful agent of social progress', and Rui Barbosa and André Rebouças were only two of the many who took up the feminist cause.[1] Britain was both the model of the good society and the source of change. 'In the confidence and mutual respect between the two sexes lies the great strength of the moral structure' of England, wrote one Brazilian.[2] Schools for girls were organized by the British in nineteenth-century Brazil, and missionaries preached sermons against marriages arranged by parents without consulting the couple.[3] Women were allowed to be active in determining the policies of Kalley's church, generally participating in its organizational life.

One way in which the British missionary raised the position of women in society was by his attack on the double standard of sexual morality. The Catholic church stressed chastity in the woman but, whether for theological or practical reasons, it laid little emphasis on equivalent behavior in the male. The British missionary was shocked by the 'immorality' of the people, and by the extra-marital relations that led to 'shame, poverty, disease, and total ruin'. One missionary wrote that 'Convenience, not rectitude, is the principle which dominates all ranks, and...lusts have free rein, with no fear of God, or even public opinion to check them...The family relation is violated on every hand... On all this Rome thrives apace and priests lead the way'.[4] In contrast, Protestant men were judged by the same standards as

[1] Alberto Brandão quoted by Stanley Stein, *Vassouras, a Brazilian Coffee County, 1850–1900*, Harvard Historical Studies, 69 (Cambridge, Mass.: Harvard Univ. Press, 1957), p. 152; also see pp. 153–8; André Rebouças, *Agricultura nacional, estudos economicos; propaganda abolicionista e democratica* (Rio: Lamoureux, 1883), p. 220; but on Rui Barbosa cf. Magalhães Júnior, *Rui, o homem e o mito*, pp. 42–4, 47n.

[2] Tobias do Rego Monteiro, *O presidente Campos Salles na Europa*, 2nd ed. (Rio: Briguiet, 1928), p. 71.

[3] *Jornal do commercio*, 1 Jan. 1850, p. 3; 1 Jan. 1871, pp. 3, 5, 7, and 8; 4 Jan. 1855, p. 3; *A provincia de São Paulo*, 22 Mar. 1884, p. 4; Kalley quoted by Rocha, *Lembranças do passado*, II, 191; Ernst Troeltsch, *Protestantism and Progress*, transl. W. Montgomery, (Boston: Beacon, 1958), pp. 93–7; Troeltsch, *Social Teaching*, II, 809.

[4] Kalley quoted by Rocha, *Lembranças do passado*, II, 191 (also see I, 292); South American Evangelical Mission, *Our Story*, p. 13. On the uses of morality by the middle class see Ronald E. Wraith and Edgar Simpkins, *Corruption in Developing Countries Including Britain until 1880* (London: Allen & Unwin, 1962), pp. 178–82, 186–7; Affonso d'Albuquerque Mello, *A liberdade no Brasil: seu nascimento, vida, morte e sepultura* (Recife: Typ. Figueroa de Faria, 1864), *passim*, esp. p. 187.

the women and were taught to consider their wives as helpmates rather than objects. In this way an attempt was made to recognize the individuality of women alongside the independence of each man.

Paradoxically, Brazilian Protestantism also provided security for the individual set adrift by the process of modernization. It did this by creating for its members a distinct sub-culture with its own customs and its own taboos. The view of society held by the British missionaries corresponds to what Richard Niebuhr has called 'Christ against culture'. They felt it was spiritually necessary to isolate themselves from their sinful environment. A colleague of Kalley during his stay in Madeira had said that 'Scottish Christians in general, seem not to realize...that they are not of this world, but sent into it by God as messengers'. In 1865 Sarah Kalley expressed these views in this hymn:

> As a stranger live I here;
> I am bound for heaven.
> This world's only a passing thing;
> I am bound for heaven.[1]

Of course, their very location demanded such an attitude, even without theological considerations. An American traveler had observed Brazilians in 1856 and concluded that 'The more I see of this people, the more distant appears the success of any Protestant missions among them. Festivals are obstacles that cannot easily be got rid of. The masses are too fond of them, and the national pulse beats in unison with them...There is no ground on which a missionary can meet the people. They avoid him as one with whom association is disreputable...Then, the climate is against the severities of northern sects. Neither stringent Methodism nor Puritanism can ever flourish in the tropics'.[2] So if they were isolated it was not always by design.

Nevertheless, their behavior distinguished the Protestants from the rest of society. This is not surprising since the emphasis upon behavioral norms was a predominant characteristic of Victorian

[1] Baillie, *Memoir of the Rev. W. H. Hewitson*, p. 257; Rocha, *Salmos e hinos com músicas*, no. 77; Rocha, *Lembranças do passado*, II, 83; cf. H. Richard Niebuhr, *Christ and Culture* (New York: Harper, 1951), pp. 45–82.   [2] Ewbank, *Life in Brazil*, pp. 238–9.

religious life. The British missionary set up ethical standards according to his own middle-class culture and was then very naturally repulsed by the degree to which Brazilians did not live up to them. A young single missionary girl wrote that

Every day one is more shocked by the total neglect of God in the lives of the people around; the devil seems to hold sway in all departments of life: in the commercial world with its fraudulency and deceit; in the home life; in the business life with its seven working days a week and Sabbath trading, and in the social life everywhere...How one misses the uplifting influences of the dear homeland.[1]

For all these vices of Brazil the missionaries naturally blamed Roman Catholicism. 'Idolatry and priestcraft are at the root of all this evil, and are responsible for the drunkenness and immorality which are destroying the people.'[2] Another missionary wrote about the area north of Santos along the coast of São Paulo, saying, 'the region is one of the oldest settled in the State, and has been blighted by generations of priestly misrule. Idolatry thrives, as does persecution, rum, impurity and illiteracy'. The conclusion was that 'South America is cursed with a baptized paganism...Romanism...has reached a depth of ignorance, superstition and filth which can find no parallel in any other continent'.[3]

Needless to say, the British missionary did not understand the ethical ideals of the local culture. One example of the failure to comprehend the efforts of Brazilian society to translate into action the precepts of Christianity is revealed in the missionary view of a charitable institution in Rio which made it a practice to accept foundlings without questioning the parentage. The Santa Casa had a revolving shelf on which they were placed; when the wheel was turned the child entered the building and no one from inside

[1] Alice V. Hurford, 'First Impressions of São Paulo', *South America*, III (1914–15), 202, 204.

[2] Bryce W. Ranken, 'Through Darkest São Paulo', *ibid.* II (1913–14), 87. Similar moralism was sometimes expressed by Brazilians, Rebouças, *Agricultura nacional*, pp. 38, 60; André Rebouças, *Diário e notas autobiográficas*, ed. Ana Flora and Inácio José Verissimo, Documentos Brasileiros, 12 (Rio: José Olympio, 1938), pp. 14, 215, 246.

[3] *South America*, II (1913–14), 13; *Illustrated Missionary News*, no. 154 (Oct. 1911), p. 150.

could tell who had placed it there. The missionary commented
with strong disapproval that 'thus the secret of crime and shame
is kept'.[1]

In the face of the 'sinful' current, the missionary had to be
especially puritanical. Even 'sons of English parents sent out by
British firms' were said to have gone 'into that moral cesspool
and down to hell'.[2] It was alleged that the entertainments common in Brazil were calculated to 'inflame the instincts of young
men and lead them irresistibly toward the satisfaction of carnal
impulses'. Therefore it was necessary to exercise rigid discipline
and constantly exhort the flock regarding the future punishment
of hell-fire and damnation. For God was a Lord of 'vengeance...
opposed to everything that is impure and depraved'. Kalley
warned one lackadaisical member of his church 'to be careful,
for I judge you in terrible and fatal danger. Satan grips you and
will draw you back into all the filth of your past, constantly
dragging you until throwing you into...'.[3] Sociologists concerned with cultural change have recently emphasized how a
complete break with society is still demanded by the Brazilian
followers of the nineteenth-century missionaries.[4]

Their studies have particularly noted how Protestants and Catholics are sharply differentiated by their observance of Sunday.
On this point Kalley had been adamant. Those who lost their
jobs because of their refusal to labor on Sunday found no sympathy in him. A member of his congregation who nevertheless
eventually became sole owner of a hat factory and one of the
wealthiest men in Rio was initially impeded from becoming a
partner in the firm because he loyally refused to work on Sunday.[5]

---

[1] *South America*, I (1912–13), 182. A more relevant criticism of the Santa Casa was that
the children frequently died, Daniel Parish Kidder and James Cooley Fletcher, *Brazil and
the Brazilians Portrayed in Historical and Descriptive Sketches* (Philadelphia: Childs &
Peterson, 1857), pp. 112–13.　　　[2] *South America*, I (1912–13), 230.

[3] Kalley quoted by Rocha, *Lembranças do passado*, II, 22, 27, 191.

[4] Emílio Willems, 'Protestantism as a Factor of Culture Change in Brazil', *Economic
Development and Cultural Change*, III (July 1955), 321–33; Gordon P. Harper, 'The
Children of Hipólito: A Study in Brazilian Pentecostalism', privately mimeographed,
Cambridge, Mass., 1963.

[5] Rocha, *Lembranças do passado*, II, 145, 175–6; Silva Júnior, *Notas históricas*, I, 22; Francisco Agenor de Noronha Santos, *Meios de transporte no Rio de Janeiro, historia e legislação*,
2 vols. (Rio: Typ. do 'Jornal do Commercio', 1934), I, 167.

'Believers', Kalley said, 'must abstain from all and any work as well as thought or conversations on mundane subjects. Sunday is a Special Day which God gives us in which to learn more of our Lord.'[1] Most Brazilians did not so consider the first day of the week. 'Sundays', wrote one observer, 'are universal seasons of recreation. Ladies laugh outright at the seriousness and alleged long faces of English families passing to church as to a funeral.'[2] Through Sunday observance and other practices the Protestants were simultaneously cut off from the connexions established within a traditional society, released, therefore, from the braking effect those ties could exert on individual mobility, and shielded from the harsh effects of the transition to urban life.

Aside from isolated converts among the elite, the bulk of Kalley's followers were working class. Even slaves were included in his congregation, and several of his early converts were employed at the Naval machine shops.[3] Kalley described his congregation as 'almost all of them poor'. Many years later the executive head of the Evangelical Union of South America wrote that 'our converts are all of the poorer class', and the congregation in the city of São Paulo was described in 1914 as 'an entirely working class one'.[4] Even the urban middle-class Protestant congregations of today are made up of people whose parents or grandparents were unprivileged, and the dynamic Pentecostal sects find their converts almost exclusively among the lower class.

Nineteenth-century British Protestantism has often been charged with a lack of concern for the plight of the working man. Some historians have pointed out that instead of social criticisms the evangelicals in England offered only 'personal reform and piety', and that the Methodists and other nonconformists 'believed that the meek and righteous would be compensated in an after life'

---

[1] Kalley quoted by Rocha, *Lembranças do passado*, II, 170.

[2] Ewbank, *Life in Brazil*, p. 238.

[3] Rocha, *Lembranças do passado*, I, 153, 154.

[4] Kalley quoted in *ibid.* III, 221; Bryce W. Ranken, 'Through Darkest São Paulo', *South America*, II (1913–14), 87; and *South America*, III (1914–15), 70; also see South American Evangelical Mission, *Our Story*, p. 11. There were some Protestants among privileged groups, e.g. José Carlos Rodrigues, an influential publicist with a somewhat mixed record for honesty, George C. A. Boehrer, 'José Carlos Rodrigues and *O Novo Mundo*, 1870–1879', *Journal of Inter-American Studies*, IX (1967), 127–44.

while attempts to 'overthrow existing inequalities' were '"infidel and irreligious"'.[1] Although in the latter part of the nineteenth century Protestantism showed greater concern in this matter, it is probably true, as Élie Halévy once suggested, that the nonconformist sects by their defense of the established order prevented social upheaval in England during the French Revolution and the years immediately following.[2]

It would be tempting to suggest that the British missionaries served the same function in Brazil, defending established authority against social upheaval. It is certainly true that the British missionaries spoke more of 'pie in the sky' and the after life than of reform. Their congregations were not only told to 'Imitate His humility, always, ever, constantly', but were also instructed: 'As His imitators, be good laborers....'[3] Furthermore, Kalley's successor linked incredulity with socialism, and later missionaries also looked askance at 'the doctrines of a Christless socialism or a cruel anarchy' which Italian immigrants were bringing to Brazil.[4] But the fact of the matter is that Brazil was not yet at the developmental stage that had required religion to play a dampening role in England, and it is only today that these churches have come to perform such a task. At that time social revolution was not even a distant threat.

What Protestantism did do was to strengthen the individualism of the worker, thus preparing him for the rude shock of being transformed into a wage earner. The shift from rural peon to urban worker would have been even harder if some had not found a new religion that made their atomism understandable in the light of an individual relationship to God, the only patron, while simultaneously protecting them from the namelessness of an urban

---

[1] G. D. H. Cole and Raymond Postgate, *The British People, 1746–1946*, 2nd ed. (New York: Knopf, 1947), p. 229.

[2] Élie Halévy, *A History of the English People in the Nineteenth Century, I: England in 1815*, transl. E. I. Watkin and D. A. Barker, 2nd ed. (London: Benn, 1949), pp. 424–5; Inglis, *Churches and the Working Classes*, pp. 254–61.

[3] Rocha, *Salmos e hinos com músicas*, no. 505, also see nos. 56, 58, 62.

[4] Rocha, *Lembranças do passado*, IV, 258; South American Evangelical Mission, *Our Story*, p. 16. Rui Barbosa eventually felt that it was the Catholic Church that must act as a dike against 'delirious social and anarchical demands', Magalhães Júnior, *Rui, o homem e o mito*, p. 18; also see pp. 6–7 and cf. Brian Harrison, 'The Sunday Trading Riots of 1855', *The Historical Journal*, VIII (1965), 219–45.

setting. There were, of course, other ways in which Protestantism was related to modernization. The spread of literacy among Brazilian Protestants has always been a subject of comment; by their opposition to gambling they may have emphasized self-reliance as against blind dependence on fate; and through these and other measures they may have aided the rise of some to a higher social status.[1] But their primary contribution was to pry them loose from fixed relationships.

Protestantism was also significant in increasing the secularization of society, ironic as it may seem in view of the religiosity of the missionary. But the pluralism implied by the mere presence of a Protestant sect weakened the traditional view of a society connected at every point to religion. It is significant that the Protestant missionaries and their converts contributed to the pressure for religious freedom. Their activities also exacerbated the Church–State conflicts of the 1870s and strengthened the anti-clericalism of the modernizers. Once it was recognized that the State would not suffer if each man were allowed to choose his own religion, secularism in other matters was not far off.[2] And once the individual began determining his own beliefs, there was no end to the process. It would be interesting to know how many pursued the same itinerary as Júlio Ribeiro: 'I was once Catholic; I was then Presbyterian; I am now an atheist. My upbringing made me Catholic; Bible reading tore me from Rome; reason made me incredulous.'[3]

From small beginnings had sprung an important movement, important not because of its numbers, but because of its part within a larger drama. Brazil was being transformed and the Protestants were part of that transformation. Through their belief in the individual, through their isolation from the otherwise traditional culture, through their break with old relationships—especially *compadresco*—and through their new regard for the place

[1] On gambling see Rocha, *Lembranças do passado*, IV, 196.
[2] Religious freedom, civil marriage, and open cemeteries are constant themes in Rocha, *Lembranças do passado;* on the ultramontanist controversy see IV, 80–1; the increasing pluralism of society also brought up the question of religious disabilities, Magalhães Júnior, *Rui, o homem e o mito*, p. 8.
[3] Júlio Ribeiro, *Cartas sertanejas*, [? ed.], Coleção Nacionalista, 3 (São Paulo: Edições e Publicações Brasil Editôra, 1945), p. 94.

of women they were unmistakably linked to the process of modernization. Although the congregations of the British missionaries were primarily made up of workers, the Protestants' significance was not in preventing social upheaval but in helping the worker adjust to an increasingly secular and impersonal urban society. The new churches also contributed to that secularization by their very existence. The British missionary, despite his limited purpose and illiberal viewpoint—blind to his own bigotry while denouncing it in others—was nevertheless an agent of modern change as surely as were the railroad builders.

DECLINING INFLUENCE

The First World War marked the end of British predominance in Brazil. Even in the years before 1914 the importance of Great Britain was beginning to pale in relation to the total Brazilian scene, first, and most importantly, because of the development of Brazil itself, and, secondly, because of the increasing competition offered by other nations. The monopoly of foreign economic power once held by the British was eroding away and the war speeded the process to its conclusion.

Brazil, because of all the changes since 1850, had been set loose in the rapids of the modernizing process and, although the country might temporarily linger in some peaceful cove or be occasionally snagged by the roots of resistance, it could not return to the starting point. Rather, the persistent pull of the current impelled it ever onward. The corporate society still hung on, not only in some parts of the country and in the beliefs of some persons, but also in some of the attitudes of most individuals; nevertheless, continual modernization was now merely a matter of expanding the geographical areas of influence, increasing the size of the groups that had already been affected, and extending within each individual the logical implications of the attitudes he had accepted or positions into which he had been placed. By 1914 Brazil had begun; the first phase of the process was over.

Most important were the changes in values, ideas, and world-views. The goal of an industrialized society had been adopted by a well-defined sector of the population. The Brazilian manufacturers increasingly emphasized the value of hard work and could point to themselves, rather than to foreigners, as a model of this virtue. Similarly, the conception of the individual as a unit to be moved about both geographically and socially according to economic needs had been firmly established as the ideal. Finally, the increasing secularization of society and especially the idea that the welfare of the state does not depend on the uniform acceptance of a particular religious belief had progressed to the point where it could not easily be reversed. It is practically inconceivable for the Brazil of 1914 to have returned to the societal structures of 1850. The British role, whether it had been positive or negative, was now unimportant since modern change would continue even if their influence were entirely removed.

The best evidence of the transformation of Brazil by this time was the fact that Brazilian industrialization had begun. The year 1914 is often pointed to as the date of its initiation because the artificial impetus provided by war-time shortages greatly accelerated the process. But the effect of the war would have been radically different if major changes had not already occurred. Brazil would have profited little if capital, equipment, attitudes, and values had not been prepared and ready. Even in 1907 Brazil was producing more than half of its needs in cottons, shoes and leather goods, hats, matches, beer, macaroni and similar products, all of which had once been entirely imported, not to mention items which had often come from abroad like bricks, earthenware, and candy.[1]

The insistent demand for protective tariffs, which clearly reflects this development, was especially directed against Great Britain since Brazilian industrialists considered it the chief opponent of their program. The manufacturers' association noted reproachfully in 1882 that France and Britain preached free trade only because they had nothing to lose and everything to gain if such policies were adopted by the countries less advanced in industrial power. Four years later an industrial leader similarly accused England of trying to foist off upon Brazil self-serving theories.[2] At the end of the century, low-tariff President Campos Sales was charged in the Chamber of Deputies with being merely

---

[1] Heitor Ferreira Lima, *Mauá e Roberto Simonsen: dois pioneiros do desenvolvimento* (São Paulo: Editôra Edaglit, 1963), p. 48.

[2] Bibliotheca da Associação Industrial, *Archivos da Exposição da Industria Nacional. Actas, pareceres, e decisões do jury geral da Exposição da Industria Nacional realizada no Rio de Janeiro em 1881* (Rio: Typ. Nacional, 1882), p. xxv; Frederico Glette, *A industria nacional e as tarifas da alfandega. Considerações* (Rio: Leuzinger, 1886), p. 9.

a tool of 'the manufacturing industries of London', his 'all consuming passion being for the London [*sic*] textile industry'. He would, it was alleged, 'make us import everything that can be made abroad, and import it all from England'.[1] Industrialists then played upon national pride, encouraging resentment against the flooding of the Brazilian market with British goods. They charged their country was still 'a nation vegetating within a colonial order, though calling itself independent: miserably exploited...and reduced to a mere trading post'.[2] By their arguments against commercial dependency and in behalf of protective tariffs these Brazilians demonstrated their emergence from traditionalism. In such a context, the British could no longer occupy the position they had once held.

The inclusion, or re-inclusion, of Brazil in the fabric of Western civilization is also revealed by the increasing eclecticism and the growing breadth with which Brazilians accepted influences from abroad. No longer was the foreigner a cause for suspicion nor were persons of only one nationality to be trusted. To be sure, the French had throughout the nineteenth century offered alternative values and inspiration to those of the British; but it is clear that by 1914 Brazil had moved much further. It received immigrants and operas from Italy, company law and philosophy from Germany, and political ideas from the United States. It was now fully a part of Western culture.[3]

Brazil also admitted increasing amounts of manufactured goods from Germany and the United States so that the British predominance in Brazilian markets was being undercut not only by Brazilian industrialization but also by the rising American and German competition. This was especially true for newer products, such as electrical equipment, which, as it was installed in factories and for urban lighting, tended to come almost exclusively from these

---

[1] Brazil, Congresso, Câmara dos Deputados, *Anais*, 1899, I, Appendix, pp. 46–7.

[2] Antonio Felicio dos Santos, *et al.* 'Auxilios á industria', *Jornal do commercio*, 6 July 1892, p. 2.

[3] Gilberto Freyre, *Introdução à história da sociedade patriarcal no Brasil, III: Ordem e progresso* ...2 vols. (Rio: José Olympio, 1959), I, 168, 178, 188, 292; II, 634, 636–7; *Jornal do commercio*, 5 July 1910; Emília Nogueira, 'Alguns aspectos da influência francêsa em São Paulo na segunda metade do século XIX', *Revista de história*, Ano IV, Vol. VII (1953), 317–42.

two countries. But older trades were also affected. British houses long specializing in coal now reported that 'steamship owners are all anxious to try American coal', concluding that 'we shall have to put American coal at our Depots for bunkering purposes in self defense as quickly as possible'.[1] A Britisher in Rio Grande do Sul reported that German import houses were everywhere taking the place of his compatriots, while Americans were purchasing old British trading firms in Rio de Janeiro.[2] One explanation was that the Germans made more effort to learn the language and were more willing to penetrate into the interior instead of remaining ensconced on the coast. Furthermore, they offered broader credits. Some of the results could already be seen in 1902: while Britain still accounted for 28 per cent of Brazil's imports, its rivals were gaining rapidly with German goods representing 12·2 per cent and American ones 11·5 per cent. France now trailed at 8·8 per cent.[3]

In shipping also the Germans now stood second only to the British and were rapidly increasing their share. Lamport and Holt was reported to be losing business to them in southern Brazil, and other British lines were encountering the same difficulty elsewhere. In 1913 the Germans carried 3·5 million bags of Brazilian

[1] F. M. Farrell to R. A. Mather, London, 29 June 1900, PWL, p. 430; but cf. p. 434 and Farrell to Mather, London, 11 May 1900, *ibid.* p. 389.

[2] London *Times*, 3 Mar. 1897, p. 15; Stanley J. Stein, *The Brazilian Cotton Manufacture; Textile Enterprise in an Underdeveloped Area, 1850–1950* (Cambridge, Mass.: Harvard Univ. Press, 1957), p. 71; *Jornal do commercio*, 1 Nov. 1891, p. 9.

[3] On German and American competition see Alan K. Manchester, *British Preëminence in Brazil; Its Rise and Decline: a Study in European Expansion* (Chapel Hill, N.C.: Univ. of North Carolina Press, 1933), pp. 329–32; Ross J. S. Hoffman, *Great Britain and the German Trade Rivalry, 1875–1914* (Philadelphia: Univ. of Pennsylvania Press, 1933); David Joslin, *A Century of Banking in Latin America; to Commemorate the Centenary in 1962 of the Bank of London and South America, Limited* (London: Oxford University Press, 1963), pp. 105–8. On electrical equipment see Wm. I. Buchanan to Joaquim Nabuco, New York, 4 Apr. 1907, JNP, Lata 11; Nelson Lage Mascarenhas, *Bernardo Mascarenhas. O surto industrial de Minas Gerais* (Rio: Gráfica Editôra Aurora, [1955?]), pp. 134, 205, 207, 209, 230–1; on German success see Tobias do Rego Monteiro, *O presidente Campos Salles na Europa*, 2nd ed. (Rio: Briguiet, 1928), pp. 2, 4; João Dunshee de Abranches Moura, *A Allemanha e a paz. Appelo do presidente da Camara dos Deputados ao Congresso Nacional do Brazil* (São Paulo: Typ. Brazil de Rothschild, 1917), p. 11; for import figures see Nelson Werneck Sodré, *História da burguesia brasileira*, Retratos do Brasil, 22 (Rio: Civilização Brasileira, 1964), p. 185. Also see Jorge Martins Rodrigues, 'A rivalidade comercial de norte-americanos e inglêses no Brasil do século XIX', *Revista de história da economia brasileira*, 1 (1953), 73–82.

coffee compared to Britain's 5·3 million and France's 1·6 million. Americans, however, were unsuccessful in their attempts to compete in this field.[1]

German and American banks also began to invade the Brazilian financial market. The Germans had long tried to elbow into this profitable business, and were offering serious competition by the turn of the century. Americans called for the establishment of their own banking facilities in Brazil to 'relieve exporters', as *Bradstreets* put it, 'of the necessity of transacting such business through London'. The American government published detailed studies of Latin American banking in order to encourage such a move.[2] Finally, in 1915, the First National City Bank of New York established a branch in Rio de Janeiro. The decline of British banking hegemony is illustrated by the loan raised in 1906 by the state of São Paulo to finance a price support program for coffee. The German coffee export firm of Theodor Wille & Co., one of E. Johnston & Co.'s main competitors, was chiefly responsible for bringing in German banks who took the lead in the venture. The First National City Bank of New York and some French banks also joined in the scheme, although eventually the British private banking firm of Schroeder & Co. came to dominate the lending consortium. The caution of the Rothschilds in this matter contrasts with their nineteenth-century liberality.[3]

The British long managed to avoid competition in the field of cable communications, but eventually the Americans successfully

[1] London *Times*, 3 Mar. 1897, p. 15; Manchester, *British Preëminence*, p. 329; Brazil, Serviço de Estatística Econômica e Financeira, *Commercio exterior do Brasil. Foreign Trade of Brazil. Commerce extérieur du Brésil. Importação...Exportação...Annos 1913–1915–1916–1917–1918*, 2 vols. (Rio: Monotypado nas officinas da Estatística Commercial, 1921–3), II, 240; Joseph R. West, 'The Foreigner in Brazilian Technology, 1808–1900' (unpub. Ph.D. diss., Univ. of Chicago, 1950), pp. 822–33; Edward N. Hurley, *Banking and Credit in Argentina, Brazil, Chile, and Peru*, U.S. Bureau of Manufacturers Special Agents Series, 90 (Washington, D.C.: Government Printing Office, 1914), pp. 38–9.
[2] Alcindo Guanabara, *A presidencia Campos Salles: politica e finanças, 1898–1902* (Rio: Laemmert, 1902), pp. 343, 345; *Bradstreets*, XIX (1891), 182; Hurley, *Banking and Credit*.
[3] Charles A. Gauld, *The Last Titan: Percival Farquhar, American Entrepreneur in Latin America* [Special Issue of the *Hispanic American Report*] (Stanford, California: Institute of Hispanic American and Luso-Brazilian Studies, Stanford Univ. 1964), p. 256; Caio Prado Júnior, *História econômica do Brasil* (São Paulo: Brasiliense, 1945), pp. 243–4; Freyre, *Ordem e progresso*, II, 440; Leon F. Sensabaugh, 'The Coffee-Trust Question in United States–Brazilian Relations: 1912–1913', *Hispanic American Historical Review*, XXVI (1946), 482n.

challenged even this monopoly. Englishmen had done a lot to destroy the peaceful isolation of traditional Brazil by building submarine telegraph lines in the 1870s. The Brazilian Submarine Telegraph Company, Ltd, had acquired the concession for trans-Atlantic communication and the Western and Brazilian Telegraph Company, Ltd, secured a similar privilege for coastal lines. The two companies then cooperated in setting rates and sharing profits, merging in 1899 to form the Western Telegraph Company, Ltd. An American enterprise had linked New York and Argentina long before that, but the British companies charged an exorbitant surtax on telegrams sent to Argentina for relay to America, thus forcing communications between Brazil and the United States to go via England. Finally, in 1917, the Americans were granted a concession for a direct cable to Brazil.[1] The British thus lost a powerful tool for maintaining their hegemony. Eduardo Prado had once observed that 'all the earth is caught up in the net of English telegraph lines', which were 'powerful invisible nerves' connecting even the most remote regions to the 'brain of the world, London'.[2] This exclusive dependence was no longer the case for Brazil after 1917.

There were other areas as well into which the Americans began to intrude. As early as 1882 a Brazilian entrepreneur complained bitterly of these changing circumstances which he was not alert enough to perceive. He had envisaged a railroad that would run south from Rio de Janeiro along the coast. After great efforts, he managed to raise the money for the initial section in London. But just as the project was about to get under way, the Brazilian government granted a concession for a line—which would compete with this section—to the Botanical Garden Rail Road Company, an American streetcar enterprise. The English backers immediately withdrew their support and the Brazilian promoter lacked

[1] Brazil, Ministerio da Agricultura, Commercio e Obras Publicas, Repartição Geral dos Telegraphos, *Memoria historica* (Rio: Imp. Nacional, 1909), pp. 66–8, 70; J. Fred Rippy, *British Investments in Latin America, 1822–1949. A Case Study in the Operations of Private Enterprise in Retarded Regions* (Minneapolis: Univ. of Minnesota Press, 1959), p. 43; Lawrence F. Hill, *Diplomatic Relations between the United States and Brazil* (Durham, N.C.: Duke Univ. Press, 1932), pp. 303–5.

[2] Eduardo Prado, 'Victoria, R.I.' in *Collectaneas*, 4 vols. (São Paulo: Escola Typographica Salesiana, 1904–5), I, 252, 255.

even the necessary funds to take his case to court.[1] Railways and urban services were no longer to be financed solely by British investors.

Other railroads were also attracting American interest. Pennsylvania-born Percival Farquhar, a would-be captain of industry, dreamed of creating a vast network of rails to link the Amazon with Rio Grande do Sul. He was well on the way to consolidating the railroads of southern Brazil—the first step of his dream—when the end of the rubber boom in the Amazon caused his financial structure to collapse. But, despite his failure, his efforts were accompanied by an increasing importation of American railway equipment.

Still other areas beckoned to the Americans. Farquhar had been intimately connected with the creation of internationally financed power plants in Rio de Janeiro and São Paulo built by a company with head offices in Canada. It greatly aided the industrialization of these two cities although its rate structure was naturally the subject of much controversy. The Farquhar interests also included land and cattle companies, while other American firms became interested in meat-packing. Meanwhile, the Germans had invested in breweries, a paper company, several foundries, textile mills, and electric companies.[2] Table 7 illustrates the point that the British did not have Brazil to themselves any longer.

In some ways the declaration of the republic in 1889 was also an assertion of Brazil's freedom from old ties with Britain. Britain's connexions with the monarchy had been so close and the apparent similarity of governmental forms so striking that the alteration seemed to signify a move toward the United States or at least an identification with the New World as opposed to the Old. The end of parliamentary government clearly set the new Brazil off from Britain in the opinion of contemporary observers, and many of the leaders of the new republic specifically

[1] *Jornal do commercio*, 5 Feb. 1882, p. 2.
[2] Gauld, *The Last Titan*, pp. 65–89, 160–97, 247–62; Simon G. Hanson, 'The Farquhar Syndicate in South America', *Hispanic American Historical Review*, XVII (1937), 324–5; Claude L. Douglas, *Cattle Kings of Texas* (Dallas: Baugh, 1939), pp. 235–42; Warren K. Dean, 'São Paulo's Industrial Elite, 1890–1960' (unpub. Ph.D. diss., Univ. of Florida, 1964), p. 86.

Declining Influence

Table 7. *Foreign Companies Authorized to Operate in Brazil, 1861–1920, by Period and Home-Office Location*[a]

Home-Office Location	1861– 1875	1876– 1890	1891– 1905	1906– 1920
Great Britain	78	99	80	171
U.S.A.	6	13	11	138
Germany	4	18	21	40
France	1	10	25	68
Belgium	none	7	21	29
Portugal	12	7	3	15
Other	2	13	19	84
Total	103	167	180	545

[a] Derived from: Brazil, Departmento Nacional da Indústria e Comércio, *Sociedades mercantís autorizadas a funcionar no Brasil, 1808–1946* (Rio: Imp. Nacional, 1947).

looked to the United States as a model.[1] But this aspect of the change must not be exaggerated. Quintino Bocaiuva (1836–1912), one of the chief republicans and a most vocal advocate of the need to identify with the other nations of the Western Hemisphere, recognized that Brazil was in 'pecuniary' need of continued good relations with England and refused to countenance rash moves to break up old connexions.[2] And indeed those relationships declined in importance only gradually.

Nevertheless, the rising prominence of the United States in world affairs was keenly perceived by Brazil's new leaders and

[1] Nícia Villela Luz, 'A monarquia brasileira e as repúblicas americanas', *Journal of Inter-American Studies*, VIII (1966), 358–70; Campos Salles to Victorino Carmillo, Geneva, 14 June 1893, in Manuel Ferraz de Campos Salles, *Cartas da Europa* (Rio: Leuzinger, 1894), pp. 202–6; Afonso Arinos de Melo Franco, *Um estadista da república (Afrânio de Melo Franco e seu tempo)*, Documentos Brasileiros, 85, 3 vols. (Rio: José Olympio, 1955), I, 350; João Pinheiro da Silva, *João Pinheiro e sua doutrina...1889–1908* (Belo Horizonte: n.p., 1935), *passim*, esp. pp. 36, 42; also note career of Alfredo Ellis, in J. F. Velho Sobrinho, *Dicionário bio-bibliográfico brasileiro*, 2 vols. (Rio: Pongetti, 1937–40), I, 213.

[2] Quintino Bocaiuva, 17 June 1890, in João Dunshee de Abranches Moura, ed., *Actas e actos do governo provisorio. Copias authenticas dos protocollos das sessões secretas do Conselho de Ministros desde a proclamação da republica até a organização do gabinete Lucena, acompanhadas de importantes revelações e documentos*, 3rd ed., Obras completas, 4 (Rio: 'Jornal do Brasil', 1953), p. 198; also see 19 July 1890, p. 217.

they took positive diplomatic steps to ally themselves with that country. Salvador de Mendonça (1841–1913) had been named the Brazilian minister in Washington in early 1889 and was maintained in that post by the new regime, remaining there until 1898. Mendonça had lived in the United States since 1875, first as consul and then as secretary of legation, and had married an American.[1] It was because of his work that the reciprocity treaty of 1891 was signed.

The greatest circumstantial evidence which suggests the Americans were gaining ground in the early days of the republic was this treaty by which both countries agreed to lower tariffs on certain products of the other. Brazil agreed to reduce the duties on American machinery and flour in exchange for continued low tariffs on Brazilian products entering the United States. It was said that the British considered the treaty a powerful threat to their position. Americans in Brazil argued that in attempting to discredit the treaty British banks forced down the value of Brazilian currency 'in their arbitrarily established daily rates'. The United States' consul in Recife reported that the British 'hate Secretary Blains [sic] "reciprocity" views as embodied in the new Tariff Bill and are determined to kill it'. But the treaty was principally unpopular among Brazilian industrialists and was hotly debated in the Rio de Janeiro Press. A new tariff law in the United States in 1894 finally dampened the controversy.[2]

It has sometimes been said that Great Britain went so far as to support revolts in Brazil because the British business community was alarmed by the reciprocity treaty and the generally favorable attitudes of the republican government toward the United States. During the period from 1892 to 1894 Brazil simultaneously faced

[1] Salvador de Menezes Drummond Furtado de Mendonça, *A situação internacional do Brazil* (Rio: Garnier, 1913), pp. 233, 245; Múcio Leão, *Salvador de Mendonça; ensaio bio-bibliográfico* (Rio: Publicações da Academia Brasileira, 1952), pp. 16–20.

[2] American minister in Rio quoted by Hill, *Diplomatic Relations*, p. 272; Stevens to Department of State, Recife, 23 Nov. 1891, NA/DS, Despatches Consuls, Pernambuco, no. 70; note American belief that the treaty would open the way for large trade relations, Merchants and Manufacturers' Association of Baltimore, *A reciprocidade commercial: Baltimore e Brazil. Um compendio de informações uteis relativas aos interesses mutuos da Republica do Brazil e da cidade de Baltimore, Estados Unidos da America* (Baltimore: Merchants and Manufacturers' Association of Baltimore, 1891).

two major revolutionary movements. One broke out in Rio
Grande do Sul provoked by regional demands for parliamentary
government, and another one, caused by the navy's sense of displaced status and fading power, erupted within the naval squadron
in Rio de Janeiro in 1893. Both movements were supported by
some who wished the return of a monarch, but it is doubtful
that either of them was monarchical in major intent. Nevertheless,
an American consul reported at the time that the revolutionaries
were strengthened 'by the monarchical element of the country
backed by the larger part of the English opinion'.[1] Later historians
have tended to repeat this American view of the British position.
The implication is that this attitude was passed on to the Foreign
Office, which then lent support to the rebellious navy. Although
the intervention of foreigners was probably not as important as has
been thought, the allegation of British involvement merits some
attention. If correct, the defeat of the revolts would have been a
major blow to Britain's place in Brazil.[2] But the evidence lends no
support to this view.

The British business community much preferred short-run
gains to be derived from uninterrupted trade in Rio de Janeiro to
the conjectural advantages of supporting the naval squadron's
effort to blockade Brazil's capital city. British businessmen unani-
mously opposed the blockade, from Leopold Rothschild and the
London & Brazilian Bank to the principal British merchants in
Rio de Janeiro. Twelve of these firms took an especially firm stand
by signing a collective letter to Hugh Wyndham, the British
minister in Rio, suggesting the need for additional protection of
British commerce from the pretentions of the insurgents.[3] In the
same tone, E. Johnston & Co. expressed the desire for protection
so they could 'resume business with greater confidence'. In late

---

[1] Burke to Department of State, Recife, 31 Jan. 1894, NA/DS, Despatches Consuls,
Pernambuco, no. 43.
[2] June E. Hahner, 'Officers and Civilians in Brazil, 1889–1898', unpub. Ph.D. diss.,
Cornell Univ. 1966, pp. 73–5, 77–85, 91, 176–81; Walter LaFeber, *The New Empire: An
Interpretation of American Expansion, 1860–1898* (Ithaca, N.Y.: Cornell Univ. Press for
the American Historical Association, 1963), pp. 210, 212.
[3] Memorandum, 21 Sept. 1893, attached to Draft Telegram, Foreign Office to Wyndham,
28 Sept. 1893, FO, 13/708, no. 14; Phipps Brothers & Co. *et al.* to Wyndham, Rio,
19 Dec. 1893, copy encl. in Wyndham to Foreign Office, Rio, 24 Dec. 1893, FO 13/707,
no. 265.

December 1893, when the revolting forces were taking an especially firm stand on the blockade, Wyndham reported that it was the opinion of the commercial community that 'armed intervention should take place to force the insurgents to cease from worrying commerce and to free the Custom House from molestation'.[1] The rebel leaders, presumably aware of this attitude, were so suspicious of the British that they accused E. Johnston & Co. of allowing government spies to use their launches in making inquisitive cruises about the bay.[2] In short, British business interests did not support the insurrection.

The Foreign Office was chiefly interested, first, in protecting British life and property from injury and, second, in being on the winning side.[3] By its wait-and-see attitude it managed to preserve considerable dignity at a difficult time, although ruffling the feathers of both contenders. The commander of the naval revolt was rebuffed by the British refusal to recognize him as a belligerent, while the legal forces felt the British were aiding the enemy since Wyndham put pressure on the government not to provoke the bombardment of the city by fortifying it.[4] Thus protests in either direction brought recriminations of one-sidedness and yet, as the British minister complained, it was 'exceedingly difficult to say from which side provocation comes'.[5] The British government insisted, nevertheless, on neutrality.

Only the British minister in Rio was apparently pro-insurgent. His feelings seem to have sprung from his revulsion at the arbitrary and illiberal actions of Floriano Peixoto. But he did not believe in the possibility of a monarchical restoration. And he leaned over backward in 1893-4 to maintain diplomatic neutrality on most occasions, despite his personal preferences. The blockade had been declared as early as September 1893, but Wyndham joined forces

[1] Wyndham to Foreign Office, Rio, 20 Dec. 1893, and following enclosure: E. Johnston & Co. to W. G. Abbot (British Consul), Rio, 18 Dec. 1893, FO 13/707, no. 259; telegram Wyndham to Foreign Office, Petrópolis, 20 Dec. 1893, FO 13/708, no. 75.

[2] Wyndham to Foreign Office, Rio, 20 Jan. 1894, and enclosures, FO 13/724, no. 25.

[3] Comments by Foreign Office staff on Wyndham to Foreign Office, 22 Sept. 1893, FO 13/705, no. 125; draft telegrams Foreign Office to Wyndham, 15 Dec. 1893, 18 Dec. 1893, FO 13/708, nos. 37, 38.

[4] Draft telegram, Foreign Office to Wyndham, 6 Oct. 1893, FO 13/708, no. 20; Wyndham to Foreign Office, Rio, 29 Sept. 1893, FO 13/705, no. 134.

[5] Wyndham to Foreign Office, Rio, 14 Nov. 1893, FO 13/706, no. 205.

with the Americans to protect commerce and see that goods continued to flow into the city. As the British had some seventy-five merchant ships in Rio to the Americans' twelve, this proved a demanding task, especially since the British had only four men-of-war while the Americans had five.[1] To Wyndham and the British naval commander the demands of the British merchants for complete protection seemed callously single-minded. They were incensed at the merchants' insistence on carrying on 'at all hazards': when the Rio de Janeiro City Improvements Co., Ltd, complained of the 'serious inconvenience and extra expense' caused by the commander's refusal to provide escort into a particularly dangerous area of the bay, the British captain replied that he saw no reason for 'the lives of H.M.'s officers and men to be needlessly risked in order that you...may not be inconvenienced in the course of business'.[2] Nevertheless, both this officer and the British minister did all they could short of actual fighting to maintain the flow of British goods into Rio de Janeiro.

In December the revolutionaries adopted much stricter and more aggressive measures which finally reduced foreign trade to a mere trickle.[3] The result was a renewed and violent outcry from the British merchants. The matter came to a head in late January 1894, over Belgian shipping under the protection of the British. The naval commanders, with the full support of the senior British officer, now proposed to use force at once. It was only at this point that Wyndham seems to have allowed his preferences for the revolting forces to influence his decisions. He counseled moderation and another final attempt to persuade the insurrectionaries to abandon their intransigent attitude. Meanwhile, he cabled the

[1] Wyndham to 'Jervoise', Rio, 23 Jan. 1890, FO 13/658, unnumbered; Wyndham to Foreign Office, Rio, 3 Oct. 1893, FO 13/705, no. 139; telegram senior naval officer to Admiralty, Rio, 7 Nov. 1893, FO 13/708, following no. 53; telegram Wyndham to Foreign Office, Rio, 28 Dec. 1893, FO 13/708, no. 80a; Wyndham to Foreign Office, Rio, 24 Dec. 1893, and comments of Foreign Office staff thereon, FO 13/707, no. 265.
[2] Telegram Wyndham to Foreign Office, Petrópolis, 20 Dec. 1893, FO 13/708, no. 75; J. V. Benest, manager Rio de Janeiro City Improvements Company, to Wyndham, Rio, 18 Nov. 1893, and W. M. Lang, senior British naval officer in Rio, to Benest, aboard *Sirius*, Rio, 23 Nov. 1893, both encl. in Wyndham to Foreign Office, Rio, 2 Dec. 1893, FO 13/707, no. 228.
[3] Wyndham to Foreign Office, Rio, 20 Dec. 1893, FO 13/707, no. 256; Wyndham to Foreign Office, Rio, 7 Feb. 1894, FO 13/724, no. 52.

Foreign Office recommending the insurgents be granted belligerent status, citing in support of his argument their impressive military gains in the south of Brazil. But he had earlier advised against such recognition and some of his despatches in this tenor were arriving in London by sea-mail at the very time the crisis was being reported by telegram.[1] Before any decision had been taken, the Americans, having dissembled their intentions before the other members of the diplomatic corps, forced the rebels with a brief exchange of shots to allow a merchantman to unload at the wharf. Then and only then did Wyndham try to arouse interest in London by suggesting the Americans were acting in alarm at the threat which would be posed to their commercial treaty by the success of the revolt.[2]

If the British had considered the insurgent cause worth supporting, they would have recognized them as belligerents. Throughout the conflict they had numerous opportunities to do so, especially after rebel forces set up a government in southern Brazil and the squadron commander in Rio placed himself under its nominal direction. Belligerent status would not only have empowered him to set up an effective blockade in Rio de Janeiro, but greatly facilitated his efforts to secure armaments in Europe. But the Foreign Office consistently refused to take this step. It could still have reversed its stand after the American action, and in this it would probably have been supported by the Germans—who had always been pro-insurgent—and the Italians. The United States would then have been isolated in its stance.[3]

[1] Wyndham to Foreign Office, Rio, 30 Jan. 1894, FO 13/724, no. 34; telegram quoted in Wyndham to Foreign Office, Rio, 2 Feb. 1894, FO 13/724, no. 37; Wyndham to Foreign Office, Rio, 2 Nov. 1893, FO 13/706, no. 189; Wyndham to Foreign Office, Rio, 28 Dec. 1893, FO 13/707, no. 273; telegram Wyndham to Foreign Office, Rio, 27 Dec. 1893, FO 13/708, no. 80.

[2] Wyndham to Foreign Office, Rio, 5 Feb. 1894, FO 13/724, no. 48.

[3] Telegram Wyndham to Foreign Office, Rio, 25 Oct. 1893, FO 13/708, no. 49; Raimundo Magalhães Júnior, *Rui, o homem e o mito*, Retratos do Brasil, 27 (Rio: Civilização Brasileira, 1964), pp 90-1; draft telegrams Foreign Office to Wyndham, 29 Sept. 1893, 27 Oct. 1893, FO 13/708, nos. 15, 27; draft telegram Foreign Office to Wyndham, 3 Feb. 1894, FO 13/728, no. 12; telegram Wyndham to Foreign Office, Rio, 21 Oct. 1893, and Foreign Office staff comment upon it, esp. memorandum by Rosebery, 23 Oct. 1893, FO 13/708, no. 46; Wyndham to Foreign Office, Rio, 19 Nov. 1893, FO 13/706, no. 211; Wyndham to Foreign Office, Rio, 30 Jan. 1894, 2 Feb. 1894, FO 13/724, nos. 34, 37.

But once again the Foreign Office held back, cabling the British minister that 'H.M.s government would prefer to protect commerce by the use of force rather than recognize the insurgents as belligerents'. When Wyndham reiterated his recommendation that they be granted belligerent status, the Foreign Office immediately queried, 'If we adopt this course, what measures do you recommend for the protection of our national commerce?'[1] Evidently the British government cannot be charged with supporting the revolt. And its defeat was caused as much by British inaction as by American interference. The incident does not mark a turning point for British hegemony.

On the other hand, this does not mean that Brazil was not, in fact, gradually moving into the American orbit. In the twentieth century the shift to the United States was emphasized by José Maria Paranhos, 2nd, *barão* do Rio Branco (1845–1912), who became Brazilian foreign minister in 1902. Although oriented toward Europe by his training and background, he recognized the necessity of strengthening Brazil's ties with the United States. In so doing he laid the foundation of subsequent Brazilian foreign policy. One indication of his position was the renewal of trade agreements with the United States in 1904, 1906, and 1910, chiefly to the detriment of manufacturers in Brazil. And he was responsible for forestalling the enactment of a really protective tariff in 1903.[2]

At the beginning of 1905 Rio Branco persuaded the American government that the legations of the two countries should be raised to the rank of embassy, and he named Joaquim Nabuco to be the first Brazilian ambassador to the United States. It has been said that Nabuco had long been an advocate of closer ties with North America, but the chapters he wrote during the 1890s reflect the greatest skepticism and even dislike for the United States.

[1] Draft telegrams Foreign Office to Wyndham, 2 Feb. 1894, 3 Feb. 1894, FO 13/728, nos. 11, 12.

[2] Frederic William Ganzert, 'The Baron do Rio Branco, Joaquim Nabuco and the Growth of Brazilian–American Friendship, 1900–1910', *Hispanic American Historical Review*, XXII (1942), 435; Aluízio Napoleão, *Rio-Branco e as relações entre o Brasil e os Estados Unidos*, Monografias da Commissão Preparatória do Centenário do Barão do Rio Branco, 2 (Rio: Ministério das Relações Exteriores, 1947), p. 212; E. Bradford Burns, *The Unwritten Alliance: Rio Branco and Brazilian–American Relations* (New York: Columbia Univ. Press, 1966), pp. 68–72, and *passim*; Reports General Manager, 1912, pp. 2–4, ARFM.

Even in 1882 he had expressed considerable contempt for James G. Blaine's Pan-American idea.[1] Nabuco also had less than cordial relationships with his pro-American predecessor in Washington. He believed that Salvador de Mendonça had been chiefly responsible for encouraging United States' support of Floriano in 1893, a course of action that Nabuco—at that time a monarchist—felt would lead to a surrender of Brazilian independence and an unseemly rendering of obeisance to America. He also thought Mendonça was illegally receiving substantial sums for placing large orders for military equipment in the United States.[2]

Now, however, Nabuco had made an about face. Confessing his 'ordinary preference for London', he recognized that 'our diplomacy should receive its principal impetus from Washington. Such a policy would be better than the largest army or navy'.[3] Once he had been made ambassador to the United States he was untiring in his efforts to bring the two countries closer together. First of all, he bent every effort to dispel, through a strenuous lecture circuit, the indifference with which Americans regarded his country. Typical of his attempt to win friends was the convocation address he delivered at the University of Chicago in which he expressed the hope that Brazil would be 'penetrated with your optimism, your self-reliance, and your energy'.[4] Secondly, Nabuco took vigorous action on the diplomatic front to strengthen the ties between the two countries. Most conspicuous was his success in gaining the presence of Elihu Root at the third Pan-American Conference held in Rio de Janeiro in 1906. This was the first time an American Secretary of State had left the United States in an official capacity.

[1] Cf. Carolina Nabuco, *The Life of Joaquim Nabuco*, transl. & ed. Ronald Hilton (Stanford, California: Stanford Univ. Press, 1950), p. 307, and Ganzert, 'Baron do Rio Branco', p. 439, with Joaquim Nabuco, *Minha formação*, [? ed.], Documentos Brasileiros, 90 (Rio: José Olympio, 1957), pp. 123–62, and Joaquim Nabuco, 'Correspondencia', *Jornal do commercio*, 8 Mar. 1882, p. 2.

[2] Joaquim Nabuco, Diary, entry for 4 Nov. 1893, JNP; Joaquim Nabuco to Francisco Ignacio de Carvalho Moreira, *barão* do Penedo, London, 7 Mar. 1891, in Joaquim Nabuco, *Obras completas*, XIII, 200–1; Hahner, 'Officers and Civilians', p. 88.

[3] Carolina Nabuco, *Life of Joaquim Nabuco*, pp. 305, 307.

[4] Joaquim Nabuco, *The Approach of the Two Americas. Convocation Address before the University of Chicago, August 28, 1908*, Bulletin of the American Branch of the Association for International Conciliation, 10 (New York: American Branch of the Association for International Conciliation, 1908), p. 5.

Rio Branco and Nabuco acted in Brazil to emphasize the value of the connexion with the United States, meanwhile giving credit to themselves for this new policy. But Salvador de Mendonça was not impressed: he noted that 'when Rio Branco sent Joaquim Nabuco to discover North America, it had already been discovered, measured, and delimited. The *barão* do Rio Branco always had the fate of breaking down open doors'. Now it was Mendonça's turn to accuse Brazil of surrendering its dignity before the American colossus, deriding Nabuco for 'firing compliments at Mr. Roosevelt at point-blank range'.[1] Nevertheless, despite the critics, the policy adopted by Rio Branco has lasted to the present time with minimal exceptions.

To understand the significance of this twentieth-century development one may well contrast the ideas of Rui Barbosa in 1894 with those he held a decade later. Irritated by American support of his enemy Floriano Peixoto, the dictatorial president, Barbosa had then said that the United States was a subject for admiration only in so far as it held true to English ideals.[2] This it was not doing: 'There is not...a free country where society and politics are developing more disrupting tendencies than in the United States.' There was in that country a 'degeneration of the democratic element, manifest in the mediocrity of its legislature, in the corruption of its assemblies, in the decadence of its finances, in the greed of its parties, and in the violence of its internal struggles'. He swept aside any suggestion that he had been pro-American in writing the constitution in 1891. 'I never urged a republican solution; I pointed to it as the coming danger if the monarchy were not reformed...My prophecy proved correct. I accepted it as an irrevocable fact. To give it a liberal structure, the United States' constitution was the only possible model.' But, Barbosa insisted, it was 'merely a variation of the English constitution. All that is substantial in it...belongs to a heritage of ancient traditions, ancient as Great Britain'. He added that if he could have converted the Braganza throne into a Hanoverian one and exchanged Pedro II for Victoria, he would have done so, but 'since

---

[1] Mendonça, *A situação internacional*, pp. 247–8, 255.
[2] Ruy Barbosa, *Cartas de Inglaterra* (Rio: Leuzinger, 1896), pp. 38, 320.

this prodigy was impossible, I was obliged to choose for the inevitable republic the most satisfactory form'.[1]

By 1906, however, Barbosa's attitude toward the United States had completely changed. He now wrote to Joaquim Nabuco saying that 'no one has greater liking for that country than I'. He claimed he had begun to admire the United States at the time of the Civil War, although confessing that 'afterwards my tendencies and studies were absorbed by England. With our revolution of '89 they turned again to the United States. You see that I support your campaign for this friendship'.[2] The fact that he now hoped to be named head of the Brazilian delegation to the second Hague Peace Conference may have particularly inspired him to support the policies so firmly enunciated by the Brazilian foreign minister.

In any case, the result of this diplomacy was an abject prostration before the new foreign idol. Brazil, said Rio Branco, looked to the Monroe Doctrine not as a unilateral policy, but as a basic statement of the solidarity of the whole continent.[3] Rio Branco's mouthpiece, João Dunshee de Abranches Moura (1867–1941), applauded the actions of the Brazilian statesmen who strove 'to strengthen day by day our longstanding friendship with the United States'. He then referred to the two countries as 'sister nations, the two greatest powers of the New World'.[4] And this was also Rio Branco's mistake: to think that without parity of power there could be real friendship.

Abranches' admiration for the United States was matched only by his love of Germany. He had been deeply affected in his

---

[1] Ruy Barbosa, *Cartas de Inglaterra*, pp. 38, 211–12, 340, 344.

[2] Barbosa quoted by Carleton Sprague Smith, *Os livros norte-americanos no pensamento de Rui Barbosa*, Separata das 'Publicações da Casa de Rui Barbosa, Conferências', 2 (Rio: Imp. Nacional, 1945), pp. 6, 7; also see Homero Pires, *Anglo-American Political Influences on Rui Barbosa*, transl. Sylvia Medrado Clinton (Rio: Casa de Rui Barbosa, 1949), p. 24.

[3] José Maria da Silva Paranhos, 2º, *barão do Rio Branco*, 'O Brasil, os Estados Unidos e o Monroísmo', in *Estudos históricos*, Obras do Barão do Rio Branco, 8 (Rio: Ministério das Relações Exteriores, 1948), pp. 129–51; Burns, *Unwritten Alliance*, pp. 146–59.

[4] João Dunshee de Abranches Moura, *Brazil and the Monroe Doctrine* (Rio: Imp. Nacional, 1915), pp. 9–10, also see p. 71; on his relationship to Rio Branco see Ganzert, 'Baron do Rio Branco', p. 434; Joaquim Vieira da Luz, *Dunshee de Abranches, e outras figuras* (Rio: privately printed, 1954), pp. 52–5. On Brazilian attitudes toward the United States the official position should be contrasted with the influence of Eduardo Prado's anti-American *A illusão americana*, 2nd ed. (Paris: Colin, 1895).

native northeast, as Sílvio Romero had been, by the Germanophile philosopher Tobias Barreto. Abranches believed 'Brazil and the United States cannot fail ever to proceed united on the [American] continent, as, likewise, the true course we should follow in view of European policy is ever increasingly to foster approximation toward Germany, which, aside from being our best friend and most cultured of the European countries, is the one which best serves our economic and social interests'.[1] What social interests he meant are not clear, but the economic ones were evident to all: manufactured goods, shipping, banks, import–export houses.

When the First World War broke out he sided heavily with Germany. During its duration he published several books in support of the German position, the most important of which was *A illusão brazileira*. He summed up his position by the vacuous argument that 'Great Britain and France have always been the nations which, since our independence, have mistreated and oppressed us the most', while 'from the Berlin governments we have not yet received to this day the smallest slight or simplest insult'. In another publication he more perceptively argued that the war was an attempt to crush the upstart economic giant.[2]

When the United States joined the war against Germany, Abranches was in a difficult position. The opinion of men like Rui Barbosa—who always advocated Brazilian support of Britain —won out, and Brazil joined the Allies. British control of Brazilian shipping and the cable system had already prepared the way. One of their first actions when war broke out was to cut the German telegraph lines to the New World, thus ensuring a virtual monopoly of all news that reached Brazil. Tons of propaganda were also shipped on the Royal Mail Line, and by November 1914 the public library in São Paulo had already placed on its shelves a British view of the causes of the war. The British also blacklisted any Brazilian merchant trading with the Germans,

[1] Abranches Moura, *Brazil and the Monroe Doctrine*, p. 68. Also see Vieira da Luz, *Dunshee de Abranches*, p. 49.

[2] João Dunshee de Abranches Moura, *A illusão brazileira* (*justificação historica de uma attitude*) (Rio: Imp. Nacional, 1917), pp. 365, 371; João Dunshee de Abranches Moura, *A conflagração européa e suas causas: discurso...na Camara dos Deputados...em 26 de setembro de 1914* (Rio: Almeida Marques, 1915); also see Abranches Moura, *A Allemanha e a paz*.

and the continuing British predominance in the export–import complex made this a serious blow. Brazil had no real alternative but to oppose Germany.[1] Yet the outbreak of the First World War marked the end of that kind of British control. Conditions that had been changing were now accelerated. The international economy which, since 1850, had formed the context of Anglo-Brazilian economic relationships was drastically altered by the conflict. Not only did the war itself interrupt the working of the previously existing system, but its effects were to radically modify the post-war world. Gone was the free flow of capital, goods, and people which had been characteristic of the pre-1914 period. Instead, there were immigration laws, tariff regulations, and shaky currency structures. So 1914 is a decisive cut-off point when viewed from the British side.[2]

In Brazil the most immediate effect of the war was to greatly weaken the British position while increasing the importance of the United States and eliminating German competition for several years. Shipping was the area most immediately affected, since the blockade of Germany and war-time transport needs seriously cut into the capacity of both European nations. Arrival of British ships in Brazilian ports dropped from 9·9 million tons in 1913 to 2·2 in 1917. Although Great Britain was able to recover its dominant position after the war and hold it until 1930, the same cannot be said for other areas of the British–Brazilian connexion.[3]

Britain's place as chief supplier of Brazilian imports was seriously

[1] Abranches Moura, *A illusão brazileira*, pp. 10, 175; H. C. Peterson, *Propaganda for War: the Campaign Against American Neutrality, 1914–1917* (Norman, Okla.: Univ. of Oklahoma Press, 1939), pp. 12–15; H. W. Leslie, '*The Royal Mail' War Book, Being an Account of the Operations of the Ships of the Royal Mail Steam Packet Co.*, 1914–1919 (London: Heinemann, 1920), p. 180; Great Britain, Foreign Office, *Correspondencia do governo britannico relativa a crise europea; apresentado [sic] ás duas camaras do parlamento por ordem de Sua Magestade, agosto de 1914* (London: Foreign Office, 1914), stamped by the then Biblioteca Publica do Estado on 24 Nov. 1914; also see Great Britain, Commissão sobre as Barbaridades Attribuidas aos Allemães, *Relatorio da commissão... presidida pelo visconde Bryce* (London: Nelson, n.d.); Brazil, Ministerio das Relações Exteriores, *Guerra da Europa: documentos diplomáticos. Attitude do Brasil, 1914–1918*, 2 vols. (Rio: Imp. Nacional, 1917), I, 116–28.
[2] Sanford A. Mosk, 'Latin America and the World Economy, 1850–1914', *Inter-American Economic Affairs*, II, no. 3 (winter 1948), pp. 53–82; William Ashworth, *A Short History of the International Economy, 1850–1950* (London and New York: Longmans, Green, 1952), pp. 186–214; Joslin, *A Century of Banking*, pp. 215–33.
[3] Brazil, Serviço de Estatística Econômica e Financeira, *Commercio exterior do Brasil... 1913–1918*, II, 307; Manchester, *British Preëminence*, p. 336.

undermined by the war. In 1913 Brazil had imported £16·4 million worth of merchandise from England; two years later this amount had fallen to £6·6 million. Although then recovering somewhat, by 1918 it was still only £10·8 million while imports from the United States amounted to £19 million. Despite a brief flurry of renewed struggle after the war, the British definitely lost out to the Americans by 1924. In fact, the Brazilian government deliberately encouraged this shift by its advertising policies. In 1926 the United States furnished 29 per cent of Brazil's imports and Great Britain only 19 per cent. The British never recovered their position, and the great depression caused the final demise of British imports from the Brazilian scene, as they fell from £16 million in 1928 to £4·5 million in 1932.[1]

The flow of British capital to Brazil was also quite naturally interrupted by the war. Subsequently the total British investment increased much more slowly than that of the Americans. It has been estimated that while British investments grew by approximately U.S. $252 million between 1913 and 1929, American investments rose by U.S. $426 million. Thus Wall Street replaced the 'City' of London as the major source of new capital. Furthermore, the British private investments of this period were directed primarily toward the expansion of existing enterprises rather than the creation of new and innovating businesses. In the case of railways, which next to public loans were the most important area of British investment, the size of the British commitment actually decreased. Although the total amount of British capital in Brazil continued until 1930 to overshadow the American investment, the United States was rapidly making up for Britain's century-long head-start.[2]

[1] Brazil, Serviço de Estatística Econômica e Financeira, *Commercio exterior do Brasil...* *1913–1918*, I, lvii; E. Lloyd Rolfe, *Report on Brazil's Trade & Industry in 1918 with Special Reference to the State of São Paulo. Hints, Information for Manufacturers & Merchants* (São Paulo: British Chamber of Commerce of São Paulo & Southern Brazil, 1919), p. 5; Brazil, Ministerio da Agricultura, Industria e Commercio, *What Brazil Buys and Sells* (Rio: Imp. Nacional, 1918); Clarence F. Jones, 'The Evolution of Brazilian Commerce', *Economic Geography*, II (1926), 571; Manchester, *British Preëminence*, pp. 334–6; Joslin, *A Century of Banking*, pp. 221–3, 231.
[2] Max Winkler, *Investments of United States Capital in Latin America*, World Peace Foundation Pamphlets, Vol. IX, no. 6 (Boston: World Peace Foundation, 1928), pp. 275, 278, 280, 283; Rippy, *British Investments*, p. 151; Joslin, *A Century of Banking*, pp. 217, 221.

Declining Influence

The depression of the 1930s sealed the tomb of British predominance in Brazil. But the financial crash only made evident its moribund condition since 1914. The British position of preeminence may legitimately be said to have come to an end at the time of the First World War. Although the British were still present, their importance was gone, partly because of the rise of Brazilian interests and partly because of the competition offered by other countries. The British phase was over by 1914.

CONCLUSION

The onset of modernization in Brazil was not caused by the British. Rather, it was the result of broad trends within which Britishers exercised an important but limited role. Change in Brazil was partly the result of the expansion of the international economy which swept Brazil into its increasingly turbulent course. The spread of new ideas and attitudes which accompanied this economic transformation was also responsible for recasting Brazilian patterns of life. In addition, modernization was the result of factors within Brazil which enabled Brazilians to respond constructively to those foreign stimuli. Thus they were able simultaneously to enjoy the benefits of rapidly increasing exports while controlling a significant portion of the resulting wealth, that is, the capital resources that were needed to develop other sectors of the economy. Similarly, absorption of ideas and attitudes from abroad did not prevent the emergence of an embryonic national consciousness. So internal and external forces combined to launch Brazil into a modernizing trajectory.

Nor were the British responsible if the promise of modern change was unfulfilled by 1914. The process which had then begun has not yet made Brazil over in the image of the modern world because of the obstacles to change presented by the old society. Furthermore, the very process of modernization, like the motion of an aircraft, created waves of opposition which seem to have mounted rapidly in strength when the speed of change increased. At that point where either progress is slowed or the barriers must be noisily broken, Brazil, perhaps because of the qualities of its cultural heritage, has often seemed to hesitate, postponing the inevitable moment of crisis. In any case, the British were not primarily responsible either for change or for the obstacles to change.

But the British became entwined in Brazilian life and their actions were thus bound up with both the forces of conservatism and of progress. Not equally, of course: they were more closely tied to the influences which impelled Brazil toward development,

319

because, to a large degree, these forces—like the British—were foreign. So, if one were to strike a balance sheet for British actions in Brazil, one would find them more often connected to disruptive and, therefore, transforming influences than to preserving ones. But they appear as well on the other side of the ledger, an ambiguity which is not surprising to any observer of the human past.

Once industrialization had begun in Brazil, the export economy —to which the British were so closely tied—often slowed the pace of change. Coffee interests were usually against tariffs, government loans to industries, crop diversification, land reform, and education. And the British strengthened these plantation interests. The British built or financed the railroads that fixed coffee monoculture on south-central Brazil. They reduced the costs of transporting this agricultural product both by rail and by sea and built the port works where the transfer was made from trains to ships. Foreign loans raised in London allowed the Brazilian government to sidestep the consequences of its over-dependence on one crop and forestall the growth of pressures for changing this relationship. Meanwhile, the human resources that were so urgently needed for the process of modernization were left relatively untouched by coffee culture.

In addition, the British acquired great power over the Brazilian economy. In attempting to reduce the risks of the coffee trade, their export houses became larger and controlled more and more of Brazil's life-blood. Brazilian shipping was almost exclusively in the hands of the British and so Brazil's international trade could be completely disrupted by British events, as was the case at the outset of the First World War. The growth of British banking firms similarly extended foreign economic power in Brazil. Note, for instance, the remarks of a jealous American in 1914 who complained that Americans throughout South America had to depend on British banks for financing their trade and providing local credit information: 'An enormous toll is annually paid to London, the center of international banking.'[1] Thus, much

---

[1] Edward N. Hurley, *Banking and Credit in Argentina, Brazil, Chile and Peru*, United States Bureau of Manufacturers Special Agents Series, 90 (Washington, D.C.: Government Printing Office, 1914), p. 66.

of the wealth that ideally should have remained in the cities of Brazil to foster further development was, instead, drained off by these unwittingly 'neo-colonial' structures.

Outright opposition to those steps that would have fostered industrialization was also evident among some Britishers. The Rothschilds forcefully opposed the industrial loans of 1892 and may have thus contributed to the lack of confidence which surrounded them. Certainly the conditions that the British banking community imposed on Brazil in 1898 in exchange for a 'funding loan' were partly responsible for the ensuing recession and consequent difficulties for Brazilian infant industries. The opposition to protective tariffs which was voiced not only by British importers but by Brazilians who copied their free-trade ideas also contributed to the difficulties industrialists encountered. But the principal threat to industrialization was the presence of low-cost mass-produced imports turned out by the well-financed and fully experienced English mills. It is no wonder that in the twentieth century industrialization came to be associated with opposition to the foreigner.

Even when the British contributed to industrialization their help was not unqualified. The railroads, for instance, were sometimes constructed at exorbitant cost and were not ideally placed to meet industrial needs. The machinery which came from Britain continued to make Brazil dependent on this industrial giant for spare parts, and sometimes—as in the case of the central sugar factories—the equipment was obsolete or otherwise unsatisfactory. The Britishers who extended credit for industrial purposes were not above demanding their pound of flesh, and the managerial and technical skills which the British supplied were often overpriced. In some cases direct British investment meant only increased difficulties for competing local industrialists without benefits to the consumers, as when J. & P. Coats bought up a Brazilian cotton-thread factory only to hurl the machinery into a river.[1]

With regard to the ideas with which the British were identified in Brazil, their hold was so strong that it was hard to discard them

[1] Stanley J. Stein, *The Brazilian Cotton Manufacture; Textile Enterprise in an Underdeveloped Area, 1850–1950* (Cambridge, Mass.: Harvard Univ. Press, 1957), p. 145.

Conclusion

once they had served their purpose. Liberalism failed to glorify national interests and, instead, advanced a dog-eat-dog philosophy of the individual. The necessary role of the government in a rapidly developing economy was subjected to injudicious criticism by men still dominated by an outdated liberal ideal. Protestants, obsessed with anti-Catholicism, failed to emphasize community goals. And neither they nor the liberals were much concerned with social justice or the overthrow of structures which doomed the masses to a sub-human existence.

Furthermore, hindsight suggests that many of the positive efforts of the British were tragically insufficient for the task at hand. Although Britishers invested in Brazilian manufacturing activities, they did not do so to the extent many modernizers would have wished. Certainly the major investments in manufacturing were not British. Nor was much of their effort directed toward heavy industries or the development of Brazil's iron resources, a step which could have meant so much for her future growth. Few converts were won over to the gospel of work, and Protestantism did not succeed in destroying the *compadre* system. The idea of progress made only halting gains. The abolition of Negro slavery still left the worker subservient to the planter. Modification of company law was not enough to make stocks as attractive as land. And so, insofar as Brazil modernized too slowly because of insufficient effort on the part of modernizing forces, the British must share the blame. It is clear that the British may be damned if they did—for doing it too slowly—and damned if they didn't.

But a thoughtful appraisal of the British role must include a recognition of the very important part they played in fostering change. The coffee-export economy pumped new life into Brazil and the railways made this coffee 'boom' possible. The British provided the initial impetus toward railroad building and then supplied the necessary technicians, loans, investment capital, 'know-how', materials, and supplies. This was their principal contribution to the onset of modernization in Brazil. The export economy was also aided by the factors we have already listed: export houses, shipping companies, insurance firms, harbor works, and banking establishments, to which should be added the importers and distributors of agricultural machinery. It was from this base of prosperity, stimulated by coffee exports, that Brazilians could begin to industrialize, and it was only after they had begun to do so that the export economy somewhat hindered progress. Moreover, the British directly aided the process of industrialization. Their railroads and their loading docks made the industrialists' work that much easier; their machinery and supplies equipped the factories; their credit facilities often enabled Brazilian manufacturers to start up; and even the importation of British goods accustomed the public to consumption patterns later exploited by Brazilian industrialists. Furthermore, the British pioneered in flour milling, contributed to apparel manufacturing, played a part in textile production, and were principally responsible for building the early sugar factories of the northeast.

The end of Negro slavery, to which the British contributed so much, helped shift power away from the decadent sugar zone and into the dynamic coffee region. It also undermined the foundations of the monarchy, a major symbol of the traditional society. Finally, it served to strengthen the cities and weaken—at least temporarily—the landed aristocracy. Not only did the British thus alter Brazil's labor system, but they wrought significant changes in that country's political structure.

The growth of cities and the introduction of new ideas there was another major aspect of the British role. The railroads transformed the urban centers upon which they converged and the industries the British strengthened drew both capitalists and workers to the cities. British imports and utility companies distinguished the urban, that is, European style of life from that of the backward countryside. Technicians and engineers in the cities learned English because the position of Britain in the industrial world demanded it. Entrepreneurs relied for support upon their financial and personal connexions with the British. Thus one may list Mauá, São Vicente, Antônio and André Rebouças, Tarqüínio, Antônio Prado, Jaceguai, Pereira Passos, Frontin, Francisco Figueiredo, Murtinho—and doubtless there were others—who were touched to one degree or another by British influence. The

British helped inculcate in them all the profit motive and the belief in an inevitable progress toward an industrial future.

Other British concepts with important implications also spread within the cities. The end of privilege for special groups and freedom for the individual to fulfill himself posed a real threat to the traditional system. Liberalism and Protestantism helped destroy the fixed position of the individual within a corporate society and free him for engagement at the most productive point within the socio-economic structure. A secular and pluralistic regime was advanced by Protestantism and it also undermined the moral bases of dependence-paternalism in the old hierarchical structure.

By 1914 Brazil had begun to move toward a modern society. The British had done a lot to bring about this onset of modernization, although they had also given some support to those forces that opposed it. Acting neither with altruism nor with malice, but driven by the ambitions and desires instilled in them by their own modernizing society, the British played a large part in initiating change in tropical Brazil.

Br. indirectly start modernization machines, RR, lib,

FINANCIAL RECORD OF THE MINAS AND RIO RAILWAY COMPANY, LTD, 1881–1902[a]

Year ending mid-	Net Revenue £	Dividend per cent per annum	Share Prices in £[b] (calendar year)	
			High	Low
1882	—	none	26·5	22·75
1883	—	none	26	23·5
1884	...[c]	none	24	20
1885	—	7	23	20
1886	1,324	7	23	21·5
1887	12,017	7	24	21
1888	25,374	7	24	22
1889	28,823	7	27·25	20
1890	17,344	7	21·5	18·5
1891	29,350	7	21·5	15
1892	12,674	7	19	12
1893	29,923	7	16·625	10·5
1894	15,012	5	17·5	10·5
1895	15,312	7	20·75	15
1896	16,252	7	19·5	13·375
1897	14,309	5[d]	14·625	11·125
1898	26,421	6	12·75	7·25
1899	16,693	4·5	11·5	9
1900	16,782	5	11·5	8·75
1901	31,829	5	15·5	9·25
1902			Opened 31 Jan.:	15·5

[a] Compiled from *Investor's Monthly Manual*, xv–xxxii (1885–1902); and London *Times*, 28 Oct. 1891, p. 11; 3 May 1889, p. 12; 12 Nov. 1897, p. 13; 6 Nov. 1901, p. 13.

[b] Ordinary shares, par value: £20.

[c] Net revenue given as Rs. 86:872$780 or 'more than £7,000'.

[d] For the first half of the fiscal year the dividend was only 4 per cent 'due to decline in value of Brazilian currency'; for the second half of the year it was only 6 per cent 'due to necessity of enlarging working capital'. No explanation was given for the failure to recover subsequently.

FINANCIAL RECORD OF THE SÃO PAULO RAILWAY COMPANY, LTD, 1865–1920[a]

Half year	Divisible Profit in £	Dividend per cent per annum	Bonus per cent	Share Prices in £[b] (entire year) High	Low
1st 1865	—	—	—		
2nd 1865	—	—	—	19	16
1st 1866	—	—	—		
2nd 1866	—	—	—	17·5	13
1st 1867	24,262	7	None		
2nd 1867	29,000	7	None	17·75	13
1st 1868	—	—	—		
2nd 1868	66,977	6·625[c]	None	19·5	17
1st 1869	—	6·625	None		
2nd 1869	—	—	—	20·5	17·5
1st 1870	—	6·625	None		
2nd 1870	—	—	—	22	18·75
1st 1871	81,882	6·625	None		
2nd 1871	68,971	6·875	None	23·25	20·5
1st 1872	—	6	None		
2nd 1872	69,375	6·5	None	24·75	20·5
1st 1873	—	7	None		
2nd 1873	80,477	7	None	24	21
1st 1874	104,140	8	None		
2nd 1874	113,149	7	None	27·5	23·375
1st 1875	138,383	12	None		
2nd 1875	108,759	7	None	30·5	24
1st 1876	—	10	None		
2nd 1876	—	7	None	30	25
1st 1877	—	9	None		
2nd 1877	—	7	None	31	27

APPENDIX B *(cont.)*

Half year	Divisible Profit in £	Dividend per cent per annum	Bonus per cent	Share Prices in £[b] (entire year)	
				High	Low
1st 1878	—	13	None		
2nd 1878	—	8	None	33	28·75
1st 1879	—	8	None		
2nd 1879	—	8	None	35·125	29·75
1st 1880	—	10	None		
2nd 1880	—	10[d]	None	36	33
1st 1881	—	10[d]	None		
2nd 1881	—	—	—	39·5	34·5
1st 1882	—	—	—		
2nd 1882	—	8	None	40·5	37·5
1st 1883	—	12	None		
2nd 1883	186,726	10	None	39·75	37
1st 1884	153,888	10	I		
2nd 1884	—	—	—	42	36·5
1st 1885	—	—	—		
2nd 1885	—	10	None	41	36·5
1st 1886	—	10	None		
2nd 1886	—	10	I	41·75	39·5
1st 1887	195,736	12	1·5		
2nd 1887	174,230	10	None	45	39·5
1st 1888	149,826	10	1·25		
2nd 1888	315,000	12	None	45	39·75
1st 1889	—	12	3		
2nd 1889	—	—	—	50·5	40
1st 1890	—	12	2		
2nd 1890	—	—	—	50	40
1st 1891	—	12	2		
2nd 1891	—	—	—	49·5	37
1st 1892	—	9	None		
2nd 1892	—	—	—	41	31·125
1st 1893	—	—	—		
2nd 1893	—	8	None	36	20

Appendix B

Half year	Divisible Profit in £	Dividend per cent per annum	Bonus per cent	Share Prices in £[b] (entire year) High	Low
1st 1894	—	4	None		
2nd 1894	—	12	—	30·75	18
1st 1895	—	12	2		
2nd 1895	222,346	12	None	44	29
1st 1896	137,902	12	2		
2nd 1896	237,267	12	None	46·25	32
1st 1897	117,454	12	1[e]		
2nd 1897	223,947	11	None	40·125	35
1st 1898	81,730	11·5	None		
2nd 1898	—	—	—	38·5	30
1st 1899	91,737	9·5	None		
2nd 1899	206,295	8	None	35	26·5
1st 1900	73,826	8	None		
2nd 1900	—	8	1	143[f]	125[f]
1st 1901	181,552	8	1		
2nd 1901	—	8	3	166	137
1st 1902	214,410	10	1		
2nd 1902	—	10	1	172·75	154
1st 1903	—	10	1		
2nd 1903	347,739	10	1	176	161
1st 1904	142,409	10	1		
2nd 1904	—	10	1	182	157·5
1st 1905	163,160	10	1		
2nd 1905	—	10	1	220	178
1st 1906	156,783	10	1		
2nd 1906	—	12[g]	...[g]	214·875	199·5
1st 1907	—	12			
2nd 1907	—	14		219·5	182·5
1st 1908	—	12			
2nd 1908	—	14		211·5	190
1st 1909	—	12			
2nd 1909	—	14		214·5	194

Appendix B

Year	Divisible Profit in £	Dividend per cent per annum	Share Prices in £[b] (entire year)	
			High	Low
1910[h]	103,635	13	214·5	198·5
1911	124,669	13	217	202·125
1912	168,717	13	262	205·75
1913	196,544	14	270	226
1914	120,942	14	249·5	215
1915	162,565	10	208	158
1916	—	10	196·5	170
1917	—	10	191·25	164
1918	—	10	202	180
1919	—	10	191·5	164·5
1920	—	10	188	122

[a] Compiled from *Investor's Monthly Manual*, III–VI (1867–70); n.s. I–L (1870–1920); and Speers, comp., *Companhia São Paulo Railway e o governo imperial*, p. 5.

[b] Ordinary shares, par value 1865–99, £20; 1900–20, £100.

[c] Although the government guaranteed 7 per cent, it would not guarantee interest on the last £100,000 invested; therefore, a portion of the amount paid by the government had to be used to pay the interest on this investment.

[d] Average of the two dividends paid during this year.

[e] Bonus of 4 shillings per share on ordinary shares plus 4·8 pence per share on new ordinary shares, making a total with the dividend of 13 per cent.

[f] In order to double the line, capital was increased during 1899 by the issue of new ordinary shares which, when consolidated with old ones, had a new par value of £100.

[g] Hereafter dividend and bonus stated as a combined percentage.

[h] Hereafter only yearly figures are given.

APPENDIX C

EXPORTS FROM GREAT BRITAIN TO BRAZIL, 1850–1909[a]

	VALUE (£) 1850–4	per cent	VALUE (£) 1855–9	per cent	VALUE (£) 1860–4	per cent	VALUE (£) 1865–9	per cent
Cottons	8,689,288	53·95	10,305,183	59·00	12,886,034	56·15	17,010,971	54·07
Woolens	1,859,432	11·54	2,053,246	9·96	1,418,981	6·18	2,563,818	7·30
Linens	1,024,063	6·36	1,246,526	6·05	1,203,832	5·25	1,970,607	6·38
Silks	112,947	0·70	178,450	0·87	102,014	0·44	67,789	0·21
Jute and bagging							158,911	0·52
Total textiles and textile manufactures	11,685,730	72·55	13,783,405	65·88	15,610,861	68·02	21,772,096	68·48
Apparel	234,409	1·45	300,083	1·46	324,490	1·41	594,287	1·92
Foodstuffs	573,687	3·56	957,371	4·65	995,185	4·34	970,079	3·14
Rubber goods								
Earthenware, etc.	382,347	2·37	539,672	2·62	519,093	2·26	619,315	2·00
Silver and jewelry	62,973	0·39	121,135	0·59	66,700	0·29	24,733	0·08
Arms and ammunition	209,324	1·31	322,051	1·56	307,111	1·34	482,359	1·56
Musical instruments	54,796	0·34	47,553	0·23	15,250	0·07	7,212	0·02
Drugs and medicine								
Leather	65,426	0·40	178,332	0·37	224,493	0·98	451,714	1·46
Total consumer goods other than textiles	1,582,962	9·82	2,466,197	11·48	2,452,322	10·69	3,149,699	10·18
Hardware, cutlery, and tools	557,891	3·46	791,292	3·84	655,356	2·86	994,188	6·22
Iron, wrought and unwrought	534,328	3·32	1,130,591	5·48	1,203,513	5·51	1,165,395	3·77
Metals other than iron	293,068	1·82	509,616	2·47	453,173	1·97	455,645	1·48
Coal and coal products	665,999	4·13	285,227	3·49	446,493	1·94	725,659	2·35
Chemicals	50,960	0·32	73,069	0·35	79,782	0·35	97,877	0·32
Machinery	137,187	0·85	411,007	1·99	412,399	1·80	394,340	1·28
Railway equipment								
Telegraph and telephone equipment								
Cement								
Seed oil	53,869	0·33	87,030	0·42	108,715	0·47	106,774	0·35
Total capital goods	2,293,302	14·23	3,287,832	18·04	3,419,431	14·90	3,939,878	15·77
Other	544,168	3·40	1,072,076	4·60	1,465,629	6·39	2,029,334	5·57
GRAND TOTAL	16,106,162	100·00	20,609,510	100·00	22,948,243	100·00	30,891,007	100·00

APPENDIX C (cont.)

	VALUE (£) 1870–4	per cent	VALUE (£) 1875–9	per cent	VALUE (£) 1880–4	per cent	VALUE (£) 1885–9	per cent
Cottons	15,624,589	45·44	14,739,775	49·11	15,751,779	47·25	13,970,172	46·99
Woolens	2,210,090	6·43	2,082,015	6·94	1,578,747	4·74	1,571,984	5·29
Linens	1,259,871	3·66	842,980	2·81	617,608	1·85	493,984	1·66
Silks	181,263	0·53	74,832	0·25	46,844	0·14		
Jute and bagging	456,792	1·33	337,760	1·13	853,158	2·56	830,562	2·79
Total textiles and textile manufactures	19,732,605	57·39	18,077,362	60·24	18,848,136	56·54	16,866,702	56·73
Apparel	499,959	1·45	334,837	1·12	417,197	1·31	383,327	1·29
Foodstuffs	886,843	2·58	425,024	1·42	276,579	0·83	349,768	1·18
Rubber goods					115,500	0·35	154,790	0·52
Earthenware, etc.	725,935	2·11	721,462	2·40	662,150	1·98	513,492	1·73
Silver and jewelry								
Arms and ammunition	373,577	1·09	333,206	1·11	474,530	1·42	285,298	0·96
Musical instruments								
Drugs and medicine	176,353	0·51	185,127	0·62	212,499	0·64	258,327	0·87
Leather	701,737	2·04	681,925	2·27	908,460	2·73	1,002,316	3·37
Total consumer goods other than textiles	3,364,404	9·78	2,681,581	8·94	3,066,825	9·26	2,947,318	9·92
Hardware, cutlery, and tools	1,295,485	3·77	1,234,954	4·12	1,204,190	3·61	1,122,335	3·77
Iron, wrought and unwrought	2,846,265	8·28	3,329,234	9·19	3,329,324	9·99	2,456,511	8·26
Metals other than iron	430,120	1·25	397,109	1·32	386,469	1·16	307,122	1·03
Coal and coal products	1,541,715	4·48	1,096,535	3·65	1,163,375	3·49	1,561,628	5·25
Chemicals	134,814	0·39	111,558	0·37	104,157	0·31	104,165	0·35
Machinery	1,099,002	3·20	1,029,228	3·43	2,173,227	6·52	2,265,757	7·62
Railway equipment							183,277	0·63
Telegraph and telephone equipment	1,453,360	4·23	297,561	0·99	245,473	0·74	93,706	0·32
Cement					194,226	0·58	153,336	0·52
Seed oil					175,208	0·53	181,437	0·61
Total capital goods	8,942,350	26·01	7,644,714	23·56	8,975,649	26·93	8,434,274	28·36
Other	2,344,418	6·82	2,179,175	7·26	2,423,138	7·27	1,483,000	4·99
GRAND TOTAL	34,383,777	100·00	30,582,832	100·00	33,313,748	100·00	29,731,294	100·00

APPENDIX C (cont.)

	VALUE (£) 1890–4	per cent	VALUE (£) 1895–9	per cent	VALUE (£) 1900–4	per cent	VALUE (£) 1905–9	per cent
Cottons	15,761,545	40·46	11,212,484	36·16	8,938,866	33·16	10,513,551	25·56
Woolens	1,951,425	5·01	1,373,775	4·43	1,015,102	3·77	1,371,257	3·33
Linens	542,421	1·39	480,078	1·55	396,435	1·47	670,654	1·63
Silks	84,796	0·22	90,316	0·29	62,355	0·23	51,585	0·13
Jute and bagging	690,687	1·77	1,458,377	4·71	1,745,644	6·48	2,154,031	5·23
Total textiles and textile manufactures	19,030,874	48·85	14,615,030	47·14	12,158,402	45·11	14,761,078	35·88
Apparel	467,113	1·20	241,001	0·78	201,303	0·75	77,505	0·19
Foodstuffs	375,507	0·97	536,847	1·73	436,668	1·62	338,411	0·82
Rubber goods	217,792	0·56	207,714	0·67	133,268	0·50	144,788	0·35
Earthenware, etc.	644,072	1·65	532,151	1·72	421,059	1·56	551,998	1·34
Silver and jewelry		—		—		—		—
Arms and ammunition	417,352	1·07	456,580	1·47	182,295	0·68	216,262	0·53
Musical instruments								
Drugs and medicine	292,949	0·75	256,898	0·83	191,578	0·71	223,712	0·54
Leather	1,171,067	3·00	782,822	2·52	315,254	1·17	340,762	0·82
Total consumer goods other than textiles	3,585,852	9·20	3,014,013	9·72	1,881,425	6·99	1,893,438	4·59
Hardware, cutlery, and tools	1,353,484	3·47	1,090,802	3·52	995,361	3·69	1,716,703	4·17
Iron, wrought and unwrought	4,027,538	10·34	3,356,598	10·83	2,364,392	8·77	4,493,796	10·92
Metals other than iron	623,635	1·60	614,800	1·97	613,771	2·28	783,875	1·91
Coal and coal products	2,735,440	7·02	2,909,613	9·39	3,748,338	13·91	4,063,356	9·88
Chemicals	331,188	0·85	348,664	1·12	451,199	1·67	763,429	1·85
Machinery	3,880,749	9·96	2,321,405	7·49	1,881,017	6·98	4,097,489	9·96
Railway equipment	587,029	1·51	522,354	1·69	164,369	0·61	411,454	1·00
Telegraph and telephone equipment	361,541	0·93	468,804	1·51	591,585	2·19	275,061	0·67
Cement	197,723	0·51	136,251	0·44	63,028	0·23	251,157	0·61
Seed oil	233,063	0·60	311,278	1·00	343,589	1·27	335,836	0·82
Total capital goods	14,331,390	36·79	12,080,569	38·96	11,216,649	41·60	17,192,156	41·79
Other	2,011,296	5·16	1,295,148	4·18	1,699,400	6·30	7,293,667	17·74
GRAND TOTAL	38,959,412	100·00	31,004,760	100·00	26,955,876	100·00	41,140,339	100·00

Source: Great Britain, Board of Trade, Customs and Excise Department, Statistical Office, *Annual Statement of the Trade of the United Kingdom with Foreign Countries and British Possessions* (London, 1853–1909). Figures are not given for the period after 1909 because the basis of the tables was changed rendering comparison difficult.

[a]

LIST OF SOURCES

ARCHIVES AND PRIVATE PAPERS

Archives of Rio de Janeiro Flour Mills and Granaries, Ltd (ARFM): Board Minutes; Directors' Reports; Minutes of the General Meetings; Reports of the General Manager. London.

Arquivo do Estado da Bahia. Salvador.

Arquivo do Estado de São Paulo. São Paulo.

Arquivo do Instituto Histórico e Geográfico Brasileiro (AIHGB). Rio de Janeiro.

Arquivo do Museu Imperial de Petrópolis (AMIP). Petrópolis.

Arquivo Histórico do Ministério de Relações Exteriores, Itamaratí (AHI). Rio de Janeiro.

Arquivo Nacional (AN). Rio de Janeiro.

Arquivo Público Estadual de Pernambuco (APEP). Recife.

Biblioteca Nacional: Seção de Manuscritos. Rio de Janeiro.

Casa de Rui Barbosa. Rio de Janeiro.

Companies Registration Office. London.

Edward Greene Papers. Letterpress Books I and II, 1892–1904 (GPL). London.

Joaquim Nabuco Papers (JNP). Rio de Janeiro.

National Archives: Department of State (NA/DS). Washington, D.C.

Papers of Knowles & Foster. London.

Papers of Rio de Janeiro Lighterage Co., Ltd: Board Minutes, 1912–18. London.

Papers of Wilson Sons & Co., Ltd: Board Minutes, 1877–1920; Letterpress Book, 1899–1900 (PWL). London.

Public Record Office: Foreign Office (FO); Board of Trade (BT). London.

PRINTED MATERIAL AND UNPUBLISHED THESES

O abolicionista: orgão da Sociedade Brasileira Contra a Escravidão. Rio. Nos. 1–14. 1 Nov. 1880–1 Dec. 1881.*

Abranches Moura, João Dunshee de, ed. *Actas e actos do governo provisorio. Copias authenticas dos protocollos das sessões secretas do Conselho de Ministros desde a proclamação da republica até a organisação do gabinete Lucena, acompanhadas de importantes revelações e documentos.* 3rd ed. Obras completas, 4. Rio: 'Jornal do Brasil', 1953.

A Allemanha e a paz. Appelo do presidente da Camara dos Deputados ao Congresso Nacional do Brazil. São Paulo: Typ. Brazil de Rothschild, 1917.

Brazil and the Monroe Doctrine. Rio: Imp. Nacional, 1915.

* Dates of publication for periodicals are given only when consulted throughout or when needed for identification.

List of Sources

Abranches Moura, João Dunshee de. *A conflagração européa e suas causas: discurso ...na Camara dos Deputados...em 26 de setembro de 1914*. Rio: Almeida Marques, 1915.

Governos e congressos da Republica dos Estados Unidos do Brasil:...apontamentos biographicos sobre todos os prezidentes e vice-prezidentes da republica, ministros de estado, e senadores e deputados ao Congresso Nacional, 1889–1917... 2 vols. São Paulo: Abranches, 1918.

A illusão brazileira (justificação historica de uma attitude). Rio: Imp. Nacional, 1917.

Abreu, João Capistrano de. *O descobrimento do Brasil*. Rio: Annuario do Brasil for the Sociedade Capistrano de Abreu, 1929.

Adalbert, Prince of Prussia. *Travels in the South of Europe and in Brazil; with a Voyage up the Amazon and its Tributary the Xingú, Now First Explored*. Transl. R. H. Schomburgk and J. E. Taylor. 2 vols. London: Bogue, 1849.

Adams, Jane Elizabeth. 'The Abolition of the Brazilian Slave Trade', *Journal of Negro History*, x (1925), 607–37.

Adams, Richard N. *et al. Social Change in Latin America Today*. New York: Harper for the Council on Foreign Relations, 1960.

Adamson, Thomas. 'Report of Consul-General Adamson...', in *Commercial Relations of the United States with Foreign Countries. 1878*. Washington, D.C.: Government Printing Office, 1879.

Afonso, João. *Três séculos de modas*. Belém: Tavares Cardoso, 1923.

Agassiz, Louis, and Elizabeth Cabot Cary Agassiz. *A Journey in Brazil*. 2nd ed. Boston: Ticknor & Fields, 1868.

Aguiar, Pinto de. *A abertura dos portos do Brasil: Cairú e os ingléses*. Marajoara, 30. Salvador: Progresso, 1960.

Albion, R. G. 'British Shipping and Latin America', *Journal of Economic History*, xi (1951), 361–74.

'Album Estrada de Ferro Santos a Jundiaí: história de uma ferrovia', *Magazine das nações*. Edição especial, Ano 10, Oct. 1957.

Albuquerque, Ulysses Lins de. *Um sertanejo e o sertão*. Rio: José Olympio, 1957.

Albuquerque Mello, Affonso d'. *A liberdade no Brasil: seu nascimento, vida, morte e sepultura*. Recife: Typ. Figueroa de Faria, 1864.

Alexander, Alec P. 'Industrial Entrepreneurship in Turkey: Origins and Growth', *Economic Development and Cultural Change*, viii (July 1960), 349–65.

Almanak [Laemmert] administrativo, mercantil e industrial do Rio de Janeiro e indicador...Obra estatistica e de consulta. Rio.

Alves, Constancio. 'Ruy Barbosa e os livros', *Revista da Academia Brasileira de Letras*, xvii (Mar. 1925), 240–6.

Alves, João Luiz. 'A questão do elemento servil. A extincção do tráfico e a lei de repressão de 1850. Liberdade dos nascituros', in *Revista do Instituto Historico e Geographico Brasileiro, tomo especial consagrado ao primeiro Congresso de Historia Nacional...(1914)*, iv, 187–258.

List of Sources

Andrade, Jorge. 'Os ossos do barão', in 'A escada' e 'Os ossos do barão'. São Paulo: Brasiliense, 1964.

Andrews, Christopher Columbus. *Brazil—Its Condition and Prospects.* New York: Appleton, 1887.

Anglo-Brazilian Chronicle. São Paulo.

Annuario politico, historico e estatistico do Brazil: 1846. Rio: Firmin Didot, [1846?].

The Art Journal Illustrated Catalogue: The Industry of All Nations, 1851. London: Virtus, 1851.

Ashworth, William. *An Economic History of England, 1870–1939.* London and New York: Methuen & Barnes & Noble, 1960.

A Short History of the International Economy, 1850–1950. London and New York: Longmans, Green, 1952.

Assier, Adolphe d'. *Le Brésil contemporain: races, mœurs, institutions, paysage.* Paris: Durand et Lauriel, 1867.

Associação Commercial do Rio de Janeiro. *Elemento servil;...representação da commissão especial...1884.* Rio: Villeneuve, 1884.

Resposta da Associação commercial do Rio de Janeiro aos quesitos da Commissão Parlamentar de Inquerito. Rio: Typ. Montenegro, 1883.

Associação do Quarto Centenario do Descobrimento do Brasil. *Livro do centenario (1500–1900).* 3 vols. Rio: Imp. Nacional, 1900–2.

Atayde, Raymundo Austregésilo de. *Paulo de Frontin, sua vida e sua obra.* Coleção Cidade do Rio de Janeiro, 11. Rio: Estado de Guanabara, Secretaria Geral de Educação e Cultura, 1961.

Athayde, Raymundo Austregesilo de. *Pereira Passos, o reformador do Rio de Janeiro; biografia e historia.* Rio: Editôra 'A Noite', [1944?].

Aubertin, J. J. 'O algodão [Carta a Fidelis Preta]', *Correio paulistano,* 21 July 1864, pp. 2–3.

Carta dirigida aos srs. habitantes da provincia de S. Paulo por...superintendente da estrada de ferro da mesma provincia. São Paulo: Typ. Litteraria, 1862.

'Carta do sr. Aubertin, Londres, 21/12/1869', *Correio paulistano,* 30 Jan. 1870, p. 1.

'Communicado. Ilms. amigos e snrs. fazendeiros de S. Paulo', *Correio paulistano,* 3 Jan. 1867, pp. 2–3.

Eleven Days Journey in the Province of São Paulo with the Americans, Drs Gaston and Shaw, and Major Mereweather. Letter Addressed to His Excellency the Baron of Piracicaba. Translated from...Portuguese by the Author. London: Bates, Hendy, 1868.

A estrada de ferro e a provincia de S. Paulo. Carta ao illmo. snr. dr. Antonio da Silva Prado. São Paulo: Typ. Americana, 1867.

O norte da provincia de S. Paulo (1866). Carta dirigida ao illm. snr. João Ribeiro dos Santos Camargo. São Paulo: Typ. Schroeder, 1866.

Aubrey, Henry G. 'Industrial Investment Decisions: a Comparative Analysis', *Journal of Economic History,* xv (1955), 335–51.

List of Sources

Azevedo, Aroldo de. *Cochranes do Brasil. A vida e a obra de Thomas Cochrane e Ignacio Cochrane.* Brasiliana, 327. São Paulo: Editôra Nacional, 1965.

Azevedo, Fernando de. *A cultura brasileira: introdução ao estudo de cultura no Brasil.* 4th ed. Obras completas de Fernando de Azevedo, 13. São Paulo: Melhoramentos, 1964.

Um trem corre para o oeste; estudo sôbre a Noroeste e seu papel no sistema de viação nacional. 2nd ed. Obras completas, 12. São Paulo: Melhoramentos, 1959.

Baillie, John. *Memoir of the Rev. W. H. Hewitson, Late Minister of the Free Church of Scotland at Dirleton.* 2nd ed. London: Nisbet, 1852.

Baleeiro, Aliomar. *Rui, um estadista no ministério da fazenda.* Rio: Casa de Rui Barbosa, 1952.

Bank of London & South America, Ltd. *A Short Account of the Bank's Growth and Formation.* London: privately printed, 1954.

The Bankers' Magazine, Journal of the Money Market, and Commercial Digest. London.

Barbosa, Rui. *Antologia.* ed. Luís Viana Filho. Rio: Casa de Rui Barbosa, 1953.

Barbosa, Ruy. *Cartas de Inglaterra.* Rio: Leuzinger, 1896.

Barbosa, Rui. *Discursos e conferencias.* Pôrto: Cia. Portugueza Editora, 1921.

Barbosa, Ruy. *Finanças e politica da republica: discursos e escriptos.* Rio: Cia. Impressora, 1892.

Liberdade commercial. O partido liberal bahiano. Discurso proferido...na Assembléa Provincial da Bahia na sessão de 27 de junho de 1878. Bahia: Typ. do 'Diario da Bahia', 1878.

Barbosa, Rui. *Mocidade e exilio. Cartas ao conselheiro Albino José Barbosa de Oliveira e ao dr. Antônio d'Araújo Ferreira Jacobina.* Ed. Américo Jacobina Lacombe. Brasiliana, 38. São Paulo: Editôra Nacional, 1934.

Obras completas. —vols. Rio: Ministério da Educação e Cultura, 1942–.

Obras seletas. 10 vols. Rio: Casa de Rui Barbosa, 1952–61.

Barbosa de Oliveira, Albino José. *Memórias de um magistrado do império.* Ed. Américo Jacobina Lacombe. Brasiliana, 231. São Paulo: Editôra Nacional, 1943.

Barreto, Plínio. *Uma temerária aventura forense (a questão entre D. Amalia de Moreira Keating Fontaine de Lavaleye e a City of San Paulo Improvements & Freehold Land Company, Limited). Allegações finaes do advogado desta ultima.* São Paulo: Revista dos Tribunaes, 1933.

Barros, Roque Spencer Maciel de. 'O germanismo nos fins do império', *O estado de São Paulo,* 12 Jan. p. 64 and 19 Jan. p. 72, 1958.

A ilustração brasileira e a idéia de universidade. Universidade de São Paulo, Cadeira de História e Filosofia da Educação, Boletim 241 (2). São Paulo: Universidade de São Paulo, 1959.

Barroso, Gustavo. *Brasil, colonia de banqueiros (história dos emprestimos de 1824 a 1934).* 6th ed. Rio: Civilização Brasileira, 1937.

List of Sources

Barzun, Jacques. *Darwin, Marx, Wagner: Critique of a Heritage.* Boston: Little, Brown, 1941.

Bastide, Roger, and Florestan Fernandes. *Relações raciais entre negros e brancos em São Paulo.* São Paulo: Anhembi, 1955.

Battaglia, Felice. *Filosofia del lavoro.* Bologna: Zuffi, 1951.

Bauer, P. T. 'Concentration in Tropical Trade: Some Aspects and Implications of Oligopoly', *Economica,* n.s. xx (1953), 302-21.

Bell, Alured Gray. *The Beautiful Rio de Janeiro.* London: Heinemann, 1914.

Bello, José Maria. *A History of Modern Brazil, 1889-1964.* Transl. James L. Taylor. Stanford, California: Stanford Univ. Press, 1966.

Bello, Júlio. *Memórias de um senhor de engenho.* 2nd ed. Documentos Brasileiros, 11. Rio: José Olympio, 1948.

Besouchet, Lídia. *José Ma. Paranhos, visconde do Rio Branco. Ensaio histórico-biográfico.* Rio: Valverde, 1945.

Mauá e seu tempo. São Paulo: Anchieta, 1942.

Bethell, Leslie M. 'Britain, Portugal and the Suppression of the Brazilian Slave Trade: the Origins of Lord Palmerston's Act of 1839', *English Historical Review,* lxxx (1965), 761-84.

Bezerra, Alcides. 'Visconde de Cayrú: vida e obra', in Brazil, Arquivo Nacional, *Publicações,* xxxiv (1937), 339-54.

Bibliotheca da Associação Industrial. *Archivos da Exposição da Industria Nacional. Actas, pareceres, e decisões do jury geral da Exposição da Industria Nacional realizada no Rio de Janeiro em 1881.* Rio: Typ. Nacional, 1882.

Bigg-Wither, Thomas Plantagenet. *Pioneering in South Brazil: Three Years of Forest and Prairie Life in the Province of Paraná.* 2 vols. London: Murray, 1878.

Boehrer, George C. A. *Da monarquia à república; história do Partido Republicano do Brasil (1870-1889).* Transl. Berenice Xavier. Rio: Ministério da Educação e Cultura, Serviço de Documentação, 1954.

'José Carlos Rodrigues and O Novo Mundo, 1870-1879', *Journal of Inter-American Studies,* ix (1967), 127-44.

Borba de Moraes, Rubens, and William Berrien. *Manual bibliográfico de estudos brasileiros.* Rio: Souza, 1949.

Borja Castro, Agostinho Victor de. *Descripção do porto do Rio de Janeiro e das obras da doca d'alfandega.* Rio: Imperial Instituto Artistico, 1877.

Bouças, Valentin F. *História da dívida externa.* 2nd ed. Rio: Edições Financeiras, 1950.

Bowle, John. *Politics and Opinion in the Nineteenth Century. An Historical Introduction.* London: Cape, 1954.

Boxer, Charles R. *The Golden Age of Brazil.* Berkeley: Univ. of California Press, 1962.

Bradstreets. New York.

Braga, Henriqueta Rosa Fernandes. *Música sacra evangélica no Brasil (contribuição à sua história).* Rio: Kosmos, 1961.

337

List of Sources

Braga, Osvaldo Melo. *Bibliografia de Joaquim Nabuco*. Instituto Nacional do Livro, Coleção B-1, Bibliografia, 8. Rio: Imp. Nacional, 1952.

Branner, John Casper. *The Railways of Brazil, a Statistical Article. Reprinted from the 'Railway Age' with Notes and Additions*. Chicago: Railway Age Publishing Co., 1887.

Brasiliense de Almeida Mello, Americo, ed. *Os programas dos partidos e o 2º império. Primeira parte: exposição de principios*. São Paulo: Seckler, 1878.

Brazil. Commissão... [de] Inquerito sobre...a Crise...de 1864. *Relatorio*. Rio: Typ. Nacional, 1865.

Commissão Encarregada da Revisão da Tarifa. *Documentos estatisticos sobre o commercio do imperio do Brasil nos annos de 1845 a 1849 que acompanhão o relatorio da commissão*...Rio: Typ. Nacional, 1853.

Commissão Encarregada da Revisão da Tarifa em Vigor. *Relatorio...que acompanhou o projecto de tarifa apresentado pela mesma commissão ao governo imperial*. Rio: Empreza Typ. 'Dous de Dezembro' de Paula Brito, 1853.

Congresso. Câmara dos Deputados. *Anais*.

Congresso. Senado. *Anais*.

Conselho de Estado [José Antonio Pimenta Bueno, *marquês* de São Vicente *et al.*]. *Trabalho sobre a extincção da escravatura no Brasil*. Rio: Typ. Nacional, 1868.

Departamento Nacional da Indústria e Comércio. *Sociedades mercantís autorizadas a funcionar no Brasil, 1808–1946*. Rio: Imp. Nacional, 1947.

Diario official. Rio.

Directoria Geral de Estatistica. *Annuario estatistico do Brazil. Annuaire statistique du Brésil. 1º anno. 1ère année. (1908–1912.)* 2 vols. Rio: Typ. de Estatistica, 1917.

Directoria Geral de Estatistica. *Recenseamento do Brazil, 1920, Vol. 1: Introducção*. Rio: Typ. da Estatistica, 1922.

Laws, statutes, etc. *Colleção das leis do imperio do Brasil*. Rio: Imp. Nacional, 1850–1909.

Ministerio da Agricultura, Commercio e Obras Publicas. *Relatorio*.

Ministerio da Agricultura, Commercio e Obras Publicas. Repartição Geral dos Telegraphos. *Memoria historica*. Rio: Imp. Nacional, 1909.

Ministerio da Agricultura, Industria e Commercio. *What Brazil Buys and Sells*. Rio: Imp. Nacional, 1918.

Ministerio da Fazenda. *Correspondencia entre o Ministerio da Fazenda e a Legação em Londres concernante ao empréstimo contraido em 1865*. Rio: Typ. Nacional, 1866.

Ministerio da Fazenda. Commissão de Inquerito Industrial. *Relatorio*. Rio: Typ. Nacional, 1882.

Ministerio da Fazenda. *Relatorio*.

Ministerio da Industria, Viação e Obras Publicas. Directoria Geral de Obras e Viação. *Estatística das estradas de ferro da união e concedidas pela união em 31 de dezembro de 1898*. Rio: Imp. Nacional, 1900.

Ministério da Justiça e Negócios Interiores. Arquivo Nacional. *Organizações e programas ministeriais. Regime parlamentar no império.* 2nd ed. Rio: Departamento da Imprensa Nacional, 1962.

Ministerio das Relações Exteriores. *Guerra da Europa: documentos diplomáticos. Attitude do Brasil, 1914–1918.* 2 vols. Rio: Imp. Nacional, 1917.

Serviço de Estatística Econômica e Financeira. *Commercio exterior do Brasil. Foreign trade of Brazil. Commerce extérieur du Brésil. Importação...Exportação...* [Vol. II adds: *Movimento maritimo...Movimento bancario...*] *Annos 1913–1915–1916–1917–1918.* 2 vols. Rio: Monotypado nas officinas da Estatistica Commercial, 1921–3.

Sovereigns, etc. *Fallas do throno desde o anno de 1823 até o anno de 1889 acompanhados* [sic] *dos respectivos votos de graças.* Rio: Imp. Nacional, 1889.

Brazilian Bulletin. New York: Brazilian Government Trade Bureau.

Brazilian Business. Rio: American Chamber of Commerce.

Briggs, Asa. *1851.* Historical Association General Series, 18. London: Historical Association, 1951.

Brinton, Crane. *English Political Thought in the Nineteenth Century.* London: Benn, 1933.

British and Latin American Chamber of Commerce. *Commercial Encyclopedia Comprising a Series of Standard Publications on the Actual and Potential Markets of the World, Compiled and Issued by Sections: Fourth Sectional Issue: South America.* Ed. W. H. Morton-Cameron. 2nd ed. London: Globe Encyclopedia Co., 1924.

British Chamber of Commerce of São Paulo and Southern Brazil. *Facts about the State of São Paulo.* São Paulo: British Chamber of Commerce of São Paulo and Southern Brazil, 1950.

Grã Bretanha: seu commercio e industria. São Paulo: Camara de Commercio Britannica de São Paulo & Sul do Brasil, 1927.

Personalidades no Brasil; Men of Affairs in Brazil. São Paulo: British Chamber of Commerce of São Paulo and Southern Brazil, 1933.

Bruno, Ernani Silva. *História e tradições da cidade de São Paulo.* Documentos Brasileiros, 80. 3 vols. Rio: José Olympio, 1954.

Buarque de Holanda, Sérgio. *Raízes do Brasil.* 2nd ed. Documentos Brasileiros, 1. Rio: José Olympio, 1948.

Buckley, Jerome Hamilton. *Victorian Temper: a Study in Literary Culture.* Cambridge, Mass.: Harvard Univ. Press, 1951.

Burmeister, Karl Hermann Konrad. *Viagem ao Brasil através das províncias do Rio de Janeiro e Minas Gerais, visando especialmente a história natural dos distritos auri-diamantíferos.* Transl. Manoel Salvaterra and Hubert Schoenfeldt. Biblioteca Histórica Brasileira, 19. São Paulo: Martins, 1952.

Burns, E. Bradford. *The Unwritten Alliance: Rio Branco and Brazilian–American Relations.* New York: Columbia Univ. Press, 1966.

Burton, Richard Francis. *Explorations of the Highlands of the Brazil; with a Full Account of the Gold and Diamond Mines. Also, Canoeing Down 1500 Miles of the Great River São Francisco from Sabará to the Sea.* 2 vols. London: Tinsley, 1869.

List of Sources

Bury, John Bagnell. *The Idea of Progress; an Inquiry into its Origin and Growth.* London: Macmillan, 1920.

Bushell, Thomas Alexander. *'Royal Mail', a Centenary History of the Royal Mail Line, 1839–1939.* London: Trade and Travel Publications, 1939.

Cairncross, A. K. *Home and Foreign Investment, 1870–1913: Studies in Capital Accumulation.* Cambridge University Press, 1953.

Caminhoá, Luiz Monteiro. *Engenhos centraes. Relatorio publicado por ordem do snr. cons. João Ferreira de Moura.* Rio: Imp. Nacional, 1885.

Campos, Bernardino de, ed. *Funding loan: o accôrdo do Brasil com os credores externos realisado pelo governo do dr. Prudente de Moraes em 15 de junho de 1898; documentos inéditos; varias apreciações.* São Paulo: Duprat, 1909.

Campos Salles, Manuel Ferraz de. *Cartas da Europa.* Rio: Leuzinger, 1894.

Da propaganda á presidencia. São Paulo: Typ. 'A Editora', 1908.

Cannabrava, Alice P. *Desenvolvimento da cultura do algodão na província de São Paulo (1861–1875).* São Paulo: Siqueira, 1951.

'Máquinas agrícolas', *O estado de São Paulo*, 6 July 1949, p. 2.

Cardoso, Fernando Henrique. 'Condições sociais da industrialização de São Paulo', *Revista brasiliense*, no. 28 (Mar.–Apr. 1960), 31–46.

Carneiro, Ennor de Almeida. *Mauá (Ireneo Evangelista de Souza).* Pequenos Estudos Sôbre Grandes Administradores do Brasil, 8. Rio: Serviço de Documentação do DASP, 1956.

Cartas de Londres. São Paulo: Duprat, 1902.

Castro Rebello, E. de. *Mauá, restaurando a verdade.* Rio: Universo, 1932.

Centre Industriel du Brésil. *Le Brésil. Ses richesses naturelles, ses industries. Extrait de l'ouvrage: 'O Brazil, suas riquezas naturaes, suas industrias'.* 2 vols. Paris: Aillaud, 1909–10.

Centro Industrial do Brasil. *O Brasil. Suas riquezas naturaes, suas industrias.* 3 vols. Rio: Orosco, 1907–8.

Le Brésil. Ses richesses naturelles, ses industries (édition pour l'étranger). 3 vols. Rio: Orosco, 1908–9.

Cerqueira Falcão, Edgard de. 'A primeira maquina a vapor introduzida no Brasil e o primeiro barco a vapor que sulcou aguas brasileiras', *Revista do Arquivo Municipal de São Paulo*, Ano I, Vol. VI (1934), 63–8.

Christie, William D. *Notes on Brazilian Questions.* London and Cambridge: Macmillan, 1865.

Clairmonte, Frederick. *Economic Liberalism and Underdevelopment: Studies in the Disintegration of an Idea.* London: Asia Publishing House, 1960.

Clapham, John Harold. *An Economic History of Modern Britain.* 2nd ed. 3 vols. Cambridge University Press, 1930–8.

Cochran, Thomas C. '"Social Attitudes, Entrepreneurship, and Economic Development": Some Comments', *Explorations in Entrepreneurial History*, VI (Feb. 1954), 181–3.

Coelho, J. Augusto. *Principios de pedagogia.* 4 vols. São Paulo: Teixeira, 1891–3.

List of Sources

Cole, G. D. H., and Raymond Postgate. *The British People, 1746–1946*. 2nd ed. New York: Knopf, 1947.

Collares Moreira, Arthur Quadros. *A Câmara e o regimen eleitoral no império e na república*. Rio: J. Leite, n.d.

Companhia Brazil Industrial. *Petição ao corpo legislativo*. Rio: Typ. Maximino, 1875.

Cooper, Clayton Sedgwick. *The Brazilians and Their Country*. New York: Stokes, 1917.

Copleston, Frederick, S. J. 'Herbert Spencer—Progress and Freedom', in Harmon Grisewood *et al. Ideas and Beliefs of the Victorians: an Historical Revaluation of the Victorian Age*. London: Sylvan, 1949. Pp. 86–93.

Corrêa Filho, Virgílio. *Joaquim Murtinho*. Rio: Imp. Nacional, 1951.

Correio braziliense ou armazem literario. London.

Correio mercantil. Rio.

Correio paulistano. São Paulo.

Costa, Emília Viotti da. *Da senzala à colônia. Corpo e Alma do Brasil*, 19. São Paulo: Difusão Européia do Livro, 1966.

Costa Aguiar, Antonio Augusto da. *O Brazil e os brazileiros*. Santos: Typ. Commercial, 1862.

Cruz Costa, João. *Contribuição à história das idéias no Brasil. (O desenvolvimento da filosofia no Brasil e a evolução histórica nacional.)* Documentos Brasileiros, 86. Rio: José Olympio, 1956.

The Crystal Palace and its Contents; Being an Illustrated Cyclopaedia of the Great Exhibition of the Industry of All Nations, 1851... London: W. M. Clark, 1852.

Cunha, Euclydes da. *A margem da história*. 6th ed. Pôrto: Lello, 1946.

Cunha, Euclides da. *Os sertões (Campanha de Canudos)*. 23rd ed. Rio: Francisco Alves, 1954.

Cunha Galvão, Manuel da. *Relatorio apresentado...sobre os trabalhos de sua commissão em Londres*. Rio: Typ. Nacional, 1871.

Cunningham, William. *The Gospel of Work: Four Lectures on Christian Ethics*. Cambridge University Press, 1902.

Dantas, Francisco Clementino de San Tiago. *Dois momentos de Rui Barbosa: conferências*. Rio: Casa de Rui Barbosa, 1951.

Darwin, Charles. *Journal of Researches into the Natural History and Geology of the Countries Visited during the Voyage of 'H.M.S. Beagle' Round the World under the Command of Capt. Fitz Roy, R.N.* New York: Appleton, 1896.

Dean, Warren K. 'São Paulo's Industrial Elite, 1890–1960'. Unpub. Ph.D. diss. Univ. of Florida, 1964.

Deane, Phyllis and W. A. Cole. *British Economic Growth, 1688–1959*. University of Cambridge Department of Applied Economics Monographs, 8. Cambridge University Press, 1962.

Denis, Pierre. *Brazil...with a Historical Chapter by Bernard Miall and a Supplementary Chapter by Dawson A. Vindin*. London: Unwin, 1911.

List of Sources

Dent, Hastings Charles. *A Year in Brazil, with Notes on the Abolition of Slavery, the Finances of the Empire, Religion, Meteorology, Natural History, Etc.* London: Kegan Paul, Trench, 1886.

Diario de Pernambuco. Recife.

Diario do Rio de Janeiro. Rio.

Dias, Arthur de Barros Alves. *The Brazil of Today; a Book of Commercial, Political and Geographical Information on Brazil; Impressions of Voyage, Descriptive and Picturesque Data About the Principal Cities, Prominent Men and Leading Events of Our Days.* Nivelles, Belgium: Lanneau & Despret, 1907.

Dias, Everardo. *História das lutas sociais no Brasil.* Temas brasileiros, 8. São Paulo: Editôra Edaglit, 1962.

Dicey, Albert Venn. *Lectures on the Relation Between Law and Public Opinion in England during the Nineteenth Century.* London: Macmillan, 1905.

Diégues Júnior, Manuel. 'O banguê em Pernambuco no século XIX', *Revista do Arquivo Público [Estadual de Pernambuco],* Anos VII–X (1952–6), nos. 9–11, pp. 15–30.

O engenho de açucar no nordeste. Documentário da Vida Rural, 1. Rio: Serviço de Informação Agrícola, Ministério da Agricultura, 1952.

Döllinger, Johann Joseph Ignaz von. *A questão religiosa. O papa e o concílio. Por Janus [pseud.].* Transl. and ed. Rui Barbosa. Rio: Brown and Evaristo, 1877.

Douglas, Claude L. *Cattle Kings of Texas.* Dallas: Baugh, 1939.

Duncan, Julian Smith. *Public and Private Operation of Railways in Brazil.* Studies in History, Economics and Public Law, 367. New York: Columbia Univ. Press, 1932.

Duque Estrada, Osorio. *A abolição (esboço histórico—1831–1888).* Rio: Leite Ribeiro e Maurillo, 1918.

Dyer, Isaac Watson. *A Bibliography of Thomas Carlyle's Writings and Ana.* Portland, Me.: Southworth Press, 1928.

The Economist. London.

Egydio de Oliveira Carvalho, Paulo. *Contribuição para a historia philosophica da sociologia.* São Paulo: Ribeiro, 1899.

Do conceito scientifico das leis sociologicas;...introducção. Volume primeiro. São Paulo: Ribeiro, 1898.

Elliott-Binns, Leonard E. *Religion in the Victorian Era.* 2nd ed. London: Lutterworth, 1946.

Ellis Júnior, Alfredo. *Populações paulistas.* Brasiliana, 27. São Paulo: Editôra Nacional, 1934.

Enock, C. Reginald. *The Republics of Central and South America, Their Resources, Industries, Sociology, and Future.* London and New York: Dent & Scribners, 1913.

Epstein, T. S. *Economic Development and Social Change in South India.* Manchester, Eng.: Manchester Univ. Press, 1948.

List of Sources

Esboço historico da escola dominical da Igreja Evangelica Fluminense, 1855–1932. Rio: Igreja Evangelica Fluminense, 1932.

Escragnolle Doria, Luiz Gastão d'. 'Cousas do passado', *RIHGB*, LXXI, Part 2 (1908), pp. 183–403.

Escragnolle Taunay, Affonso d'. *Pequena história do café no Brasil (1727–1937).* Rio: Departamento Nacional do Café, 1945.

'Subsídios para a história do tráfico africano no Brasil', *Anais do Museu Paulista*, X, 2.ª parte (1941), pp. 1–311.

O estado de São Paulo. São Paulo.

Ewbank, Thomas. *Life in Brazil; or, a Journal of a Visit to the Land of the Cocoa and the Palm...* New York: Harper, 1856.

Ewbank da Camara, José. *Caminhos de ferro estratégicos do Rio Grande do Sul.* Rio: Typ. Americana, 1874.

Expilly, Charles. *Les femmes et les mœurs du Brésil.* Paris: Charlieu et Huillery, 1864.

Faria, Alberto de. *Mauá—Ireneo Evangelista de Souza, barão e visconde de Mauá, 1813–1889.* 2nd ed. Brasiliana, 20. São Paulo: Editôra Nacional, 1933.

Farias Brito, Raimundo de. *A base physica do espirito; historia summaria do problema da mentalidade como preparação para o estudo da philosophia do espirito.* Rio: Francisco Alves, 1912.

Fay, Charles R. *Great Britain from Adam Smith to the Present Day. An Economic and Social Survey.* London: Longmans, Green, 1928.

Palace of Industry, 1851. A Study of the Great Exhibition and its Fruits. Cambridge University Press, 1951.

Fernandes Pereira de Barros, José Mauricio. *Apontamentos de direito financeiro brasileiro.* Rio: Laemmert, 1855.

Ferns, Henry S. *Britain and Argentina in the Nineteenth Century.* Oxford: Clarendon, 1960.

Ferreira Cesarino Júnior, Antonio. 'A intervenção da Inglaterra na suppressão do tráfico de escravos africanos para o Brasil', *Revista do Instituto Histórico e Geográfico de São Paulo*, XXXIV (1938), 145–66.

Ferreira de Rezende, Francisco de Paula. *Minhas recordações.* Documentos Brasileiros, 45. Rio: José Olympio, 1944.

Ferreira Vianna, Pedro Antonio. *A crise commercial do Rio de Janeiro em 1864.* Rio: Garnier, 1864.

Festinger, Leon. *A Theory of Cognitive Dissonance.* Evanston, Ill. and White Plains, N.Y.: Row, Peterson, 1957.

Ffrench, Yvonne. *The Great Exhibition, 1851.* London: Harvill, 1951.

Fialho, Anfriso. *Processo da monarquia brasileira; necessidade da convocação de nova constituinte.* Rio: Typ. da 'Constituinte', 1886.

Um terço de seculo (1852–1885): recordações. Rio: Typ. da 'Constituinte', 1885.

Forsyth, W. B. *A União Evangélica Sul-Americana.* São Paulo: União Evangélica Sul-Americana, 1960.

List of Sources

Fox, Daniel Makinson. *Description of the Line and Works of the São Paulo Railway in the Empire of Brazil...with an Abstract of the Discussion upon the Paper.* Ed. James Forrest. London: Clowes, 1870.

Fox, James J. 'Natural Law', *The Catholic Encyclopedia,* IX (1910), 76–9.

Franco, Afonso Arinos de Melo. *Um estadista da república (Afrânio de Melo Franco e seu tempo).* Documentos Brasileiros, 85. 3 vols. Rio: José Olympio, 1955.

Franco de Almeida, Tito. *Conselheiro Francisco José Furtado. Biografia e estudo da história política contemporânea.* 2nd ed. Brasiliana, 245. São Paulo: Editôra Nacional, 1944.

Freire, Felisbello Firmo de Oliveira. *Historia constitucional da republica dos Estados Unidos do Brasil.* 2nd ed. 3 vols. Rio: Typ. Aldina and Typ. Moreira Maximino Chagas, 1894–5.

Freitas, Caio de. *George Canning e o Brasil, influência da diplomacia inglêsa na formação brasileira.* Brasiliana, 298. 2 vols. São Paulo: Editôra Nacional, 1958.

Freyre, Gilberto. *Inglêses.* Rio: José Olympio, 1942.

Inglêses no Brasil: aspectos da influência britânica sôbre a vida, a paisagem e a cultura do Brasil. Documentos Brasileiros, 58. Rio: José Olympio, 1948.

Introdução à história da sociedade patriarcal no Brasil, III: Ordem e progresso. Processo de desintegração das sociedades partriarcal e semi-patriarcal no Brasil sob o regime de trabalho livre: aspectos de um quase meio século de transição do trabalho escravo para o trabalho livre; e da monarquia para a república. 2 vols. Rio: José Olympio, 1959.

The Mansions and the Shanties (Sobrados e Mucambos): the Making of Modern Brazil. Transl. Harriet de Onís. New York: Knopf, 1963.

The Masters and the Slaves (Casa-grande & Senzala): a Study in the Development of Brazilian Civilization. Transl. Samuel Putnam. New York: Knopf, 1956.

Ordem e progresso (see *Introducão à história,* above).

'Social Life in Brazil in the Middle of the Nineteenth Century', *Hispanic American Historical Review,* v (1922), 597–630.

'Traços da influência inglêsa sôbre a vida brasileira na primeira metade do século XIX...', *Revista da Sociedade Brasileira de Cultura Ingleza,* no. 2 (1939).

Frick, João. *Abolição da escravatura. Breve noticia sobre a primeira sociedade de emancipação no Brazil (Fundada na cidade do Rio Grande do Sul em março de 1869).* Lisbon: Lallemant Frères, 1885.

Friedman, John. 'Intellectuals in Developing Societies', *Kyklos...International Review for Social Sciences,* XIII (1960), 513–44.

Fuchs, Carl Johannes. *The Trade Policy of Great Britain and Her Colonies Since 1860.* Transl. Constance H. M. Archibald. London: Macmillan, 1905.

Furtado, Celso. *The Economic Growth of Brazil: a Survey from Colonial to Modern Times.* Transl. Ricardo W. de Aguiar and Eric Charles Drysdale. Berkeley and Los Angeles: Univ. of California Press, 1963.

Gallagher, John, and Ronald Robinson. 'The Imperialism of Free Trade', *Economic History Review,* 2nd series, VI (1953), 1–15.

List of Sources

Galvão Alcofarado Junior, José Bernardo. *Discursos proferidos nas sessões de 27 de julho e 20 de agosto de 1886*. Rio: Imp. Nacional, 1886.

Gama, Luiz. 'Questão juridica: subsistem os effeitos manumissores da lei de 26 de janeiro de 1818, depois da de 7 de novembro de 1831 e 4 de outubro de 1850?', *A provincia de São Paulo*, 18 Dec. 1880, p. 5.

Ganzert, Frederic William. 'The Baron do Rio Branco, Joaquim Nabuco and the Growth of Brazilian–American Friendship, 1900–1910', *Hispanic American Historical Review*, XXII (1942), 432–51.

Garcia Redondo, Manuel Ferreira. 'A primeira concessão de estrada de ferro dada no Brasil', *Revista do Instituto Historico e Geographico de São Paulo*, VI (1900–1), 1–11.

Gaston, James McFadden. *Hunting a Home in Brazil. The Agricultural Resources and Other Characteristics of the Country; also, the Manners and Customs of the Inhabitants*. Philadelphia: King & Baird, 1867.

Gates, Paul. *The Illinois Central Railroad and its Colonization Work*. Harvard Economic Studies, 42. Cambridge, Mass.: Harvard Univ. Press, 1934.

Gauld, Charles A. *The Last Titan: Percival Farquhar, American Entrepreneur in Latin America* [Special issue of the *Hispanic American Report*]. Stanford, California: Institute of Hispanic American and Luso-Brazilian Studies, Stanford Univ. 1964.

Gayer, Arthur D. *et al. The Growth and Fluctuation of the British Economy, 1790–1850*. 2 vols. Oxford: Clarendon Press, 1953.

Gerschenkron, Alexander. 'Social Attitudes, Entrepreneurship and Economic Development', *International Social Science Bulletin*, VI (1954), 252–8.

Gillin, John P. 'Some Signposts for Policy', in Richard N. Adams *et al.*, *Social Change in Latin America Today*. New York: Harper for the Council on Foreign Relations, 1960. Pp. 14–62.

Ginsberg, Morris. *The Idea of Progress, a Revaluation*. Boston: Beacon, 1953.

Girão, Raimundo. *A abolição no Ceará*. Fortaleza: Fentenele, 1956.

Glette, Frederico. *A industria nacional e as tarifas da alfandega. Considerações*. Rio: Leuzinger, 1886.

Gobineau, Joseph Arthur, comte de. *D. Pedro II e o conde de Gobineau (correspondências ineditas)*. Ed. and transl. Georges Raeders. Brasiliana, 109. São Paulo: Editôra Nacional, 1938.

Góes e Vasconcellos, Zacarias de. *Da natureza e limites do poder moderador*. 2nd ed. Rio: Laemmert, 1862.

Gomes, Alfredo. 'Achegas para a história do tráfico africano no Brasil—aspectos numéricos', in Instituto Histórico e Geográfico Brasileiro, *Anais do IV Congresso de História Nacional (1949)*, V (1950), 29–78.

Gomes, Eugênio. *Influências inglêsas em Machado de Assis (estudo)*. Bahia: Regina, 1939.

Prata de casa (ensaios de literatura brasileira). Rio: Editora 'A Noite', [1953?].

Goulart, Maurício. *Escravidão africana no Brasil (das origens à extinção do tráfico)*. São Paulo: Martins, 1949.

List of Sources

Gouveia, Maurílio. *História da escravidão*. Rio: Gráfica Tupy, 1955.

Rui—o apóstolo do direito (estudo biográfico). 2nd ed. Rio: Gráfica Tupy, 1952.

Graham, Gerald S. 'The Ascendancy of the Sailing Ship, 1850–1885', *Economic History Review*, n.s. IX (1956–7), 74–88.

Graham, Richard. 'A British Industry in Brazil: Rio Flour Mills, 1886–1920', *Business History*, VIII (1966), 13–38.

'Os fundamentos da ruptura de relações diplomáticas entre o Brasil e a Grã-Bretanha em 1863: "A questão Christie"', *Revista de história*, XXIV (Jan.–June 1962), 117–38, 379–402.

Grampp, William D. *The Manchester School of Economics*. Stanford, California, and London: Stanford Univ. Press & Oxford Univ. Press, 1960.

Great Britain. Board of Trade. Customs and Excise Department. Statistical Office. *Annual Statement of the Trade of the United Kingdom with Foreign Countries and British Possessions*. London: H.M. Stationery Office, 1853–1910.

Commercial Reports Received at the Foreign Office from Her Majesty's Consuls. London: Harrison & Sons, 1862–70.

Commissão sobre as Barbaridades Attribuidas aos Allemães. *Relatorio da commissão...presidida pelo visconde Bryce*. London: Nelson, n.d.

Foreign Office. *Correspondencia do governo britannico relativa a crise europea; apresentado [sic] ás duas camaras do parlamento por ordem de Sua Magestade, agosto de 1914*. London: Foreign Office, 1914.

Foreign Office. *Diplomatic and Consular Reports on Trade and Finance. Annual Series*. Nos. 1–. 1886–.

Parliament. *Hansard's Parliamentary Debates*.

Parliament. House of Commons. *Sessional Papers*. Readex Microprint Edition. Ed. Edgar L. Erickson.

Reports from Her Majesty's Consuls on the Manufactures, Commerce, etc. of Their Consular Districts. London: Harrison & Sons, 1872–86.

Grisewood, Harman, *et al. Ideas and Beliefs of the Victorians: an Historical Revaluation of the Victorian Age*. London: Sylvan, 1949.

Guanabara, Alcindo. *A presidencia Campos Salles: politica e finanças, 1898–1902*. Rio: Laemmert, 1902.

Haas, Werner, *et al. Os investimentos estrangeiros no Brasil*. Rio: privately mimeographed, 1958.

Haddad, Jamil Alamansur. *O romanticismo brasileiro e as sociedades secretas do tempo*. São Paulo: Siqueira, 1945.

Hagen, Everett E. *On the Theory of Social Change: How Economic Growth Begins*. Homewood, Ill.: Dorsey, 1962.

Hahner, June E. 'Officers and Civilians in Brazil, 1889–98'. Unpub. Ph.D. diss. Cornell Univ. 1966.

'The Role of the Military in Brazil, 1889–1894'. Unpub. Master's thesis, Cornell Univ. 1963.

List of Sources

Halévy, Élie. *A History of the English People in the Nineteenth Century, I: England in 1815.* Transl. E. I. Watkin and D. A. Barker. 2nd ed. London: Benn, 1949.

Hanson, Simon G. 'The Farquhar Syndicate in South America', *Hispanic American Historical Review*, XVII (1937), 314–26.

Haring, Clarence H. *Empire in Brazil: a New World Experiment with Monarchy.* Cambridge, Mass.: Harvard Univ. Press, 1958.

Harper, Gordon P. 'The Children of Hipólito: a Study in Brazilian Pentecostalism'. Unpub. paper, Cambridge, Mass., 1963.

Harrison, Brian. 'The Sunday Trading Riots of 1855', *The Historical Journal*, VIII (1965), 219–45.

Hawkshaw, John. *Melhoramento dos portos do Brasil: relatorios.* Rio: Leuzinger, 1875.

Heindel, Richard Heathcote. *The American Impact on Great Britain (1898–1914). A Study of the United States in World History.* Philadelphia: Univ. of Pennsylvania Press, 1940.

Help for Brazil: Occasional Papers. Nos. 1–50, 1893–1907.

Henderson, William Otto. *Britain and Industrial Europe, 1770–1870. Studies in British Influence on the Industrial Revolution in Western Europe.* Liverpool: Liverpool Univ. Press, 1954.

Hill, Lawrence F. 'The Abolition of the African Slave Trade to Brazil', *Hispanic American Historical Review*, XI (1931), 169–97.

Diplomatic Relations between the United States and Brazil. Durham, N.C.: Duke Univ. Press, 1932.

Hirschman, Albert O. *The Strategy of Economic Development.* New Haven: Yale Univ. Press, 1958.

Hobhouse, Christopher. *1851 and the Crystal Palace; Being an Account of the Great Exhibition and its Contents.* 2nd ed. London: Murray, 1950.

Hobson, Charles K. *The Export of Capital.* Studies in Economic and Political Science, 38. London: Constable, 1914.

Hoffman, Ross J. S. *Great Britain and the German Trade Rivalry, 1875–1914.* Philadelphia: Univ. of Pennsylvania Press, 1933.

Hofstadter, Richard. *Social Darwinism in American Thought.* 2nd ed. Boston: Beacon, 1955.

Hollowood, Bernard. *The Story of Morro Velho.* London: St John d'El Rey Mining Company, Ltd, 1955.

Homem de Mello, Randolpho. 'A agua em S. Paulo', *Revista do Arquivo Municipal de São Paulo*, XIV (1935), 164–6.

Horder, William Garrett, comp. *Worship-Song.* London: Elliot Stock, n.d. [before 1902].

Hoselitz, Bert F. 'Entrepreneurship and Capital Formation in France and Britain since 1700', in Universities—National Bureau Committee for Economic Research, *Capital Formation and Economic Growth, a Conference.* Princeton, N. J.: Princeton Univ. Press, 1955. Pp. 291–337.

Sociological Aspects of Economic Growth. Glencoe, Ill.: Free Press, 1960.

347

List of Sources

Houghton, Walter Edwards. *The Victorian Frame of Mind, 1830–1870.* New Haven: Wellesley College and Yale Univ. Press, 1957.

Hughes, J. R. T. *Fluctuations in Trade, Industry, and Finance. A Study of British Economic Development, 1850–1860.* Oxford: Clarendon Press, 1960.

Humphreys, R. A. 'The Fall of the Spanish American Empire', *History: the Journal of the Historical Association,* n.s. XXXVII (1952), 213–27.

Humphries, A. E. 'Modern Developments in Flour Milling', Royal Society of Arts, London, *Journal,* LV (1906–7), 109–26.

Hunt, Bishop Carleton. *The Development of the Business Corporation in England, 1800–1867.* Cambridge, Mass.: Harvard Univ. Press, 1936.

Hurford, Alice V. 'First Impressions of São Paulo', *South America,* III (Feb. 1915), 202–4.

Hurley, Edward N. *Banking and Credit in Argentina, Brazil, Chile and Peru.* U.S. Bureau of Manufacturers Special Agents Series, 90. Washington, D.C.: Government Printing Office, 1914.

Ianni, Octavio. *As metamorphoses do escravo. Apogeu e crise da escravatura no Brasil meridional.* Corpo e Alma do Brasil, 7. São Paulo: Difusão Européia do Livro, 1962.

Igreja Evangélica Fluminense. *Artigos orgânicos da Igreja Evangélica Fluminense seguidos da breve exposição das doutrinas fundamentais do cristianismo recebida pela mesma igreja.* Rio: Estab. Gráfico 'Apollo', n.d.

Illustrated Missionary News. London.

'Importação—Manifestos', *Jornal do commercio,* 1 Jan., p. 2; 3 Jan., p. 3; 5 Jan., p. 3; 8 Jan., p. 7; 11 Jan., p. 3; 17 Jan., p. 3; 23 Jan., p. 3; 24 Jan., p. 3; 25 Jan., p. 3; 28 Jan., p. 3, 1850.

In Memoriam. Conde Francisco Matarazzo. São Paulo: Orlandi, 1937.

Inge, William Ralph. *The Idea of Progress.* The Romanes Lecture. Oxford: Clarendon Press, 1920.

Inglez de Souza, Herculano Marques. 'O commercio e as leis commerciais do Brasil', *Jornal do commercio,* 2 Oct. 1915, pp. 2–3.

Inglis, K. S. *Churches and the Working Classes in Victorian England.* London and Toronto: Routledge and Kegan Paul & Univ. of Toronto Press, 1963.

Investor's Monthly Manual, a Newspaper for Investors. I–VI, 1864–70; n.s. I–L, 1871–1920.

Ivan, Mauro. 'Fenianos nasceram na luta pela república', *Jornal do Brasil,* 27 Jan. 1965 (Caderno B), pp. 1–3.

Jaceguay, Arthur Silveira da Motta, *barão de. De aspirante a almirante,* [*Vol. IV:*] *1860–1902. Minha fé de officio documentada, 1893–1900.* Mendes, R. J.: Typ. Cia. Industrial Santa Rita, 1906.

Reminiscencias da guerra do Paraguay. Rio: 'A Noite', 1935.

John, A. H. *A Liverpool Merchant House: Being the History of Alfred Booth and Company, 1863–1958.* London: Allen & Unwin, 1959.

List of Sources

E. Johnston & Co. *One Hundred Years of Coffee*. London: E. Johnston & Co., 1942.

Jones, Clarence F. 'The Evolution of Brazilian Commerce', *Economic Geography*, II (1926), 550–74.

Jones, G. P., and A. G. Pool. *A Hundred Years of Economic Development in Great Britain (1840–1940)*. London: Duckworth, 1940.

Jones, Wilbur Devereux. 'The Origins and Passage of Lord Aberdeen's Act', *Hispanic American Historical Review*, XLII (1962), 502–20.

Jordão, Vera Pacheco. *Maneco, o byroniano*. Rio: Ministério da Educação e Cultura, 1955.

Jornal do commercio. Rio.

Jornal do commercio: Retrospecto commercial. Rio: Villeneuve, 1874–80.

Jornal do Recife. Recife.

José, Oiliam [*sic*]. *A abolição em Minas*. Belo Horizonte: Itatiaia, 1962.

Joslin, David. *A Century of Banking in Latin America; to Commemorate the Centenary in 1962 of the Bank of London and South America, Limited*. London: Oxford Univ. Press, 1963.

Joyce, Lillian Elwyn (Elliot). *Brazil, Today and Tomorrow*. New York: Macmillan, 1917.

Kaufmann, William W. *British Policy and the Independence of Latin America, 1804–1828*. Yale Historical Publications Miscellany, 52. New Haven: Yale Univ. Press, 1951.

Kidder, Daniel Parish, and James Cooley Fletcher. *Brazil and the Brazilians Portrayed in Historical and Descriptive Sketches*. Philadelphia: Childs & Peterson, 1857, and 9th ed. Boston: Little, Brown, 1879.

Klingberg, Frank J. *The Anti-Slavery Movement in England*. London & New Haven: Milford and Oxford & Yale Univ. Press, 1926.

Knowles & Foster. *The History of Knowles & Foster, 1828–1948*. London: Knowles & Foster, 1948.

Koebel, William Henry. *British Exploits in South America. A History of British Activities in Exploration, Military Adventure, Diplomacy, Science and Trade in Latin America*. New York: Century, 1917.

Krischke, George Upton. *História da Igreja Episcopal Brasileira*. Rio: Gráfica Tupy, 1949.

Lacerda, João Baptista de. 'The *Metis*, or Half-breeds, of Brazil', in *Papers on Inter-racial Problems Communicated to the First Universal Races Congress Held at the University of London, July 26–29, 1911*, ed. G. Spiller. London and Boston: King & World's Peace Foundation, 1911.

Lacombe, Américo Jacobina. *Rui Barbosa e a primeira constituição da república*. Rio: Casa de Rui Barbosa, 1949.

LaFeber, Walter. *The New Empire: An Interpretation of American Expansion, 1860–1898*. Ithaca, N.Y.: Cornell Univ. Press for the American Historical Association, 1963.

List of Sources

Lafer, Celso. 'O problema dos valores n'Os lusiadas', *Revista camoniana*, II (1965), 9–44.

Landes, David S. '"Social Attitudes, Entrepreneurship, and Economic Development": a Comment', *Explorations in Entrepreneurial History*, VI (1954), 245–72.

Landor, Arnold Henry Savage. *Across Unknown South America*. 2 vols. London and New York: Hodder & Stoughton, 1913.

Latourette, Kenneth Scott. *A History of the Expansion of Christianity*. 7 vols. New York and London: Harper, 1937–45.

Lauterbach, Albert. *Enterprise in Latin America: Business Attitudes in a Developing Economy*. Ithaca, N.Y.: Cornell Univ. Press, 1966.

Law, Henry. *Exposição das questões entre o presidente da provincia de Pernambuco, o...dr. Henrique Pereira de Lucena, e a Companhia Recife Drainage*. Rio: Winter, 1873.

Leão, Múcio. *Salvador de Mendonça: ensaio bio-bibliográfico*. Rio: Publicações da Academia Brasileira, 1952.

Leite, Aureliano. 'Inglêses em São Paulo', *Jornal do comércio*, 30 Jan. 1944, and 30 Apr. 1944.

Lemos, Miguel, and Raimundo Teixeira Mendes. *Nóssa inissiassão no pozitivismo. Nóta retificativa ao 'Rezumo istórico do movimento pozitivista no Brazil' publicado en 1882*. Rio: Apostolado Pozitivista do Brazil, 1889.

Léonard, Émile-G. 'O protestantismo brasileiro. Estudo de eclesiologia e de história social', *Revista de história*, II (Jan.–June 1951), 105–57, 329–79; III (July–Dec. 1951), 173–212, 411–32; IV (Jan.–June 1952), 165–77, 431–75; V (July-Dec. 1952), 129–87, 403–43.

Lerner, Daniel, and Lucille W. Pevsner. *The Passing of Traditional Society: Modernizing the Middle East*. Glencoe, Ill.: Free Press, 1958.

Leslie, H. W. '*The Royal Mail*' *War Book, Being an Account of the Operations of the Ships of the Royal Mail Steam Packet Co., 1914–1919*. London: Heinemann, 1920.

Levin, Jonathan. *The Export Economies, Their Pattern of Development in Historical Perspective*. Cambridge, Mass.: Harvard Univ. Press, 1960.

Levy, Marion J. 'Some Social Obstacles to "Capital Formation" in "Underdeveloped Areas"', in Universities—National Bureau Committee for Economic Research, *Capital Formation and Economic Growth, a Conference*. Princeton, N. J.: Princeton Univ. Press, 1955. Pp. 441–501.

Lewis, William Arthur. *The Theory of Economic Growth*. London: Allen & Unwin, 1955.

Lima, Heitor Ferreira. *Mauá e Roberto Simonsen: dois pioneiros do desenvolvimento*. São Paulo: Editôra Edaglit, 1963.

Lima Sobrinho, Alexandre José Barbosa. *Artur Jaceguai, ensaio bio-bibliográfico*. Coleção Afrânio Peixoto, 3. Rio: Publicações da Academia Brasileira de Letras, 1955.

'Linhas Para Coser—Empire of Thread', *Brazilian Business*, XXXIX, no. 7 (July 1959), pp. 34–5.

List of Sources

Lisboa, Alfredo. 'Portos do Brasil', in Instituto Historico e Geographico Brasileiro, *Diccionario historico, geographico e ethnographico do Brasil (commemorativo do primeiro centenario da independencia)*. 2 vols. Rio: Imp. Nacional, 1922, I, 560–710.

Lisboa, Bento da Silva, and J. D. de Attaide Moncorvo. 'Juizo sobre a obra intitulada "Histoire des rélations commerciales entre la France et le Brésil", par Horace Say', *RIHGB*, I (1839), 320–6.

Lloyd, Christopher, *The Navy and the Slave Trade; the Suppression of the African Slave Trade in the Nineteenth Century*. London: Longmans, Green, 1949.

Lloyd, Reginald, *et al.* eds. *Twentieth Century Impressions of Brazil: Its History, People, Commerce, Industries, and Resources*. London: Lloyd's Greater Britain Publishing Co., 1913.

Lloyd, William. *Caminho de ferro de d. Isabel da provincia do Paraná a de Matto Grosso. Considerações geraes sobre a empresa pelo visconde de Mauá; relatorio por William Lloyd*. Rio: Leuzinger, 1875.

Lobo, Helio. *Docas de Santos, suas origens, lutas e realizações*. Rio: Typ. do 'Jornal do Commercio', Rodrigues, 1936.

London, Great Exhibition of the Works of Industry of All Nations. *Official Catalogue*. 2nd ed. London: Spicer & Clowes, 1851.

Lopes, João Fernandes. *Colonias industriaes destinadas á disciplina, correção e educação dos vagabundos regenerados pela hospitalidade e trabalho*. Recife: Typ. d'A Provincia, 1890.

Luz, Nícia Villela. *Aspectos do nacionalismo econômico brasileiro. Os esforços em prol da industrialização*. Coleção 'Revista de história', 16. São Paulo: 'Revista de história', 1959.

'O industrialismo e o desenvolvimento econômico do Brasil', *Revista de história*, XXVII, no. 56 (Oct.–Dec. 1963), pp. 271–85.

'A monarquia brasileira e as repúblicas americanas', *Journal of Inter-American Studies*, VIII (1966), 358–70.

'O papel das classes médias brasileiras no movimento republicano', *Revista de história*, XXVIII, no. 57 (Jan.–Mar. 1964), pp. 13–27.

Lyra, Heitor. *História de D. Pedro II, 1825–1891*. Brasiliana, 133. 3 vols. São Paulo: Editôra Nacional, 1938–40.

Machado, Sylvio Marcondes. *Ensaio sôbre a sociedade de responsabilidade limitada*. São Paulo: n.p., 1940.

Machado de Assis, Joaquim Maria. *Quincas Borba*. N.p.: Instituto de Divulgação Cultural, n.d.

McNairn, A. Stuart. *Three Republics: A Study in Contrasts*. London: Evangelical Union of South America, n.d.

Madureira do Pinho, Péricles. *Luís Tarquínio, pioneiro da justiça social no Brasil*. Salvador: Imp. Vitória, 1944.

Magalhães Júnior, Raimundo. *Rui, o homem e o mito*. Retratos do Brasil, 27. Rio: Civilização Brasileira, 1964.

List of Sources

Magalhães Júnior, Raimundo, ed. *Três panfletários do segundo reinado: Francisco de Sales Torres Homem e o 'Líbelo do povo'; Justiniano José da Rocha e 'Ação; reação; transação'; Antônio Ferreira Vianna e 'A conferência dos divinos'*. Brasiliana, 286. São Paulo: Editôra Nacional, 1956.

Manchester, Alan K. *British Preëminence in Brazil; Its Rise and Decline: A Study in European Expansion*. Chapel Hill, N.C.: Univ. of North Carolina Press, 1933.

'Dom Pedro Segundo, the Democratic Emperor', in Lawrence F. Hill, ed., *Brazil*. Berkeley and Los Angeles: Univ. of California Press, 1947.

Mangabeira, João. *Rui, o estadista da república*. Documentos Brasileiros, 40. Rio: José Olympio, 1943.

Mansfield, Charles Blackford. *Paraguay, Brazil and the Plate; Letters Written in 1852–1853 ...with a Sketch of the Author's Life by the Rev. Charles Kingsley*. Cambridge, England: Macmillan, 1856.

Marchant, Anyda. 'A New Portrait of Mauá the Banker: a Man of Business in Nineteenth-Century Brazil', *Hispanic American Historical Review*, XXX (1950), 411–31.

'A sorte não o permitiu', *RIHGB*, CXCII (1946), 46–59.

Viscount Mauá and the Empire of Brazil: a Biography of Irineu Evangelista de Sousa (1813–1889). Berkeley and Los Angeles: Univ. of California Press, 1965.

Marshall, Leon S. 'The Emergence of the First Industrial City: Manchester, 1780–1850', in Caroline Ware, ed., *The Cultural Approach to History*. New York: Columbia Univ. Press, 1940. Pp. 140–61.

Martin, Percy Alvin. 'Causes of the Collapse of the Brazilian Empire', *Hispanic American Historical Review*, IV (1921), 4–48.

'The Influence of the United States on the Opening of the Amazon to the World's Commerce', *Hispanic American Historical Review*, I (1918), 146–62.

'Slavery and Abolition in Brazil', *Hispanic American Historical Review*, XIII (1933), 151–96.

Martins, Luís. *O patriarca e o bacharel*. São Paulo: Martins, 1953.

Marvin, Francis Sydney, ed. *Progress and History*. London and New York: Milford and Oxford University Press, 1916.

Mascarenhas, Nelson Lage. *Bernardo Mascarenhas. O surto industrial de Minas Gerais*. Rio: Gráfica Editôra Aurora, [1955?].

Mathieson, William Law. *Great Britain and the Slave Trade, 1839–1865*. London: Longmans, Green, 1929.

Mauá, Irineo Evangelista de Souza, visconde de. *Autobiografia ('Exposição aos credores e ao público') seguida de 'O meio circulante no Brasil'*. Ed. Claudio Ganns. 2nd ed. Rio: Valverde, 1942.

Correspondência política de Mauá no Rio da Prata (1850–1885). Ed. Lídia Besouchet. 2nd ed. Brasiliana, 227. São Paulo: Editôra Nacional, 1943.

Maxwell. 'Robert Reid Kalley, the Founder of the "Help for Brazil" Mission', *South America*, II (1914), 207–11, 226–8.

List of Sources

Mayrink, Francisco de Paula. *O cambio, a producção, o governo; artigos publicados na imprensa da corte em maio de 1881.* Rio: Typ. do Cruzeiro, 1881.

Meen, J. G. 'Conditions in the Roman Catholic Church To-Day as Compared with Twenty-five Years Ago', *South America,* III (Dec. 1914), 169.

Mendonça, Carlos Sussekind de. *Sílvio Romero, sua formação intelectual, 1851–1880; com uma indicação bibliográfica.* Brasiliana, 114. São Paulo: Editôra Nacional, 1938.

Mendonça, Renato. *Um diplomata na côrte de Inglaterra; o barão do Penedo e sua época.* Brasiliana, 219. São Paulo: Editôra Nacional, 1942.

Mendonça, Salvador de Menezes Drummond Furtado de. *A situação internacional do Brazil.* Rio: Garnier, 1913.

Menucci, Sud. *O precursor do abolicionismo no Brasil (Luiz Gama).* São Paulo: n.p., 1938.

Merchants and Manufacturers' Association of Baltimore. *A reciprocidade commercial: Baltimore e Brazil. Um compendio de informações uteis relativas aos interesses mutuos da Republica do Brazil e da cidade de Baltimore, Estados Unidos da America.* Baltimore: Merchants and Manufacturers' Association of Baltimore, 1891.

Milet, Henrique Augusto. *O meio circulante e a questão bancária.* 2nd ed. Recife: Typ. do Jornal do Recife, 1875.

Mill, John Stuart. *On Liberty.* 3rd ed. London: Longman, Green, Longman, Roberts & Green, 1864.

Millikan, Max F., and Donald L. M. Blackmer, eds. *The Emerging Nations, Their Growth and United States Policy.* Boston: Little, Brown, 1961.

Miranda, Floresta de. *Ruy Barbosa and England. A Short Talk at the Brazilian Society of English Culture on 5th November, Ruy Barbosa's Birthday.* Reprint from Casa de Rui Barbosa, Conferências, IV. Rio: Casa de Rui Barbosa, 1954.

Momsen, Jr., Richard P. *Routes over the Serra do Mar: the Evolution of Transportation in the Highlands of Rio de Janeiro and São Paulo.* Rio: [privately printed?], 1964.

Monbeig, Pierre. *Pionniers et planteurs de São Paulo.* Collection des Cahiers de la Fondation Nationale des Sciences Politiques, 28. Paris: Colin, 1952.

Monteiro, Tobias do Rego. *O presidente Campos Salles na Europa.* 2nd ed. Rio: Briguiet, 1928.

Monteiro de Barros Lins, Ivan. *História do positivismo no Brasil.* Brasiliana, 322. São Paulo: Editôra Nacional, 1964.

Moraes, Evaristo de. *A campanha abolicionista (1879–1888).* Rio: Leite Ribeiro, Bastos, Spicer, 1924.

—— *A escravidão africana no Brasil (das origens a extinção).* Brasiliana, 23. São Paulo: Editôra Nacional, 1933.

Morgan, John. *The Paraguassú Steam Tram-Road, in the Province of Bahia, Empire of Brazil...* London: Smith, Elder, 1866.

Morse, Richard M. *From Community to Metropolis: a Biography of São Paulo, Brazil.* Gainesville, Fla.: Univ. of Florida Press, 1958.

List of Sources

'Some Themes of Brazilian History', *The South Atlantic Quarterly*, LXI (1962), 159–82.

'Toward a Theory of Spanish American Government', *Journal of the History of Ideas*, XV (1954), 71–93.

Mosk, Sanford A. 'Latin America and the World Economy, 1850–1914', *Inter-American Economic Affairs*, II, no. 3 (winter 1948), pp. 53–82.

Moura, Clovis. *Rebeliões da senzala (quilombos, insurreições, guerrilhas)*. São Paulo: Zumbi, 1959.

Mulhall, Michael George. *The English in South America*. Buenos Aires: 'Standard' Office, 1878.

Murtinho, Joaquim. *Introducções aos relatorios do dr. Joaquim Murtinho*. [Probably ed. José Carlos Rodrigues]. N.d., n.p. [probably Rio, 1901 or 1902].

Nabuco, Carolina. *The Life of Joaquim Nabuco*. Transl. & ed. Ronald Hilton. Stanford, California: Stanford Univ. Press, 1950.

Nabuco, Joaquim. *O abolicionismo*. [2nd. ed.?] Rio & São Paulo: Civilização Brasileira & Editôra Nacional, 1938.

The Approach of the Two Americas. Convocation Address before the University of Chicago, August 28, 1908. Bulletin of the American Branch of the Association for International Conciliation, 10. New York: American Branch of the Association for International Conciliation, 1908.

'Correspondencia', *Jornal do commercio*, 4 Mar. 1882, p. 3; 8 Mar. 1882, p. 2; 1 April 1882, p. 3; 28 July 1882, p. 3; 13 Aug. 1882, p. 2; 26 Aug. 1882, p. 2; 5 Dec. 1882, p. 3; 24 Dec. 1882, p. 2.

'Um darwinista alemão', *O Globo*, 15 Aug. 1875, p. 1.

Um estadista do imperio, Nabuco de Araujo. Sua vida, suas opiniões, sua época. [2nd ed.?] 2 vols. Rio & São Paulo: Civilização Brasileira & Editôra Nacional, 1936.

'Manifesto da Sociedade Contra a Escravidão, 1880', in Osvaldo Melo Braga. *Bibliografia de Joaquim Nabuco*. Instituto Nacional do Livro, Coleção B–1: Bibliografia, 8. Rio: Imp. Nacional, 1952, pp. 14–22.

Minha formação. [? ed.] Documentos Brasileiros, 90. Rio: José Olympio, 1957.

Obras completas. 14 vols. São Paulo: Instituto Progresso Editorial, 1949.

'O 1º de Maio', *Jornal do Brasil*, 10 June 1891, p. 1.

Napoleão, Aluízio. *Rio-Branco e as relações entre o Brasil e os Estados Unidos.* Monografias da Commissão Preparatória do Centenário do Barão do Rio Branco, 2. Rio: Ministério das Relações Exteriores, 1947.

Nascimento Brito, José do. 'Bernardo Pereira de Vasconcelos e a verdadeira origem das estradas de ferro no Brasil', *Engenharia*, VIII (1950), 556–64.

Meio século de estradas de ferro. Rio: Livraria São José, 1961.

Nery, Fernando. *Rui Barbosa, ensaio biográfico.* 2nd ed. Rio: Casa de Rui Barbosa, 1955.

Niebuhr, H. Richard. *Christ and Culture.* New York: Harper, 1951.

The Social Sources of Denominationalism. New York: Holt, 1929.

List of Sources

Nogueira, Emília. 'Alguns aspectos da influência francêsa em São Paulo na segunda metade do século XIX', *Revista de história*, Ano IV, Vol. VII (1953), 317–42.

Nogueira, Rubem. *O advogado Rui Barbosa: momentos culminantes de sua vida profissional*. Rio: Gráfica Olímpica, 1949.

Nogueira Matos, Odilon. 'A evolução ferroviária de São Paulo', in IX Congresso Brasileiro de Geografia, *Anais*, 5 vols. Rio: Conselho Nacional de Geografia, 1941–4, IV (1940), 556–68.

Normano, J. F. *Brazil, a Study of Economic Types*. Chapel Hill, N.C.: Univ. of North Carolina Press, 1935.

Noronha Santos, Francisco Agenor de. *Indice alphabetico do livro 'Contractos e concessões', Prefeitura do Distrito Federal*. Rio: Typ. do Instituto Profissional, 1902.

Meios de transporte no Rio de Janeiro, historia e legislação. 2 vols. Rio: Typ. do 'Jornal do Commercio', 1934.

Northrop, F. S. C. *The Meeting of East and West: an Inquiry Concerning World Understanding*. New York: Macmillan, 1947.

The Northwestern Miller. Minneapolis, Minn.

'Noticiario. O sr. Aubertin e a producção do algodão em S. Paulo', *Correio paulistano*, 6 May 1869, p. 1.

'Noticiario. Plantação do algodão', *Correio paulistano*, 14 Oct. 1868, p. 1.

Novaes, Maria Stella. *A escravidão e a abolição no Espírito Santo: história e folclore*. Vitória: Departamento de Imprensa Oficial, 1963.

Oakenfull, J. C. *Brazil (1913)*, Frome, England: Butler & Tanner, 1914.

Oliveira, João Gualberto de. *Conselheiro Francisco de Paula Mayrink; as ferrovias paulistas, a vila Mayrink, seu fundador, pioneiros*...São Paulo: Bentivegna, 1958.

Oliveira Lima, Manoel de. *Memorias (estas minhas reminiscências)*. Rio: José Olympio, 1937.

Oliveira Vianna, Francisco José de. 'O povo brasileiro e sua evolução', in Brazil, Directoria Geral de Estatística, *Recenseamento do Brazil, 1920, Vol. I: Introducção*. Rio: Typ. da Estatistica, 1922, pp. 279–400.

Orico, Osvaldo. *O tigre da abolição*. Edição Comemorativa do centenário de José do Patrocínio. Rio: Gráfica Olímpica, 1953.

Ottoni, Christiano Benedicto. *Autobiografia...Maio, 1870*. Rio: Typ. Leuzinger, 1908.

Esboço historico das estradas de ferro do Brazil. Rio: Villeneuve, 1866.

'Estrada de ferro do Parahyba', *Jornal do commercio*, 7 June, p. 2; 10 June, p. 2; 14 June, p. 2; 17 June, p. 2; 22 June, p. 1, 1855.

Ottoni, Theophilo Benedicto. *Circular dedicada aos srs. eleitores pela provincia de Minas-Geraes no quatriennio actual e especialmente dirigida aos srs. eleitores de deputados pelo 2º districto eleitoral da mesma provincia para a proxima legislatura*. 2nd ed. Rio: Typ. do Correio Mercantil, 1860.

List of Sources

Parker, Barry, and Raymond Unwin. *The art of building a home: a collection of lectures and illustrations*. 2nd ed. London, etc.: Longmans, Green, 1901.

Pedro II. *Diário da viagem ao Norte do Brasil*. Ed. Lourenço Luiz Lacombe. Bahia: Univ. da Bahia, 1959. .

Penedo, Francisco Ignácio de Carvalho Moreira, *barão* do. *O empréstimo brasileiro contraido em Londres em 1863*. Paris: n.p., 1864.

Relatorio sobre a exposição internacional de 1862. London: Brettell, 1863.

Pereira, Lúcia Miguel. *Machado de Assis (estudo crítico e biográfico)*. 5th ed. Documentos Brasileiros, 82. Rio: José Olympio, 1955.

Pereira da Silva, Clodomiro. *A evolução do transporte mundial (enciclopédia dos transportes)*. 6 vols. São Paulo: Imp. Oficial do Estado, 1940–6.

Pernambuco. Governador. *Mensagem*.

Presidente. *Falla*.

Presidente. *Memoria*.

Presidente. *Relatorio*.

Peterson, H. C. *Propaganda for War: the Campaign against American Neutrality, 1914–1917*. Norman, Okla.: Univ. of Oklahoma Press, 1939.

Phipps, E. Constantine W. 'Report...on the Trade and Commercial Relations of Brazil and on Finance (24 June 1872)', C636, in Great Britain, Parliament, House of Commons, *Sessional Papers*. Readex Microprint Edition, ed. Edgar L. Erickson, 1872, LIX, 625–72.

Picanço, Francisco. 'Estradas de ferro', *Imprensa fluminense*, 20 May 1888, p. 2.

Pinheiro, Xavier, ed. *Francisco Octaviano, carioca illustre nas letras, no jornalismo, na politica, na tribuna, e na diplomacia*. Rio: Edição da Revista de Lingua Portuguesa, 1925.

Pinheiro da Silva, João. *João Pinheiro e sua doutrina...1889–1908*. Belo Horizonte: n.p., 1935.

Pinto, Adolpho Augusto. *Historia da viação publica de São Paulo (Brasil)*. São Paulo: Vanorden, 1903.

Pinto, Estevão. *História de uma estrada-de-ferro do nordeste (contribuição para o estudo da formação e desenvolvimento da empresa 'The Great Western of Brazil Railway Company Limited' e das suas relações com a economia do nordeste brasileiro)*. Documentos Brasileiros, 61. Rio: José Olympio, 1949.

Pinto Junior, Joaquim Antonio. *Liberdade do commercio*. Rio: Typ. Imperial Instituto Artistico, 1869.

Santos e S. Vicente de 1868 a 1876. Rio: Santos, 1877.

Pires, Homero. *Anglo-American Political Influences on Rui Barbosa*. Transl. Sylvia Medrado Clinton. Rio: Casa de Rui Barbosa, 1949.

Pires de Almeida. 'A escola byroniana no Brazil (suas origens, evolução, decadencia e desapparecimento)', *Jornal do commercio*, 17 July 1904, p. 2; 5 Feb. 1905, p. 4; 26 Feb. 1905, pp. 3–4; 22 Mar. 1905, p. 3; 8 June 1905, p. 4; 13 July 1905, p. 3; 20 Nov. 1905, pp. 3–4.

Pontes, Carlos. *Tavares Bastos (Aureliano Candido), 1839–1875*. Brasiliana, 136. São Paulo: Editôra Nacional, 1939.

List of Sources

Prado, Eduardo. *Catalogue de la bibliothèque Eduardo Prado.* São Paulo: Typ. Brasil de Rothschild, 1916.

Collectaneas. 4 vols. São Paulo: Escola Typographica Salesiana, 1904–5.

A illusão americana. 2nd ed. Paris: Colin, 1895.

Prado, Nazareth, ed. *Antonio Prado no imperio e na republica: seus discursos e actos colligidos e apresentados por sua filha.* Rio: Briguiet, 1929.

Prado, Paulo. *Retrato do Brasil. Ensaio sôbre a tristeza brasileira.* 5th ed. São Paulo: Brasiliense, 1944.

Prado Júnior, Caio. *História econômica do Brasil.* São Paulo: Brasiliense, 1945.

A provincia de São Paulo. São Paulo.

Putnam, Samuel. *Marvelous Journey. A Survey of Four Centuries of Brazilian Writing.* New York: Knopf, 1948.

Raffard, Henri, ed. *O Centro da Industria e Commercio de Assucar do Rio de Janeiro.* Rio: Cia. Typ. do Brazil, 1892.

Raiz, Jovino da. 'O trabalhador negro no tempo do banguê comparado com o trabalhador negro no tempo das uzinas de assucar', *Estudos afro-brasileiros. Trabalhos apresentados ao 1º Congresso Afro-brasileiro reunido em Recife em 1934.* Rio: Ariel Editôra, 1935, pp. 191–4.

Ramalho Ortigão, Antonio de Barros. 'Surto de cooperativismo', *Revista do Instituto Historico e Geographico Brasileiro, tomo especial: Contribuições para a biographia de D. Pedro II.* Rio: Imp. Nacional, 1925. Pp. 289–311.

Ranken, Bryce W. 'Through Darkest São Paulo', *South America,* II (Aug. 1913), 87.

Rebouças, André. *Agricultura nacional, estudos economicos; propaganda abolicionista e democratica.* Rio: Lamoureux, 1883.

Ao Itatiaya. Rio: Lombaerts, 1878.

Diário e notas autobiográficas. Ed. Ana Flora and Inácio José Veríssimo. Documentos Brasileiros, 12. Rio: José Olympio, 1938.

Melhoramento do porto do Rio de Janeiro. Organização da Companhia das Docas de D. Pedro II (nas enseadas da Saude e Gamboa): colleção de artigos publicados. Rio: Typ. Nacional, 1869.

'Noticia sobre a organização da Companhia das Docas de D. Pedro II', *Revista de engenharia,* IV (1882), 42.

Soccorros publicos; a sêcca nas provincias do norte. Rio: Leuzinger, 1877.

Rebouças, André, and José Rebouças. *Ensaio de indice geral das madeiras do Brazil.* Rio: Typ. Nacional, 1877.

Rebouças, Antonio. *Apontamentos sobre a via de communicação do Rio Madeira.* Rio: Typ. Nacional, 1870.

Relatorio da commissão de estudos do abastecimento d'agua desta capital. Rio: Typ. Nacional, 1871.

Reclus, Élisée. 'Le Brésil et la colonisation. I. Le bassin des Amazones et les indiens. II. Les provinces du littoral, les noirs et les colonies allemandes', *Revue des deux mondes,* May–June (pp. 930–59) and July–August (pp. 375–414), 1862.

23-3

List of Sources

Reed, Edward T. 'Off to the Putumayo', *South America*, I (Jan. 1913), 209.

Revista da Academia Brasileira de Letras. Rio.

Revista de engenharia. Rio. Vols. I–XII. 1879–1891.

Revista de história. São Paulo.

Revista do Arquivo Municipal de São Paulo. São Paulo.

Revista do Arquivo Publico [Estadual de Pernambuco]. Recife.

Revista do Instituto Histórico e Geográfico Brasileiro. Rio.

Ribeiro, Júlio. *A carne*. São Paulo: Teixeira, 1888.

Cartas sertanejas. [? ed.] Coleção Nacionalista, 3. São Paulo: Brasil Editôra, 1945.

Ribeiro Lamego Filho, Alberto. *O homem e a serra*. 2nd ed. Biblioteca Geográfica Brasileira, A–8: Setores da Evolução Fluminense, 4. Lucas, GB: Conselho Nacional de Geografia, 1963.

Ricciardi, Adelino R. 'Parnaíba, o pioneiro da imigração', *Revista do Arquivo Municipal de São Paulo*, Ano IV, Vol. XLIV (1938), 137–84.

Rio Branco, José Maria da Silva Paranhos, 2º, barão do. 'O Brasil, os Estados Unidos e o Monroísmo', in *Estudos históricos*, Obras do Barão do Rio Branco, 8. Rio: Ministério das Relações Exteriores, 1948.

O visconde do Rio Branco. Ed. Renato Mendonça. Rio: 'A Noite' Editora, n.d.

Rio de Janeiro Lighterage Company Limited. *Memorandum and Articles of Association; Date of Incorporation, the 28th day of December, 1911*. London: privately printed, 1911.

Rio de Janeiro (state). Governador. *Mensagem...*

The Rio Mercantile Journal. Rio, 1847–56.

Rio News. Rio, 1874–1901.

Rippy, J. Fred. *British Investments in Latin America, 1822–1949. A Case Study in the Operations of Private Enterprise in Retarded Regions*. Minneapolis: Univ. of Minnesota Press, 1959.

Rizzini, Carlos. *Hipólito da Costa e o 'Correio braziliense'*. Brasiliana, Grande Formato, 13. São Paulo: Editôra Nacional, 1957.

Rocha, João Gomes da. *Lembranças do passado. Ensaio histórico do início e desenvolvimento do trabalho evangélico no Brasil, do qual resultou a fundação da 'Igreja Evangélica Fluminense' pelo dr. Robert Reid Kalley*. 4 vols. Rio: Centro Brasileiro de Publicidade (Vols. I–III), 'O Cristão' (Vol. IV), 1941–57.

'Robert Reid Kalley', *Rio News*, 24 Feb. 1888, p. 3.

Rocha, João Gomes da, et al. comps. *Salmos e hinos*. [? ed.]. São Paulo: Imp. Metodista, 1965.

Salmos e hinos com músicas sacras. 5th ed. Rio: Igreja Evangélica Fluminense, 1952.

Rodrigues, Jorge Martins. 'A rivalidade comercial de norte-americanos e inglêses no Brasil do século XIX', *Revista de história da economia brasileira*, I (1953), 73–82.

List of Sources

Rodrigues, José Carlos. 'Religiões acatholicas', in Associação do Quarto Centenario do Descobrimento do Brasil. *Livro do centenario (1500–1900)*. 3 vols. Rio: Imp. Nacional, 1900–2. Vol. II, Section 3.

Resgate das estradas de ferro do Recife a S. Francisco e de outras que gozavam da garantia de juros: relatorio...Rio: Imp. Nacional, 1902.

Rodrigues, José Honório. *Conciliação e reforma no Brasil. Um desafio histórico-político*. Retratos do Brasil, 32. Rio: Civilização Brasileira, 1965.

Notícia de vária história. Rio: Livraria São José, 1951.

Rolfe, E. Lloyd. *Report on Brazil's Trade & Industry in 1918 with Special Reference to the State of São Paulo. Hints, Information for Manufacturers & Merchants*. São Paulo: British Chamber of Commerce of São Paulo & Southern Brazil, 1919.

Romero, Sylvio. *Doutrina contra doutrina: o evolucionismo e o positivismo no Brasil*. Rio and São Paulo: Livraria Classica de Alves, 1895.

Romero, Sílvio. *História da literatura brasileira*. 6th ed. 5 vols. Rio: José Olympio, 1960.

Rössler, Augustine. 'Woman', *The Catholic Encyclopedia*, XV (1912), 687–94.

Rostow, W. W. *British Economy of the Nineteenth Century*. Oxford: Clarendon Press, 1948.

Royal Society of Arts. *Journal*.

Ruggiero, Guido de. *The History of European Liberalism*. Transl. R. G. Collingwood. Boston: Beacon, 1959.

Sabóia, Edith. 'Francisco Rangel Pestana (notas biográficas por ocasião do centenário do seu nascimento, 1839–1939)', *Revista do Arquivo Municipal de São Paulo*, Ano VI, Vol. LXI (Sept.–Oct. 1939), 23–42.

Sacramento Blake, Augusto Victorino Alves. *Diccionario bibliographico brazileiro*. 7 vols. Rio: Typ. Nacional, 1883–1902.

Saldanha Marinho (I), Joaquim. *A monarchia; ou, a politica do rei*. Rio: Leuzinger, 1885.

Santos, Antonio Felicio dos, *et al.* 'Auxilios á industria', *Jornal do commercio*, 6 July 1892, p. 2.

Santos, Antonio Felicio dos. 'Discurso na Camara dos Deputados', *Diario official*, 25 Apr. 1882, pp. 3–4.

Santos, Francisco Martins dos. *Historia de Santos*...*1532–1936*. 2 vols. São Paulo: Grafica 'Revista dos Tribunaes', 1937.

Santos, Joel Rufino dos, *et al.* *Da independência à república*. Coleção História Nova, 7. Rio: Campanha de Assistência ao Estudante, Ministério da Educação e Cultura, 1964.

Santos, José Maria dos. *A politica geral do Brasil*. São Paulo: Magalhães, 1930.

Os republicanos paulistas e a abolição. São Paulo: Martins, 1942.

Santos Werneck, Antonio Luiz dos. *O positivismo republicano na Academia*. São Paulo: Seckler, 1880.

São Paulo de ontem, de hoje, e de amanhã. São Paulo. Vols. V–VII, 1945–7.

List of Sources

São Paulo (state). Assembléia Legislativa. *Anais.*

São Paulo Railway Company. *São Paulo Railway Company como successora da Companhia Bragantina: documentos relativos ao prolongamento de Bragança a Socorro.* São Paulo: São Paulo Railway Company, 1904.

São Vicente, José Antonio Pimenta Bueno, marquês de. *Companhia de Navegação do Amazonas. Discurso proferido no Senado na sessão de 8 de outubro de 1877.* n.p., n.d.

Memoria justificativa dos planos apresentados ao governo imperial para o prolongamento da Estrada de Ferro de S. Paulo. Rio: Imp. Nacional, 1876.

Saul, Samuel Berrick. *Studies in British Overseas Trade, 1870–1914.* Liverpool: Liverpool Univ. Press, 1960.

Sawyer, John E. 'In Defense of an Approach: A Comment on Professor Gerschenkron's "Social Attitudes, Entrepreneurship, and Economic Development"', *Explorations in Entrepreneurial History*, VI (1954), 273–86.

Say, Horace Émile. *Histoire des relations commerciales entre la France et le Brésil et considérations générales sur les monnaies, les changes, les banques, et le commerce extérieur.* Paris: Guillaumin, 1839.

Schapiro, J. Salwyn. *Liberalism and the Challenge of Fascism. Social Forces in England and France (1815–1870).* New York: McGraw-Hill, 1949.

Schoenrich, Otto. *Former Senator Burton's Trip to South America, 1915.* Carnegie Endowment for International Peace, Division of Intercourse and Education, Publication 9. Washington: Carnegie Endowment for International Peace, 1915.

Scully, William. *Brazil: Its Provinces and Chief Cities; the Manners and Customs of the People; Agricultural, Commercial, and Other Statistics, Taken from the Latest Official Documents; with a Variety of Useful and Entertaining Knowledge, Both for the Merchant and the Emigrant.* London: Murray, 1866.

Sensabaugh, Leon F. 'The Coffee-Trust Question in United States–Brazilian Relations: 1912–1913', *Hispanic American Historical Review*, XXVI (1946), 480–96.

Serpa, Phocion. *Francisco Otaviano; ensaio biográfico.* Rio: Publicações da Academia Brasileira, 1952.

Sierra y Mariscal, Francisco. 'Idéas geraes sobre a revolução do Brazil e suas consequencias [Lisbon, 10 Nov. 1823]', in Biblioteca Nacional do Rio de Janeiro, *Anais*, XLIII–XLIV (1920–1), 49–81.

Silva Júnior, Ismael de. *Notas históricas sôbre a missão evangelizadora do Brasil e Portugal.* 3 vols. Rio: Souza, 1960–1.

Silveira da Motta, José Ignácio. *Degeneração do sistema representativo [discurso na Conferência Radical, 25. 4. 1869].* Rio: Typ. Americana, 1869.

Simonsen, Roberto. 'As consequências econômicas da abolição', *Revista do Arquivo Municipal de São Paulo*, Ano IV, Vol. XLVII (1938), 257–68.

Siqueira, Edmundo. *Resumo historico de The Leopoldina Railway Company, Limited.* Rio: Gráfica Editora Carioca, 1938.

Smelser, Neil J. *Social Change in the Industrial Revolution: an Application of*

List of Sources

Theory to the British Cotton Industry. Chicago: Univ. of Chicago Press, 1959.

Smiles, Aileen. *Samuel Smiles and His Surroundings.* London: Hale, 1956.

Smiles, Samuel. *Life and Labour, or Characteristics of Men of Industry, Culture and Genius.* [? ed.] London: Murray, 1916.

Self-Help with Illustrations of Conduct & Perseverance. [? ed.] London: Murray, 1958.

Smith, Carleton Sprague. *Os livros norte-americanos no pensamento de Rui Barbosa.* Separata das 'Publicações da Casa de Rui Barbosa, Conferências', 2. Rio: Imp. Nacional, 1945.

Smith, Herbert Huntington. *Brazil, the Amazons and the Coast.* New York: Scribner's, 1879.

Smith, John. 'Memoria...por parte dos herdeiros Bowman, sobre melhoramentos introduzidos na producção do assucar desta provincia', in Sociedade Auxiliadora d'Agricultura de Pernambuco, *Acta da sessão solemne da Assembléa Geral de 28 de setembro de 1882 e relatorio annual do gerente Ignacio de Barros Barreto.* Recife: Typ. Central, 1882, pp. 110–17.

Smith de Vasconcellos, Rodolpho Smith de Vasconcellos, 1º barão, and Jayme Luiz Smith de Vasconcellos, 2º barão Smith de Vasconcellos. *Archivo nobiliarchico brasileiro.* Lausanne, Switzerland: La Concorde, 1918.

Soares, Álvaro Teixeira. *O gigante e o rio. Ação de Mauá no Uruguai e Argentina, 1851–1878.* Rio: Cia. Brasileira de Artes Gráficas, 1957.

'Mauá, o Uruguai e o Brasil (1851–1875)', *RIHGB*, ccix (1950), 3–213.

Sociedade Auxiliadora d'Agricultura de Pernambuco. *Acta da sessão solemne da assembléia geral...1877–1882.* Recife: Typ. Central, 1877–82.

Boletim, Sept. 1882.

Society of Arts, Manufactures and Commerce. *Lectures on the Results of the Exhibition.* London: Bogue, 1852.

Sodré, Nelson Werneck. *História da burguesia brasileira.* Retratos do Brasil, 22. Rio: Civilização Brasileira, 1964.

Sousa, Octavio Tarqüínio de. *História dos fundadores do império do Brasil.* 10 vols. Rio: José Olympio, 1957.

Sousa Sá Vianna, Manoel Alvaro. 'O trafico e a diplomacia brasileira', in *Revista do Instituto Historico e Geographico Brasileiro: tomo especial consagrado ao primeiro Congresso de Historia Nacional (1914).* Vol. v, pp. 539-84.

South America. The Magazine of the Evangelical Union of South America. I–III, 1912–15.

South American Evangelical Mission. *Our Story, Being a Short Retrospect of the Work of the South American Evangelical Mission, with a Brief Reference to Our Field of Labor.* Liverpool: South American Evangelical Mission, 1908.

South American Evangelical Mission and Union of Prayer Circles. *Annual Report,* 1904–10.

The South American Journal and Brazil and River Plate Mail. London.

361

List of Sources

Souza, Antônio Cândido de Mello e. *Formação da literatura brasileira (momentos decisivos)*. 2 vols. São Paulo: Martins, 1959.

O método crítico de Sílvio Romero. 2nd ed. Universidade de São Paulo, Cadeira de Teoria Literária e Literatura Comparada (1), Boletim, 266. São Paulo: Universidade de São Paulo, 1963.

Souza, T. Oscar Marcondes de. *O estado de São Paulo: physico, politico, economico e administrativo*. São Paulo: Universal, 1915.

Souza Rego, Antonio José de, comp. *Relatorio da segunda exposição nacional de 1866*. Rio: Typ. Nacional, 1869.

Speers, William, comp. *Companhia São Paulo Railway e o governo imperial. Reproducção dos artigos sob essa epigraphe publicados no jornal pelo dr. Engenheiro Fiscal d'esta estrada de ferro com as respostas dadas aos ditos artigos pela respectiva superintendencia e os documentos a que os mesmos se referem*. São Paulo: Typ. a vapor de Jorge Seckler, 1889.

Spencer, Herbert. *Education: Intellectual, Moral, and Physical*. New York and London: Appleton, 1920.

Essays, Scientific, Political and Speculative. 3 vols. New York: Appleton, 1891.

First Principles. New York: Appleton, 1898.

'From Freedom to Bondage', in *Essays, Scientific, Political and Speculative*. 3 vols. New York: Appleton, 1891. Vol. III, pp. 445–70.

The Principles of Sociology. System of Synthetic Philosophy, 6–8. 3 vols. New York: Appleton, 1889.

'Progress: Its Law and Cause', in *Essays, Scientific, Political and Speculative*. 3 vols. New York: Appleton, 1891. Vol. I, pp. 8–62.

'Reasons for Dissenting from the Philosophy of M. Comte', in *Essays, Scientific, Political and Speculative*. 3 vols. New York: Appleton, 1891. Vol. II, pp. 118–44.

Social Statics: or, the Conditions Essential to Human Happiness Specified, and the First of Them Developed. London: Chapman, 1851.

The Statesman's Year-Book. London: Macmillan.

Stein, Stanley J. *The Brazilian Cotton Manufacture; Textile Enterprise in an Under-developed Area, 1850–1950*. Cambridge, Mass.: Harvard Univ. Press, 1957.

'The Brazilian Cotton Textile Industry, 1850–1950', in Simon Kuznets, *et al.* eds. *Economic Growth: Brazil, India, Japan*. Durham, N.C.: Duke Univ. Press, 1955. Pp. 430–47.

Vassouras, a Brazilian Coffee County, 1850–1900. Harvard Historical Studies, 69. Cambridge, Mass.: Harvard Univ. Press, 1957.

Stevenson, Carlos W. 'Os bandeirantes das ferrovias', in Instituto de Engenharia de São Paulo. *1º Centenario da locomotiva. Commemoração 1825–1925*. São Paulo: Gordinho Braune, 1925?

Storck, John, and Walter Dorwin Teague. *Flour for Man's Bread: a History of Milling*. Minneapolis: Univ. of Minnesota Press, 1952.

List of Sources

Tarquinio, Luiz. *Direitos de importação em ouro. Cartas dirigidas ao Ministro da Fazenda cons. Ruy Barbosa e ao dr. Aristides Galvão de Queiroz, seguidas de considerações sobre as tarifas do Brazil e da União americana.* Salvador: Imp. Popular, 1890.

A solução da crise; artigos publicados na imprensa da capital federal. Salvador: Imp. Popular, 1892.

Tavares, Raul. 'Almirante Arthur Jaceguay', in Arthur Silveira da Motta, barão de Jaceguay, *Reminiscencias da guerra do Paraguay.* Rio: 'A Noite', 1935. Pp. 5–80.

Tavares Bastos, Aureliano Cândido. *Cartas do Solitário.* 3rd ed. Brasiliana, 115. São Paulo: Editôra Nacional, 1938.

Os males do presente e as esperanças do futuro. 2nd ed. Brasiliana, 151. São Paulo: Editôra Nacional, 1939.

A provincia: estudo sobre a descentralização no Brasil. 2nd ed. Brasiliana, 105. São Paulo: Editôra Nacional, 1937.

O valle do Amazonas: a livre navegacão do Amazonas. Estatistica, producções, commercio, questões fiscaes do valle do Amazonas. 2nd ed. Brasiliana, 106. São Paulo: Editôra Nacional, 1937.

Tenorio d'Albuquerque, A. *O imperialismo britanico no Brasil.* Rio: Grafica Labor, 1941.

Thadani, J. N. 'Transport and Location of Industries in India', *Indian Economic Review*, I, no. 2 (Aug. 1952), 19–42.

Thomas, Arthur H. M., and Hermann Moraes Barros. 'Cia. Melhoramentos do Paraná formerly Cia. de Terras Norte do Paraná', mimeographed, *ca.* 1955.

Times. London.

Tischendorf, Alfred. *Great Britain and Mexico in the Era of Porfirio Díaz.* Durham, N.C.: Duke Univ. Press, 1961.

Todd, Geoffrey. 'Some Aspects of Joint Stock Companies, 1844–1900', *Economic History Review*, IV (Oct. 1932), 46–71.

Tôrres, João Camillo de Oliveira. *A democracia coroada: teoria política do império do Brasil.* 2nd ed. Petrópolis, R.J.: Editôra Vozes, 1964.

A formação do federalismo no Brasil. Brasiliana, 308. São Paulo: Editôra Nacional, 1961.

Trevelyan, George M. 'Macaulay and the Sense of Optimism', in Harman Grisewood, *et al. Ideas and Beliefs of the Victorians: an Historical Revaluation of the Victorian Age.* London: Sylvan, 1949. Pp. 46–52.

Trilling, Lionel. *The Liberal Imagination; Essays on Literature and Society.* Garden City, N.Y.: Doubleday, 1953.

Troeltsch, Ernst. *Protestantism and Progress.* Transl. W. Montgomery. Boston: Beacon, 1958.

The Social Teaching of the Christian Churches. Transl. Olive Wyon. Halley Stewart Publications, I. 2 vols. Glencoe and New York: Free Press & Macmillan, 1931.

List of Sources

Tschudi, Johann Jacob von. *Viagem às províncias do Rio de Janeiro e São Paulo.* São Paulo: Martins, 1953.

U.S. Department of State. *Commercial Relations of the United States with Foreign Countries.* 1862–1902.

Department of State. *Reports from the Consuls of the United States on the Commerce, Manufactures, etc. of Their Consular Districts.* 1880–.

Universal Races Congress, 1st, London, 1911. *Papers on Inter-racial Problems Communicated to the First Universal Races Congress, Held at the University of London July 26–29, 1911.* Ed. G. Spiller. London and Boston: King & World's Peace Foundation, 1911.

Universities—National Bureau Committee for Economic Research. *Capital Formation and Economic Growth, a Conference.* Princeton, N.J.: Princeton Univ. Press, 1955.

Varella, Carlos Arthur Busch. *Conferencia sobre a lei de 7 de novembro de 1831, realisada no dia 9 de março de 1884 a convite do Club Abolicionista Sete de Novembro.* Rio: Typ. Central de Evaristo Rodrigues da Costa for the Confederação Abolicionista, 1884.

Vargas, Getúlio. *A nova política do Brasil.* 11 vols. Rio: José Olympio, 1938–47.

Velho Sobrinho, J. F. *Dicionário bio-bibliográfico brasileiro.* 2 vols. Rio: Pongetti, 1937–40.

Veríssimo, Inácio José. *André Rebouças através de sua autobiografia.* Documentos Brasileiros, 20. Rio: José Olympio, 1939.

Viana Filho, Luís. *A vida de Rui Barbosa.* (Centenary edition.) [6th ed. ?] São Paulo: Editôra Nacional, 1952.

Vianna, Hélio. *D. Pedro I e D. Pedro II: acréscimos às suas biografias.* Brasiliana, 330. São Paulo: Editôra Nacional, 1966.

'Instruções de D. Pedro II ao marquês de Olinda e ao visconde de Abaeté', *Jornal do comércio*, 5 June 1964.

'Instruções de D. Pedro II ao presidente do conselho, marquês de Olinda', *Jornal do comércio*, 22 May 1964.

'Instruções de D. Pedro II ao visconde de Abaeté e Silva Ferraz', *Jornal do comércio*, 12 June 1964.

'Instruções de D. Pedro II aos presidentes do conselho, Zacarias e Furtado', *Jornal do comércio*, 3 July 1964.

'Programa de governo, por D. Pedro II, dado ao visconde de Paraná (1853)', *Jornal do comércio*, 16 Oct. 1964.

'Relações do Poder Moderador com o poder executivo, conforme D. Pedro II', *Jornal do comércio*, 31 May 1964.

Vianna de Lima, Cezar Augusto. *Estudo sobre o ensino primario no Reino Unido da Grã-Bretanha e Irlanda.* Rio: Imp. Nacional, 1885.

Vieira da Luz, Joaquim. *Dunshee de Abranches, e outras figuras.* Rio: privately printed, 1954.

List of Sources

von Binzer, Ina (pseud. for Ulla von Eck?). *Alegrias e tristezas de uma educadora alemã no Brasil.* Transl. Alice Rossi and Luisita da Gama Cerqueira. São Paulo: Anhembi, 1956.

Walsh, Robert. *Notices of Brazil in 1828 and 1829.* 2 vols. Boston and New York: Richardson, Lord and Holbrook & Carvill, 1831.

Wanderley Pinho, José. *Cotegipe e seu tempo: primeira phase, 1815–1867.* Brasiliana, 85. São Paulo: Editôra Nacional, 1937.

Watts, Alfredo J. 'A colônia inglêsa em Pernambuco', *Revista do Instituto Arqueológico e Geográfico de Pernambuco,* XXXIX (1944), 163–70.

Weber, Max. *The Protestant Ethic and the Spirit of Capitalism.* Transl. Talcott Parsons. New York: Scribner's, 1930.

Webster, Charles K., ed. *Britain and the Independence of Latin America, 1812–1830: Select Documents from the Foreign Office Archives.* 2 vols. London and New York: Oxford University Press for the Ibero-American Institute of Great Britain, 1938.

Wells, James William. *Exploring and Travelling Three Thousand Miles Through Brazil from Rio de Janeiro to Maranhão. With an Appendix Containing Statistics and Observations on Climate, Railways, Central Sugar Factories, Mining, Commerce and Finance; the Past, Present and Future, and Physical Geography of Brazil.* London: Low, Searle, & Rivington, 1886.

West, Joseph R. 'The Foreigner in Brazilian Technology, 1808–1900'. Unpub. Ph.D. diss., Univ. of Chicago, 1950.

Whyte, William F., and Allan R. Holmberg. 'Human Problems of U.S. Enterprise in Latin America', *Human Organization,* XV, no. 3 (fall 1956), pp. 1–40.

Wileman, J. P., comp. *The Brazilian Year Book, 1908–1909.* 2 vols. Rio and London: Brazilian Year Book & McCorquodale, n.d.

Willems, Emílio. 'Protestantism as a Factor of Culture Change in Brazil', *Economic Development and Cultural Change,* III (July 1955), 321–33.

Williams, Mary Wilhelmine. *Dom Pedro the Magnanimous, Second Emperor of Brazil.* Chapel Hill, N.C.: Univ. of North Carolina Press, 1937.

Wilson Sons & Co., Ltd. *Wilson Sons & Co. Ltd, 1837–1946: an Historical and Descriptive Account of the Organization Built in One Hundred and Ten Years' Happy Trading.* London: Wilson Sons & Co., 1946.

Wingfield-Stratford, Esmé Cecil. *Those Earnest Victorians.* New York: Morrow, 1930.

Winkler, Max. *Investments of United States Capital in Latin America.* World Peace Foundation Pamphlets, Vol. IX, no. 6. Boston: World Peace Foundation, 1928.

Winter, Nevin Otto. *Brazil and Her People of To-Day: an Account of the Customs, Characteristics, Amusements, History and Advancement of the Brazilians, and the Development and Resources of Their Country.* Boston: Page, 1910.

List of Sources

Woodward, Ernest L. *The Age of Reform, 1815–1870*. Oxford History of England. Oxford: Clarendon Press, 1946.
Wraith, Ronald E., and Edgar Simpkins. *Corruption in Developing Countries Including Britain until 1880*. London: Allen & Unwin, 1962.
Wright, Mrs Marie Robinson. *The New Brazil: Its Resources and Attractions, Historical, Descriptive and Industrial*. 2nd ed. Philadelphia: Barrie, 1907.

ADDENDA

Brazil. Instituto Brasileiro de Geografia e Estatística. Conselho Nacional de Geografia. *Tipos e aspectos do Brasil*. 7th ed. Rio: Conselho Nacional de Geografia, 1963.
Coutinho, Afrânio, ed. *A literatura no Brasil*. 3 vols. Rio: Editorial Sul Americana, 1955–9.
Duncan, T. Bentley, 'Uneasy Allies: Anglo-Portuguese Commercial, Diplomatic and Maritime Relations, 1642–1662.' Unpub. Ph.D. diss., Univ. of Chicago, 1967.
Garcia Redondo, Manuel Ferreira. 'A primeira concessão de estrada de ferro dada no Brasil', *Revista do Instituto Historico e Geographico de São Paulo*, VI (1900–1), 1–11.
Marques Guedes, Armando, *A aliança inglesa (notas de história diplomática), 1383–1943*. Lisbon: Enciclopédia, 1943.
Martins, Luiz Dodsworth. *Presença de Paulo de Frontin*. Rio and São Paulo: Freitas Bastos, 1966.
Palhano de Jesus, J. 'Rapida noticia da viação ferrea do Brasil' in Instituto Historico e Geographico Brasileiro, *Diccionario historico, geographico e ethnographico do Brasil (commemorativo do primeiro centenario da independencia)*. 2 vols. Rio: Imp. Nacional, 1922. Vol. I, pp. 723–56.
Parker, Barry. 'Town Planning Experiences in Brazil', *Architects Journal*, LI (1920), 48–52.
'Two Years in Brazil', *Garden Cities and Town Planning*, n.s. IX (1919), 143–51.
Rugendas, Johann Moritz. *Malerische Reise in Brasilien*. Paris: Engelmann & Cie: Mülhausen, 1835.
Smith, T. Lynn. *Brazil: People and Institutions*. 3rd ed. Baton Rouge: Louisiana State Univ. Press, 1963.
Tavares, Luís Henrique Dias. 'As soluções brasileiras na extinção do tráfico negreiro', *Journal of Inter-American Studies*, IX (1967), 367–82.

INDEX

Index

Banks (*cont.*)
interest in, 198, 199; rural credit, 209; company law regarding, 222–3, 225; Murtinho's interest in, 238; American, 302, 320; French, 302; German, 302. *See also* N. M. Rothschild & Sons

Banks, British: and export–import complex, 94, 323; discussed individually, 95–9; practices of, 97; and industrialization, 136, 323; and exchange rate, 306; faced American competition, 320; predominance of, 320; and funding loan of 1898, 321; mentioned, 111

Baptists: influence in Brazil, 285–6

Bar Association of Recife: and company law, 225

Barbacena, Felisberto Caldeira Brant Pontes, second *visconde* de, 225

Barbosa, Rui: and funding loan of 1898, 105; and liberalism, 260, 267, 271–6; life, 268; and republicanism, 268; and individualism, 268, 271, 272–3, 274–6; British influence upon, 269; influence of in Brazil, 270; and Pedro II, 271; and federalism, 272; and education, 272; and democracy, 273, 274–6; and labor, 273–4; and social welfare legislation, 273–4; and Carlyle, 274–6; and J. S. Mill, 275; and Protestantism, 283; and position of women, 290; and the United States, 313–14; position of during First World War, 315

Baring, House of, 85

Barra do Piraí, 54

Barreto, Tobias: and Romero, 240; German influence upon, 315

Barros, Roque Spencer Maciel de, 18

Bastos, Aureliano Cândido Tavares. *See* Tavares Bastos, Aureliano Cândido

Beets: competition with cane sugar, 24

Belém, Pará: population of, 32; urban services in, 118; branch of Mauá bank in, 190

Belgium: company law in, 228; investments from, 305; British protection of its shipping, 309

Bentham, Jeremy, 107, 216, 224, 262

Bento de Souza e Castro, Antônio, 173

Bibles: sale of, 119, 281, 283

Biblioteca Pública do Estado de São Paulo, 315

Birmingham, England, 116, 180

Blaine, James G., 306, 312

Blair, James Edward, 151

Blockade: of Rio de Janeiro by revolting navy, 307–11

Blount, John, 92–3

Blue Books, 176

Blue Star Line, 90

Bocaiuva, Quintino, 305

Booth Steamship Company, 90

Botanical Garden Rail Road Company, 303

Bowman, David William, 142

Boxwell, John Harvey, 74

Bradshaw, Wanklin & Co., 85

Bragantina, Estrada de Ferro, 64

Braganza dynasty, 313

Brant Pontes, Felisberto Caldeira, 225

Brazilian and Portuguese Bank, 96

Brazilian Imperial Central Bahia Railway, 71

Brazilian Submarine Telegraph Company, Ltd, 201, 303

Brazilian Sugar Factories Company, Ltd, 151

Brazilian Warrant Co., Ltd, 80

Breweries, 33, 44, 299, 304

British and Foreign Anti-Slavery Society, 168, 176, 180, 184

British and Foreign Bible Society, 282, 283

British Bank of South America, 96, 136

British colony: in Rio de Janeiro, 120

Brito, Raimundo de Farias, 241–2, 243

Brougham, Henry Peter, Lord, 179, 262

Bruderer, John Gasper, 201

Bruderer & Co., 195

Brunlees, James, 61, 62

Bueno, José Antônio Pimenta, *marquês* de São Vicente, 61, 197–8, 323

Buenos Aires, 89, 93, 96, 128, 189, 190

Bureaucracy: inefficient, 28, 205; increase of, 32; attitudes of, 37

Burton, Richard, 12, 289

Buxton, Thomas, 179, 180

Byron, Lord, 260

Cable communications: effect upon import firms, 84; Mauá's interest in, 201; British interest in, 302–3; American interest in, 302–3; British control of during First World War, 315 .

Caldeira Brant Pontes, Felisberto, *visconde* de Barbacena, 225

Calvinism, 285

Campinas, São Paulo, 32, 190, 192, 196

Campos, Rio de Janeiro: iron foundry there, 143; port works there, 92; and flight of slaves, 172, 173, 175

Index

Index

trade, 79; carried in British ships, 88, 90; insured by British companies, 91; and free trade, 108, 110, 247, 306; and Rebouças's dock company, 194; carried on German ships, 302; did little to develop human resources, 320

Coffee interests: of São Paulo, 31; modernizing concerns of, 31; dissatisfied by imperial government in 1880s, 39; opposed urban ones, 43, 47; predominance of in government after 1894, 47; opposed education, 49, 320; included brokers, 78; organized warehousing company, 80; and shipping companies, 89; and exchange rate, 98; and price support program, 101; and funding loan of 1898, 105; and Campos Sales, 110; and slavery, 160–1, 163, 171, 172, 175, 186; and agricultural loans of 1888 and 1889, 185; of Pereira Passos, 196; of Prado brothers, 196; investments in industry, 206; against tariffs, 320; opposed land reform, 320; against government loans to industries, 320

Coffee processing: mechanized by 1914, 45, 46; importation of British machinery for, 82, 84, 86–7; manufacture of machinery for, 141

Coffee production: backward techniques of in 1850, 13; yield, 14; along Paraíba river, 27, 53; in São Paulo, 27, 60; spreading area of after Paraguayan War, 29, 30; spreading area of because of railways, 29, 51, 58, 59, 60; in Minas Gerais, 58, 59; on British-owned plantations, 78

Colégio D. Pedro II, 17, 237

Combination Acts of 1824 and 1825, 253

Comissários, 78, 80, 97

Commerce: international, 3, 4; internal, 14, 15, 97; external, 15; contempt for, 16; dominated by foreigners, 26; balance of trade in 1865–80, 31; Portuguese colonial restrictions upon, 82; effect of First World War upon, 316

Commercial Code of 1850, 25

Compadre system, 288–9

Companhia Brasil Industrial, 131

Companhia Cantareira de Aguas e Esgôtos, 117

Companhia das Docas de D. Pedro II, 193–4, 266

Companhia das Docas de Santos, 93

Companhia de Navegação do Amazonas.

See Amazon Steam Navigation Company

Companhia de Obras Hydraulicas no Brasil, 199

Companhia Empório Industrial do Norte, 195

Companhia Estrada de Ferro Leopoldina, 56–7. *See also* Leopoldina Railway Company

Companhia Estrada de Ferro Mogyana, 56, 136

Companhia Estrada de Ferro Paulista. *See* Paulista, Estrada de Ferro Companhia

Companhia Fabrica de Juta, 141

Companhia Florestal Paranaense, 194

Companhia Industrial, 145

Companhia Paulista de Armazens Geraes, 80

Companies. *See* Stock companies, Legislation on companies

Comte, Auguste: influence, 36; and Spencer, 233, 234, 235, 240, 241, 242

Conciliação, 27, 255

Conde d'Eu, Estrada de Ferro, 70, 192

Conde d'Eu Railway Company, Ltd, 70, 192

Confederação Abolicionista, 175, 181

Conscription: during Paraguayan War, 29; opposed by Republicans, 36

'Conselheiro', Antônio, 43

Conservative Party: defeated in elections of 1861, 224

Constant, Benjamin: influence on Brazilian constitution, 20

Constant, Benjamin (Brazilian). *See* Magalhães, Benjamin Constant Botelho de

Constitution: of 1824, 20, 255; of 1891, 268, 272, 313; of United States used as model, 313

Copper: production predicted, 71; importation of, 84

Corcovado Railway, 197

Corn laws: repeal of in 1846 in England, 106

Corporations. *See* Stock companies, Legislation on companies

Corrêa, João Artur de Souza, 102, 104

Correio braziliense, 218

Correio mercantil, 260

Correio paulistano, 241

Costa, João Cruz, 234, 242

Cotegipe, barão de, 175

Cotton: cultivation, 67–8, 71; transported by rail, 71, 126; exports, 75, 76; handled by modern ports, 127

Index

Index

Index

France (cont.)
fluences of upon Brazil, 300; banking interests of, 302; investments from, 305; and Abranches Moura, 315
Franco de Almeida, Tito, 259
Free Church of Scotland, 286
Free enterprise: defended by Rebouças brothers, 208; urged by Otaviano, 261
Free trade: advocated by British, 105-10, 299, 321; advocated by modernizers before 1875, 106; advocated by Murtinho, 247
Freyre, Gilberto, 114, 249 n. 3
Frontin, André Gustavo Paulo de: and Spencer, 237, 240; life of, 238; and railways, 240; and laissez faire, 246; as abolitionist, 249; British influence upon, 323
Fundição Aurora, 142
'Funding loan' of 1898, 102-5, 110, 238, 321
Furniture: changing styles of, 115-16

Gama, Luís, 182
Gas companies, 118, 188
George Harvey & Silva, 113
Germany: exports to on British accounts, 76; imports from, 84, 300-1; influence of, 203, 240, 300, 314-15, 316; company law in, 230; and Barreto, 240; shipping of, 301; banking interests of, 302; investments from, 304, 305; and naval revolt, 310; and Abranches Moura, 314-15; Brazil's position toward, 315-16
Ginásio Anglo-Brasileiro, 214
Gladstone, William, 167, 263, 268
Glasgow, 279
Glass industry, 44, 196
Góes e Vasconcelos, Zacarias de. See Zacarias de Góes e Vasconcelos
Gold, 2, 71
Gospel of work, 48, 209-13, 298, 322
Government: use of Britain as model, 4, 304; Church–State relations, 18, 19, 37, 38, 39, 40, 42, 262, 263, 272, 296; in 1850, described, 20; illiberalism of, 21, 255, 264-5; local, 21, 268; stability of, 27, 29, 31; centralized, 28, 166
Great Britain: expansionist tendency, 1, 4; production of coal in, 2; production of steel in, 2; production of iron in, 2; industry, 2, 3; railways, 2, 3; international trade, 2, 3, 4, 5; capital accumulations, 3; export of capital, 3, 4, 5; economic growth, 3, 7; company law

in, 3, 221, 225, 227; governmental ideals, 4; shipping, 4; population trends, 6; entrepreneurial attitudes, 7
Great Exhibition of the Works of Industry of All Nations, 1851, 7, 8
Great Western of Brazil Railway, 70, 139
Greene, Edward: joined E. Johnston & Co., 77; proposed retailing business, 78; created Brazilian Warrant Co., 80; and exchange rate, 98; and funding loan of 1898, 104
Grinders: importation of for sugar cane, 87
Guarantee of interest for railways: instituted 1852, 51; not always sufficiently attractive, 52; curtailed by Republican government, 59; increased by province of São Paulo, 60; dispensed with by São Paulo Railway, 65
Guarantee of interest for sugar factories, 150, 154
Guardian Assurance Company, 91
Guinness, H. Grattan, 286

Hague Peace Conference, Second (1907): and Barbosa, 268, 270, 272, 314
Halévy, Élie, 295
Hardware: production of after 1889, 44; importation of, 84, 87, 88, 134, 135, 330-2
Hargreaves, Henry Edward, 141, 192
Harrison Line, 90
Harvey & Silva, 113
Hats: manufacture of, 33, 44, 293, 299; importation of, 115
Hawkshaw, Sir John, 92, 93, 137
Health: yellow fever, 48, 114, 147; British investments and, 124
Hegel, Georg Wilhelm Friedrich, 242
Help for Brazil Missionary Society, 281, 282
Henry Rogers Sons & Co., 86, 87, 132
Hides: exportation of, 75
History: philosophies of, adopted by modernizers in Brazil, 35
Holden, Richard, 287
Holman, William Henry, 199
Home and Colonial Marine Insurance Company, Ltd, 91
House of Commons: mimicked in Brazil, 20; and Brazilian slavery, 184
Houses: of taipa, 10
Hugh & William Nelson, Ltd, 90
Hugh Wilson & Son, 151
Hungary, 146
Hymns: translated by the Kalleys, 280; reflected theology, 286

Index

Immigrants: Portuguese, 16; in Brazilian commerce, 26, 32; as modernizers, 44; on coffee plantations, 81; German, 113; in coal mines, 129; used wheat flour, 148; and abolition of slavery, 175; said to introduce socialism, 295

Immigration: and Republicans, 40; and Pedro II, 41; increase after 1884, 44; financed by British loans, 101; and Tavares Bastos, 109; discouraged by slavery, 160, 161; and coffee planters, 162; to United States, 273; decline after First World War, 316

Imperial Brazilian Collieries, Ltd, 129

Imperialism: Brazilian economic, 190; and Spencer, 250

Import firms, American, 301

Import firms, British: and export firms, 81, 84; predominance of, 83; interests of, 84–5; and British shipping, 88, 89; and port works, 92, 193; offered credit, 94, 134; and British banks, 96–8; on exchange rate, 99; dealing in coal, 128; and industrialization, 134, 140–1; and slavery, 184; and Mauá, 187; and Rebouças, 193; and Tarqüínio, 195; and naval revolt, 1893–4, 307; aided export economy, 323

Import firms, German, 84, 129, 301

Importation: to Britain, 5; from Britain, 81–8, 111, 317, 323, 330–2; statistics regarding, 82–3, 330–2; of port equipment, 92; and urban life, 112–16; and modernization, 124; of consumer goods, 124; of coal, 127–8; of iron, 129–30; of machinery, 130–3, 142, 154, 321; changing nature of, 133–4; of capital goods, 134, 135; of shoes, 145; of wearing apparel, 145; of flour, 146; of textiles, 195; from Germany, 300–1; from the United States, 300–1, 306, 317; and industrialization, 321

Independence of Brazil, 19, 163

Independence of Latin America, 4

Indians: missionary work among, 281

Individualism: in Britain, 7; earlier lack of, 9, 254; and *caudillismo*, 22; and modernization, 35, 276; and slavery, 160, 266; and entrepreneurship, 217; and Spencer, 236; and liberalism, 252, 256, 274, 322; Iberian heritage of, 258; and Barbosa, 268, 271, 272–6; and J. S. Mill, 275; and Protestantism, 277–97, *passim*; accepted by 1914, 298; spread by British, 324

Industrialists: new group of, 33; dissatisfied with imperial policies, 39; opposed coffee planters, 47; and tariffs, 47, 306, 311; considered British credit terms unfair, 94; and funding loan of 1898, 105; included British ex-importers, 140–1; and slavery, 162; and Barbosa, 270

Industrialization: extent of, 14, 25, 44, 50, 299; slowed by earlier attitudes, 16; stimulated by Paraguayan War, 28, 29, 33; and export economy, 31, 320, 323; and slavery, 42, 162; and transport, 45, 111, 125–7, 323; and the British, 73, 125, 300; and port works, 94, 111, 125, 127, 323; and British credit, 96, 134, 136, 321, 323; and government development loans of 1892, 102, 103, 321; and foreign public loans, 105; and tariffs, 106, 110, 311; and imports, 124, 129, 130, 131, 133–4, 321, 323; and British technicians, 137; and British workers, 137–8; and direct British investments, 142–57; and labor relations, 157–9; stimulated by Republic, 195; and Protestantism, 278, 283, 291, 294, 295; aided by power plants, 304; and British competition, 321; and funding loan of 1898, 321; and the cities, 323

Industrialization, idea of: lacking among capitalists in 1850, 14; accepted by 1914, 48, 298; and the British, 81, 140, 324; Mauá's derived from England, 199; among entrepreneurs, 207, 208; and Rebouças brothers, 209; and Spencer, 236, 246–7; and Murtinho, 247

Insurance companies: in 1866, 25; increase in number after Paraguayan War, 32; British ones, 91; aided export economy, 111, 322

International economy: Brazil swept into it, 24; and railway development, 67; and sugar production, 69; and cotton production, 69; and modernization, 71, 319; altered after 1914, 316

Investments: American, 303, 304, 305, 317; German, 304, 305; Belgian, 305; French, 305; Portuguese, 305

Investments, British: extent of, 5, 316, 317; in a stagecoach company, 26; in railways, 52, 54, 56, 57, 58–72, 127, 191; in coffee plantations, 78; in urban services, 116–18; in port works, 127, 194; in coal mines, 129; in industries, 134, 136, 142–57; welcomed by Brazilian entre-

Index

Index

Monroe Doctrine: Brazil's position re, 314
Monteiro, Tobias do Rego, 110
Montevideo, 89, 128, 190
Morality: and British missionaries, 290, 292, 293, 296
Moreira, Francisco Inácio de Carvalho. *See* Penedo, Francisco Inácio de Carvalho Moreira, *barão* do
Mota, Artur Silveira da. *See* Jaceguai, Artur Silveira da Mota, *barão* de
Mota, José Inácio Silveira da, 227
Moura, João Dunshee de Abranches. *See* Abranches Moura, João Dunshee de
Mules, 14, 30, 65, 119
Murtinho, Joaquim Duarte: and *laissez faire*, 219, 246, 247; life of, 238; and Spencer, 239; and social welfare legislation, 245; and change, 248; and race, 248; and imperialism, 250; British influence upon, 323

Nabuco, Joaquim: on urban life, 33; and the British, 176–180, 183, 184, 186, 266–7; and slavery, 176–86, 265, 266; and his father, 177; political ideas of, 179, 260, 263–7; and Christie, 183; and Mauá, 208; and pragmatic spirit of the British, 214; on evolution, 234; on science and religion, 243; on race, 249; and Bagehot, 264; on labor, 265; and Spencer, 265; and Frederick Youle, 266–7; business interests of, 266–7; and Penedo, 266, 267; and Alfred de Rothschild, 267; and the Prince of Wales, 267; as first Brazilian ambassador to United States, 311–14; and Mendonça, 312, 313; and Barbosa, 314; mentioned, 276
Nabuco de Araújo, José Tomás: and Joaquim Nabuco, 177; and slavery, 182, 259; on company law, 225–9 *passim*; and the British, 259
Nathan Brothers, 84, 128
National Bank of Brazil, Ltd, 199
Nationalism: economic, 140, 201, 321; and Protestantism, 284
Navy: revolt, 66, 306–11; civilian employees, 294
Navy, British. *See* Admiralty
Neate, Charles: and port works, 92, 93; as consulting engineer for coal company, 129; long life of in Brazil, 137; influence of upon André Rebouças, 200
Negroes: and sugar factories, 157–8; and work, 212

Nelson Line, 90
New Orleans, 77, 90
New York: shipping connexions to, 90; and coffee trade, 77, 79, 97; branch of Mauá bank there, 189; cable connexions to, 303
Niterói, 32, 149, 172, 181, 279
Nitrates, 71, 84
North Brazilian Sugar Factories, Ltd, 151
Northeastern Brazil: economic conditions, 12, 13, 50, 69–70, 156–8
Nova Cruz, Estrada de Ferro, 69

Ocean Coal Company, Ltd, 128
Oeste de Minas, Estrada de Ferro do, 54
Oliveira Carvalho, Paulo Egydio de, 241
Oliveira Vianna, Francisco José de: and Spencer, 237, 239; and railways, 239; and social Darwinism, 250
Otaviano de Almeida Rosa, Francisco: life of, 260; British influence upon, 260; liberalism of, 260–1; mentioned, 276

Pacific Steam Navigation Company, 90, 128
Palmerston, Lord, 164
Pan-American Conference, 3rd, in 1906, 312
Paper: production of after 1889, 44
Paraguassú Steam Tram-Road, 70
Paraguayan War: effects of, 27, 28, 29, 33; André Rebouças in, 204; mentioned, 23, 144, 187, 254
Paraíba, state, 192
Paraíba river and valley: sugar production in, 13; coffee production in, 13, 25, 53–4, 107; transport to, 26, 27, 52, 53–4; decline of, 30, 160; governmental influence of region, 39; and abolition of slavery, 160
Paraná: and London and Brazilian Bank, 95; railroads in, 189, 191, 192; lumber resources of, 194; and Figueiredo, 199; landed interests in, 204; Protestants in, 280
Paranhos, José Maria da Silva, 1st, *visconde* do Rio Branco, 34
Paranhos, José Maria da Silva, 2nd, *barão* do Rio Branco. *See* Rio Branco, José Maria Paranhos, 2nd, *barão* do
Parker, Barry, 120
Passos, Francisco Pereira. *See* Pereira Passos, Francisco
Patrocínio, José do, 177

378

Index

Index

Republican Manifesto of 1870: issued, 29, 255; and conscription, 29; attacked privilege, 35–6; on Church–State relations, 38; and liberalism, 256

Republican Party: filled by bitter planters after 1888, 39

Republicanism: and Paraguayan War, 28; and coffee planters, 31; supported by both conservative and progressive forces, 39; and modernization, 40; and revolution, 40; and industrialization, 145, 195; and *laissez faire*, 219; and Spencer, 238, 248; and Pedro II, 257; and Irish example, 259; and Nabuco, 263–5; and Barbosa, 268; and the American model, 313–14

Revolutions: before 1849, 20, 27, 258; republican, 40, 43, 60, 230, 304; of 1892–4, 66, 306–11; avoided in Britain, 294–5; French, 295

Ribeiro, Júlio. *See* Ribeiro [Vaughan], Júlio César

Ribeiro [Vaughan], Júlio César: and evolution, 240, 244; as abolitionist, 249; and social Darwinism, 250; and Protestantism, 296

Ricardo, David, 107, 253

Rio Branco, José Maria da Silva Paranhos, 1st, *visconde* do: on science and industry, 34

Rio Branco, José Maria da Silva Paranhos, 2nd, *barão* do: and the United States, 311, 313, 314; and Salvador de Mendonça, 313; and the Monroe Doctrine, 314

Rio Claro, São Paulo, 60, 71

Rio Claro São Paulo Railway, 58, 60, 196

Rio de Janeiro (city): transport serving, 14, 27, 51, 54, 303; schools in, 17, 19, 214, 237; urban services in, 48, 116, 118, 188; contrasted with São Paulo, 49; as commercial center, 74, 77, 79, 83, 86, 128, 211, 301; and shipping connexions, 88, 89, 90; as financial center, 91, 95, 302; port works in, 92, 93–4, 105, 127, 194, 199; borrowed in London, 100; compared to Recife, 117; British colony there, 120; as industrial center, 126, 145; seat of Mixed Commission Court, 167, 168; and abolition of slavery, 172, 173, 175, 181; Pereira Passos, prefect of, 197; and politics, 227, 307; Protestants in, 279, 288; power plants serving, 304; Pan-American Conference at (1906), 312; mentioned, 104, 108, 113, 121, 133, 141, 260, 264, 268, 282, 306

Rio de Janeiro (province and state): German traveler in, 12; sugar production in, 13; coffee production in, 25, 30; governor of, 78, 260; borrowed in London, 117; sugar factories there, 150, 151; and slavery, 164, 176

Rio de Janeiro Central Sugar Factories, Ltd, 151

Rio de Janeiro Chamber of Commerce, 98

Rio de Janeiro City Improvements Company, Ltd, 116, 309

Rio de Janeiro Flour Mills and Granaries, Ltd. *See* Rio Flour Mills

Rio de Janeiro Lighterage Company, 90, 128

Río de la Plata, 190

Rio Flour Mills, 146–9; and funding loan of 1898, 104; equipment, 132; and labor, 138–9; and tariff, 140; contrasted with sugar factories, 153; and Figueiredo, 199

Rio Gas Company, 199

Rio Grande (city), 129

Rio Grande do Norte, 151

Rio Grande do Sul: and port works, 92, 206; and banks, 95, 190; urban services in, 118; coal deposits, 129; retail outlet in, 145; emancipation of slaves in, 184; transportation in, 188, 304; German import firms, 301; revolution in, 307

Rio News, 57

Roads, 14, 26

Robert Sharpe & Sons, 62

Rodrigues Pereira, Lafayette: and Mauá, 228

Rogers Sons & Company, Henry, 86, 87, 132

Romero, Sílvio: and Spencer, 240–1; on race, 248; on slavery, 249; German influence upon, 315

Root, Elihu: visits Rio, 312

Rosa, Francisco Otaviano de Almeida. *See* Otaviano de Almeida Rosa, Francisco

Rothschild, Alfred de: and Souza Corrêa, 102; and funding loan of 1898, 104; and Nabuco, 267

Rothschild, Leopold: opposed blockade of Rio, 307

Rothschild, Lionel de, Baron: and Penedo, 101

N. M. Rothschild & Sons: and São Paulo Railway, 62; bankers to Brazil, 101–5; and sugar factories, 150, 152; opposed industrial loans of 1892, 246, 321; caution regarding price support program, 302

Index

Royal Insurance Company, 91
Royal Mail Steam Packet Company, 88–9; and Charles Miller, 122; as model, 198; and British propaganda, 315
Rubber: exports of, 75, 76, 304
Ruggiero, Guido de, 258
Rural life: in colonial Brazil, 10; its values carried to city, 49; contrasted with results of industrialization, 157–9
Russell, John, Lord, 168, 169, 176

St John d'El Rey Mining Company: labor policies of, 139, 184
Sales, Alberto, 235
Sales, Manuel Ferraz de Campos. *See* Campos Sales, Manuel Ferraz de
Salvador, Bahia: as railhead, 27; population of, 32; port works in, 92; urban services in, 117, 118; Wilson Sons & Co. branch, 128; iron foundry in, 142; Protestants in, 288. *See also* Bahia
San Paulo (Brazilian) Railway Company, Ltd. *See* São Paulo Railway
San Paulo Central Sugar Factory of Brazil, Ltd, 151
San Paulo Gas Company, Ltd, 118
Santa Casa de Misericordia, 292
Santos, Antônio Felício dos, 213
Santos, José Maria dos, 173
Santos, São Paulo: as railhead, 27, 29, 60, 72, 119; as commercial center, 30, 32, 77, 79, 80, 98, 128; and shipping connexions, 89, 90; as financial center, 91, 95, 96, 190; dock company in, 93; urban improvements in, 101, 117, 118; flour milling there, 149; and abolition of slavery, 172, 173; Protestants there, 282, 292; mentioned, 12
Santos a Jundiaí, Estrada de Ferro. *See* São Paulo Railway
São Francisco river, 69, 70
São Paulo (city): population, 32; urban improvements, 48, 101, 117, 118; described, 49; rail connexion, 51, 54; as financial center, 96, 136, 190, 198; schools in, 108, 214, 260, 268; as commercial center, 113, 128; compared to Recife, 117; British colony in, 122; as industrial center, 126, 132, 141, 145, 149; and abolition of slavery, 172; Antônio Prado as prefect of, 197; Spencerians in, 241; Protestants in, 281, 282, 288, 294; power plants serving, 304; public library, 315

São Paulo (province and state): railways in, 27, 29, 54, 60; agricultural production in, 30, 67, 69, 86; attitudes of population, 39, 212, 217, 247; agricultural school, 46; population, 50; government of borrowed in London, 100–1, 196; government of to operate urban services in capital, 117; textile milling, 131, 144; sugar factories there, 151; ascendancy, 160–1; and immigration, 162; and slavery, 171, 173, 175, 176; Protestants in, 280, 282, 292; government of and coffee price supports, 302
São Paulo Alpargatas Company, 145
São Paulo e Rio, Estrada de Ferro, 54
São Paulo Railway, 60–6; effects of, 27; completed 1868, 29; and coffee, 67, 71; and cotton, 67–8; and port of Santos, 93; and urban change, 118–19, 123; and industrialization, 126; and bank, 136; and labor, 158; and slaves, 174; and Mauá, 189, 190; and Pereira Passos, 197; and São Vicente, 198; and Aubertin, 211; described by Ribeiro, 240; and Nabuco, 267; chapel in connexion with, 279; financial record of, 326–9; mentioned, 58
São Vicente, José Antônio Pimenta Bueno, *marquês* de, 61, 197–8, 323
Sapucaí, Estrada de Ferro do, 54
Saunders Brothers, 74
Schapiro, J. Salwyn, 274
Schools: of law, 17, 19, 196, 213; medical, 17, 196; vocational, 18; military, 18, 191, 196, 214; engineering, 33, 47, 137, 191, 196, 209, 238–9, 244; agricultural, 41, 46; of law in São Paulo, 108, 260, 268; secondary, 214, 237, 272; of law in Recife, 261; for girls, 290
J. H. Schroeder & Co.: and valorization scheme, 101, 302
Science: acceptance of, 9, 18, 48, 49, 243; agricultural, 12, 46; in law schools, 19; and Positivism, 36; and industrialization, 232; and progress, 232, 234; and Spencer, 240; and Protestantism, 284
Scotland, 137, 188, 291
Scotland, Church of, 285
Scotland, Free Church of, 286
Scottish Bible Society, 282–3
Scully, William, 24, 184
Secularization: of early modern Portugal, 9; threat to established order, 37; and Protestantism, 277, 296, 324; far-reaching by 1914, 299

382

Index

Index

Sugar factories: and earlier techniques of manufacture, 13, 142; effect of creation of, 50; and railways, 70, 156; British-owned, 125, 149–56, 323; fuel for, 128, 154; and bagging factory, 141; expectations for, 149–50; and André Rebouças, 149–50, 209; law of 1875 regarding, 150; owned by Brazilians, 150, 156, 157; supply of cane to, 152, 155; causes for failure, 152–6; and traditional society, 153, 156; and Nabuco, 266; equipment of, 321

Sunday observance, 293–4

Supreme Court, 62

Taipa (packed mud) houses, 10, 50

Tanneries, 44

Tariff: revision of in 1853, 85, 107; as source of revenue, 99; of 1844, 107, 188; under the Republic, 145; of 1891, 195, 306; in the United States, 306

Tariff, protective: debate on, 47, 110, 299–300; and Tavares Bastos, 109; opposition to, 109, 209, 320, 321; and the British, 140, 299–300, 321; and machinery, 142; failure to maintain, 142, 205, 311; and shoe industry, 145; and Tarqüínio, 209; in world at large after 1914, 316; and coffee interests, 320

Tarqüínio, Luís: and abolition of slavery, 162; and Bruderer, 195, 201; as entrepreneur, 195, 203, 206; British influence upon, 201, 202, 323; belief in industry, 209; and gospel of work, 212; and government aid to industry, 220; mentioned, 187

Taubaté, São Paulo, 141, 144

Tavares Bastos, Aureliano Cândido, 108–10; and slavery, 176–7; and gospel of work, 212; and private enterprise, 217; on company law, 227; and democracy, 257–8; and Otaviano, 260

Taxes: import. *See* Tariff

Technology: in Britain, 1–3, 4, 7, 8, 24; admiration for, 8; of sugar manufacturing, 10, 13, 149; agricultural, 12, 45, 49; of coffee processing, 13, 14, 46; backwardness of, 15, 16, 28; expertise imported from Great Britain, 52–3, 63, 136–40, 206, 323

Teixeira Mendes, Raimundo, 37

Telegraph lines, 205

Textile manufacturing: in 1866, 25; in 1870s, 33; after 1889, 44; and British competition, 85, 86; British investments in, 125, 143–4; and railways, 126; British equipment for, 131; and British banks, 136; and labor, 137–8, 139, 158; and Hargreaves brothers, 141; Tarqüínio's, 195; and André Rebouças, 206, 209; German investments in, 304; British contribution to, 323

Textiles: in Britain, 2; importation of, 84–5, 195, 330–2

Theodor Wille & Co., 302

Theology: of missionaries, 284–7

Timber company, 194

The Times, 59

Tools, 16

Toronto, Canada, 281

Trade. *See* Commerce

Traditional society: in colonial Brazil, 9, 10; in 1850, 10, 16–19; and Catholicism, 37–8, 277; and use of wheat flour, 148; and sugar factories, 153, 156; and labor, 157–9; and slavery, 160; as obstacle to entrepreneurs, 204–5; and gospel of work, 209–10; and *laissez faire*, 216; and restrictive economy, 220; and idea of progress, 234; and social mobility, 254; and individualism, 254, 324; and women, 289

Transportation: in Britain, 2; in 1850, 14; companies to supply, 25, 32; and André Rebouças, 206; and company law, 227; British influence upon, 320. *See also* Railways, Roads

Treaties, commercial: Anglo-Portuguese (1702), 82; Anglo-Brazilian (1810), 82, 278; attempts by British to renew, 107–8; with the United States, 306, 310, 311

United States: merchants from, 26, 76, 77; cotton production in, 67, 69, 87; Civil War in, 67, 87, 170, 314; as Brazil's best customer, 74, 76, 77, 88, 109; shipping of, 88, 89, 301; and Tavares Bastos, 109; imports from, 137, 146, 300–1; dock companies there, 192; and Spencer, 236; and race, 249; as political model, 257, 268; immigration to, 273; and Protestantism, 277, 285, 287, 288; influences from, 300, 304–6, 311–14, 316; and cable companies, 302; and banking interests, 302, 320; investments from, 303, 304, 305; and naval revolt, 307, 308, 310; and Rui Barbosa, 313–14

Index